The Techniques of Rug Weaving

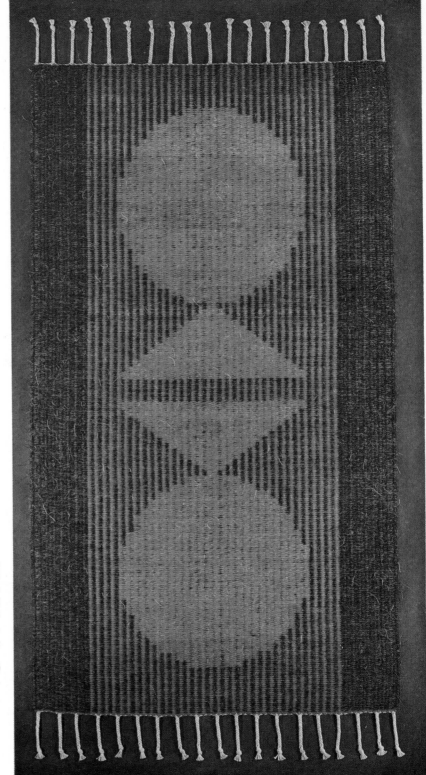

I.
Weft-face rug in wool
and horsehair on linen warp,
using the shaft shifting
principle applied to a
Four-Shaft Block Weave,

see page 327

(designed by the author)
and woven by Jill Maguire.

THE TECHNIQUES OF
RUG WEAVING

Peter Collingwood

FABER AND FABER
London

First published in 1968
by Faber and Faber Limited
3 Queen Square, London WC1
Reprinted 1970, 1972 and 1976
Printed in Great Britain by
Whitstable Litho Ltd, Whitstable, Kent

ISBN 0 571 08333 1

To the late Alastair Morton

Contents

3.   General Rug-Weaving Techniques

4.   Weft-face Rugs in Plain Weave
Part One: Techniques in which the Weft runs from Selvage to Selvage

5. Weft-face Rugs in Plain Weave
Part Two: Techniques in which the Weft does not run from Selvage to Selvage

6. Weft-face Rugs in Plain Weave
Part Three: Techniques giving a Raised Surface Decoration

7. Weft-face Rugs in Multishaft Weaves
Part One: Techniques giving All-over Effects

8. Weft-face Rugs in Multishaft Weaves
Part Two: Techniques giving Block Designs controlled by Shafts

9. Weft-face Rugs in Multishaft Weaves
Part Three: Techniques giving Block Designs controlled by Pick-up Methods

10. Weft Pile Techniques

12. Rugs in which both Warp and Weft contribute to the Surface

13. Weft and Warp Twining

14. Rug Finishes

Plates

143. Warp-face plain weave
144. Warp-face plain weave. Spots of weft brought to the surface
145. Warp-face twill. Weft brought to the surface
146. Warp-face plain weave combined with weft twining and weft-face plain weave
147. Part of a Bedouin Saha
148. Mohair warp-face rug showing raised surface and unraised reverse
149. Warp-face 2/2 twill, with various colour sequences in the warp
150. Warp-face form of block weave using three-end block draft
151. Warp-face form of block weave based on straight three-shaft draft
152. Warp-face form of block weave using single end spot draft
153. Pick-up based on weave shown in Plate 150
154. Warp-face version of six-shaft shadow weave
155. Matting sample. Seagrass and jute weft across coir and sisal warp
156. Matting sample. Seagrass weft across a warp of plastic tubing, 2/2 twill
157. Honeycomb weave, warp and weft being 6-ply rug wool
158. Plain weave double cloth, warp and weft being 6-ply rug wool
159. Matting sample. Seagrass weft across warp of plastic-covered wire
160. Mat woven of unspun jute, dyed sisal and cotton
161. Matting sample. Plaited rush, dyed coir and cotton across cotton warp. Woven by Brian Knight
162. Matting sample. Rayon tow, unspun flax, unspun delustred rayon and cotton across linen warp
163. Matting sample. Seagrass and cotton across cotton warp threaded on alternate two-shaft blocks
164. Matting sample. Rope, coir, unspun jute and raffia across a spaced hemp warp
165. Block of weft twining on a background of 2-and-2 stripes
166. Weft twining. Wefts encircling one, two and three ends
167. Weft twining. Taniko technique
168. Weft twining. Part of rug in twined tapestry, from Abyssinia
169. Open shed weft twining
170. Warpway stripes in Navajo selvage technique

Text Figures

Preface

This book is written from the point of view of a professional, not a hobby, weaver. Most readers will fall into the latter category, more through lack of time and opportunity than through any lack of ability. But it is hoped they will agree that the one-rug-per-year weaver should aim as high, both in design and technique, as the weaver who makes one or two a week. Many ideas, methods and attitudes only occur to the weaver who lives with his work. Complete control over and insight into a technique often comes only after it has been repeated many times. It is one of the purposes of this book to pass on this sort of knowledge.

The possibilities in rugweaving are immense. It may seem at first to have very obvious boundaries; but greater familiarity forces these to recede and eventually disappear, until finally the field of possibilities is seen to be so vast that the difficulty becomes one of selection. To describe these techniques in an orderly way, I have had to adopt an arbitrary sequence. It moves mainly from the simple to the complex, from few shafts to many shafts, from one weft to many wefts, but this does not mean that the techniques occurring early in the book are necessarily the easiest, or vice versa. Often a weave of complex construction, using many shafts, is simple in the actual weaving.

Because some of these techniques are original and others have no names, I have had to christen many of them for ease of reference. I have endeavoured to use descriptive rather than fanciful names, being grateful to the clear-headed lead given in this direction by Irene Emery in *The Primary Structure of Fabrics,* and to helpful advice from Harriet Tidball.

Most of the samples photographed have been especially woven in contrasting colours in order to illustrate their structure. Some are the work of students to whom I am very grateful.

The diagrams have been drawn solely to convey information. To this end various aspects have had to be distorted, such as relative size of warp and weft. It is hoped that this will be thought justified by the resulting clarity.

Once or twice in the course of writing this book, I have wondered whether by being too explicit I was not perhaps robbing the readers of the pleasure of personal discovery. But the thought has been banished when I realized its implicit arrogance—that the book contained all there was to discover. There is of course a great deal more. The information contained in this book can serve as a foundation on which I hope readers will continue to build for some time to come.

The majority of the photographs are by A. J. A. M. van Helfteren, except for
Nos. 2, 104, 114, 125, 130, 134, 138, 148 by the Council of Industrial Design
Nos. 53, 98, 112, 119, 131, 137, 161 by John Arthur
No. 159 by Flair Photography
No. 160 by the Architectural Review.

All the diagrams are by the author.

1 · Equipment for Rug Weaving

1. THE LOOM

A. Rug looms in use today

INTRODUCTION

Weaving is the interlacing of two sets of threads, the active weft crossing the passive warp at right angles. For the easy manipulation of the warp and the easy beating down of the weft, it is essential that the warp threads be kept under tension. Basically, a loom is nothing but a device to produce this necessary warp tension; indeed some simple rug looms do very little else. All the complexities that have been added to the loom are only to save time or effort or to make intricate weave structures possible. They do not alter the fundamental function of a loom as a warp-stretcher.

At least four different ways are still used to achieve this tension:

the horizontal ground loom, in which the warp is stretched between two beams, fastened to pegs in the ground.

the warp-weighted loom, in which weights are attached to a vertically-hanging warp.

the horizontal and vertical frame looms, in which the warp is stretched between two beams, which are themselves part of a rigid horizontal or vertical framework.

the back-strap loom, in which the warp is stretched between the weaver's body and some fixed point.

All except the last method are used for rug weaving and will be described in detail.

(i) THE HORIZONTAL GROUND LOOM

The very earliest portrayal of any loom shows a horizontal ground loom. It is a drawing inside a shallow dish from the Badarian civilization in Egypt, and is dated about 4400 B.C. Many details can be plainly seen, including the four pegs at the corners, three picks of weft and some cross sticks, presumed to be a shedding mechanism.

The earliest representation of this loom being used to weave a floor-covering is more recent and is found in one of the famous Beni Hassan tomb paintings, dated about 1900 B.C. A stiff weft, possibly rush, is being woven and is seen protruding at the selvages. The weaver squats on the part already woven. Of about the same date is a small wooden model of a weaver's workshop, found at Thebes in Egypt, which includes a loom of this type, at which two weavers sit.

Today the horizontal ground loom is used by nomads, such as the Bedouin in Jordan and the Kashkai in Persia, as its portability makes it ideal for their way of life. At any point in the weaving of a rug, the pegs can be uprooted, the completed section of the rug, plus the warp, rolled up on one of the beams and the whole loaded onto a camel. Such nomads weave kilims, flidjs (strips of goathair material for tent making), warp-face rugs, the decorative saha and even knotted rugs. But the simplicity and cheapness of the loom commend it to more static weavers, such as the weavers of durries (cotton kilims) in India and many others.

The warp is wound in a continuous figure-of-eight between the two beams, see Fig. 1. Its tension can be adjusted by altering the lashings between the two beams and

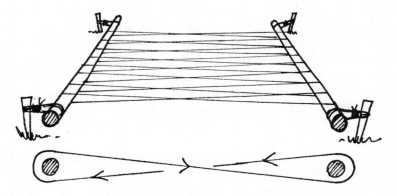

Fig. 1. Horizontal Ground Loom

the four pegs. The two sheds are obtained by means of a shed stick and leashes. The shed stick takes an over-one-under-one course through the warp, and the leashes encircle each end that passes under this stick. The leashes are generally made from a continuous thread and are attached to a rod as they are made. One shed is obtained by twisting the shed stick on its edge or if it is a thick rounded stick by pulling it towards the weaving. The counter-shed is obtained by raising the rod to which the leashes are attached and pushing the shed stick away from the weaving. Some provision may be made for holding the leash-rod in its raised position, such as posts or a pile of stones on either side of the warp. Sometimes the weaver erects over the loom a large wooden tripod, from which is suspended the leash-rod. The weaver sits or squats on the completed part of the rug and so works in a rather cramped position.

(ii) THE WARP-WEIGHTED LOOM

The warp-weighted loom is first portrayed on a Greek vase of about 600 B.C.; though a very schematic representation on an earlier urn from Oedenburg, Hungary, may also be of this loom. But traces in the shape of loom weights and post holes are found from as early as 2500 B.C., for example, at Troy. It is on this loom that the Neolithic and Bronze Age fabrics were woven in Europe. From that time to the present day the loom has been in use, in a practically unchanged form. It now only survives in Scandinavia. A settlement of Lapps in northern Norway still use it for the production of *grene*, flat-woven woollen rugs.

For a very full account of this loom, see *The Warp-Weighted Loom* by Marta Hoffman.

(iii) a. THE VERTICAL FRAME LOOM

At its simplest the vertical frame loom consists of a rectangular framework, an upper and lower beam between which the warp is stretched and two side pieces. The latter hold the two beams apart, thus taking over the function of the ground in the horizontal ground loom.

Its earliest portrayal is in a tomb painting at Thebes of about 1400 B.C. Two centuries later, the tomb of the head weaver of Thebes was similarly decorated. In Europe, drawings of the loom first appear around A.D. 1000, generally as illustrations in psalters, Bibles, etc.

The vertical frame loom has always been the type most favoured for weaving knotted rugs. It is easy to knot onto a vertical warp. The rug fork can be used to full advantage in this position. The fact that the weft has to be slowly passed, not thrown, through the shed is immaterial, as this takes up such a small proportion of the total weaving time. Its very simple design lends itself to the building of massive looms on which the largest carpets can be woven in one piece.

It still exists in three forms, which in the order they are described below would seem to present a possible line of development.

(i) With warp arranged in a continuous figure-of-eight between the two beams.

This is just the horizontal ground loom upended, see Fig. 2 (a). It has three disadvantages; the weaver's bench has to be raised as the work proceeds, the weaving becomes progressively more difficult as the upper beam is approached, and the rug can be no longer than the loom is high. The contemporary Navajo loom is a refinement of this type.

In this and the following type, the warp is given its final tightening by driving wedges between the lower beam and the sockets cut for it in the side pieces.

A variation of this type has nails or pegs in the upper and lower beams and the warp is carried around these instead of around the beams themselves.

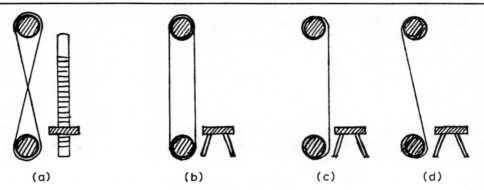

Fig. 2. Types of Vertical Frame Loom

(ii) With warp arranged in a continuous spiral around the two beams.

Only the layer of warp nearest the weaver is woven in this type, see Fig. 2 (b). After every foot or so of weaving, the tension of the warp is slackened and the warp slipped round the two beams and re-tensioned. Thus the weaver can work at one level and the carpet can be almost twice as long as the loom is high.

When beating the weft, there is a tendency for the warp to slip as it is only held by the friction between it and the two beams. This can be overcome if a stick, woven in with the first few picks, is tied to one or other of the beams to prevent this movement.

Warp-face rugs are often woven on this type of loom.

(iii) With warp wound round upper beam and the carpet rolled onto lower beam.

With this type, see Fig. 2 (c) and (d), there is no longer any limitation on the length of the rug that can be woven and, having two revolving beams, it lends itself to far more sophisticated ways of adjusting warp tension. As Fig. 2 (d) shows, the warp can be tilted away from the weaver, giving a more comfortable working angle, if it is wound in the opposite direction on the upper beam.

This loom exists in very many forms, from the relatively light upright rug loom sold to handweavers, to massive looms which have to be built into a workshop, some of which can weave carpets up to 48 feet wide. They all have two features in common, great strength to withstand the high warp tension and some mechanism for producing and adjusting this tension. These two features are somewhat at variance with each other, because the greater the diameter of the two beams, the more difficult it is to exert enough force on them to tighten the warp. This can ideally be solved with metal gearing, but on more primitive looms levers have to be used. Fig. 3 shows one solution from an eighteenth-century French workshop. From the end of a long lever, attached to the upper beam, a rope passes to a winch on a nearby wall. The latter is tightened until the warp tension is correct and then the long lever is lashed to the side frame. Fig. 4 shows another method in which levers from upper and lower beams are connected by chain and turnbuckle. Tightening the latter naturally tightens the warp.

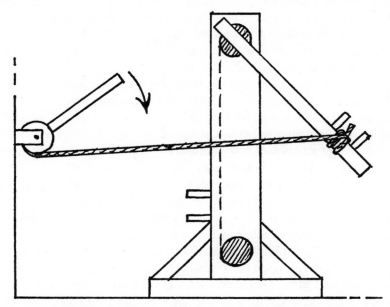

Fig. 3. Eighteenth-century French method of tightening a rug warp

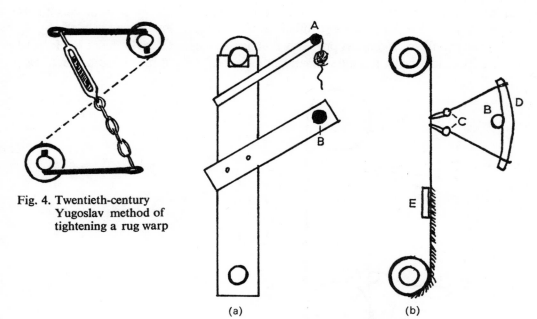

Fig. 4. Twentieth-century Yugoslav method of tightening a rug warp

(a)

(b)

Fig. 5. Typical Vertical Frame Loom

Fig. 5 (a) shows the side view of a typical primitive loom of this type, as found in India and Persia. The massive side frame is seen, with a socket at the top for the warp beam and a hole at the bottom for the cloth beam. The upper arm supports a rod, A, that stretches the width of the loom and from which are hung bobbins or balls of wool for knotting. Sometimes the bobbins are put on pegs on a board that is similarly placed. The lower, much heavier, arm supports a very strong pole, B, that also stretches the width of the loom. Two leash-rods, C, are used, each with its set of leashes, see Fig. 5 (b). These can be thought of as two very primitive shafts; pulling one forward raises the even numbered ends, pulling the other forward raises the odd-numbered ends. At several points across the width, a cord from each rod goes to either end of a strong stick, D, which lies vertically, hard up against the pole, B. This is comparable to a heddle horse on a horizontal loom. By manipulating it, one or other of the leash-rods can be pulled forward. E is a temple on the back of the rug. One advantage of a vertical frame loom is that a temple can easily be inserted in this position, where it does not interfere with the knotting.

Although the above loom has been described as typical, there is an infinite variety among vertical frame looms used for rug weaving, many depending on what material is locally available and almost all involving a good deal of improvisation.

At first it can be a little shaming to a Western weaver to realize that rugs of un-equalled beauty and quality have been, and are being, produced on such simple looms and he may wonder which parts of his gadget-loaded loom are really essential. But when the element of time is taken into consideration, most additions to the present day hand loom become justified, as time-savers.

The vertical frame loom has probably reached its highest development in Holland. See Fig. 6 which shows a diagrammatic side view of this all-metal loom. Each warp

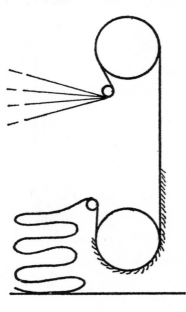

Fig. 6
Dutch Vertical Frame Loom

end comes from a separate bobbin held in a creel (not shown) which is part of the loom. These ends pass under a metal bar and then over the upper beam. The latter has a specially roughened surface, so that the warp is gripped through contact with its large circumference and cannot slip. The warp then drops vertically to the lower beam, which is covered with small spikes so that it grips the back of the knotted rug. The latter then passes over a bar to lie in folds on the floor behind the loom. Both beams are turned by gear wheels, the lower having a worm gear. The two strong shafts are moved by chains controlled by a metal wheel at the side of the loom. The shed obtained is so deep that a whole ball or tube of weft can literally be thrown across. A reed is used for spacing the warp but the weft is beaten with a heavy rug fork. As will be understood, this loom banishes any warping problems and makes possible the weaving of rugs of any length or shape without their building up on the cloth beam. A rug is started by tying the warp to a stick which is attached to an apron impaled on the spikes of the cloth beam.

Between the two extremes of the primitive Indian loom and the highly developed Dutch loom, comes the vertical rug loom as sold to handweavers. It has two shafts operated by pedals, which may be duplicated if the loom is very wide, to enable several weavers to work side by side. Exceptionally, four shafts are fitted. It has a batten which may slide on runners on the side frame or may be pivoted at the back. The batten is generally held up by springs but the back-pivoted type may have its swords prolonged backwards to support a counterweight. This is preferable as the weaver does not have to beat against the pull of the springs. Sometimes the batten is held up by a catch which is released by pressing a third pedal. It then falls with its own weight and has to be lifted back to engage with the catch.

(iii) b. THE HORIZONTAL FRAME LOOM

The horizontal frame loom has now become the normal type. It has many advantages; the shafts, which can be of any number, are operated by the feet, leaving the hands free: the shuttle can be thrown easily from side to side of a wide warp: there is a superstructure from which to hang a batten and the working position is comfortable.

From the evidence of surviving textiles, this loom was known in Syria before A.D. 256. It is first mentioned in European sources in about A.D. 1100 and it is generally, and conveniently, assumed to have first appeared in Europe around A.D. 1000. It then quickly supplanted the warp-weighted loom and was the mainspring of the terrific expansion in the cloth trade that followed. The earliest pictures of the horizontal frame loom date from the thirteenth century. Some of these look like horizontal ground looms on stilts, i.e. there is very little frame-work above the warp level and the pulleys for the shafts are sometimes shown attached to the workshop ceiling. In the early examples the reed was very light and was either not attached to the loom or hung on cords. In either case, it was the weaver who had to ensure that the beat was straight.

Later, when a heavier frame was built (and this was nearly always of the four-poster type), a proper rigid batten was hung from it. The harness always consisted of pulleys. Small pedals, sometimes no bigger than shoes, were tied directly to the lower half of each shaft. It is obvious from examining these pictures that the early horizontal frame loom was not strong enough for rug weaving.

Later looms became sturdier and the typical peasant loom was evolved on which could be woven all the textiles required by the household, from fine linen sheets to heavy rugs. The latter would be flat-woven, either weft-face, or warp-face, or woven with a rag weft. The vertical frame loom was still regarded as the proper type for knotted rugs.

This division still exists in the East where, as already mentioned, almost all knotted rugs are produced on the vertical frame loom, but flat-woven rugs are produced on the horizontal ground loom or horizontal frame loom. The latter sometimes has two

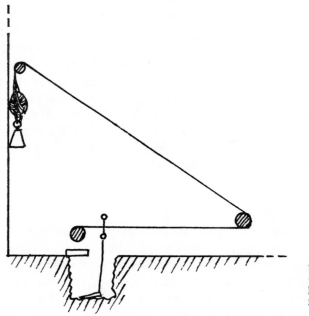

Fig. 7
Middle Eastern
pit-loom for
rug weaving

special features. The warp is almost at ground level and the weaver sits on a plank across a specially dug pit, with his feet in this pit working the pedals, see Fig. 7. The warp passes under the back beam and then up over a bar or hook on the wall above the weaver's head, to end in a ball or chain of warp. To the latter is attached a heavy weight. When the warp is turned on, a little more is let off the ball. Thus the warp is never beamed and small adjustments to tension can be made as weaving proceeds.

It is in Scandinavia that the horizontal frame loom has become most accepted for weaving both pile and flat rugs. This may have a historical basis. The earliest written record of Scandinavian pile fabrics is in a MS. of 1451, and these together with those subsequently mentioned are all bed covers. So although the structure was basically similar to that of knotted Eastern rugs, they were not thought of as rugs, and it was natural to weave them on horizontal looms. Later, when they were woven in a heavier form suitable for the floor, the same loom was used.

In Great Britain, the newly developed techniques such as Wilton (cut warp pile), Brussels (uncut warp pile), Kidderminster (plain weave double cloth) and Chenille rugs were all originally woven on hand looms. These were exceedingly heavy horizontal frame looms of the four-poster type. Sometimes the whole frame was of metal. The Brussels carpet loom had a drawloom mechanism and the leashes controlling the various sheds were pulled by a drawboy standing at the side of the loom. He also had to insert a wooden 'sword' to hold open the shed so formed. The weaver then inserted a wire into the shed, the drawboy withdrew the sword and the weaver wove some picks of weft. It was essential to keep the number of pile tufts per inch constant, so that the pattern would match on two strips of carpet sewn edge to edge. So a bell was made to ring after the number of tufts that should exist in a quarter yard had been woven. The weaver could then measure his work and either repeat the last row of pile or omit a row, if he had woven less or more than nine inches from the last point the bell rang. A weaver could produce about five yards a day on this loom, compared with the twenty-five yards produced by the earliest power-driven Brussels carpet looms.

B. The Requirements of a Modern Horizontal Rug Loom

The two essentials for rug weaving, a high warp tension and a heavy beat, dictate most of the features in an ideal rug loom.

(i) THE LOOM FRAME

The loom frame must be exceedingly strong. This applies especially to all cross members, i.e., warp and cloth beams, breast and back beams, knee bar. They have to be completely rigid, for if each of them gives at its centre even a fraction of an inch, the result will be a progressive slackness of the warp towards its centre. Obviously the wider the loom, the stronger these parts must be; and to avoid woodwork of immense and cumbersome proportions, metal should be introduced appropriately on very wide looms. If the batten is overslung, the upper part of the loom frame must be strong enough to support the extra weights fixed to the batten for rug weaving.

The length from front to back of the loom should be as great as possible. This enables the sheds to be easily made although the warp is at high tension. The apparent length of the loom can be increased by having a back beam that can revolve or is made of polished metal. Then the fixed end-point of the warp threads is the warp beam itself, and the threads can move slightly around the back beam when a shed is opened. The length from breast beam to the front shaft should be about twenty inches to allow a good weaving space.

(ii) THE CONTROL OF WARP TENSION

The warp and cloth beams are generally controlled by pawl and rachet wheels. A ratchet wheel with a few large teeth is adequate for the warp beam. But for the cloth beam a much finer adjustment is necessary, especially when an inelastic warp like linen or hemp is being used.

The ideal is for the cloth beam to be furnished with a toothed wheel which meshes with a worm operated by a crank handle. A more usual way is to add an extra pawl to the existing ratchet, in such a position that when one pawl engages with the ratchet, the other pawl is halfway between two teeth, see Fig. 8. In this way the ratchet gives

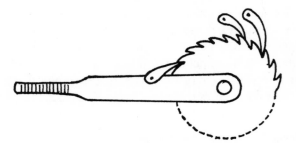

Fig. 8
Lever for turning cloth beam; also showing ratchet with two pawls

as much adjustment as one with twice as many teeth. Sometimes the same principle is used, but with a pawl and ratchet at each end of the cloth beam.

Some way has to be found of applying sufficient force when tightening the cloth beam. A turning handle with spokes is the usual device, but it should have more than two spokes, otherwise it will often happen that these are awkwardly placed for applying force. With any spoked handle, the weaver's knee may have to be used, pushing down on a spoke on one side of the handle while the hands pull up a spoke on the other side. The knee also helps when one hand has to be free to disengage the pawl when releasing tension. A good way of applying force is the lever shown in Fig. 8. This is a metal or wood strip with a handle at one end and a hole at the other through which passes the cloth beam's axle. A pawl is attached to it, engaging with the ratchet, so as this lever is pumped up and down the cloth beam is turned. The longer the lever, the greater the force that can be applied.

Because of the high warp tension, there is a great strain thrown on the fixings of the pawl and ratchet. The former should be bolted, not screwed, to the loom frame. There are many ways of fixing the latter. Screwing the ratchet into the end of the cloth beam, see Fig. 9 (a), is not very satisfactory, as the screws go into the end-grain of the wood and will eventually tear out. This type of fixing can be greatly strength-ened by bolting two heavy metal angle-pieces as shown in Fig. 9 (b). Sometimes the ratchet is itself attached to a metal sleeve which slides over the end of the beam and is screwed into position, see Fig. 9 (c). Another method is to screw the ratchet to the centre block of the turning handle, see Fig. 9 (d). This obviously necessitates a thick axle as shown; it has the advantage that the ratchet is outside the loom frame and so is not in the way when weaving at full width.

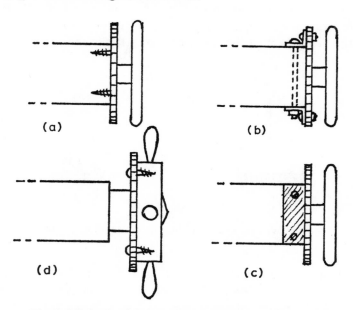

Fig. 9. Methods of fixing ratchet to cloth or warp beam

(iii) THE BATTEN AND THE REED

The ability of the batten to compact the weft depends on its momentum when it strikes the fell of the cloth. Its momentum is simply the product of its speed and its weight. In other words, the heavier it is, the slower it need be swung to produce a given effect. Conversely, a light batten has to be swung with great speed to produce the same effect. The matter is not quite as simple as this because the batten is not swinging freely, but has the added pull of the weaver. It is however true that a batten must be specially weighted for rug weaving. On the old Wilton hand looms, the whole of the batten, except for the part gripped by the hand, was of metal; this is the sort of weight to be aimed at.

Metal strip, ⅜ or ½ inch thick, is suitable. Fig. 10 (a) shows how it can be fixed to the underside of the batten, with a bolt at each end. To avoid it whipping when beating, bend the strip into a very slight bow and bolt it with the convex curve uppermost.

Fig. 10 (b) shows an alternative method. Two strong angle brackets are screwed to the batten as shown and the strip fits tightly between the front of the batten and the vertical arms of the brackets. As different widths and types of rug require different weights, it is advisable to have two strips both the full length of the batten but one strip half the width of the other and therefore half the weight. Then by using them singly or together, three different weightings of the batten are possible. As an example, the wider strip for a 5 foot wide batten might weigh about 22 lb.

Horizontal rug looms are made with either overslung or underslung battens; the majority of the large professional looms have the former type.

Because of the heavy beat, a rug loom has to be fastened to the floor to prevent it

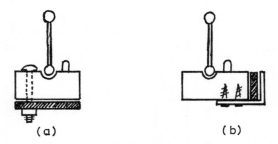

Fig. 10. Two methods of adding extra weight to the batten

slipping. A pad of foam rubber under each corner post is a simple expedient, but something more permanent is preferable, such as floor blocks. To prevent distortion and weakening of the frame of a four-poster loom, brace the upper part against nearby walls.

As with everything else in rug weaving, the reeds need to be especially strong. Most manufacturers have a range of different gauge metal for the wires and the thickest gauge, suitable for the required dentage, should be chosen. Normal reeds can be used, but if for example a rug warp is spaced out in 12-dents-per-inch reed, the latter will become so distorted after a few rugs have been woven that it will no longer be fit for normal fine weaving. Remember that if a reed is being specially ordered, it does not need to have a whole number of dents to the inch. It could, for instance, have $3\frac{1}{2}$ dents per inch. There is a considerable difference between a setting of 3 and 4 ends per inch and it is useful to be able to bridge the gap in this way.

(iv) THE SHEDDING MECHANISM

Because a highly tensioned and often inelastic warp is being used, it is far easier to obtain a given depth of shed with a system that raises some shafts and lowers others than with one that only raises shafts. In the former, the shafts have only to move two inches above or below the normal warp line to give a four inch shed; in the latter, they have to move four inches above the line. In other words, a counterbalanced or countermarch loom is very suitable. When at rest, the shafts of a jack loom are so positioned that the heald eyes are below the line from breast to back beam. To keep them in this position, when a highly tensioned warp is being used, they have to be specially weighted. Otherwise they will rise and decrease the depth of the shed.

The countermarch loom has the advantage that any number of shafts can be used and a perfect shed is obtained however many or few shafts are lifted at a time. Its drawback is the amount of tying up required. But this can be greatly simplified as in the Cyrus loom or by using the method described in the *Quarterly Journal of the Guilds of Weavers, Spinners and Dyers, number 49.*

All the cording connected with the shafts, lams and pedals should be of thick loom cord or it can be replaced where possible with chains.

String healds are best as every kind of warp can easily be threaded through the eyes. If only weft-face rugs are to be woven, then the normal wire healds are adequate.

(v) THE PEDALS

Pedals pivoted at the back of the loom are better than those pivoted at the front, because of the force needed to open the shed, especially with a wide warp.

(vi) APRON, FRONT AND BACK STICKS

A strong canvas apron from cloth beam to front stick is preferable to cords. Cords strong enough for rug weaving would have to be very thick and therefore tend to build up unevenly on the cloth beam. Whatever is used, make sure it is long enough. (See Marking the Length and Viewing the Rug in Chapter 3.)

Front and back sticks should be of metal, especially if the loom is wide. The front stick must be very strong if a narrow rug is being woven on a wide loom, as there is a tendency for the central pull of the warp to bow the front stick and thus curve the starting edge of the rug.

(vii) THE SEAT

A bench seat that is part of the loom and stretches its full width is preferable to a separate stool. It provides a useful shelf while weaving, but it really comes into its own when knotting a wide rug or weaving a kilim, when the weaver does not only want to sit centrally. Some looms have the added refinement of a small upholstered trolley seat which runs on wheels along the bench. The height of the bench should be adjustable.

(viii) PROTECTING THE WOVEN RUG

Some looms are fitted with a narrow strip of wood that rests in slots just in front of the breast beam. This is useful because as the woven rug passes between the strip and the breast beam, it is protected from being rubbed by the weaver as he moves from side to side. See Fig. 11. The underside of the rug, as it passes from the breast beam to the knee bar, will collect wool fluff, unless a cloth is fixed as shown in Fig. 11. It can be attached to a metal rod that is fixed to the far under-edge of the breast beam.

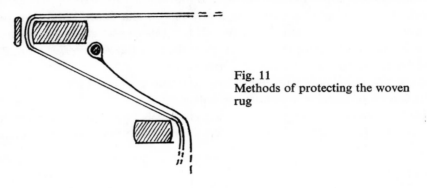

Fig. 11
Methods of protecting the woven rug

(ix) AN EXTENSION FOR DIFFICULT WARPS

Some warps are very difficult to manage on a normal warp beam, e.g., sisal and coconut yarns. The following simple extension to a loom makes their use very easy; it also 'corrects' a badly-made warp of any material.

Fig 12 (a) shows the side view of a loom. Two strong wooden beams, A, are bolted to the side frame, as shown, a little below the warp line. At their far end, they each have a small upright, B, to support their weight. C is a cross bar that fits between the

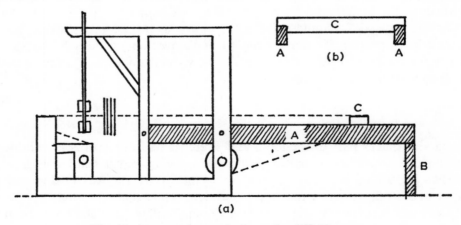

Fig. 12. An extension to the loom for difficult warps

two beams and can slide along them. See Fig. 12 (b). Some device such as large clamps (not shown) are used to fix the cross bar in any desired position. The top of each beam is marked off in inches.

The warp comes from the warp beam, passes backwards around the cross bar and then forwards into the loom as shown. Whenever the warp has to be turned on, the cross bar is simply moved the appropriate distance towards the loom. The warp beam is not touched throughout the weaving. If the beams, A, extend, say, 4 feet beyond the loom, then a rug nearly 8 feet long can be woven. As long as the initial tying to the front stick is accurately done, the warp tension will be perfect throughout the weaving, because the total length of required warp is exposed.

A one-rug warp need not be beamed. One end can be looped round the back stick on the warp beam to tether it and the rest carried round the sliding cross bar as described.

To ensure that threads lie parallel, pass a raddle down the warp before starting to weave.

From the above description of an ideal rug loom, the weaver will know whether his own loom is adequate and, if not, where and how it should be strengthened. To withstand the high warp tension and heavy beating, a rug loom should look *unnecessarily* strong.

(x) VERTICAL AGAINST HORIZONTAL FRAME LOOMS

The vertical rug loom takes up less room,
>—is cheaper,
>—is slower to operate with weaves in which the weft passes regularly from selvage to selvage,
>—generally only has two shafts so makes complex weave structures impossible,
>—is specially made for rug or tapestry weaving and so is not suitable for other types of weaving,
>—cannot give such a heavy beat, unless a rug fork is used.

2. ADDITIONAL EQUIPMENT

A. Shuttles

For a horizontal loom, a shuttle that will slide easily through the shed is essential and the type generally known as a 'ski-shuttle' is without doubt the best. Two views of this are shown in Fig. 13 (a), with approximate measurements. The weft is wound around the two wooden hooks in a circular manner As the shuttle is only $1\frac{1}{4}$ inches high, it can find its way through a very shallow shed. Also as the tips of the shuttle curve up to the same level that the hooks curve down, it is impossible for the latter to catch on the warp.

To avoid unnecessary winding and rewinding, at least twelve of these shuttles are needed per weaver. Occasionally sandpaper the shuttle where it strikes the reed, otherwise a roughened, thread-catching area will develop.

A normal throwing shuttle is useful for finer wefts, e.g., plain weave binding picks. The best size is about 14 inches long as this takes a cardboard tube as a bobbin. The type without rollers slides better across the fairly open rug warp than that with rollers.

For a vertical loom, the most useful feature in a shuttle is its length, so that it can if possible be passed from hand to hand, without being poked through the shed. A very long stick shuttle with one end fashioned like a netting shuttle works well, see Fig. 13 (b).

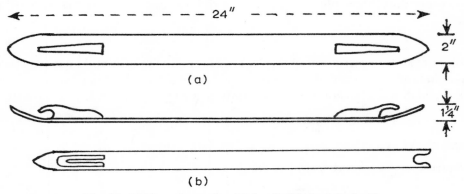

Fig. 13. (a) Two views of a ski-shuttle (b) A stick shuttle

For making narrow samples, stick shuttles notched at both ends or smaller versions of the above are quite adequate.

B. Temples

To make a weft-face rug with really firm and straight edges, it is essential to use a temple from the first woven pick to the last. The temple needs to be of stronger construction than those usually supplied, and the type shown in Fig. 14 (a), consisting of two similarly-shaped halves, is better than the conventional type shown in Fig. 14 (b). One half of the latter, (B), is weaker and tends to bend under the strain of rug weaving. The two halves of the upper type are held together by a bolt, those of the lower type by a pin.

The length of any type of temple should be as finely adjustable as possible. The best way to achieve this, without having so many holes that the temple is weakened, is to use the vernier system. In one half, (B), make holes every $\frac{1}{2}$ inch for the whole of its

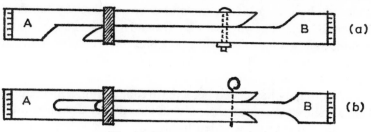

Fig. 14. Two types of temple

usable length. In the other, (A), make just four holes, $\frac{3}{8}$ inch apart, where the bolt or pin is to be. By this means the length of the temple can be altered by increments of $\frac{1}{8}$ inch. It greatly helps inserting the bolt or pin, if there is an incised line, on the upper surface of the temple, over each hole. Such marks on A and B can be aligned and the bolt pushed through.

C. Rug Forks or Beaters

Rug forks are chiefly used to beat the weft on a vertical loom, but they can be used to supplement the batten on a horizontal loom if a particularly close beat is wanted. The fork can weigh $\frac{1}{2}$ to $1\frac{1}{2}$ lbs.

The two essentials in a rug fork are to have weight and to have it in the right place, i.e., as near the tines of the fork as possible. It is an item of equipment that has never become standardized and there are many types. If made of metal, the fork can be cast in one piece from brass, or constructed of strips of metal bolted together at the handle. If made of wood, the fork is generally weighted with lead; or it may have a wooden handle with metal tines. Sometimes the handle is set at an angle to the body of the fork, presumably to facilitate beating.

There is no real need for the number of tines per inch on the fork to correspond with the ends per inch in the warp. Forks are usually made with 3–5 tines per inch. The tines should be smooth and polished to prevent damage to the warp.

D. Yarn Winder

If rug weaving is carried out on any scale, some method of winding yarn, other than into balls by hand, is essential. Most rug and carpet wool is bought in hank form, so the first requisite is a strong skeiner. The wooden umbrella-type skeiner from Scandinavia is adequate and works best if set up so the axle is horizontal. More useful is an expanding metal skeiner as used in industry. This is also set up with its axle horizontal. In addition, it can be used for making skeins from cones and tubes, etc. Remember that carpet wool hanks are larger than normal ones, so make sure the skeiner will expand sufficiently.

The most easily obtainable forms of yarn winder are those made for use with home knitting machines. These clamp to a table and are worked by hand. The majority wind neat, but small balls. The yarn can be drawn from the centre, so such balls can be placed together in a box and they will not roll about while being unwound. Others are made to wind the normal industrial paper or plastic cones and these are preferable as the cone is the ideal yarn package for the rug weaver.

As ½ to 1 lb. of wool may be needed per square foot of rug, a mechanical winder is a great help. Fig. 15 shows diagrammatically an electrically-driven winder that can be used for cones, tubes and small wooden bobbins.

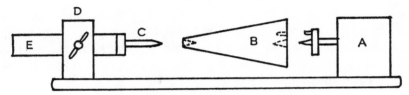

Fig. 15. Electrical yarn winder

A is the electric motor from which the driving axle emerges at the left. This has a tapered point and a disc near its end with a small pin fixed as shown. B is a piece of wood shaped to receive the cones. At its base, (right-hand end), it has a central hole and another smaller one off-centre to receive the axle and its pin. At its left-hand end, it also has a central hole. This is to receive C, a small axle, similar to that of the motor. It is housed so that it can revolve—for instance, in a ball bearing. It is attached to the end of the arm, E, which can slide through the upright block, D, and can be fixed in any position with a butterfly screw.

B has a strip of sandpaper or rubber material running down its length to anchor the cones to it. It may be necessary to cut the points off the cones to allow C to pass through.

The speed of the motor is controlled by a foot-operated rheostat, so that both hands are free. When winding tubes or wooden bobbins, C is moved in until the two tapered axles grip them.

On this simple piece of apparatus the yarn is guided on by hand; there is quite an art in winding a firm cone. (See Chapter 3).

More complex industrial machines, which automatically wind perfect cones or cheeses, are well worth the investment if much rug weaving is to be done. The split-drum type is fairly slow, so a machine which will wind several separate cones at once is suitable. With high-speed, more expensive types, a single head machine is adequate.

The large metal drums, (used in Scandinavia for winding warp yarn), are very useful for any type of yarn which cannot be wound on cones, e.g., horsehair, sisal and seagrass. One is shown in Fig. 16. It has a special hand-operated winder. Due to its large diameter and the gearing in the winder, it winds yarn at high speed. It holds a great weight of yarn.

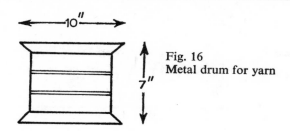

Fig. 16
Metal drum for yarn

It is very difficult to wind cones of such a slippery yarn as mohair, e.g., for the warp of a warp-face rug. However carefully the yarn is guided on by hand, it slips off the top of the cone in loops as it is unwound. For this purpose it is necessary to use some type of flanged bobbin. Flanged cardboard tubes are made but more easily obtainable are so-called warper's bobbins, used in industry and made of wood or plastic. They should have a flange about 4 inches in diameter and be up to 8 inches in length. Choose a size that can be fitted onto the winder described above.

E. Miscellaneous Items

A number of other items of equipment are useful, such as a doubling stand (see Colour Plying in Chapter 4), a magnet fixed to the loom to hold darning needles, and a clip also fixed to the loom to hold designs. A mousetrap screwed to the upper cross bar of the loom frame serves well for the latter purpose.

Suppliers for most of the equipment described above are given in the appendix at the end of the book.

2 · Warp and Weft Yarns

1. WARP YARNS

A. For Weft-face Rugs

In a weft-face rug, the warp only appears at the two fringes. Elsewhere it is hidden, running through the centre of the fabric, where it contributes nothing to the appearance of the rug but considerably affects its handle and the way it lies on the floor.

Yarns used for the warp are cotton, wool, linen, hemp, jute, ramie, synthetics and others.

A 7/7s cotton yarn is often used by beginners as it is easy to obtain and easy to use. But it is a very soft yarn with little body. The various cotton twines, used in the fishing industry for net-making, are more tightly-spun and greatly preferable. They are produced in a large range of counts. Cotton is easy to use because of its elasticity; so an imperfectly made warp will weave satisfactorily. It is also easy to dye, if the weaver wants the fringe in some colour other than its natural white.

Wool is the traditional warp for Eastern knotted rugs and it would be more used by present day rug weavers if a suitable yarn were available. The yarn needs to be worsted-spun from a long staple, coarse, fibre. The latter could be goat or camel hair, not necessarily wool. It must be tightly spun so that it does not fluff in the reed. The warp yarn used by tapestry weavers is of this type. The commercially used belting yarns make a good warp but have the disadvantage that they are so springy that any rug finish will soon work loose—even an overhand knot will not hold. A satisfactory warp can be made from the 6-ply wool, sold as rug weft.

Linen (and the other inelastic fibres) gives a firmness to the rug, lacking in those with cotton or wool warp. In its unbleached state, it has a pleasant neutral colour and so can be used for most rugs without having to be dyed. The best type has a fairly rough surface, i.e., it is spun from tow. Line yarns (spun from long fibres) are often so smooth and glossy that there is no cohesion between them and the weft. However tightly beaten, the latter will tend to slide on the warp. A count of 6/10s lea or 4/8s lea will be found suitable. A linen warp has to be perfectly made.

The above remarks also apply to hemp, jute and ramie. Jute is the least satisfactory of the three, as it is generally loosely spun, rubs in the reed, rots if damp and becomes a darker colour after long exposure. Hemp was used as the warp for the first knotted rugs produced in England.

Synthetics tend to be too slippery for the warp of weft-face rugs, but in time a suitable synthetic yarn is bound to be produced

B. For Warp-face Rugs

Warp-face rugs can have a warp of 2-ply carpet wool, 6-ply rug wool, belting yarns, mohair, goathair, in fact all the materials suitable for the weft of weft-face rugs. If the mohair is to be brushed, the amount of twist in the yarn is critical. It has to be high enough to give the yarn strength for the weaving process and yet low enough to allow a few surface fibres to be brushed out without tearing.

C. For Warp- and Weft-face Rugs

All the materials described for weft-face rugs are suitable, with the addition of the synthetic netting twines, (nylon, polypropylene, polythene) and sisal and coir, (coconut fibre yarn).

2. WEFT YARNS

A. For Weft-face Rugs

Wool is the most used fibre. It can be easily compacted by the beater to give a smooth, hardwearing surface and is very easy to dye. The yarn should be worsted-spun, with medium twist, from fairly coarse fibres. The 2-ply wool used in the carpet trade with a count of about 2/50s, (the 50 here means 50 yards per ounce), is quite suitable and can generally be obtained in a large range of colours. The same yarn is sometimes made up in a 6-ply form specifically for rug weaving, but the 2-ply yarn has more flexibility in use.

The Norwegian yarn, spun entirely from the fleece of the Spaelsau sheep, is ideal, giving a heavy, strong, practical rug.

A singles yarn, spun from a mixture of wool and cowhair, is specially produced in Scandinavia for the weaving of weft-face rugs. It lacks the springiness of an all-wool yarn, but is cheaper and at least as hardwearing.

Other tougher animal fibres, such as goat- and horsehair, are eminently suitable, especially for rugs that are going to receive a great deal of hard wear. Due to their incompressibility, they probably need to be combined with wool yarns to produce a structure that is entirely weft-face.

Ideally, a different type of yarn should be used for all cut-pile techniques, (knotting, corduroy, etc.). The need here is for a long staple fibre, worsted-spun, giving a yarn which after some wear acquires a paintbrush-like tip. A woollen-spun yarn will shed fluff until it is almost completely worn away. Scandinavian suppliers produce special yarns for this purpose, called rya yarns and flossa yarns. The Spaelsau yarn, mentioned above, and the various belting yarns are very suitable.

Other weft materials include unspun fleece, thick cotton, linen (and the other bast fibres) and synthetics. Due to their varying elasticity, it is difficult to combine two such materials in one rug. See Chapter 4, for details of handspun weft yarns.

B. For Warp-face Rugs

A heavy thick yarn, such as horsehair, thick cotton or 6-ply wool, is needed.

C. For Warp- and Weft-face Rugs

The field is large here. Sisal, coir, cane, seagrass, various ropes, unspun hemp and jute, rayon tow can all be used, in addition to materials already mentioned.

This is only an outline of the materials that can be used for weaving rugs. There are, for instance, many excellent yarns employed in industry, which are difficult for the handweaver to obtain, but which are well worth searching for.

Suppliers for most of the yarns described above are given in the appendix to this book.

Weight of Yarn used in Rug

A flat-woven rug uses about $\frac{1}{2}$ lb of weft per square foot.

A pile rug uses $\frac{3}{4}$ lb upwards of weft per square foot.

A $3' \times 5'$ rug uses about $\frac{3}{4}$ lb of warp.

3 · General Rug-Weaving Techniques

1. MAKING AND BEAMING A WARP

A. Using Warping Mill or Frame

It is extremely important that a rug warp should be as perfectly mounted in the loom as possible; that is, with every end at an equal and high tension and of an equal length. In a weft-face rug, there is no take-up of the warp in weaving, so a loose thread or group of threads will remain loose throughout the rug. Such looseness may not seem important when the rug is stretched on the loom but once it is off and lying on the floor, the loose areas may bulge and prevent the rug lying flat.

A ONE-MAN METHOD OF BEAMING A WARP OF ANY WIDTH

Make the warp on a mill or frame, with a cross at both ends. Raddle it. Attach warp to backstick on warp beam. Mount raddle on the back beam of the loom and work at the back of the loom. So the warp is passing in the wrong direction over the back beam, (see Fig. 17 (a), where the arrow is pointing to the front of the loom).

Turn the warp beam once, applying no tension to the warp. Then tighten the warp by picking up 1- or 2-inch-wide sections and pulling on each in turn. This is done all across the warp, always picking up the same number of threads and always pulling with an equal force. Give the beam another complete turn and tighten again.

Sometimes tighten from the right to left, sometimes from left to right, sometimes from the centre outwards, in order to cancel out any inequality in the force applied. The simplest way to apply an equal force is to pick up the section and lean back with one's full weight. This becomes quite a rhythmic sequence of movements: pick up section, comb ends out through fingers to equalize their length, lean back, lean forwards, repeat.

If the warp is being beamed tightly enough, the hand holding the sections will soon develop blisters. So carry a small 1 inch thick rod in that hand, and each time twist the warp once around it, then pull on the rod, see Fig. 17 (b).

Roll in warp sticks where required. After sticks have been inserted, give the beam two turns before tightening, otherwise they will slip.

Headless nails knocked into the beam, the width of the warp apart, will stop it spreading. (See Fig. 352 (a) in Chapter on Warp-Face Rugs.)

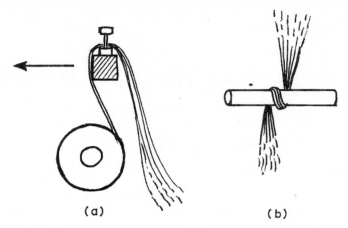

Fig. 17. (a) Beaming a warp by the one-man method (b) Method of gripping the warp sections

The warp wound on the beam should feel hard and solid. Remember that if the warp is beamed at a tension lower than that used when weaving, it will bite into itself and any semblance of equal tension will be lost. Once the warp is wound on, reverse its direction around the back beam and thread the shafts normally.

B. Using Sectional Warp Beam

A sectional warp beam is ideal for rug warps. It is quicker, very efficient and guarantees a warp of perfectly even tension for as long a rug as is wanted. The beam itself should be very strong with metal pins, (about $\frac{1}{4}$ inch diameter) every 2 inches, to separate the sections.

Though a conventional tension box may be adequate, a slightly more complex one has advantages. See Fig. 18 where (a) is a cross-section and (b) a view from above.

The ends come from a creel and enter the tension box through a collecting plate at the right. They then pass over bar A, under B, over C and through a section of reed D. They now pass under bar E, around the drum F, under G, through the adjustable reed H and over bar I to the warp beam.

The drum F, is a wooden cylinder about 4 inches diameter and as long as the box is wide. It turns on a central axle. It is covered for most of its length with some material, e.g., thick rubber, to prevent the warp ends slipping (shaded in Fig. 18(b)). The rest of its length is uncovered and over this part runs a leather strap, (dotted line in Fig. 18 (a), labelled in Fig. 18 (b)). One end of the strap is fastened to the floor of the box, the other passes over a wheel under the collecting plate and then hangs free. Weights can be attached to its free end. Thus when the drum is turned by the warp ends (as they are wound on to the sectional beam), the weighted strap acts as a simple friction brake, and as high a tension as is wanted can be applied to the warp. As the ends cannot slip

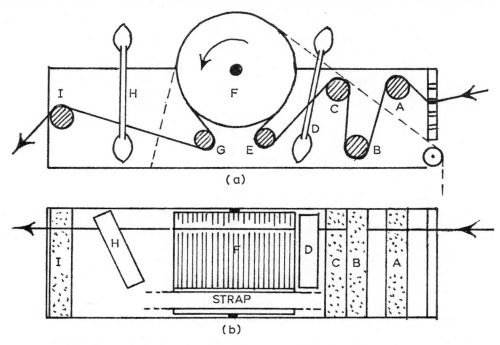

Fig. 18. Tension Box for sectional warping. (a) Side view (b) View from above

on the drum, the latter also ensures that an equal length of each end is delivered to the beam. The final reed H is mounted so that it can swing to give minute adjustments to the width of the sections.

Most of the warps for weft-face rugs described in the following chapters have six ends to the inch. So only twelve ends at a time have to be dealt with by the tension box.

C. Putting a Warp on a Vertical Rug Frame

In the normal method of putting a spiral warp (see Fig 2 (b)) on a simple vertical frame, a ball or cheese of yarn is continually carried around the upper and lower beams. But there is an ingenious method, used in the Middle East, whereby the package of yarn is never moved; the warping is done entirely with a blind *loop* of yarn.

It is simpler if there are two workers, who stand on opposite sides of the frame. To the left side piece of the frame a thick stick is tied so that it projects horizontally and nearly reaches the right side piece. See Fig. 19. The ball of yarn lies on the floor beside the worker on the near-side of the frame. He ties the end of it to the stick, then passes a *loop of yarn* over the upper beam to the far-side worker. The latter draws the loop down the back of the frame and passes it, under the lower beam, to the near-side

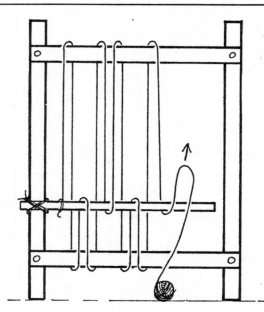

Fig. 19
A method of warping a
vertical rug frame

worker, who slips it on the stick. The near-side worker then puts the yarn (that runs to the ball) behind the stick and passes a second loop of yarn upwards as before. This is repeated, always working towards the right, until the full width has been warped. The final end of the yarn is then knotted to the stick. Fig. 19 shows diagrammatically the course taken by the yarn as the third loop is begun. The stick is untied from the side piece and serves as a firm foundation for the weaving that starts directly above it. Whenever the warp is moved on, the stick is naturally carried round with it. When the rug is finished, the stick is slid out leaving loops of warp at both ends of the rug.

Note—That each time a loop is passed around the frame, two ends have been warped.
   —That the way the warp loops wrap around the stick (upward and downward loops alternating in strict succession) establishes their order.
   —That throughout the whole process, the ball of yarn lies on the floor.

2. TYING TO FRONT STICK

After the warp is drawn in and sleyed, it has to be tied to the front stick, and the method that wastes least warp is the following.

Pick up a 2 inch wide section of the warp. Comb the fingers through it, so that all the ends it contains are of equal tension. Divide it into halves and knot these two halves around the front stick with a reef (square) knot. At either selvage, tie a much smaller group of ends, i.e., those that come through the first two dents of the reed.

As each knot is tied, test the resulting warp tension, always comparing it with that of the first part of the warp that was tied. If it is compared with the adjacent section, which was tied last, there is far less control and the tension may gradually increase with each successive knot.

After the first tying, push the cross sticks back to the back beam and secure them and make sure every end is running in a straight line from that beam to the reed. Tighten the knots where required.

Now tie a piece of heavy cord to one end of the front stick and thread it through the

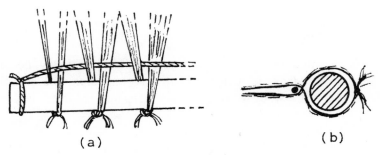

Fig. 20. Tying warp to front stick

warp as shown in Fig. 20 (a) i.e., pass it over the ends that pass over the stick and under the ends that pass under the stick. Pull it tight and tie to the opposite end of the front stick. This brings all parts of the warp to the same level, see cross-section at Fig. 20 (b). This is important as the front stick, to be strong enough, may have to be an inch thick.

3. OPENING OUT WARP GROUPS

However the warp is knotted to the front stick, its ends are crowded together at each knot, and they have to be opened out to the spacing that exists at the reed. The simplest way to do this, is to weave three or four picks (in plain weave sheds if possible) of some very heavy material, such as warp linen used six to eightfold. These are thrown and only beaten after the *final* pick. It may need several blows with the batten to drive these picks up against the front stick. The warp should then be evenly spaced or it may need two or three more picks woven in the same manner.

This manœuvre also shows up any loose ends, which will loop upwards over the picks, or any loosely knotted groups. The latter reveal themselves by a curving of the fell away from the front stick.

These preliminary picks (and those put in at the far end of the rug) also act as temporary weft protectors for the finished rug, before a proper rug finish is carried out.

The temple is fixed into these picks before the weaving of the rug proper begins.

4. WEAVING THE HEADING

Whatever weave is used for the main part of the rug, it is best to begin and end with a heading of plain weave. Naturally this is not possible with some threadings, such as a straight draft on three shafts. The heading can be $\frac{1}{2}$–2 inches in depth and can be woven of one of the weft yarns used in the rug. It provides a firm basis against which to carry out any of the rug finishes and an opportunity to use any of the two-shuttle patterns.

5. STARTING THE WEFT

If the thick weft used in a weft-face rug is begun in the normal way, i.e., an end, left hanging out in the first pick, is tucked into the second pick, the resulting double thickness of weft will not beat down to cover the warp and the latter will show at this point.

In Fig. 21 (a), the weft has been thrown from left to right. Split the weft into two halves. Here the weft is fourfold so each half consists of two threads. Bring one half, A, out of the shed a little short of the selvage. Wrap the other half, B, twice round the selvage thread. Reintroduce it into the same shed and bring it out two raised warp ends beyond A.

> *Note*—That B passes over two ends as it re-enters the shed.
> —That the only extra thickness of weft is between the emerging points of A and B and here the thickness is only increased by a half.
> —As this is the beginning of the rug, A and B have to be darned upwards (i.e., away from the weaver).

The same diagram can serve as an illustration of finishing the final weft in a rug. Where thinner wefts are used, the normal ways of starting and finishing are possible.

6. JOINING WEFTS

As with starting and finishing wefts, the aim here is to avoid too much extra thickness of weft. This is done by tapering both wefts where they overlap.

In Fig. 21 (b), two wefts consisting of four threads are joined. The white (old) weft has been thrown from left to right. Half, A, is brought out under end 11 and half, B, some inches away under end 3. The black (new) weft is also thrown from left to right. Half of it, C, is brought out two raised ends away from A, and the other half, D, two raised ends away from B.

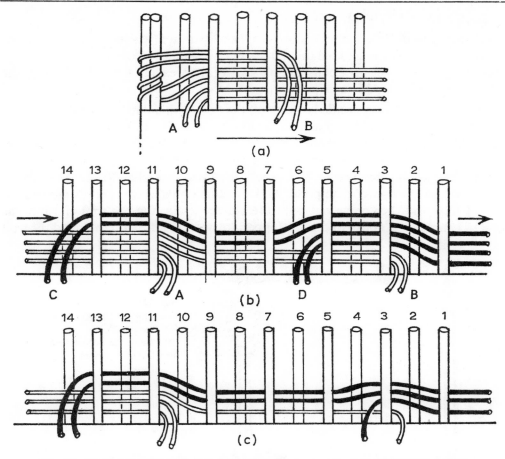

Fig. 21. (a) Starting the weft (b) and (c) Joining two wefts, fourfold and threefold

Note—There are two places where the weft thickness is increased by a half.
— The number of ends brought out depends on the number that it is practical to darn into the rug in one place. Two ends of normal 2-ply carpet wool can be darned in easily, so two have been brought out together.

Fig. 21 (c), in which the two wefts consist of three threads each, shows how it is still possible to bring the ends out in pairs.

Almost all colour changes in a rug can be carried out as weft joins. It is not necessary, for instance, to finish one colour at one selvage and start the next colour at the opposite selvage. Weft joins can be made anywhere across the width of the rug. If for any reason the rug needs building up slightly at one side, then make all the weft joins at this point: and make them so that there is more extra weft thickness than shown in Fig. 21 (b) and (c).

7. DARNING IN THE WEFT

All short lengths of weft that protrude from the rug surface (whether due to weft joins or knots in the weft), must be darned in as the weaving proceeds.

As this process takes up a considerable part of the weaving time of a flat rug, the following quick method is a help.

A 4 inch long packing needle is required, the type with a flattened curved end, see Fig. 22 (a). Blunt the point on a stone or file. Make a fine wire noose, as shown in Fig. 22(b). It can be twisted from a dismantled wire heald. The noose itself should be small enough to slide easily through the eye of the needle.

Thread the noose into the eye of the needle and using it as a handle, push the needle into the rug at the appropriate point. Make it slide down in front of a warp end for about ¾ inch and then come out onto the surface again. Put the weft end into the noose. Then pull the noose to the left (upper arrow in Fig. 22 (b)) to thread the weft

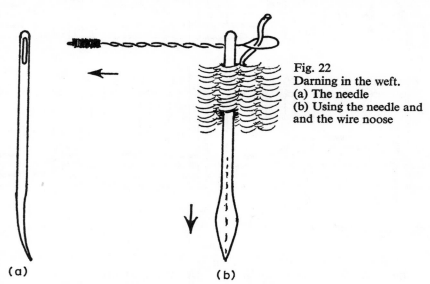

Fig. 22
Darning in the weft.
(a) The needle
(b) Using the needle and
and the wire noose

(a)   (b)

into the needle, and pull the needle downwards (lower arrow) to darn the weft into the rug. Then trim the darned-in weft threads by pulling on them and cutting them flush with the rug.

Note—The needle moves down towards the weaver.

     —The needle is blunted so that it will slide down in front of a warp end and not pierce it.

     —A piece of weft only ½ inch long or shorter can be darned in, using scissor points to push it into the wire noose.

     —It is important always to give the weft end a pull before darning it in, as there is often unwanted slack in the weft near its point of emergence.

It is important to darn the weft down the correct warp end. Where two weft threads emerge at the same point, darn them down the warp end they would next cross if they were weaving in normal plain weave sequence. Thus, referring back to Fig. 21 (b), weft A is darned down end 10, weft B down end 2, C down 14 and D down 6.

Where two wefts emerge from either side of an end (see end 3 in Fig. 21 (c)) then they are darned together down this end.

Always try to space out weft joins evenly over the surface of the rug, so that any slight unevenness caused by the darning is well distributed. When darning in a tough yarn, such as horsehair, unply and untwist the protruding piece with the needle's point, pulling out any loose fibres. This reduces its bulk to a tapering bunch of fibres, that can be unobtrusively darned in.

8. WEAVING

A. Warp and Weft Tension

Always weave with the warp as tight as possible, because the tighter (i.e., the more rod-like) the warp ends are, the easier it is to beat successive picks of weft close against each other.

In a weft-face rug, the warp ends run in a straight line through the centre of the structure, and the weft curves over and under these ends. Therefore it is necessary that each pick be laid in the shed with enough slack or extra length to make this serpentine course possible. This is why waving (also called bowing, bubbling and curving) the weft is necessary, with every pick of a weft-face rug.

WAVING THE WEFT

I. Throw the shuttle from right to left. Hold the right selvage thread with the right hand and pull the weft with left hand. This both pulls in the small amount of slack that always exists in the previous pick and ensures that the weft fits tightly round the selvage. Leave the weft well towards the reed at the left selvage, so that slack can easily be drawn into the shed.

II. Keeping the shed open, work from right to left (i.e., following the direction of the shuttle's flight) waving the weft thus:

Grip the weft between right thumb and index at point A (Fig. 23), i.e., where the crest of the first wave is to be. Push down the weft at point B with a finger of the left hand to make the trough of the wave. Repeat for points C and D, E and F. It is important that the weft be gripped as described. Otherwise making the second wave will just draw in slack from the first and flatten it.

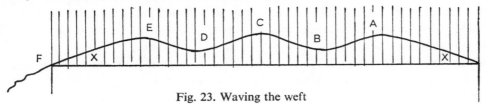

Fig. 23. Waving the weft

Note—There should be approximately one wave for each foot width of the rug.

—Keep the troughs of the waves at least 2 inches from the fell of the rug, otherwise the weft will loop out at this point when beaten. But make the last wave join the fell of the rug at the left selvage.

—Although the shed must be open while waving the weft, slightly diminishing its depth does help to control the positioning of the waves. So raise the appropriate pedal a small amount while waving the weft.

—Steep-sided curves are hardly ever necessary. This applies especially at the selvages, where angle X should be small, and so overcome the tendency for the weft to be slack at either selvage. More slack is always needed at the centre of the rug than at the selvage.

—The size of the waves varies with the weave being used. The more intersections of warp and weft, the bigger the waves should be and the more waves there should be. Thus plain weave needs more waves than a twill with the same warp set.

—The waves also vary with the type of weft yarn used. Thus with an elastic yarn, like wool, one wave per foot width of rug is satisfactory. But with a non-elastic yarn, like linen, it will be found better to make more and smaller waves. Also the more inelastic a yarn is the more accurately the waves must be made. A slight excess of yarn in any place will loop out.

—It is easy to have a perfect-seeming face to the rug but with loops of weft protruding at the back, so inspect the back periodically.

III. Having waved the weft successfully, change the shed and beat. Beating on the opposite shed helps to even out the extra length of weft across the full width of the rug.

Then repeat the above sequence. This time the shuttle will be thrown from left to right. So after the weft has been tightened around the left selvage the waving is carried out from left to right and the hands switch roles. The left hand now grips the crests of the waves and the right hand pushes down the troughs.

Change shed and beat.

As every pick of weft has to be curved in this way before being beaten in, it is very important to develop the ability to do it both quickly and accurately. Exactly the same amount of slack must go into each pick, hour after hour, day after day. An apparently well woven rug will, in use, gradually show by its undulating selvage how and where the weft tension varied. However, if two yarns of differing elasticity are being woven in stripes, it is practically impossible to so adjust the tension that the selvages remain straight.

When weaving on an upright loom and beating with a rug fork, start by making one large curve from selvage to selvage. The curve can be kept in position by almost closing the shed. Beat this curve in its centre, making two half-width curves. Beat these two curves in their centres making four quarter-width curves. Continue thus, beating each curve in its centre, until all the weft is dealt with.

B. Beating

As already mentioned the batten should be weighted with metal, the wider the rug the heavier the piece of metal.

For greater efficiency the batten should be handled in such a way that the last pick is squeezed up against the preceding picks; it should not be used as a hammer dealing the weft sharp blows and then rebounding. So grip the batten with both hands and then lean back on the loom seat, adding the weaver's weight to that of the batten. This is far less tiring than sitting upright and pulling the batten with the arm muscles.

As the last pick is always beaten with the shed changed, it should stay in position.

C. Cone Winding

The difficulty in learning to wind a cone by hand is that in order that the cone be firmly wound, it has to revolve at a high speed, and the beginner finds it hard to control the thread at this speed.

Begin by passing the yarn once round (in the direction the cone is going to turn), so that it is caught under the part coming from the hank, see Fig. 24 (a). Then as soon as the cone starts to revolve, move the hand that is guiding the yarn quickly backwards and forwards, so that the yarn does not build up in any one place. This is to ensure that the first few turns of yarn grip the cone securely. Thereafter the guiding hand can move more slowly.

Never bring the yarn nearer than 1 inch from the top of the cone and nearer than $\frac{1}{4}$ inch from the bottom of the cone. These furthest extremes of the yarns traverse should be reached almost as soon as winding begins, and each succeeding traverse should be shorter. The pear-shaped outline shown in Fig. 24 (b) is a good one to aim at. Do not try to save time by overfilling cones.

(a)   (b)

Fig. 24. Cone Winding. (a) How to start (b) Shape to aim at

When winding a cone at full speed, the wool passes so quickly through the fingers that to avoid burning them, they just guide the yarn and in no way grip it. The necessary tension in the yarn is best obtained by having some simple friction brake on the skeiner, e.g., a weighted leather loop hung on the axle. Such brakes are supplied with industrial skeiners and are also useful as the skeiner stops almost immediately the winding does and so does not overrun.

When winding slippery yarns, first wind a few turns of ordinary yarn to provide a foundation, and move the guiding hand more quickly than normal as the slippery yarn is wound on top.

A badly-wound cone with loops of yarn coming off the top can best be unwound from the base rather than the top. Keep handy a dowel rod with a wooden block fastened at one end, see Fig. 25 (a). Pass this up through the centre of the cone. Then, holding this rod, let the yarn be pulled off, as shown in Fig. 25 (b), straight onto a fresh cone. The ballooning of the yarn prevents it fouling the cone's base until the latter is practically empty.

A yarn, such as camel belting yarn, that kinks as it dries after scouring or dyeing, can be wound onto cones while still slightly damp. Drying thus, under tension, it develops no kinks.

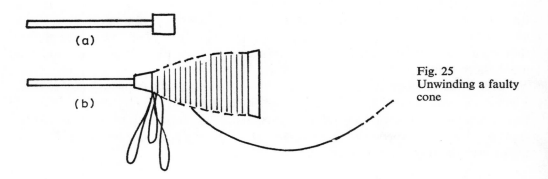

(a)

(b)

Fig. 25
Unwinding a faulty cone

D. Shuttle Winding and Throwing

Assuming the various weft yarns are wound on cones, stand these on the floor with their ends hanging over a warp stick, or a stretched piece of string, so they do not get tangled. Try to arrange them so that colours that will be wound together on the shuttle stand close to each other. If this is not possible, the weft threads can be led up through a reed supported on two chairs, to ensure that each thread comes off vertically, see Fig. 26 (a).

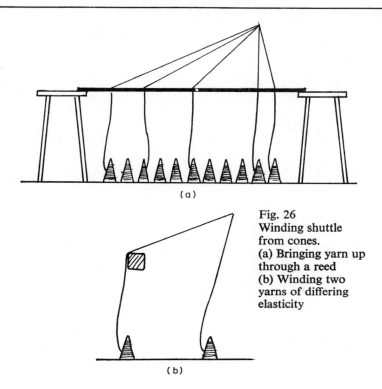

(a)

Fig. 26
Winding shuttle
from cones.
(a) Bringing yarn up
through a reed
(b) Winding two
yarns of differing
elasticity

(b)

It is a false economy to overfill shuttles. Wind on so much weft that the shuttle can be thrown, not poked, through the shed right from the start. If a weft has to be joined during winding, tie either a reef knot or the overhand slip knot shown in Fig. 29 (a).

If two wefts of unequal elasticity are being used, wind the less elastic one under a higher tension. Assuming both wefts come from cones, then the less elastic one can drag over some bar as shown in Fig. 26 (b), and the other weft can go straight from cone to shuttle. Without some such precaution, there will always be some extra slack in the inelastic weft when the shuttle is thrown.

The one disadvantage of a ski-shuttle is its length. So throw it like a normal shuttle, with an index finger on its point giving the final flick, but catch it in its centre. To catch it at its end stretches the arms unnecessarily. With practice the shuttle can be caught thus without looking. Unwind from the ski-shuttle only the minimum amount of weft that will allow it to be thrown across the width of the rug.

If several shuttles are being used in a certain sequence, put down the shuttle that has just been thrown in a place that accords with that sequence. Thus if shuttle A and B are being thrown in a pick-and-pick sequence, when A has been thrown it is placed next to the weaver, so B is close to the fell of the rug and at hand to be picked up. When B is thrown it is placed next to the weaver, pushing A up towards the fell.

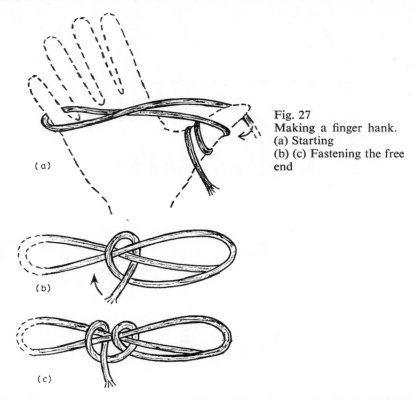

Fig. 27
Making a finger hank.
(a) Starting
(b) (c) Fastening the free
end

More complex sequences demand more complex placings of the shuttles but there is always a logical way which will save time and tangles.

With a very wide rug, the weaver may not have sufficient stretch to both throw and catch the shuttle without shifting his position on the seat. In such a case, throw normally but catch the shuttle as it emerges at the opposite selvage by suddenly closing the shed. Then move across and pick it up.

E. Making Finger Hanks

It is often useful to have weft wound in small packages, and not on a shuttle, for instance, in soumak, and the other hand-manipulated techniques. Finger hanks (also called Butterflies) are made in the following way from cones or hanks or balls of yarn.

First carry the end of the yarn or yarns twice round the thumb to anchor it, see Fig 27 (a). Then wind the yarn in a continuous figure-of-eight between the thumb and little finger, with the hand stretched wide open.

When enough yarn has been wound, cut the yarn from its source. Finish by carrying it around the thumb and tying the end round the waist of the figure-of-eight with two hitches. These are shown in Fig. 27 (b) and (c), and they are tied with the left hand while the finger hank is still on the right hand.

Remove the finger hank from the little finger first, then from the thumb. The end of yarn wrapped round the thumb, is the end that is used and it will pull out of the finger hank, without tangling. As long as the final knot follows a turn round the thumb, as described above, it will undo itself as the finger hank finishes.

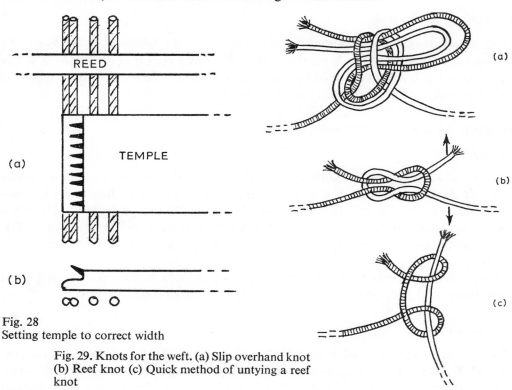

(a)

REED

TEMPLE

(a)

(b)

∞ O O

Fig. 28
Setting temple to correct width

(a)

(b)

(c)

Fig. 29. Knots for the weft. (a) Slip overhand knot
(b) Reef knot (c) Quick method of untying a reef
knot

F. Temple

Set the width of the temple, by holding it upside down over the warp as it emerges from the reed. The bases of the temple's pins should be in line with the first warp interspace at each side. See Fig. 28 where (a) is a view from above and (b) is a cross-section.

Use the temple right from the start of the rug, inserting it first into the preliminary picks of thick yarn which open out the warp groups.

Move the temple up after every half inch of weaving. Insert it so that it is as close to the fell of the rug as possible and ensure that the pins are really embedded in their correct position before the two halves of the temple are pushed down and locked.

By slightly varying the temple setting it is possible to counteract the effect on the selvage of yarns of differing elasticity, i.e., set it wider for a stripe of the more elastic yarn. This can be very important, if a large rug is being woven in strips and absolutely straight selvages are therefore essential. The amount by which the temple setting is altered can only be found by trial and error.

Always release the temple if a rug is being left for any length of time, otherwise it will cause a bulge at the selvage.

G. Turning on the Warp

With a well-designed loom about 6 inches can be woven before the warp has to be turned on. First release the tension on the cloth beam, then let off another 6 inches from the warp beam and finally tighten the cloth beam. Before resuming weaving, beat the weft hard several times and retighten the cloth beam.

H. Knots Encountered in Weaving

IN THE WEFT

Beat the pick, then untie the knot. If it is the overhand slipknot, shown in Fig. 29 (a), just pull the two free ends. If it is a reef, capsize the knot by pulling either the two parts that point to the right (arrows in Fig. 29 (b)) or the two parts that point to the left. In either case it becomes·a slip knot and can be quickly undone, see Fig. 29 (c). Bring out the two ends of the weft on either side of a raised warp end and darn them in later.

If yarn is bought with knots in it, they are generally weaver's knots. It is simpler to leave these, and later pick them undone with a needle's point and darn the ends in.

IN THE WARP

The warp of a weft-face rug is such that it should not break under normal circumstances. However, a badly thrown shuttle may foul the warp and break an end. Mend it by knotting a new piece of warp (with a weaver's knot), to the far part of the broken end, and darning it into the rug down beside the near part of the broken end. After 3 inches of darning, bring the thread to the surface and fasten it round a stout pin, set in the rug. Because a warp end runs straight through a weft-face rug, there are no curves in its course to anchor it (as in a 50/50 plain weave structure), so it is best to leave this pin in position until the rug is finished.

I. Marking the Length of the Rug

It is as well to make a habit of marking the length of a rug every 6 inches as it is woven. This is not always essential; but it can be, as in the case of a large rug being woven in strips, when some motif or stripe has to tally across the joins.

Keep a curved needle threaded with warp yarn by the loom. Only put in a marker when the warp is slack, i.e., do it while the warp is being turned on.

At 6 inches, tie a reef knot.
At 1 foot, tie one overhand knot.
At 1 foot 6 inches, tie a reef.
At 2 foot, tie two overhand knots.
Carry on thus, tying as many overhands as there are feet in length, and tying a reef at each intermediate 6 inch mark.
At 5 feet, tie two overhand knots on top of each other. This makes a double-size knot.
At 6 feet, tie the above double overhand, plus a normal overhand.
At 10 feet, tie two double overhand knots, and so on.

One way to ensure that the markers are accurately spaced is to make two notches, 6 inches apart, on a strip of wood, see Fig. 30. Place this on the edge of the slack rug, so that the last marker is in one notch, and then insert the threaded needle down into the rug through the other notch.

If accuracy of length is essential, test the markers by inserting one every yard in the following way. Release the cloth beam ratchet, so that a loop of rug can be pulled out towards the weaver. Into this loop, put a strong bar with cords at each end which are

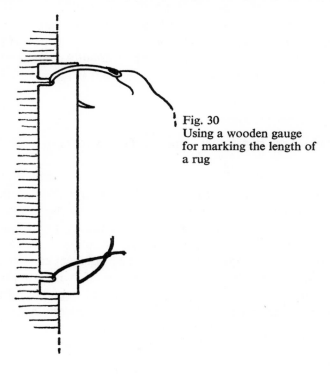

Fig. 30
Using a wooden gauge
for marking the length of
a rug

tied to something solid, e.g., a wall. Pull out enough rug, so that a yard is exposed, see Fig. 31. Using a wooden or steel yard measure (not a tape measure which can be very inaccurate), put in the next marker, say, for 6 feet, 1 yard from the 3 foot marker. These yardly checks cancel out any inaccuracies in the 6 inch markers.

In order to be able to put the first yard marker in thus, the apron or strings, stretching from cloth beam to front stick, have to be longer than usual. But this is in any case desirable, see below.

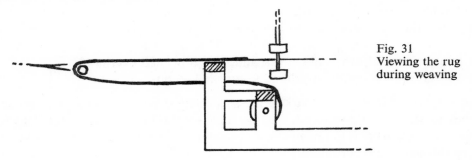

Fig. 31
Viewing the rug
during weaving

J. Viewing the Rug during Weaving

It is often used as an argument against weaving rugs on a horizontal loom, as compared with a vertical loom, that so little of the finished work can be seen. But at least a yard of the finished rug can be quickly exposed in the manner described above. Much more, say 6 foot can be exposed if a really long rug is being woven. If the weaver then stands on the breast beam of the loom or something equally high, he can obtain a true view of that section of the finished rug.

K. Taking the Rug from the Loom

After the final pick of the rug proper, weave about six picks of a heavy weft, as used at the beginning.

Turn the warp on, until the fell of the rug is at the breast beam. Now the rug finish to be used dictates where the warp is to be cut. The minimum length for even the simplest rug finish is about 8 inches. So draw a line across the warp at least 8 inches from the end of the rug. A wax crayon drawn along the edge of a warp stick, pushed hard onto the warp, will make a sufficient mark.

Now, every 3 or 4 inches across the warp, cut two adjacent ends at the marked line and tie them in a half-knot or a bow. This is simply a safety measure to hold the thick picks in position until the rug receives its proper finish. Then cut all the way across, following the marked line, knotting the far ends so that they do not fall back through the reed.

As the rug is unwound from the cloth beam, examine its reverse side carefully and

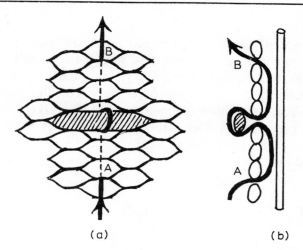

Fig. 32
Darning in a weft float.
(a) Front view
(b) Longitudinal section

(a)   (b)

darn in any weft threads that need it. Where a weft thread floats instead of weaves it can be darned in thus. Fig. 32 (a), shows a weft (shaded), floating over three ends where it should be passing over one, under one, in plain weave sequence. Thread a short length of warp on the darning needle, only a single thickness even if the warp is being used double in the rug. Insert it into the rug about 1 inch below the float, point A in Fig. 32 (a), and slide it along the warp end that the float should have passed under, bringing it out under the float. Carry the thread over the float as shown, re-enter it into the rug beyond the float and slide it up the same end as before, for a further 1 inch or so to emerge at point B. Pull the entering and emerging ends of this thread apart and slide the thread up and down a few times. The float will sink back into the rug, and disappear into the weave. The very diagrammatic longitudinal section in Fig. 32 (b) will make this clear.

When all repairs have been completed on the back of the rug, untie the rug from the front stick, again tying a knot every 3 or 4 inches to keep the initial thick picks in position.

This is the time to weigh the rug for costing, before parts of the warp are trimmed off as the rug finish is completed.

L. Problems Connected with Weaving a Large Rug in Strips

As no weaver will ever have a loom big enough to weave in one piece the largest rugs required of him, it is best to develop a technique of weaving rugs in strips and later joining them. This has the advantage that any sized rug can be woven by one weaver on one loom.

WARP TENSION

A warp equally tensioned is essential. If as weaving proceeds, the warp becomes slack, say, on the right side and nothing is done to correct this, then the right side of the finished rug will be longer than the left, and the rug will lie on the floor in a slight curve. If it is straightened, the right side will buckle. So either start with a perfectly made warp or correct any tension inequalities the moment they arise. It sometimes happens that a warp becomes progressively slacker towards one side (as if the warp beam were conical rather than cylindrical), this is generally due to a badly placed warp stick. It can be corrected thus.

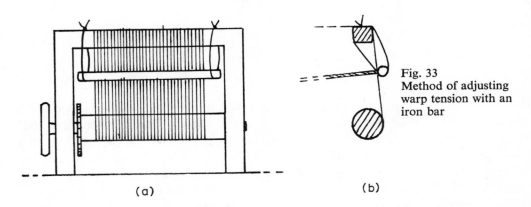

Fig. 33
Method of adjusting warp tension with an iron bar

(a)   (b)

Hang a strong metal bar half-way between the back beam and the warp beam, see Fig. 33 (a) and (b). Attach a thick cord to each end of the bar and bring these cords forward and tie them to some upright of the loom frame. Then if the warp is slacker towards the right side shorten the right-hand cord.

LENGTH OF STRIPS

Measure accurately as already described. It is safest to weave a few extra inches and then adjust the length as the strips are sewn up. See below.

WEAVING THE STRIPS

There is probably an overall design or plan for the rug, but this may not show every slight colour change. So as the first strip is woven, make a note of where each colour change is made. For simplicity give each colour a number, and use these numbers rather than names, in the notes. Then follow the notes when weaving subsequent strips. If a rug has pick-and-pick stripes, say, in black and white, remember that if one strip has a black stripe at its selvage, then the next strip must have a white stripe.

JOINING THE STRIPS

The following sequence ensures accurate results.

(1) Fringe all the strips at one end.

(2) Sew the strips together, starting from the fringed ends. Stop a few inches short of the unfringed ends.

(3) Make a plan of the rug, the actual size, on the floor, chalking or otherwise marking the rectangle exactly.

(4) Put the rug on the plan with its fringed end along the appropriate chalked line and the sides of the rug along the side lines. Then the fourth chalked line shows exactly where the other rug fringe should be.

(5) Unweave the end of the rug to bring the fringe to the right place. As the initial picks (heading) are probably different from the main part of the rug, unpick the correct amount of the main part, then slide the heading along the warp ends into its new position.

(6) Bring the sewing right up to the corrected ends of the strips and fringe these ends.

This method may sound over-complex, but experience shows it is necessary. It is very easy otherwise to make a large rug that proves to be more a parellelogram than a rectangle.

Always try to obtain a plan of the site for the rug, for this will show which of its dimensions are absolute (e.g., wall-to-wall,) and which can be exceeded or diminished by an inch or so.

The sewing is best done with a large curved needle. If the stitches will be quite invisible, as with a pile rug, use ordinary warp yarn; but if they may show, as with a flat woven rug, dye the warp yarn an appropriate colour.

The stitch used is shown in Fig. 34 (a). Kneel on the floor, moving backwards as the sewing proceeds. Insert the needle downwards into the first warp interspace of one strip and bring it out between the two strips, see Fig. 34 (a). Then insert it downwards into the first warp interspace of the other strip and up again between the strips. Keep the stitches tight by holding the emerging thread with the non-sewing hand.

An alternative method is to enter the needle into the weft loops only, as they turn around the selvage. The needle slides down beside the selvage thread for $\frac{1}{4}$ to $\frac{1}{2}$ an inch, then emerges between the strips. It then enters the weft loops of the other strip, see Fig. 34 (b). This join is quite invisible but less secure.

Join on a new length of yarn with a reef knot. Capsize the knot as shown in Fig. 29 (b) and (c), slide it down snug against the rug, then uncapsize it. Begin and finish the sewing with a knot and darn all ends into the rug.

Note—It is wise before sewing to join the two strips every 2 foot or so with a temporary tie. This will stop the strips shifting while sewing.

—That a strip newly cut from the loom should never be joined to a strip completed some days previously. This is because it takes some time for the rug to assume its final length. According to the elasticity of the warp this will be a varying number of inches shorter than its off-loom length.

—When joining strips of pile rug, work from the back, i.e., have the pile downwards. Use the scissor points to tuck the pile of each strip out of the way, so that it does not foul the sewing thread.

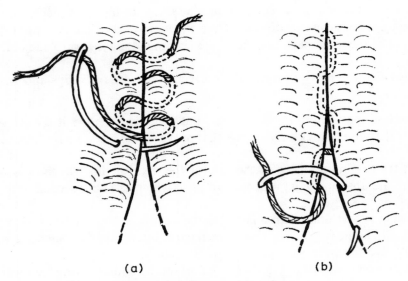

(a)　　　　　　　(b)

Fig. 34. Joining two strips of rug

4 · Weft-face Rugs in Plain Weave

PART ONE: TECHNIQUES IN WHICH THE WEFT RUNS FROM SELVAGE TO SELVAGE

1. GENERAL DETAILS

A. Introduction

In weft-face plain weave rugs, the surface is made up entirely by closely beaten weft, on which therefore the colour, design and texture all depend. The warp lies hidden in the middle of the thickness of the rug and only appears at the fringes. It is like an invisible skeleton which the weft clothes with flesh. In the finished rug, the warp ends lie as straight parallel lines, but the weft takes a serpentine course, curving over and under the warp. So a cross-section of the rug is as shown in Fig. 35. This gives the clue

Fig. 35. Cross-section of a weft-face rug

to two essentials in weaving weft-face rugs, a very tight warp to allow the weft to be well beaten down and a very loose weft to allow of its serpentine course. With slight exceptions, these rugs are identical on both sides and so are fully reversible in use.

B. Warp and Weft Settings

In England during this century, there has risen a convention that the warp for a rug (generally a 7/7s cotton used double) is always set at 3 ends per inch and that the weft is always a 6-ply rug wool. This is firmly established and manufacturers advertise a reed with 3 dents per inch as a rug reed. Although this does give a possible texture for a rug, it is certainly not the only one, as the following will show.

In describing warp settings in rugs, one difficulty is often encountered. This is that the warp is very often used twofold, threefold or even fourfold, simply because a yarn thick enough to be used singly is not easily available. So there is a difference in the number of ends per inch on the warp beam and the number of actual *working* ends per inch in the weaving.

By a working end is meant the warp unit that works independently in the weaving, be it a single thread or many threads working as a single thread. So the number of working ends per inch gives the number of dents and healds per inch needed. Also, in the case of plain weave, it gives the number of warp/weft intersections per inch, which is the chief factor in controlling the texture of the rug. The best way to avoid confusion is to speak of a rug warp with, say '12 ends per inch, double in the heald, therefore 6 working ends per inch'. This method of describing warp settings will be used throughout this book. To give another example, if a standard warp with 6 ends per inch is used, this can be arranged double in the heald to give 3 working e.p.i., or alternately double and single in the heald to give 4 working e.p.i., or 4 single, 1 double in the heald to give 5 working e.p.i., or singly in the heald to give 6 working e.p.i.

The use of a multiple warp is so much a habit that it is well to remember that there is no special virtue in it, and that a single thicker yarn is, if anything, better being more compact. In the latter case, the ends per inch in the warp and the working ends per inch in the weaving would be the same number. However, two advantages go with a multiple warp. A long warp can be put on the loom and then split into different numbers of working e.p.i. as is required by each successive rug, following the examples given above. A corollary to this is that the weaver need only keep a stock of one standard warp yarn for weft-face rugs.

Coming to actual settings of the warp and weft, the rule governing weft-face plain weave is that the more warp there is per inch (i.e., the thicker the working ends are or the more ends there are), the finer the weft must be that crosses it. If the correct relationship between warp and weft is obtained, a rug of any desired thickness can be woven and it will possess a firm practical texture. A table can be constructed to give a rough guide to this relationship, see Fig. 36. As materials, a warp of 6/10s lea linen is taken and a weft of 2/50s carpet wool; the settings for other materials can be worked out from this basis.

Note—That the first column shows working ends per inch, the actual ends per inch in the warp are obtained by multiplying this by the number in the second column.

—Where alternatives are given in the warp and the weft columns, the higher numbers will always give a firmer rug, but they may need heavier beating than some weavers can muster. So if the loom or the weaver is not made for heavy beating, use the lower numbers.

Working e.p.i.	Warp 6/10s *linen*	Weft 2/50s wool	Character of Rug
3	2–3 fold	4–6 fold	THICK
4	2 fold	3–4 fold	
5	1–2 fold	2 fold	
6	1 fold	1 fold	THIN

Fig. 36 Table showing relationship of warp and weft in a weft-face rug

The table illustrates the rule already mentioned, that the more warp there is per inch the finer the weft must be. But it also shows that there are always three variables, which must be correctly related to each other to give a satisfactory rug, namely, the working e.p.i., the warp thickness and the weft thickness. Once the rigidity of this table is departed from, it is necessary to juggle with these three variables. The problem can arise in several forms.

For instance, a certain specific weft may have to cross a certain specific warp. Then the third variable, the working e.p.i., has to be adjusted until a suitable texture is achieved. Or the loom may be set up with a certain warp set at so many working e.p.i. and the problem then is to vary the weft thickness until the correct texture is produced. Or again, an unusually stiff and stubborn weft may be encountered, and then both warp thickness and its setting have to be varied to reach a satisfactory solution. Remember all the time, the aim is to make a firm-textured rug.

The above juggling with variables implies the weaving of experimental samples. This, rather than following recipes and books, is the best way to acquire an insight into the problem. If this principle of three variables is understood, then the two most obvious faults in weft-face rugs will be avoided. These are either having the warp too thin for the weft (or vice versa) giving a spongy, sleazy, rug that a finger can poke through, or having the warp too thick for the weft (or vice versa), giving a hard, board-like rug which will not lie flat and in which the weft barely covers the warp.

Apart from the thickness, there is another property in yarns which affects the warp/ weft relationship. This is their firmness or degree of compressibility. For example, to judge from its visible diameter alone, a horsehair yarn used two- or threefold might be thought suitable for the weft. But its lack of compressibility will prevent it beating down and covering the warp and so it may have to be used singly. Though really obvious, this is mentioned to emphasize how rough a guide the table is. It is based on a certain warp and weft, and a different table could be constructed for any combination of other warp and weft yarns.

Most weft-face rugs woven by western hand weavers nowadays, have a weft far thicker than the warp. But the reverse relationship is the one typical of these rugs in the past and among most weavers in the East today.

These have a different surface, with strong warpway ribs made by the fine weft curving over the thick solid warp ends. It might be thought that this relationship would have the disadvantage of slowness in weaving as there are so many more picks per inch. But as the fine weft can be wound onto normal bobbins and thrown in ordinary shuttles, this is not so. Also as the warp makes up so much of the weight of the rug, it means there is less weft per square yard than in the more normal type, an advantage if, as is likely, the weft is a more expensive yarn than the warp. The reduced time needed to dye the weft is another advantage.

An all-wool rug of this type can be made with a warp of 6-ply rug wool, 4 e.p.i., single in the heald, therefore 4 working e.p.i., and a weft of 2-ply carpet wool used singly. Another type has a 6/10s linen warp, 12 e.p.i., double in the heald, therefore 6 working e.p.i., and a weft of 2-ply carpet wool used singly or a tapestry worsted yarn used double or treble.

C. Selvages

In rugs, selvages have considerable importance, because, unlike a piece of cloth that is cut and shaped before it is finally used, a rug is used as made. Its selvages, good or bad, are always on view. They have to stand a great deal of hard wear. A rug generally begins to wear out somewhere on its periphery, either at the selvages or at the fringes.

In some rugs woven on primitive equipment (for instance, kilims woven on a horizontal ground loom) the selvages curve and waver. A rug may lose a foot in width between its starting and final end. This may have a certain charm to sophisticated eyes but it is only the result of weaving without the physical help of a batten and temple, and without the mental concept of parallel selvages. It should not be cited as an excuse for irregular selvages on a rug woven on a better equipped loom.

The rule for the warp at the selvage is to increase its thickness and to set it closer in the reed. Thus if the main part of the rug has a warp formula of 6 e.p.i., double in the heald, therefore 3 working e.p.i., at the selvage have one or two working ends in which the warp yarn is used threefold instead of twofold, and place these thicker working ends closer together. This is shown diagrammatically in Fig. 37, where such a warp is seen sleyed in a reed with 6 dents per inch. Generally, the wider the rug, the more thickened selvage ends are needed: but the limit is about three such ends at each selvage.

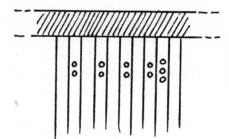

Fig. 37
Method of sleying selvage in the reed

It will be seen that using a reed with more dents than are actually needed, e.g., a reed with 6 dents per inch instead of 3, has the advantage that the selvage spacing can be more finely adjusted. Also there need never be two selvage working ends in one dent where they tend to catch on each other in the shedding.

A selvage setting as described, combined with correct weft tension and the use of a temple, should give perfectly satisfactory edges to the rugs, They will be firm and strong, and need no extra overcasting with weft as is sometimes advised.

All the points described in Chapter 3 apply to the weaving of weft-face rugs and the weaver should be conversant with them before trying the following techniques.

2. ONE-SHUTTLE TECHNIQUES

A. Colour Blending

Colour blending is the making of an area of colour more alive and interesting by using mixtures of different shades of that colour. This can be used by itself or to enhance the interest of other rug techniques.

If, for example, a red rug is to be made, many reds are used (instead of using one shade throughout) some lighter and some darker, with perhaps excursions into purples and pinks. This can be done in two main ways. Assume that the warp is set up so that a 2-ply carpet wool used fourfold is the appropriate weft.

(i) One way is to wind several shuttles each carrying only one colour, i.e., four threads of colour A on one shuttle, and four threads of colour B on another, etc. Then in the weaving, use these shuttles in some order, such as 1 inch of A, $2\frac{1}{2}$ inches of B, $1\frac{1}{4}$ inches of C and so on. So that the result is irregular stripes of different, but closely-related colours. Such irregular stripes can be woven without a pre-arranged plan, merely letting what has just been woven suggest the colour to use next. An arrangement of colours like this is always more interesting than regularly repeating stripes or a scientific grading from one colour into another. Its unpredictability is its strength: such a rug cannot be 'solved' at a glance.

(ii) The other type of colour blending starts as the shuttles are being wound. Instead of each shuttle holding only one red, it now holds a mixture of different reds. A shuttle could be wound with four different reds and the whole rug woven of that particular mixture. But it is more interesting to wind each shuttle with a different mixture and then to use these shuttles in the irregular way described above. So in the first method, the weaving mixes plain colours, but here it mixes mixtures and gives the possibility of richer effects.

Colours can be changed during the winding of a shuttle, e.g., one of the four threads can be broken and a different colour knotted on. But as it is difficult to judge where this new colour will appear in the weaving, the weaver has less control and this method should not be used to excess.

It will be noticed that the weft used for the first method could have been some single yarn whose thickness was similar to that of a 2-ply carpet wool used fourfold and this single thread could have been wound on the shuttles. But for the second method, the finer yarn is essential.

Though ideas about colour slip through any net of words, some things can perhaps be said. If colours very close to each other are mixed, a new colour will be produced, especially when the rug is seen at its proper distance, i.e., on the floor, not on the loom. Mixed dark colours will enrich each other, mixed light colours tend to become muddy. If, instead of a rich mixture a flecked one is wanted, then colours very dissimilar in depth are mixed, the extreme case being black and white. For very gentle grading of colour, change only one of the four colours in each successive mixture. Colours which look well together when seen in the mass, i.e., in hanks, may not be so successful when they are finally mixed on a shuttle, so when choosing colours always hold single threads together.

The practical side to colour blending is mentioned in Chapter 3, where Fig. 26 (a) shows the cones of different colours arranged on the floor with their threads being led up through a horizontal reed to prevent tangling. The reed is only necessary if many colours are being used. If only about twenty cones are being used, they can just be stood in a group on the floor, as a thread will pull off the top of a cone at quite an oblique angle; a vertical pull-off is not essential.

The different colours are wound on to the shuttle without any attempt to twist or arrange them. The fact that they are not twisted adds to the haphazard effect. If black and white are used, a different result can be produced by arranging the cones either as in Fig. 38 (a) or in Fig. 38 (b), the latter giving a finer fleck than the former.

Apart from the visual effect, colour blending has two practical advantages.

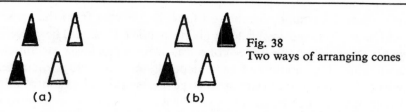

Fig. 38
Two ways of arranging cones

(a) (b)

(a) A wool whose colour is too crude or dull to be used by itself can often be employed very satisfactorily in a mixture.

(b) A small amount of wool of one colour, not sufficient for a whole rug, can be used up in a mixture. Even threads only a few inches long can be laid in, in addition to the normal weft, and so not be wasted.

B. Colour Plying

This really differs from colour blending only in that some control is exercised over the way the different colours are arranged as they are wound on the shuttle.

Though yarns can obviously be plied on a spinning wheel, not many fliers have a large enough opening to take the thickness of yarn being dealt with here. So one of two other methods can be used.

(i) The first is that shown in Fig. 39. Put one colour on a cone and stand it on a reed supported in some way. Put the other colour on a cone on the floor, and lead its thread up through the horizontal reed and through the centre of the first cone. As the

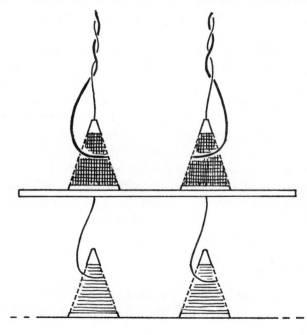

Fig. 39
Plying two yarns to give
Z twist and S twist

two threads are wound together on to a shuttle, that from the upper cone will wrap round that from the lower cone giving a plied thread. The direction of twist will depend on whether the upper cone was wound clockwise or anticlockwise, so it is controllable. The amount of twist depends on the average diameter of the cone, a small cone giving more twist than a large one, so this is less controllable. But packages other than cones can be used to vary the amount of twist, e.g., pirns or tubes, if fixed upright, can replace the upper cone; or a cone can stand on a large warping drum on the floor, the thread from the drum twisting round that from the cone. The former arrangement will give far more twist than the latter.

(ii) In the second method, both the yarns to be used are wound together on to a cone. Then, as they are drawn off, they twist around each other. If more twist is needed they are wound onto another cone, and if necessary then on to yet another. So the twist in this method is more controllable than in the first method.

This technique can be put to various uses, such as the following:

(i) s and z twist stripes

If the warp requires a weft used fourfold and black and white are the colours chosen, then wind some cones with white twofold, and some with black twofold. But wind the cones of one of the colours, say, black, so on some the yarn lies in a clockwise spiral and on others in an anticlockwise spiral. Put a black cone of each type on the horizontal reed, with white cones underneath, see Fig. 39. A shuttle wound from the right-hand cones will have the black and white yarns Z-twisted and one from the left-hand cones will have them S-twisted.

If an inch or so is woven with one shuttle, then an inch or so with the other, vague stripes will appear. In one stripe, indistinct black and white streaky lines will be seen inclining up to the right, in the next stripe the lines incline up to the left. The effect naturally varies with the amount of twist; the less twist, the vaguer the lines. With exactly the right amount of twist—and only experiment will show what this is—a fairly rigid effect can be obtained, looking very like a rug woven in twill, with reverses in the twill direction. The thicker the weft, the better this will show. So if using a warp with 3 working e.p.i., a weft of two threefold carpet yarns twisted together will give a better effect than the same yarns used twofold as described above. But this will require a very hard beat in the weaving. It will be realized that 2-ply carpet wool used threefold is about as thick as 6-ply rug wool. This latter will be more convenient to use for this technique, if a solid, rather than a mixed, colour is wanted.

(ii) plying unequal thicknesses

Assuming a weft of 2-ply carpet wool used fourfold is needed, cones can be wound with many threefold mixtures and then these be plied with one colour, wound singly on to a cone. In other words, the cone of threefold weft will be on the floor and the cone of single weft will be on the reed. The colour of the single yarn can be something a little different in depth or tone from that of the threefold mixtures, so that it is seen as a regular small fleck against a changing background. This idea can naturally be combined with S and Z twist stripes. It can also be reversed, so that the threefold mixture is a constant colour, and the single yarn changes its colour.

(iii) PLYING DIFFERENT MATERIALS

Many combinations of materials can be tried, e.g., wool and linen, wool and cotton, wool and jute, horsehair and linen, and so on. In most cases, these materials will weave together more successfully if plied than if merely wound together onto a shuttle.

C. Handspun Wefts

Very few rug weavers now spin their own materials, either warp or weft. A rug uses much yarn in proportion to its size, e.g., 6 to 8 lb. of weft for a rug 3 foot x 5 foot, so the days spent in spinning for it would far outnumber the days spent in weaving it. But for those for whom this is not a deterrent, the hand-spun weft-faced rug offers many possibilities.

The spinning should be of the worsted, not woollen, type, both for strength and for resistance to fluffing out in use. Also it is quite inappropriate to spin a light woollen yarn and then beat it up close in the weaving and obliterate its characteristics. The long staple lustre fleeces are the best therefore, if wool is to be used. A tightly spun 2-ply yarn should be aimed at. This can be used two, three or fourfold in the weaving, which is far easier and more controllable than spinning a very thick yarn to be used single.

Many different materials can be used alone or in combination, such as wool, hairs (horse, camel, goat, alpaca, mohair), linen, hemp, jute and synthetics. When spinning together materials whose fibre length is very dissimilar, cut the longer one to the staple length of the shorter before carding. Plate 1 shows a sample spun of black and white delustred rayon with hemp and jute. For this, the hemp and jute were cut into 6-inch lengths because the rayon happened to have a 6 inch staple. These were all carded together, but only to give a slight mixing of the materials. They were then roughly combed by pulling through the hands and tightly spun. In subsequent cardings, different proportions of black to white rayon and of hemp to jute were used, so that the yarn produced would not be uniform and therefore the rug would have a more interesting surface. So here the rug is being designed in the spinning.

There are many variations possible, such as dyeing the fibre and mixing different colours during spinning. Because the yarn is tightly spun and will be tightly beaten in the weaving, fibres can be spun together which are very dissimilar in such physical properties as elasticity and resilience. An example is a yarn spun from wool, rayon and shreds of raffia, which gives a very interesting texture to both hand and eye when woven. There is obviously a large field for experiment in the spinning of rug yarns and many as practical as the commercially produced wool and hair yarns could very likely be designed.

Because the aim is a tightly spun 2-ply yarn, the initial singles must be very tightly spun. And as this will be thicker than normal hand spun yarn, it is often difficult to spin it on a wheel. The problem is that the thicker a yarn is, the less twists per inch it needs to become tightly spun. This implies that the hands have to move very fast, controlling the entry of the wool into the spinning area, in relation to the speed of the pedalling. Another difficulty is to so adjust the wheel that it will draw in the thick tightly spun yarn quickly and easily before it is overspun.

The historically older great wheel, in which a metal spindle is driven by a large hand-turned wheel, overcomes both these difficulties. Very few weavers have such a wheel but they all have a bobbin winder and this can be used in exactly the same way, as described below.

Tie some strong yarn onto the spindle of the bobbin winder near its thicker end. Rotate the spindle and guide the yarn up to its tip. If the spindle continues to rotate, the yarn will slip off the tip at each revolution, and with each revolution one more twist will be put into the yarn. To prevent damage to the yarn, hold it at an oblique angle, not a right angle, to the spindle. Now attach the prepared fibres to the piece of yarn, rotate the spindle and start spinning. One hand controls the bobbin winder, the other the fibres. The latter hand, the spinning hand, naturally draws further and further away from the spindle as the yarn is spun. At the limit of stretch, reverse the spindle sufficiently to unwind the yarn from the tip of the spindle. Then rotate it in the normal direction, but with the spinning hand guiding the yarn so that it is wound on to the spindle. When the yarn is nearly all wound on, again lead it up to the tip and continue spinning.

Continue thus until the spindle is full and then wind the yarn to await plying. Alternatively, a tube can be fixed on the spindle before spinning and the yarn wound on to this as it is spun. This tube is then simply slipped off when full and replaced with an empty one. Plying is done in the same way, but rotating the spindle in the opposite direction.

With practice a thick single yarn can be spun on a bobbin winder. If woven without being plied this unexpectedly gives the appearance of twill lines. With a Z twist yarn these lines incline up to the right.

D. Tie and Dye Wefts

The various tie and dye techniques offer almost limitless scope to the handweaver. Perhaps the reason for their being so little used is that the weaver, on seeing complex examples in museums, decides that such meticulously accurate work is beyond him. There are, however, some very simple applications of the technique to rug weaving which are quick to prepare and interesting to weave.

Repeating Designs

In this method, the whole of the design of the rug comes from the tying and dyeing of the weft. Its special feature is that the weft is dyed whilst still in hanks.

As the weft is wound straight on to the shuttle from the hank, the latter must have yarn of the correct thickness for weaving, e.g., it could be a hank of 6-ply rug wool, if the warp is to be set at 3 or 4 working e.p.i. The technique can be best understood if one example is described in detail.

Tie the hank so as to exclude its outer quarters from the dye, see Fig. 40 (a). A thick, but soft, cotton yarn is the best to use, and the tying must be as tight as possible. A time-saving alternative is to slip sections of rubber tube over the outer quarters, as these only have to be tied at one end, see Fig. 40 (b).

Dye the hanks, say, black, suspending them in the bath by the tied portions. After dyeing, rinse and untie, and then dry the hanks. They will now consist of yarn in which a length dyed black follows an equal length which is undyed, see Fig. 40 (c).

If this were woven on a warp as wide as the hank is long, a rug as in Fig. 40 (d)

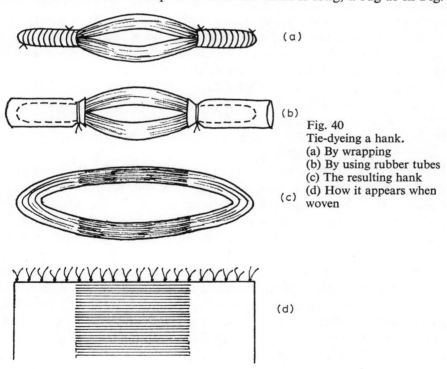

(a)

(b)

Fig. 40
Tie-dyeing a hank.
(a) By wrapping
(b) By using rubber tubes
(c) The resulting hank
(d) How it appears when
woven

(c)

(d)

would be the result. The black and white parts of each pick would lie exactly over the black and white parts of the preceding pick. This suggests possible rugs with warpway stripes and blocks. But here, use a warp whose width is *slightly more or slightly less* than the hank length, i.e., if the hank when stretched measured 36 inches, then use a warp 1 or 2 inches wider or narrower. This is done so that in each pick the black and white parts do not lie exactly over each other, but a little to one side. This shift becomes greater with each succeeding pick.

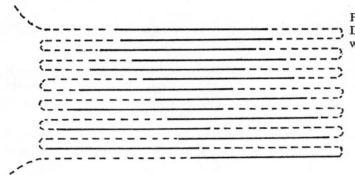

Fig. 41
Detailed plan of tie-dyed
weft to show colour shift

Assuming that the warp is wider than the hank length, Fig. 41 shows diagrammatically what happens to the weft. Three areas are produced, namely, a triangle of solid black in the centre, two triangles of solid white at the sides, and two triangles of black and white, pick-and-pick, in between. These triangles become diamonds as the weaving continues. Plate 2 shows the completed rug.

Once the right width of warp has been found—and a little trial and error is necessary to establish this—the weaving is perfectly straightforward. If at any point the pattern jumps, due perhaps to a loose thread in the hank, take up the slack by winding the weft once or twice round the selvage threads. Overcome other small irregularities in the hank, by varying the weft waving.

It will be understood that the closer the hank length approaches the warp width, the smaller will be the colour shift in each succeeding pick and therefore the bigger, in the warp direction, the diamonds will become. Another facet of this principle is that by varying the size of the weft waves or their tension, the size of the diamonds can be varied in the course of one rug. But for practical reasons, this should only be done within narrow limits.

It will be obvious that because of this hank size/warp width relationship, a bought hank may have to be rewound to the desired size. Do this either on a skeiner adjusted so that its circumference is twice the required hank length or by finding a combination of pegs on a warping board that gives the correct length and winding the yarn round these by hand. In both methods be very careful to keep the tension of the yarn constant and avoid it building up on itself.

Other Developments of this Method

(a) A tie and dye weft can be combined with a normal weft in some such sequence as two picks of one then two picks of the other. The normal weft could be one of the colours of the tie and dye weft, or it could be a colour mixture that changes throughout the rug and robs the repeating design of some of its severity.

(b) Two tie and dye wefts can be used at once in a pick-and-pick sequence. This will give bigger diamonds in the warp direction and diamonds of cross stripes will replace those of pick-and-pick stripes.

(c) Instead of tying and dyeing a hank of 6-ply wool, a hank can be made of three or four differently coloured 2-ply yarns, i.e., all three or four yarns are run on to the skeiner together. Make the hanks with different mixtures of colours, say, reds, then tie and dye them all in black or very dark red. The rug will then have a play of reds against a constant black.

(d) The hanks can be tied in some different way, for instance, to exclude the dye from one half only (giving a rug like the right hand half of Fig. 41) or to exclude the dye from the outer sixth of the hank (giving a rug with a large dyed central diamond alternating with a small undyed one).

The beauty of this method is that as long as the hank is the correct size, it will result in some sort of repeating design based on diagonal lines, in whatever manner it is tied up before dyeing. There is, therefore, great scope for experiment.

Non-Repeating Designs

The tying and dyeing of hanks which do not have the above relationship to the warp width can be used as an alternative method of colour blending or to produce haphazard two-colour effects. The simplest and quickest way is to tie very tight overhand knots in the hank itself. Due to the bulk of the material, it is generally difficult to tie more than two.

With this method there is not the crisp boundary between dyed and undyed portions obtainable with normal tie and dye methods. But these blurred boundaries, which may appear as a third colour some way between the other two, add variety to the yarn. Such a yarn can be used by itself (or mixed with another) where an area consisting of two colours intimately mixed is required. The effect is quite different from that obtained if yarns of the two colours had been blended in the usual way; it is a coarser-grained mixture.

Plate 3 shows the result of tying a hank of red wool in three places in the normal way and then dying it black. The hank was 36 inches long and the sample about 9 inches wide. It was while trying to produce this effect on a full-sized warp that the technique described above was chanced upon.

E. Twisted Wefts

In Coptic tapestries there are often areas woven with a weft consisting of a purple and white thread. This generally gives an over-all speckled appearance but occasionally by chance the two strands lie in such a way as to give an ordered sequence. The present technique sprang from the idea of making this chance happening deliberate, and led to the finding of other variations not present in the Coptic textiles.

As these are all small scale effects, they show best when the two colours used differ widely in tone. Black and white are suitable for trying the technique. Assuming the warp to have 3 working e.p.i., wind a 6-ply yarn of each colour on to the same shuttle. This means that the combined weft is equivalent to six 2-ply yarns, whereas four has been given earlier as a normal amount. But if this extra thick yarn can be beaten in, it will give a better effect and will prove easier to handle.

The various effects that can be produced are now described.

(i) HORIZONTAL LINES

Throw the shuttle, arrange the two colours so that the black is nearest to the fell of the rug, all across the width of the warp. Beat.

In the next pick, make the white nearest the fell of the rug. Beat.

Repeat these two picks.

Note—That this gives straight horizontal lines, quite unlike the wavy lines if two picks of black alternate with two picks of white. See Fig. 42 (a).

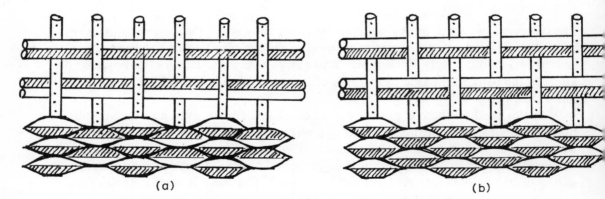

(a)   (b)

Fig. 42. Twisted Wefts (a) Giving horizontal lines (b) Giving spots

(ii) SPOTS

Arrange wefts so that either black or white is nearest the fell of the rug in every pick. See Fig. 42 (b).

(iii) COMBINED LINES AND SPOTS

(*a*) *An Area of Spots on a Background of Lines*

In the first pick arrange the colours so that the white is nearest the fell of the rug. Insert the fingers through the top of the shed and twist the middle portion of both wefts so that the position of the colours is here reversed.

In next pick, make the black nearest the fell on the rug, all the way across. Do not twist the central portions.

Repeat these two picks. See Fig. 43 and Plate 4.

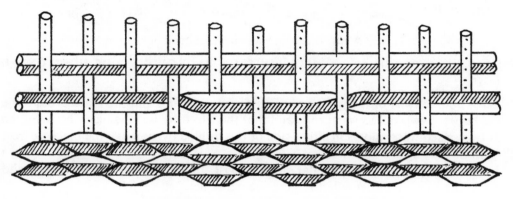

Fig. 43. Twisted Wefts. Area of spots on background of lines

Note—That the size and shape of the area of spots is completely controllable by the amount of weft which is twisted in the first pick of each repeat.
—That there can be several such areas across the width of the warp, not just one in the centre as described and illustrated.

(*b*) In an exactly similar way, an area of lines can be produced on a background of spots. Arrange the wefts to make the black nearest the fell of the rug in every shed, and twist the central part of the weft in every other shed.

(iv) DIAGONAL LINES ON BACKGROUND OF HORIZONTAL LINES

Arrange the wefts as for horizontal lines but twist the central portion, thus reversing the colours, in every shed. Make the twist so one colour, say, the black as in Fig. 44, is always on top where the yarns cross. Twist a progressively larger amount of weft in each pick, so that the crossing points move outwards. Do this carefully, making sure the black crosses the white in between two raised warp ends, as in Fig. 44, which shows only one diagonal line. Plate 5 shows both black and white diamonds produced in this way.

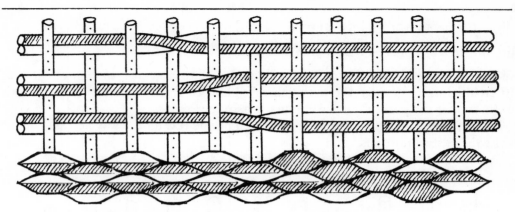

Fig. 44. Twisted Wefts. Diagonal lines on background of horizontal lines

(v) VERTICAL BLACK AND WHITE LINES ON BACKGROUND OF HORIZONTAL LINES

Make a double twist of the wefts as in Fig. 45 (a), ensuring that the black crosses the white between two raised warp ends and that the white crosses the black between the next two raised warp ends. On either side of this double twist, make the black nearest the fell of the rug.

In the next pick, make a similar double twist, but in the reverse direction, and arrange the weft on either side to make the white nearest the fell.

Repeat these two picks making the twists in exactly the same place, see Fig. 45 (a) and Plate 6 (lower half).

> *Note*—The lines need not be vertical. They can be moved to either side by changing the position of the twists.
> —There can be many lines across the width of the warp.

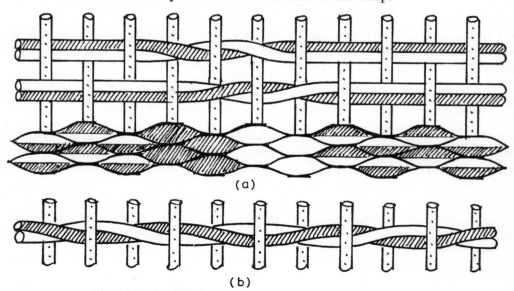

(a)

(b)

Fig. 45. Twisted Wefts
(a) Vertical lines on background of horizontal lines
(b) Twisting wefts at centre

(vi) MULTIPLE TWISTS

(a) Uncontrolled

Throw the shuttle; then, with the shed still open, insert the index finger and thumb of both hands through the centre of the raised warp ends. Picking up the wefts in the centre, twist them several times in one direction, either away from or towards the fell of the rug. Close shed and beat. The weft will now be twisted so that half is S-twist and half Z-twist, see Fig. 45 (b).

Repeat this for about 2 inches of weaving, always twisting in the same direction. Then weave another 2 inches but twist the weft in the reverse direction.

The result is an area with vague concentric oval lines see top of Plate 6. The more twist that is put in, the more obvious the lines will be. On the back of the rug, there is a vague cross shape.

(b) Controlled

This is really an extension of (v). Throw the shuttle. Twist the weft many times in the centre of the pick so that a different colour comes up between each pair of raised warp ends, see Fig. 46. Arrange the weft on either side of the twisted area to give the black nearest the fell of the rug.

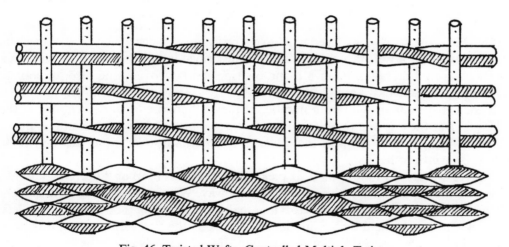

Fig. 46. Twisted Wefts. Controlled Multiple Twists

In the next pick, twist the central part in the same direction, and arrange the colours to produce diagonal lines. Arrange the weft on either side to give the white nearest the fell.

Continue thus, always twisting in the same direction and always arranging the colours so that the diagonal lines are built up. To reverse the direction of the diagonal lines, reverse the direction of the twist. Plate 7 (lower half) shows a rectangle produced in this fashion. Another variation is to twist the wefts in the opposite direction in each successive pick, and to arrange the colours so that vertical lines are built up. These lines have a characteristic zigzag appearance, as seen in the upper half of Plate 7. Both of these controlled twist effects are very similar to those obtained with weft twining (see Chapter 13).

> *General Note*—Although all of these techniques have been described as being woven with a black and white weft on one shuttle, some of them may be easier to weave with the two wefts on separate shuttles.

3. TWO-SHUTTLE TECHNIQUES

By using two shuttles carrying different colours and always throwing them from selvage to selvage, three basic effects can be obtained. These are weftway or cross stripes, warpway or pick-and-pick stripes and spots. In the following descriptions the two wefts will be called A and B.

A. Weftway or Cross Stripes

Start weft A at the left selvage, and weave two picks. Start weft B at the right selvage and weave two picks. Repeat these four picks.

The thin cross stripes produced will have a wavy appearance which is characteristic of such stripes in a weft-face weave. The one described is called a 2-and-2 stripe. In a similar way, a 4-and-4 stripe or a 6-and-6 stripe can be woven; and also, of course, uneven stripes, such as 2-and-4, and 4-and-6.

If each stripe contains an even number of picks, there are no complications at the selvages. But there is one thing to notice. After 2, 4 or 6 picks of A, when B is introduced it forms a small loop at the selvage between its last pick and this new pick. Pull the yarn tight here.

If there is a stripe of more than six picks of A, then this loop of B becomes a weakness and should be dealt with in the following way Weave weft A from left to right normally Then catch it around weft B and make the returning pick from right to left. Weft B will then be held by and hidden by weft A as the latter loops around the selvage. This may be understood by referring to Fig. 47, and also perhaps by imagining that B is glued to the selvage thread on its side, so whatever A does in relation to the selvage, it does the same in relation to B. This gives a slight extra thickness to the right selvage but it is hardly noticeable. However, if stripes of many picks are to be woven, it is better visually and economically (the above procedure slows down the rhythm of weaving) to finish off each colour at the end of its stripe, and then start it again at the beginning of its next stripe.

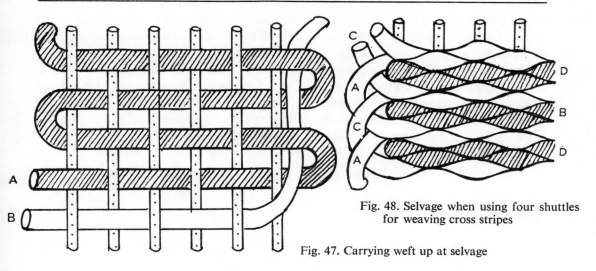

Fig. 48. Selvage when using four shuttles for weaving cross stripes

Fig. 47. Carrying weft up at selvage

The small loop at the selvage when weaving 2-and-2 stripes adds strength and substance to the edge of the rug. But it can be made use of even when not weaving stripes. For instance, instead of using one shuttle in an area of solid colour, use two shuttles each carrying the same colour and weave two picks with one and two picks with the other, remembering to start them from opposite selvages as described above.

A development of this uses four shuttles, though not necessarily four colours, and gives a decorative edge, see Fig. 48, which shows a left-hand selvage. Two wefts A and C (white) have started from the left selvage, and two other wefts B and D (shaded) have started from the right selvage. The picking order is two picks A, two picks B, two picks C and two picks D, repeat. Notice how A and C twist round each other. B and D twist similarly at the right selvage. A begins its first pick by passing over C, then under the first warp thread, and ends its second pick by passing over the same warp thread and under C.

B. Warpway or Pick-and-Pick Stripes

If two colours are used alternately, i.e., pick-and-pick, in a weft-face weave, they give thin lines of the two colours in the warp direction. If the warp has 3 working e.p.i. there will be three such lines to the inch: in other words, each line lies over a warp thread. These lines are a characteristic feature of weft-face weaving and have been known and used for centuries in rugs and tapestries. They can be used all across a rug or in small areas. The same principle can lead to warpway stripes in more complex weaves, e.g., twills and block weaves.

The extreme simplicity of the technique is slightly offset by the difficulties that arise at the selvage. In ordinary weaving, the fine wefts are generally locked round each other at the selvage when weaving pick-and-pick. The same method using thick rug wefts leads to untidy lumpy edges.

The correct method will be described in detail together with suggestions for speeding up the process. In essence, it is to let one of the wefts not weave with the selvage thread at all, and to wind the other weft round the selvage to make up for the thickness of the missing weft. The exact manipulation of threads depends on the number of working ends in the warp. It is different for an odd and even number.

(i) WITH ODD NUMBER OF WORKING ENDS

Fig. 49 shows a miniature warp with seven working ends. The sequence of the four picks in the repeat is thus.

Start with two wefts, A (shaded) and B (white) both at the right selvage, the last pick having passed *over* the selvage thread. See arrow in Fig. 49.

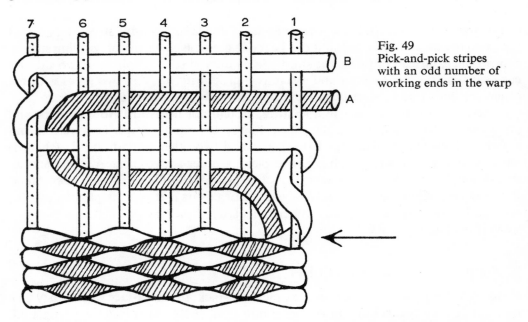

Fig. 49
Pick-and-pick stripes
with an odd number of
working ends in the warp

Lift odd-numbered ends, throw A from right to left. Note that A does not weave with the selvage thread at all. It misses it completely, jumping up vertically from its preceding pick and leaving a small loop at the back of the rug between the first and second working end.

Lift even-numbered ends, wrap B twice around selvage thread in a downwards direction, then throw from right to left.

Lift odd-numbered ends, throw A from left to right as before. It now leaves a loop at the back between the sixth and seventh working ends.

Lift even-numbered ends, wrap B twice around selvage thread in a downwards direction and then throw from left to right.

Repeat these four picks.

Be careful of the weft tension. Do not pull A too tight or its loop will kink the weft B and bring it onto the surface of the rug. Pull tight the twists of B around the selvage thread before allowing the usual slack for waving the weft. The number of twists can be increased if necessary to make level the fell of the rug.

The top surface of the rug will be perfect but the reverse will have small 'jump-up' loops of weft A visible at each selvage. When first practising this technique, frequently examine the underside of the rug to make sure these loops are regular.

Always wrap weft B in the correct direction, otherwise it will cause a float over two ends at the selvage.

Always start with the picks exactly as in Fig. 49. If the sequence is started with both wefts at the right selvage but with the last pick going *under* the selvage thread, the loops of weft A, where it misses the selvage, will be on the top surface of the rug. Also the twists of weft B round the selvage will have to be in the opposite direction to those described, i.e., upwards instead of downwards.

As will be imagined, the twisting of weft B twice round the selvage thread is time-consuming, but there are ways of quickening the process. Note that the only effect of the first downward twist is to make the weft B lie under the selvage thread instead of over it. So if, when weft B is thrown, the hand catching the shuttle lifts the selvage thread (normally down where B is thrown in either direction) the shuttle will pass under it instead of over it. Weft B will now lie under the selvage thread. Throw weft A normally. Weft B now only needs *one* downward twist before it is thrown back, and made to pass under the selvage thread on the opposite side. This method is a help, but can be developed further by using a floating selvage.

Floating Selvage

A floating selvage is one which is not threaded through any heald, but is sleyed normally through the reed. So it is unattached to any shaft. When a shed is made, e.g., for plain weave, half the threads rise and half fall but the floating selvage on each side stays unaltered, lying horizontally in the neutral position of the warp, bisecting the angle of the shed. It is shown as a dotted line in Fig. 50 (a). This means that there are two openings through which the shuttle can be entered, X above the floating selvage and Y below the floating selvage. Naturally at the opposite side the shuttle will always tend to leave the shed *below* the floating selvage.

Using the floating selvage, the sequence is thus:

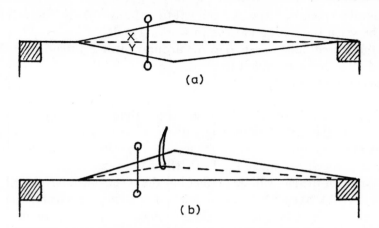

Fig. 50. Floating Selvage. (a) With rising and falling shed (b) With rising shed only

Lift odd-numbered ends, throw A right to left, entering it *under* right floating selvage, and catching it from *under* left floating selvage.

Lift even-numbered ends, wrap B *once* downwards round right selvage thread, throw it right to left, entering it *over* right floating selvage and catching it from *under* left floating selvage.

Lift odd-numbered ends, throw A from left to right, entering it *under* left floating selvage and catching it from *under* right floating selvage.

Lift even-numbered ends, wrap B *once* downwards around left selvage thread, throw it left to right, entering it *over* left floating selvage and catching it from *under* right floating selvage.

Repeat these four picks.

Note—That A always enters under floating selvage.
    —That B always enters over floating selvage.
    —That both A and B always leave shed under floating selvage.

It will be obvious that a floating selvage is only possible with a loom which has a rising and falling shed as shown in Fig. 50 (a). This is produced by a counter-balanced or counter-march loom or by a jack loom, in which the warp line when the shafts are at rest is well below the line from breast beam to back beam. A table loom, which generally has a rising shed only, and a warp line which is horizontal at rest, is not suitable as it stands. But it can be made suitable by fixing the floating selvage with a string loop to the upper frame of the loom, so that it is always in a half raised position, as in Fig. 50 (b).

Such a string loop may also be necessary with a rising and falling shed, so that the height of the floating selvage can be exactly adjusted. It should be at such a level that the shuttle leaving the shed just passes under it, and so that at the same time there is as much space as possible over it for the entering shuttle. The deeper the over-all shed, the easier it is to strike this balance.

There is a simpler, quicker, but less tidy way of using the floating selvage in pick-and-pick areas. In this, each shuttle always enters the shed *over* the floating selvage and always leaves it *under* the opposite floating selvage. Fig. 51 shows that one weft A

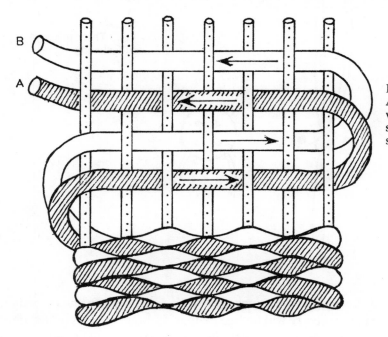

Fig. 51
Alternative method of weaving pick-and-pick stripes with a floating selvage

(shaded) floats over two ends at each selvage and the other weft B floats under two ends at each selvage, thus slightly blurring the pick-and-pick stripes at the selvage. The obvious danger is that the weaving at the selvage will become slack, as there are fewer warp/weft intersections than in the rest of the rug. This can be overcome if the two outer threads are set very close together.

Adjustable Floating Selvage

While weaving pick-and-pick, the floating selvage is a great help, but it will be a nuisance if in the same rug areas of one colour or stripes of 2-and-2, are wanted, so a simple method is used to allow the selvage either to float or behave normally, rising and falling with the rest of the warp. See Fig. 52 (a).

Assume the selvage thread should be drawn in on shaft 1. Do not draw it in, but encircle it with a loop of strong cotton twine, the ends of which go through the eye of an empty heald on shaft 1 and then up to the shaft above. Bring one end up behind the

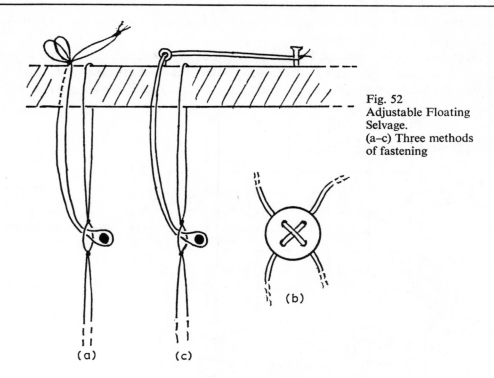

Fig. 52
Adjustable Floating
Selvage.
(a–c) Three methods
of fastening

shaft, the other in front. Leaving about 6 inches of slack, knot the two ends together.

If this loop is left slack, the selvage will be free to float. If, however, it is pulled tight (and fastened with a slip knot above the shaft), the selvage thread will be pulled tight up against the heald eye and will then have to move as if it were threaded through this eye. So for areas of pick-and-pick the loop is left slack, and for any other area it is pulled tight.

There are two alternatives to a slip knot for tightening the loop. One is to thread the twine through the four holes of a button, as shown in Fig. 52 (b) then slide the button up or down as required. There is enough friction in this system to fix the button in any position. But if many rugs needing the adjustable floating selvage are to be woven use the second, more permanent, method, as in Fig. 52 (c). Pass the ends of the twine through a screw eye fixed in the top of the shaft vertically above the selvage. About 6 inches away from the screw eye, fix a screw or nail also in the top of the shaft. Bring the ends of the twine round this screw, pull them tight and knot, making the knot of such a size that it cannot pass through the screw eye. With the cord in this position the selvage is tight against the heald and will work with it; to make it float, just slip the twine off the screw.

(ii) WITH EVEN NUMBER OF WORKING ENDS

A pick-and-pick rug looks better with an odd number of working ends, as the same colour or type of yarn forms the selvage on both sides. But there may be occasions when an even number has to be used, e.g., when making a rug to an exact width or when making a rug in two strips, to be later sewn together. The sequence of events is then different. Fig. 53 shows a miniature warp of six ends with the four picks that make up the repeat not beaten down.

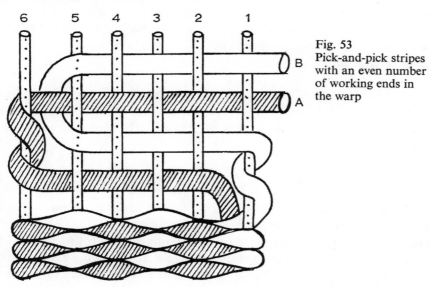

Fig. 53
Pick-and-pick stripes with an even number of working ends in the warp

The procedure is as follows. Start with both wefts at the right selvage, the last pick (white) having gone over the selvage thread.

(a) With Normal Selvage

Lift odd-numbered ends, throw A from right to left, noting that it misses right selvage.

Lift even-numbered ends, wrap B twice *downwards* around right selvage thread, then throw from right to left.

Lift odd-numbered ends, wrap A twice around left selvage in an *upwards* direction, then throw from left to right.

Lift even-numbered ends, throw B from left to right, noting that it misses left selvage.

Repeat these four picks.

It will be seen that only the third and fourth pick differ from the sequence used with an odd number of warp ends.

(b) With Floating Selvage

Lift odd-numbered ends, throw A from right to left, so that it enters shed *under* right selvage and leaves shed *over* left selvage.

Lift even-numbered ends, wrap B once *downwards* around right selvage and throw from right to left, so that it enters shed *over* right selvage and leaves it *under* left selvage.

Lift odd-numbered ends, wrap A once *upwards* round left selvage, and throw from left to right so that it enters shed *under* left selvage and leaves shed *under* right selvage.

Lift even-numbered ends, throw B from left to right, so that it enters shed *under* left selvage and leaves shed *under* right selvage.

Repeat these four picks.

The only slightly awkward pick is the first, as the left floating selvage has to be pushed downwards by the hand that catches the shuttle, to allow the shuttle to pass over it. Naturally the adjustable floating selvage can also be used with an even number of warp ends.

Design Possibilities

When using pick-and-pick, two wefts appear in close association and the colour or material of both are under the weaver's control.

The prominence of the warpway stripes can be finely controlled by the contrast between the two wefts. Take as an example, a rug set at 3 working e.p.i., so that each weft consists of four 2-ply carpet wools. If one shuttle has 4 threads of colour A and the other shuttle has 4 of colour B, the stripes will be at their most apparent. But if one shuttle has 3 A and 1 B and the other 2 A and 2 B, the stripes will hardly read at all; there are several stages between these two extremes.

An area of pick-and-pick in two colours, A and B, is often used as a transition between a cross stripe of solid A and one of solid B. If this is combined with varying the proportions of the two colours in the pick-and-pick area, as described above, a very gradual transition can be managed.

If the colour of one weft is kept constant while the colour of the other weft changes either gradually or suddenly, a unity will be given to the latter colours not obtained if used by themselves.

C. Spots

Spots are produced by weaving one pick of colour A and two, three, four or more of colour B and then repeating this sequence.

If there is an odd number of picks of B, the spots in each row will lie vertically above those in the previous row.

If there is an even number of picks of B, the spots in each row will lie to one side of those in the previous row.

(i) WITH ODD NUMBER OF PICKS

If there are three or five picks of B, use the same principle as described for pick-and-pick stripes.

Start with weft A at right selvage and weft B at the left selvage, exactly as in Fig. 54.

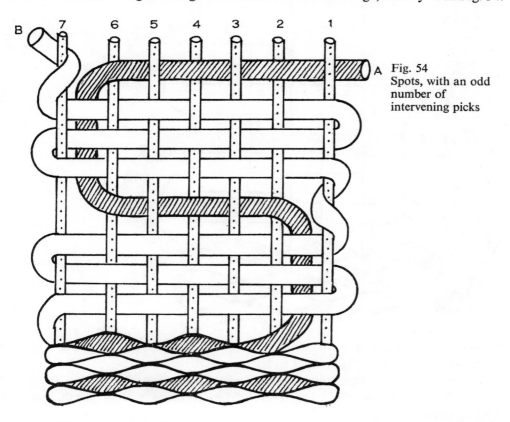

Fig. 54
Spots, with an odd number of intervening picks

Weave three or five picks of B, ending with a double downward twist around right selvage.

Weave one pick of A from right to left, missing selvage thread. The 'jump-up' loop on the reverse of the rug is over three or five picks of B.

Weave three or five picks of B, ending with a double downward twist at left selvage.

Weave one pick of A from left to right, missing left selvage thread.

Repeat this sequence.

The loops of A on the reverse become impractically long, if more than five picks of B are woven. In this case, catch A in the loops of B as they turn round the selvage thread, as described for cross stripes.

(ii) WITH EVEN NUMBER OF PICKS

Start as above with B at left selvage and A at right selvage, see Fig. 55.

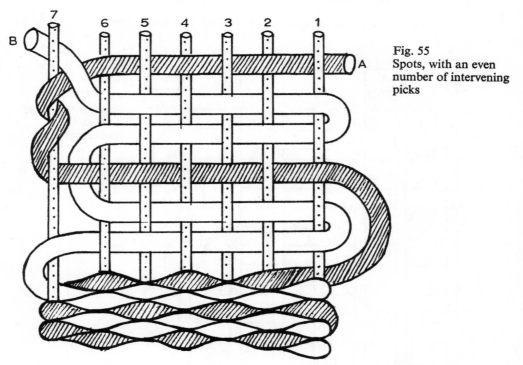

Fig. 55
Spots, with an even number of intervening picks

Weave two picks of B.

Weave one pick of A from right to left.

Weave two picks of B, noting that it misses left selvage.

Twist A twice downwards and then throw from left to right. Note that this begins by floating over two ends.

Pass B over this float and under the selvage thread exactly as in Fig. 55.

Repeat this sequence.

Variations

Much can be done using just these three elements, cross stripes, pick-and-pick stripes and spots, see Plate 8. Difficulties may be encountered at the selvage, when combining the different elements or playing variations upon them, but by following the principles explained above they can be solved.

Take as an example the reversing of colours in a pick-and-pick area. At the bottom of Fig. 56 stripes of colour A (shaded) lie over the even-numbered warp ends. At the top of Fig. 56, colour A lies over the odd-numbered ends.

The switch-over is managed thus:

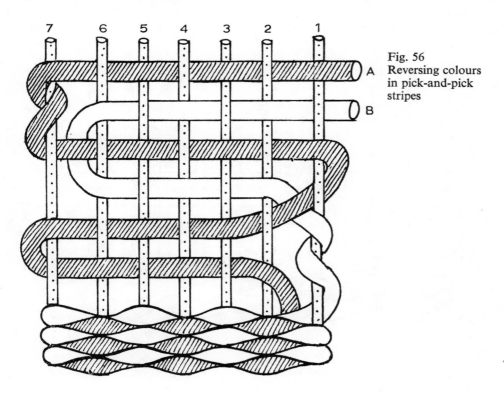

Fig. 56
Reversing colours
in pick-and-pick
stripes

Weave two picks of A.

Twist B twice downwards around right selvage thread then throw from right to left. Note that it floats over two ends at right selvage.

Take A over this float, then under right selvage thread and throw from right to left.
Weave one pick B from left to right, missing left selvage.
Twist A twice downwards around left selvage then throw from left to right.

Continue thus with B missing the selvage and A wrapping round it, i.e., the reverse of what is occurring at the bottom of Fig. 56.

The switch-over can be done similarly but starting with two picks of B instead of A.

D. Crossed Wefts

(i) IN CONTRARY MOTION

In *Costumes of the Bronze Age in Denmark* by H. C. Broholm and M. Hald, there are details and diagrams of a strange characteristic of these textiles. This is the frequent occurrence of several separate wefts in each shed. Each weft travels in the opposite direction to its neighbour (i.e., in contrary motion) and when two neighbouring wefts meet, they cross each other as in Fig. 57 (a), and then continue on in their original

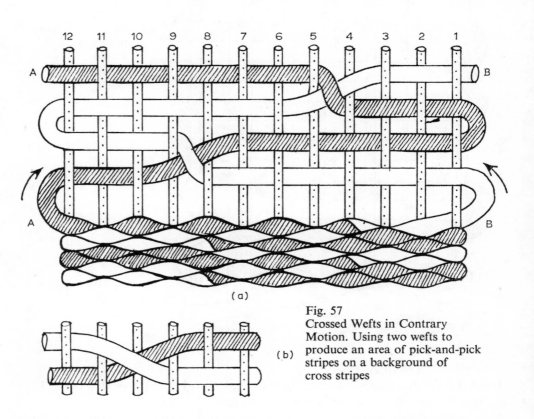

Fig. 57
Crossed Wefts in Contrary Motion. Using two wefts to produce an area of pick-and-pick stripes on a background of cross stripes

direction in the next shed. As some of the Bronze Age cloths are over four feet wide, the supposition is that two or more weavers were employed simultaneously at one loom and that the use of several wefts saved time. All the wefts are identical and the weave is a 50/50 plain weave, but there are interesting results if the wefts are of different colours and the weave is weft-face plain weave. The resulting technique can employ two, three or more wefts.

(a) *Using Two Wefts*

Two wefts, A (shaded) and B (white), start from opposite selvages, A from the left, B from the right, see arrows in expanded part of Fig. 57 (a).

Lift the even-numbered ends.
Take A across in this shed, from left to right, for a little way, then bring it out of the shed between the raised ends 8 and 10.
Take B across in the same shed, from right to left, and also bring it out between ends 8 and 10.

Lift odd-numbered ends.
Put A into this shed down between raised ends 9 and 7, and take straight across to right selvage. Note that in entering shed, A crosses two ends, 8 and 9. This float cannot be avoided but it is tied down by the next move of B.
Put B in the same shed between ends 9 and 7 and take it across to left selvage. At this crossing point, B is lying almost parallel to the warp.

Lift even-numbered ends.
Take A across in this shed, from right to left, for a short distance, then bring it out between raised ends 4 and 6.
Take B across in the same shed, from left to right, and also bring it out between ends 4 and 6.

Lift odd-numbered ends.
Put B into this shed down between raised ends 3 and 5 and take it across to right selvage. Note that this floats over ends 4 and 5.
Put A into the same shed down between ends 3 and 5 and carry it across to left selvage. Here it is A which is sharply angled as it ties down the float of B.

Repeat this sequence.
The result of these manoeuvres is to give an area of 2-and-2 stripes on either side, and an area of pick-and-pick stripes in the centre, see lower part of Fig. 57 (a). As this pick-and-pick area is bound by the weft crossings and these can be made anywhere at will, it is clear that this is a way of weaving a pick-and-pick area of any desired shape on a background of 2-and-2 stripes. See Plate 9.

Note—In this description B crosses A in the first crossing, and A crosses B in the second crossing. But there is nothing special about this arrangement; equally well, both crossings could have been A over B or B over A.
—A common fault is to contrive two floats at the crossing, both over two ends, as in Fig. 57 (b). This is the result of putting the second weft to move (white in Fig. 57 (b)) down between the wrong two ends. It is an obvious weakness and should be avoided.

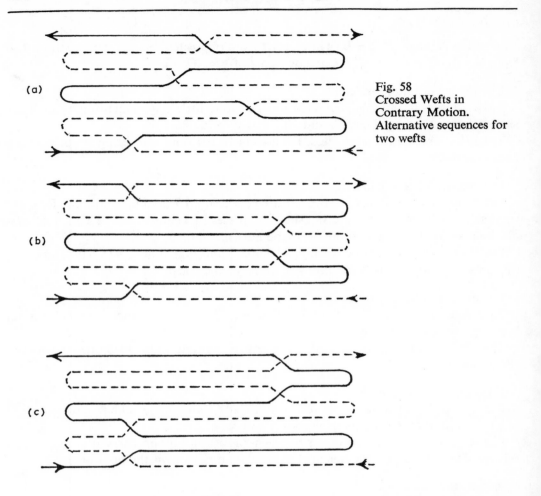

Fig. 58
Crossed Wefts in
Contrary Motion.
Alternative sequences for
two wefts

Fig. 57 (a) gives a detailed view of this technique, but in the following descriptions, simplified diagrams will be used. Fig. 58 (a) as an example, shows how to weave a triangular pick-and-pick area on a background of 2-and-2 stripes. Notice that the crossing points occur alternatively on the right and left boundary of the pick-and-pick area. This is the general rule, but by disobeying it, other effects can be obtained, as the following two examples show.

To reverse colours in a pick-and-pick area, make the crossing points twice on one side, then proceed normally, see Fig. 58 (b).

To make quite a different two colour pattern in the central area, make the crossing points twice on the right boundary of the area, and then twice on the left and repeat this sequence, as in Fig. 58 (c).

Many other variations of this type are possible.

(b) Using Three Wefts

Fig. 59 shows a possible arrangement of three wefts, black, white and shaded. The difficulty when using more than two wefts is starting correctly, because in the first shed each weft must move in the opposite direction to its neighbour.

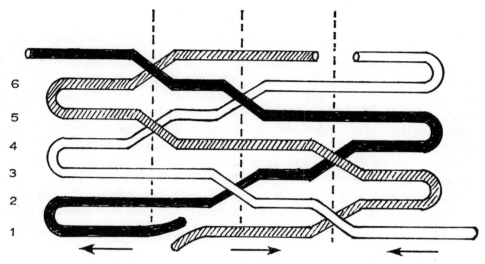

Fig. 59. Crossed Wefts in Contrary Motion. Using three wefts

Looking at the first pick in Fig. 59, the white weft begins from right selvage, but the black and shaded wefts have to start within the shed to fulfil the above conditions. Overlap their free ends as when joining two wefts.

Note—That there are three places where wefts cross, left, right and centre.
    —That the shaded weft takes a symmetrical course through the fabric. All its crossing points are at the right or left and never at the centre.
    —That the black and white wefts have crossings at all three points, but only cross each other at the centre.

When weaving with three or more colours, it becomes more important to decide which colour moves first at any crossing point. The rule is always to move the weft which will go into the correct opening and this is found by counting ends.

For example, imagine that at a crossing point two wefts have been brought out between raised ends 4 and 5, counting from the left selvage, see Fig. 60 (a). The shed is then changed, see Fig. 60 (b). The correct weft to move first is the one which will go naturally into the opening between the *new* fourth and fifth raised ends. This is the white weft; the black, if moved first, would go into the opening between third and fourth raised ends. So the white moves first and the black crosses it in the normal way.

Plate 10 shows a sample using three wefts, black, white and grey. These three

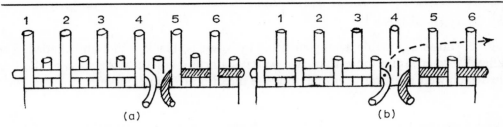

Fig. 60. Crossed Wefts in Contrary Motion. Determining correct point to enter wefts after crossing

colours appear as cross stripes at either side. The central area (bounded by right and left crossing points as in Fig. 59) has discontinuous pick-and-pick stripes. The outline of this area can of course be altered by shifting the right and left crossing points. The two small rectangles of spots were obtained by moving the central crossing point from side to side, so that the black and white weft (see Fig. 59) alternately cross a little to the right and a little to the left of the centre. These two new crossing points defined the boundaries of the spotted area, thus three distinct areas with controllable boundaries are obtained. It will be understood that the areas differ because, although in one complete repeat each area must have two picks of all three colours, the sequence of these three colours varies from one area to the next due to the weft crossings between them.

(c) *Using Four Wefts*

Fig. 61 shows a possible plan using four wefts. Each of the wefts follows a similar course through the fabric, always crossing at all three possible points (right, left and centre) on its passage from selvage to selvage. In the first pick, the black and white weft start from the selvages but the two other wefts start from the centre of the shed. This is in order to preserve the contrary motion of the four wefts.

Nothing very interesting results if wefts of four different colours are used, the central area being a mixture of spots of all four colours. More is obtained by limiting the colours, but still using four wefts. For instance, in the first pick the two right-hand

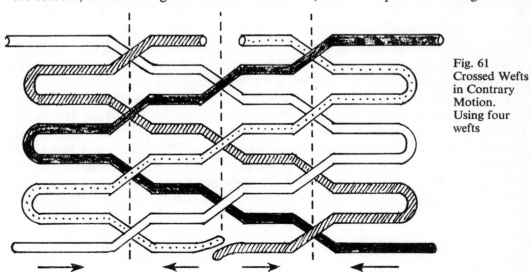

Fig. 61
Crossed Wefts
in Contrary
Motion.
Using four
wefts

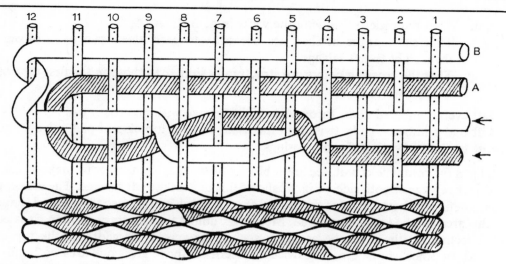

Fig. 62. Crossed Wefts in Parallel Motion. Using two wefts to produce an area of cross stripes on a background of pick-and-pick stripes

wefts could be black and the two left-hand wefts white, see Plate 11.

There are probably many more variations waiting to be discovered in this slow but rewarding technique.

(ii) IN PARALLEL MOTION

Seeing and analysing an American Indian textile brought the realization that there is another type of Crossed Weft technique, one in which both wefts start from the same side, i.e., they move in parallel motion. This opens many more possibilities, some of which are described below.

(a) The first example gives an area of 2-and-2 stripes on a background of pick-an-pick stripes. Referring to Fig. 62, start weft A and B from right selvage, see arrows.

Lift even-numbered ends. Take A across in this shed then bring it out of the shed between raised ends 4 and 6.

Lift odd-numbered ends, take B across similarly and bring it out between raised ends 3 and 5.

Lift even-numbered ends, continue B across inserting it down between ends 4 and 6 and bringing it out again between ends 8 and 10. Note that it forms a float over ends 4 and 5.

Lift odd-numbered ends, continue A across, inserting it down between ends 3 and 5, and taking it out again between the ends 7 and 9. Note that this ties down the float of B.

Lift even-numbered ends, insert A down between ends 8 and 10 and bring it out at the left selvage. Note that it forms a float over ends 8 and 9.

Lift odd-numbered ends, insert B down between ends 7 and 9, tying down above float, and carry it on to left selvage.

Note—That the order of moving the wefts is A, B, B, A, A, B.

That six changes of shed are necessary to carry these two picks of weft from right to left selvage.

That the crossing points are structurally similar to those in the first type of crossed wefts.

Lift even-numbered ends, throw A to right selvage with no crossings.

Lift odd-numbered ends, twist B in the usual way for a pick-and-pick selvage and throw to right selvage with no crossings.

This is the complete repeat, see lower block in Plate 12. Remember to make a pick-and-pick selvage at both sides; Fig. 62 shows this only at the left selvage. The crossing points define the boundaries of the central area of 2-and-2 stripes, so the size and shape of this area can be easily controlled. Moreover, unlike the Contrary Motion Crossed Weft technique, there can be as many such areas across the width of the rug as desired. In other words, crossing twice as described above gives one area of 2-and-2 stripes, crossing four times gives two such areas, crossing six times gives three such areas, see Fig. 63. This applies to all the variations described below, so therefore there is much more scope for design with this method.

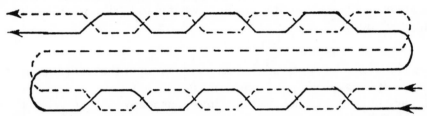

Fig. 63. Crossed Wefts in Parallel Motion. Producing many areas across width of rug

(b) This is the type seen in the American Indian textile mentioned above. The sequence is the following:

Take both wefts from right to left twisting as described above.
Take both wefts from left to right also twisting as above.
Then weave one pick of A, right to left, with no twisting.
Weave one pick of B, right to left, with no twisting.
Weave one pick A, left to right, with no twisting.
Weave one pick B, left to right, with no twisting.
Repeat this sequence; see upper block in plate 12.

(c) The same central block can be woven but with 4-and-4 stripes at the side instead of pick-and-pick stripes. Fig 64 (a) shows the sequence. The result is similar to that produced by one of the four weft variations of the Contrary Motion Crossed Weft technique, but it is much simpler to carry out; see Plate 13.

(d) The first type described under the Contrary Motion Crossed Weft technique, i.e., a block of pick-and-pick stripes on a 2-and-2 stripe background, can also be produced. Fig. 64 (b) shows the sequence. The advantage of using the Parallel Motion method is that many such blocks, instead of only one, can be produced in the width of the rug.

(e) There are many other variations. They all result from varying the order or number of the twisting picks and the normal non-twisting picks. The reader who has understood and tried the variations described will be able to discover new ones for himself.

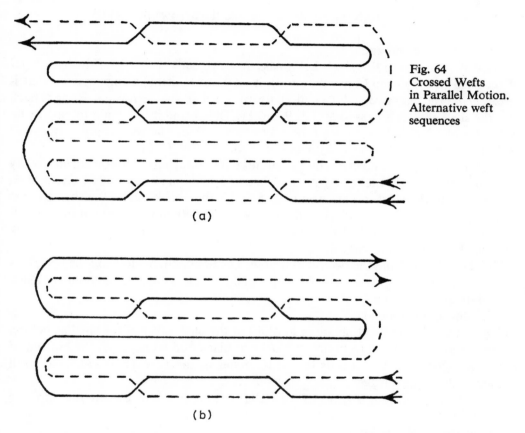

(a)

Fig. 64
Crossed Wefts
in Parallel Motion.
Alternative weft
sequences

(b)

In conclusion, note that there are two main differences between the Contrary Motion and the Parallel Motion varieties of the Crossed Weft technique.

(1) Many wefts can be used in the former technique, the more wefts, the more complex it becomes; whereas all the variations of the latter technique are produced with only two wefts.

(2) If both techniques are limited to two wefts, then the former only gives one block, but the latter gives any number of blocks across the width of the rug.

E. Skip Plain Weave

This is a traditional Middle Eastern technique for rugs. It is also found in Peruvian textiles, but with an approximately equal warp and weft count, i.e., not as a weft-face weave.

The basis of this technique is plain weave, with two wefts in each shed. Both wefts travel from selvage to selvage but they pass in and out of the back layer of the shed, forming floats on the reverse of the rug. Where one weft is in the shed, the other is floating.

The two wefts start from the right selvage, see the arrows in Fig. 65 (a).

Lift even-numbered ends.

Insert A (black) into this shed. Let it pass *over* two ends (1 and 3) of the back layer of the shed in the normal way, then push it backwards through this layer so that it passes *under* the next two ends (5 and 7), forming a float on the reverse. Bring it back into the shed and let it pass *over* ends 9 and 11. Then bring it out again to pass *under* ends 13 and 15. Continue thus all the way across, taking the weft alternately over 2 and under 2 ends of the back layer of the shed. See Fig. 65 (a).

Still with the even-numbered ends lifted, take B (white) across following an exactly opposite course to that taken by A. So it begins by passing *under* ends 1 and 3, then comes up into the shed to pass *over* ends 5 and 7 then back out of the shed to pass *under* ends 9 and 11 and similarly, all the way across. Wherever A was in the shed, B floats on the reverse, and vice versa. Fig. 65 (b) shows a cross section through the back layer of the shed at this stage.

The shed is closed and the two picks beaten. The floats slip behind and the two picks combine to give the appearance of a single pick, which is coloured alternately black and white along its length.

Lift odd-numbered ends.

Pass A from left to right, going in and out of the back layer of the shed as before.

Presuming it is desired to build up blocks of black and white, as at the bottom of Fig. 65 (a), then take A over ends 18 and 16, under 14 and 12, over 10 and 8, etc. until it reaches the right selvage.

In the same shed take B from left to right, making it follow exactly the opposite course to A.

This is the whole repeat.

Note—That as B does not weave at the left selvage, it has to be caught in the returning loop of A. The way it is caught looks awkward in the diagram, but in practice it is an effective method. The two wefts will be similarly caught together at the right selvage, before the next two picks.

—That there are two picks, one of A and one of B, for each change of shed.

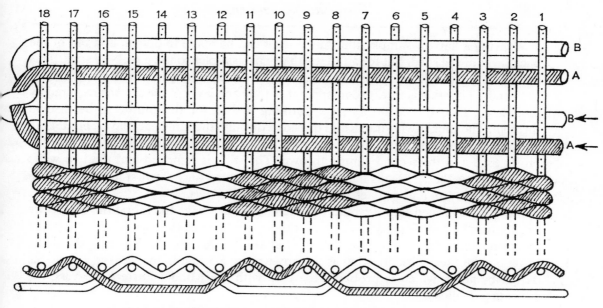

Fig. 65. Skip Plain Weave. (a) General view (b) Cross section

The above describes the weaving of a very simple pattern with this technique. But depending on the course the wefts take through the back layer of the shed, a great range of complex designs is possible. One colour should always be the 'leader' in this technique. In the above description, it was A, the black weft. Whatever course A takes, dictated by the design required, B takes exactly the opposite course.

The limiting factor in designs is the length of float on the reverse of the rug, which should not exceed about 1½ inches. This means that there should not be an area of one colour on the face wider than 1½ inches. If a larger area is wanted, then spot it or stripe it with the other colour, so that the floats of the latter do not go right across the width of the area. It is this avoidance of long floats which gives some of the special character to designs in this technique. See Plates 14 and 15.

But the really special feature is the opportunity it gives the weaver of producing the finest possible lines, in both the vertical and diagonal directions. Even using conventional tapestry techniques, such lines are very difficult to produce. This is therefore the chief feature to exploit when using the technique.

Because of the floats on the reverse, it is not practical to use this technique all over a rug, unless of course it is to be used purely as a decorate textile. So it is best to alternate stripes of this technique with stripes of plain weave. A warp with 6 e.p.i. is suitable, threaded straight on four shafts, single in the heald. Then for the plain weave stripes, lift 12 and 34 and use a weft of three to four thicknesses of 2-ply carpet wool. For the stripes of skip plain weave, lift 13 and 24, and use wefts consisting of two thicknesses of 2-ply carpet wool. Woven thus, the floats will not give too much extra thickness in the skip plain weave sections.

Weaving a narrow sample, the shuttle itself can be made to dive in and out of the back layer of the shed, but for a full width rug it is simpler to use a pick-up stick. This should be flat and have a cross section of about 2 inches by $\frac{1}{4}$ inch and be pointed at both ends. The stick is threaded in and out of the back layer of the shed as required by the design, then turned on its edge, forming a shed for the shuttle to be thrown through. The stick is withdrawn and threaded through the same back layer, but taking an exactly opposite course, using the weft just thrown as a guide. It is then turned on its edge and the second shuttle thrown. The stick is removed and the two wefts beaten up together. Threads seldom need to be counted once the first few picks of the design are woven, and can act as a guide to what follows.

It could be argued that it would be much easier to weave the fabric the other way up, so that the shuttle goes in and out of the *upper* layer of the shed, and is therefore more convenient for the weaver to manipulate. But the drawback is that the floats (now on the face) obscure what is already woven. So unless the weaver knows his design by heart, which is probably the case with the Middle Eastern weavers, the advantage is illusory.

Three wefts can be used instead of two and are often found in Eastern examples of this technique. The introduction of the third weft makes the avoidance of long floats more difficult than usual. At any one point in the weaving, one of the three wefts is lying in the shed and the other two are floating on the reverse. Plate 16 shows an example using three colours.

If the weave is mentally turned through a right angle, so that what was the black and white weft becomes the warp, the structure is now warp-face and is identical with the 'saha' technique, described in Chapter 11. This is one of the many instances where a certain weave structure, in which one of the thread elements predominates, can be woven either as a warp-face or as a weft-face textile.

F. Technique for Weaving Letters and Figures

Occasionally the weaver may want to record his own initials on a rug or the date it was woven. Or a rug woven for presentation may have to include some reference to the donor. For these purposes, the following simple method is useful. It is satisfying because it is a real woven technique not an embroidered one.

The technique is basically a stripe of pick-and-pick weaving which is distorted to produce letters or figures by floating the wefts over or under three ends in appropriate places. So the rug has to have an end border of pick-and-pick weave in two contrasting colours. See Plate 17 and Fig. 66. The latter shows the details of producing the letter 'P'.

Beginning just above the full-stop at the foot of the letter, it will be seen that the black weft has floated over three ends for four picks, labelled 1 to 4. The white weft floats correspondingly under three ends in this position. These floats are produced by

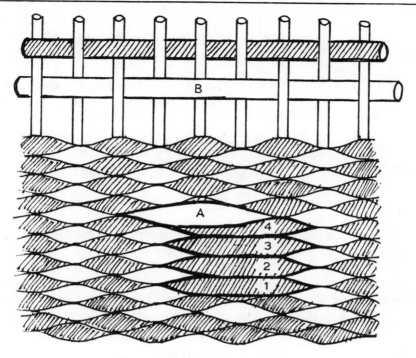

Fig. 66. Weaving letters and figures

bringing the shuttle out of the front (or the back) of the shed, and passing it over (or under) one end before returning it into the shed. The net result is a solid area of black on the face and of white on the reverse.

To produce the lower part of the loop of the 'P', the white weft has to float over three ends. This float is labelled A in Fig. 66; there is of course a corresponding black float on the reverse of the rug. The upper part of the loop is shown in the expanded section of the diagram and is labelled B. Note the float of black weft passing under three ends above it. When these are beaten down, the letter 'P' will be completed and should be followed with a few picks of black weft only.

In this technique it is best if one of the colours, e.g., white, always initiates the changes of outline by floating where necessary. Then the other colour always follows the white's lead, floating on the reverse where the white floats on the face and vice versa.

5 · Weft-face Rugs in Plain Weave

PART TWO: TECHNIQUES IN WHICH THE WEFT DOES NOT RUN FROM SELVAGE TO SELVAGE

INTRODUCTION

In all the techniques described so far the wefts have passed from selvage to selvage, even though this course may have been interrupted for some reason, e.g., twisting.

The characteristic of the techniques described in the present chapter is that the wefts never take a simple selvage to selvage course, they either weave within the confines of a small area, or if they do pass from selvage to selvage they take a complicated zigzag course. These methods lead to a far greater freedom in design.

1. MEET AND SEPARATE TECHNIQUE

Meet and Separate is the convenient name given to a technique which is basically only a special application of *hatching*, a method used in tapestry. In tapestry it is generally used to shade from one colour to another, i.e., to give an area of mixed colours, A and B, between areas of solid A and solid B. In this technique it is used with two contrasting colours so that the hatched area is not just a half-way stage, but becomes an important element in itself.

A. Normal Method

(i) USING TWO COLOURS

The normal method is shown in Fig. 67 and the sequence is as follows:

Lift even-numbered ends, insert the two wefts A and B, from opposite selvages (see arrows) and bring them both out of the shed between raised ends 6 and 8.

Lift odd-numbered ends, insert A and B down into the shed between raised ends 7 and 9 and let each return to its own selvage. So the wefts have met and then separated, leaving a small slit in the rug at the meeting point, X.

Lift even-numbered ends, insert wefts into this shed as before, but this time bring them out of the shed, between raised ends 2 and 4.

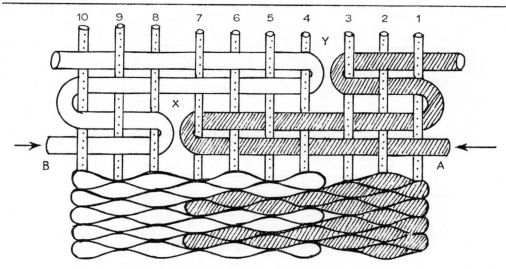

Fig. 67. Meet and Separate Weave, normal method. Using two wefts

Lift odd-numbered ends, insert wefts down between raised ends 3 and 5 into the shed, and let them return to their own selvages. There is now a small slit at this new meeting point, Y.

If these four picks are repeated, with the meeting points alternating between positions X and Y, the result will be as at the bottom of Fig. 67, i.e., an area of solid black to the right, an area of solid white to the left, and, in between, a striped area made up of two picks of black alternating with two picks of white. Note that two shuttles are giving three areas.

It will be immediately apparent that the outline of this central striped area can be altered by changing the position of the meeting points, X and Y; for it is these points which establish its right and left boundary. Thus to enlarge the area X must move to the left and Y to the right.

Once this principle is learnt, a shape of any complexity can be woven. Fig 68 (a) shows the weft plan for weaving the triangle seen in Fig. 68 (b).

One obvious variation is to make the wefts meet twice at X and then twice at Y, so that the central area is made up of four picks of black alternating with four picks of white.

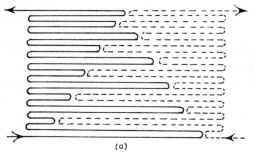

(a)

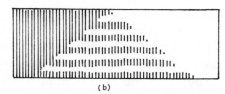

(b)

Fig. 68. Meet and Separate Weave, normal method. (a) Weft plan for weaving a triangle (b) The result

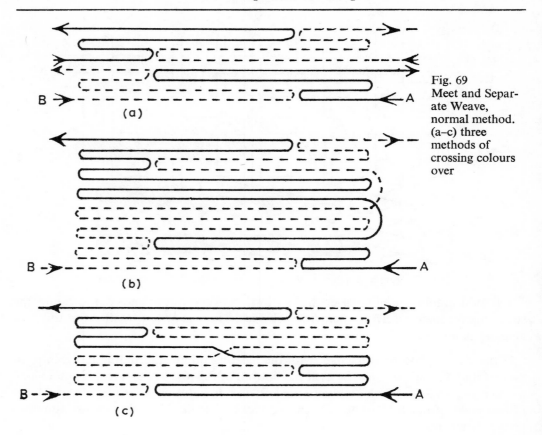

Fig. 69
Meet and Separate Weave, normal method. (a–c) three methods of crossing colours over

Crossing Colours Over

The need will probably be felt to switch the two colours over, i.e., to bring the black over to the left and the white to the right, otherwise one side of the rug will be darker than the other. It is difficult to do this without destroying the continuity of the central area. In fact the only perfect way is to cut both wefts when they are at their selvages and then start them again at the opposite selvages. The next meeting place will then have to be at the same side as the one before the colour change, in order to preserve the striped sequence, see Fig. 69 (a).

Amongst other ways which upset the striped sequence, but seem a little less contrived, are the following.

(a) Start with both wefts at their own selvages and then weave three picks of B from selvage to selvage, followed by three picks of A from selvage to selvage. Then continue normally, the next meeting point being on the same side as the one before the colour change, see Fig. 69 (b). This gives a black and white stripe at the point of colour change.

(b) Bring both wefts out at the centre, not at either of the normal meeting points. Change shed and then instead of letting them return to their own selvage, cross them exactly as in the Crossed Weft technique. The next meeting point is on the opposite side to the one before the colour change. This method gives a row of spots in the central area, see Fig. 69 (c), but if it is used at the point of a striped triangle, there will be no spots. Plate 18 shows the two above methods.

So far the meeting points, X and Y, have been ordered in a precise way, but a rug of quite a different character can be woven if the meeting points are more or less haphazard. Fingers of colour from each side reach varying distances into the opposite colour, giving more movement and variation.

(ii) USING THREE COLOURS

Just as two wefts can give three areas, so three wefts can give five areas. Plate 19 shows a simple design using three wefts. Note that there are three areas of solid colour and two striped areas. The two outside wefts (black) move in relation to the striped area on their side exactly as in the method described above. But the central weft (white) takes a more complicated course, being involved in both the striped areas and in the central white area; it never reaches either selvage.

Fig. 70 will help to explain this. Note that in the first shed, each of the three wefts is moving in the opposite direction to its neighbour, see arrows. Weft A moves to the left, B to the right and C to the left. The sequence is thus:

Pick 1, B meets A at right boundary of right-hand striped area (point Q), and C passes to the selvage.

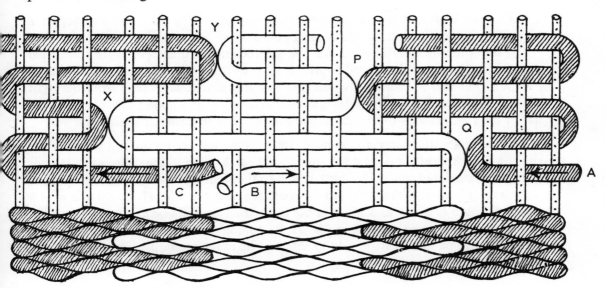

Fig. 70. Meet and Separate Weave, normal method. Using three wefts

Pick 2, B meets C at left boundary of left-hand striped area (point X), and A passes to the selvage.

Pick 3, B meets A at left boundary of right-hand striped area (point P), and C passes to the selvage.

Pick 4, B meets C, at right boundary of left-hand striped area (point Y), and A passes to the selvage.

These four picks constitute the repeat and if continued will produce the five areas seen at the bottom of Fig. 70. Note it is always best to move the central weft first in each shed, as it establishes where the meeting points are to be.

To alter the outline of the two striped areas all four meeting points may have to be shifted. To achieve the effect in Plate 19, points X and Y have gradually to separate, as do points P and Q. Then points X and Y must gradually approach each other as also do points P and Q. Some difficulties arise because the four meeting points are one pick ahead of each other. So the two striped areas cannot change outlines simultaneously, one must precede the other.

Interchanging Colours with Three Wefts

Any two adjacent colours can be interchanged using the Crossed Weft technique. For example, A and B could be crossed at P or Q, and B and C could be crossed at X or Y. So the two outside colours could be switched over, but it would have to be done in stages, needing four picks.

B. Method Using Clasped Wefts

(i) USING TWO COLOURS

The Clasped Weft method has an interesting application to the Meet and Separate technique, greatly increasing its range of possibilities.

For this, the two wefts involved must be half the normal thickness. If they consisted above of 2-ply carpet wool used fourfold, they must here be 2-ply carpet wool used twofold. One weft A (black) is wound on a shuttle and it will weave from the right selvage. The other colour B (white) is wound as a ball or on a cone and is placed to the left of the rug, perhaps on the floor, see Fig. 71. The sequence is as follows:

Throw the shuttle (carrying the black weft) to the left across the full width of the rug. At the left selvage take out the shuttle and catch it round the white weft. Do not change the shed, but throw the shuttle back to the right selvage. The returning black weft drags a loop of white weft into the shed, see pick 1 in Fig. 71. So there is now a doubled length of black and white in the shed, the two wefts being looped into each other (clasped) at some point, X in Fig. 71. By pulling on the two free ends of the weft, this point can be moved from side to side and its exact position adjusted before the weft is beaten.

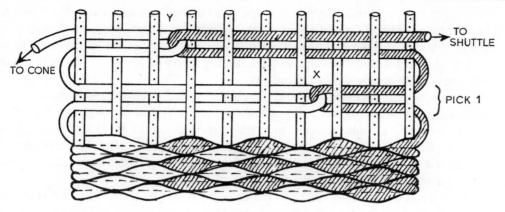

Fig. 71. Meet and Separate Weave, method using clasped wefts

Change the shed and repeat the above procedure.

Note—Tension is put on the wefts to move their meeting point to the required position, so remember to wave the wefts after this stage and before beating.

—The fact that there are always doubled wefts in the shed explains why these wefts must begin by being half the normal thickness.

—A simple way to catch one weft round the other at the left selvage is to suspend a loop of wire from the loom framework on the left so that it is to the side of, and a bit above, the level of the fell of the rug. Then lead the white weft up from the cone on the floor, through the loop and then to the rug, see Fig. 72. Catch the shuttle with the hand under the part marked X. Withdraw the shuttle, pass it over X and back into the shed. This can be done very quickly.

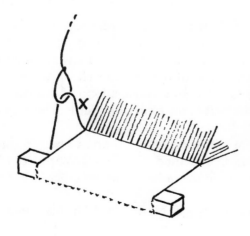

Fig. 72
Meet and Separate
Weave, method using
clasped wefts. View of
loom

Now if the meeting points (labelled X and Y as before) are alternated from side to side as in the normal Meet and Separate technique, the central area, instead of consisting of 2-and-2 stripes, will consist of pick-and-pick stripes, as at the bottom of Fig. 71. If this is not understood, compare the top parts of Fig. 67 and Fig. 71. The former shows four picks, the latter only two.

If the meeting point is twice at X and then twice at Y, the central area will consist of 2-and-2 stripes as before. If it is twice at X then once at Y, and the sequence repeated, the central area will have black spots on a white ground. So the great advantage given by the Clasped Weft method is the possibility of varying the striping of the central area. In fact it will be discovered that by varying the meeting points appropriately any two-weft pattern can be produced in the central area.

Another variation specially suited to the Clasped Weft method is to use two colours for one of the side areas. In other words, have two cones holding different colours on the floor to the left of the rug. When the shuttle comes across, it can catch either one or other of them. If it catches them alternately, then the left hand area instead of being a solid colour will show pick-and-pick stripes. Any other sort of striping can be produced in this area. See Plate 20.

The above variations show there is an endless field for exploration here.

(ii) USING THREE COLOURS

Three colours can be used to give five areas as with the normal method for Meet and Separate technique. There are two possible methods.

(a) The two outer colours are on cones at their respective sides, and the central colour is on a shuttle which lies at the centre of the warp. This shuttle passes down into the shed and to the left selvage, picks up a loop of that colour and then goes straight across to the right selvage. Here it picks up a loop of the other colour and returns to the centre where it leaves the shed. All this takes place in one shed. The procedure is repeated in the next shed.

(b) The two outer colours are on shuttles and the central colour is in a ball or in some convenient form. The right-hand shuttle is thrown across to the left selvage, a loop of the central weft is pushed down into the shed so that on the return of the right-hand shuttle its weft picks up a loop of the central weft. In the same shed, the left-hand shuttle is thrown across to the right selvage, a loop of central weft pushed down as before and picked up by the weft of the returning shuttle. The shed is changed and the sequence repeated.

A simple implement, made from stiff wire, with a loop at one end, and another about 6 inches away, will help with this method, see Fig. 73. Yarn from the central ball is threaded through the two loops in the order shown and then goes to the fell of the rug.

Throw the right shuttle to the left selvage. Now introduce this implement down through the centre of the warp, passing over the pick just thrown (marked A in Fig. 73), and as close to the reed as possible. Throw the right shuttle back and draw out the implement. The weft from the right shuttle will now be looped around the central weft. Repeat this manœuvre with the left shuttle. Note that the implement remains threaded all the time, yarn being paid out from the ball, through the wire loops and into the weaving area.

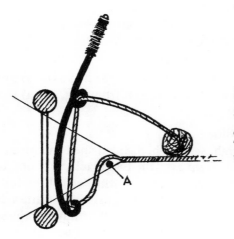

Fig. 73
Meet and Separate
Weave, method using
clasped wefts.
Technique for using
three colours

An alternative method is to have the central weft in a ball or cone underneath the warp and pull a loop up instead of pushing one down. Either way needs some development to make it more practical.

However it is carried out, this is a slow process and necessitates a small float of the central float between each pick, but it has more design possibilities than when using three colours in the normal Meet and Separate technique.

2. COMPENSATED INLAY

In the various inlay methods used in fine weaving, the inlay weft is an extra element added to certain parts of the cloth. So in these parts there is an increased thickness of weft. But in a weft-face technique, there has to be equal thickness of weft throughout, so it is only possible to inlay a weft, if some method is found of compensating for its added thickness.

A. Basic Method

Fig 74 (a) shows the basic idea.

Weave two picks of the white weft (the inlay weft), where required in the centre of the warp.

Weave the black weft (the background weft) from the right selvage up to the right edge of the inlay.

Change shed, take the black weft to the right selvage.

Change shed, take it right across to the left selvage.

Change shed, take it up to the left edge of the inlay area.

Change shed, take it back to the left selvage.

This characteristic zigzag course of the black weft is the means of compensating for the added thickness of the inlay weft. It will be seen from Fig. 74 (a) that there are now three picks of weft all the way across.

There are now two main possibilities.

(i) Return the black weft to the right selvage in the next shed and repeat the process over again. That is, take the white weft up over the two black picks and behind end 5 into the next shed, see Fig. 74 (b). Weave two picks of white as before, followed by the black as before. This will give a central inlay block consisting of alternate stripes of inlay weft and ground weft. It will be seen from the way the inlay weft jumps up that it naturally gives a vertical right edge to the inlay block. See Plate 21.

(ii) Leaving the black weft at the left selvage, weave two more picks of inlay weft. It can be inserted into the shed, either by carrying it over two warp ends (5 and 4 in Fig. 74 (c)), or by carrying it vertically upwards as in Fig. 74 (d). In either case it naturally gives an inclined right edge to the inlay block, sloping up to the right in Figs. 74 (c) and (d). After these two inlay picks, bring the ground weft back to the right selvage following the same zigzag course as before, see Fig. 74 (d). Here the weft sequence in the inlay block is two picks of inlay weft followed by one of ground weft. In other words it will be spotted as seen in Plate 22.

Thus the block can consist of either stripes or spots, depending upon which of the above two methods is used. Naturally, the two types can be combined in one block, e.g., by alternating repeats of the two methods.

It will be seen from Plates 21 and 22 that the successive jump-ups of the inlay weft, where it floats over some warp and weft, build up into a ridge. This is vertical in the case of a striped block and angled in the case of a spotted block. But there is no ridge when the jump-up is made as in Fig. 74 (d), and obviously there is no such ridge on the reverse of the rug. Note that the angled ridge can slant either way.

So far attention has been focused on the right-hand edge of the inlay block and the manner in which the jump-up of the inlay weft controls its outline. But the left-hand edge of the block is under no such control for the two inlay picks can weave as far as desired to the left. So the left outline can be exactly as the weaver wishes. This leads to many design possibilities such as alternating long and short inlays to the left in an ordered way, see Fig. 75 (a). There are then two areas suggested, one of which has only half the normal quota of inlay picks.

It will be understood that the inlay weft jumps up on the right of the block simply because its first pick began on this side, see Fig. 74 (a). It could equally well have begun on the left. So it is simple to control on which side of the block the jump-up ridges

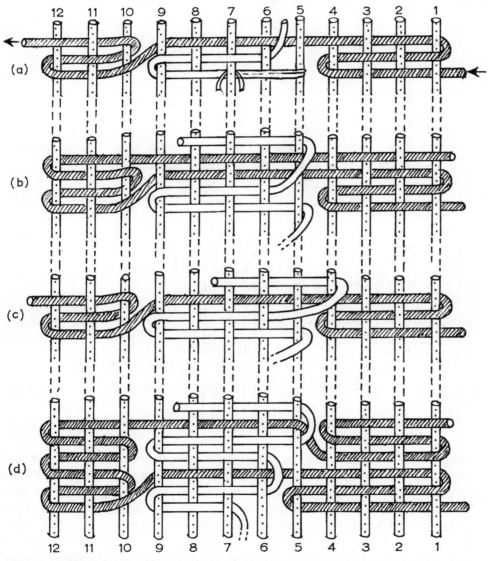

Fig. 74. Compensated Inlay. (a)–(d) Methods of jumping from one inlay to the next

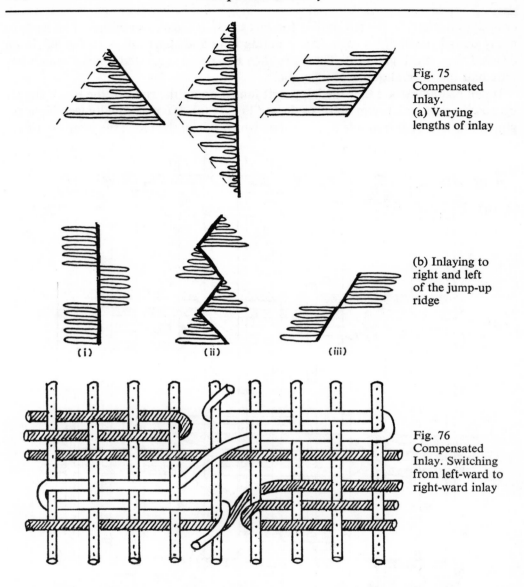

Fig. 75
Compensated
Inlay.
(a) Varying
lengths of inlay

(b) Inlaying to
right and left
of the jump-up
ridge

(i)   (ii)   (iii)

Fig. 76
Compensated
Inlay. Switching
from left-ward to
right-ward inlay

are to appear. This is important as they form a quite marked feature of the result-ing design. In a certain type of design, due to the placing of successive blocks the ridge appears alternately to right and left, see Fig. 75 (b). The inlay weft is carried to the left for several repeats to make the first block. Then it is carried to the right to make the second block. The ridge (shown as a thick line) becomes a kind of spine from which the inlay stripes radiate to right and to left. Fig. 76 shows in detail the switch from left-ward to right-ward inlay, such as occurs at the mid-point in Fig. 75 (b) (iii). It should be emphasized that it is impossible to move the ridge from one side to the other of a block simply by putting in a single inlay pick. This sounds as if it would work, but it is essential for the correct sequence of sheds that there should always be two picks (or some other even number) of inlay wefts.

B. Inlaying Several Blocks

One beauty of this technique is that however many inlay blocks there are across the width of the rug (each of course needing its own weft) only one ground weft is needed for all the intervening areas. But the ground weft has to take an increasingly zigzag course to compensate for each extra inlay block. Fig. 77 shows diagrammatically two

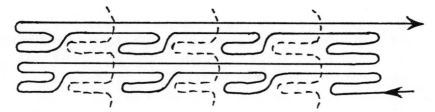

Fig. 77. Compensated Inlay. Weft plan when inlaying several blocks

complete repeats when there are three striped inlay blocks. Plates 21 and 22 show a hollow square and a hollow diamond. Naturally when weaving the middle third of these blocks, two inlay wefts have to be used and the jump-up ridge of the second weft can be seen to the left of each central hollow. Plate 23 shows a small sample woven with two inlay wefts. The weft forming the right half of the motif jumps up on its left, the weft forming the left half jumps up on its right. Because the method shown in Fig. 74 (d) was used, there are no ridges, just small vertical flicks of weft which give a toothed edge to the motif where it borders the central hollow. These teeth do not show on the reverse.

C. Two Inlay Wefts in One Block

In this development of the technique, two inlay wefts work in Contrary Motion within one block, see Fig. 78.

A convenient way to begin is to place the centre of a length of weft in the first shed so that there is weft to work with, hanging out of the left and right end of this pick.

Change shed, bring both wefts in towards the centre then bring them out of the shed in the space between raised warp ends 2 and 4.

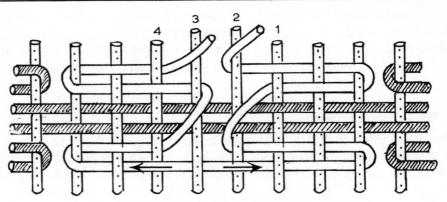

Fig. 78. Compensated Inlay. Using two wefts in one block.

Weave the ground weft, here inserted to give a striped block.

Carry both inlay wefts up over the ground weft, as shown, and down into the shed between raised ends 1 and 3. The wefts then separate in the first inlay shed and approach each other again in the second inlay shed.

> *Note*—When making a spotted block, the method of working is similar to the above.
> —As the inlay weft jump-up is at the centre of the block, both left- and right-hand edges of the block are controllable, and can assume any outline. So this method gives far greater freedom of design, see Plate 24.
> —The ridge formed by the two wefts jumping up can be moved about the centre of the block to give vertical or inclined lines as in Plate 24, and becomes a prominent part of the design. With a striped block the ridge tends to be vertical, and with a spotted block, diagonal. A block in which a repeat as for stripes alternates with one as for spots has a very steeply angled ridge of pleasant texture, see Plate 27. The effects shown in Fig. 75 (a) for one weft can be applied to both the inlay wefts in this technique, see Plate 25.

There are other variations using two inlay wefts in one block, such as the following.

(a) There is, of course, no necessity for the two inlay wefts in the second pick to meet at the point they started from in the first pick. In other words, the jump-ups can be in a different place in each repeat, so that instead of their building up into a solid ridge, they appear as isolated elements dotted about the block.

(b) Instead of the two inlay wefts lying parallel at the jump-up point, they can cross over each other. This works best in a spotted block. Fig. 79 shows these crossed jump-ups. Note that they have been arranged haphazardly to illustrate the point made in (a) above. See Plate 26.

(c) The two inlay wefts forming a block can be of different colours, which either keep to their own side throughout the block or are switched over by means of crossed jump-ups.

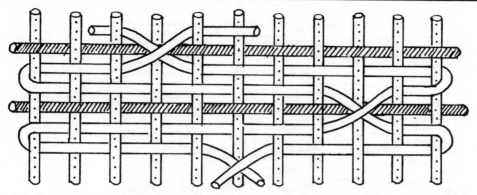

Fig. 79. Compensated Inlay. Using two wefts in one block and crossing them as they jump up

D. Four Inlay Wefts in One Block

Fig. 80 shows a block using four inlay wefts. It is really a pair of two-weft blocks side by side. To avoid a break in the centre, the two inner wefts are locked, and this lock is shifted from side to side to avoid any lumpiness. Note there are now two ridges which can be moved independently, see Plate 27. This variation gives the possibility of using up to four colours in one block.

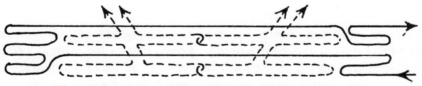

Fig. 80. Compensated Inlay. Using four wefts in one block

E. Several Blocks with One Inlay Weft

In this variation, both inlay weft and ground weft take a zigzag course from selvage to selvage. The chief advantage is that any number of blocks can be woven with just one inlay weft and one ground weft.

As with normal compensated inlay there are two main types of block.

(i) SPOTTED BLOCKS

Fig. 81 (a) shows the course taken by the two wefts to produce two spotted blocks. It will be obvious that the weft sequence in the blocks is three picks white, one pick black (which will appear as black spots on a white ground) and in the intervening areas it is three picks black, one pick white (which will appear as white spots on a black ground). Fig. 81 (b) shows this diagrammatically. The way wefts are disposed all over the rug means that the blocks are not greatly differentiated from the background. See Plate 28 where the central block seems to merge into the ground weave.

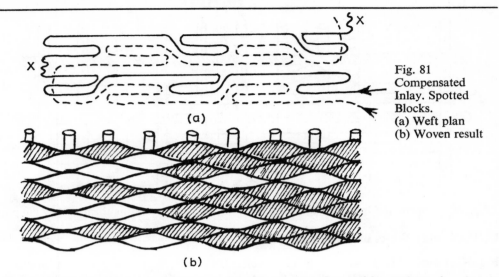

Fig. 81
Compensated
Inlay. Spotted
Blocks.
(a) Weft plan
(b) Woven result

Note—Blocks and intervening areas should consist of an odd number of ends.
　—The selvages are managed as described under 'Spots' in Chapter 4. The double twist of the ground weft around the selvage is indicated by X on Fig. 81 (a).

(ii) STRIPED BLOCKS

Here there is an extra pick of each weft which runs straight from selvage to selvage. That of the inlay weft occurs before its zigzag pick, that of the ground weft after its zigzag pick, see Fig. 82 (a). This method gives blocks and background areas even less differentiated than in the previous method. They both consist of stripes, the blocks having four picks white, two picks black and the background areas having four picks black, two picks white, see Fig. 82 (b).

Naturally these two types can be combined in one block.

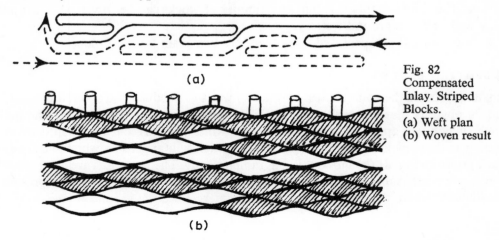

Fig. 82
Compensated
Inlay. Striped
Blocks.
(a) Weft plan
(b) Woven result

3. TAPESTRY TECHNIQUES

The essence of all tapestry techniques is that a weft-face textile is built up of a mosaic of small areas, each of which is woven with its own differently coloured weft. No weft as a rule, passes from selvage to selvage; but at any moment in the weaving, there will be a number of discontinuous wefts which together span the total width of the textile.

A. Slit Tapestry or Kilim

INTRODUCTION

It should be noted that in *The Primary Structure of Fabrics*, Irene Emery casts doubt on the use of the word 'kilim' as a synonym for slit tapestry. This is probably true when the whole field of tapestry weaving is considered, but in the field of rugs the word is a useful abbreviation for a 'slit tapestry-woven rug', and will be here used with this meaning.

Knotted pile, kilim and soumak are the three great techniques that have been traditionally used for rug weaving. Of the three, knotted rugs have achieved considerably more importance, and are collected and prized as works of art. Much is known of their history, and they can be dated and assigned a place of manufacture with some certainty. Until fairly recently, kilims, with none of the appeal of a rich pile, have been thought of as inferior by Western buyers. This has had one advantage: no kilims in the Middle East have been specially woven with an eye on the export market. They have been woven for home consumption only and so tend to be more 'genuine' and less influenced by Western tastes. Their official standing can be gauged by the fact that the exhibition of Near Eastern Kilims held in the Textile Museum, Washington, in 1965, claimed it was the first entirely devoted to this type that had ever been held anywhere. But anyone who has really looked at and studied kilims knows that some of the finest rugs in the world are of this type.

The word 'kilim' (also spelt kelim, khelim, ghilleem) is supposedly related to the Arabic word for curtain, suggesting that their early use was as a decorative hanging textile. Kilims have also been used as blankets, horse trappings, bed covers, saddlebags, and as a strong material for wrapping around goods, so necessary in nomadic life.

In fact, their typical feature, the slit between adjacent colour areas, does not make them ideally suitable for Western floor-coverings; though the more sturdy varieties can take a great deal of hard wear.

HISTORY

The earliest known kilim was found in 1960 by James Mellaart at Dorak, a site near ancient Troy. It lined a king's tomb, and fitted it so exactly that it was probably made especially for that purpose. Although it fell to dust on contact with the air, the wool fragments still had sufficient colouring for the design to be reconstructed with certainty. This was in yellow, red, blue and black and was made up of those simple geometric motifs still found in kilims today. As it was dated definitely before 2500 B.C., the implication is that a span of 4,500 years has not greatly altered the appearance of this type of rug. This fact loses some of its surprise when it is realized to what extent the design of a kilim is controlled by technical limitations. The ancient weaver arrived at the same solutions to the same problems and from these solutions arose the design limitations which cut right across styles and cultures.

Though this is the earliest evidence of a kilim so far discovered, there is other evidence which suggests its history may reach back a further 4,000 years in time. Pottery found in Hacilar in S. Anatolia and dating from the sixth millennium B.C., is painted with simple geometric motifs typical of those found on kilims. The inference, supported by many other examples from other cultures, is that these motifs were derived from contemporary kilims. The astonishing finds made at Catal Huyuk, in 1961, included some wall paintings with similar kilim-like motifs. These are dated from the second half of the seventh millennium B.C.

So certainly for 4,500 years, and maybe for twice as long, this type of textile has been produced in the Middle East. In this time, many types have flourished, such as the silk kilims of Kashan, enriched with gold and silver threads, dating from the sixteenth and seventeenth century A.D., and the Sehna kilims which represent the finest produced in the last two centuries. More recent types have included bride kilims from Baghdad made as part of the trousseau, the boldly-patterned Kurdish kilims, and the Allepo and Malatia kilims with their fine intricate details. The classification and description of the various types is not the concern of this book but will be found in books intended for collectors, a selection of which appear in the Bibliography.

Other countries, apart from Asia Minor, with a considerable history of weaving kilims and still producing them are Rumania (with its famous Oltenian kilims), Yugoslavia, Bulgaria, Poland, Denmark, Sweden, north coast of Africa, India, North and South America; in fact the technique seems universal.

TECHNIQUE

The essence of kilim technique is that the design is built up of small areas of solid colour, each of which is woven with its individual weft, and that between two such adjacent areas the respective wefts never interlock. The result is a vertical slit, which may be up to $\frac{3}{4}$ inch long. See Plates 29 and 30.

It is the ordering of the colour areas to avoid excessively long slits that results in the characteristic diamond, triangle and lozenge shapes.

As will be imagined, so universal a technique has many variations both of structure and of actual weaving processes. It is important to have a basic understanding of the technique before these are embarked upon. So to begin with, the weaving of a triangle of one colour on the background of another will be described in detail.

(i) WEAVING A TRIANGLE

(a) *Detailed Description*

Referring to Fig. 83 it will be seen that three wefts are necessary. One for the triangle (black), one for the background to the right of the triangle and one for the background to the left (both white). These are easier to handle as finger hanks than on shuttles.

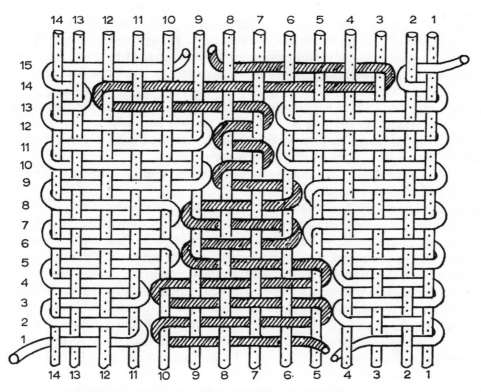

Fig. 83. Kilim. Weaving a triangle with wefts in contrary motion

The sequence is as follows:

Pick 1. Begin the three wefts in the first shed (even-numbered ends raised) so that each is running in the opposite direction to its neighbour. In Fig 83, the triangle's weft moves to the left, and the two background wefts move to the right. The triangle's weft is weaving under ends 6, 8 and 10, The background wefts weave under ends 2 and 4 on the right side and under 12 and 14 on the left.

Pick 2. Change shed. Return each weft back across its prescribed area, the triangle's weft going under ends 9, 7 and 5, and the background wefts going under 3 and 1, and 13 and 11.

It is very important that the triangle's weft should be weaving across an even number of warp ends at the base of the triangle. This is to ensure that when the tip of the triangle is reached, two ends still remain to weave on. Starting with an odd number at the base, there would only be one end at the tip on which it is impossible to weave. So as the second pick begins, move the triangle's weft first and ensure that it enters the shed down between raised ends 9 and 11, thus making the base of the triangle weave on six ends. If it enters down between raised ends 11 and 13, which from every other point of view it could equally well do, the base of the triangle will span an odd number of ends, i.e., seven. The left background weft enters the shed between the same two raised ends, i.e., 9 and 11, and moves to its own selvage. The right background weft moves in from its selvage.

Note that a small slit is left between ends 10 and 11 because as the two wefts turn round these ends to begin their second picks, they do not interlock.

Pick 3. Change shed. The three wefts repeat the first pick exactly. Note that the two wefts concerned leave a small slit between ends 4 and 5.

Pick 4. Change shed. The three wefts repeat the second pick, and the slit between ends 10 and 11 grows longer.

Four picks have now been completed with the triangle's weft weaving with six ends. Note that the three wefts are completely independent of each other. It is as if three miniature rugs are being woven, side by side, each with its own warp and weft. Obviously if this continued, the two slits would become impractically long; so in order to prevent this, the triangle's weft will begin to weave on only four ends in the next pick, i.e., the triangle will begin to taper. The background wefts will move inwards and now include the two warp ends (5 and 10) abandoned by the triangle's weft. Thus they weave across the top of the slit on their own side, and effectively close it.

Pick 5. Change shed. Weave the triangle's weft under ends 6 and 8. Weave the left background weft under ends 14, 12 and 10, closing the slit on its side, and weave the right background weft under ends 4 and 2.

Pick 6. Change shed. Weave the triangle's weft to right, entering the shed down between raised ends 9 and 11 and weaving under ends 9 and 7. Weave the right background weft, passing under ends 1, 3 and 5, thus closing the slit on its side. Weave the left background weft to its selvage, leaving a new slit between ends 9 and 10. Note that, as the very first pick of the triangle's weft began towards the left, the left side of the triangle is always one move ahead of the right, e.g., the triangle tapers first on the left, and the left slit is closed before the right. This is inevitable. No tapering of the triangle can be accomplished in just one pick. It always needs two picks, one to the left to alter its left boundary, and one to the right to alter its right boundary.

Pick 7. Change shed. Weave the triangle's weft to left, entering the shed down between raised ends 4 and 6. Enter the right background weft in same space and weave to its own selvage. A new slit between ends 5 and 6 now begins to appear. Weave the left background weft inwards to meet the triangle's weft.

Pick 8. Change shed. This is exactly as Pick 6. The slit between ends 9 and 10 lengthens.

Four picks have now been woven with the triangle's weft weaving with four ends. To complete the triangle its weft must weave another four picks with the two central ends, 7 and 8. These four picks are exactly comparable with picks 5 to 8, so will not be described in detail. The slits produced in the last four picks are closed and two new slits appear on either side of the two central ends. This completes the weaving of the triangle.

From this simple example it will be seen that the angular junction between colours in a kilim is the direct result of the need to avoid over-long slits. The colour junction, i.e., the slit, is forced to step up to right or left, before it becomes an impractical feature in the rug. So colour junctions in a kilim can only be horizontal (as in ordinary cross stripes) or at an angle, never in a straight vertical line. This is the technical detail which controls kilim designs.

(b) *Direction of Wefts*

If Eastern kilims are examined, it will often be found that at any change of outline two wefts come together in one shed. This is because they are usually woven with all wefts going from right to left in one shed, and all returning from left to right in the next shed; whereas in the above description, each weft moves in the opposite direction to its neighbour in any one shed. Fig. 84 shows in detail what happens when all the wefts move in the same direction in the same shed, in weaving a triangle.

Where the triangle tapers, its weft and the background weft lie together in the same shed; these points are marked X in Fig. 84. Compare with Fig. 83. This small overlap of the two wefts does not really matter, but where there is a sudden large change of outline, as at the top of Fig. 83 and Fig. 84, the difference between the two methods becomes more obvious. From Fig. 83 it will be seen that with this first method, no difficulty is encountered. Any change of shape can be accomplished with ease. But Fig. 84 shows how in its movement from right to left, the triangle's weft has to lie in

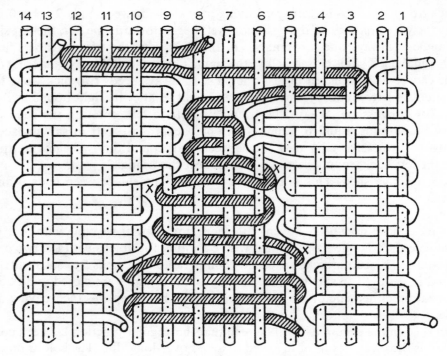

Fig. 84. Kilim. Weaving a triangle with wefts in parallel motion

the same shed as the background weft on both sides. Why this is the traditional method, may be explained by the three following facts.

(1) It can be used for any possible sort of design. Consider the introduction of the motif in Fig. 85, a common one in kilims, if it were to be woven with contrary motion of the wefts. The arrows show the direction of the wefts in one of the sheds. So starting

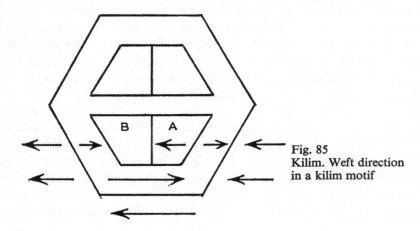

Fig. 85
Kilim. Weft direction
in a kilim motif

from the bottom, the background weft moves to the left in this shed. When the base of the motif is reached, its weft moves to the right, and both the background wefts move to the left.

When the two areas A and B are reached, only one of the new wefts, say, the one in A, can obey the rule and move in the opposite direction to its weft on the right. Whichever way the weft in area B moves, it will be the same as that of one of its neighbouring wefts.

In other words there are exceptions to the method using contrary motion of the weft. So it is simpler to use the method with no exceptions.

In some kilims with wefts moving in the same direction in the same shed, two wefts in a shed are avoided by having a float of weft at the back, see Fig. 86. This only works

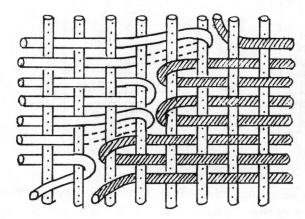

Fig. 86
Kilim. Method of
avoiding two wefts in
a shed when weaving
with parallel motion

if the colours are stepping up over an even number of ends (two in Fig. 86). The white weft is shown with dotted outline where it floats at the back passing behind three warp ends. Naturally this is not very practical and the Yugoslav kilims which have this feature are probably intended for decorative use only.

(2) In Eastern kilims the weft threads are finer than the warp. So a double thickness of weft at any point is not a great drawback; it does not mean that the warp will fail to be covered. Where the weft is much thicker than the warp, this does not apply.

(3) Visually, two wefts in a shed, give a very clear straight-line boundary between the colours involved, quite different from the usual wavy boundary line.

(c) Controlling Angle of Colour Junction

The exact angle of a colour junction can be varied within wide limits. This can be done in two ways.

(i) In Fig. 83, there were four picks before the triangle began to taper. There could equally well have been only two or any number over four that still kept the slit to a practical size. The former would give a small triangle with flat sides, the latter a tall triangle with steep sides. The stepped character of the colour junction would be more obvious in the latter.

(ii) In Fig. 83, the triangle's weft only moved in one warp thread each side when it tapered. It could have moved in two or more.

By combining these two methods, a curved colour junction can be woven.

It is impossible to say at what angle the slits become impractical, because it is related to the number of ends per inch. This is shown in Fig. 87 where (a) has twice as many

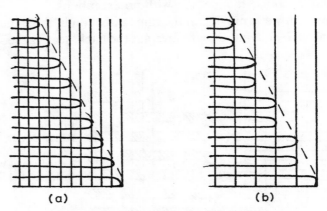

Fig. 87. Kilim. Angle of weft junction

ends as (b). So to achieve the same angle, the weft in (a) can have twice as many steps. This means it has twice as many slits, therefore they are half as long as those in (b).

45° or less is a practical angle to aim at. This is found in the heavier and more durable kilims from Scandinavia and the East.

(d) Two Methods of Weaving

In the above description of weaving a triangle, each weft was moved in each successive shed. Kilim rugs often consist of many motifs across their width, and to take up the finger hank for each weft in turn and weave just one pick would be a laborious process. So kilims are generally woven motif by motif, colour area by colour area. For instance, in Fig. 83 or Fig. 84, the central triangle would be woven first until it stood up as a complete shape with empty unwoven warp ends on either side. Then each of the background areas would be completely woven, one after the other. In weaving thus, the finger hank can be quickly passed from hand to hand across the width of each area, until it is completed.

Note—That once the triangle has been woven, the batten cannot be used for beating the background wefts. Its swing would be halted by the tip of the triangle long before it reached the background weft. So in this method, some type of rug fork has to be used for all areas except the first one woven. With practice it will be found possible to weave four or six picks and then beat them all down together with the fork.

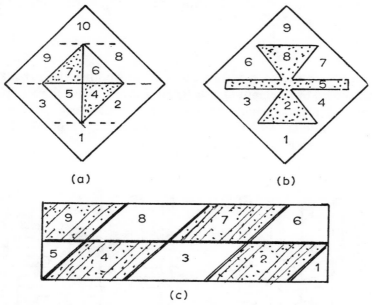

(a)   (b)

(c)

Fig. 88. Kilim. Sequence of weaving areas in typical kilim motifs

—That this method dictates a certain sequence of weaving the motif. For instance, in Fig. 83 or Fig. 84, the triangle has to be woven first. If the background areas had been woven first, the triangle's weft could only have been darned in with a needle. Fig. 88 shows some typical kilim motifs with the areas numbered in the order in which they could be woven.

(ii) PRACTICAL DETAILS

(a) Beginning and Finishing the Wefts

With so many small areas being woven, it is important to know how to start and finish off the many wefts involved.

Beginning:

A weft can be begun in the normal way, i.e., splitting it into two, bringing one half out of the shed, and taking the other half round the outer thread of the area concerned, and back into the same shed. However, if the weft is thin enough, its end can be left hanging out and be woven into the next shed. This, of course, gives two picks in a shed but as explained above, this need not matter

In some circumstances, neither way is very feasible, for instance when starting the point of a diamond. Here there are only two warp ends to weave on, so the normal method is quite impossible. The second method is often seen on Eastern kilims and provided the weave is very tight, is fairly practical. It is probably safest to leave the weft hanging out and later darn it down beside the appropriate warp end.

Finishing:

When finishing a weft, the normal way can be used. Another way is really the reverse of the second method of beginning a weft, see Fig. 89. After the last pick has been woven, it is pushed up away from the fell of the rug to allow enough room for the weft to be darned back into the *preceding* shed. This is a neat way, provided the warp and weft settings allow two picks in a shed.

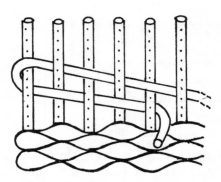

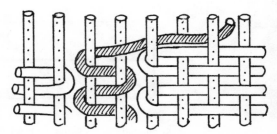

Fig. 90. Kilim. Finishing weft at tip of triangle
by running it into surrounding weave

Fig. 89. Kilim. Finishing a weft by
inserting into previous shed

As above, there are times when neither method is feasible, for instance when finishing the tip of a triangle. The problem here is how to finish on two ends. The second method just described, is often seen but there are three other possibilities.

(1) Let the weft end run into the background colour for a short distance, see Fig. 90. This flick of colour coming from the tip of the triangle can be made a feature of the design.

(2) Darn the weft down beside the appropriate warp end.

(3) If the triangle has been built up separately, lay the weft at an angle down one side of it, in the same shed as the triangle's final pick. Then as the background weft is woven on that side, this end of the weft becomes firmly held between it and the triangle. See Fig. 91.

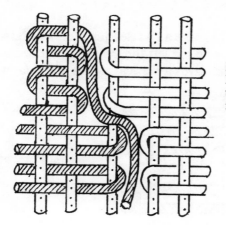

Fig. 91
Kilim. Finishing weft at
tip of triangle by running
it down side of triangle

(b) *Weft Tension*

In a kilim most wefts weave only across a small area, so in general it will not be found necessary to wave the weft to any extent. In fact, when weaving over only two or four warp ends, the weft has to be consciously tightened to avoid an over-loose texture. If a rug consists of stripes made up of kilim motifs alternating with normal cross stripes, the tension must be watched very carefully, otherwise due to the difference in tension, the selvage will bulge opposite each kilim stripe.

(c) *Warp and Weft Settings*

A warp of 6 e.p.i., double in a heald, therefore 3 working e.p.i., has often been mentioned for the various plain weave techniques described so far. This is possible for kilims, but there is a tendency for the slits to gape open at this setting. A closer setting, e.g., 4 to 6 working e.p.i., is more practical. A kilim with more of the traditional warp/weft relationship can be woven using 6-ply rug wool as the warp, set at 4 e.p.i., and 2-ply carpet wool used singly as the weft.

(iii) WEAVING VERTICAL COLOUR JUNCTIONS

Although the angled colour junctions are the most typical in kilims, there are occasions when a vertical colour junction is needed, such as between the borders and central field of an Eastern kilim. As mentioned earlier, this cannot be a straight-line vertical junction, unless as in tapestry weaving the long slit thus produced is later sewn up. So various methods are used to achieve a junction as near vertical as possible.

(a) Zigzag Junction

The most obvious way to do this is to make an angled junction which inclines to the right for a few steps and then inclines to the left for the same number of steps, as in Fig. 92. As shown at the bottom, this gives a vertical zigzag junction, which can be

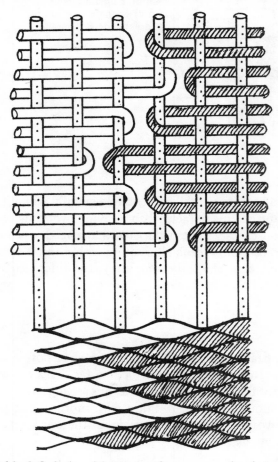

Fig. 92
Kilim. Vertical Colour
Junctions

continued indefinitely without causing any weakening of the fabric. This type of junction is often found in Rumanian kilims. In actuality, there would probably be more than two picks per step.

A development of this is shown at Fig. 93 (a), where, due to the sequence of picks, a curved black weft always meets a curved white weft at the line of junction. This gives a clean-edged boundary between the two colours, not a stepped boundary as in the above method.

The first method could be woven either by moving both of the wefts in each successive shed, or by building up an area at a time in the sequence shown in Fig.   3 (b).

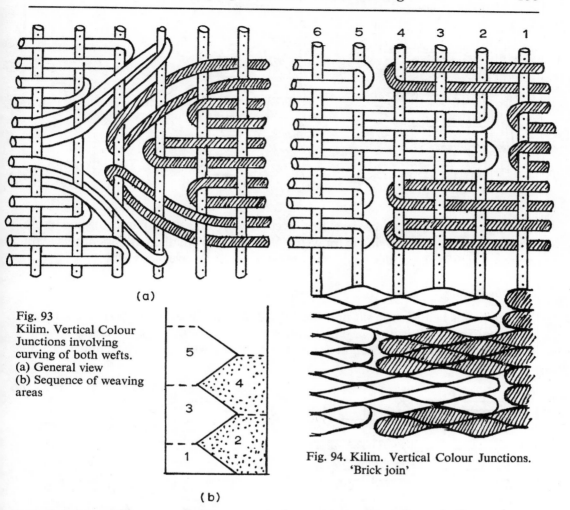

(a)

Fig. 93
Kilim. Vertical Colour
Junctions involving
curving of both wefts.
(a) General view
(b) Sequence of weaving
areas

(b)

Fig. 94. Kilim. Vertical Colour Junctions.
'Brick join'

The second method can only be woven as in Fig. 93 (b), a complete 'wedge' of black
being woven, then a complete 'wedge' of white.

(b) 'Brick Joining'

The vertical junction can be based on the idea of alternating the colour junction, and
therefore the slit, between a right and left-hand position. See Fig. 94 where the slit
between black and white wefts alternates from between ends 1 and 2, to between ends
4 and 5. The lower half of Fig. 94, shows how this appears when woven. The two
colours overlap each other as do successive courses of bricks in a wall; hence it is
sometimes called 'brick joining'. In actuality more than four picks would be woven
before moving the slit.

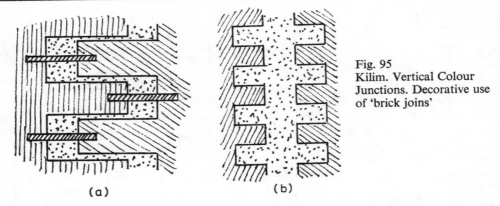

Fig. 95
Kilim. Vertical Colour
Junctions. Decorative use
of 'brick joins'

This practical idea can be developed decoratively. Figs. 95 (a) and (b) show more elaborate junctions involving extra wefts. Note that the small cross bars of this extra weft in Fig. 95 (a), besides being decorative, prevent an over-long slit.

(c) Dovetailing

Dovetailing is neither true slit nor interlocked tapestry but is described here for convenience. Though it is used in tapestry, it is not often found in rugs. As Figs. 96 and 97 show, both wefts weave round a common warp end where the two colours meet. So

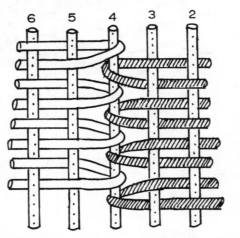

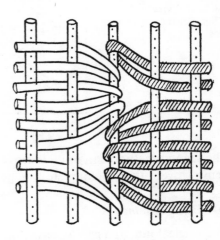

Fig. 96. Kilim. Vertical Colour Junctions.
Single Dovetailing

Fig. 97. Kilim. Vertical Colour Junctions.
3/3 Dovetailing

this end has double the normal number of weft picks passing round it. If this vertical junction is continued too long in the same position, there is a tendency for the rug to buckle or not lie flat. But if junctions of this type are staggered they are quite feasible and their characteristic toothed outlines can be an interesting element in the design.

In single (or 'comb-tooth') dovetailing, two picks of each colour are woven alter-ately, see Fig. 96. They both include warp end 4 in their passage, so this is the end bearing twice the normal number of wefts. The two colours are finely intermingled at the junction and appear as very small teeth, hence the name.

The two wefts concerned can turn round the common warp, so that it bears two loops of one, then two of the other (2/2 dovetailing), or three loops of one then three loops of the other (3/3 dovetailing). The latter is shown in Fig. 97. When beaten down these types give a much coarser toothing at the junction; hence they are sometimes called 'saw tooth' dovetailing.

(d) *Method Found in Sehna Kilims*

A combination of toothed and brick joining is seen on Sehna kilims, and as might be expected with this type of rug it involves curving the weft.

As Fig. 98 (a) shows, at each slit, four picks of one colour face eight picks of the other colour. For instance, at the slit between ends 1 and 2 (marked X) four white picks on the right come up against eight black picks on the left. It is this preponder-ance of one weft over the other at each colour junction that causes the curving of the weft. Note that ends 2 and 3 and ends 6 and 7 have twice the normal number of picks weaving with them. So this extra 'load' of weft is spread over more ends than in the types of dovetailing already described.

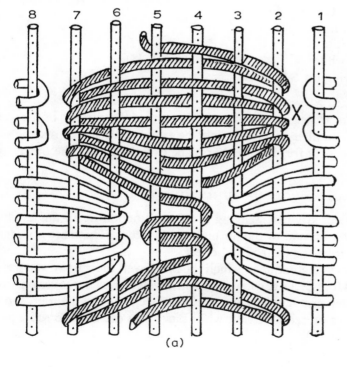

Fig. 98(a)
Kilim. Vertical Colour
Junctions. Method
used in Sehna Kilims.
(a) General view

(a)

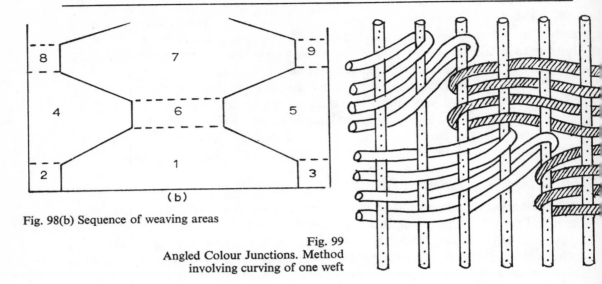

Fig. 98(b) Sequence of weaving areas

Fig. 99
Angled Colour Junctions. Method
involving curving of one weft

Fig. 98 (b) shows the outline this join assumes when beaten down. The numbers indicate the order in which the blocks are woven, thus:

Eight picks black (weaving on 6 ends)
Four picks left-hand white
Four picks right-hand white
Eight picks left-hand white
Eight picks right-hand white
Four picks black (weaving on two ends)
This sequence is repeated.

It is when the eight picks areas are being beaten down that the curving of the wefts appears. In actuality, the number of picks might be twelve and six, or sixteen and eight, nor is there any necessity for one number to be exactly double the other.

(iv) VARIATIONS OF ANGLED COLOUR JUNCTIONS

Several techniques can be used when weaving a colour junction at an angle which gives it a serrated character instead of the normal regular steps. These are not structurally necessary but are used for their visual effect.

(a) Fig. 99 shows one such technique in which the black weft moves two warp ends along at each step and has four picks per step. The white weft however, moves only one warp end along in each step and has only two picks per step. As the diagram shows, the four black picks always precede the four white picks thus causing the white picks to tilt upwards.

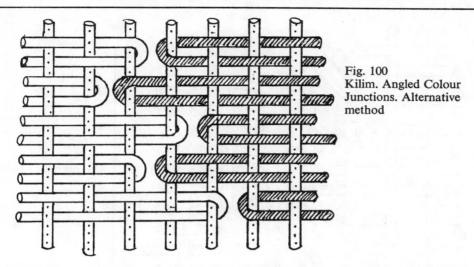

Fig. 100
Kilim. Angled Colour
Junctions. Alternative
method

(b) Fig. 100 shows another technique. It will be seen that the steps move over two ends to the left and then move back over one end to the right. This is repeated so that the sum effect is a slow movement to the left. In actuality there would be more than two picks per step, so this is really the brick-joining made at an angle.

(c) Fig. 101 (a) shows yet another, slightly more complicated, method, which brings an angled section of both wefts into contact with one another. A finer weft of another colour can be woven in between the two main wefts as shown in Fig. 101 (b). Three picks of this fine weft follow each six picks repeat of black or white, giving an intricate zigzag line which emphasizes the character of this colour junction.

Obviously these overlapping junctions make it impossible to build up one complete motif before another in the manner already described. A few picks of each colour in turn have to be woven all across the width of the rug.

(v) 'LAZY LINES'

In a kilim it is always easier to weave a small colour area (e.g., up to 6 inches in width) than a wider one. With the small area, the weft can be passed from hand to hand in each succeeding shed; it does not have to be awkwardly poked along the shed for some distance between its point of entry and exit.

For this reason, a large area of one colour is often broken up into small sections, each of which is a typical kilim shape, i.e., triangle, diamond, or lozenge. The only visible evidence that an area has been woven in this way are the faint diagonal lines, sometimes called 'lazy lines', where one small section meets another. These may be better seen when the rug is held against the light. Fig. 102 shows how a large, one-colour area, to the left of a central motif, might be dealt with. The sections could be

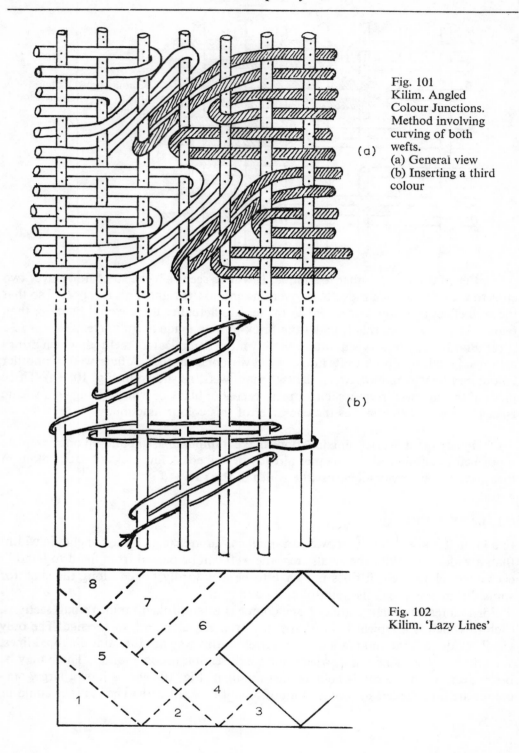

Fig. 101
Kilim. Angled
Colour Junctions.
Method involving
curving of both
wefts.
(a) General view
(b) Inserting a third
colour

(a)

(b)

Fig. 102
Kilim. 'Lazy Lines'

woven in the order they have been numbered. The dotted boundaries between these sections represent the 'lazy lines'.

(vi) OBLIQUE AND CURVED WEFTS. ECCENTRIC WEFTS

Wefts lying in curves or obliquely (often called Eccentric Wefts), are found almost everywhere that the tapestry technique has flourished. Thus they are seen in early Peruvian tapestries and in modern Polish, Swedish and Norwegian tapestries. They are known to French tapestry weavers as *ressaut* or *crapaud*. However, it was the Copts who exploited this method to its fullest in their small tapestry panels. Examination with a magnifying glass often shows that there is hardly a single weft lying at right angles to the warp. The picks outline shapes and fill in areas with a complete freedom that gives additional life and movement to the already lively designs. As a result of the inclined wefts, and their sequence of weaving, the warp ends are pulled out of the vertical and curve this way and that under the influence of the varying tensions. That this also adds to the liveliness of the tapestries is undeniable, but it is questionable whether it was consciously intended. While the tapestries were being woven, the warp was held under tension and so these eccentric warps probably appeared only when the tapestries were taken from the loom.

In the field of kilim weaving, it is the rugs made by the Kurds near Sehna in West Iran (now known as Sinneh) that have made most use of this technique. In addition to this feature, old Sehna kilims are often exceedingly fine and represent the result of a very highly-developed weaving skill. Curved wefts are also a marked feature of the Rumanian kilims from Oltenia.

(a) Outlining Areas

The idea of laying in wefts obliquely and in curves follows naturally from using the method of kilim weaving in which one complete motif or colour area is woven at a time. For instance, in Fig. 103 (a), a small triangle has been woven. Now before the background areas are woven, weave some picks of another weft (black in diagram) right across the top of the triangle, travelling from end 1 to 6 and back again. Then weave in the background areas.

The curved weft will appear as a thin black outline to the triangle.

Note—A minimum of two picks is necessary to give a curved line. One pick will only give spots.

—Great care must be taken with the curved weft so that it will lie correctly tensioned when the background weft has been beaten in beside it.

—The curved weft can only be poked into place with the fingers or a stick, a rug fork is not much help.

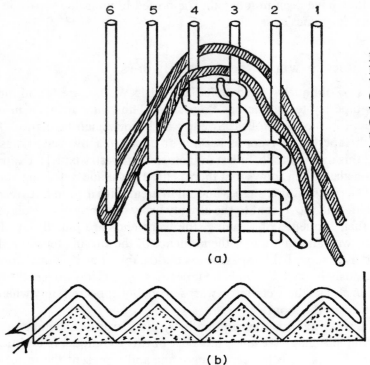

Fig. 103
Kilim. Curved
Wefts.
(a) Outlining a
woven triangle
(b) Outlining several
triangles with one
weft

(a)

(b)

   —If the angle of the weft is less than 45° to the vertical, this technique becomes impractical. The oblique weft lies too loosely and does not bed in with the surrounding weft.

    This sort of outlining can be carried right across the width of a rug, if, as in Fig. 103 (b), a series of triangles have been woven to receive it.

(b) *Building Up Whole Areas*

In the above example it was an extra weft that lay obliquely, but the ordinary wefts used in building up kilim motifs can lie obliquely or in curves for part of their course. This has one definite result, in that it avoids stepped outlines at angled colour junctions, and one possible result in that it may reduce the number of finger hanks needed to weave certain motifs.

    Both results appear in Fig. 104 which shows in detail the weaving of interlocking black and white triangles, and whose sequence is as follows.

    Start the black weft at the right selvage (lower arrow). Weave a small triangle. In

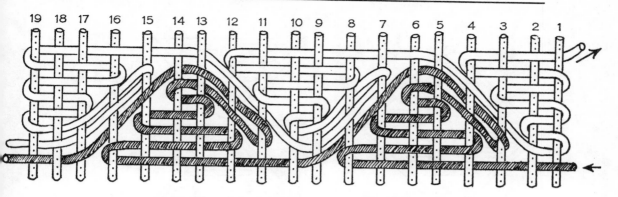

Fig. 104. Kilim. Using curved wefts to weave interlocking triangles

the diagram only the bare bones of the weaving have been shown, obviously more picks will be needed to build up a reasonably-sized triangle.

When the weft has reached the top of the triangle (weaving on ends 5 and 6) take it down the right side of the triangle to end 3, i.e., one end beyond the base of the triangle. Then in the next shed take it up the right side and down the left side of the triangle and carry it on to start weaving the base of the second triangle. Weave the second triangle exactly as the first. The black weft ends at the left selvage (lower arrow).

Start the white weft from the left selvage (upper arrow). Take it up the side of the left-hand triangle and down again, then start weaving normally. When the weft is level with the top of the triangle, take it over the top and down into the dip between the two black triangles, then up the side of the right-hand triangle and down again. Fill in the dip with normal weaving. Finally take the weft over the top of the right-hand triangle, and down to the right selvage. Weave normally, until the white weft ends at the upper arrow.

Note—Wherever the oblique wefts of the two colours lie together, the sheds are in the correct sequence. This will always happen and is independent of the sides from which the two wefts begin.

—Despite the oblique wefts, there are eight picks weaving with every end in the diagram. This is not always easy to arrange but is obviously the ideal to aim at.

—Only two wefts have been used for weaving five areas.

After this detailed description, the more diagrammatic representations in Fig. 105 will be understood. In these, only the course taken by the motif weft is indicated. The warp and the background weft are both omitted. One diagram shows an alternative method of weaving interlocking triangles.

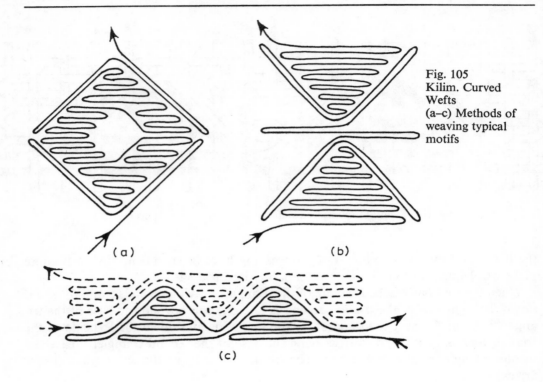

Fig. 105
Kilim. Curved
Wefts
(a–c) Methods of
weaving typical
motifs

(a)

(b)

(c)

(c) *Motifs Consisting Entirely of Curved Wefts*

Complete motifs such as ovals can be built up entirely from curved wefts.

The sequence of weaving an oval is shown in Fig. 106 (a). First weave the left and right half of the 'socket' to receive the oval, i.e., the background below the oval's mid-point. Then weave the oval itself, followed by the background above its mid-point. The 'socket' should be as curved as possible. So leave a flat base (ends 6, 7 and 8 in Fig. 107) and then step up the weft on either side in such a way as to make a gentle curve.

The principle of weaving the oval is shown diagrammatically in Fig. 106 (b). Start the weft at the mid-point on the left, dip right down into the 'socket' and up the other side, change the shed and return the weft. Continue thus with the weft travelling less far in each successive pick, until half the oval has been woven. At this point, two conditions should be fulfilled. The weft should be weaving on the central ends of the oval and the oval should, at its deepest point, have as many picks as have the sides of the 'socket'. These two conditions are not automatically fulfilled. For instance, if the picks have decreased in length too slowly, a shape as in Fig. 106 (c) will be woven by the time the central ends are reached. Alternatively, if they have decreased too quickly, the opposite fault, as in Fig. 106 (d), will be seen. Both of these are quite valid shapes

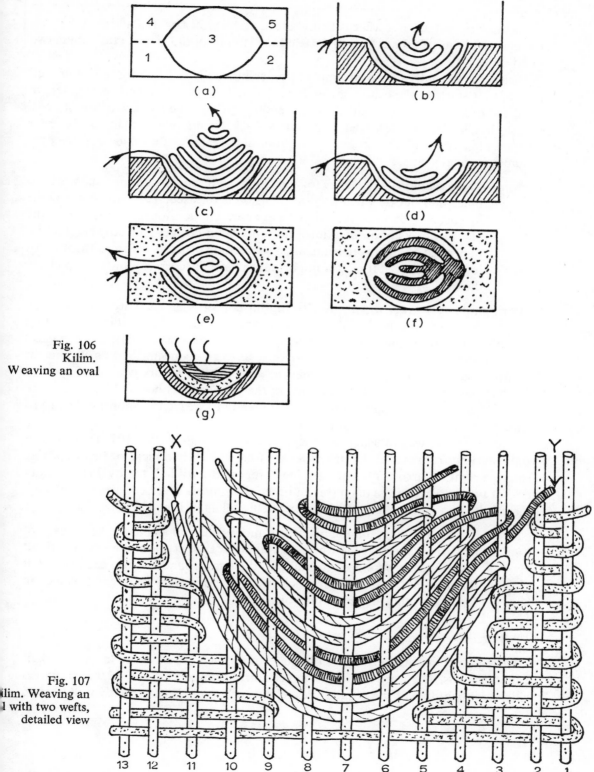

(a)

(b)

(c)

(d)

(e)

(f)

Fig. 106
Kilim.
Weaving an oval

(g)

X

Y

Fig. 107
Kilim. Weaving an
oval with two wefts,
detailed view

13 12 11 10 9 8 7 6 5 4 3 2 1

in themselves, but are not what is being aimed at. So either by trial and error or by a simple calculation, find out how to decrease the lengths of the picks to fulfil these two conditions.

Weave the top half of the oval simply by reversing the steps taken for the lower half. So the weft starts at the centre. From here it weaves picks of ever-increasing length until the oval is completed with the weft ending on the side from which it started, i.e., the left, see Fig. 106 (e). Then weave in the background, repeating in reverse order the picks that made up the 'socket'. It is not until these picks are woven that the oval assumes its final shape.

> Note—There is always a tendency for such an oval, or any area of oblique wefts, to bulge and buckle when the warp tension is released. This can be overcome by ensuring that the curved picks are correctly tensioned. For instance, the first few picks of an oval must not only be at correct tension when laid in, they must be at this tension when succeeding picks have forced them down into the 'socket'. It is also important to have the correct number of picks in the oval.

For simplicity's sake, the above description concerns an oval woven with only one weft. Such an oval shows a slightly curved grain to the weft, but it is obvious that it is only when two or more wefts are being used that the curved nature of the picks can be brought out. Such wefts can be woven so as to give concentric ovals of different colours. Fig. 106 (g) shows diagrammatically the state of affairs when half such an oval has been woven. Note that the ends of the four wefts concerned have not been darned-in but are left hanging out and so are ready to weave the appropriate curved stripe as the top half of the oval is completed.

A very effective way of using two wefts is shown in detail in Fig. 107. Two picks of white starting from the left (at arrow X) are followed by two picks of black starting from the right (at arrow Y). This striping is repeated until half the oval is woven (a total of twelve picks in the diagram) and then the process reversed in the usual way. The result is an interlocking black and white figure as in Fig. 106 (f).

> Note—That in the diagram, the black weft moves one end less to the left in each of its stripes, and that the white weft similarly moves one end less to the right.
> —Twelve picks were used to build up the background area on each side, but there are not exactly twelve picks weaving with every warp end involved in the half oval. This seems unavoidable.

(d) Wedge-Weave Rugs

There is a technique relying on oblique wefts which is found in Navajo blankets from the 1880s. These are known as 'pulled warp' or 'wedge-weave' blankets, names which highlight two of the peculiarities of this technique. It can equally well be used

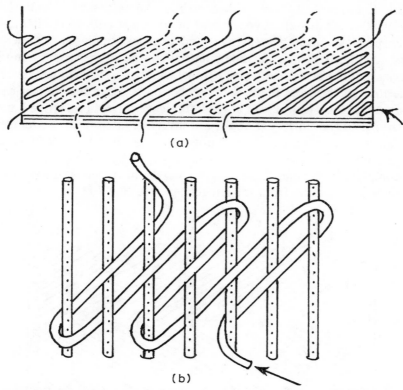

Fig. 108. Wedge-Weave Rugs. (a) Arrangement of wefts in first woven band (b) Detail of one stripe within the band

for floor rugs and is interesting because of the very close connection between the method of weaving and the designs produced.

The technique is as follows:

Start with a few picks of normal weaving from selvage to selvage, see Fig. 108 (a). Then begin weaving at the right selvage (see arrow), first on only a few warp ends, but gradually including more and more as the work grows upwards. So the right-hand extremity of each pick is always the right selvage, but the left-hand extremity moves in some orderly way towards the left, i.e., it includes two (or four, or six) more ends every two picks. As this is beaten down with a rug fork, not the batten, the fell of the rug will tilt down to the left as shown. So in effect, a right-angled triangle or wedge is being woven, with all the picks lying parallel to its longest side. When this triangle is 2 or 3 inches high, stop weaving with this weft, leaving it hanging out at the top of the wedge for later use. Do not darn it in.

Now weave a number of oblique stripes of varying colours, following the angle set by the weft in the triangle. In each of these stripes, the weft (starting at the bottom as shown in Fig. 108 (a)) includes two (or four or six) more ends to the left at its lower end each second pick, and stops weaving round a similar number at its upper end each second pick, see Fig. 108 (b). Thus the upper boundaries of the stripes join to make a straight horizontal line across the warp, parallel with the first starting picks of the rug.

Continue thus right across the rug, remembering to leave the weft of each stripe hanging out at the top. The last weft at the left selvage cannot be a stripe but has to be a triangle similar to the starting triangle, but inverted, i.e., the left extremity of each pick is the left selvage, but the right extremity moves to the left every two picks. Stop weaving this final weft at the left selvage as shown in Fig. 108 (a).

Having completed this band of oblique stripes, the next step is to repeat the whole process exactly, but starting from the left selvage, see Fig. 109.

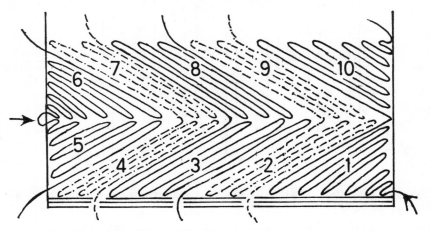

Fig. 109. Wedge-Weave Rugs. Arrangement of wefts in first two woven bands

With the weft from the final triangle in the first band, start to build up a triangle or wedge at the left selvage (see arrow at left). Weave this in exactly the same way as the first triangle in the first band. The weft will slope down to the right instead of to the left. The weaving stops when it exactly covers the triangle below it. Leave the weft hanging out at the top of the triangle.

Now pick up the weft from stripe 4 in the first band and weave a similar stripe above it, No. 7. Then pick up the weft from stripe 3 and weave stripe 8 above it. Continue thus all the way across to the right, ending with an inverted triangle as before (No. 10).

These two bands with stripes sloping in opposite ways can be repeated for the whole length of the rug. Or such bands may be interrupted by stripes of normal selvage to selvage weaving. Note that there are always an odd number of picks in each oblique stripe, as the weft always begins at the lower boundary and ends at the upper.

Distortion of the Warp

As might be expected with such large areas of oblique weft, the warp becomes distorted. Each succeeding band of stripes tends to pull it out of its true line, first to one side then to the other, hence the alternative name for this technique, 'pulled warp'. For instance, the first band in Fig. 109, pulls the warp to the left to the extent that it crosses each weft almost at right angles. The second band pulls it to the right in a similar way.

Fig. 110 (a) shows the path taken by a few ends as they pass through four bands of stripes. This is not very obvious in the body of the rug, but it means that the edges of the rug bulge to give the wavy or scalloped outline, typical of this technique.

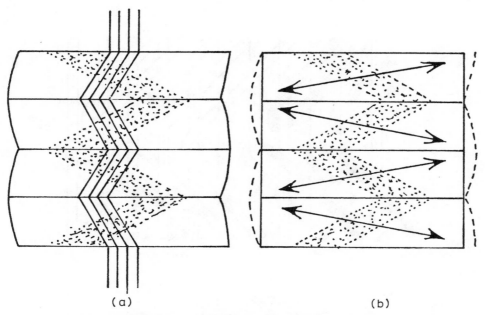

(a) (b)

Fig. 110. Wedge-Weave Rugs. Explanation of warp distortion

Another way to look at this feature is to consider each band separately. In Fig. 110 (b) the bottom band has wefts sloping down to the left. So when forces are exerted on the sides of the rug in use (e.g., when shaking it) it can only stretch in the direction shown by the diagonal arrow. This is like stretching a bit of cloth on the bias. It cannot stretch along the other diagonal as this is the direction in which the wefts lie, and they will resist any pull. Taking the next band, the same reasoning shows that it can only stretch in the opposite direction as indicated by its arrow; and so on, through all the bands. The net result will be that the edges bulge as shown by the dotted lines.

Junction Between Bands

The horizontal junction between two bands tends to be a point of weakness as weft, and to a lesser degree, warp change direction along this line. It can be strengthened if the wefts of the second band loop round different warp ends from those used by the first band. See Fig. 111 (a) which shows this line of junction at the point where two colour stripes meet. This arrangement of the wefts also gives a sharper point to the angle where two stripes meet.

The steeper the angle of the wefts, the greater this weakness will be, and also the more the selvages will bulge and the less likely the rug is to lie flat. A weft angle of about 20° to 30° to the horizontal is a good one to aim at.

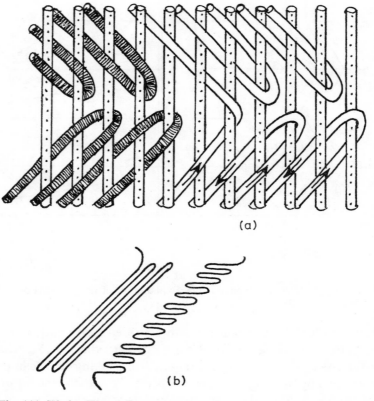

(a)

(b)

Fig. 111. Wedge-Weave Rugs
    (a) Detail of junction between bands
    (b) Comparison of narrow, angled stripe when woven
normally and when woven with oblique weft

Design

It will be understood that the purpose of weaving in this way is to produce stripes that zigzag down the length of the rug, though, conceivably, a rug woven in only one colour might have an interesting surface 'grain' due to the angling of weft and warp. Such zigzag stripes can, of course, be woven in the normal kilim way but there are two differences.

(i) A narrow oblique stripe, which, in wedge-weave needs only five picks, would require many more picks if woven as in normal kilim, see Fig. 111(b). So wedge weave is a quicker method. For the same reason, while two 1-inch stripes in wedge weave take the same time to weave as one 2-inch stripe, they take twice as long in normal kilim.

(ii) The junction between adjacent colours is a clean one, not a stepped one as in normal kilim.

So on this basis, it is fine oblique stripes which should be exploited if this technique is to be used to its fullest.

B. Interlocked Tapestry

The distinguishing feature of the vertical colour junction in slit tapestry is the absence of any interlocking of the two wefts involved. But there is a well-developed and much used method of interlocking, which allows the weaving of vertical junctions of any length without the formation of a slit.

The Swedish word, rölakan, is sometimes used for this technique of interlocked tapestry. It is derived from rygglakan, the name of a textile hung on the wall behind a seat. This textile has interlocked wefts as do the modern Swedish rölakan rugs.

Because there is no slit, vertical colour junctions can be used freely in the design. In some traditional textiles the design is built up entirely of small squares of colour, so there are no angled colour junctions at all. In other weaves, such as in Navajo blankets, angled and vertical colour junctions are combined. It is, of course, in true tapestry weaving that this combination is exploited to the fullest and a technique is achieved which imposes practically no limitations on the designer. Against the great freedom in design must be set this technique's slowness of execution.

The interlocking of wefts is found in early tapestry-woven textiles from Peru and North America. In the East, slit tapestry has always been used more than interlocked tapestry, but the latter is found in some rugs from this area.

There are two types of interlocked tapestry:

Single Interlocked Tapestry or Norwegian Rölakan

Double Interlocked Tapestry or Swedish Rölakan

(i) SINGLE INTERLOCKED TAPESTRY

This is much the more used and is almost certainly the older of the two types. It produces a completely reversible rug, with no ridge or extra thickness where the wefts interlock.

(a) Scandinavian Method of Weaving

The following description is the classical Scandinavian one, but as will be seen later, it need not be regarded as the only possible method.

Referring to Fig. 112 note that each area must have an even number of warp ends.

Starting in the shed that lowers the left-hand end of each area, enter each weft from the left and carry it across to the right boundary of its particular area, see Fig. 112 (a). Deal with each weft's end either by putting it into the next shed (if weft is thin enough to allow this) as shown in diagram, or by the normal method of starting wefts. There will now be a whole series of picks across the width of the rug, all going from left to right. Only two wefts are shown in the diagram.

Change sheds. Starting from the right selvage, weave the extreme right-hand weft (black) with its allotted warp ends and then bring it out of the shed and lay it across the next weft to the left (white), see Fig. 112 (b).

Now pick up the white weft and weave it across its colour area. Note that as it enters the shed, its returning loop catches round the black weft, see Fig. 112 (c). Bring the white weft out of its shed and lay it across the next weft to the left (not shown in diagram).

Carry on thus right across the rug until the left selvage is reached. Wave each weft according to the width of its colour area. Each weft should now be coming from the left boundary of its area and should be looped around the next weft to the right, see Fig. 112 (c).

Change sheds. Starting from the left selvage, weave each weft in succession across its own area, but do *not* interlock, see Fig. 112 (d). The important feature of this pick is to tension each weft so that the previous interlock lies flat and causes no looseness or lumpiness in the weave. So after each weft is carried across its own area, put a finger of the left hand over the relevant interlock and pull the weft to the right until the interlock feels tight and lies centrally between the two ends that flank it. It is sometimes difficult both to do this and to leave sufficient slack in the weft for the normal waving. But it should be persevered with as the good looks of the rug depend on the proper adjustment of the interlock.

This sequence is repeated, locking when the wefts go to the left but not locking when the wefts return to the right.

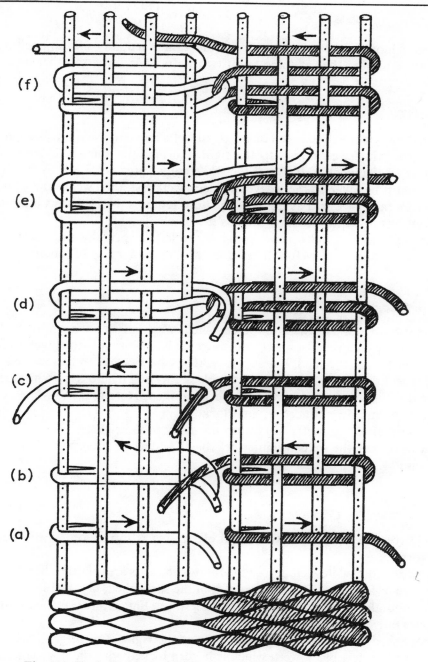

Fig. 112. Single Interlocked Tapestry. Scandinavian Method.
(a)–(d) Stages in weaving
(e) and (f) Moving colour area to right and to left

Changing Outline of Design

As all wefts move in the same direction in the same shed, any shift in position of the colour areas implies that at some point two wefts have to lie together in a shed.

To Move Colour Area to Right

This is naturally done in the shed in which all wefts move to the right. See Fig. 112 (e) in which the white weft moves to the right. Normally in this shed, the white weft weaves before the black weft. But if the white colour area is to shift to the right, this sequence must be reversed. So weave the black weft first, then weave the white carrying it across the black area as far as the pattern requires. Note that as it does so, the white weft has to lie in the same shed as the black.

In the next shed, all wefts move from right to left as normally, interlocking as they go. The black and white weft will interlock at their new point of junction.

To Move Colour Area to the Left

This is naturally done in the interlocking shed, when all wefts move to the left. See Fig. 112 (f) in which the black weft moves to the left. Normally the black weft moves before the white in the shed, but as above, this sequence has to be reversed. So first weave the white to the left, then weave the black carrying it across the white area as far as desired. This brings two wefts into the same shed. Note that the white and black wefts cannot, and do not need to, interlock.

In the next shed, the wefts will return normally to the right.

In the next shed, the wefts will interlock, black and white doing so at their new point of junction.

To Introduce a New Colour Area

Figs. 113 (b) and (c) show how a small black area is introduced in the centre of a white area.

First weave the white weft across the full width of its area, in the shed in which all wefts move to the right. Then on top of it in the same shed, lay the black weft where required and also another white weft to its left, see Fig. 113 (b). Ensure that the two new wefts move to the right.

In next shed, weave normally beginning at the right. The original white weft is locked with the new black weft, which is in turn locked with the new white weft, see Fig. 113 (c). Weaving then proceeds normally.

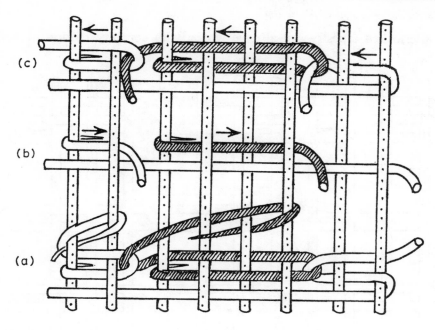

Fig. 113. Single Interlocked Tapestry. Scandinavian Method.
      (a) Finishing off a colour area
      (b) and (c) Introducing a new colour area

To Finish a Colour Area

Always do this in the shed in which all wefts move to the right. Having tightened the interlocks, push the wefts up away from the fell of the rug, so that the free ends can be darned back into the previous shed.

In Fig. 113 (a), the black weft and the left-hand white weft are both being finished off in this way. In the next shed, the original white weft can carry across the full width of its area again. As a colour area both starts and finishes in the same shed (i.e., when wefts move to the right), it must always contain an odd number of picks.

Note that the single interlocked colour junction is not a clean one but is slightly blurred, rather like that produced by single dovetailing.

The smallest possible unit of pattern is that spanning two ends. When weaving such a small area, great attention has to be paid to weft tension. No weft waving is necessary and the interlocks on either side of the area must be pulled tight to avoid a loose patch in the weave.

(b) Alternative Method of Weaving

Single interlocked tapestry can also be woven with contrary motion of wefts, see Fig. 114.

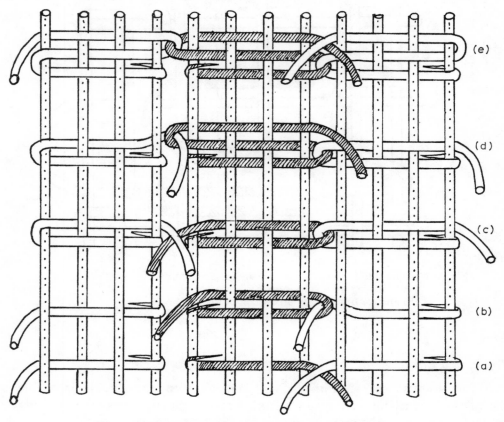

Fig. 114. Single Interlocked Tapestry. Alternative Method.
(a–e) Stages in weaving

In the first shed, start each weft in the opposite direction to its neighbour, making sure that the weft on the extreme right moves in from the selvage, see Fig. 114 (a).

All the way across the rug, there will now be, at intervals, two adjacent wefts coming out of the shed together, e.g., black and right-hand white in Fig. 114 (a). Fig. 115 (a) shows how this appears on the full width of a rug. Note that the pairs of wefts come out from every *other* colour junction; and, because in this example there is an odd number of colour blocks, there is one single weft at the left selvage.

Change sheds. Starting from the right, weave each of these pairs of wefts in turn. First, weave the weft from the left-hand of the two adjacent blocks (i.e., black). As it enters the shed it catches the other weft of the pair, see Fig. 114 (b). Secondly, weave the weft from the right-hand block (white), see Fig. 114 (c). Pull these two wefts against each other to tighten the interlock.

Repeat this with the next pair of wefts to the left and so on all across the warp, dealing with each pair in turn, until finally the odd weft at the left selvage is woven in.

The positions of the pairs of wefts are now as in Fig. 115 (b). Note they are now

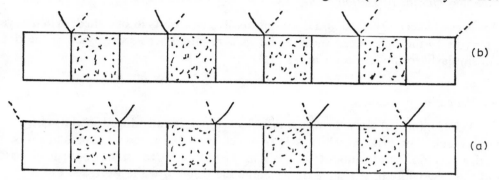

(b)

(a)

Fig. 115. Single Interlocked Tapestry. Alternative Method.
(a) and (b) How wefts emerge from design blocks

emerging from different colour junctions and that the odd single weft is at the right selvage.

Starting from left, weave each of the pairs in turn. First, weave the weft from the right-hand of the two adjacent blocks (i.e., black). Note that this is the weft moved first in the last shed. In fact it is always the weft from the even-numbered block that is moved first, see Fig. 114 (d). Secondly, weave weft from the left-hand block (i.e., white), see Fig. 114 (e). Pull the wefts apart to tighten the interlocks.

Repeat with the next pair of wefts to the right and continue thus across the warp until the single weft at the right selvage is reached and woven in.

This is the complete repeat.

Note—That on emerging from the shed, the free ends of two adjacent wefts cross each other in a certain way. The weft from the odd-numbered block (white) always lies on top. This happens quite naturally if the above description is followed exactly. A very awkward, bulky interlock, as at Fig. 116 (c), will result if this is not done correctly.

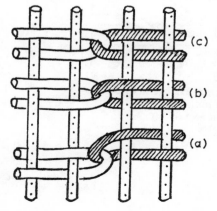

(c)

(b)

(a)

Fig. 116
Single Interlocked Tapestry. Methods of weft interlock.
(a) In Scandinavian Method
(b) and (c) Correct and Incorrect Types in Alternative Method

—That in this method, interlocking takes place in every shed. Each particular weft locks with the weft to its left in one shed and with that to its right in the next shed.

Changing Outline of Design

This is easily accomplished and does not involve two wefts in one shed. When a weft is moving to the right it can move as far as is required across the block to the right, and similarly to the left, see Fig. 117 (c).

Introducing a New Colour Area

Fig. 117 (a) and (b) show how a small black block is introduced in the centre of a white block. The original white weft is woven part way across its area. In the same shed, a new black and white weft are laid in. The black moves in the opposite direction and the new white in the same direction as the original white weft, see Fig. 117 (a). Weaving proceeds normally; Fig. 117 (b) shows the next pick.

A colour area is stopped in the same way as described above.

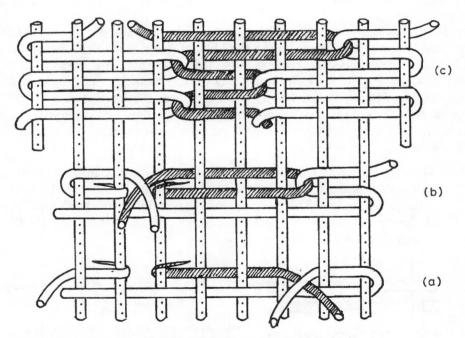

Fig. 117. Single Interlocked Tapestry. Alternative Method.
(a) and (b) Introducing a new colour area
(c) Moving a colour area to right and to left

The only objections to weaving interlocked tapestry in this way would seem to be:

(i) that it is slightly less orderly. There is not a specific interlocking shed and a tightening shed, as in the Scandinavian method.

(ii) that a design can be encountered which upsets the contrary motion of wefts. This has been discussed in connection with kilims.

The main advantage is the ease with which colour areas can be moved and new colour areas introduced without each time having two picks in a shed.

Fig. 116 compares the different ways adjacent wefts are locked in single interlocked tapestry.

(a) is found in the Scandinavian method.

(b) represents the correct way in the alternative method.

(c) represents the incorrect way in the alternative method.

(ii) DOUBLE INTERLOCKED TAPESTRY

Whereas with single interlocked tapestry, the vertical colour junction is flat and unobtrusive, with the double interlock it is in the form of a definite ridge. This lies on the upper surface as the textile is being woven; Fig. 118 shows the various stages in weaving double interlocked tapestry.

Begin as for single interlock, i.e., with all wefts going to the right in the first shed, see Fig. 118 (a). The blocks can span an odd or even number of warp ends. The white and black span three ends in Fig. 118.

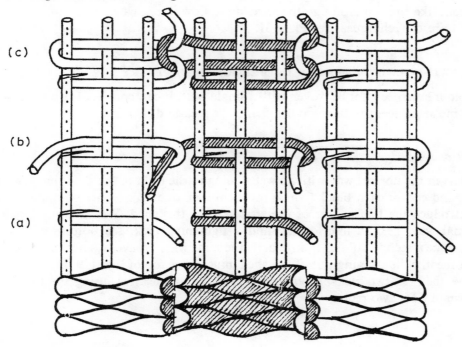

Fig. 118. Double Interlocked Tapestry.
(a–c) Stages of weaving

Change shed. Beginning at the right selvage, move each weft in turn, making an interlock, see Fig. 118 (b).

Change shed. Beginning at the left selvage, move each weft in turn, also making an interlock, see Fig. 118 (c).

Continue thus, locking in every shed.

As the diagram shows, each colour junction has a ridge made up of interlocking loops of both wefts. When beaten down this ridge appears as at the bottom of Fig. 118, but on the back of the rug there is a perfectly clean join.

The technique is sometimes used in tapestry. The great strength of the join is useful when a large tapestry is hung, as is common practice, with the weft lying vertically. Also it is suitable for the intricacies of a tapestry design, as a weft can be woven spanning a single warp end.

Though strength of construction is desirable in rugs, the ridge is a definite disadvantage and the single interlock variety is always used.

But there is one interesting application of double interlocked tapestry to rugs, in which the ridge becomes the chief feature of the design. This is woven with several wefts, but all of the same colour, and the upper side as woven is the upper side as used. So the rug has vertical ridges lying on flat areas. The ridges can be moved to left or right in exactly the same way as colour areas are shifted in interlocked tapestry. Similarly a ridge can be started, or discontinued.

There are not many techniques which give the weaver a freely-controllable vertical element like this, so although the weaving is slow it is a worthwhile addition to the repertoire of techniques. See Plate 31.

(iii) TWO-COLOUR AREAS IN INTERLOCKED TAPESTRY

A colour area need not be woven with a single weft. It can consist of two wefts woven in some sequence, producing cross stripes or pick-and-pick stripes.

(a) *2-and-2 Stripes*

Start in the normal way with all wefts going to the right in the shed that lowers the left-hand end of each block (which must contain an even number of ends).

Introduce the first colour of the stripe, A, in this shed. Weave two picks in the normal way, i.e., an interlocking and a tightening pick, see bottom of Fig. 119. Introduce a second colour, B, in exactly the same way. Weave two normal picks using B, A meanwhile hanging out of the shed unused, see top of Fig. 119. Bring A back to weave the next two picks, leaving B unused. Continue thus, using the two colours alternately for two picks.

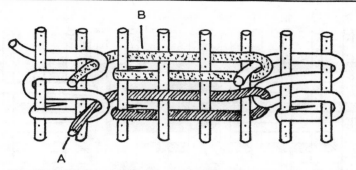

Fig. 119. Single Interlocked Tapestry. Weaving an area with two wefts in cross stripes

Note—That as each weft begins a new stripe, it has to be brought up at an angle over the preceding stripe. For example, in Fig. 119, A will have to be carried across the stripe of B before it can weave its next stripe. This gives a slight downward slant to the left-hand of each stripe.

(b) Pick-and-Pick Stripes

There are several ways of weaving a block of pick-and-pick stripes, all of them fairly complicated. Fig. 120 shows diagrammatically one such method. Note that only one of the wefts involved (black) locks with the wefts of the surrounding area.

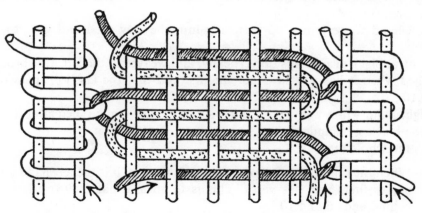

Fig. 120. Single Interlocked Tapestry. Weaving an area with two wefts in pick-and-pick stripes

A pick-and-pick area can be woven in a far simpler way if one of its colours is also the colour of the areas on either side, see Fig. 121. In this case, every other pick goes right across the warp.

Referring to the bottom of Fig. 121, weave the shaded weft from left to right across the full width of the warp. (Pick 1)

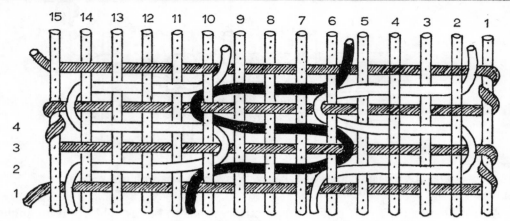

Fig. 121. Weaving areas of pick-and-pick stripes which share one weft

Change shed. Introduce three tapestry wefts as shown. (Pick 2)

The right-hand white weft passes under ends 6, 4 and 2.

The central black weft passes under ends 10, 8 and 6.

The left-hand white weft passes under ends 14, 12 and 10.

Change shed. Weave shaded weft to the left, first making a pick-and-pick selvage at the right. (Pick 3)

Change shed. Weave the three tapestry wefts towards the left, starting with the left-hand one. (Pick 4)

The left-hand white jumps up vertically into the new shed and goes to the left selvage.

The central black also jumps up vertically, and weaves to the left. It is brought out of the shed when it has passed under the first end that the last weft passed under, i.e., end 10.

The right-hand white weaves to the left similarly, leaving the shed after it has overlapped the black weft under end 6.

This is the whole repeat.

> *Note*—When the tapestry wefts weave towards the left, it is the left hand one which moves first, and vice versa. This is to ensure that they overlap correctly behind ends 6 and 10.
>
> —This is not true interlocked tapestry, as the tapestry wefts are locked by passing vertically over the selvage-to-selvage weft, and are not locked with each other.
>
> —The selvage-to-selvage weft is shown shaded for clarity. Naturally, it would have to be white to make the two side areas a solid colour.

C. Tapestry Techniques not in Plain Weave

The following techniques can conveniently be described here.

(i) TWILL TAPESTRY

The tapestry principle, i.e., a textile woven of discontinuous wefts, can be applied to structures other than plain weave. 2/2 twill is a commonly used weave for this purpose and may be a simple diagonal twill or a diamond twill.

With a simple twill, the weaving is very similar to plain weave tapestry, except that it requires four picks, not two, to make a solid line of colour. The twill lines may be used as diagonals along which colour junctions can be made, see lower half of Fig. 122 where the colour areas slope up to the right, following the twill lines. In the upper half, the twill has been reversed to allow the colour areas to change direction. In a more complex weave of this type, the sheds are finger- not shaft-controlled. This means that the twill only needs to reverse where the design demands it and the reverse need not take place right across the width of the textile as in Fig. 122. Thus, far more intricate designs can be woven. The twill lines can run parallel with the axis of each motif helping to emphasize it.

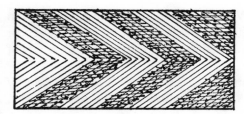

Fig. 122. Twill Tapestry. Colour areas following twill lines

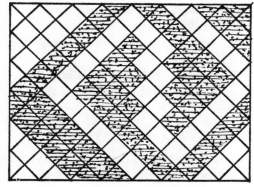

Fig. 123
Diamond Twill Tapestry. Showing rug surface made up of mosaic of diamonds

Another method for more complex designs is to use a diamond twill as this provides diagonals in both directions along which colour junctions can be made. The surface of the rug is made up of a mosaic of small diamonds, as indicated in Fig. 123, and shown in greater detail in Fig. 124. These diamonds are the unit of design and each one consists of a solid colour. Where adjacent diamonds are of different colours, the wefts can be interlocked along the dividing line. Plate 32 shows a sample whose warp was threaded (4,3,2,1,2,3) repeat. The shafts were lifted 23, 12, 14, 12, 23, 34, 41, 34, repeat. The first four lifts give the lower two diamonds in Fig. 124, the last four lifts the upper two diamonds. Note that the pick when 23 is raised is both the last pick of one row of diamonds and the first pick of the next row. If different colours are used for the first four and second four lifts, the rows of diamonds at either end of the sample appear automatically. The central motif was built up in diamond twill tapestry technique a

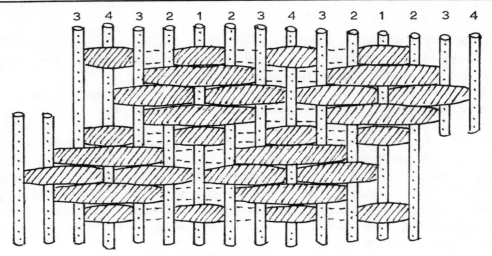

Fig. 124. Diamond Twill Tapestry. Detail of weave

separate weft being used for each colour area. Visually the result is little different from plain weave tapestry and it is certainly more difficult to weave. With a warp set at 5 or 6 working e.p.i. and a weft of 2-ply carpet wool used threefold, the resulting rug is of good texture.

For further details of this and related techniques see *Cultivation and Weaving of Cotton in the Prehistoric South West United States*, mentioned in the Bibliography.

(ii) TAPESTRY OF WEAVES

In normal tapestry, the design areas are distinguished from each other by the colour of the various wefts used. In this technique, the design areas are produced by varying the weaves. The rug could, in fact, be of one single colour, the areas only being distinguished by the differing surface textures, resulting from the different weaves. So it is a tapestry of textures rather than of colours.

Weaves which can be combined are plain weave, hopsack, straight and broken 2/2 twill. Each area is built up separately using its own weft, the number of picks required per inch depending on the weave used. Plate 33 shows a sample in which the central motif is woven in straight 2/2 twill, the triangles at each side in broken 2/2 twill and the intervening areas in plain weave. The technique has great possibilities but is naturally very slow.

6 · Weft-face Rugs in Plain Weave

PART THREE: TECHNIQUES GIVING A RAISED SURFACE DECORATION

INTRODUCTION

All the techniques described so far (with the exception of double interlocked tapestry) produce a rug which is flat on both sides. So it can equally well be used either way up, though there may be very slight differences of design between the two sides. In the methods described in this Chapter, there is some sort of surface decoration or texture on the upper side of the rug as it is woven, so the rug definitely has a right and a wrong way up. In some cases, however, both sides are equally practical to use.

1. SOUMAK OR WEFT WRAPPING

The word Soumak is said to derive from Shemakha, which was once the capital of the Khanate of Shirvan in the Caucasus, but is now in the province of Azerbaidzahn, U.S.S.R. This region was the source of the classical soumak rugs which though produced in smaller quantities than knotted and kilim rugs, were in no way inferior in quality or beauty.

HISTORY

The technique itself can be traced back at least to 2000 B.C. which is the approximate date of some famous linen fragments found in a lake dwelling at Irgenhausen, Switzerland. These show a two colour design in soumak and include a very complicated use of it in the formation of a border. Other early examples come from Egypt (1500 B.C.), from Peru in neolithic times and from Persia (eleventh century A.D.). The technique is said to have reached Sweden in late Roman times and there still exist some splendid wall hangings dating from the twelfth or thirteenth century, which were found in churches at Skog, Dal and Overhogdal. These use the soumak technique (known as snärjevävnad in Sweden) to represent very stylized people and animals and they tell a story in the way the Bayeux tapestry does. The decorative use of the technique has also been discovered by many primitive people, such as the Ainu of Japan, and the inhabitants of New Caledonia and of Guiana.

A. General Technical Details

As with most methods in this Chapter there are basically two wefts. One is the ground weft which weaves with the warp to make a normal weft-face structure, the other is the soumak weft which crosses the warp at intervals, wrapping round its ends, more in the manner of an embroidery stitch than of weaving. So the soumak weft adds little to the structure of the rug but is predominantly decorative, forming a ridge raised above the level of the surrounding plain weave.

  Fig. 125 (a) shows one row of soumak following two picks of plain weave. The

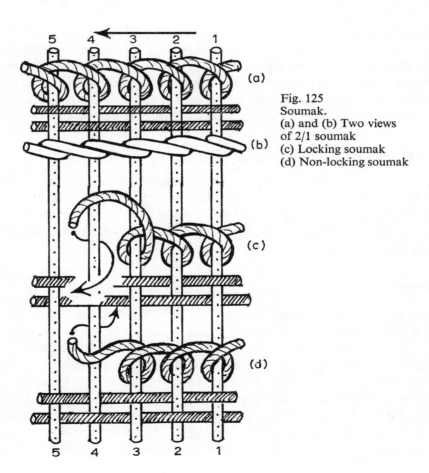

Fig. 125
Soumak.
(a) and (b) Two views
of 2/1 soumak
(c) Locking soumak
(d) Non-locking soumak

soumak weft is white, the ground weft is shaded. As the arrow indicates, the soumak weft is moving to the left. The soumak weft passes forward over two warp ends and then backwards under one, taking a wrapping course around the warp similar to that found in backstitch or stem stitch.

This is the simplest form of soumak and can be called 2/1 soumak. There are many other types in which the soumak weft wraps round a different number of warp ends, e.g., 4/2 soumak, where it passes forwards over four ends and backwards under two, 3/2 soumak, 6/3 soumak, and 9/3 soumak (as used in the Skog hanging). But it is 2/1 soumak which gives the closest texture and has been most used in rugs and saddlebags. Note that the soumak weft engages with all the warp ends, i.e., no shed is opened when the soumak is worked. It is carried out on the flat warp ends.

B. Surface Angling

Fig. 125 (a) shows that the forward-moving portions of the soumak weft do not lie at right angles to the two warp ends they cross, but at a definite angle, in this case slanting upwards to the left. These are the only parts of the soumak weft visible in a well-beaten rug and this angling gives the characteristic surface to a soumak rug, see Fig. 125 (b).

Whether this angle slants up the the left or right depends on two things, the exact way the soumak weft is wrapped around the warp and the direction in which the soumak weft is moving.

(i) METHOD OF WRAPPING GIVING LOCKING AND NON-LOCKING SOUMAK

The normal way of wrapping is shown in Fig. 125 (c). Place a loop of soumak weft over warp end 4, then pass it backwards under this end. Bring it up in the interval between its forward-moving portion and the last pick of ground weft, as shown by the arrow. Pull the soumak weft tight. As it now lies in the form of a half-hitch round the warp end, it will stay tight. For this reason, this type will be called *locking* soumak. Note that when locking soumak is worked from right to left (as in Fig. 125 (c)), its surface weft spans slant up to the left.

The alternative method is shown in Fig. 125 (d). Place the soumak weft over warp end 4 and pass it backwards under this end. But here, bring it up beyond its forward-moving portion, as shown by the arrow. Tighten. As in this case the weft makes no form of knot with the warp, it can easily become loose again, hence it is the less-used method. For this reason, this type will be called *non-locking* soumak. Note that when non-locking soumak is worked from right to left (as in Fig. 125 (d)) its surface weft spans slant up to the right, i.e., in the opposite direction to locking soumak.

(ii) DIRECTION IN WHICH SOUMAK IS WORKED

If one row of locking soumak made from right to left is followed by another row from left to right (with some ground weft in between), the weft spans of the first row will slant up to the left and those of the second row up to the right, see Fig. 126 (a). As working alternately to left and to right would seem to be the simplest and most natural way to carry out soumak, the resultant alternation of the surface angling can be regarded as normal, see Fig. 126 (b). It is the method found in most classical soumak rugs. A similar result is naturally obtained if non-locking soumak is worked alternately to left and to right.

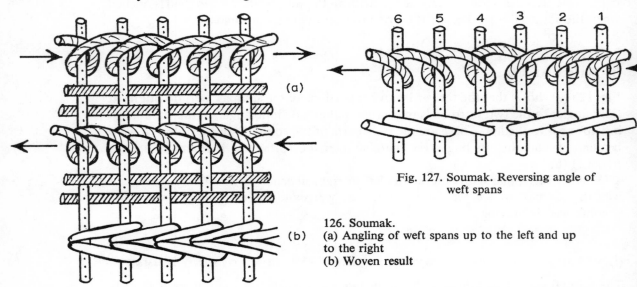

(a)

(b)

Fig. 127. Soumak. Reversing angle of
weft spans

126. Soumak.
(a) Angling of weft spans up to the left and up to the right
(b) Woven result

If, however, several rows with identical angling are wanted, there are two possible ways of producing this. One is to keep the normal right to left, left to right sequence, but to use locking and non-locking soumak in alternate rows. The other is to work, with only one type of soumak but always move from left to right or always right to left. In other words the soumak weft will either have to be finished off at the end of each row or returned to its starting selvage in a plain weave shed.

From the above it will be understood that the surface angling is always under the control of the weaver. Moreover the angling can be reversed in the middle of a row of soumak, by changing from the locking to the non-locking type, or vice versa. Fig. 127 shows such a reversal. The soumak (going to the left as shown by the arrow) is non-locking around ends 1–3 and locking around ends 4–6 In this way, blocks of soumak with opposite surface angling can be produced.

C. Types of Soumak

(i) SINGLE AND DOUBLE SOUMAK

So far, only single soumak has been described, in which the weft makes a single wrapping movement around one or more warp ends. Double soumak in which the weft wraps around two separate warp ends, or groups of warp ends, gives a much thicker ridge.

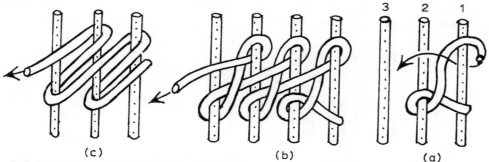

Fig. 128. Soumak. (a) and (b) Double locking soumak (c) Double non-locking soumak

Referring to Fig. 128 (a), wrap the weft round end 2 as in normal locking soumak. Then carry the weft backwards and wrap it round end 1, again in the locking manner, as shown by the arrow. Now wrap the weft round end 3, then carry it backwards and wrap around end 2.

So in each complete repeat, the weft wraps once around a new, unused, end and once around the end just used. Fig. 128 (b) shows several repeats and indicates why this is also called figure-of-eight soumak.

Fig 128 (c) shows several repeats of double non-locking soumak. This gives a far less prominent ridge.

Once the principle of double soumak is understood, other variations of this type will occur to the weaver.

(ii) BUSHONGO TYPE OF SOUMAK

The raffia cloths from the Bushongo tribe in central Africa are decorated with areas of raffia pile and with thin lines carried out in a variation of soumak. Both of these were embroidered on the finished cloth. But this soumak variation can be carried out when weaving and was extensively used in the Shiant rugs, designed by Jean Milne and woven in the Scottish islands. Fig. 129 shows how it is carried out. Comparison with Fig. 125 (c) will show how it differs from normal locking soumak. Note that each loop is tightened by pulling the soumak weft to the *right* in Fig. 129. This type of soumak

Fig. 129. Soumak. Bushongo type

gives a thin ridge that stands up well above the ground weave. It is often used to give a ridge lying at an angle to the fell of the rug.

(iii) TWO-COLOUR SOUMAK

Any of the types of soumak described so far can be carried out with two soumak wefts of different colours. The simplest sort, two-colour single soumak, is occasionally seen on Eastern knotted rugs as a decorative line across the knotless plain weave strip at either end. It is shown in Fig. 130 (a).

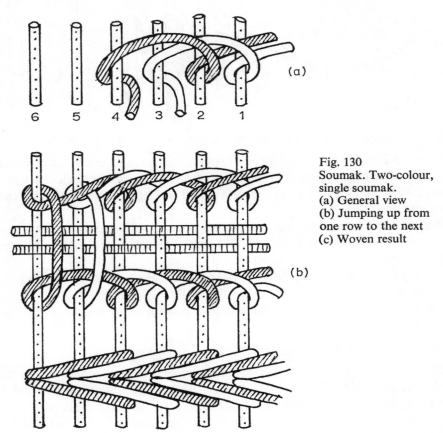

Fig. 130
Soumak. Two-colour, single soumak.
(a) General view
(b) Jumping up from one row to the next
(c) Woven result

Wrap the white weft in the locking manner around end 5 and then bring it down over the already-woven rug. Then wrap the shaded weft similarly around the next end, 6, and bring this weft down over the rug.

This gives a ridge in which the angled weft spans are alternately of two colours. If a second row of two-colour soumak is added, the two wefts are carried up as in

Fig. 130 (b). The lower part of this diagram shows that this will appear as chevrons of the two colours. This is, however, only one of several possibilities.

If the second row is made in non-locking soumak, its weft spans will lie at the same angle as those in the first row. If, again, in the jump-up from one row to the next, the two colours are crossed (so that the white weft in the second row is wrapping round the ends used by the shaded weft in the first row and vice versa), then the colour positions will be reversed. By playing with these variables, the weft spans can be made to appear as vertical or oblique stripes of the two colours. This is exactly comparable to the effects given by two-colour weft twining, illustrated in Chapter 13. In fact anything possible in the latter technique is also possible in two-colour single soumak.

Fig. 131 shows one of the forms two-colour double soumak can take.

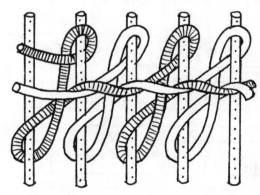

Fig. 131
Soumak. Two-colour,
double soumak

(iv) GAUZE SOUMAK

The angled weft spans of normal soumak show only on the upper surface of the rug. Gauze soumak was the result of trying to discover some type of weft wrapping which would show equally on both sides.

Referring to Fig. 132 (a), take the soumak weft forwards over two ends, backwards under one and over one, then forwards under two ends. Repeat.

As the cross-section in Fig. 132 (b) makes clear, this gives a weft span over two ends on both sides of the rug. This is not angled.

A simpler way to work this type involves twisting the warp, hence the name gauze soumak.

Of the next two warp ends to be wrapped around (7 and 8), twist the left-hand over the right-hand, and through the opening thus formed, pass the soumak weft, see Fig. 132 (a). Make the two ends untwist, either with the fingers, or by beating, and if the weft was at the correct loose tension it will now lie in the form of gauze soumak. With practice several repeats can be worked before beating.

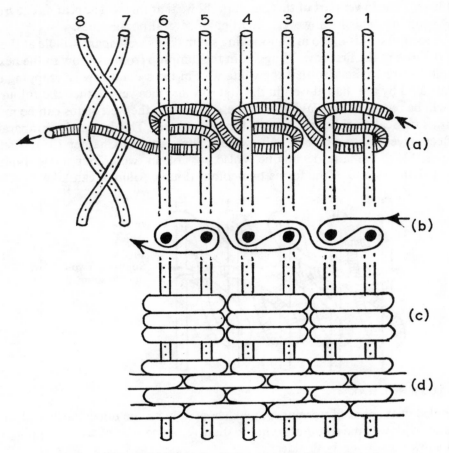

Fig. 132. Gauze Soumak. (a) Method of production (b) Cross-section
(c) and (d) Methods of arranging weft spans in successive rows

Note—The two warp ends could equally well be twisted right over left, if this is
found more convenient.
—Gauze soumak is very simple to undo. Simply pull the weft from both ends,
thus crossing all the pairs of warp ends. The weft, now lying in a straight
line, can be easily withdrawn.

As shown in Fig. 132 (c) and (d), the weft spans lie end to end, rather like bricks in a
wall. If the next row of gauze soumak is worked round the same pair of warp ends
(with, of course, some plain weave in between) the result will be as in Fig. 132 (c). If
alternate rows of soumak use different warp ends, then the result will be as in Fig.
132 (d).

D. Uses of Soumak

(i) RIDGES

The simplest use of soumak is to make raised ridges across the width of a rug. The prominence of these varies with the thickness of the yarn and the type of soumak used. The tension of the soumak weft should be carefully adjusted or the rug will be pulled in by each soumak row.

Such a soumak ridge need not lie parallel with the fell of the rug, but can slope upwards at an angle and is made thus.

Make one wrapping of soumak. Then weave a few picks of plain weave with the ground weft from selvage to selvage. Make one more soumak wrapping, repeat the plain weave. See Fig. 133.

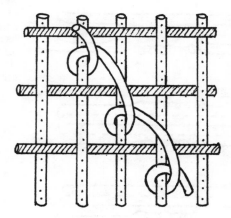

Fig. 133
Soumak. Forming a ridge at an angle

The more picks of plain weave, the steeper the angle at which the soumak will lie. In Fig. 133 only one pick of ground weft has been shown for simplicity's sake.

A sloping ridge of soumak can be used to outline a kilim motif. First weave the motif, say, a triangle, then carry the soumak up one side and down the other. Then weave in the background area. This is comparable with outlining a kilim motif with plain weave, e.g., the black weft shown in Fig. 103 (a) in Chapter 5.

(ii) BLOCKS

A more interesting use of soumak is to make soumak blocks (whose shape is always controllable) on a plain weave ground, so the soumak stands out as a raised and textured area lying on a flat plain weave background. This can be done in several ways.

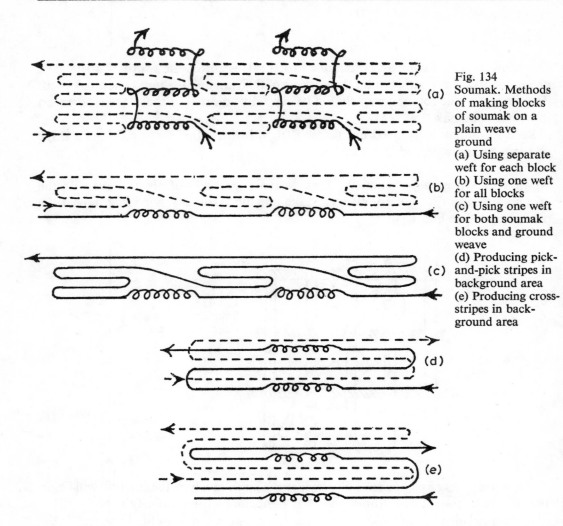

Fig. 134
Soumak. Methods of making blocks of soumak on a plain weave ground
(a) Using separate weft for each block
(b) Using one weft for all blocks
(c) Using one weft for both soumak blocks and ground weave
(d) Producing pick-and-pick stripes in background area
(e) Producing cross-stripes in background area

(a) Separate Soumak Weft for Each Block

Referring to Fig. 134 (a), carry each soumak weft across its prescribed area. Then weave with ground weft as shown. Make the second row with each soumak weft, then the ground weft as before.

The compensatory zigzag course of the ground weft may not be necessary after every row of soumak. If the soumak weft is thin, the ground weft can sometimes go straight from selvage to selvage. Do whatever gives a level fell to the rug.

(b) With One Soumak Weft for All the Blocks

Referring to Fig. 134 (b), start soumak weft at the right selvage, see arrow. Carry it in a plain weave shed up to the edge of the first proposed block. Then bring it out of the shed, and, on a closed shed, work it in soumak across the width of the block. Re-open the same shed and insert the soumak weft, carrying it up to the edge of the next block. Continue thus all the way across the rug to the left selvage.

At this point two things can be done, either introduce a ground weft and weave as shown in Fig. 134 (b), or let the soumak weft act as the ground weft as in Fig. 134 (c). In either case the compensatory zigzag course may not be necessary if the soumak weft is not too thick. In both cases repeat the whole process, taking the soumak weft in its partly woven, partly wrapped, course across the warp, followed by plain weave.

Note—That in the second method, one soumak weft can make any number of blocks across the width of the rug.

—That each time the soumak weft is carried across there is the possibility of altering the boundaries of the block. So their shape is constantly under the weaver's control.

—That in the type shown in Fig. 134 (b), the plain weave ground will show spots of the soumak weft colour on the ground weft colour. Other two-colour effects can be obtained in this area, e.g., pick-and-pick stripes as in Fig. 134 (d), and 2-and-2 cross stripes as in Fig. 134 (e). These sequences will probably have to be interrupted at intervals with compensatory zigzag picks.

—Making soumak blocks becomes far quicker if the soumak is carried out on the *raised* ends of an open shed. There is then no need for any compensatory picks. The ground weft can pass from selvage to selvage in the normal way.

If when using 4/2 soumak, a very crisp edge to the block is wanted, start with one repeat of gauze soumak (putting right-hand warp over left, if working from right to left). Then continue with 4/2 soumak to the edge of the block. Fig. 135 shows this being used to make the smallest possible block, i.e., spanning four ends as it is in 4/2 soumak. If a similar block is made when the soumak weft returns, they will combine to form a small raised spot as in Fig. 135.

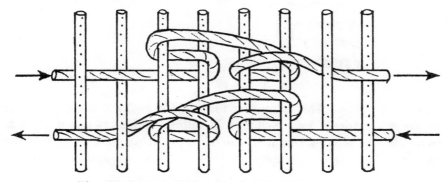

Fig. 135. Soumak. Using Gauze soumak to start a block

(iii) ALL-OVER SOUMAK

The classical soumak rugs are covered with the weft spans of closely packed rows of soumak. No plain weave is visible. Each soumak weft is worked from the right edge to the left of its own colour area and then back again, exactly as a tapestry weft is woven. But because of the ground weft (weaving from selvage to selvage), one soumak motif cannot be built up ahead of the rest, as is often done in tapestry. So the soumak weft of every colour area, all the way across the rug, has to be worked before the ground weft can be woven and the whole process repeated. This may explain why the design on the right side of a soumak rug rarely gets out of step with that on the left side, a thing that can easily happen with a kilim.

Designs of an intricacy approaching those found in knotted carpets can be produced with all-over soumak, see Plate 34. This is partly due to the high number of ends per inch found in soumak rugs and saddlebags, e.g., 14 to 18 e.p.i. Fine vertical lines are obtained by wrapping the weft round a single warp end. The only effect knotting can give which is unobtainable with soumak is a single spot of colour (one knot). The inside of a soumak saddlebag shows the short cuts taken by the weaver. Where several areas of the same colour are required, the soumak weft is looped across behind the intervening areas to avoid the use of several separate wefts.

A loop is also found on the back where a motif suddenly changes its outline. In Fig. 136, the dotted line shows where the soumak weft would have a loop at the back

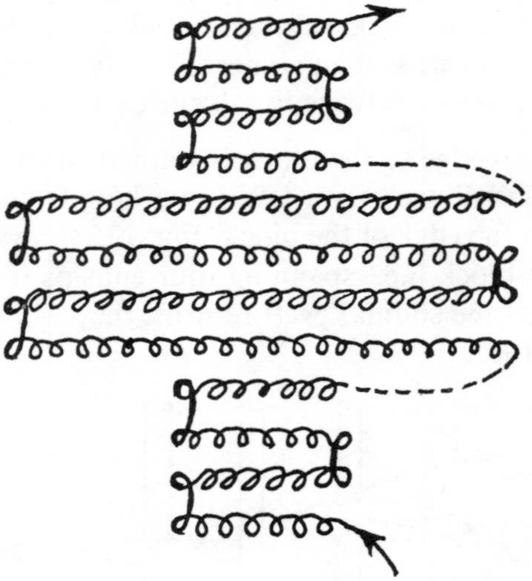

Fig. 136
Soumak. Showing weft loops at the back when working a cross shape in soumak

in the weaving of a cross. This is another form of the problem met with in tapestry technique where a sudden change of a motif's outline can lead to two wefts in a shed.

In such an all-over soumak rug, there are naturally many places where the soumak weft from the end of one row jumps up to start the next row and in so doing passes

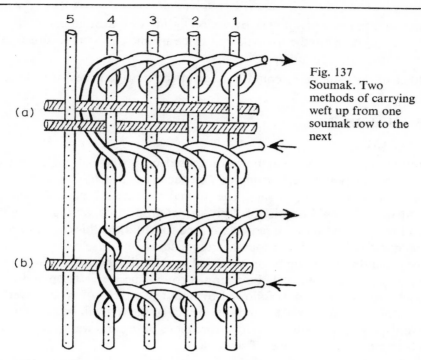

Fig. 137
Soumak. Two
methods of carrying
weft up from one
soumak row to the
next

over the intervening plain weave picks. Many methods are used, one of which is that shown in Fig. 139, in connection with selvages. Another is shown in Fig. 137 (a).

Complete the row of soumak by wrapping the weft around end 4. Push the weft between ends 4 and 5 through to the back. Weave two picks of ground weft. Bring the soumak weft forward between ends 4 and 5 and start the second row of soumak.

A third method which does not give such a regular edge to the motif is shown in Fig. 137 (b). It is generally associated with only one pick of ground weft.

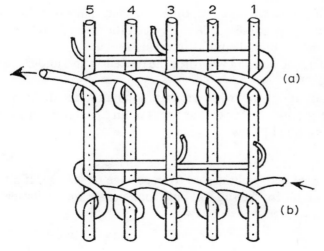

Fig. 138
Soumak.
(a) Starting a
soumak weft
(b) Finishing a
soumak weft

Complete the row of soumak by wrapping the weft around end 4 and then weave the ground weft. Wrap the soumak weft twice around end 4 in the direction shown and begin the soumak around end 3.

Either of these methods could be used at the selvage instead of the one shown in Fig. 139.

E. Practical Details

(i) GENERAL

As soumak is basically a decoration imposed on a weft-face rug, the remarks concerning the warp and weft setting of weft-face rugs in Chapter 4 apply to the warp and ground weft of soumak rugs. The soumak weft itself is generally thicker than the ground weft. It could consist of 2-ply carpet wool used sixfold to eightfold, if the ground weft consisted of the same yarn used fourfold. Its thickness naturally controls the boldness with which the soumak ridges stand out.

The ground weft should be on a normal rug shuttle, the soumak weft should be in a finger hank, which can easily be wrapped round successive warp ends.

If each row of soumak is followed by about two picks of ground weft, the former will completely hide the latter and the surface of the rug will be made up of the slanting weft spans of the soumak weft. More picks of ground weft will give some separation between successive rows of soumak.

(ii) STARTING AND FINISHING SOUMAK WEFTS

(*a*) *Starting*, See Fig. 138 (a)

Work a row of soumak to the left leaving the starting end of the soumak weft hanging out at the right end of the row. Open the plain weave shed which raises the first warp end included in the soumak (No. 1 in Fig. 138 (a)) and tuck the soumak weft around this end into the shed, bringing its threads out at intervals as shown.

(*b*) *Finishing*, See Fig. 138 (b)

Having finished a row of soumak to the left, open the shed that raises the last warp end included in the soumak (No. 5 in Fig. 138 (b)). Tuck the soumak weft around this end into the shed, bringing its threads out at intervals.

In both cases the subsequent weaving will force the tucked-in end under the soumak so that it is well hidden.

Note that these methods apply only when separate soumak wefts are being used for blocks on a plain weave ground, or for colour areas in an all-over soumak rug. The more usual method is described below.

(iii) SELVAGES

It is best not to work the soumak right across from selvage to selvage. If a few warp ends at each selvage are excluded, the rug will both look neater and lie flatter. Exactly how this is done will depend on the number of picks of ground weft between each row of soumak, how the surface angling of the soumak is being arranged, and many other factors.

Fig. 139 shows a typical example in which two rows of plain weave separate each row of locking soumak.

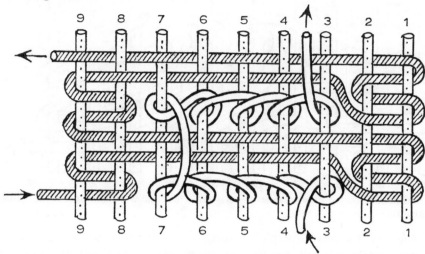

Fig. 139. Soumak. Showing how selvages are woven, when a separate plain weave weft is used

Start soumak round end 3 and carry across to end 7. Starting from the left, weave the ground weft up to the edge of the soumak, then back to the left selvage. These two picks on ends 8 and 9 compensate for the thickness of the absent soumak. Weave ground weft straight across to the right selvage, noting that it dips down as it reaches ends 2 and 1.

Weave up the edge of the soumak and back to the right selvage. These two picks on ends 1 and 2 compensate, as at the opposite selvage, for the absence of the soumak.

Then weave the ground weft straight across to left selvage. The fell of the rug should now be quite level.

Pick up the soumak weft and, beginning around end 7, carry it across to end 3.

Fill in the ground weft exactly as before. The extra compensatory picks around the two outer ends may not always be necessary.

The jump-up of the soumak weft from one row to the next which looks so prominent on the expanded diagram, is small and inconspicuous in actuality.

Soumak is sometimes woven with a single weft which acts as both a ground and a soumak weft. Fig. 140 shows how the selvage is managed in this case.

Starting at the right selvage (see bottom arrow) weave with the first three ends in a plain weave shed. Close the shed then work the weft in soumak around ends 4 to 7.

Open the same plain weave shed and weave in this to the left selvage.

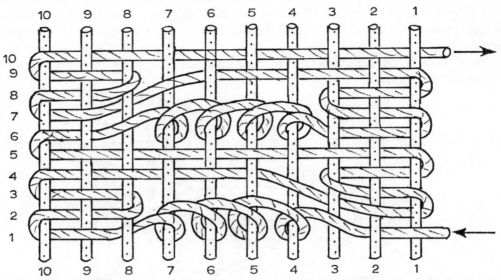

Fig. 140. Soumak. Showing how selvages are woven, when one weft is used for both soumak and ground weave

Then weave for the next four picks exactly as in the previous example. This brings the weft back to the left selvage. Repeat the process from that side, beginning with pick No. 6.

> *Note*—That if picks 5 and 10 were omitted, i.e., if only one pick of plain weave separated each soumak row, the soumak would always be moving from right to left. This would result in the weft spans of successive rows all slanting in the same direction. It would also occur if an extra pick of plain weave were woven.

For other methods of carrying up the soumak weft from one row to the next, see Figs. 137 (a) and (b).

F. Types of Vertical Soumak

(i) VERTICAL SINGLE SOUMAK

It has already been mentioned that a ridge of soumak can slope up at an angle to the fell of the rug. The ridges can also lie vertically; and in this present technique, vertical soumak ridges completely cover the surface of the rug.

The principle will be understood from Fig. 141, where a series of parallel soumak wefts are seen moving up the surface of the rug, with picks of plain weave separating their points of attachment to the warp. In actuality, the soumak wefts are of such a thickness that their upward-moving spans completely cover the plain weave, thus giving a characteristic angled surface to the rug, see Plate 35. The method is as follows:

Begin the rug with some picks of plain weave. Then make a sufficient number of finger hanks of soumak weft to cover its surface, remembering that a few ends at each selvage will carry plain weave only, as in Fig. 141. So if the warp had four working e.p.i. and the soumak wefts are to wrap around two ends, two finger hanks for every 1 inch width of the rug are needed. They need not all be of the same colour.

Tuck each weft under a pair of warp ends from right to left. The starting end of each weft hangs out from the right side of each warp pair, see bottom of Fig. 141.

Weave $\frac{1}{2}$ to 1 inch of plain weave with a separate weft. At both selvages, compensate for the absence of thickness of the soumak weft by some extra picks, as shown in Fig. 141.

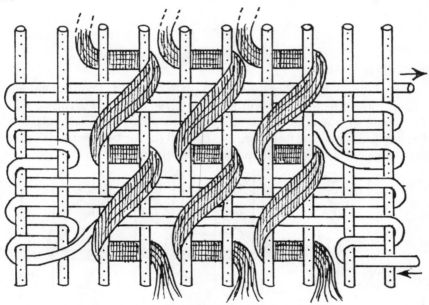

Fig. 141. Vertical Single Soumak. General view

Take each soumak end in turn and wrap it around the same two ends and in the same direction as before. This will produce surface spans of the soumak wefts which all slant up to the right and completely cover the plain weave.

Continue thus, alternating a plain weave section with a step-up of all the soumak wefts, to the end of the rug.

As the soumak wefts are very thick (two to four times the thickness of the ground weft), the finger hanks, if they are to contain enough weft for the whole rug, will be very bulky and hard to handle. Again due to their thickness, a join in the wefts can never be unobtrusive or very neat. Fig. 142 shows such a join. The finishing ends of the old wefts have been laid to the left in one shed and the beginning ends of the new wefts have been laid to the right in the next shed.

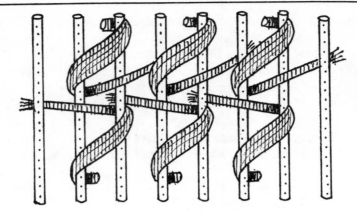

Fig. 142
Vertical Single Soumak.
Starting and finishing
soumak wefts

VARIATIONS

(a) Angle of Weft Spans

There is no need for all the weft spans to slant up to the right. They can equally well be made in the reverse direction, see bottom of Fig. 144 (b). So one rug could use both types; this would give a faint stripe in a monochrome rug. The angle can also be changed at any point in a rug (see Figs. 143 (a) and (b) for two methods), giving more possibilities, e.g., checks with weft spans at opposite angles.

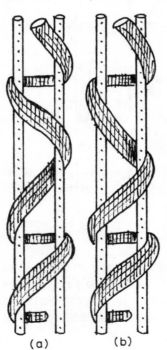

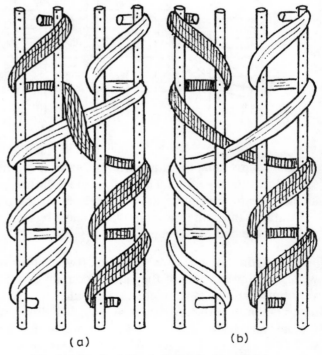

(a)   (b)

Fig. 143. Vertical Single
Soumak. Changing
angle of weft spans

(a)   (b)

Fig. 144. Vertical Single Soumak. (a) and (b)
Changing two adjacent colours

(b) Switching Colours

If two adjacent columns of soumak weft are of different colours, they can easily be switched over. The centre of Fig. 144 (b) shows how this is done if the weft spans of the two colours are at opposite angles. Fig. 144 (a) shows the procedure if the weft spans slant in the same direction. Note that in this case, there has to be a long and a short weft span, so use the short to bind down the centre of the long.

(c) Combination with Flat Areas

There is no need to cover a rug with the soumak wefts. Warpway stripes of plain weave can alternate with warpway stripes of this technique. Moreover the stripes need not be parallel to the warp. As is shown in Fig. 145 (a), if the weft is wrapped around more ends (three) than it passes over (two), the stripes will slant up in one direction, and if as in Fig. 145 (b) it is wrapped around fewer ends (one) than it passes over (two), the stripe will slant up in the opposite direction. Which actual direction it takes depends on whether the weft spans themselves are angled up to the right as shown or up to the left. By this means warpway stripes of the technique can be angled at will across the surface of the rug giving considerable freedom of design.

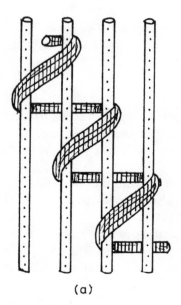

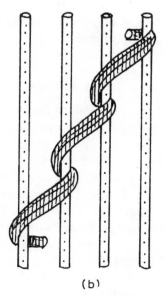

(a)   (b)

Fig. 145(a) Vertical Single   Fig. 145(b) Vertical Single
      Soumak. Angling   Soumak. Angling
      the soumak   the soumak
      stripes   stripes

(d) Cutting the Soumak Wefts

At any point weft spans can be left very loose and later cut to produce a pile. As the weft is not in any way knotted to the warp, the security of the pile depends on how tightly the plain weave grips the soumak wefts. So it is only safe to cut the soumak weft at intervals, for instance after it has stepped up three times in the normal way. Plate 35 shows a sample with cut pile.

A line of pile across the rug can be used as a method of finishing one set of wefts and starting a new set, in place of the method shown in Fig. 142. Obviously, at any such point, a soumak weft of a new colour can be introduced. Normally with this technique, any colour stripes in the soumak wefts have to run the length of the rug. But with a line of pile across the rug at intervals (at which every weft has the opportunity of being changed) this is no longer necessary and a far greater freedom is achieved.

Practical Details

Anything from 3 to 6 working e.p.i. can be used for the warp. Use the appropriate thickness of plain weave weft to produce a firm weft-face weave. The thickness of soumak weft necessary to cover the plain weave depends on the angle at which its weft spans lie. The more nearly parallel they are to the fell of the rug, the thinner the weft need be. The angle of the weft spans is governed by two factors.

(1) The amount of plain weave between each step-up of soumak wefts.

(2) The number of ends around which the soumak wefts are wrapped.

(ii) VERTICAL DOUBLE SOUMAK

This is similar in principle to the last technique but, as the vertical ridges formed by the soumak wefts have a pleasant angular character, the technique is probably better employed in forming distinct ridges alternating with plain weave rather than as an all-over technique. See Plate 36.

The idea was derived from one of the Argatch techniques described in the section on knotted pile in this Chapter, but it can also be considered as vertical double soumak. Compare Fig. 146 (a) with Fig. 128 (a).

Each vertical ridge needs its own separate weft wound as a finger hank.

Begin as in Fig. 146 (a) by wrapping the free end of the weft around a warp that was raised in the last plain weave shed, e.g., end 2.

Weave three picks of plain weave.

Wrap the weft around the next warp end to the right, No. 1 in Fig. 146 (a). Note that this too was raised in the last plain weave shed.

Weave three picks of plain weave.

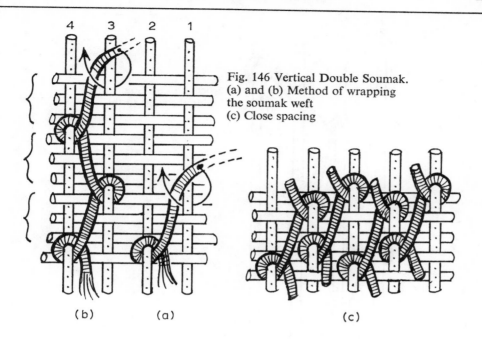

Fig. 146 Vertical Double Soumak.
(a) and (b) Method of wrapping
the soumak weft
(c) Close spacing

(b)　　　(a)　　　　　　(c)

Continue thus, alternating three picks of plain weave with one wrapping movement of the soumak weft, which moves from left to right of the two warp ends that carry the ridge, see Fig. 146 (b).

Because the weft is wrapped around an end raised in the last plain weave shed, it slides down over the plain weave weft and does not seem to add any extra bulk to the weave at that point. Hence the plain weave can always pass from selvage to selvage and not take a compensatory zigzag course, thus saving much time.

Ridges can be made on every two adjacent warp ends across the rug's width. But these will not cover the plain weave surface as did the ridges in the last technique. In order to cover the plain weave, the wefts have to be placed closer still so that every warp end is wrapped around by two adjacent wefts, see Fig. 146 (c).

Fig. 147 shows how a ridge can be carried sideways to the right. Starting from the bottom of the diagram, the weft is wrapped around end 3, then 4, then carried across to the right and wrapped around end 2, then 3. Always make the sideways movement when the weft is in any case moving in that direction.

In Plate 36, the yarn used for both ground weft and soumak weft was of the same thickness. This gives compact and practical ridges.

The starting and finishing ends of the soumak wefts can either all be laid in a plain weave shed or left hanging out to form an additional fringe to the rug or be darned in along warp ends in the normal manner for wefts.

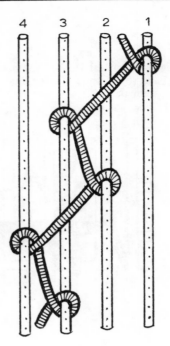

Fig. 147
Vertical Double Soumak.
Moving the ridge to the right

2. WEFT CHAINING

Most weavers know how to chain a warp as it is taken from the mill, manipulating it in a manner similar to crocheting. The same idea, combined with twisting, is applied to single warp threads by some primitive people, as a simple way of making what is more or less a 3-ply thread.

It is surprising that the idea has not been applied to the weft until relatively recent times, as it has an effect rather like soumak and is far quicker to carry out. There are two types, both of which need a chaining weft and a ground weft.

A. First Type

(i) USING ONE CHAINING WEFT

Of the two types, the first to be described is more like soumak, in fact one row of this type looks very like two rows of soumak.

Referring to Fig. 148, begin by weaving the chaining weft with a few ends at the right selvage to anchor it. Then pass it *under* the warp all the way to the left selvage. In Fig. 148 (a) it has woven with ends 1 to 4, then passed under ends 5 to 12 to the left selvage.

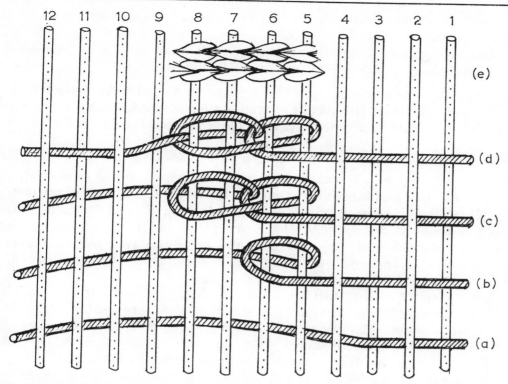

Fig. 148. Weft Chaining. (a–c) Stages in forming the chain (d) Locking the chain (e) Actual appearance

Hold the weft at the left selvage with the left hand. With the right hand pull up a loop of it between ends 4 and 5, see Fig. 148 (b).

Put the right finger and thumb through this loop and pull up another loop of the weft, drawing it up between ends 6 and 7, see Fig. 148 (c).

Continue thus, always picking up a new loop of weft and drawing it up between two new warp ends and up through the previously made loop.

As each new loop is made, pull it to the right to tighten the previous loop. The slack that consequently enters the new loop makes it over-large. So reduce its size by pulling on the free end held in the left hand, before the next loop is pulled up. This control of tension is very important as there is a tendency for the loops to become larger and looser as the work proceeds.

A few ends before the left selvage is reached, lock the chaining by pulling the free end of the weft (instead of a loop), up through the previous loop and then laying the weft in a plain weave shed to the selvage, see Fig. 148 (d). If it is not locked, the chained weft will undo just as easily as does a chained warp.

Now weave three or more picks of ground weft, and repeat the above sequence. The ground weft will occasionally have to take a compensatory zigzag course as described under soumak.

When the chaining is worked from left to right it is naturally the left hand which pulls up the loops and the right hand that holds the free end.

The result is a bold raised ridge which overlaps the ground weft immediately preceding and following it. Its structure is identical with chain stitch, either as produced by hand in embroidery or automatically by the single-thread sewing machine.

Relationship of Weft Thickness to Spacing of the Chained Loops

The weaver must ensure that the ridge is tight and compact enough to be practical, yet is not so tight that it pulls in the selvage. The necessary balance depends on the correct relationship between the thickness of the chaining weft and the spacing of the loops. In the above description, the loops were pulled up between every other warp end. But they could equally well have been pulled up between every pair, i.e., between ends 4 and 5, 5 and 6, 6 and 7, etc., or between every third pair, i.e., between 4 and 5, 7 and 8, 10 and 11, etc., or in some other sequence.

A weft of such a thickness that it gave a correct chain when pulled up as in Fig. 148, would, when pulled up between *every* pair of ends, give an over-tight, bulky ridge that would probably not lie flat. The same weft when pulled up between every third pair of ends would either pull in the selvages if the loops were correctly tightened or would give a loose chain, not affecting the selvages, if the loops were left slack.

So either decide on a thickness of weft and find by trial and error the correct spacing of the loops to suit it, or decide on a spacing of loops and adjust the thickness of the weft to suit that. In the first case it may be necessary to space loops in an irregular sequence to achieve exactly the right result.

Fig. 148 (e) shows the appearance of two rows of weft chaining when the loops are pulled up between every pair of ends. The similarity to four rows of soumak is obvious. Plate 37 shows weft chaining carried out in rope with a ground weft of sisal and hemp yarn.

(ii) USING TWO CHAINING WEFTS

This technique is well suited to all-over weft chained rugs. There are basically two methods; in the first, each row of weft chaining consists of alternate loops of the two colours, in the second, loops are pulled up in such a way that a completely free, two-colour design can be produced.

(a) Start both colours (black and white in Fig. 149) at the right selvage in successive sheds and then pass both of them under all the warp ends to the left selvage, see Fig. 149 (a).

Between ends 4 and 5 pull up a loop of the weft which is nearest to the fell of the cloth (white) with the right hand, see Fig. 149 (b). Insert the fingers of the right hand

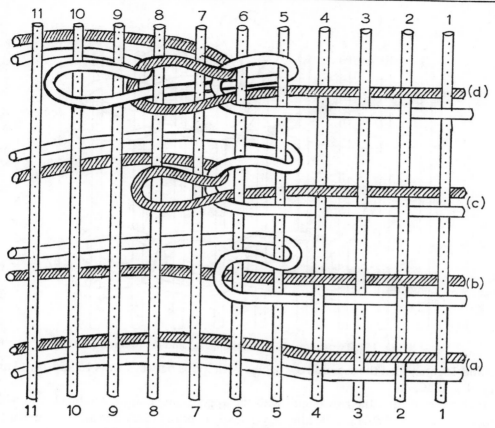

Fig. 149. Two-colour Weft Chaining. (a–d) Method I

down through this white loop and down between ends 6 and 7 and pull up a loop of the other weft (black), see Fig. 149 (c). Tighten the white loop by pulling on the white weft with the left hand at the left selvage.

Now through the black loop, pull up a loop of white weft, drawing it up between ends 8 and 9, see Fig. 149 (d). Tighten black loop by pulling on black weft at left selvage.

Continue thus, pulling up a black weft through a white loop, and a white through a black. After pulling up a black weft tighten the white, after pulling up a white, tighten the black. Finish by locking the chain. If the last loop pulled up was white, then pull the whole of the black weft up through this loop to lock it.

Insert the black weft in a plain weave shed, followed by the white in the next plain weave shed. Then weave some plain weave picks.

In the returning row, pull the loops up in different warp interspaces from those used in the first row. So if the first row ended with loops between ends 11 and 12, 13 and 14,

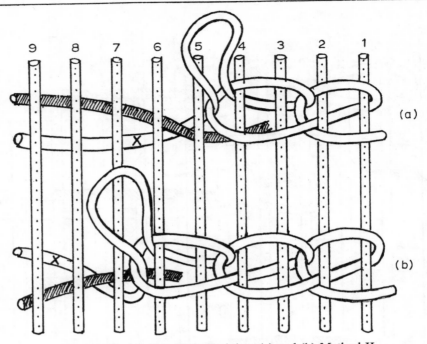

Fig. 150. Two-colour Weft Chaining. (a) and (b) Method II

15 and 16, etc., then the second row begins with loops between ends 15 and 14, 13 and 12, 11 and 10, etc.

If this is done and the row begun with the appropriate colour, the black and white loops of the second row will lie almost vertically over the black and white loops of the first row. In the third row pull the loops up in the original warp interspaces. The fourth row is exactly like the second.

The result is wavy warpway stripes of the two colours, as seen in Plate 38. Other effects are easily obtained by positioning the loops and colours differently.

(b) The second method begins exactly as the first. If the design dictates there should be an area of white, start normal chaining with the white weft only. But something has to be done to prevent a long float of the black weft at the back.

So before each loop of white is pulled up, cross the white weft *behind* the black, with the left hand, see Fig. 150 (a). Now pull up a loop of white between ends 6 and 7. Again cross white behind black, but this time in the reverse direction, see Fig. 150 (b), otherwise the black and white wefts will tangle around each other at the back of the warp. Pull up a loop of white between ends 8 and 9.

Where the design demands black, just reverse the procedure, i.e., bring up a black loop and then continue chaining with the black weft catching the white weft at the back, as explained above.

Plate 39 shows examples of this technique. In one, the colour boundaries are at an angle, and this was done by bringing the loops up in different warp interspaces in each alternate row. Note the characteristic toothed outline to the motif. In the other, the loops were pulled up in the same warp interspaces in each row, and this lends itself more to vertical colour boundaries.

B. Second Type

The second type of weft chaining gives a ridge which closely resembles a chain lying on the surface of the rug.

As with the first type, anchor the chaining weft in a plain weave shed at the right selvage, see Fig. 151 (a). Then bring it out of the shed so that it lies *above* the warp.

With the left hand pass a loop of the weft under end 6, see Fig. 151 (b). Then through this loop pull another loop of weft and immediately pass the new loop under end 8, see Fig. 151 (c). This can be done in one movement if the fingers of the left hand work correctly. Tighten each loop by pulling on the free end of the weft held in the right hand.

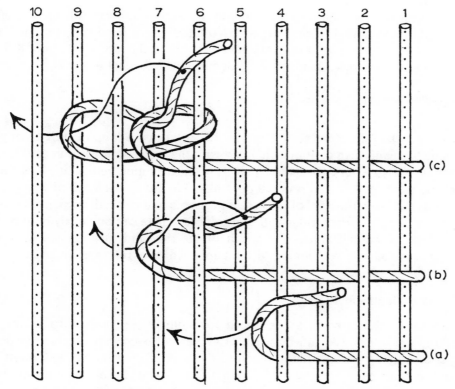

Fig. 151. Weft Chaining. Second Type. (a–c) Method of production

Finish row by locking the last loop and laying the weft in a plain weave shed at the left selvage exactly as for the first type. If tensioned correctly, the chaining should look as in Fig. 152.

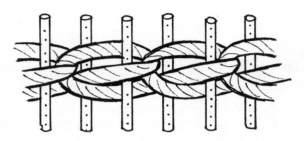

Fig. 152
Weft Chaining.
Second Type. Actual
appearance

Note—That in the above description the loops are only inserted under the even-numbered warp ends, so the chaining can be worked on the open shed in which these ends are raised. This is also the shed in which the chaining weft lies at either selvage.

—The loops can be inserted under every end, or at every third end or at any desired interval. If they are inserted under every third end, e.g., under 6, 9 and 12 in one row and then under 7, 10, 13 in the next row, under 8, 11, 14, in the next row, there will be a definite twilled effect in the surface texture.

One possible variation is as follows.

Having reached the stage shown in Fig. 151 (c), draw a loop of weft through the last-made loop and then continue chaining with the fingers but without attaching the chain to the warp. After two or three repeats of this chaining 'in the air', tuck the last-made loop under end 10 and proceed normally. The result is a knob of chained weft, that stands out from the level of the rug. If in subsequent rows, the process is repeated in the same place, a vertical ridge will be produced. There can obviously be as many of these ridges as wanted across the width of the rug, and they do not have to lie vertically; appropriate positioning of the knobs will give ridges at an angle.

C. Practical Details and Uses

The practical details are all as described for soumak, i.e., any warp setting from 3 working e.p.i. upwards can be used. However, all-over weft chaining (especially using two chaining wefts) adds so much to the bulk of the rug that with a setting as low as 3 working e.p.i., the rug may be too heavy. So 4 or 5 working e.p.i. are better. The ground weft is always of a thickness appropriate to the warp setting.

Weft chaining can be used to make ridges which can be straight, oblique or curved, to make raised blocks of any shape, or to cover completely the surface of a rug. Remember that if several blocks are made across the width of the rug, the chaining weft has to be locked as each one is finished.

Though all-over weft chaining is not commonly used, it can be a very effective technique, e.g., when using thick sisal as the chaining weft or when using two chaining wefts. Always begin and end each chaining row with the weft lying for some distance in a plain weave shed, as this will prevent the rug from curling up at the edges.

3. WEFT LOOPING

The idea of decorating or thickening a textile with loops made during weaving is an ancient one. Some hold the opinion that it preceded the technique of knotted pile, because the yarn in a looped pile would presumably wear better than the cut ends of a knotted pile and durability would, in early times, be the first consideration. This is partly supported by the fact that several of the methods of producing a knotted pile involve first making a weft loop, then cutting it. When the decorative aspect of such textiles became more important, the weft loop had to yield to the knot, as the latter is by far the more flexible technique, imposing hardly any limitations on the designs that can be carried out with it.

The loops may be made either from the weft lying in a shed, e.g., pulled-up and wrapped loops, or from an extra yarn, e.g., Sehna loops and many unnamed varieties.

A. Pulled-Up Weft Loops

HISTORY

One of the earliest finds using a pulled-up weft loop is a patterned towel from Deir el-Bahri, Egypt, dated about 2160 B.C. Both warp and weft are of linen. In certain areas, every other pick is of a much thicker yarn and it is this that is pulled up in loops to give various patterns. Later, in Egypt, wool was used for the weft loops and later still, short lengths of different-coloured wools were laid in the same shed and loops pulled up so that a polychrome looped design was produced (A.D. 400 to 500).

Strangely, weft loops were a technique not much exploited in Peruvian weaving. They are sometimes seen in pictorial tapestries where, for instance, a furry animal may be represented entirely in pulled-up loops.

Its use in heavier fabrics is now found in the rugs of the Alpujarras region, south of Granada, in Spain, in Sardinian rugs, in some gravecloths of Eastern Europe, and in Scandinavian rugs. They are sometimes called boutonné rugs.

(i) GENERAL TECHNICAL DETAILS

The sequence is as follows:

Referring to Fig. 153 (a), throw a weft and keep the shed open. Beginning at the selvage from which the shuttle was thrown (right in Fig. 153 (a)), pull up loops of this weft between every other pair of the raised warp ends, e.g., between 4 and 6, 8 and 10, and so on. If the yarn is of the correct spin and springiness, the loops will probably twist once or twice as in Fig. 153 (b).

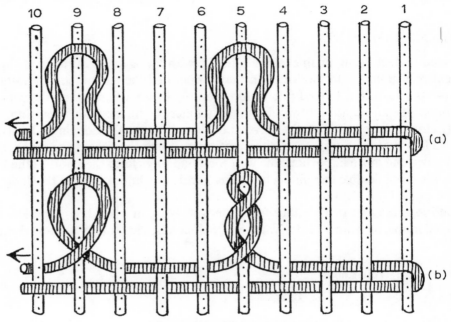

Fig. 153. Pulled-up Loops

When the row is completed, weave some picks of plain weave using either the same or another weft.

Then repeat the row of loops, followed by more plain weave.

There could be one, two, three or more picks between each row of loops, or two rows of loops could be followed by two picks of plain weave, or some such sequence.

It is the plain weave surrounding the loops that holds them in place, so it must be tightly woven. It is also for reasons of security that the loops are not pulled up between every pair of raised ends.

To achieve regularity of size, each loop can be slipped over the end of a smooth stick. This is slid in from the right by the right hand while the left hand pulls up the loops. Do not slide out the stick until the plain weave that follows has been woven. The hand positions are, of course, reversed when the loops are begun from the left side.

(ii) PLACING THE LOOPS

If there is an odd number of plain weave picks between each looping row, the latter will always lie in the same shed. If there is an even number, each looping row will lie in a different shed to its predecessor. Which of these two alternatives is chosen depends on the effect and design required.

(a) With the loops always coming from the same shed there are two possibilities. Either pull up the loops from the same warp interspace in each row, which gives vertical rows of loops, see Fig. 154 (a). Or pull them up from different warp interspaces in successive rows. This is a common method and gives a good regular coverage of loops over the rug, see Fig. 154 (b).

(b) When the loops are pulled up from different sheds, there are more possibilities, because there are four positions in which a loop can be pulled up. Fig. 154 (c) shows loops pulled up successively in these four positions to give angled lines of loops. If

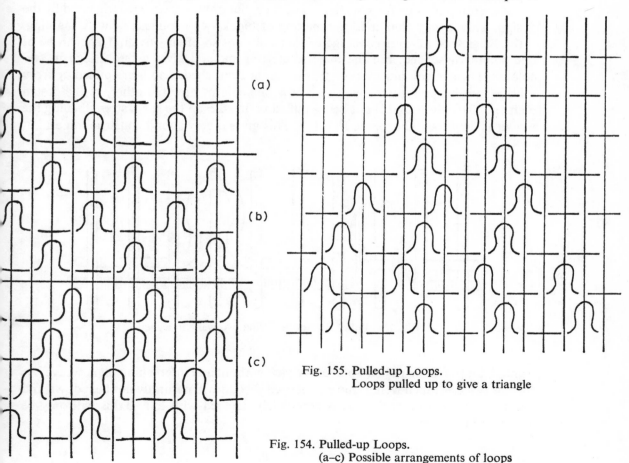

(a)

(b)

(c)

Fig. 155. Pulled-up Loops.
Loops pulled up to give a triangle

Fig. 154. Pulled-up Loops.
(a–c) Possible arrangements of loops

the lower two rows in Fig. 154 (c) were repeated several times, vertical rows of loops would result, wider than the rows in Fig. 154 (a). Fig. 155 shows how a triangle of loops can be built up. Note that, starting at the tip, there are two rows with only one loop, two rows with two loops, two rows with three loops, etc. In the whole of Figs. 154 and 155 the plain weave has been omitted for the sake of clarity.

There tends to be a weakness in the rug under each loop, especially if the warp is widely set. So an extra weft is often run in the same shed as the looping weft to overcome this.

(iii) USES

(a) Pulled-up loops are very commonly used in monochrome rugs, whose design depends entirely on the contrasting areas of loops and of plain weave. In other words, loops are not pulled up from selvage to selvage, but only in those areas dictated by the design. This is very similar to the making of blocks with soumak or weft chaining.

(b) Rugs with all-over coverage of loops are not so often woven. They can be of one colour or striped, but the most interesting method gives a free design in two colours. The two colours are both thrown in the *same* shed. Loops are pulled up from selvage to selvage in each row, using now one colour, now the other, as the design dictates. The colour that is not being pulled up just lies in the shed, strengthening the weave as described above, see Fig. 156. This gives a very sound construction and, if

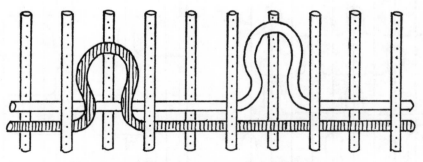

Fig. 156. Pulled-up Loops. Using two wefts in a shed

wanted, loops can be pulled up in every pick without any intervening plain weave. As there is twice as much weft as normal in each shed, it will naturally not beat down and cover the warp. But as the rug is completely covered with loops, this will only be apparent on the back

(iv) PRACTICAL DETAILS

The warp could have from 3 to 6 working e.p.i. according to the thickness of rug required.

The looping weft should be springy, so the loops will stand up again when trodden on, and have enough spin in it to ensure that the loops twist into a compact form as suggested in Fig. 153 (b). To achieve the latter requirement, extra spin may have to be added to the yarn as bought, either on a spinning wheel or on a bobbin winder, as described in Chapter 4. If this is combined with very long loops, something resembling a pile is produced, see Fig. 157.

With unsuitable yarns, pulled-up weft loops can appear very sad and slack.

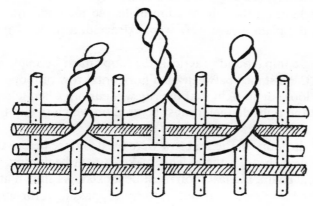

Fig. 157
Pulled-up Loops.
Appearance of loops
made from highly
twisted yarn

(v) CHAINED LOOPS

In this interesting development, pulling up weft loops is only the first of two stages. In the second stage, the loops are themselves chained into each other to give rows resembling weft chaining, but lying in the warp direction, see Fig. 158.

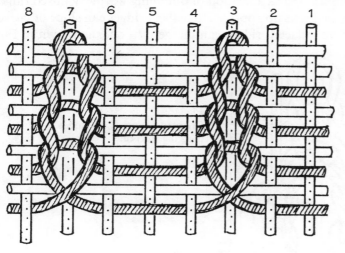

Fig. 158
Chained Loops.
General view

First pull up weft loops between ends 2 and 4, 6 and 8, etc., then throw some picks of plain weave.

Repeat this several times, to make vertical rows of loops.

Then, using the fingers or an improvised hook, work on the right-hand vertical row of loops, pulling the second loop through the first, the third through the second, the fourth through the third, and so on. Then move to the next row and do likewise.

The two vertical chains thus produced lie flat on the rug and as the loops are all interlocked there is not the danger of their being pulled out, always present in other types of pulled-up loops. For this reason loops can be pulled up between every pair of warp ends with perfect safety, see Figs. 161 and 162.

As an interesting sidelight on the interrelation of textile methods, note that if in Fig. 158 the warp and the plain weave weft were extracted, a piece of normal weft knitting would be left.

To make the chaining compact and practical, the loops must be made exactly the right size in relation to the distance between each horizontal row of loops. Otherwise the chain will either be loose or so tight that the rug will curl up when taken from the loom. So a stick of just the right diameter must be used on which to slip the loops as they are made.

Note that in Fig. 158 the loops in the first row were twisted once before the loops in the second row were pulled through them. This makes a neat beginning.

At the end of a vertical chain, the last loop must be locked. As shown at the top of Fig. 158, this is done by bringing a weft out of the shed, passing it through the final loop of the first chain and then back into the shed as far as the final loop of the next chain. This weft cannot be on a shuttle as the latter will not fit through the final loops.

Possibilities of Chained Loops

(a) Chained loops can be used as a method of obtaining warpway raised ridges on a flat ground. By pulling the loops up appropriately these ridges can slope or curve or lie parallel to the warp. Two adjacent ridges can merge into one, as shown in Fig. 159.

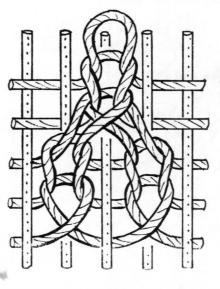

Fig. 159
Chained Loops. Two ridges
merging into one

(b) When used as an all-over technique, it gives a design which depends on the controlled placing of the loops from two coloured wefts. An effective method is shown in Plate 40, in which black and white loops have been pulled up to give alternate stripes of the two colours, whose angular direction is decided by the weaver. These stripes are then chained, as already described. Fig. 160 shows diagrammatically (and without plain weave) four such stripes sloping up to the right.

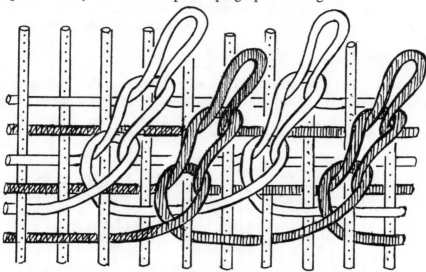

Fig. 160. Chained Loops. Using two colours to make oblique stripes

(c) Figs. 161 and 162 show two of the many other possible all-over uses of chained loops. Alternate rows of loops (pulled up at every available warp interspace) are made of two colours. An even number of plain weave picks, not shown in diagram, are woven between each row of loops. The loops can then be chained, either as in Fig. 161 or as in Fig. 162, the surface texture being quite different in the two cases.

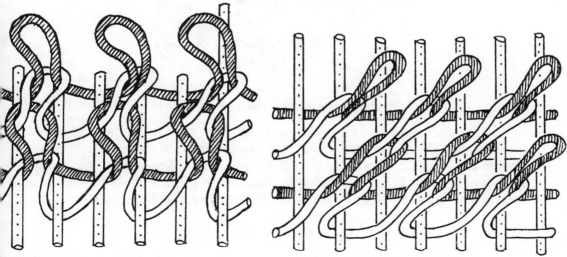

Fig. 161. Chained Loops. Another method of using two colours

Fig. 162. Chained Loops. Another method of using two colours

(d) Another variation is to twist each loop in the chaining stage, just as the first loop is twisted in Figs. 158, 159 and 160.

This is applicable both to vertical ridges and all-over chained loops. The twists which may be single or multiple can be either in the S or Z direction. Contrasting the two directions of twist in the same rug is another possibility.

The relation to weft knitting has already been mentioned and a study of knitting methods might lead to the discovery of other variations of this technique.

B. Wrapped Weft Loops

This is the second type of loop made from a weft lying in the shed and again it can be traced back at least 2,000 years. In the earliest finds, it was used to make a looped pile of wool.

Fig. 163 (a) shows how it differs from a pulled-up loop.

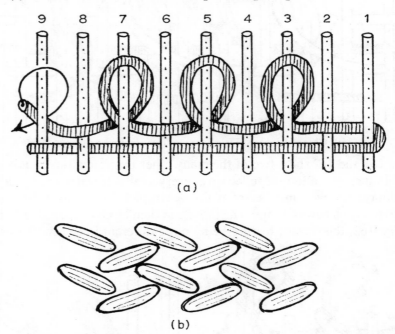

(a)

(b)

Fig .163. Wrapped Loops. (a) General view. (b) View from above

Open the shed which raises the odd-numbered warp ends. Insert the weft from the right selvage under the first two raised ends, 1 and 3, and then bring it out of the shed between ends 3 and 5. Cross it to the right over end 3, and re-insert it into the shed between ends 3 and 1. Pass it under ends 3 and 5 and bring it out of the shed again between ends 5 and 7. Wrap it round end 5 as before and re-insert into the shed.

Continue thus across the warp. The result is a row of loops which wrap round ends 3, 5, 7 and so on.

This is naturally much slower to work than pulled-up loops, but it produces more firmly held loops. For this reason, the loops can be made more closely together (compare with Fig. 153 (a)). Another advantage is the absence of the structural weakness found behind each pulled-up loop, so there is never any need to run another weft in the same shed.

Practically all the remarks made about pulled-up loops also apply to wrapped loops. They can be made on a rod to control their size, they need plain weave to hold them in position, they can be spaced as in Figs. 154 and 155, their uses are identical, and they can be chained.

Because of the way they are made, the loops all have a slight tilt when looked at from above. When worked from right to left, the loops tilt up to the right, see bottom row in Fig. 163 (b). When worked in the opposite direction, they tilt up to the left, see next row in Fig. 163 (b). A pleasant texture can therefore be produced by looping from right to left in one shed and from left to right in the next shed and then weaving two picks of plain weave, or some such sequence. Plate 41 shows wrapped loops of coir.

The wrapped loop is related structurally to the one-warp knot, described later in this Chapter. If, in Fig. 163 (a), the loops were made by pulling forward the parts of the weft lying in the shed (not the parts wrapping round the warp ends) and if these loops were cut, the result would be a row of one-warp knots.

C. Sehna Loops

Loops of this type, both in linen and wool, are found in Egyptian textiles dated about A.D. 400 and in earlier finds at Dura-Europas on the Euphrates. A woollen textile from Jericho, dating back to the second century A.D., has Sehna loops on *both* sides, those on the face being a different colour from those on the back. There also exists a large fragment of a Coptic rug in this technique. It is used today in the making of Tibetan rugs.

The name, Sehna loop, is based on the fact that if the loop is cut, the yarn is attached to the warp as in a Sehna knot. There is, however, a slight difference which will be explained later.

Unlike wrapped and pulled-up loops, Sehna loops are not made from a weft lying in the shed but from a separate extra weft.

Begin by fixing this looping weft in a shed at the right selvage, then bring it out of the shed so that it lies on top of the warp ends, see Fig. 164 (a).

With the shed still open (even-numbered ends raised) pull a loop of the weft under, end 4 as shown by arrow in Fig. 164 (a). Note that the loop passes *forwards* (i.e., in the direction the work is moving), and points down to the left. Slip this loop, shown in

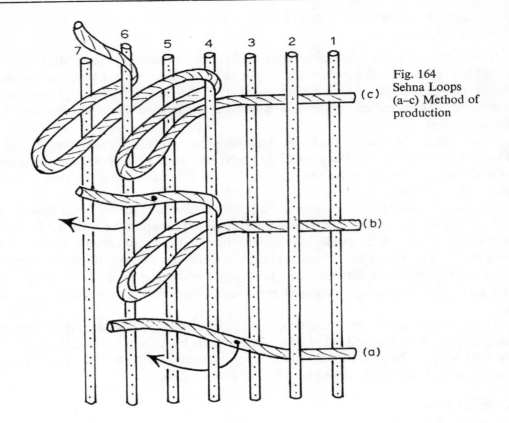

Fig. 164
Sehna Loops
(a–c) Method of
production

Fig. 164 (b), onto a stick. Pull another loop under the next raised end, No. 6, and also slip it onto the stick. See Fig. 164 (c).

Continue thus, pulling loops under the raised ends until the left selvage is reached. Then enter the weft into the shed to fix it. Plain weave picks now follow.

As shown in Figs. 165 (a) and (b), the loops can be pulled in the reverse direction that is, they pass *backwards* under the raised ends and then point downwards to the right. The right- and left-inclined Sehna loop is directly related to the right- and left-hand Sehna knot.

There is no reason, apart from convenience, for making these loops on the raised ends of an open shed. They can equally well be made on a closed shed, in which case a loop can be made around every warp end as in Fig. 165 (c), or around two ends as in Fig. 165 (d), or around more. When made around every end, the Sehna loop gives the closest form of looping available.

All these types are very securely held.

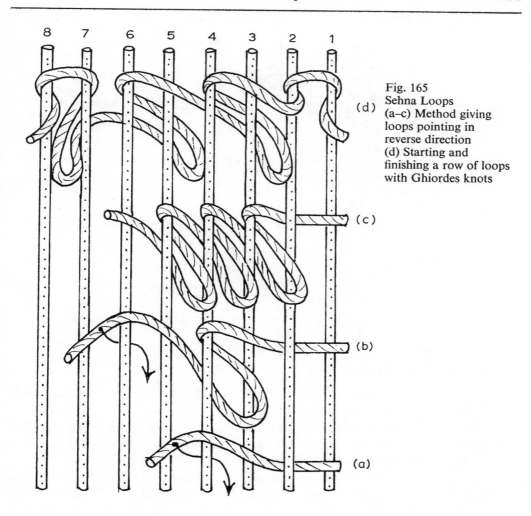

Fig. 165
Sehna Loops
(a–c) Method giving loops pointing in reverse direction
(d) Starting and finishing a row of loops with Ghiordes knots

An alternative way of beginning and ending a row of Senha loops is with a Ghiordes knot, as found in Tibetan rugs, see Fig. 165 (d).

An extremely well-tethered loop that can be regarded as a development of the Sehna loop, is shown in Fig. 166. Working from right to left, make a Sehna loop around end 2. See Fig. 166 (a), where the loop has been pulled upwards for clarity's sake.

Now take the same weft loop around end 1 as shown by the arrow and pull it tight.

The loop will now hang down as in Fig. 166 (b). It will be found that the path taken around end 2 and 1 by the weft loop is exactly the same as that taken by a free end of weft in double locking soumak.

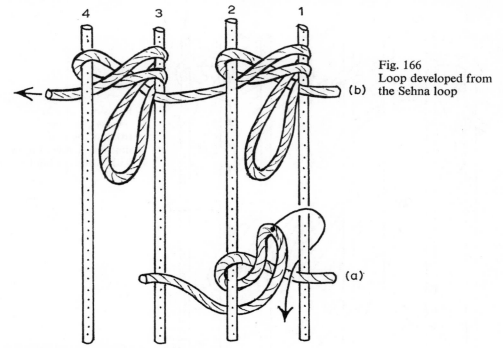

Fig. 166
Loop developed from
the Sehna loop

D. Pulled-Up Loops Based on Soumak

This type of loop is pulled up from the normal soumak structure, so is extremely secure. There are several varieties.

(i) Fig. 167 (a) shows loops based on 4/2 soumak. Normal locking 4/2 soumak is worked to the left. From that part which passes backwards under two ends, pull up a loop, as shown by the arrow between ends 5 and 6.

(ii) Fig. 167 (b) shows normal 3/1 soumak. As indicated by the arrows, the loops are drawn from the weft as it passes forward. The result, see Fig. 167 (c), is that the weft wraps around one end and then has a blind loop tucked under the next end, and this sequence is repeated. In working this type it is easier to make these two movements alternately, rather than trying to make the soumak and then pull a loop from it.

(iii) A loop can be based on gauze soumak, see Fig. 168 (a)

Work the soumak to the left. Of the next pair of warp ends, cross the left over the right. Pass the weft forwards through the opening so formed. Then pull a loop of the weft backwards through the opening and round to the front as shown by the arrow in Fig. 168 (a). This will both form a loop and untwist the warp ends. Note that the forward-moving weft and backward-moving loop take a different path through the opening between the crossed warps. It is easy to make the loop with the right hand. Put the index and third finger through the opening from behind forwards. Take hold of the weft and pull a loop through to the front.

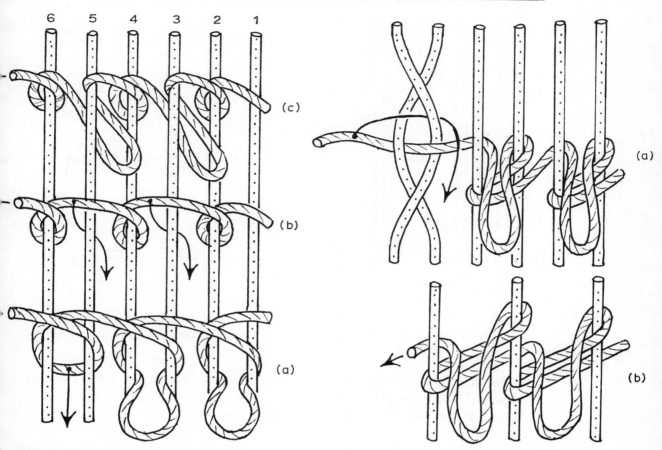

Fig. 167. Pulled-up Loops based on (a) 4/2 soumak (b–c) 3/1 soumak

Fig. 168. Pulled-up Loops based on gauze soumak. (a) Method of production (b) Close spacing

Very close loops can be made this way if, of the two warp ends crossed, one is a new one, and one is the left-hand of the two just used, see Fig. 168 (b).

E. Loops Based on the Ghiordes Knot

Both of the types included here are on the borderland between knots and loops, in fact if the first type is cut, it gives a perfect Ghiordes knot.

The arrow in Fig. 169 (a) shows how a loop is pulled from a yarn lying over the warp and wrapped around two ends, to give the configuration seen in Fig. 169 (b). This really amounts to tying a Ghiordes knot with a blind loop of yarn.

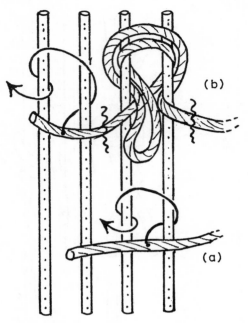

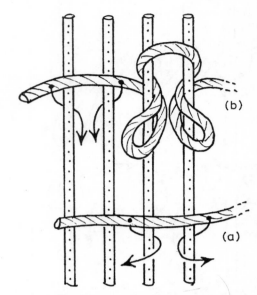

Fig. 169. Loop based on Ghiordes knot   Fig. 170. Loop based on Ghiordes knot

In the other type, the weft is pulled in two places, as shown in Fig. 170 (a), to give symmetrical loops emerging from between adjacent ends, see Fig. 170 (b).

Both of these types are found in old Swedish ryas.

4. KNOTTED PILE

HISTORY

More has been written about the history of knotted pile rugs than about any other type of rug. But it is out of place in this book to attempt a summary of this large mass of information. The reader is referred to the Bibliography, especially to those books written for collectors of carpets.

The Earliest Physical Evidence of Knotted Pile Rugs

In 1953, Russian archaeologists discovered a series of tombs in Pazyryk, in the Altai mountains of southern Siberia. For some reason, these had become filled with perpetual ice, so that their contents were perfectly preserved. It is to this freak occurrence that the Pazyryk rug owes its remarkable survival from about 500 B.C. to the present day. The rug, now in the Hermitage Museum, Leningrad, measures 6 by 6½ feet. It is of such assured and developed design, with a central field and five main borders, that it is obviously representative of a long tradition of carpet weaving, of which absolutely nothing is known at the present time. The rug is knotted of fine-spun wool in various natural colours using the Ghiordes knot.

There is a gap of 800 years until the date of the next known rugs. These are merely fragments which were found at Dura-Europas on the Euphrates and at Loulan in E. Turkistan, but they already show a great variety of knotting techniques. Knots of the three main types appear and one piece even has pile on both sides.

Earliest Written Evidence

The first written record concerning a carpet is an Oriental manuscript which states that the Arabs, on conquering Ktesiphon, then capital of Persia, in A.D. 635, found a huge and magnificent carpet. This has been called the Spring or Winter Carpet of Chosroes, the king of Persia. It is thought to have been 84 feet square, and represented a garden with paths, flower beds, water courses, and shrubs, and was the inspiration for many Garden Carpets that were later woven.

The Scandinavian Ryas

Probably the best documented piece of rug history is that of the ryas in Finland and Sweden, where over the last few centuries a development can be traced from the use of pile textiles merely for warmth and thickness (as bedcovers), to their use as decorative, fine art products. The earliest are made with uncut loops and are either monochrome or striped. Later, in the sixteenth century, knotted types appear but with a thick yarn tied in widely spaced knots, often on both sides of the rug. These could be quickly and easily made by the members of a household for their own use. Then as the decorative qualities were developed, the pile became shorter and more closely set to allow of greater detail and precision in the design, until some ryas approached the texture of Eastern rugs. More recently, when richness of colour and texture, rather than complexity, became the aim of the rya designers, the pile again became long but remained fairly closely set.

This shows how a basically simple technique can be adapted to the needs of the moment. It may also give an indication of the development of carpet weaving which led up to the Pazyryk rug, a development which will probably always remain conjectural.

A. Types of Knots

(i) GHIORDES, SMYRNA OR TURKISH KNOT

Ghiordes and Smyrna are both towns in northern Irak from which have come rugs knotted in this manner.

The Ghiordes knot is now the one most used for attaching a pile weft to the warp. Of the three main types, it is the most secure and so lends itself to long-pile rugs or to the use of unusual materials.

It is a symmetrical knot tied round two warp ends and can be produced in a number of ways.

(a) *Knotting from Continuous Pile Yarn and Cutting each Knot as it is Tied*

Wind the yarn to be used in some convenient form, e.g., a finger hank. Pass the free end down between the two warp ends and bring it up to the right of the right-hand end. The pile weft is now looped round one end as shown in Fig. 171 (a).

Now take it across both ends, to the left, down behind the left-hand end and finally up between the two ends, as shown by the arrow. The result is as Fig. 171 (b).

Hold the free end of weft so that it gives the required length of pile, and tighten the knot by pulling on the part that runs to the finger hank. Then cut this latter part at the appropriate point, indicated by wavy line in Fig. 171 (b), and the knot will appear as in Fig. 171 (c).

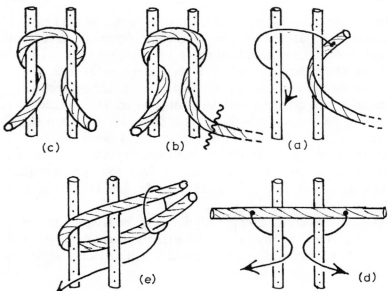

(c)　　　　　(b)　　　　　(a)

(e)　　　　　(d)

Fig. 171. Ghiordes Knot. (a–c) Knotting from continuous yarn
(d) and (e) Knotting with cut yarn

With practise the knot can be tied in this way with some speed, say, 10 to 15 knots a minute. The actual finger movements are as follows.

The middle finger of the left hand raises and parts the two ends that are to carry the knot. The fingers of the right hand tie the right half of the knot, pass the yarn to the thumb and index finger of the left hand which tie the left half of the knot.

Carry the scissors in the right hand all the time. If weaving scissors are used (these have a spring to keep the blades open and only one fingerhole), wear them on the fourth finger, see Plate 42. The thumb, index and middle finger are then left free for the knotting. If using normal scissors, a pair about 5 inches long is best. Put the fourth finger of the right hand in one of the fingerholes and carry the scissors in the hand, as a surgeon does, see Plate 43. As above, this leaves the thumb and next two fingers free. When a knot is to be cut, slip the thumb into the scissors' other fingerhole. It is probably easier to cut a thick pile yarn with ordinary scissors than with weaving scissors.

It is an advantage to become used to this method of holding a pair of scissors, as it can help in several other techniques, e.g., corduroy.

The finger hanks of the various colours needed lie on the already woven rug and are picked up as required.

The Eastern carpet weaver holds a small curved knife in the right hand to cut the weft after each knot is tied. A hook at its end is sometimes used to assist in the second stage of tying the knot. The yarn usually comes from a series of large bobbins, one of each colour needed, held on a crossbar above the weaver's head.

(b) *Knotting with Cut Lengths of Pile Yarn*

The method by which the yarn is first cut into equal lengths and then knotted may have arisen in Scandinavia. It is slower but lends itself to very subtle colour changes.

The pile yarn is wound around a long square-section stick. This stick, whose size determines the pile length, has a groove running down one of its long sides. It may be attached to the spindle of a spinning wheel, to a bobbin winder, or may be housed on a special stand with a turning handle. By turning the stick, the yarn is wound spirally on it with no overlapping. When a knife is run down the groove, the yarn falls off in equal lengths. Each colour is treated in this way and then put into the compartments of a tray or some convenient holder.

The method of knotting is as follows.

Select the colours required for one knot and place the yarns over two warp ends as in Fig. 171 (d). Wrap the two free extremities of the yarns around the warp ends as shown by the arrows and pull them tight. This can be done very quickly if both hands move together and symmetrically, as follows.

Raise and separate the two warp ends with the middle fingers and hold the yarns across them with the thumbs and index fingers. Then roll the yarns under the warp ends with the index fingers, and pick them up again between the warp ends, and tighten.

As with most manual techniques, words do not convey the simple, smooth movement involved.

An alternative method is shown in Fig. 171 (e).

Loop the cut pile yarn around both warp ends and hold it sideways with the right hand. Pass the middle finger of the left hand down between the two ends and up to the right of the right-hand end. Catch the pile yarn on this finger and draw it back up between the two warp ends as shown by the arrow in Fig. 171 (e). Tighten.

If many yarns are used together for each knot, this method is probably easier than the first one described in this section.

Generally no trimming is done after the knot is tied, so the free ends are bound to be slightly irregular, a feature found in Scandinavian ryas.

(c) *Knotting over a Guide Rod*

Forming Ghiordes knots over a guide rod is a relatively recent innovation and of only limited usefulness. It may save time when a large area of one colour is to be knotted. Each guide rod will only give pile of one length, so a number of various sized rods is necessary if the weaver is not to be limited to this one length. The chief feature of this method is that it automatically gives a pile of even length. So, as no trimming is needed, there is no wastage of yarn.

The guide rod is a flat strip of metal with a groove along o ne edge and sometimes with a handle at one end. The pile yarn is wound in a fingerhank. Note that in this method it is the finger hank and not its free end that is carried round the warp ends to form the knot.

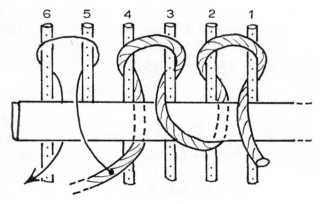

Fig. 172
Ghiordes Knot. Knotting over a guide rod

Referring to Fig. 172, make a knot around ends 1 and 2. Then pass the pile weft under the rod, up over it, and make a knot round ends 3 and 4. Repeat. Tighten each knot as it is made. When the row is complete and the plain weave picks have been inserted, turn the rod on its edge so that the groove is uppermost and slice through the loops with a knife.

(d) Cutting Weft Loops

Ghiordes knots can be produced by cutting the first type of loop described in Section 'E', under 'Weft Looping', see Fig. 169 (b). As the yarn is doubled in the tying, a yarn of half the normal thickness must be used. It could be cut only where indicated by wavy lines, in Fig. 169 (b), in which case one end of the knot will be formed by a loop of yarn and the other by two cut ends, thus combining a cut and looped pile.

(e) Mechanical Methods of Tying Ghiordes Knots

The various mechanical devices for tying knots have all concentrated on reproducing the Ghiordes knot. The simplest is a small Swiss tool which is held in one hand. By pressing a plunger, a knot is tied with yarn fed to it by the other hand.

A much more elaborate power-driven machine exists which can tie knots in any one of twenty-one colours. The colour for each successive knot is selected by the weaver, who presses any one of the twenty-one typewriter-like keys on the machine, as it passes slowly across the warp. It can work at a speed of over a knot per second, and at a great variety of knot densities.

Also, at any point, knots can be tied in by hand if another colour, or special effect, is wanted. The plain weave picks are woven by hand. It can be regarded as a very sophisticated tool, rather than as a machine, because it is entirely under the weaver's control.

There also exist completely automatic power looms which tie the Ghiordes knot. These are generally used to make very high quality carpets of one colour or of simple design.

Direction of Pile

Because of the way the knot is tied the pile weft always slopes down towards the weaver. The shorter the pile, the more regularly the cut ends slope in this direction. As the colour of a yarn always looks many tones darker when viewed end on, i.e., when looking at the cut end, a short pile rug when tied with Ghiordes knots appears much darker and richer when viewed from the end at which the weaver started. So simply by walking round such a rug, the starting and finishing ends can be distinguished. Naturally with a long pile, as in a rya, this one-way slope of the pile weft is somewhat obscured.

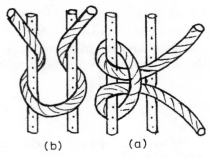

Fig. 173
Ghiordes Knot. Knotting
in reverse direction and
sideways

(b)   (a)

The Ghiordes knot is sometimes found knotted sideways on one warp end in old Finnish ryas, see Fig. 173 (a). It can also be inserted upside down, with the pile sloping away from the weaver, see Fig. 173 (b). So by using knots tied in these various ways, the direction in which the pile weft lies can be altered at will and thus become another element in the design of a knotted rug.

(ii) SEHNA OR PERSIAN KNOT

Despite its past importance, the Sehna knot is little used by weavers today; but it has features which make it quite distinct from other knots and it is therefore worth studying.

The features that commended it to Eastern weavers were the fact that it gave an even distribution of pile over the surface of the rug (i.e., one end of the pile yarn protrudes in the gap between every warp thread, whereas with the Ghiordes knot two ends protrude in one gap and no ends in the next gap), and the fact that more knots per square inch could be tied with it.

It can be tied in three main ways.

(a) Wind yarn into a finger hank. Take the free end down between the two warp ends that are to carry the knot, and up to the right as shown in Fig. 174 (a). Then, as arrow in Fig. 174 (a) carry it to the left over the right-hand end and under the left-hand end. The knot is now as in Fig. 174 (b). Pull the free end to the required length, tighten the other end and cut it as shown by the wavy line. The knot will now lie as in Fig. 174 (c).

Note that both ends point to the left so this can be called a left-hand Sehna knot. By a similar but opposite procedure a right-hand Sehna knot can be tied, see Fig. 174 (d).

As with the Ghiordes knot, the right half of the knot is tied by the fingers of the right hand, the left by those of the left hand. Being a simpler knot it is quicker to tie and is only a little less secure.

(b) The Sehna knot can also be tied from a cut length of yarn as shown in Fig. 174 (e).

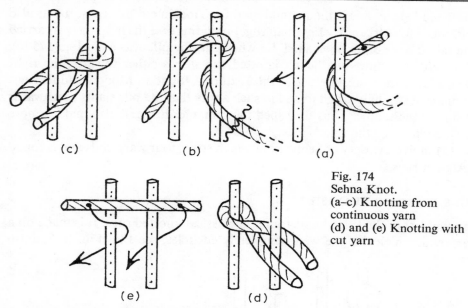

Fig. 174
Sehna Knot.
(a–c) Knotting from
continuous yarn
(d) and (e) Knotting with
cut yarn

(c) It can also be tied using a guide rod, exactly as was the Ghiordes knot. But a far quicker way is to make Sehna loops over a guide rod and then cut these. If the loops shown in Fig. 165 (c) were cut, the result would be Sehna knots as in Fig. 175 (a). Note that the knots overlap each other, giving twice the normal number (shown in Fig. 175 (b)). Each warp end is involved in two knots instead of only one.

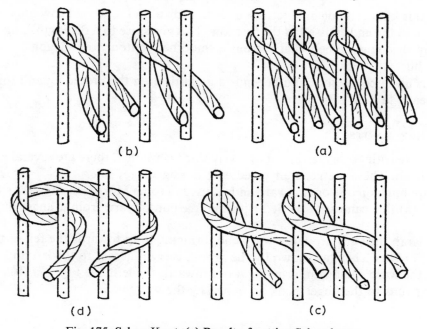

Fig. 175. Sehna Knot. (a) Result of cutting Sehna loops
(b) Spacing of normally tied knots
(c) Knotting on raised warp ends
(d) Variety found in Afghan rugs

As mentioned before, this is the method used for Tibetan cut pile rugs. It was also used on a famous fourth century Egyptian rug, but in this case the looping was carried out on the raised ends of an open shed. So when cut, the pile was as in Fig. 175 (c).

The pile weft of a short pile Sehna knotted rug slopes either towards the right selvage or the left. An interesting use of this feature is found in Mongol saddle rugs. These are made in two halves and joined in such a way that the pile slants downwards on either side of the saddle. Thus they shed the rain and dust and also make a more comfortable contact for the rider's legs.

Fig. 175 (d) shows a variety of Sehna knot which spans four warp ends and is found in some Afghan rugs.

(iii) SINGLE WARP OR SPANISH KNOT

This is the simplest of the three knots found in classical knotted rugs. It is made on a single warp end, which the pile weft completely encircles, see Fig. 176. In Spanish

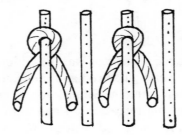

Fig. 176
Single Warp Knot

carpets this knot is made on alternate ends as shown. In the second row the knots are made round the ends missed in the first row. This gives rise to a distinguishing feature in the finished rug, namely that there is a smoother contour to a diagonal than to a vertical line.

This is an insecure knot and depends a great deal on the preceding and following plain weave to hold it in place.

(iv) OTHER KNOTS

When a pile with no suggestion of one-way slope is wanted, there are several knots to choose from. These are generally used with a long shaggy pile.

A clove hitch on one or two warp ends is used in some Morrocan rugs. As shown in Fig. 177 (a) this can easily be tied with the free end of yarn from a finger hank.

First wrap the yarn around a warp end, bringing it up towards the fell of the rug, see Fig. 177 (a). Then, as shown by the arrow, carry it across to the left and wrap it around the warp end again, bringing it out towards the left. See Fig. 177 (b). Cut the part that runs to the finger hank as shown by the wavy line.

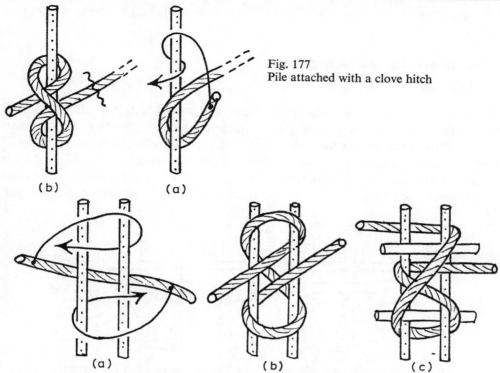

Fig. 177
Pile attached with a clove hitch

(b)　(a)

Fig. 178. (a) and (b) Very secure pile knot (c) Related knot used in Danish Bronze Age

A more complicated knot, as shown in Fig. 178 (a) and (b), is best tied with a cut length of yarn.

Pass this under two warp ends, see Fig. 178 (a). Then, as shown by the arrows, carry each end of the yarn across the two warp ends and up between them. See Fig. 178 (b).

This is extremely secure and is closely related to a knot thought to have been used in the Danish Bronze Age, see Fig. 178 (c).

Another knot of this type is shown in Fig. 179 (a). It is rather like a Ghiordes but with the right-hand end turned upwards instead of downwards. It can also be regarded as a cut soumak knot, for as shown in Fig. 179 (b), it can be made by cutting every

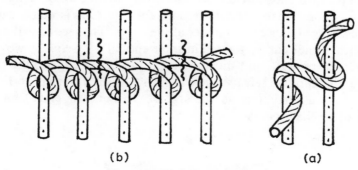

(b)　(a)

Fig. 179. Cut Soumak Knot

other weft span of a 2/1 soumak. This knot has been found on a nineteenth-century Kazak rug.

B. Construction of a Knotted Rug

General Details

A knotted rug whether it has a silk pile so short it looks and feels like velvet or a thick woollen pile many inches long, always has the same basic construction. This consists of rows of knots made across the width of the rug alternating with a certain number of plain weave picks. See Fig. 180. The length of the pile, the material of the pile yarn, the amount of plain weave, and the spacing of the knots are some of the elements that can be endlessly varied to produce rugs of different thickness, resilience, texture and weight.

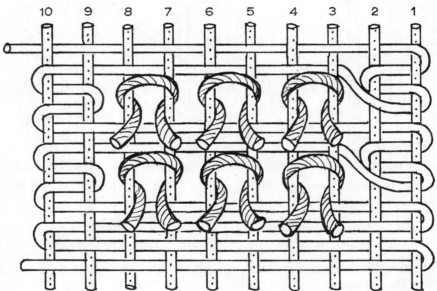

Fig. 180. General view of knotted rug

It will be seen at once from Fig. 180 that the knots stop short at both sides of the rug So there are warp ends at each selvage which, for the whole length of the rug, never carry any knots. There are two reasons for this. One is that a carpet knotted right up to the selvage tends to curl under at the edges. The second is that carrying no knots these selvage ends can be treated in some special way, e.g., be woven or bound with a separate strong weft, and thus provide a protective edge to the rug.

This feature, the knotless selvage ends, is such a distinct concept to Eastern carpet weavers, that it has a Persian name, the argatch. In Fig. 180, ends 1 and 2 and ends 9 and 10 constitute the argatch

There are many ways of treating the argatch, which will be described later, but as Fig. 180 shows, the simplest is to weave extra picks on these ends to make up for the thickness of the absent knots, exactly as was done for soumak.

(i) LENGTH OF PILE

Not many weavers nowadays produce a rug with a pile as short as that found in the classical Eastern carpets. Such a short pile implies very few plain weave picks, e.g., one to three, between the rows of knots and consequently a very slow technique.

A pile a little longer, say, up to half an inch, is characteristic of the type called flossa in Sweden. This name, together with rya (meaning a long pile rug), are sometimes used as if they represented quite distinct and different techniques. But this distinction only exists if the techniques are taught and used in a traditional and set way. Once it is realized that the pile can vary from $\frac{1}{2}$ inch up to, say, 6 inches, with every possible gradation in between, it will be understood there are no hard boundaries between a flossa and a rya rug. The words are, however, useful as a convenient way of referring to a short pile knotted rug and a long pile knotted rug.

Especially with a flossa rug, the knots as cut will have to be trimmed to produce a smooth even pile. This is best done every few rows on the loom. Bang the rug to make the pile stand up, then trim any long ends with a pair of long-bladed scissors.

The large scissors used for Eastern rugs are usually curved along their long axis. The finger holes are wrapped with fur for the comfort of the right hand and there may also be finger grips projecting from the pointed end of each blade so the left hand can assist in managing this heavy tool.

Some rugs, e.g., Chinese and Tibetan, have another cutting operation when they are completed and off the loom. This is 'outlining', the cutting of a groove in the pile around some of the motifs. It is done with a smaller pair of scissors and gives a sculptured surface to the rug.

In rugs of the rya type, with much weaving in between each row of knots, the latter appear in definite stripes across the rug. If not wanted, this effect can be mitigated by tying each knot so that one end is longer than the other.

(ii) MATERIAL OF PILE YARN

Rugs have been made with a knotted pile of almost every material, e.g., cotton, linen, mohair, raffia, jute, hemp and nylon, but the traditional material, wool, is still most used.

Old Eastern rugs used a yarn of a lustre and quality not obtainable commercially today. They may well have been spun from wool plucked selectively from certain parts of the sheep and not from a whole fleece. It is essential that the yarn be worsted-spun (i.e., with the fibres running lengthwise) from a long staple wool. The cut end of such a yarn wears so that it has a tapered tip rather like a paint brush. This feature is very obvious in old ryas.

Materials which, due to their differing elasticity, are difficult to combine as wefts, e.g., wool and linen, can be easily combined in a knotted pile, where this characteristic does not matter. Also materials of differing texture or lustre or resilience can be used to add variety to the pile of a rug.

(iii) AMOUNT OF WEAVING BETWEEN KNOT ROWS

The number of picks of plain weave between rows of knots is related to two factors, the length of the pile and whether this pile is required to lie flat or stand upright. The longer the pile, the more picks are needed; but this number is increased to allow the pile to lie flat and is reduced to force the pile to stand upright. So with a medium length pile, say, 2 inches, there should be about $1\frac{1}{2}$ inches of plain weave, if this pile is to lie flat and in obvious rows. But if the pile is to stand upright, this amount could be reduced to as little as $\frac{1}{2}$ inch.

A very short pile is generally required to stand upright so the minimum of plain weave is used. In Eastern rugs, only one row was used on the fine rugs from Sehna and Tabriz and four rows on coarser rugs, such as Kazaks, but the average was two rows.

Where very few picks are used, the majority of the body of the rug is made up of the knots themselves. If they were removed, a very open and loose plain weave textile would be left. Where more picks are used, they constitute a definite stripe of weft-face weaving between each knot row. The greater the number of picks, the more nearly the textile becomes a weft-face rug embellished with occasional rows of knots. So in the first case, the weft yarn is not very important, and in fact is often found to be of rather poor quality in Eastern rugs. But in the latter case the weft yarn's quality is of great importance.

In Eastern rugs, the plain weave weft often consists of two single ply yarns run in together as they beat down better than a 2-ply yarn. Sometimes these two yarns are spun in opposite directions to prevent any tendency of the rug to curl up. Where there is considerable space between the knot rows, use the thickness of weft appropriate to the warp setting, i.e., that which will give a firm weft-face weave.

There is, of course, no necessity for the picks between the knot rows to be in plain weave, though where the knot rows are close together it obviously provides the safest method of interlacement. Where the rows are not so close together, a twill or hopsack or simple fancy weave can equally well be used. This can be done either to provide increased firmness to the woven part of the rug, or from a decorative point of view. The latter must have been the reason for the two colour weaves seen on the backs of Swedish eighteenth and nineteenth-century ryas. Such weaves are effective if combined with a sparse pile through which the intricate designs can be half seen.

(iv) SPACING OF THE KNOTS

So far, it has been assumed that the knots (except for the single warp type) are tied around every available warp end between the right and left argatch, but this is by no means necessary. There are many other ways in which the knots can be disposed over the warp.

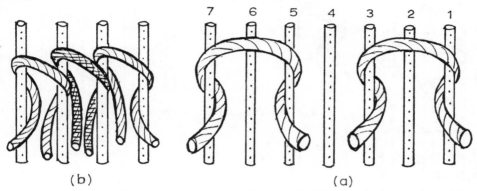

Fig. 181. Spacing of knots. (a) Knotting on open shed (b) Close spacing

For instance, as in Fig. 181 (a), the knots can be tied around every other warp end and this is obviously done by knotting on an open shed, i.e., with the odd-numbered ends raised. One advantage of this method is that the knots slide down in front of the plain weave weft, so at the argatch no extra picks are needed to make up for the absent thickness of the knots. It is, therefore, the method to use in a rug with alternating areas of ground weave and pile, as the time-consuming, zigzag course of the weft is avoided.

Fig. 181 (b) shows the closest that Ghiordes knots can be tied, each warp end being wrapped round by two adjacent knots. Fig. 182 (a) shows knots on two adjacent ends with an intervening missed end. As shown, this lends itself to a twill arrangement of the knots. In Fig 182 (b) two ends have been missed between the knots, and

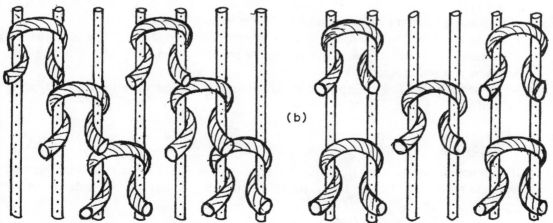

Fig. 182. Spacing of knots. (a) Giving arrangement in twill lines (b) Giving counterchange arrangement

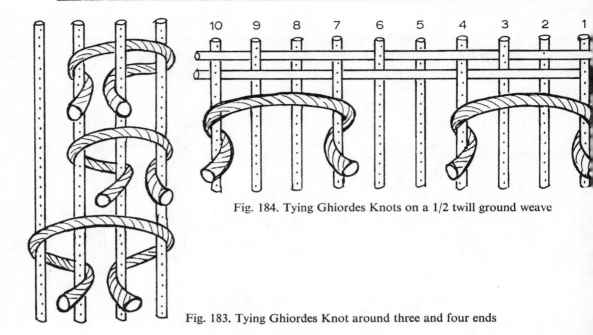

Fig. 184. Tying Ghiordes Knots on a 1/2 twill ground weave

Fig. 183. Tying Ghiordes Knot around three and four ends

here the latter could be arranged in vertical or angled rows or in the counter-change sequence as shown. Fig. 183 shows ways that a Ghiordes knot can be tied around three and four ends.

When a twill weave is used between the knot rows, the knots are tied around the ends raised for one of the twill sheds. Fig. 184 shows the knots tied when ends 1, 4, 7, 10, are raised with a 1/2 twill weave. Figs. 185 (a) and (b) show ways knots can be tied on an open shed of a 2/2 twill weave, with ends 3 and 4, and 7 and 8 raised.

When tying knots on every adjacent pair of warp ends, and using plain weave between knot rows, it saves time to have two extra pedals tied up to raise the ends in these pairs, i.e., to raise shafts 1 and 2, and shafts 3 and 4. These pedals are used alternately to present the warp in pairs to the weaver's hands.

There is no need for the knots to be evenly spaced all over a rug. The combination of areas of close and of sparse pile is another source of variety in a knotted rug, and can give it a sculptured look.

These are only a few examples; there are obviously endless variations in the spacing of knots.

Warp Setting and Knot Counts

The closer the warp is set, the closer the knots can lie in the horizontal direction and thus the more intricate and finely drawn are the designs that can be rendered. In the

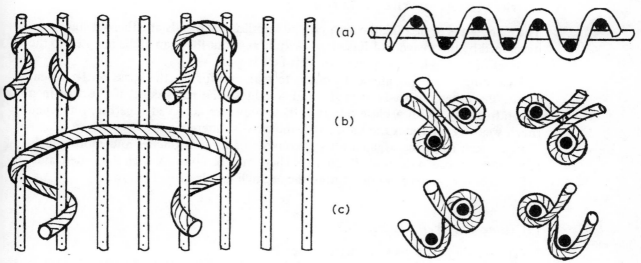

Fig. 185. Two ways of tying Ghiordes knots on an open shed of a 2/2 twill

Fig. 186. (a) Cross-section to show two levels of warp
(b) Effect on Ghiordes knot
(c) Effect on Sehna knot

sixteenth and seventeenth century, when Persian rugs probably reached their peak, warp settings as high as 54 e.p.i. were used, which implies twenty-seven knots for every inch width of the rug. Such settings are exceptional, but 10 to 20 e.p.i. are quite common on Eastern rugs produced today.

With settings of this order, it is difficult to accommodate the warp threads side by side in one plane, so they are generally woven on two levels. As the cross-section in Fig. 186 (a) shows, the picks of weft take a straight and sinuous course alternately, and only half the total number of warp ends are visible on the back of the rug. The two levels of warp affect the knots, e.g., the Ghiordes knot is tilted to one or other side, see Fig. 186 (b), and the Sehna knot (whose wrapping loop is always made round the upper warp end) has its pile still further angled towards right or left, see Fig. 186 (c).

Knotted rugs today are generally made with warp settings between 4 and 10 e.p.i., i.e., between two and five knots per inch width of the rug. Short pile rugs are often woven so that there are the same number of knots in the warp and in the weft direction. This makes it easy to translate a design made on squared paper as one square represents one knot. Thus a rug set at 10 e.p.i. will have 5 x 5 = 25 knots per square inch. The latter figure, the knot count, is obviously an expression of the closeness of the knotting and so the fineness of the rug. In Eastern rugs, where there are often more knots in the warp direction than in the weft, as many as one thousand knots per square inch have been counted. In such a rug, the knot has to be tied with the yarn threaded on a needle. The average knot count of Eastern rugs is between fifty and a hundred, and of ryas between one and twenty.

(v) TREATMENT OF THE ARGATCH

The many ways of treating the argatch (the knotless warp ends at either selvage) were developed by the weavers of Eastern short-pile rugs but they can all be adapted to the selvages of long-pile rugs or even of weft-face rugs.

Two things are being aimed at, one is to make up for the thickness of the absent knots, the other is to add strength and weight to the rug's edge, if possible in a decorative way. With a close-pile rug, these aims are achieved together, but when much weaving separates the knot rows, the case is different.

In Eastern rugs, the argatch always consists of threads thicker and more widely spaced than those in the body of the rug. There may be up to six such thickened ends.

Some of the many ways of treating the argatch are described below.

(a) *Using One Weft*, see Fig. 187

   (1) Weaving extra picks at argatch, see Fig. 187 (a).
   (2) Overcasting or wrapping round the argatch, see Fig. 187 (b).
   (3) Figure-of-eight wrapping round argatch, see Fig. 187 (c).

Any of these can be used to make up for the thickness of the absent knots and repeated according to the thickness of the knots.

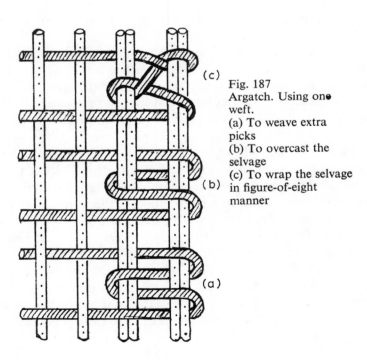

Fig. 187
Argatch. Using one weft.
(a) To weave extra picks
(b) To overcast the selvage
(c) To wrap the selvage in figure-of-eight manner

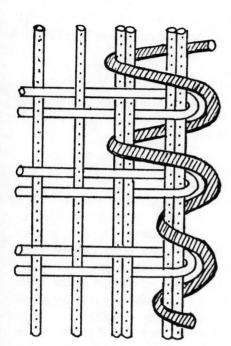

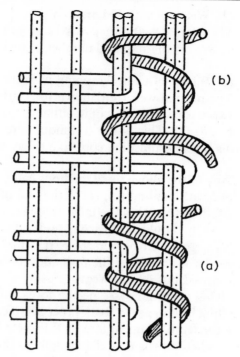

Fig. 188. Argatch. Using extra weft to overcast the selvage

Fig. 189. Argatch using extra weft.
(a) To overcast the selvage
(b) To weave with it

(b) *Using an Extra Weft*, see Figs. 188 and 189.

(1) Overcasting or wrapping round the argatch. This can be done in several ways. The normal weft can extend right to the selvage and the extra weft wrap around one or more of the argatch threads, see Fig. 188. Or the normal weft can stop short of the outermost thread and the wrapping weft include this thread with the last one woven on, see Fig. 189 (a). The proportion of plain weave picks to the number of wrapping turns is, of course, infinitely variable.

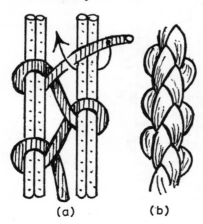

Fig. 190
Argatch. Figure-of-eight wrapping.
(a) Method
(b) Appearance

(2) Weaving with the argatch

The normal weft either weaves up to the selvage or stops short of it, and the extra weft weaves the required number of picks with the argatch threads, see Fig. 189 (b).

(3) Figure-of-eight wrapping with the argatch

The normal weft (not shown for clarity in Fig. 190 (a)) weaves up to the selvage; between each two picks of it, either one or two figure-of-eight wrappings are made, see Fig. 190 (a). This is the technique already described as vertical double soumak. It gives a very handsome cord-like ridge, as shown in Fig. 190 (b).

Any of the above three methods can be used as selvage strengtheners in a rya, combined with method (*a*), (1) at the end of each knot row.

Method (*b*), (1) is the most frequently used and is often applied to weft-face rugs. The yarn should be lustrous and worsted-spun, for instance, long staple wool, or alpaca, goat hair or horsehair. It is best to use several fine threads together, as they spread out and cover the normal weft better than a single thick yarn. This type can be carried out during weaving using a finger hank for each side of the rug, or after weaving using a coarse needle threaded with the yarn. One advantage of the latter method is that, as the work proceeds, it can be seen if the extra weft is going to prevent the rug from lying flat and its thickness be adjusted accordingly. That this cannot be seen when the rug is stretched tight on the loom is shown by the buckled argatch often seen on Eastern rugs.

Such a wrapping yarn can be started by weaving two picks a short distance into the body of the rug, as shown in Fig. 191 (a). The normal weft (white) stops short of the selvage by the same distance. In the same way the wrapping weft can be finished off at the end of a rug. Fig. 191 (b) shows how a join between two wrapping yarns can be made.

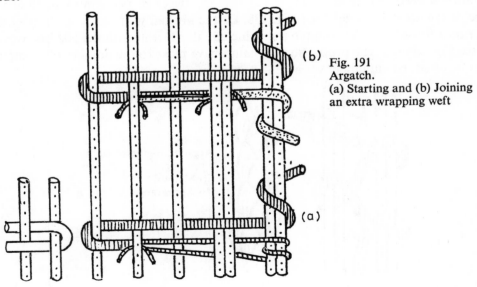

(b)

Fig. 191
Argatch.
(a) Starting and (b) Joining
an extra wrapping weft

(a)

(c) *Using Two or More Extra Wefts*

(1) Weaving with two argatch threads.

Fig. 192 (a) shows how the two extra wefts are carried round the argatch threads, labelled 1 and 2.

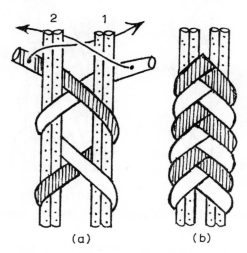

Fig. 192
Argatch. Using two extra wefts pick-and-pick
(a) Method
(b) Appearance

Beginning at the foot of the diagram, carry black over end 2 and under 1, and carry white over 1 and under 2. The normal weft (not shown) then weaves across to the selvage. Then carry white over end 2 and under 1 and black over end 1 and under 2 and follow with the normal weft.

Note that the movement of the two extra wefts always begins from the same side (in this description, from the left). Fig. 192 (b) shows the result which looks like a braid, but is in effect two wefts weaving pick-and-pick with two ends.

(2) Figure-of-eight wrapping.

There are at least two ways in which two colours can be used in this technique. Fig. 193 (a) shows three stages of one type, which are worked as follows.

In Stage 1, wrap black to the left, and white to the right and follow with the plain weave picks.

In Stage 2, wrap white to the left, and black to the right and again follow with the plain weave.

This is the whole sequence, which is then repeated. Note that the colour that moved last in one stage moves first in the next stage. Fig. 193 (b) shows the result, a raised ridge with the two colours appearing across it in oblique stripes.

Another type is seen in Fig. 193 (c) and is worked as follows.

In Stage 1, wrap white to right and to left and follow with plain weave picks.

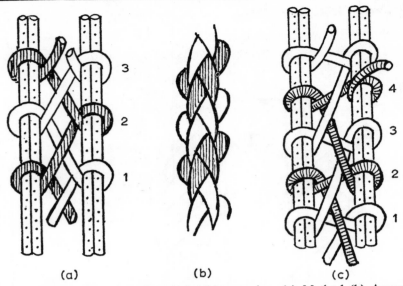

Fig. 193. Argatch. Two-colour figure-of-eight wrapping. (a) Method (b) Appearance (c) Alternative method

In Stage 2, wrap black to left and to right and follow with plain weave.

This is the whole repeat, so Stages 3 and 4 are exactly the same as Stages 1 and 2. It gives a ridge with a slightly more complex structure, with the two colours running vertically down its centre.

(3) Weaving in checks.

Fig. 194 shows a complex argatch with five ends (four of double thickness, one of quadruple thickness). There are two extra wefts (black and white) each weaving on two of the ends and a third yarn wrapping around the very thick outside warp end.

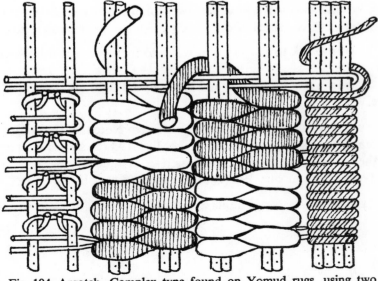

Fig. 194. Argatch. Complex type found on Yomud rugs, using two extra wefts and one wrapping weft

After every eight picks, the black and white wefts switch positions to give a check pattern. The switch is easily accomplished in the following way.

Starting with the stage shown at the top of the diagram, carry the white to the right, weaving with all four threads, then carry the black to the left weaving with the two left-hand threads and the white to the left weaving with the two right-hand threads, and continue weaving normally.

The normal plain weave weft alternately stops short of the argatch and carries right across to the selvage, as indicated at the top of the diagram.

This type of argatch found on Yomud rugs is really a strip of kilim attached to either side of a knotted pile rug, and it illustrates how decoratively an argatch can be treated.

(d) Using an Extra Weft in Kilim Fashion

Fig. 195 shows how the argatch is sometimes treated on a rya. The weaving of the extra weft is only confined to the argatch at the end of each knot row. But between knot rows, the picks reach progressively further inwards until the half-way point between two knot rows is reached, when the picks become progressively shorter again. This gives a pointed projection of the extra weft into the normal weft, as shown in Fig. 195.

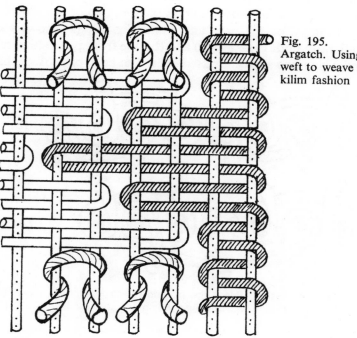

Fig. 195.
Argatch. Using extra
weft to weave in
kilim fashion

Note—That here, the extra weft is the same thickness as the normal weft, not thicker.

—That the extra weft, where it weaves, completely replaces the normal weft, i.e., there are no picks of normal weft reaching to the selvage, as present in all other methods.

This method is generally used from the point of view of colour. The extra weft can be of a colour that suits the pile of the rug, whereas the normal weft is probably a standard one used for all rugs, no matter what the design or colouring. Or it can be of several colours in sequence to give a variegated edge to a simple pile rug. The edge can, of course, be far more complex, using two or three colours together to build up a composite kilim motif between each row of knots.

C. Double-Sided Pile Rugs

Textiles with a knotted pile on both sides have been produced in Scandinavia for at least two centuries and in the East for far longer. In Sweden and Finland, where the rya was originally a bed-covering, it was obviously done to provide extra warmth. In the East, carpets have been made with a completely different design on the two sides, presumably as a technical tour-de-force. Today rugs with a long pile on both sides are sometimes woven, both for their very luxurious feel and for the two different designs they show.

In the case of the old double-sided ryas, there were fewer rows of pile knots on the back than on the front, and the pile on the back was consequently left longer than at the front. Figs. 196 (a) and (b) show, in cross-section, two of the ways in which the pile knots were arranged on the back and front. Fig. 197 (a) shows such a rug in longitudinal section. In both Figs. 196 (a) and (b), the front pile (white) has been tied on an open shed, using two adjacent raised ends. The back pile (black) has been tied

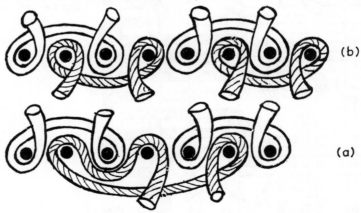

Fig. 196. Double-sided Pile Rugs. (a) and (b) Cross-sections showing two methods of arranging the knots

on the ends missed by the front pile, i.e., on the lowered ends of the same open shed. In Fig. 196 (b), the back pile uses two adjacent ends and in Fig. 196 (a) three adjacent ends. Tying the back pile thus is difficult on a horizontal loom, so presumably these rugs were woven on a vertical frame. The weaver had then only to walk round to the back of the loom to tie the back pile knots. This would only have to be done after every second or third row of front knots.

The method in Fig. 196 (b) is also the one used in Eastern rugs, but in this case there would be a row of back pile knots combined with every row of front pile knots. In this connection, a vertical rug loom pivoted at top and bottom, has been described, so that the weaver stayed stationary and the loom was turned to and fro to present him the two sides of the rug for knotting.

On a horizontal loom it is simpler to weave a double-sided rya by arranging the back and front pile knots in separate rows.

Make a row of knots on the front, using all the warp threads, followed by half the normal amount of plain weave. Then make a row of knots on the back, using all warp threads, again followed by half the normal amount of plain weave.

This can be repeated or the back row of knots could be omitted between the next two rows of front pile. The first of these alternatives is seen in longitudinal section, see Fig. 197 (b).

It is easiest to tie a back pile knot with a cut length of yarn. Fig. 198 (a) shows one method.

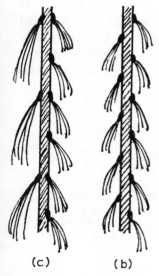

(c)   (b)

ig. 197. Double-sided Pile Rugs.
(a) and (b) Longitudinal sections showing two methods of arranging rows of knots

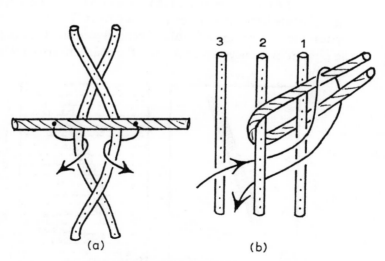

(a)   (b)

Fig. 198. Double-sided Pile Rugs.
(a) and (b) Two methods of tying a Ghiordes knot to show on back of rug

Cross the two warp ends that are to carry the knot. Lay the pile yarn over them and then wrap its two extremities under them as shown by the arrows. Tighten the knot and push the pile through to the back.

Another way is shown in Fig. 198 (b).

Loop the pile yarn around the two warp ends concerned (1 and 2), and hold it towards the right. Put a finger of the left hand down between ends 2 and 3 and up between ends 1 and 2 (top part of arrow). Then catch the pile yarn on this finger and draw it back under end 2 (as bottom part of arrow). Tighten and push the pile through to the back.

Naturally, the pile at the back can only be trimmed when the rug is finished and off the loom.

D. Design

Knotted pile is the rug technique giving the greatest freedom of design. Theoretically, every single knot can be tied with a different coloured yarn. And if the knotting is close enough, i.e., if there is a high knot count, every conceivable shape, line and curve can be produced. But the majority of weavers today favour the long pile rug of the rya type, both for the speed of production and for the opportunities it affords to exploit rich colours and textures. This type has definite design limitations which increase with the length of the pile and consequent distance between knot rows.

(i) DESIGN LIMITATIONS IN RYAS

One of the limitations is illustrated in Fig. 199, where (a) shows two lines at different angles on the paper design and (b) shows how they will appear on the rug. The dotted lines indicated the spacing of the knot rows. It will be seen at once that the nearly vertical line can be fairly faithfully reproduced; its yarn is shifted one or two knots to the right in each successive row. But the nearly horizontal line is distorted into a series of steps.

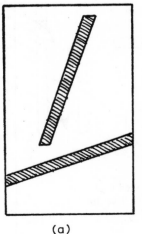
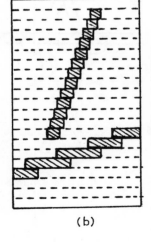

Fig. 199
(a) Two lines as designed
(b) The same two lines as they appear on a rya rug with widely spaced knot rows

(a)   (b)

So if a rya with really long pile is being woven, avoid lines and curves that approach the horizontal. Conversely if a design with lines and curves that approach the horizontal has to be knotted, make it a short-pile rug with a small distance between knot rows.

The difficulty is due to the fact that in a rya there are more knots in the weft than in the warp direction. Take, for instance, a rug with a warp set at 6 e.p.i. This will give three knots per inch in the weft direction. But such a rug could easily have an inch between each row of knots and therefore only one knot per inch in the warp direction. The difficulty does not arise if the knots are evenly spread over the rug, i.e., as many per inch in the warp and weft directions. In this case, the two lines in Fig. 199, could be produced with equal accuracy.

Another design limitation in ryas is more obvious and concerns size of motif. Due to its length, the pile lies in a haphazard manner on the finished rug. So any carefully knotted motif which is too small in scale becomes lost, e.g., several vertical stripes of different colour, each being only two knots wide, will probably read as a blur instead of as distinct lines. But if knotted on a short pile rug, they will appear as definite stripes.

(ii) COLOUR BLENDING IN RYAS

From the point of view of colour, the rya has one great advantage. Because many threads (e.g., four to twelve) go into each knot, and because each thread could be of a different colour, there is a great opportunity for blending. This can lead to a very rich effect if several colours of the same tone are used together in a knot. It also means that the passage from one colour to another can be so gradual that no hard boundary can be seen between them. This is more true of a colour change across the rug, i.e., in the weft direction, due to the higher number of knots in this direction, than in the warp direction, It is colour changes across the rug which are now considered.

Take, for instance, the extreme case of moving from black to white and assume that knots consisting of six threads are being tied. Knots with five intermediate mixtures of black and white can be placed between the knots of solid black and of solid white, thus giving seven possible colours for the knots, labelled A to G below.

6 Black	A
5 Black, 1 White	B
4 Black, 2 White	C
3 Black, 3 White	D
2 Black, 4 White	E
1 Black, 5 White	F
6 White	G

The transition can be sudden if only one knot of each mixture is tied, or gradual if many knots are tied. It can be made still more gradual by elaborating the sequence of the mixtures, as below.

A,B,A,B,C,B,C,D,C,D,E,D,E,F,E,F,G,F,G

With two colours not as disparate as black and white, fewer intermediate mixtures need be used. With two close colours (Y and Z) no mixtures are necessary, for by switching two knots at the colour boundary, the latter can be successfully blurred. So instead of knotting in the sequence, Y,Y,Y,Z,Z,Z, use the sequence Y,Y,Z,Y,Z,Z. The haphazard way in which the pile lies naturally helps in blurring such colour boundaries.

The pile of a flossa rug usually contains only one or two threads per knot and these are often both of the same colour. So if a gradual passage from one colour to another is wanted, it can only be achieved by dyeing the intermediate colours.

From the foregoing remarks it will be understood that a long pile rug lends itself to large-scale motifs, rich colour mixtures and indefinite boundaries, whereas a short pile rug is more suited to clear cut (and, if desired, small) motifs and solid unmixed colours.

(iii) RELATING THE PAPER DESIGN TO THE KNOTTED RUG

There are two main ways of relating the paper design to the knotted rug.

(a) Using a Knot Diagram

In this method it is assumed that the knot rows occur at very exact intervals and a diagram indicating the colour for every knot is made from the original design. The weaver then reads the colour for each knot directly from the diagram.

If the rug has as many knots in the warp as in the weft direction, then the knots will appear as squares on the diagram. If there are more in the weft than the warp direction, they will appear as oblongs. Fig. 200 (a) shows the diagram for a rug with four knots per inch in each direction. Each square is coloured or marked with a number indicating a colour. Fig. 200 (b) shows the diagram for a rug with three knots per inch in the weft direction and one per inch in the warp direction. Each oblong is marked with a number which corresponds to a mixture of colours, as indicated by a key placed somewhere on the diagram.

In this method the weaver becomes a mere technician whose only virtue is the accuracy with which he follows the knot diagram.

(b) Using a Coloured Sketch

In the second method, a coloured sketch of the rug is made to perhaps half, or quarter, scale. This is mounted on a board as shown in Fig. 201 between two scales in inches. A

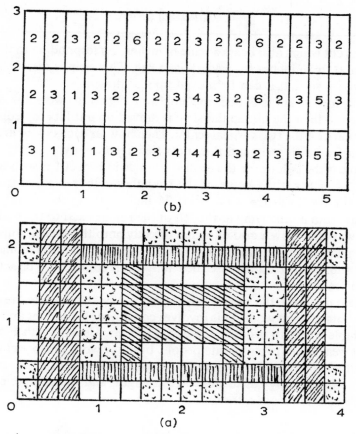

Fig. 200. Knot Diagrams. (a) For rug with equal number of knots in warp and weft direction (b) For rug with three times as many knots in weft than warp direction

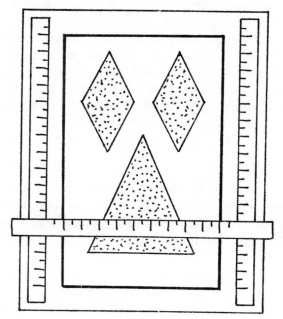

Fig. 201
Method of knotting
rug direct from
coloured sketch

strip of card is cut which also bears a scale in inches, corresponding to the width of the rug, i.e., from 0 to 36 inches for a yard-wide rug. This strip is fastened in some way across the board, so that it can be moved up and down.

Before each row of knots is tied, the length of rug so far woven is measured. Say this is $10\frac{1}{2}$ inches, then the horizontal strip is moved up until its top edge is level with the $10\frac{1}{2}$ inch mark on the two vertical scales. Then how far each colour area extends can easily be read from this strip and the knots tied accordingly.

For example if the colour for the central triangle in Fig. 201 is seen to extend from 16 inches to 24 inches, then knots of the triangle's colour are tied from a point 16 inches from the right selvage, to a point 24 inches from this selvage, taking these measurements from a tape lying at the fell of the rug or fixed to the batten.

A simpler way is to draw a grid of inches directly onto the sketch, but this spoils the sketch and makes it difficult to use the same design for a rug of similar proportions but different size. In the method described above, this could easily be accomplished by changing the scales.

In both these methods, the weaver has to decide how to translate the colours on the sketch into knots of dyed wool. This involves considerable thought and skill in blending the available wools to produce the desired result. Usually with Finnish ryas, the designer and weaver are two separate people, but they work in close collaboration, as an unsympathetic or unskilled weaver could spoil an excellent design. The knots are tied from wool previously cut to the correct length, and the component threads for each knot are selected from a tray.

(c) *Some Eastern Methods*

Several methods of following a pattern are used in the weaving of Eastern rugs. These consist of following a knot diagram, copying a sample specially woven by a master weaver and copying an old rug. An interesting and now almost extinct method is the singing of the pattern. This was done by a *ma'allem*, or carpet conductor, who intoned the colours of each knot in a row, beginning at one selvage and working all the way across to the other. He was sometimes blind, but in any case had an excellent memory and might hold over a hundred designs in his head. The intoning of each row was done without a break, so there was no time to correct a mistake. Any mistake had to be adjusted as well as possible in the succeeding row.

(d) *General Points*

(1) After each row has been knotted and before the ground weave is added, stand back and make sure nothing needs altering. A knot can be removed from a completed rug and another of different colour substituted (using a large needle threaded with the yarn) but it is much easier during the weaving.

(2) If a rug is considered in longitudinal section, it will be seen that the pile in each row lies at an angle, see Fig. 202. This is because it is pushed forward where it overlaps the pile in the preceding row. The thickness of the rug at any point is also due to this overlapping of succeeding rows. But the first knot row in a rug (arrowed in Fig. 202) has nothing to overlap, so its pile tends to lie very flat and the rug is thinner at this point. To overcome this admittedly minor failing, some weavers increase the number of threads in each knot of the first row, as indicated in Fig. 202.

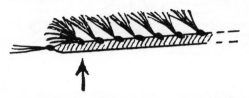

Fig. 202. Increasing amount of yarn in first row of knots

(3) It is sometimes helpful to have an odd number of ends in the warp. Then according to the requirements of the design, the knots of one row can either be on the same pair of warp ends as the preceding row or they can shift along one end to right or to left. The latter arrangement allows a very fine movement of a motif line in a nearly vertical direction.

E. Variations in Knotted Pile Rugs

So far, rugs with an all-over knotted pile have been dealt with, but there are other types.

(i) COMBINING FLAT-WOVEN WITH KNOTTED PILE AREAS

This is a well-established way of making rugs especially in Scandinavia. It is called half-flossa when a short pile is used, and half-rya when a long pile is used. The rug is formed by areas of knotted pile and pileless areas where the ground weave constitutes the surface. So the knotted areas stand out in relief against the flat ground weave areas. Such a rug is often made in one colour only, relying on the contrasts of level and texture, and the shapes of the knotted areas, to give sufficient interest. So the pile yarn and the ground weave yarn are often of the same colour.

If the knots are tied on every available warp end in the areas concerned, the ground weave has to take a compensatory zigzag course to make up for the thickness of the knots absent from the intermediate areas, see Fig. 203. But if the knots are tied on the raised ends of an open shed, this is not necessary and the ground weft can be thrown from selvage to selvage in the normal way.

When designing such a rug, especially if it is to be long, consider what is going to happen on the cloth beam. For instance, a rug consisting of wide warpway stripes of

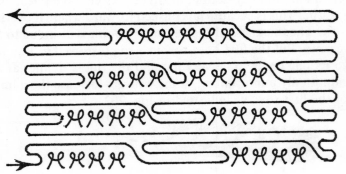

Fig. 203
Course of weft when
weaving knotted areas
on plain weave back-
ground

knotted pile and ground weave will build up very unevenly on the beam, see Fig. 204. Unless rags or paper are wound in to pad out the ground weave stripes, the warp tension will become impossibly uneven. But if the stripes are at an angle or the design is in checks, this problem will not arise.

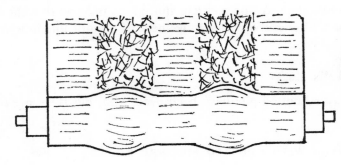

Fig. 204
Build-up of rug
on cloth beam if
weaving warpway
stripes of pile

(ii) COMBINING CUT AND UNCUT PILE

If Ghiordes knots are made continuously over a guide rod, as in Fig. 172, or if Sehna loops are made, there is the opportunity of cutting some loops to form cut pile and leaving others as loops. This can be done in such a way as to form a definite design, which like the preceding method, will be on two levels. If carried out in only one colour, there will not only be a contrast in texture between cut and uncut areas but also of depth of colour. The cut areas will appear much darker than the uncut.

(iii) UNCUT GHIORDES KNOTS PRODUCING A RIDGE

The Ghiordes knots can be tied continuously but without using a gauge. The loop connecting one knot with the next knot is pulled tight, so the yarn lies as in Fig. 205 (a).

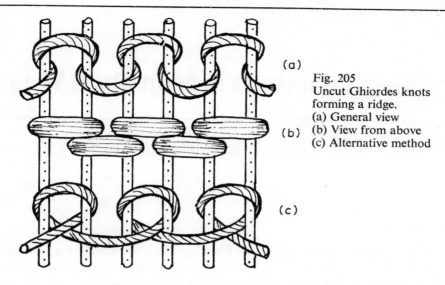

(a)

Fig. 205
Uncut Ghiordes knots
forming a ridge.
(a) General view
(b) (b) View from above
(c) Alternative method

(c)

When beaten down, this looks as in Fig. 205 (b). It gives a good, tight ridge which can be used in any of the ways described under Soumak and Weft Chaining. By the way in which successive rows are worked it can give various brick patterns. It can also be made as shown in Fig. 205 (c).

Note—That as Fig. 205 (a) shows, the uncut Ghiordes knot is structurally identical with a row of 2/1 soumak in which the locking and non-locking type has been used alternately.
—That this wrapping method is used in the Wrapped Edge, see Chapter 14.

(iv) UNCUT GHIORDES KNOTS LYING VERTICALLY OR AT AN ANGLE OR AS A BRAID

These methods have been pioneered by Mary Allard, to whose book the reader is referred, see Bibliography.

7 · Weft-face Rugs in Multishaft Weaves

PART ONE: TECHNIQUES GIVING ALL-OVER EFFECTS

INTRODUCTION

All the techniques described so far have been based on the simplest warp/weft interlacement, i.e., plain weave. They have resulted from manipulating the weft in some way, or from using many wefts, or from adding surface textures.

The techniques that follow are still weft-face but the warp/weft interlacements are more complex, needing 3–8 shafts. With the exception of the pick-up weaves, the weft is thrown without any interruption from selvage to selvage. This increases the speed of weaving but brings with it more limitations of design than exist with the earlier techniques.

These techniques have been divided into three parts.

PART 1—Techniques giving all-over effects, i.e., designs or textures which run from selvage to selvage. This group consists chiefly of twills, but also consists of double-faced weaves and texture weaves.
PART 2—Techniques giving block designs, controlled by shafts.
PART 3—Techniques giving block designs, controlled by pick-up methods.

Any classification tends to create hard boundaries where in fact none exist and the above is no exception. Mention will always be made where techniques are interrelated.

EXPLANATION OF WEAVE DIAGRAMS

For most weaves the details will be given in diagrammatic form according to the following convention, see Fig. 206.

(1) The threading draft, at the top. Starting at the right, the first warp end goes in a heald on the fourth shaft, the second end goes in a heald on the third shaft, the third end goes in a heald on the second shaft, the fourth end goes in a heald on the first shaft, the fifth end goes in a heald on the fourth shaft, and so on.

(2) Weave plan, below the threading draft. Each horizontal line represents one

pick. These are numbered on the left in the order of weaving, that is pick No. 1 is at the bottom. A filled-in or shaded square means that at this point warp crosses weft. Starting with the first pick, at the bottom of the weave plan, the weft is seen to pass over ends threaded on shafts 3 and 4 and under ends on shafts 1 and 2. The second pick passes over ends on shafts 4 and 1 and under ends on shafts 2 and 3, etc. The weave plan will normally show only one repeat of the pattern.

> *Note*—That with a weft-face weave, a filled-in square does not mean that at this point the warp is *visible*. The weave plan is purely a diagram of the warp/weft interlacements and gives little idea of the appearance of the rug.

(3) Lifts, at the right of the weave plan. To the right of each pick is indicated the shafts that have to be lifted to obtain that pick. So for the first pick, shafts 1 and 2 have to be lifted, for the second, shafts 2 and 3, and so on. As weavers may be trying these techniques on table looms, jack looms, counterbalanced looms, countermarch looms and even dobby looms, this method has been chosen rather than tie-up diagrams or pegging plans, which would vary with the type of loom. Sometimes a colour sequence is indicated. In Fig. 206, the first pick is of colour A, the second pick of colour B, the third of A, the fourth of B.

Because there is little relationship between the weave plan and the actual appearance of the rug, in some cases an actual thread interlacement diagram will also be given.

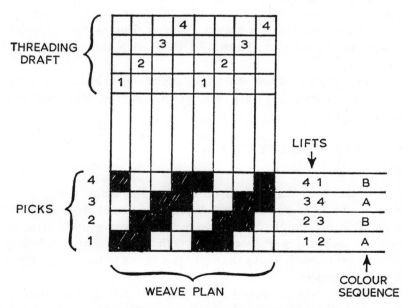

Fig. 206. Explanation of Weave Diagrams

This will show, at the top, an expanded view and, when considered necessary, at the bottom the appearance when the weft is beaten. For the sake of simplicity, these will be referred to as the expanded and beaten view.

In the text, a threading draft will be written thus (1,2,3,4), a lifting sequence will be written thus (12,23,34,41) and a colour sequence will be written thus (A,B,A,B). In each case the brackets enclose one repeat.

NOTE ON THE NOMENCLATURE OF TWILLS

Twills are referred to numerically in the following manner, e.g., 2/1, 1/2, 2/2, 3/1. Of the two figures separated by the stroke, the first refers to the number of ends each weft pick passes under in one repeat of the twill, and the second to the number of ends it passes over. In an even twill, these two numbers are the same, e.g., 2/2, and both faces of the fabric show warp and weft to an equal degree. In an uneven twill, these two numbers are different, e.g., 3/1, and one face of the fabric will show warp floats, the other weft floats.

This system can perhaps be most easily understood if the stroke between figures is made into a horizontal line, thus $\frac{2}{1}$, $\frac{1}{2}$, $\frac{3}{1}$. Then the line represents the weft pick and the figures represent the number of warp ends it passes over and under. This makes clear the fact that if a 2/1 twill is turned over, the reverse face is a 1/2 twill. In more complex twills, such as are produced on six and eight shafts, there may be more than two figures involved, e.g., 3/1/1/1, or 4/2/1/1.

Note that adding the figures together gives the total ends in the repeat, and therefore the total picks, as all regular twills have an equal number of ends and picks in a repeat. In other words their weave plan is always a square. This in turn gives a number of shafts necessary for the weaving. Thus a 2/1 twill needs three shafts, a 2/2/1/1 twill needs six shafts.

In museum usage, the stroke between the figures is angled according to the direction of the twill, i.e., / or \ (or ∧ if a warp herringbone), but this refinement will not prove necessary in this book.

1. THREE-SHAFT DRAFTS

HISTORY

It is thought that the wool-weavers in Syria at some time before A.D. 250 were the first in our half of the world to add an extra shaft to the two-shaft horizontal loom and thus make possible the simplest twill weave. The fewer warp/weft interlacements enabled them to weave a weft-face fabric with simple selvage-to-selvage shuttle throwing, whereas with plain weave the weft tension has to be very carefully adjusted to produce such a fabric.

This technique was soon developed into a pointed draft on three shafts, which enabled a simple type of double-faced cloth to be woven, the two sides of which showed different colours. At the same time, the loom had some harness of the draw loom type added, for by the fourth century A.D., repeating patterns in two colours, using this double-faced weave, were being produced.

This interlacement, see Fig. 214, was used to make a weft-face fabric, but if the weave is turned through a right angle it gives the interlacement of a reversible warp-face weave. The latter is found in silk textiles from the Han Dynasty (205 B.C.–A.D. 220) and is seen in a simpler form in a textile from the Shang-Yin Dynasty (1500–1000 B.C.). So it is probable that the Syrian weavers were adapting to their traditional materials a silk weave imported from China.

The earliest find of a three-shaft twill in northern Europe dates from the seventh century and comes from Sweden. In ancient Peru, three-shaft twills were used in a characteristically ingenious way, producing a motif in 1/2 twill on a ground of 2/1 twill, (i.e., the weft yarn preponderated in the motif and the warp yarn in the background). True Kashmir shawls are tapestry-woven using a three-shaft twill.

A. Twills and Other Weaves Using a Straight Three-Shaft Draft

The simplest three-shaft twill is obtained with a straight draft, i.e., threaded (1,2,3), repeat, and by lifting the shafts singly in sequence, i.e., (1,2,3), repeat. The resulting twill is of necessity unbalanced, on the face of the fabric the weft floats over two ends and under one, giving a 1/2 twill, and on the reverse the warp floats over two picks and under one, giving a 2/1 twill, see Fig. 207 (a). So as normally woven, one side always

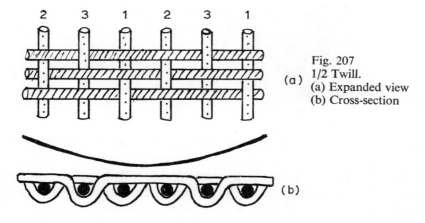

Fig. 207
1/2 Twill.
(a) Expanded view
(b) Cross-section

shows a predominance of weft and the reverse a predominance of warp. When beaten down to give a weft-face weave, the face shows weft floats passing over two ends and the reverse weft floats passing over one end, as shown in the cross-section in Fig. 207 (b). Due to the unopposed pull of the floats over two ends, this weave will have a strong tendency to curl up as indicated by the line above Fig. 207 (b). In fact the weave is impractical for that reason except when used for narrow stripes.

But if it is woven so that a pick with floats on the face alternates with a pick with floats on the reverse, the result will be both stable and more solid. There are several varieties of this weave.

(i) DOUBLE-FACED 2/1 TWILL

This first weave is a simple pick-and-pick combination of a 2/1 and a 1/2 twill. Fig. 208 shows both the conventional diagram and an expanded interlacement view. From

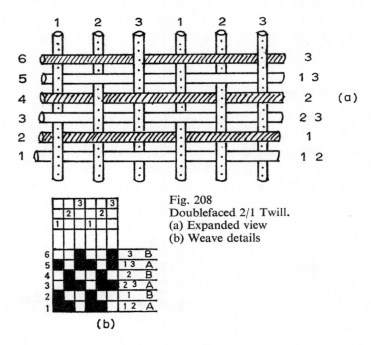

Fig. 208
Doublefaced 2/1 Twill.
(a) Expanded view
(b) Weave details

the latter it will be seen that picks 1, 3 and 5 float under two ends on the reverse of the rug and that picks 2, 4 and 6 float over two ends on the face.

It will be noticed that when beaten, the second pick will slide down in front of the first pick completely obscuring it; similarly the fourth pick will obscure the third, and the sixth obscure the fifth. So the face of the rug will be made up of the shaded picks (2, 4 and 6) and the reverse will be made up of the unshaded picks (1, 3 and 5). Thus if two wefts are used alternately a rug completely different on the two sides can be woven. Due to the twill order of lifting, both sides will show ridges running up obliquely.

This colour sequence can be simply described as (A,B,A,B), repeat, where A and B indicate any two colours. If the colour sequence were (A,A,B,B), repeat, the result would be twill lines of colours A and B on both sides of the rug, running up to the left on the face. This can best be understood by considering the even-numbered picks only, i.e., those which form the face of the rug. Their colour sequence will be A,B,A,B, as seen in Fig. 209 at the top. When these are beaten down, the floats of A join up and

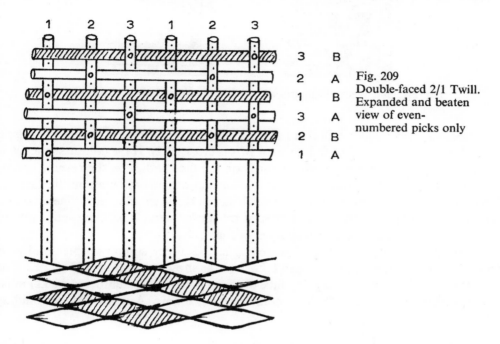

3	B	Fig. 209
2	A	Double-faced 2/1 Twill.
1	B	Expanded and beaten
3	A	view of even-
2	B	numbered picks only
1	A	

those of B join up as shown at the bottom of the diagram to give oblique lines of even thickness of the two colours. Naturally exactly the same occurs with the odd-numbered picks forming the reverse of the rug.

A four colour sequence of (A,B,C,D) will give twill lines of colours A and C on one side of the rug, and of B and D on the other. A sequence of (A,B,A,B,B,A,B,A), repeat, gives thin 'beaded' stripes of the two colours on both sides. Many other sequences can be found.

(ii) TWO RELATED DOUBLE-FACED WEAVES

These two weaves use four of the six lifts needed for the above weaves. Details of the first weave are seen in Fig. 210. The colour sequence is shown at the side, (A,A,B,B), repeat. This again gives a double-faced rug, colour B on the face, colour A on the reverse, but here the surface texture resembles hopsack not twill. Also spots of colour A show through on the face, and spots of colour B show through on the back. This weave is very like one of the double weaves used on Navajo saddle blankets.

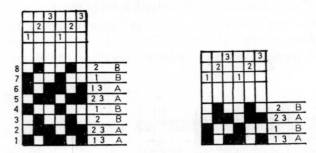

Fig. 210, 211. Weave Diagrams of two Double-faced three-shaft Weaves

The second weave which will recur later in this book is seen in its simplest form in Fig. 211 and in Fig. 212. The sequence of lifts is (13,1,23,2). If the colour sequence is (A,B,A,B), repeat, then a rug with colour B on the face and A on the reverse is produced, as indicated at the top of Fig. 212. The surface has no twill lines but the flatness of the texture is broken by depressions which run in the warp direction. These correspond to the gap between the ends threaded on shafts 1 and 2, so are evenly spaced across the warp. (Indicated by wavy lines in Fig. 212.)

By altering the colour sequence, warpway stripes (very similar to pick-and-pick stripes obtained with plain weave) can be woven, as shown at bottom of Fig. 212. For this the weft responsible for, say, the face of the rug (i.e., even-numbered picks) must be alternately of two colours. So if the colour sequence were (A,B,A,C) there would be

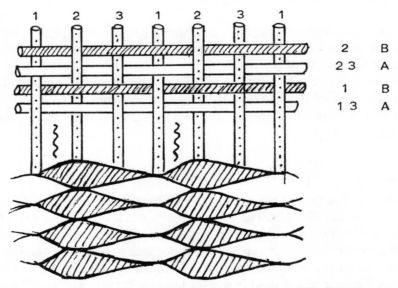

Fig. 212. Expanded and beaten view of weave in Figure 211

stripes of B and C on the face of the rug while the reverse would be of colour A all over. If the sequence were (A,A,B,B), stripes of A and B would show on both sides.

There is a tendency with this weave for the colour from one side of the rug to show through as small spots on the other side, and especially so if, say, one side is black and the other white. With closer colours the spots are hardly visible.

Practical Details for the Above Three Weaves

The three weaves above can be woven with a warp set at 4 working e.p.i. and a weft of 2-ply carpet wool used two or threefold. As with all multishaft weaves, especially when using two or more shuttles in some sequence, it is best to solve selvage problems with a floating selvage. This means that the first and last end of the warp (which will naturally be doubled or trebled to strengthen it) is not drawn through any shaft, but is treated normally in the reed. These ends therefore remain horizontal when the others rise or fall with successive sheds, i.e., they float. Every shuttle enters a shed over the floating selvage and leaves the shed under the floating selvage at the opposite side. Thus every weft is caught round the outermost end on both sides.

With the last weave described, the floating selvage is not necessary, if (a) two shuttles are always used alternately (they can of course be of the same or different colours), (b) the threading is started and ended with ends threaded on the first and second shafts.

If these two conditions are fulfilled, both wefts catch naturally at the selvage.

B. Twills and Other Weaves Using a Pointed Three-Shaft Draft

So far only a straight draft on three shafts has been considered, but there are further possibilities using a pointed draft, i.e., threading thus, (2,1,2,3) repeat, see Fig. 213. It will be seen at once that, unlike the straight draft, this can give plain weave, i.e., by lifting 2 and 13 alternately. As it is always best to start and end a rug with some firm plain weave, this is an advantage; and it is also used in some of the weave structures that follow.

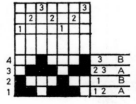

Fig. 213
Weave Diagram of Double-faced
Weave based on a weft course of
over 3, under 1

(i) DOUBLE-FACED WEAVE BASED ON A WEFT COURSE OF OVER THREE, UNDER ONE

This weave is the one referred to in the historical note. Fig. 213 shows that the shafts are lifted in the sequence (12,1,23,3). This gives odd-numbered picks which float under three ends and over one, and even-numbered picks which float over three ends and under one.

It would therefore seem that the former would appear predominantly on the reverse and the latter predominantly on the face of the rug. But as will be seen from the expanded view in Fig. 214, the second pick when beaten will slide down to obscure the first completely, see cross-section view at bottom of diagram, and the fourth to obscure the third. Therefore the face of the cloth is made up entirely of the even-numbered picks and the reverse entirely of the odd-numbered picks. So with two colours used alternately in the weft, a rug showing one colour on each side can be woven. The surface of such a rug is like plain weave, as shown in the beaten view in Fig. 214, but the weft floats are longer and looser, passing over three ends instead of

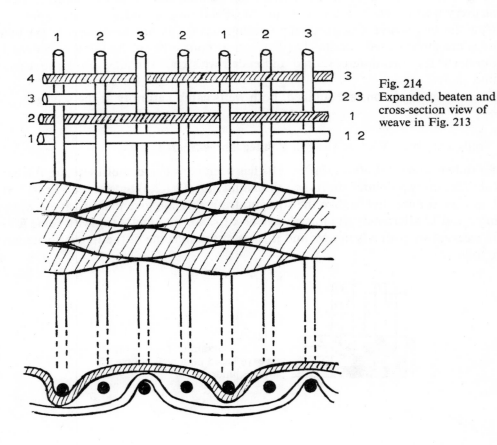

Fig. 214
Expanded, beaten and cross-section view of weave in Fig. 213

one. It will be obvious that with a colour sequence such as (A,B,A,C) or (A,A,B,B) pick-and-pick stripes can be produced on the face of the rug. In fact any of the two-weft patterns described in Chapter 4 can be woven on both sides or one side only.

The structure is not very firm and needs occasional picks of a finer weft in plain weave to strengthen it. So the sequence could be, e.g.,

Lift 12, 1	Thick weft
Lift 2, 13	Thin weft in plain weave
Lift 23, 2	Thick weft
Lift 2, 13	Thin weft in plain weave.

Or there could be just one plain weave pick between each two of the thick picks.

Practical Details

A warp setting of 5 or 6 working e.p.i. is suitable, with a weft of 2-ply carpet wool used three or fourfold for the floats and used singly for the plain weave. The plain weave picks are practically invisible being hidden by the floats. If the threading begins and ends on shaft 3 or on shaft 1, there is no need for a floating selvage (unless a complex shuttle sequence is used). The weave can be produced from many other threadings, including that normally used for Summer and Winter weave.

(ii) DOUBLE-FACED WEAVE BASED ON A WEFT COURSE OF OVER THREE, UNDER ONE, OVER ONE, UNDER ONE

The threading for this second type of double-faced rug is shown in Fig. 215. It can be thought of as a pointed draft on three shafts, though in the chapter on block weaves, it will be found that it is really the foundation of an interesting and useful threading system, that can be extended to any number of shafts. Picks 1 and 2 float over three ends on the face of the rug, and then weave with the next three ends, see Fig. 216; picks 3 and 4 behave similarly and float over three ends on the reverse of the rug and then weave with three ends. When beaten down, the floats almost completely hide the woven parts, so the face of the rug is made up of the floats of picks 1 and 2

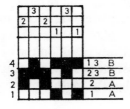

Fig. 215
Weave Diagram of Double-faced Weave based on a weft course of over 3, under 1, over 1, under 1

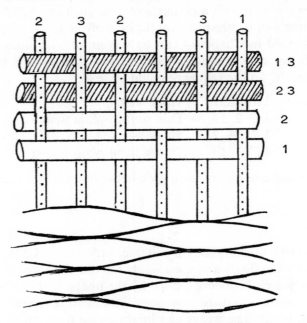

Fig. 216. Expanded and beaten view of weave in Figure 215

and the reverse of those from picks 3 and 4. If therefore the colour sequence is (A,A,B,B) the rug will be colour A on the face and colour B on the reverse.

Note—That no plain weave is necessary.
—That an alternate picking order is 1,4,2,3 with a colour sequence of (A,B,A,B) but this does not beat down so well.

The floats on either side appear in vertical rows and the weave looks very like weft-face plain weave but greatly magnified, see beaten view at bottom of Fig. 216. The interesting thing from the point of view of design is that it also behaves as plain weave in that any of the two-shuttle patterns (pick-and-pick, cross stripes and spots, see Chapter 4) weavable with weft-face plain weave, are also weavable in these floats. For instance, a colour sequence of (A,C,B,B) will give pick-and-pick stripes of colours A and C on the face of the rug and solid colour B on the reverse.

So the face and reverse of the rug can be completely different and each side can either show any of the two-shuttle patterns or just plain colour. This gives a great deal of freedom. Plate 44 shows a sample which is entirely black on the back but has pick-and-pick areas in grey and white (with some cross stripes) on the front. It will be seen that the black shows through the front colours slightly. With closer colours, this effect would be absent.

Note—That this technique allows all the two shuttle designs to be woven on a larger scale. The pick-and-pick stripes here are over ½ inch wide, those woven in plain weave would be ⅓ inch wide at the most.

—No plain weave is possible on the threading, but lifting 23 and 1 gives a two up, one down weave all the way across.

Practical Details

Warp—5 working e.p.i.
Weft—2-ply carpet wool used two or threefold.
  Use a floating selvage.
  See Chapter 8 for the four-shaft block weave version of this technique.

(iii) THREE-SHAFT KROKBRAGD

A more common use of a pointed three-shaft draft is the Norwegian weave called krokbragd. The shafts are either lifted in the sequence (1, 2, 3), repeat, i.e., a 1/2 twill or (12, 23, 31), repeat, i.e., a 2/1 twill. The resulting fabric with floats on one side and a tight weave like plain weave on the other, is the same in both cases, but with the former sequence the floats appear on the top as woven and with the latter they appear on the back. As it is the tight weave which is really the front of the rug, the second sequence is to be preferred.

With this sequence of lifts endlessly repeating, two or three wefts are used to give patterns of the type shown in Plate 45. The more conventional three colour krokbragd shapes are seen at the bottom and some of the many other possibilities, using only two colours, are seen at the top. As the weave plan in Fig. 217 (a) shows, every third pick is in a plain weave shed, i.e., when 31 is lifted. This has an important effect on the

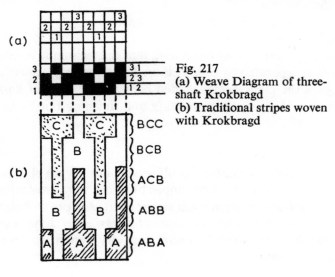

Fig. 217
(a) Weave Diagram of three-shaft Krokbragd
(b) Traditional stripes woven with Krokbragd

stability of the weave and counteracts the tendency of the rug to curl up due to the weft floats on the reverse. The plain weave pick is completely hidden by these floats, but is the most important weft on the face, coming to the surface twice as often as do the other two picks. So it is the cause of the apparently mysterious difference of design on the two sides of a krokbragd rug, see Plate 46 which shows the reverse of the sample in Plate 45. However complex and fussy a design is produced purposely on the face, there is generally something simple produced unconsciously on the reverse. Many of these krokbragd motifs can be produced with a straight draft on four shafts, but in that case they appear on both sides of the rug, see broken 2/2 twill, later in this chapter.

   Note—That the design on the back looks superficially as if it is woven in plain weave.

The traditional way of using the technique is to weave interlocking stripes of the type shown in Fig. 217 (b), employing many colours, but never more than three at any one time. Thus starting at the bottom, the colour sequence would be (A,B,A). Then it would change to (A,B,B), then to (A,C,B) always keeping the lifts in the (12, 23, 31) sequence. However it is much better for the weaver to work out the colour sequences for himself at the loom, rather than follow blindly a printed sequence. As each shed is opened it is obvious where the weft in that shed will come to the surface, so simply use the colour which is wanted in that position. Working in this way, the weave will be really understood and many new possibilities will be discovered.

Practical Details

Warp—5 or 6 working e.p.i.
Weft—2-ply carpet wool used twofold.
   Use a floating selvage.
   The type of all-over, small scale patterning that the technique gives can be effective if confined to stripes separated by solid colour. The threading is a useful one for knotted rugs, as it gives the plain weave wanted between the rows of knots and also the opportunity for weaving a complex starting and finishing border in the krokbragd technique.

   Weaving on three shafts presents no problems on most types of loom, the exception being the counterbalanced loom. The simplest but not very satisfactory method is to tie shafts 3 and 4 together and treat them as one shaft. A more complex but mechanically perfect way is shown in *The Technique of Weaving* by John Tovey (see Bibliography). It would be interesting to know how the Syrian weavers overcame this problem nearly 2000 years ago.

2. FOUR-SHAFT DRAFTS

A. Twills and Other Weaves Using a Straight Four-Shaft Draft

(i) WOVEN AS A STRAIGHT 2/2 TWILL

History

The 2/2 twill is probably the most used of all the possible twills. The earliest evidence of this interlacement dates from about 2000 B.C., and is the impression given by a floor mat on the base of a pot, found in the Balkans. The earliest surviving fabric woven in 2/2 twill is thought to be an oval cloak from Gerum, Sweden. There is some doubt over the date which is given as about 1000 B.C. Certainly by the sixth and seventh century B.C., 2/2 twill was beginning to be woven as is shown by the finds in some Swiss graves. In the Iron Age in Europe it was a popular weave for woollen garments.

Colour and Weave Effects with Weft-Face 2/2 Twill

There is an important difference between twills as normally used (with both warp and weft visible) and as used here in a weft-face technique. In the former case, see Fig. 218,

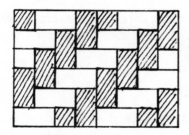

Fig. 218
Production of coloured twill lines in a normal 2/2 twill material

the twill lines are made up alternately of warp floats (shaded) and weft floats (white). Even if both warp and weft are of the same colour, the twill lines still show, though less obviously, due to the different direction in which the two sets of threads lie.

In a weft-face technique, however, the warp is completely hidden, so the twill lines must be produced without its visible aid. If only one weft is used, fine oblique ridges will be seen running across the textile in the direction of the twill. But if two or more colours are used in some special sequence, they can give rise to bold oblique lines running in the opposite direction to that of the twill lines.

This is explained in Fig. 219, where at the top the weft floats of a 2/2 twill are seen in lines running up to the right. Every third pick has been shaded (i.e., numbers 3, 6, 9 and 12). If the weft is beaten down, as at the bottom of the diagram, it will be seen that the shaded weft floats join up to form lines running up to the left. The picks are numbered correspondingly in the expanded and beaten views.

The colour sequence in the above example was (A,A,B), i.e., white, white, shaded. So it repeated every three picks. The sequence of lifts, (12, 23, 34, 41), repeated every four picks. Therefore in each lift sequence, colour B goes in a different shed.

Consider the lift and colour sequence for twelve picks. Thus

12 23 34 41 12 23 34 41 12 23 34 41
A   A   B   A   A   B   A   A   B   A   A   B

It will be seen that the pick with colour B first appears when shafts 3 and 4 are lifted
then when shafts 2 and 3 are lifted
then when shafts 1 and 2 are lifted
then when shafts 4 and 1 are lifted

After that the sequence repeats itself. So the sequence of lifts for colour B is 34, 23, 12, 41. These are the normal 2/2 twill lifts but in the opposite order to that used for the weave above. In other words colour B will appear as an oblique line, but running in the opposite direction to that of the twill it is woven in.

Taking the idea further. If the colour sequence had repeated every four picks (e.g., if it had been A,A,A,B or some such), then colour B would always have coincided with the same lift in the four-pick sequence of lifts. Hence this colour would always appear in the same spot and give not an oblique line but a vertical, warpway line. So to produce a twill colour and weave effect, the colour sequence must repeat on some number of picks other than 4, e.g., on 3, 5, 7, etc. Some of the many possibilities of this interesting technique are now described.

(a) Three-pick Colour Sequences

Using two colours this can be either (A,A,B) which gives a thin oblique line of colour B and a thick line of colour A, see Fig. 219, or (A,B,B) which gives a thick line of colour B and a thin line of A.

Many effects can be obtained by changing from one sequence to the other. Plate 47 (top) shows a sample using this idea, together with reversing the sequence of lifts to give a horizontal herringbone effect. Such reverses can be made at any point in the weave; but it is perhaps simplest to reverse at the pick of colour B in the A,A.B sequence and at the pick of colour A, in the A,B,B sequence. Thus:

↓
12 23 34 41 12 23 12 41 34 23 12
A   A   B   A   A   B   A   A   B   A   A

where the arrow shows the pick at which the lift sequence is reversed. If this is not done, make sure that the colour sequence and the lift sequence both reverse at the same point.

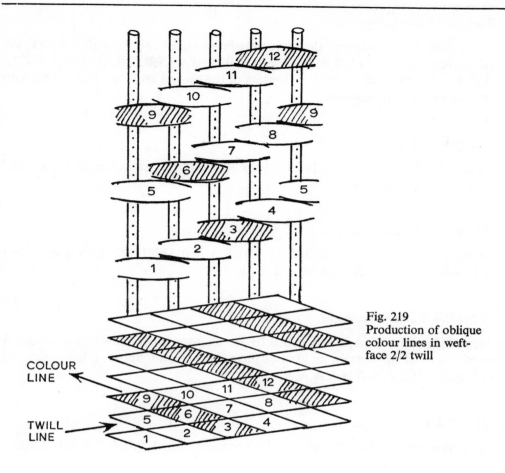

Fig. 219
Production of oblique
colour lines in weft-
face 2/2 twill

When three colours are used in the sequence (A,B,C), they appear as oblique lines of equal thickness. There are many variations in which the three colour sequence is thrown out by either omitting a colour, i.e., by weaving (A,B,C,A,C,A,B,C) or by adding an extra pick, i.e., by weaving (A,B,C,A,B,B,C,A,B,C) or by altering the colour sequence, i.e., by weaving (A,B,C) for several inches, then (A,C,B), see Plate 47 (bottom).

(b) *Four-Pick Colour Sequences*

As already explained, in whatever way colours are arranged in a four-pick sequence, they will appear in some sort of warpway stripe, not as oblique lines. These will be described in detail in the next section on broken 2/2 twill.

(c) Five-Pick Colour Sequences

The more picks in the sequence the more possibilities there are. So with five picks the colour sequence could be (A,B,A,B,A) or (A,B,B,B,A) or (A,B,C,B,A) or (A,A,B,C,C) or (A,B,A,C,A). Plate 48 shows four repeats of the second sequence alternating with one repeat of the first sequence.

(d) Six-Pick Colour Sequences

Any six-pick colour sequence is just the sum of two three-pick colour sequences and there are many possibilities.

(e) Seven-Pick Colour Sequences

These include (A,A,B,B,A,A,B) and (A,A,B,A,A,A,B), both of which give a steep jagged twill. Plate 49 shows the second sequence.

(f) Nine-Pick Colour Sequences

An interesting one is (A,A,B,A,A,B,B,B,B), which gives small diamonds of colour A. Plate 50 shows at the bottom an area of this sequence and, above, a derivative, viz. (A,A,B,A,A,B,B,B,B,A,A,B,A,A,A,A).

(g) Ten-Pick Colour Sequences

The one illustrated in Plate 51 has a colour sequence of (A,B,B,A,B,A,B,B,A,A).

(h) Twelve-Pick Colour Sequences

The one in the Plate 52 is (A,B,B,A,A,B,A,A,A,B,B,B) and it can be thought of as all the possible three-pick sequences one after the other. It gives one of the boldest patterns obtainable with 2/2 twill, resembling an area of small tapestry-woven triangles.

Practical Details for 2/2 Twills

2/2 twills can be woven with 3, 4, 5 or even 6 working e.p.i. The first gives an exceedingly thick and solid weave, using 2-ply carpet wool threefold or fourfold as th weft. It is, if anything, too spongy and if a thick but practical rug is wanted a better setting is 4 working e.p.i. The weft will then be 2-ply carpet wool used two or threefold.

For a finer rug 5 working e.p.i. is the best setting, with a weft of 2-ply carpet wool used single or double. This gives a very firm strong weave. Its only disadvantage is that it may have as many as sixty picks to the inch (compared with twenty-five to thirty for the 3 working e.p.i., and thirty to forty for the 4 working e.p.i. settings), so it is very slow to weave.

Always use a floating selvage.

The weft waves need not be so large as those used for plain weave.

(ii) WOVEN AS A BROKEN 2/2 TWILL

A 2/2 broken twill has the same four lifts as a normal 2/2 twill, but the order of the last two is reversed, thus (12, 23, 41, 34). This breaks the twill sequence, so that there are no oblique lines running up the textile. In fact, as Fig. 220 (a) shows, the first two picks begin to form a twill line running up to the right, then the next two picks start a line running up to the left, so they effectively cancel each other out.

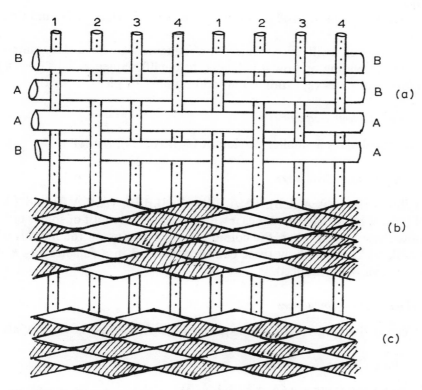

Fig. 220. Broken 2/2 Twill. (a) Expanded view (b) and (c) Beaten views when a colour sequence of (A,A,B,B) is started differently

In a normal 2/2 twill lifting, each end in succession stays up for two picks, but with a broken twill there are two points in the sequence (between lifts 23 and 41, and between lifts 34 and 12) when all the raised ends are lowered and all the lowered ends are raised. These two points of what is really hopsack weave make broken twill a very satisfactory weave for rugs; it is both firmer and better interlaced than a straight 2/2 twill.

Colour and Weave Effects

With the designs described above, it does not matter on which of the four lifts a colour sequence is begun. The result will be identical because of the regularity of the normal 2/2 twill lifts, but with a broken twill the matter is quite different. Consider the colour sequence (A,A,B,B). If this is started with the first lift in the sequence, i.e., 12, as shown at the right side of Fig. 220 (a), then thick lines of colour A and B appear in the rug, see Fig. 220 (b). But if the colour sequence is started on the second lift, i.e., 23, as shown on the left side of Fig. 220 (a), then the result is thin lines of colour A and B, as shown in Fig. 220 (c).

Thick lines will again be produced if the sequence is started on 41, and thin lines, if started on 34.

So with a broken twill the same colour sequence can have two quite different appearances, depending on how it is related to the lift sequence. This does not apply to the colour sequences repeating on an odd number of picks.

(a) Three-Pick Colour Sequences

(A,B,A) repeated gives a smaller version of (A,B,A,B,A), see (c).

(b) Four-Pick Colour Sequences

The possibilities are (A,A,A,B), (A,A,B,B), (A,B,B,B), (A,B,A,B) and (A,B,B,A). If any of these is repeated a few times it will give a vertical motif of some sort. Fig. 221 shows how these appear when the colour sequence begins on the first lift of the lift sequence. Plate 53 shows how these can be combined in a full-size rug and how a third colour can be introduced.

(c) Five-Pick Colour Sequences

The interesting design given by the sequence (A,B,A,B,A) is shown in Plate 54.

(d) Seven-Pick Colour Sequences

Plate 55 shows the sequence (A,A,B,B,A,A,B).

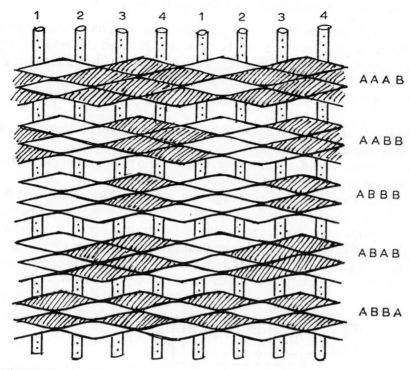

Fig. 221. Broken 2/2 Twill. Beaten view of various four-pick colour sequences

(e) *Eight-Pick Colour Sequences*

Combining two of the four-pick sequences viz. (A,A,A,B) and (A,B,B,B) and repeating them gives vertical rows of diamonds in the two colours. See plate 56 which is the result when the colour sequence begins with the first lift. Plate 57 shows the result when it begins on the second lift. The latter has been further varied by alternating (A,A,A,B,A,B,B,B) with (A,A,A,B,B,A,B,B).

(f) *Twelve-Pick Colour Sequences*

Jagged vertical stripes are produced when the colour sequence (A,B,B,B,A,A,B,B, A,B,A,B) is started on the first lift of the sequence, see Plate 58. Plate 59 shows the quite different result when the same sequence is started on the second lift. In the top half of the photo the small arrowhead motifs have been made to point to the left instead of to the right, by reversing the colours of the last two picks in the sequence.

Other Possibilities for Both Straight and Broken 2/2 Twill

These colour sequences, for both straight and broken twill, have been given to show the great variety of designs which can be obtained. But they are only the beginning. Many more variations await the enquiring weaver. These can be achieved in a number of ways.

(1) Combining colour sequences, e.g., alternating a four-pick and a seven-pick sequence.

(2) Changing from straight 2/2 twill to broken 2/2 twill and back again, while keeping the colour sequence unchanged.

(3) Reversing the lift and colour sequences at certain points, as in Plate 47. This can lead to much larger motifs and a far more lively design.

(4) Not using a straight threading draft but a pointed draft. The weft float over three ends which is associated with a pointed draft would give a weak spot in the rug so avoid it by skipping a shaft at the point of the draft. Therefore thread as in Fig. 222 (b), not as in Fig. 222 (a). This is a regular pointed draft, the threading reversing every five ends. Fig. 222 (c) shows an irregular pointed draft, the threading reverses coming after eight, six, four and six ends which could give a more varied design.

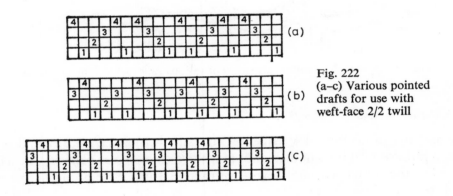

Fig. 222
(a–c) Various pointed drafts for use with weft-face 2/2 twill

(5) Using three or more colours. Colour has not been considered so far, but obviously closer weft colours will convert the blatant designs in the plates into something more subtle and so more interesting. By varying these colours and introducing a third or fourth colour, the range of possibilities is immediately widened.

(6) The most important road to discovery is to design at the loom. As each shed is opened and it is seen where the next pick will come to the surface, choose which colour is wanted in that position and weave accordingly.

Analysis of Straight and Broken 2/2 Twill

It is easy to discover the colour sequence in a weft-face 2/2 twill rug. Find the *woven* twill line and simply record the colours of the successive picks that make up this line, until the sequence begins to repeat itself, see Fig. 223. One twill line has been heavily

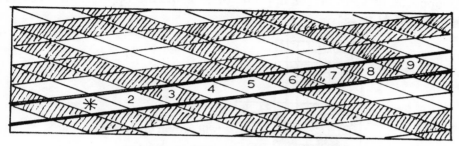

Fig. 223. Analysis of a weft-face **2/2** twill

outlined in this diagram. The colour sequence (beginning with the asterisked pick) is (A,A,B,A,A,B,B,B,B); the sequence then repeats itself. Whichever twill line had been selected and whichever pick had been used as a starting point, the same sequence would be arrived at.

It is far more difficult to analyse a broken twill as the picks do not lie in a straight line. Fig. 224 (a) and (b) show how eight picks in straight and in broken twill respec-

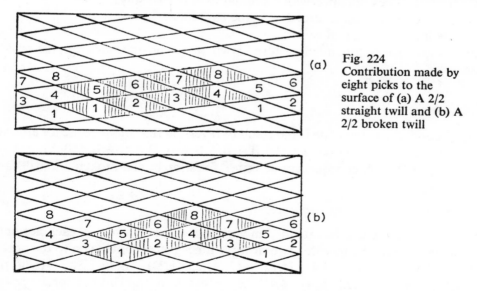

(a)

Fig. 224
Contribution made by eight picks to the surface of (a) A 2/2 straight twill and (b) A 2/2 broken twill

(b)

tively contribute to the surface of a weft-face rug. On this basis, the theoretically minded can work out on paper how a certain colour sequence will appear when woven.

(iii) 2/2 TWILL 'WOVEN ON OPPOSITES'

A twill 'woven on opposites' is based on the normal sequence of twill lifts. But after every one of these normal lifts, there is interposed its 'opposite'. By the opposite lift is mean that lift which reverses the position of the shafts existing in the normal lift. So the opposite of 12 is 34, the opposite of 23 is 41, the opposite of 34 is 12 and the opposite of 41 is 23.

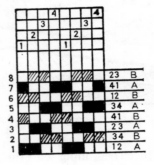

Fig. 225
Weave Diagram of 2/2
twill 'woven on opposites'

Fig. 225 shows the weave in diagrammatic form. The picks resulting from the normal lifts have been shown as solid and the picks resulting from the opposite lifts as shaded, in the weave plan. From this it will be understood that if the colour sequence in the weft is (A,B,A,B) the weave will appear as oblique lines of these two colours. They differ from the lines obtained with a normal twill in two ways,

(a) they run in the same direction as the twill lines,
(b) the lines are of equal width.

Plate 60 shows a sample combining normal twill woven on opposites with the variation below.

Variations

(a) A good zigzag twill line is the result of reversing the colour sequence after each repeat of the lifting sequence, i.e., (A,B,A,B,A,B,A,B; B,A,B.A,B,A,B,A).

(b) Any of the colour sequences described for straight and broken 2/2 twill can be tried.

(c) Extending the Lifting Sequence

The lifting sequence can be extended in various ways. For instance, each normal lift and its opposite can be repeated two or three times before moving on to the next lift. Thus: (12,34,12,34; 23,41,23,41; 34,12,34,12; 41,23,41,23). Another way is to lift thus: (12,34,12; 23,41,23; 34,12,34; 41,23,41), i.e., repeat the normal lift but not its opposite. Used with a colour sequence of (A,B,A,B) this gives oblique lines of the two colours of equal thickness, running in the opposite direction to the twill line. The lines are inclined more steeply than those resulting from normal twill woven on opposites. Warpway stripes with clear cut interesting outlines are produced by using just the first half of the latter sequence and with the same colour sequence, i.e., (12,34,12; 23,41,23), repeat. This is seen in Plate 61 where the colour sequence has been varied to (A,B,A,A,B,A,A,B,A,B,A,B,B,A,B,B,A,B) just once in the centre to give a zigzag.

Twill woven on opposites (which is really the simplest form of a weave known in industry as a weft corkscrew) has a good structure for rugs. The constant alternation of normal and opposite lifts means that warp and weft are well interlaced and there will be little tendency for the weft to slip on the warp.

(iv) WOVEN AS STRAIGHT 2/2 TWILL, BUT USING ONLY THREE LIFTS

An interesting weave results from missing out one of the four lifts in the straight 2/2 twill sequence, thus (12,23,34) repeat.

If this is used with two colours, pick and pick, oblique lines of equal thickness running in the opposite direction to the twill lines are produced, even though this does not look likely from the weave plan, see Fig. 226.

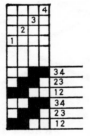

Fig. 226
Weave Diagram of weave
omitting one of the 2/2
twill lifts

If the colours are used in the order (A,A,B) repeated several times and then (B,B,A) repeated several times, blocks as in Plate 62 are produced which link together in a pleasant way as shown.

(v) DOUBLE-FACED 3/1 TWILL

All the weaves described above have been constructed from the four lifts of a 2/2 twill arranged in some order, together with special colour sequences in the weft. But there are also the eight lifts of 1/3 twill and 3/1 twill which can be used.

An excellent rug weave, which combines these lifts, gives a double-faced rug with a twill texture on both sides.

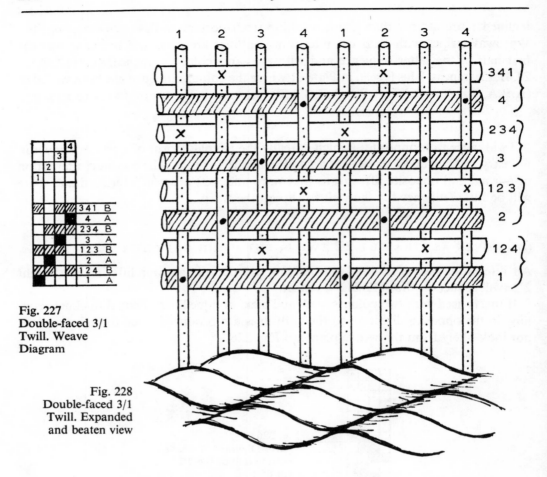

Fig. 227
Double-faced 3/1
Twill. Weave
Diagram

Fig. 228
Double-faced 3/1
Twill. Expanded
and beaten view

It is shown diagrammatically in Fig. 227 and in extended and beaten view in Fig. 228. From these it will be clear that the first pick floats over three ends and under one end (marked with a spot in Fig. 228) and the second pick floats under three ends and over one end (marked with a cross in Fig. 228). After each two picks, bracketed in Fig. 228, the interlacement moves along one end to the right. It will be seen that the second of these two picks will slide down behind the first, in each of the four bracketed pairs. Thus the picks woven when shafts 1, 2, 3 and 4 are raised will form the face of the rug (and it is these which are seen in the beaten view in Fig. 228) and those woven when 124, 123, 234 and 341 are raised will form the reverse of the rug. So with a colour sequence of (A,B,A,B) repeat, the face of the rug would be in colour A, the reverse in colour B.

The weave is the four-shaft version of the weave shown in Fig. 208 in the section on three-shaft twills. It will be met again as a block weave on eight shafts and as a pick-up weave, see Chapters 8 and 9. It gives the very tough yet flexible structure ideal for a flat rug. Because of the nature of the weave the two sides of the rug can be completely different, perhaps one side striped, the other plain. The pronounced twill ridges, seen in the beaten view in Fig. 228, give a play of light and shade on the surface, absent from a plain weave rug.

The many colour and weave effects obtained with 2/2 twill are not possible with this weave. If, however, the weft forming the front of the rug changes colour every two picks, these two colours will appear as interlocking diamonds.

A simplification of this weave is to use only picks 1, 2, 5 and 6, omitting the other four. This is identical with the weave shown in Fig. 215, obtained with a pointed three-shaft draft.

Practical Details

The aspect of a weft-face rug weave most influencing the choice of warp setting is the size of weft floats it contains. So far most weaves have had floats over only two ends, but here every pick floats over or under three ends. To reduce these to a practical size, it is necessary to have a warp setting of 6 working e.p.i. The floats will therefore be about ½ inch long, i.e., the same length as those in a 2/2 twill set at 4 working e.p.i.

The correct weft thickness is 2-ply carpet wool used threefold.

Use a floating selvage.

(vi) THREE-WEFT DOUBLE-FACED WEAVES

There are various types of double-faced rugs, which use three not two wefts. The third weft appears neither on the face or the reverse of the rug, but weaves in the centre of the rug giving firmness to an otherwise loose weave structure.

Fig. 229 shows two of these weaves. Each repeats every six picks and has a colour sequence of (A,B,C) repeat. In both cases, colour A will show on the face of the rug,

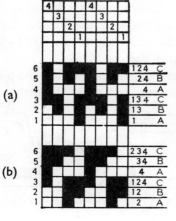

Fig. 229
Double-faced rugs with hidden weft
(a) Weave Diagram of type with hidden weft in plain weave
(b) Weave Diagram of type with hidden weft in hopsack

colour C on the reverse and colour B will be hidden. In the weave shown in Fig. 229 (a), colour B interlaces in plain weave order in the centre of the rug. This is best understood from a cross-section of the rug, see Fig. 230. The circles represent cross-sections of the warp ends, the numbers showing the shafts they are threaded on. Picks 1–3 in the sequence are shown at Fig. 230 (a) and the plain weave interlacement of the second pick, colour B, is plainly seen.

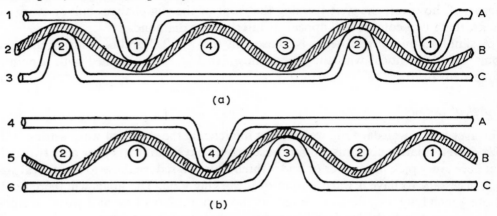

Fig. 230. (a) and (b) Cross sections of the six picks in Fig. 229 (a)

Note—How pick 1 floats over three, under one, and pick 3 floats under three over one.

—How these floats are so related to the plain weave pick that, when all three are beaten down, they will slide over each other. Pick 1 slides *in front of* pick 2 and hides it from the front, pick 3 slides *behind* pick 2 and hides it from the back.

Fig. 230 (b) shows the remaining three picks of the sequence. Notice that colour B is in the opposite plain weave shed to that used above, and that the floats of A and C are tied down at different points. The ends on shafts 1 and 2 tie down the floats of A and C in the first three picks, the ends on shafts 3 and 4 tie them down in the second three picks. So all ends are responsible for tying down one of the floating picks and there will therefore be equal warp take-up across the rug.

The weave shown in Fig. 229 (b) is very similar except that the hidden weft interlaces in hopsack order. Fig. 231 shows a cross-section of the first three picks.

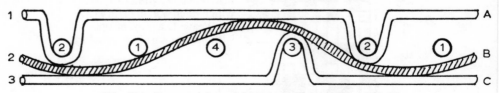

Fig. 231. Cross section of first three picks in Fig. 229 (b)

Practical Details

The wefts float over three ends, so a warp set of 6 working e.p.i. is necessary. The two wefts that form the face and the reverse of the rug are of 2-ply carpet wool used three-fold. The third hidden weft can be of varying thicknesses. If it is of 2-ply carpet wool used singly, it will be completely hidden; if used twofold it will show slightly; if used threefold it will show more prominently. So its thickness depends on whether it is to be merely structural or whether it is to contribute to the colour of either surface of the rug. A floating selvage will be necessary. Start all three wefts from the same side.

The eight-shaft block weaves developed from the above two weaves are described in Chapter 8, where is also described a further four-shaft reversible weave using three wefts.

(vii) OTHER WEAVES

(*a*) *Treating a Straight Four-Shaft Draft as a Pointed Three-Shaft Draft*

It will be seen from Fig. 232 that there is only one small difference between a straight draft on four shafts and a pointed draft on three shafts. This is the position of the fourth, eighth, twelfth end, etc., which has been indicated by a circle. Use can be made of this similarity, and a four-shaft straight draft can be regarded as a three-shaft pointed draft simply by lifting the second and fourth shafts together. Thus three-shaft krokbragd can be woven as shown in Fig. 232 (b) by lifting (124, 234, 13). Compare with the normal lifts shown in Fig. 232 (a) and note that wherever a 2 appears in Fig. 232 (a), a 2 and a 4 appear in Fig. 232 (b). This principle will appear again with weaves on six and eight shafts.

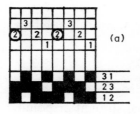

(a)

Fig. 232
Treating a straight four-shaft draft as a pointed three-shaft draft

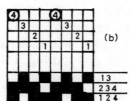

(b)

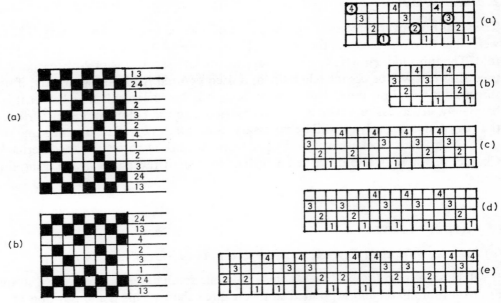

Fig. 233. Two weave
diagrams of a woven
ridge

Fig. 234. (a) Straight four-shaft draft (b–e) Skip
Twills derived from (a)

(b) Woven Ridge

A ridge can be made across a plain weave rug, by weaving several picks which float
over three ends, i.e., by using the lifts of a 1/3 twill in some sequence. Fig. 233 shows
two ways this can be done. In the upper weave, the floats form a horizontal herringbone and when beaten down slightly resemble two rows of soumak. In the lower weave
the sequence is that of a broken 1/3 twill.

The ridge will stand up more boldly if a thicker weft is used for it than for the plain
weave preceding and following it.

B. Four-Shaft Skip Twills

Skip twill drafts can be thought of as normal straight or pointed drafts from which
certain ends have been excluded in some regular order. Fig. 234 (a) shows a normal
straight draft on four shafts. If every third end is excluded (i.e., the encircled ends) the
draft becomes as in Fig. 234 (b). This is the simplest skip twill there is. Fig. 234 (c)
shows a draft constructed by excluding every fifth end and Fig. 234 (d) shows another
in which the sixth and fourth ends alternately are excluded. Fig. 234 (e) is more complex. The initial draft is a pointed one which reverses after every fourth and fifth end
alternately. From this, every seventh end has been excluded

The general effect of a skip draft on the designs obtained is that they are extended sideways compared with similar designs woven on a straight draft. So an oblique line becomes wider and lies at a flatter angle and vertical lines become broader and more widely spaced. In other words, the scale of the motifs is increased but only in the weft direction, not the warp direction. In the following descriptions only a few of the many possible colour and weave effects are mentioned.

(i) SKIP-TWILL REPEATING ON EIGHT ENDS

Fig. 235 shows that when this weave is lifted as for a 2/2 twill the weft does not only

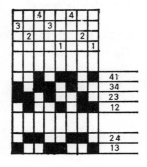

Fig. 235
Weave Diagram of Skip
Twill repeating on eight ends

pass over and under two ends, in places it passes over and under one end. So in the first pick, the weft passes under two, over one, under one, over two, under one, over one; and subsequent picks are similar. So there is more interlacing of warp and weft than with a straight draft, thus giving a good firm weave for rugs. Also the surface has a more interesting texture than has a normal 2/2 twill rug. By its very nature a skip draft cannot give plain weave, but as shown at the bottom of Fig. 235, this particular one can give hopsack by lifting 13 and 24.

Colour and Weave Effects

(*a*) *With Straight 2/2 Twill Lifts*, i.e. (12, 23, 34, 41)
  (1) Colour sequence of (A,A,B) repeat or (A,B,B) repeat.
  This gives oblique lines of the two colours. See Plate 63.
  (2) Colour sequence of (A,A,A,B) repeat or (A,B,B,B) repeat.
  It will be noticed how similar these are to the motifs obtained with a straight draft and similar colour sequences, but the scale is much bigger. See Plate 64.
  (3) Colour sequence of (A,B,A,B,A).
  This gives a vague but large-scale oblique line.

(b) *With Broken 2/2 Twill Lifts*, i.e. (12, 23, 41, 34).
Colour sequence of (A,B,A,B,A) or (A,B,A,B,A,B,A).

(c) *With Lifts of a 2/2 Twill Woven on Opposites*

Using two colours pick-and-pick, this gives oblique lines of the two colours with a pleasant stepped appearance quite unlike the dead straight lines obtained with a normal straight draft.

If between each pair of lifts in the above sequence, the two lifts, 13 and 24 are inserted, and the colour sequence of (A,B,A,B) is maintained, the irregular warpway stripes seen in Plate 65 are the rather surprising result. No trace of the twill on opposites is visible. So the lifting order becomes (12,34,13,24; 23,41,13,24; 34,12,13,24; 41,23,13,24).

If the inserted lifts are reversed, i.e., changed to 24, 13, but the pick-and-pick colour sequence preserved, the stripe moves over to the intermediate position. See top of Plate 65.

Practical Details

As for other twills, a warp set at 4 working e.p.i. and a weft using 2-ply carpet wool three or fourfold is suitable.

(ii) SKIP-TWILL REPEATING ON SIXTEEN ENDS

From Fig. 236, it will be seen that the 2/2 twill lifts make each weft go under two ends and over one for a short distance, then over two ends and under one for a similar

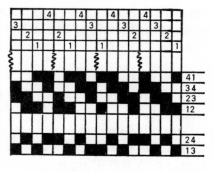

Fig. 236
Weave Diagram of Skip
Twill repeating on sixteen
ends

distance. Lifting 13 and 24 gives a combination of plain weave and hopsack. Slight grooves run down the surface of the weave corresponding to the points in the draft where an end has been excluded, see wavy lines in Fig. 236.

Colour and Weave Effects

(a) With Straight 2/2 Twill Lifts

(1) Colour sequence of (A,A,B) or (A,B,B).

This gives oblique wavy lines, see Plate 66. The waviness is more obvious at the centre of the Plate where the weave has been reversed.

(2) Colour sequence of (A,B,B,A,A,B,A,A,A,B,B,B)

A very striking warpway stripe results from this sequence. See Plate 67 and compare with the motif produced by a similar colour sequence on a straight draft shown in Plate 52.

(3) Colour sequence of (A,A,B,A,A,B,B).

This gives a jagged twill line, the boldest so far obtained. See Plate 68.

(b) With Broken 2/2 Twill Lifts

Colour sequence of (A,A,B,B,A,B,A,B,A,B,B,B) starting with a lift of 12.

Another warpway stripe is the result of this sequence. See Plate 69 and compare with Plate 58 which shows the result of the same colour sequence worked on a straight draft.

Practical Details

A warp set at 4 working e.p.i. and a weft of 2-ply carpet wool used threefold is suitable.

(iii) SKIP-TWILL REPEATING ON TWENTY-FOUR ENDS

The 2/2 twill lifts in Fig. 237 show that the weft in this weave takes a very irregular course passing over and under one and two ends as before, but also over and under three ends. When it is remembered that this skip-twill is derived from a pointed draft, these larger weft floats are to be expected. They are the cause of weaving this draft at 5 working e.p.i., not 4.

Lifting 13 and 24 gives a mixture of plain weave and hopsack. The wavy lines in Fig. 237 show where longtitudinal grooves run down the surface of the rug.

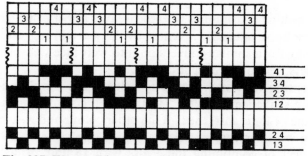

Fig. 237. Weave Diagram of Skip Twill repeating on twenty-four ends

Colour and Weave Effects

(a) *With Straight 2/2 Twill Lifts*

(1) Colour sequence of (A,A,B).
This gives oblique lines which have a tendency to break as they cross the grooves mentioned above.
(2) Colour sequence of (A,B,B, A,A,B, A,A,A,B,B,B).
As Plate 70 shows this gives a similar motif to that obtained with a straight draft and the same colour sequence, but much increased in scale.
(3) The bold, stepped stripes shown in Plate 71 were the result of the following colour sequence, starting on the 12 lift.

$$(A,A,B,B) \times 5$$
$$(A,B,B,B) \times 5$$
$$(A,B,B,A) \times 5$$
$$(B,B,B,A) \times 5$$
$$(B,B,A,A) \times 5$$
$$(B,B,A,B) \times 5$$
$$(B,A,A,B) \times 5$$
$$(B,A,B,B) \times 5$$

Repeat the above sequence.

Note an interesting subtlety in the design which results entirely from the threading. The black and white stripes are of single or double-thickness, e.g., at bottom of Plate 71 there is a double-thick black stripe at the right corner and another to the left of the centre. Whereas the stripes all step upwards to the left, these double-thick black stripes appear on a diagonal going up to the right.

Practical Details

A warp set at 5 working e.p.i., with a weft of 2-ply carpet wool used two or threefold is suitable.

The rather astonishing possibilities of these weaves (most of which can be found in an industrial weave book or can be invented by the weaver) suggest that there may be many others waiting for a similar conversion into weft-face weaves. Here is a fruitful and almost limitless field of investigation.

When experimenting with such a weave, first try the simplest colour and weave effect, i.e., a lifting sequence of (12,23,34,41), and a colour sequence of (A,A,B). If this gives a twill line of some sort, then all the other colour and weave effects described above will also be worth trying.

Try also the effect of combining these lifts with 13 and 24, as was done in the simplest skip-twill above. This can completely transform a design.

There are also the possibilities of using three colours, reversing the lift sequences and reversing the threading drafts to be investigated.

C. Twilled Overshot Blocks

There are many twill derivatives, but only one will be described in detail here. This is shown in Fig. 238 and can be described as 'four-end overshot blocks in twill order'. It

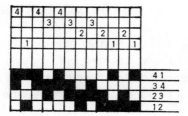

Fig. 238
Weave Diagram of
four-end overshot blocks
in twill order, lifted as
for 2/2 twill

is the simplest member of a class of threading which forms the basis of the double corduroy technique and so will be met with later.

As the weave plan shows, when lifted for a straight 2/2 twill, it gives weft floats over and under four ends. Because of this, plain weave picks are essential to give strength to the weave and these are obtained by lifting 13 and 24.

(i) TWILL RIDGES

Using a thick weft (2-ply carpet wool used fourfold) for the twill lifts (shown in bold type) and a thin weft (2-ply carpet wool used twofold) for the plain weave lifts, then the following sequence could be used: **12**, 13, 24; **23**, 13, 24; **34**, 13, 24; **41**, 13, 24. If the two wefts are of different colours then the ridges and intermediate flat areas will be of different colours. In the bottom of Plate 72, the ridges are a mixture of grey and white and the plain weave is black. As will be seen this weave gives a twill with a very gentle angle.

However, if, in the above sequence, the first three picks are repeated twice, then the next three picks repeated twice, and so on, a much bolder and steeper ridge is produced. This is seen in the middle of Plate 72.

Note that these twill lines are quite different from all the previous ones described. Here there is a series of floats of one colour on a plain weave ground of another colour. These floats form a ridge standing above the level of the surrounding plain weave. In the other twills, the whole surface of the rug was made up of small floats of two or more colours, and the twill lines resulted from the sequence in which these colours were used. There were no ridges.

(ii) WARPWAY STRIPES

The stripes at the top of Plate 72, were produced with this sequence of lifts:

12, 14—Thick weft (white)
13, 24—Thin weft (black)
34, 14—Thick weft
13, 24—Thin weft.

Then the whole sequence was repeated. If two thick wefts of different colours had been used, the stripes could have been made more complex. As before, the thick weft can be 2-ply carpet wool used fourfold and the thin weft 2-ply carpet wool used twofold.

A simpler form of stripe can be woven just by repeating over and over again the first four picks of the above sequence. Plate 73 shows a sample in this weave. The threading here was the normal double corduroy one. The thick weft was 2-ply horsehair used sixfold and the thin weft was either black or white 2-ply carpet wool used singly. Due to the thickness of the horsehair, the warp could not be covered and its appearance contributes considerably to the interest of the stripes.

Practical Details

4 working e.p.i. is a good setting for this threading but 5 or 6 working e.p.i. can be used. The latter settings naturally reduce the length of the weft float which is a point in their favour, but against this is the fact that they make it harder for the weft to cover the warp completely.

D. Four-Shaft Shadow Weave

The shadow weave system worked out by Mary Atwater is designed for a fabric with an approximate equal number of ends and picks per inch, the design depending on the interplay of the colours of the two elements. But it can be adapted as a weft-face weave (and also as a warp-face weave, see Chapter 11) in which case it is only the two *weft* colours which contribute to the design.

In Fig. 239 (a), three repeats of the eight-end threading unit are shown. The sequence in the third repeat has been reversed to give a point draft. The normal lifts are those of a 2/2 twill woven on opposites as shown, with a pick-and-pick colour sequence, i.e., (A,B,A,B). The weave this gives, as shown in the weave plan, is a large scale twill which looks as if it needs more than four shafts.

The draft for the sample in Plate 74 was reversed in the centre. The bottom section is the weave as shown in Fig. 239 (a) and it is seen to give a rather small scale flattened diamond. The scale can be made more interesting in the following way.

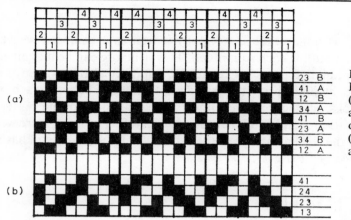

Fig. 239
Four Shaft Shadow Weave.
(a) Weave plan when lifted
as 2/2 twill 'woven on
opposites'
(b) Weave plan when lifted
as 2/2 twill

Fig. 240 (a) shows the eight lifts written out. These have been bracketed in fours, and the brackets labelled 1–4. Repeat the lifts in each bracket twice. As the brackets overlap, the last two lifts of one bracket become the first two lifts of the next. Keep the pick-and-pick colour sequence. Plate 74 (top) shows that this weave gives strongly stepped oblique lines.

Another variation is to bracket the lifts in pairs as in Fig. 240 (b) (i.e., in pairs of opposites) and repeat each pair, say, four times, then move on to the next pair. Plate 75 shows a sample in this technique and it will be seen it gives oblique lines of very complex character.

The lifts and weave plan in Fig. 239 (b) show that the threading can be used to give a 2/2 twill. The direction of twill reverses after every fourth thread, and the twill line 'clean cuts' at each reversing point. So any of the 2/2 twill colour and weave effects can be tried out on this threading. The sample in Plate 76 shows some of the many possibilities. It includes two weaves used in unequal stripes:

(1) The lifts as shown in Fig. 239 (b) with an (A,A,B) colour sequence.

(2) The lifts for a 2/2 twill woven on opposites with a pick-and-pick colour sequence. The diamonds in the design occur naturally at the junction between one weave and the other.

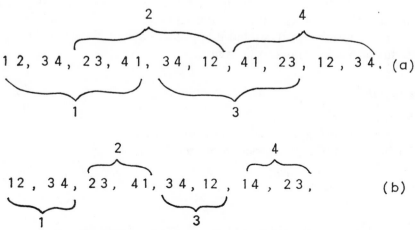

Fig. 240. Various lift sequences for four-shaft shadow weave

E. Four-Shaft Honeycomb

The cellular weave known as honeycomb is normally woven as a balanced weave. Long floats of warp and weft outline each square cell. This structure can be magnified and adapted as a rug weave and it appears in Chapter 12. But it can also be woven as a completely weft-face fabric, by interposing two picks of plain weave between each of the normal honeycomb picks. So the long weft floats appear as in a normal honeycomb but the long warp floats are hidden by the plain weave weft. The latter increases the stability, but decreases the cellular nature of the fabric which, however, still has a very deeply textured surface, see Plate 77.

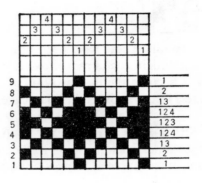

Fig. 241
Four-Shaft Honeycomb.
Weave Diagram

Fig. 241 shows the details. The weave plan only shows the normal honeycomb picks; between each one of these, two picks of plain weave (on lifts 13 and 24) are woven. Two wefts are used, a thick one for the honeycomb picks and a finer one for the plain weave picks. It will be noticed that the third and seventh picks are woven with shafts 1 and 3 lifted, i.e., in a plain weave shed. So both the honeycomb and the plain weave weft lie together in this shed. This often results in the warp not being completely covered at this point, see the white spots in Plate 77.

The weave is shown up well if the plain weave weft is a different colour or tone from the honeycomb weft. It was darker in the sample photographed, in which there is also another slight variation. This is the use of a separate weft of a much brighter colour for the fifth pick of each repeat, so that it appears as a spot. Such variations in colour can make this into a very interesting weave.

Practical Details

Warp—5 working e.p.i.
Weft—For plain weave, 2-ply carpet wool used singly.
       For honeycomb, 2-ply carpet wool used fourfold.

F. Single End Spot Weave

In the *Domestic Manufacturer's Assistant* written by J. and R. Bronson and published at Utica, U.S.A. in 1817, eleven out of the thirty-five weaves described are of one special type. As this is a spot weave the threading system is generally known as Bronson Spot Weave. The characteristic of this weave is warp and weft floats spanning five threads. These are too long for a rug weave, so for the present purpose the threading has been reduced and is shown in Fig. 242. It is an adaptable threading for rugs and can also be developed as a block weave, see Chapter 8.

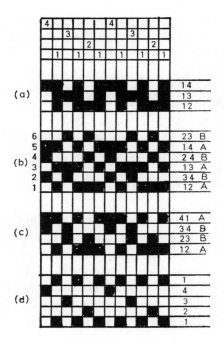

Fig. 242
Single End Spot Weave.
Weave Diagram with several weave plans

(i) At Fig. 242 (a) is shown the weave plan when the shafts are lifted in the sequence (12, 13, 14). This gives a very simple twill, but it only becomes feasible for a rug weave when woven as a twill on opposites, i.e., as in Fig. 242 (b) where the sequence is (12,34; 13,24; 14,23). This gives weft floats over three ends, forming oblique ridges, on both sides of the rug. If the colour sequence is (A,B,A,B) repeat, as shown in Fig. 242 (b), then the ridges on the face will be in colour B and those on the reverse in colour A. The ridges are separated by spots of the colour from the opposite side of the rug. This is seen in Plate 78. In the centre section, the sequence has been altered to (A,B,A,B,B,A) repeat, which makes the vertical stripes appear. The firm flexible weave obtained looks far more complex than it really is.

(ii) A development of the above weave is only to use the first four picks of the sequence but to keep to the pick-and-pick colour sequence. So the sequence is lift 12 colour A, lift 34 colour B, lift 13 colour A, lift 24 colour B. The result on the face of the rug is warpway stripes of colour B separated by thin lines of colour A; on the reverse of the rug the same applies, but with the colours interchanged.

Naturally the colour sequence could be (A,B,A,C) in which case the warpway stripes would be composed of colours B and C.

Exactly the same effect would be obtained by weaving picks number 3, 4, 5 and 6 repeated, or picks number 5, 6, 1 and 2 repeated; the stripe would merely appear in a different position, slightly shifted over to the left.

(iii) The last sentence suggests another weave in which the stripe, reduced to a small unit, is made to appear in all three positions in succession. So the sequence becomes

$$\left.\begin{array}{l}(12,34;\ 13,24)\times 2\\(13,24;\ 14,23)\times 2\\(14,23;\ 12,34)\times 2\\(14,23)\end{array}\right\}\text{Repeat}$$

With a pick-and-pick colour sequence, this gives a stepped twill.

(iv) Another stepped twill can be woven by taking the picks of the twill woven on opposites in pairs and repeating them several times, e.g.,

$$\left.\begin{array}{l}(12,34)\times 3\\(13,24)\times 3\\(14,23)\times 3\end{array}\right\}\text{Repeat}$$

Plate 79 shows how this appears with a pick-and-pick colour sequence.

(v) When this weave is lifted as for a straight 2/2 twill, it does not give any twill lines, but it yields a good firm weave very much like the weave described under (ii) above. If the colours are arranged thus, lift 12 colour A, lift 23 colour B, lift 34 colour B, lift 41 colour A, then the warpway stripes of B, and the thin lines of A will appear as in (ii). The only difference is that the thin lines appear more as a succession of spots. Plate 80 shows this weave. A black, grey and white mixture has been used as the main weft, but there are two sections, one where an all-white and one where an all-black weft has been combined with it, as in the above sequence, to give the vaguely showing white and black thin lines.

(vi) An unexpected possibility of this weave is the production of pronounced ridges across the rug. Two of the possible lifting sequences are: (1,2,3,4,1,2,3,4,1) see Fig. 242 (d) and (1,2,3,4,1,4,3,2,1). In both cases the picks with lifts 2, 3 and 4 form the floats of the ridge and so can be in a thicker yarn. These ridges could be combined with one of the above weaves or with plain weave, obtained by lifting 1 and 234, alternately.

To make a ridge on both sides of the rug lift thus, (2, 123, 3, 134, 4, 124). If continued, these lifts produce a double-faced twill weave. As the weft floats span five ends, the warp would have to be set closer than normal to make this into a practical weave.

Fig. 243 (a) shows how this threading can be developed as a pointed draft, reversing twice on the fourth end (arrowed).

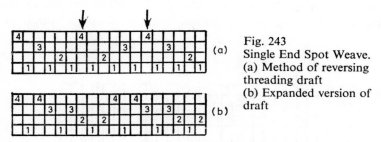

Fig. 243
Single End Spot Weave.
(a) Method of reversing threading draft
(b) Expanded version of draft

The original Bronson Spot Weave can be extended onto any number of shafts, each additional shaft giving one more controllable 'spot' in the design. Single End Spot Weave can be extended, but as it is woven quite differently this does not bring any great increase in its scope. The weave can be expanded slightly as shown in Fig. 243 (b). This gives similar effects to Single End Spot Weave, but without the possibility of plain weave.

Single End Spot Weave is one of the weaves which can be produced on a straight six-shaft draft, as it repeats every six ends, see Fig. 252.

Practical Details

A warp of 5 working e.p.i. is suitable, due to the many floats over and under three ends. A weft of 2-ply carpet wool should be used twofold, though it can be used threefold if the rug is beaten very hard.

G. Alternated Two-Shaft Blocks

A very simple rug weave consisting of plain weave and floats can be woven on any of the threadings in Fig. 244. A double-faced weave can be woven on the threading shown at Fig. 244 (a).

As the weave plans show, they all give plain weave when shafts 13 and 24 are lifted alternately and weft floats in two positions when shafts 12 and 34 are lifted. The length of this float depends on the number of ends on the front two or back two shafts in each group.

A floating pick with a thick weft is followed by one or two picks of plain weave with a finer weft. As the latter has to cover the warp, there cannot be more than about 6 e.p.i. This warp setting would make the weft floats in the threading in Fig. 244 (a) $\frac{1}{2}$ inch long and in the threading in Fig. 244 (b) $\frac{2}{3}$ inch long, both of which are within practical limits.

There are basically two ways to weave this.

(i) To alternate one of the floating picks, say, on lifting 12, with two picks of plain weave. This will give warpway stripes consisting alternately of the floats and of plain weave. Even using the same colour for both wefts, the stripes show up strongly, because the floats bulge forwards, forming prominent warpway ridges in contrast to the intervening stripes of flat plain weave. Using different colours, the contrast between the two stripes can of course be emphasized. Plate 81 shows a sample in black and white.

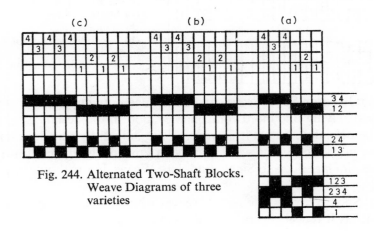

Fig. 244. Alternated Two-Shaft Blocks. Weave Diagrams of three varieties

(ii) To weave the two floating picks alternately, with two plain weave picks either after every one floating pick or after every two floating picks. So the lifting sequence could be (12,13,24; 34,13,24) repeat or (12,34; 13,24) repeat. The floats will here cover the surface of the rug, hiding the plain weave completely. By using two colours alternately for the floating picks, warpway stripes or checks can be produced. This is probably best woven with the threading shown in Fig. 244 (a), i.e., with the shortest floats.

Practical Details

Warp—5 or 6 working e.p.i.
Weft—For the floats, 2-ply carpet wool used three or fourfold.
    For the plain weave, 2-ply carpet wool used singly.

The double-faced weave referred to above is obtained by lifting (1, 4, 234, 123), see Fig. 244 (a) at bottom. This is identical with a weave described in the section on Three-Shaft Weaves. Note that the threading shown in Fig. 244 (a) is simply another form of the draft used for Four-Shaft Honeycomb, i.e., a pointed four-shaft draft, see Fig. 241. So using the same lifts, the threading used for honeycomb will serve equally well. The use of this weave for warp- and weft-face rugs is described in Chapter 12.

3. SIX-SHAFT DRAFTS

Weavers tend to ignore six-shaft weaves; if they do have a multishaft loom they jump straight from four-shaft to eight-shaft weaves. But especially in the field of colour and weave effects with twills, six shafts have a great deal to offer. Only a few of the possibilities will be described but maybe they will be enough to encourage the reader to venture into this territory.

A. Using a Straight Draft

(i) 2/2/1/1 TWILL

This is the first multiple twill met in this book. According to the nomenclature of twills, it will be understood that in each pick the weft goes under two ends, over two, under one, over one, hence 2/2/1/1. So the interlacing is a mixture of hopsack and plain weave, but in twill order, see Fig. 245 (a). Due to this close interlacing, no plain

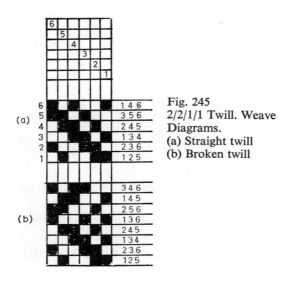

Fig. 245
2/2/1/1 Twill. Weave
Diagrams.
(a) Straight twill
(b) Broken twill

weave is needed to strengthen the fabric, thus distinguishing this from other six-shaft twills. The weft floats over two ends form oblique ridges running up to the left, as would be expected from the weave plan. These give an interesting, though small scale, surface texture and together with the good interlacing make this an ideal rug weave. A few of the many colour and weave effects are described below.

Colour and Weave Effects

(*a*) *With Straight 2/2/1/1 Twill Lifts*

A colour sequence of (A,A,B,B) gives oblique toothed lines running in the opposite direction to the twill ridge, see Plate 82. A colour sequence of (A,A,A,B,B) and (A,A,B,B,B) is seen in Plate 83, where the former sequence is shown at the top. Another colour sequence that produces good results is (A,A,B,A,A,B,B,B); and another is (B,B,B,B,B,A,B,B,B,B,A,A,B,B,B,A,A,A,B,B,A,A,A,A,B,A,A,A,A,A) repeat, but there are many others to be discovered.

(*b*) *With the Lifts of a 2/2/1/1 Twill woven on Opposites*

Between each lift as shown in Fig. 245 (a) the opposite lift is inserted. So the sequence now becomes:

$$
\begin{array}{ll}
125 & A \\
346 & B \\
236 & A \\
145 & B \\
134 & A \\
256 & B \\
245 & A \\
136 & B \\
356 & A \\
124 & B \\
146 & A \\
235 & B
\end{array}
$$

If two colours are used pick-and-pick as indicated, the oblique lines shown in Plate 84 are the result. Note the spots of black and white running up between each black and white line. This is a very firm weave.

(*c*) A rather similar weave has two wefts weaving pick-and-pick. They both work on the six lifts of the 2/2/1/1 twill but whereas one weft begins on the first pick of the cycle, i.e., with a lift of 125, the other weft begins on the fourth pick, i.e., with a lift of 245. So the sequence is:

$$
\begin{array}{ll}
125 & A \\
245 & B \\
236 & A \\
356 & B \\
134 & A \\
146 & B \\
245 & A \\
125 & B
\end{array}
$$

356 A
236 B
146 A
134 B

This gives oblique lines of equal thickness, without the spots found with the above weave. In Plate 85, the pick-and-pick sequence has been occasionally altered to show some of the possibilities of this weave.

(d) With Broken 2/2/1/1 Twill Lifts

A broken twill could be made just by weaving the picks in Fig. 245 (a) in the order 1,2,3,6,5,4. However, the three samples in Plate 86 were woven on a slightly more elaborate broken twill shown in Fig. 245 (b) with the following colour sequences.
Bottom sample—(A,A,B,B).
Middle sample—(A,B,A,B,B,A.B,A) starting on pick 1.
Top sample—(A,B,A,B,B,A,B,A) starting on pick 3.
   The difference between the last two shows how important it is to start a broken twill on the correct pick of the lifting sequence.

Practical Details

Warp—4 working e.p.i.
Weft—2-ply carpet wool used threefold.

(ii) 1/3/1/1 TWILL

Whereas the face and the reverse of all the above weaves was identical, this weave is quite different on the two sides. It has weft floats over three ends on the front which do not appear on the reverse, see Fig. 246 (a). It is best woven with two picks of plain weave (lifting 135 and 246) between each twill pick. If the plain weave weft is a different colour from the twill weft, it will show up the twill lines. See Plate 87, where a white plain weave weft was used. The reverse of the rug is also interesting showing twill lines made of the plain weave weft and spots of the twill weft.

Practical Details

Warp—4 or 5 working e.p.i.
Weft—For plain weave, 2-ply carpet wool used singly.
      —For twill, 2-ply carpet wool used three or fourfold.

An interesting double-faced rug can be woven based on this weave, 1/3/1/1 twill,

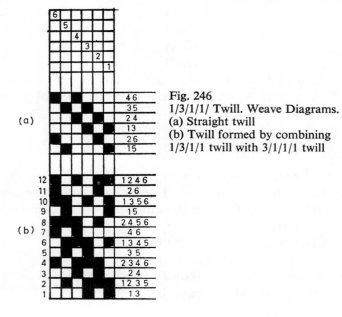

Fig. 246
1/3/1/1/ Twill. Weave Diagrams.
(a) Straight twill
(b) Twill formed by combining
1/3/1/1 twill with 3/1/1/1 twill

which gives floats on the front of the rug, together with a 3/1/1/1 twill which gives identical floats on the reverse of the rug. A pick of 1/3/1/1 twill alternates with a pick of 3/1/1/1 twill throughout, see Fig. 246 (b). Two wefts are used pick-and-pick. The result is a rug with marked oblique ridges on both sides; on the face they are of colour A (with spots of colour B also appearing) and on the reverse of colour B. As Plate 88 shows, stripes and other effects can be obtained by altering the pick-and-pick sequence of the two colours.

The warp should be set at 5 working e.p.i. and the weft should consist of 2-ply carpet wool used three or fourfold. This gives a thick but flexible rug.

The same result is obtained if the picks, as numbered in Fig. 246 (b), are woven in the following order, 1,3,4,6,5,7,8,10,9,11,12,2, and the colours used in an (A,A,B,B) sequence instead of pick-and-pick.

(iii) 3/3 TWILL

This is the most obvious six-shaft twill but due to the small amount of interlacing between warp and weft it is not very suitable for rugs. There has to be a plain weave weft, which shows up prominently between the twill weft floats. Two picks of plain weave are used between each twill pick. This gives an opportunity for small scale effects by using two differently coloured wefts for the plain weave and arranging them in pick-and-pick or 2-and-2 order, see Plate 89.

Practical Details

Because of the long floats a setting of 5 working e.p.i. is best with a weft of 2-ply carpet wool, used three or fourfold for the floats and used singly for the plain weave. For a heavier but looser weave, set the warp at 4 working e.p.i. and use 2-ply carpet wool fourfold for the floats and twofold for the plain weave.

(iv) COMBINATION OF 3/3 TWILL WITH 2/2/1/1 TWILL

An interesting weave often results from combining two other weaves, so that a pick from one alternates with a pick from the other. This can be done by combining 3/3 twill and 2/2/1/1 twill, see Plate 90 and Fig. 247. In Fig. 247, the odd-numbered picks are taken from a 2/2/1/1 twill and are in colour A, and the even-numbered picks are taken from a 3/3 twill and are in colour B. The different way the two weaves are filled in on the weave plan helps to clarify this. In the plate, the white weft corresponds to colour A.

As will be seen this gives oblique lines of the two colours, colour B giving a thicker line. Note how the character of the lines alters when they slope up to the left; their edges become broken and less smooth. This is because only the 3/3 twill was reversed in direction, the 2/2/1/1 twill continued on unaltered. So where the lines slope up to the right, the two twills are working in harmony, in the same direction (as in Fig. 247), but where the lines slope up to the left they are working against each other.

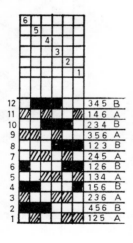

Fig. 247
Weave Diagram of twill formed by combining 3/3 twill with 2/2/1/1 twill

Practical Details

Warp—4 working e.p.i.
Weft—2-ply carpet wool used fourfold for the 3/3 twill picks and used threefold for the 2/2/1/1 twill picks.

(V) WEAVE BASED ON A THREE-SHAFT WEAVE

Fig. 248 shows a weave based on a three-shaft weave described earlier in this chapter, see Fig. 211. When lifted as for the lower weave plan, i.e., 2356, A; 36, B; 1245, A; 14, B; the rug will be colour B on the face and colour A on the reverse. But when lifted as in the upper weave plan, there will be narrow warpway stripes of the two colours, the colour B stripes will lie over the ends threaded on shafts 4, 5 and 6 and the colour A stripes over the ends threaded on 1, 2 and 3, see Plate 91. The wavy lines at the top of Plate 91 were the result of lifting as for the stripes but changing the colour sequence to (A,B,A,A,B,A,B,B). There are probably many more possibilities here with varied colour sequences.

Practical Details

Warp—4 working e.p.i.
Weft—2-ply carpet wool used threefold.

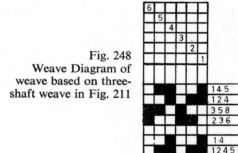

Fig. 248
Weave Diagram of
weave based on three-
shaft weave in Fig. 211

145	B
124	A
358	B
236	A
14	B
1245	A
36	B
2356	A

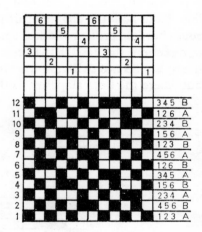

345	B
126	A
234	B
156	A
123	B
456	A
126	B
345	A
156	B
234	A
456	B
123	A

Fig. 249. Six-Shaft Shadow
Weave. Weave Diagram

B. Six-Shaft Shadow Weave

The threading for a six-shaft shadow weave is shown in Fig. 249. An end on one of the front three shafts is always followed (shadowed) by an end on one of the back three shafts. There are twelve ends in one unit of the threading. The lifts are as for a 3/3 twill woven on opposites, and the colour sequence is (A,B,A,B) repeat. As the weave plan shows, the structure is rather similar to that of a four-shaft shadow weave, and the woven result is also similar, though more complex.

Plate 92 shows a sample which has a reverse in the threading in the centre. At the bottom is seen the weave as shown in Fig. 249. Above this is seen a sample in which the numbered picks were taken in the following order, the colour sequence remaining the same.

$$\left.\begin{array}{l} 1, 2, 1, 2, 1, 2 \\ 3, 4, 3, 4, 3, 4 \\ 5, 6, 5, 6, 5, 6 \\ 7, 8, 7, 8, 7, 8 \\ 5, 6, 5, 6, 5, 6 \\ 3, 4, 3, 4, 3, 4 \end{array}\right\} \text{Repeat}$$

At the top of Plate 92 is a sample in which the picks were woven in the following order

1, 2, 3, 4, 5, 6, 7, 8,
3, 4, 5, 6, 7, 8, 9, 10,
5, 6, 7, 8, 9, 10, 11, 12, etc.

These three examples show the range of possibilities this threading can give.

Practical Details

Warp—4 working e.p.i.
Weft—2-ply carpet wool used threefold. Use a floating selvage. No plain weave is
    possible.

C. Six-Shaft Skip Twills

There are many skip twills possible on six shafts. Fig. 250 (a) shows one on which two

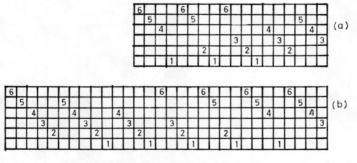

Fig. 250. Two six-shaft skip twills

ends are excluded after every three included. Because two consecutive ends are excluded, plain weave is possible with this skip twill. Plate 93 shows two of the many possibilities. At the bottom is a 2/2/1/1 twill woven on opposites using two colours, pick-and-pick, and at the top a broken 2/2/1/1 twill using a colour sequence of (A,B,B,A,B,A,A,B). Compare these with the results that similar lifting and colour sequences give with a straight draft. As these weaves contain weft floats over one, two and three ends, it is a little difficult to find a correct warp setting; probably 5 working e.p.i. is the best with a 2-ply carpet wool weft used three or fourfold.

Fig. 250 (b) shows another skip twill in which two ends are excluded after every five ends included, and there are many more to be investigated.

D. Six-Shaft Honeycomb

The longest weft floats in four-shaft honeycomb, which are over or under five ends (picks 1 and 5 in Fig. 241), limit the usefulness of this weave, for the weft at these points can very easily be caught by furniture or feet. So it is only suitable for a bedroom rug, which does not have much heavy traffic over it.

But if honeycomb is woven on a six-shaft straight draft, each of these floats over five ends can be replaced by two separate floats over four ends, see picks 1 and 2, and 6 and 7, in Fig. 251 (a). This makes a more practical weave. As Plate 94 shows there is little difference in the texture of the two types of honeycomb.

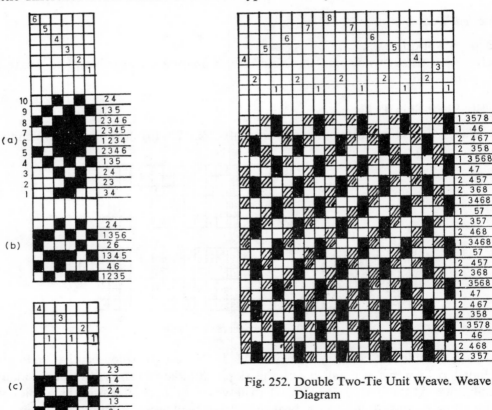

Fig. 252. Double Two-Tie Unit Weave. Weave Diagram

Fig. 251. (a) Six-Shaft Honeycomb. Weave Diagram
(b) Producing any weave that repeats on six ends with a straight six-shaft draft

In this example, the plain weave weft and the honeycomb weft for picks 9, 10, 1, 2, 3 and 4, are both white. The honeycomb weft for the remaining four picks (which form the base of the 'cell') is grey, which has the effect of emphasizing the depth of the cell.

Practical Details

Warp—5 working e.p.i.
Weft—For honeycomb, 2-ply carpet wool used fourfold.
    For plain weave, 2-ply carpet wool used singly.

E. Other Weaves

Any weave that repeats every six ends can be woven on a straight six-shaft draft. Fig. 251 (b) and (c) show the identical weave produced both from the Single End Spot Weave threading and from a six-shaft straight draft, with the respective lifts. The same applies to a pointed four-shaft draft, i.e. (2,3,4,3,2,1) repeat. So a simple honeycomb weave or a 2/2 twill vertical herringbone can both be woven on a straight six-shaft draft. Obviously such a draft would not be chosen for producing these various four-shaft weaves. But knowing these perhaps, unexpected, possibilities of a six-shaft draft, certainly widens its scope.

4. EIGHT-SHAFT DRAFTS

It is not proposed to deal in detail with eight-shaft twills and their numerous variations, as the subject is practically endless. A weaver who has understood the principles involved in the twills on three, four and six shafts will be equipped to find his own way among those on eight shafts. It is always wise to avoid weft floats that pass over more than three ends, so a good one to start with might be 2/1/1/2/1/1 twill or 2/2/1/1/1/1 twill. Always try and find a weave that has characteristics not present in weaves on fewer shafts, otherwise there is no point in using the extra shafts.

Double Two-Tie Unit Weave

An interesting interlacement system is shown in an eight shaft version in Fig. 252. Every other end is alternately on shafts 1 and 2. The other ends which can extend over any number of shafts (here on shafts 3–8), can be arranged in a straight order or in a pointed order as in Fig. 252.

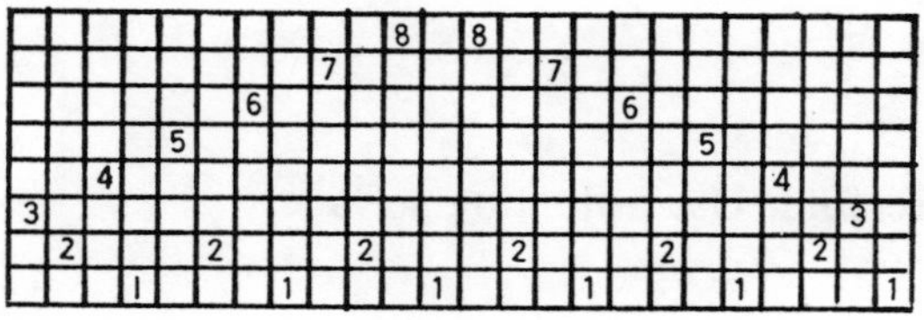

Fig. 253
Alternative method of threading for Double Two-Tie Unit Weave

This system gives a large range of weaves, including complex designs in 2/2 twill and it is the latter which are relevant here. As will be seen from the lifts, the ends on shaft 2 stay up for two picks and then the ends on shaft 1 stay up for two picks, throughout the design. The corresponding parts of the weave plan have been filled in with solid squares. On this skeleton of marks on point paper, a design such as the one shown can be built up, in which the areas differ from each other only in the direction of the twill lines. The other squares (representing warp controlled by shafts 3–8) have been shaded.

To show up this design as a weft-face fabric it is probably best to weave it on opposites, with two colours used pick-and-pick. This means that every lift shown in Fig. 252, using colour A, is followed by the opposite lift, using colour B. So starting at the bottom, the first few lifts are:

2357	A
1468	B
2468	A
1357	B
146	A
23578	B
13578	A
246	B, etc.

So the actual sequence of lifts numbers forty-eight, twice the twenty-four lifts shown. Plate 95 shows a sample woven in exactly this manner.

The same sequence of lifts but with other colour sequences will lead to more complex patterns but always contained in diamonds. Other lifts will give areas of the two directions of twill, but arranged in squares or triangles, not diamonds.

If the reverses in the threading draft had been arranged as in Fig. 253, a different type of diamond would have been produced, as using the lifts given above will show. There is almost endless scope here.

The only drawback is the large number of lifts. The above design would need fourteen pedals, two of them just controlling shafts 1 and 2, and the other twelve controlling the twelve different combinations of shafts 3–8 that need to be lifted. Both feet would be in action all the time. It is really a type of design more suitable for weaving on a dobby loom.

Plain weave can be obtained by lifting 12 and 345678, and hopsack by lifting 1357 and 2468.

Practical Details

Warp—4 working e.p.i.
Weft—2-ply carpet wool used threefold. Use a floating selvage.

8 · Weft-face Rugs in Multishaft Weaves

PART TWO: TECHNIQUES GIVING BLOCK DESIGNS CONTROLLED BY SHAFTS

INTRODUCTION

All the weaves in the preceding chapter gave small scale motifs that repeated themselves across the rug, i.e., twill lines, small warpway stripes, and others. The size of these motifs could not be increased, except to a very slight extent by setting the warp more openly. Only with skip twills were motifs of larger scale produced. In fact some of the skip-twill threadings are closely related to those of the block weaves.

The block weaves are generally woven with two colours and give rectangular blocks of these two colours, the colours reversing on the back of the rug. The important point is that the width of these blocks, i.e., their weftway dimension, is the direct result of the threading plan. So depending on the threading plan, blocks of any width can be woven. This immediately increases the design possibility of these weaves. They offer great scope for two-colour designs of almost any type.

Block weaves are of two types:

(i) THE TWO-TIE UNIT CLASS

In this class, shafts 1 and 2 control the 'tie-down' warp ends, i.e., the ends that tie down the weft floats, which form the face and the reverse of the rug.

The remaining shafts (3 and 4 in the case of a four-shaft weave) control the pattern blocks, i.e., they determine whether at any point in the weave a certain weft shall float on the face or on the reverse of the rug.

By using more of these block-controlling shafts, more design blocks can be woven and it is a characteristic of this class that each new such shaft introduced into the draft gives one more controllable design block. So with four shafts, two blocks can be woven; with five shafts, three blocks can be woven; with six shafts, four blocks can be woven and so on. There are many weaves of this type Three are described here and they have been named according to the number of ends in one threading block. Other weaves can be constructed using three tie-down shafts.

(ii) The other block weaves do not have the above property of giving an extra pattern block for each extra shaft used. Most of them have to be extended onto eight shafts to increase the blocks they can control.

1. FOUR-SHAFT BLOCK WEAVES

Part 1. Two-Tie Unit Drafts

A. Three-End Block Draft

The simplest block draft is a development of the double-faced three-shaft weave shown in Fig. 212, in the last chapter. The blocks are produced by threading units of (1,2,3) repeated ad lib. for one block, and then threading units of (1,2,4) repeated ad lib. for the next block. This is repeated right across the rug. Fig. 254 shows a very simple example threaded (1,2,3)×2, (1,2,4)×2, (1,2,3)×2. Note the additional 1,2 added at the left after the final 1,2,3 block. This is important, as it causes both wefts to catch properly at the selvages. The weave plan at Fig. 254 (a) and the corresponding ex-

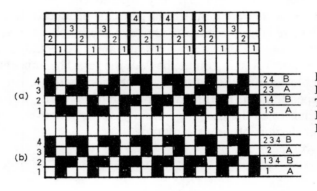

Fig. 254
Block Weave using
Three-End Block
Draft. Weave
Diagram

panded thread diagram at Fig. 255 show that the wefts are either passing over two ends and under one, or under two ends and over one. In the former case the weft will only show on the face of the rug, in the latter case it will only show on the reverse of the rug.

Looking at pick No. 1 (white weft in Fig. 255) it will be seen that in the two outer blocks, threaded on 1,2,3 it passes under two and over one end, so it will appear on the reverse. But in the central block, threaded on 1,2,4, it passes over two and under one end and thus it will appear on the face.

Pick No. 2 (black weft) does exactly the opposite, i.e., it passes over two and under one end in the two outer blocks and so appears on the face, but passes under two and over one end in the central block and so here appears on the reverse. When beaten, these two picks slide over each other, black sliding down in front of the white in the outer blocks and sliding down behind the white in the central block.

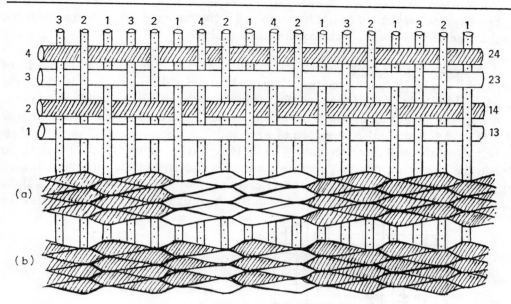

Fig. 255. Expanded and beaten views of Block Weave using three-end Block Draft

Pick 3 is similar to pick 1, but with the floats shifted one end to right or left. Pick 4 is similar to pick 2 with the floats similarly shifted. Picks 3 and 4 slide over each other in a similar way to picks 1 and 2. So when all four picks of the repeat are beaten down, there are two outer black blocks corresponding to the 1,2,3 threading and a central white block corresponding to the 1,2,4 threading, see beaten view at Fig. 255 (a). So simply by lifting (13,14,23,24) and weaving two colours pick-and-pick, the blocks appear automatically.

Note—That the floats of picks 2 and 3 are tied down by ends on shaft 1, and those of picks 1 and 4 by the ends on shaft 2. Hence their shift in position.

If the same colour all the way across, back and front of the rug, is wanted, then weave as for the blocks, but with two shuttles of the same colour. If only one shuttle is used the selvages will not catch properly.

To weave one colour all across on the front, but another colour all across on the back, lift as in Fig. 254 (b) and use two wefts pick-and-pick. So the sequence is:

$$1 \quad A,$$
$$134 \quad B,$$
$$2 \quad A,$$
$$234 \quad B.$$

The front of the rug will then be of colour A, floating over two ends, under one all the way across, and the back will be of colour B, floating under two ends, over one all the way across

These two weaves can of course be combined in the same rug. Only change from one to the other after the four pick sequence is completed.

If the foregoing has been understood it will be seen that any number of blocks of any width can be woven. As the threading predetermines the placing and width of the blocks, a large part of the designing of a rug in this technique is in the threading draft.

A warp setting of 4 e.p.i. is normal for this technique, so each repeat of the (1,2,3) or (1,2,4) threading unit takes up $\frac{3}{4}$ inch of warp width. If a sample rug 12 inches wide is to be woven, this will therefore have $\frac{4}{3} \times 12 = 16$ repeats of either (1,2,3) or (1,2,4). So design the blocks on squared paper, using an area sixteen squares wide, so that each square represents either a (1,2,3) or a (1,2,4) unit. See Fig. 256, which shows three possible arrangements. From this diagram the threading can be read directly as the

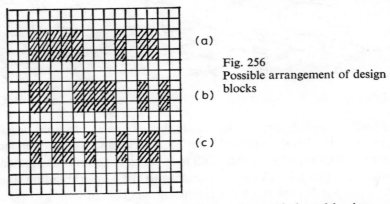

(a)

Fig. 256
Possible arrangement of design
blocks

(b)

(c)

shaded blocks represent the (1,2,4) threading units, and the white intervening areas represent the (1,2,3) threading units. Thus (a), starting from the right, reads

$$(1,2,3) \times 2$$
$$(1,2,4) \times 2$$
$$(1,2,3) \times 1$$
$$(1,2,4) \times 1$$
$$(1,2,3) \times 3$$
$$(1,2,4) \times 5$$
$$(1,2,3) \times 3$$

Note—That no plain weave is possible with this threading. Lifting 12 and 34, gives a two up, one down weave all across, similar to picks 2 and 3 in Fig. 255 (a).

VARIATIONS

(1) *Using Two Colours but Varying their Sequence*

So far only a pick-and-pick colour sequence has been considered. This gives blocks of solid colour. But consider the result of changing the sequence from (A,B,A,B) to

(A,B,B,B). This will change pick 3 in Fig. 256 from white to black. Now the picks which appear on the front of the central block in Fig. 255 are numbers 1 and 3. So this central block will now have alternately white and black picks forming its surface. These when beaten down will give warpway stripes of the two colours, see the beaten view in Fig. 255 (b). There will of course be similar stripes on the back of the two outer blocks. So simply by altering the colour sequence, a block of solid colour can be changed into an area of warpway stripes. Plate 96 shows the use of these stripes at either end of a block of solid colour. Plate 97 shows how they can be used within a block.

Note—Once the pick-and-pick weft sequence is broken, the selvage will not automatically weave correctly with each pick. So use a floating selvage, if any other sequence is employed.

(2) *Using Three or More Colours*

It is only one step from the above idea to using three colours in a sequence of (A,B,C,B). Pick 1 and 3 will now be of colour A and C alternately, so the central block in Fig. 255 will consist of warpway stripes of colour A and C, flanked as before by blocks of solid colour B. This provides a useful way of introducing variation into a block. If colour A and C are fairly close, then the occasional change from (A,B,A,B) to (A,B,C,B) will give slight striations in the colour of the block. These striations can of course be shifted to one side by using a sequence of (C,B,A,B), a further refinement.

A further possibility is a colour sequence of (A,B,C,D) which would convert each block into stripes of two colours, and suggests a different type of non-block design.

(3) *Varying Weft Thickness*

If both wefts are of the same thickness (which is the normal condition), they each tend to appear slightly as spots showing through the blocks of the other colour, i.e., in the central block of Fig. 255 which is white, there will be small spots of black showing through. This is only obvious when the colours are as different as black and white; with closer colours, the spots blend into the surrounding colour. They can always be obliterated with very heavy beating of the weft.

A feature can, however, be made of them by using wefts of different thickness. If in Fig. 255 a thick white and a thin black weft were used, then in a white block there would be no black spots, but in a black block there would be quite prominent white spots.

(4) *Altering Lifting Sequence*

The order of the lifts can be changed to (13,23,14,24). The weft does not beat down quite so well with this sequence. With a colour sequence of (A,A,B,B), blocks are produced but they are vague and less solid-looking than the blocks obtained with the normal lifting sequence. It has one advantage, in that, to make one colour show all across on back and front, only a single shuttle need be used, as it catches at both selvages (due to the alternation of shafts 1 and 2 in the lifts).

PRACTICAL DETAILS

The following warp formula is suitable, 6 e.p.i., alternately single and double in the heald, therefore 4 working e.p.i. 2-ply carpet wool used threefold is the correct weft thickness for this warp setting. Remember to add an extra 1,2 after the final 1,2,3 block, as mentioned above. Begin and finish the threading with a treble thickness warp end (i.e., three in a heald). If sleyed in an 8 reed, arrange the right selvage as in Fig. 257 (d) and finish at the left selvage in a similar manner.

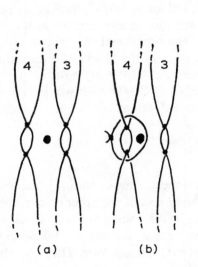

(a)   (b)

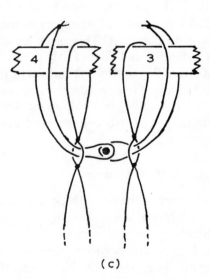

(c)

Fig. 257
(a–c) Methods of Shaft Switching

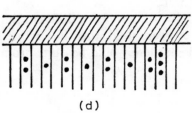

(d)

Only use a floating selvage if some other weft sequence than pick-and-pick is wanted. Begin the two wefts from opposite selvages, i.e.:

lift 13—throw weft A from right to left.

lift 14—throw weft B from left to right.

lift 23—throw weft A from left to right.

lift 24—throw weft B from right to left.

So after each repeat of the four lifts, the two shuttles are back at the sides they started from.

There is another way of making the two pick-and-pick wefts catch at both selvages. This is to start the threading at the right with 2,3 before the first 1,2,3 block, and to end at the left with an extra 1, after the final 1,2,3 block. The advantage of this method is that the face colour completely covers the reverse colour at both selvages, whereas with the normal method described above both colours are visible as they turn round the selvage threads.

If the threading units are taken as (2,3,1) and (2,4,1), not as (1,2,3) and (1,2,4), then this type of selvage occurs automatically, without adding extra ends.

If very long rugs in this technique are to be woven (i.e., over 12 feet long) it may be necessary to use two warp beams. This is because the ends threaded on shafts 3 and 4 tend to become slacker than those threaded on the front two shafts, due to the weave structure. So these two sets of ends are beamed separately.

DEVELOPMENTS OF THIS TECHNIQUE

(1) *Shaft-switching*

In this simplest of block weaves, it will be noticed that the only difference between the threading of the two blocks is the presence of an end on shaft 3 or 4. If these ends are mentally extracted from Fig. 255, it will be seen that plain weave on ends 1 and 2 is left, with two picks in each shed, one black and one white. In other words the function of the ends on shafts 3 and 4 is to separate the two picks in each shed and so allow the second to slide down in front or behind the first. But however they achieve the result, it is obvious that it is the ends on shafts 3 and 4 which control the weft's appearance either on the face or on the reverse of the rug.

So if some way could be found for, as it were, switching ends from shaft 3 to shaft 4, or vice versa, *during* the actual process of weaving a rug, then much freer designs than simple blocks could be woven. In fact, if the switching were simple enough, a completely free design could be woven.

There are several ways of doing this:

(a) Do not thread an end on shaft 3 or 4, but enter it between an empty heald on shaft 3 and an empty heald on shaft 4, see Fig. 257 (a). Then the end can be tied to one or other heald, as the design demands with a small loop of warp yarn. See Fig. 257 (b) where it has been tied to a heald on shaft 4. This is a rather primitive method, and is not suitable if many changes of many ends are required by the design.

(b) A slightly more sophisticated method is based on the floating selvage idea, see Fig. 257 (c). Loops of yarn threaded through the empty healds on shafts 3 and 4 surround the unthreaded warp end, and then go up to their respective shafts and are knotted. Now if the loop attached to shaft 4 is tightened (either with a slipknot or a button as suggested for the floating selvage) and the loop on shaft 3 allowed to hang loose, then the warp end will move as if actually threaded on the shaft 4. Similarly if the loop on shaft 3 is tightened and the loop on shaft 4 loosened, the end will move as if threaded on shaft 3. Though the preparation of loops takes time, this is a much easier method to operate, as all adjustments are made on top of the shaft, not amongst the healds at warp level, as in the first method.

The most economical use of methods (a) and (b) is in rugs designed specially for them. Such a design can be based on blocks, but may have variations in it resulting from shaft-switching. For instance, it only needs one switch to convert a block into two smaller ones, see Fig. 259 (a); two switches to convert a solid block into a hollow one, see Fig. 259 (b); and three switches to convert a block into an H-shape, see Fig. 259 (c). Such variations requiring only a little switching, rob a block design of its regularity, and so add much to its interest. If the design is planned carefully on paper beforehand, only those ends which are going to change shafts need be threaded in this special way. See Plate 98 for a rug with a few changes.

(c) A very simple addition to the loom makes the above method of shaft switching so easy that completely free designs can be woven with speed and accuracy. As will be seen, it is only possible on a loom in which the shafts are raised by cords, not on a jack loom in which they are pushed up from below.

Two strips of wood are needed as long as the shafts are wide. They should be about $\frac{1}{4}$-inch thick and about 3 to 4 inches wide. These are suspended above shafts 3 and 4 as shown in Fig. 258. A short length of cardboard tube is threaded on the cords which raise shaft 3 and one strip of wood (A) is passed between the cords above the tube, so that it lies above the shaft and parallel to it. A full-length tube is threaded similarly on the cords of shaft 4 and the other strip of wood (B) put above it. See Fig. 258, where the tubes are shown spotted.

The string loops controlling the shaft-switching are attached to these two strips of wood in the following way. Along the top edge of each strip, small nails are inserted every $\frac{3}{4}$ inch, and along the bottom edge, small screw eyes are similarly spaced, see Fig. 258. The spacing is related to the warp setting. Every third end of this particular weave can be switched and assuming the warp to be set at 4 working e.p.i., this means these ends are $\frac{3}{4}$-inch apart and hence the nails and screws are similarly spaced.

String loops are made of two sizes, short ones to be used between strip A and shaft 3 and long ones between strip B and shaft 4. Each has to be of such a size that when threaded through the screw eye, with its knotted end over the nail above (see Fig. 258),

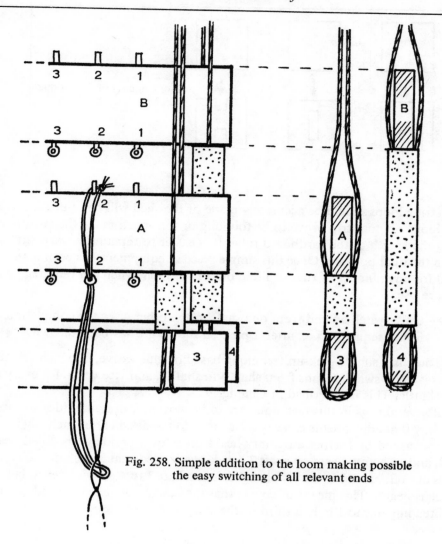

Fig. 258. Simple addition to the loom making possible
the easy switching of all relevant ends

its lower looped end just reaches the heald eye below. This is the tight position of the loop. To loosen a loop, just lift it off its nail; its knotted end prevents its slipping through the screw eye. Number each nail and screw eye similarly on both strips of wood, see Fig. 258. Then when a loop is *on* nail 6 on strip A it must be *off* nail 6 on strip B. Switching a shaft only entails lifting a loop off its nail on one strip and replacing the corresponding loop on its nail on the other strip, a procedure which takes a few seconds. It will be obvious that the two strips A and B are placed at different heights so that they are both within full view and easy reach of the weaver as he switches the shafts.

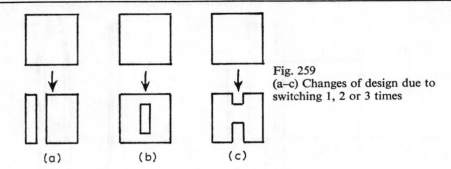

Fig. 259
(a–c) Changes of design due to switching 1, 2 or 3 times

(a) (b) (c)

The string loops should be accurately made or the shed will be of uneven depth. If all the loops on one strip prove to be too long or too short, make the adjustment by altering the length of the cardboard tube. It is easier to thread the warp with all the loops in the tight position. Once this simple piece of equipment has been made, it can be used for any number of rugs or lifted out of the loom when not required and kept for future use.

Note—Only switch an end from one shaft to the other after the completion of the lifting sequence, i.e., after a pick on the 24 lift has been thrown.

(d) There is a simple pick-up technique based on this weave, in which the pick-up stick, as it were, switches ends from shaft 3 to shaft 4, and vice versa, for every throw of the shuttle. This is described in Chapter 9.

(2) If several rugs in this technique are to be woven, it is a good idea to thread in such a way that adjustments can easily be made to the design after each rug is cut off. This is managed by leaving an empty heald on shaft 4 beside every filled heald on shaft 3, and an empty heald on shaft 3 beside every filled heald on shaft 4. Then when a rug is cut off, an end is simply changed from shaft 3 to 4, or vice versa, before the next rug is begun. This means of course that the design could be changed completely by rethreading at most only a third of the warp.

Other Weaves Using this Block Draft

It will be obvious that if shafts 3 and 4 are always lifted together, this threading draft can be treated as a straight draft on three shafts. So the weaves described for the latter in Chapter 7 can all be woven with this draft. Wherever a 3 occurs in the lifting sequence of these weaves, add a 4. So the lifts for the double-faced 2/1 twill weave in Fig. 208 change from (12, 1, 23, 2, 13, 3) to (12, 1, 234, 2, 134, 34). Another way is to tie shafts 3 and 4 together and lift exactly as for the three-shaft weaves.

B. Four-End Block Draft

This threading system is well known as it is the one used for Summer and Winter weave. The analysis of two Coptic double-faced fabrics from the fourth century A.D. shows that they could have been woven on such a threading. It is interesting that they were woven as weft-face fabrics, exactly as one of the rug techniques to be described.

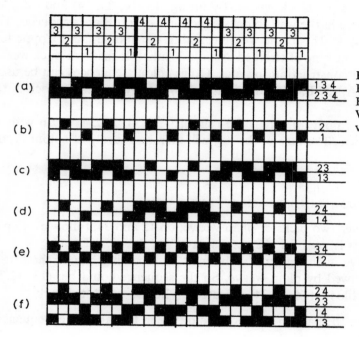

Fig. 260
Block Weave using
Four-End Block Draft.
Weave Diagram with
various weave plans

Fig. 260 shows at the top how the blocks are threaded. Two repeats of the four-end threading unit have been used in each block. It will be noticed that it is very similar to the three-end block draft. The addition of an extra 3 or 4 to each unit has two effects, (1) it makes plain weave possible and (2) it make the weft float over or under three ends, instead of two.

Below the threading draft is shown how warp and weft interlace with various lifts. In all of them it will be seen that the weft either passes over three and under one end, or under three and over one end. One of these interlacings can either go right across as at (a) and (b) or the interlacing can change from block to block as at (c) and (d).

Note—As with the previous weave, the floats forming the surface in each block can be placed in two positions. This is due to the two tie-down ends on shafts 1 and 2.

—That at the junction between two blocks the weft floats over only two ends or under two. This can be converted into a float of three ends by threading two ends on the first shaft at the beginning of each block, as was apparently done in one of the Coptic fabrics referred to above.

(i) BLOCK WEAVE NOT REQUIRING PLAIN WEAVE

Fig. 260 (f) shows this simple block weave. By lifting (13, 14, 23, 24) and using an (A,B,A,B) colour sequence in the weft, blocks of colours A and B are produced. The colours reverse on the back. This is the weave found in the double-faced Coptic textiles; it was also used in one type of checked Navajo blanket. It makes a thick weave, but it is not a very good construction for rugs. Other colour sequences can be used, e.g., (A,B,C,B) or (A,B,A,B,C,B,C,B); the first gives warpway stripes in block 2, the second weftway stripes.

To produce the same colour all across the rug, lift (1, 134, 2, 234) again with an (A,B,A,B) colour sequence. The face of the rug will then be entirely of colour A, the reverse of colour B.

(ii) BLOCK WEAVES REQUIRING PLAIN WEAVE

In all the following weaves two picks of plain weave, on 12 and 34, follow every pattern pick. A thinner weft is used for the plain weave, see Practical Details.

(a) The simplest weave in this group is obtained by repeating one of the lifts in Fig. 260 (c) or (d), followed by plain weave. So the sequence could be: (**13**, 12,34) repeated ad lib for one block, (**14**, 12,34) repeated ad lib for opposite block.

Note—That the lift for the pattern weft is in bold type in this and other sequences.

One of the blocks then appears as vertical ridges of floats which completely hide the plain weave and the other block as predominantly plain weave but with vertical rows of spots, see Plate 99 (top). So it is the difference in colour between the pattern weft and the plain weave weft that makes the two blocks more or less distinct from each other.

This is not a very satisfactory weave, all the pattern floats in a block are tied down under the same end which can lead to warp tension troubles. So it is better to use the two possible positions of floats for each block. Thus the sequence could be:

$$\left.\begin{array}{l} \textbf{(13,} 12,34) \times 4 \\ \textbf{(23,} 12,34) \times 4 \end{array}\right\} \text{Repeated ad lib for one block.}$$

$$\left.\begin{array}{l} \textbf{(14,} 12,34) \times 4 \\ \textbf{(24,} 12,34) \times 4 \end{array}\right\} \text{Repeated ad lib for the other block.}$$

There could, of course, be more or less than four repeats. As in the first weave above, this weave can be obtained all the way across the rug. If lifted (**1**, 12,34)×4;

(**2**, 12,34)×4, the pattern floats will appear all across the face of the rug. If lifted, (**134**, 12,34)×4; (**234**, 12,34)×4, the floats will appear all the way across the reverse of the rug.

By combining some of these lifts, a motif can be woven as in Plate 100. It also shows another possibility. At the junction between the two possible float positions within a block, the two picks of plain weave are distorted into a wavy line. If different colours, in this case white and black, are used for the plain weave in these positions, a feature can be made of the waviness of these lines. The plain weave picks to be differently coloured are underlined in the following sequence: **13**, 12,34; **13**, 12,34; **23**, 12,34; **23**, 12,34. (Note that the warp in this sample has been set too close and so the weft does not beat down completely and cover it.)

(b) A sequence of (**14**, 12,34, **13**, 12,34) repeated ad lib with two colours pick-and-pick for the pattern weft, gives two blocks each consisting of vertical ridges of floats of one colour, see Plate 99 (bottom). A sequence of (**24**, 12,34, **23**, 12,34) gives a similar weave, but the junction between blocks is a little different. To obtain one colour all across on the front and another on the back, lift (**1**, 12,34; **134**, 12,34) or (**2**, 12,34; **234**, 12,34). The crossbars in the Plate were woven thus.

(c) A slight variation is the sequence (**14**, 12,34, **23**, 12,34) repeat or (**24**, 12,34, **13**, 12,34) repeat, with a pick-and-pick pattern weft sequence.

Here the ridges of floats in one block are separated by spots of the colour from the opposite block, see Plate 101. For one colour all across on the front and another on the back, use the sequence (**1**, 12,34; **234**, 12,34) repeat, or (**2**, 12,34; **134**, 12,34) repeat. As the Plate shows, one of these sequences has been used at the top and bottom of the sample shown.

In both the above weaves, the surface of the rug on both sides is covered by floats. The colours of the blocks are changed simply by altering the weft sequence from (A,B,A,B) to (B,A,B,A).

(d) Probably the best block weave on this threading for rugs is the following: (**13**, 12,34, **23**, 12,34) repeated ad lib for one block; (**14**, 12,34, **24**, 12,34) repeated ad lib for the other block. It gives one block in which the pattern weft floats completely hide the plain weave and an alternating block predominantly plain weave but with spots of the pattern weft showing through in vertical rows. By using one colour for all the pattern picks, a solid block of floats is produced which alternates with a block of spots of the same colour.

But if two wefts of a different colour are used for the pattern picks, there are many more possibilities. Using these two colours alternately, their floats appear as warp-way stripes (just like pick-and-pick stripes in plain weave) within the block. See Plates 102 and 103, where the effect has been enhanced by the plain weave weft being the same colour (black in 102, white in 103) as one of the pattern wefts. Thus the black areas in the right-hand block in Plate 102 are made up partly of the black plain weave and partly of the spots of black pattern weft, the two combining visually into a single area. Note how in the alternating blocks there are corresponding warpway stripes of spots (these blocks appearing like the ghosts of the main blocks). Plate 104 shows a black and white rug in this technique.

Any of the other two-shuttle patterns described in Chapter 4, can be produced in the main blocks, i.e., cross stripes and spots, with a corresponding ghost of the pattern in the alternating blocks. This is a very firm weave and excellent for rugs; its only disadvantage is the number of plain weave picks, which make it much slower to weave than the three-end block draft weaves.

PRACTICAL DETAILS

A warp setting of 5 working e.p.i. is suitable. Of the two wefts, the plain weave weft should be 2-ply carpet wool used singly and the pattern wefts should be the same yarn used fourfold.

Always use a floating selvage. This is for the benefit of the pattern weft not the plain weave weft. Assuming there is an even number of working ends in the warp, take care at the beginning of the rug to start the plain weave weft from the correct side in relation to the shed used. This is the side at which the last *threaded* end (the one nearest the floating end) is raised. The shuttle is then inserted between this raised end and the floating end and it is withdrawn at the opposite side between the lowered end and the floating selvage. If the shuttle starts from the wrong side, the plain weave weft will weave over two, under two at both selvages. For weave (a), the block weave not needing plain weave, a setting of 6 working e.p.i. is probably better, with a weft of 2-ply carpet wool used three or fourfold.

C. Six-End Block Draft

This weave is a development of one of the double-faced three-shaft weaves described in Chapter 7.

The threading draft is shown in Fig. 261, where two repeats of the six-end unit are used in each block. Note how the ends on shafts 1 and 2 are regularly spaced across the threading. The draft can be lifted in two ways, either to give the same colour all across (and another colour all across on the back) or to give blocks of two colours.

Fig. 261 (a) shows the first possibility. Picks 1 and 2 alternately float over three ends, and weave with three ends, all the way across the face of the rug, picks 3 and 4 behave similarly on the back of the rug, floating under three ends, then weaving with three ends all the way across. With a colour sequence of (A,A,B,B) the rug will be colour A on the face and colour B on the reverse.

Fig. 261 (b) shows the lifts that give a block weave. Picks 1 and 2 float over three ends in Block 1 and under three ends in Block 2, therefore colour A will show on the front in Block 1 and on the back in Block 2. In picks 3 and 4, the opposite happens, so colour B shows on the back in Block 1, and on the front in Block 2.

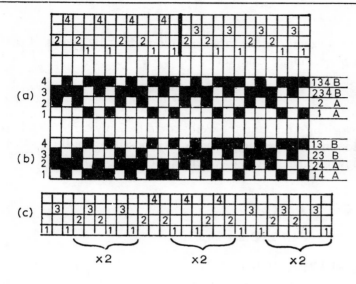

Fig. 261
Block Weave using Six-End Block Draft
(a) and (b) Weave Diagrams
(c) Method of joining threading blocks when $2\frac{1}{2}$ repeats of draft are used

So a colour sequence of (A,A,B,B) will give two blocks, each of a solid colour. But as was explained in the three-shaft version, any of the two-shuttle designs possible in weft-face plain weave can be woven in the surface floats of these blocks. So one or both blocks can have any of these two-shuttle designs in any combination. This gives great possibilities of design.

The three Plates hint at these. In Plate 105 blocks of pick-and-pick stripes and blocks of cross stripes alternate in chequer fashion, the colour sequence would be: (A,B,A,A)×4,(A,B,B,B)×4, repeat, for the first row with pick-and-pick blocks on the outside; and (A,A,A,B)×4, (B,B,A,B)×4, repeat, for the second row which has a single pick-and-pick block in the centre.

In Plate 106, the design has been limited to pick-and-pick stripes all across, but by using three colours a great deal of variety is introduced. Sometimes a colour appears all the way across, sometimes it is confined to one block.

In Plate 107, a block of solid colour alternates with blocks of two-shuttle designs. Three colours were used again.

The blocks in all these samples consisted of $2\frac{1}{2}$ repeats of the threading unit. This was done so that there were an odd number (five) of pick-and-pick stripes in each block and a motif could therefore be easily centred in the block. When the threading unit is split in this way, the sequence of ends on shafts 1 and 2 must not be broken between blocks; so the second block has to begin on 2,4,2 instead of 1,4,1. This is shown in Fig. 261 (c).

DEVELOPMENT

This weave can be developed exactly as the three-end block draft by means of shaft-switching. For the pick-up version see Chapter 9.

PRACTICAL DETAILS

The warp should have 5 working e.p.i., and the weft should be 2-ply carpet wool used two or threefold. Use a floating selvage. No plain weave is possible, but lifting 12 and 34 gives a two up, one down weave all the way across the rug.

FOUR-SHAFT BLOCK WEAVES

Part 2. Other Drafts

A. Draft Based on Single End Spot Draft

An interesting block weave can be based on the Single End Spot draft described in Chapter 7. As shown in Fig. 262, the first threading block is exactly as the Single End Spot draft and is repeated ad lib. There is then a 'linking' end on shaft 1 (encircled). The second threading block is threaded (3,4,3,1,3,2) repeated ad lib, followed by a 'linking' end on shaft 3 (encircled). Block 3 is exactly like Block 1, Block 4 is exactly like Block 2, etc. Each block has only two repeats of the threading in Fig. 262. It will be seen that the threading of Block 2 is of the same type as Block 1, except that here every other end is on shaft 3, not shaft 1.

The weave plans in Fig. 262 show that the weaves are a combination of plain weave

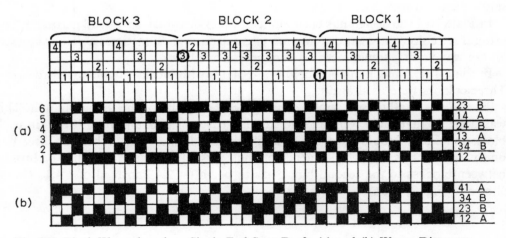

Fig. 262. Block Weave based on Single End Spot Draft. (a) and (b) Weave Diagrams

and floats over and under three ends. The latter floats more or less cover the portions in plain weave. So the surface of the rug is formed by these floats. Obviously a weft shows on the surface when floating over three ends and on the back when floating under three ends.

The blocks can be woven in various ways.

(i) Fig. 262 (a) shows the weave plan when the lifts are as for twill woven on opposites, see Chapter 7. If the colour sequence is (A,B,A,B,A,B) colour A will show on the face, in the central block (Block 2), and on the reverse in Blocks 1 and 3 (picks 1 and 5); and colour B will show on the face in Blocks 1 and 3 and on the reverse in Block 2 (picks 2 and 6).

But picks 3 and 4 are of a different type. Pick 3 gives floats all the way across on the reverse and pick 4 gives floats all the way across on the face of the rug. So colour A will appear only on the reverse on pick 3 and colour B will appear all the way across the face on pick 4.

This means that whereas Blocks 1 and 3 will show floats of colour B only (appearing in twill order), Block 2, though mainly of colour A, will have spots of colour B appearing on it. These spots join together to form a vertical stripe.

Alternatively the colours on pick 3 and 4 can be reversed, so that Block 2 is solid colour A and Blocks 1 and 3 though predominantly colour B will have spots of colour A. By combining these two colour sequences (A,B,A,B,A,B) and (A,B,B,A A,B), the blocks can be made more interesting. See Plate 108, where the alternative sequence has been twice used to give dark spots on the white blocks.

(ii) When lifted as for a 2/2 twill with a colour sequence of (A,B,B,A), see Fig. 262 (b), Blocks 1 and 3 are of colour B with thin warpway lines of colour A running down them, and Block 2 is of colour A with thin lines of colour B. See Plate 109.

A variation of this is to lift as for a broken twill with a colour sequence of (A,B,A,B). This gives a very similar result except that the thin line is more continuous and less like a succession of spots. Plate 110 shows this block woven with an (A,B,C,B) colour sequence.

(iii) If picks 1 and 2 of the twill woven on opposites are repeated up to four times, then picks 5 and 6 repeated similarly, a block with very interesting characteristics is produced. So the sequence is:

$$\left.\begin{array}{l}(12,34)\times 4 \\ (14,23)\times 4\end{array}\right\} \text{repeated ad lib}$$

The pick-and-pick sequence of colours A and B is maintained throughout. Plate 111 shows these blocks. This is the least firm of the weaves, which is why it is suggested that each pair of picks should only be repeated four times.

If a rug is woven using several of these different blocks, use the 2/2 twill weave as the ground weave. Always connect the ground weave with a block weave and vice

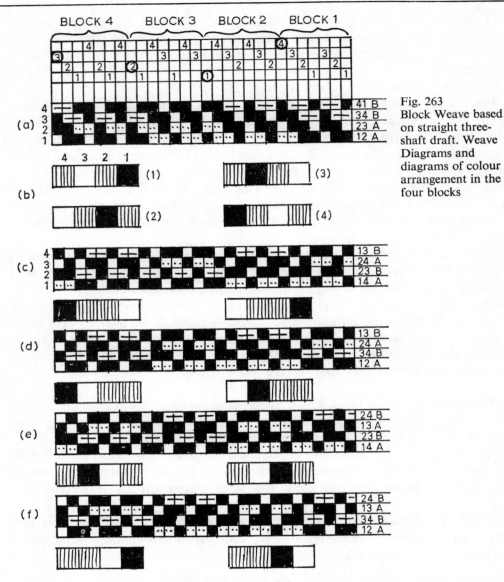

Fig. 263
Block Weave based
on straight three-
shaft draft. Weave
Diagrams and
diagrams of colour
arrangement in the
four blocks

versa in the way that least affects the lift sequences. For instance, to change from the
last weave to the ground weave, weave thus:

14, 23, 14, 23,　34, 41, 12, 23, 34, 41.

i.e., after the final 23 of the block weave, start the ground weave on the lift that
normally follows 23 in *its* sequence. This is not always simple to do.

RIDGES

As the threading stands, ridges all the way across the rug are not possible. If the positions of the ends on shafts 2 and 4 are reversed in Block 2 (so threading becomes 3,2,3,1,3,4) then lifting 1,2,3,4 will give a ridge, but this upsets the block weaves. With the threading in Fig. 262, lifting shaft 1 gives long floats in Block 2, and lifting shaft 2 gives long floats in Blocks 1 and 3 and these could possibly be worked into the block weaves.

PRACTICAL DETAILS

These are exactly as for the Single End Spot draft, i.e., a warp with 5 working e.p.i. and a weft of 2-ply carpet wool used twofold.

B. Draft Based on a Straight Three-Shaft Draft

This draft is based on a straight three-shaft threading. In each threading block, the draft is started on a different end so, as four shafts are being used, there are four threading blocks. As shown in Fig. 263, Block 1 is threaded (1,2,3) ad lib, followed by a 'linking' end on 4, Block 2 is threaded (2,3,4) ad lib, followed by a 'linking' end on 1, Block 3 is threaded (3,4,1) ad lib, followed by a 'linking' end on 2, Block 4 is threaded (4,1,2) ad lib, followed by a 'linking' end on 3. Only two repeats of the threading are shown in each block. (Note that if only one repeat of each block is threaded this becomes identical to the skip twill in Fig. 234 (c) in the last chapter.)

The special feature of this weave is that it not only gives blocks of two solid colours but a third block consisting of warpway stripes of these two colours. The relative position of these three areas can be changed at will, as the following details will show.

(i) WITH STRAIGHT 2/2 TWILL LIFTS

Fig. 263 (a) shows the weave plan when the lifts are (12,23,34,41).

> *Note*—That for all four picks the weft passes under two ends, over one for two adjacent blocks, then over two ends and under one for the next two blocks. It will appear on the face of the rug in the latter part and on the reverse of the rug in the former part. Thus pick 2 will appear on the face in Blocks 3 and 4, and on the reverse in Blocks 1 and 2.
> —That in each block, two of the picks (of the four pick repeat) appear on the surface and the other two on the back but which picks in the sequence do which varies from block to block. Thus, in Block 1, picks 3 and 4 come to surface, in Block 2, picks 1 and 4 come to the surface, in Block 3, picks 1 and 2 come to the surface, in Block 4, picks 2 and 3 come to the surface.

Now consider what happens if a colour sequence of (A,A,B,B) is used. Block 1 whose surface is formed by picks 3 and 4 will appear as solid colour B. Block 3 whose surface is formed by picks 1 and 2 will appear as solid colour A. But in Block 2 and Block 4, colours A and B will alternately come to the surface. When these are beaten down they will form warpway stripes, exactly like pick-and-pick stripes in plain weave.

To make this easier to understand, the weft floats (which form the surface of the rug) have been marked in Fig. 263 (a). Dotted lines represent the floats of colour A, and straight lines those of colour B. If these floats alone are concentrated upon (being the only visible elements in the rug as woven) the make-up of the different blocks will become clear.

This arrangement of the colour areas can be put diagrammatically as in Fig. 263 (b) (1), assuming colour A to be white, and colour B to be black. The colour areas can be shifted relative to the threading blocks simply by beginning the colour sequence (of A,A,B,B) on different lifts of the lifting sequence.

Thus if it is begun on 23, instead of 12, the colour areas all shift to the left, see Fig. 263 (b) (2). So in this case the sequence becomes:

12, 23, 34, 41
B   A   A   B

If the sequence is started on 34, the areas shift to the positions shown in (3), and if started on 41, they shift to the positions shown in (4).

Note—That in all these positions, the relation between the solid black, solid white and striped areas is constant, i.e., a striped area always separates two solid areas.

This weave can be produced equally well by lifting as for a 2/2 broken twill and using the two colours pick-and-pick.

(ii) The possibilities of this weave are still further increased by introducing the two lifts, 13 and 24. As will be seen from picks 3 and 4 in Fig. 263 (c), which use these two lifts, the interlacing still consists partly of over two, under one and partly under two, over one, but here the interlacing changes from one variety to the other at *every* junction between blocks.

The four weaves in Fig. 263 (c)–(f) consist of two of the twill lifts (either 12 and 34 or 23 and 41) plus the two lifts 13 and 24. By altering these and the colour sequences, eight more possible arrangements of the colour areas are possible. In all cases the colour sequence is pick-and-pick, either (A,B,A,B) or (B,A,B,A).

Looking at Fig. 263 (c) (where the weft floats have been drawn in as before) it will be seen that Block 1 will be all white, Block 4 all black, and Blocks 2 and 3 will both be striped. This has been shown in the left-hand diagram below the weave plan. The right-hand diagram shows the exact opposite, i.e., what happens if the colour sequence is changed to (B,A,B,A).

Similarly Fig. 263 (d), (e) and (f) show all the other possible arrangements of the colour areas.

Note—That in this weave the solid black and white areas are adjacent and that the striped area spans two adjacent blocks.

—That weave (c) is identical with weave (e) except for the reversed order of picks 3 and 4. The same applies to weaves (d) and (f),

—That the colour diagrams below each weave plan represent on the left the result when (A,B,A,B) is the colour sequence in the weft, and on the right when (B,A,B,A) is the colour sequence.

The above two weaves show the very many possibilities offered by this threading. Any of the colour arrangements, of which there are twelve, can be used separately or in combination. Plate 112 shows a rug with five threading blocks (the fifth being the same as the first) which uses only one of the 2/2 twill sequences throughout. Plate 113 shows a sample in which a design block has been built up of three different colour arrangements. Note how the stripes move slightly to one side when the colour arrangement is changed. Plate 114 shows a rug threaded with three complete repeats of the threading. Each time a design block appears, the relative positions of the solid and striped areas is changed.

Shaft Switching

The shaft switching principle can be applied to this block weave. Looking at Fig. 263, it will be seen that there is only a slight difference between the threadings of any two adjacent blocks. Thus Block 1 is threaded 1,2,3,1,2,3,1,2,3, and Block 2 is threaded 2,3,4,2,3,4,2,3,4. So it is only the ends on shafts 1 and 4 which differentiate the two blocks; the ends on shafts 2 and 3 are exactly the same for both blocks.

So ends have to be switched from shaft 1 to 4 to make an area, threaded as in Block 1, weave as if threaded as in Block 2. Similarly they have to be switched from shaft 4 to 1 to have the reverse effect. The same can be done with any two adjacent blocks.

Between Blocks 2 and 3, the switch is from shaft 1 to 2, or vice versa.

Between Blocks 3 and 4, the switch is from shaft 2 to 3, or vice versa.

Between Blocks 4 and 1, the switch is from shaft 3 to 4, or vice versa.

This enormously enlarges the scope of an already versatile block weave.

Plate 115 shows a rug using this technique, as does the colour frontispiece.

(iii) This draft can be thought of as a skip twill, as well as one based on a straight three-shaft draft. As a skip twill based on a four-shaft straight draft, it excludes every fourth end within a block but it excludes the fifth end at the junction between blocks. The following weaves are based on its identity as a skip twill.

(*a*) With a pick-and-pick weft sequence and lifted as a twill woven on opposites, the weave gives a twill line. It is so flat as to be nearly a horizontal stripe, and is of little use. But if this twill is reversed at frequent intervals, it gives an interesting block weave. The sequence can be:

12, 34, 14, 23, 34, 12, 14, 23,   Repeat
A B A B A B A B

From Fig. 264 it will be seen that the weft floats under Blocks 1 and 2 are predominantly colour A and those under Blocks 3 and 4 are predominantly colour B. Hence the appearance of the blocks, neither of which is a solid colour.

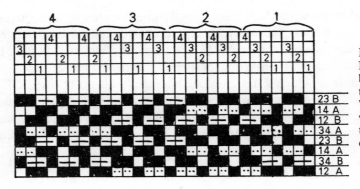

Fig. 264
Block Weave based on straight three-shaft draft. Weave plan when woven as twill 'on opposites'

(*b*) With straight 2/2 twill lifts and a colour sequence of (A,A,B) or (A,B,C) flat twill lines are obtained.

(*c*) Some weaves are achieved also by using the three pairs of opposites repeated several times, i.e. (13, 24) repeated ad lib; (12, 34) repeated ad lib; (23, 14) repeated ad lib, but they are not very sound structurally.

PRACTICAL DETAILS

A warp formula of 6 e.p.i. threaded alternately single and double in the heald, therefor 4 working e.p.i. is suitable, with a weft of 2-ply carpet wool used threefold or some yarn of equivalent thickness. Always use a floating selvage and arrange the selvage ends as for the first block weave described in this chapter.

C. Traditional M's and O's Draft

This interesting draft gives two things. Two blocks of different colours but identical weave and also two blocks of differing weaves which are shown up by the use of two or three colours in the weft

As Fig. 265 shows, the threading of one block is (1,2,3,4) repeat, and of the alternating block (1,3,2,4) repeat. So it is a reduction of the normal M's and O's draft.

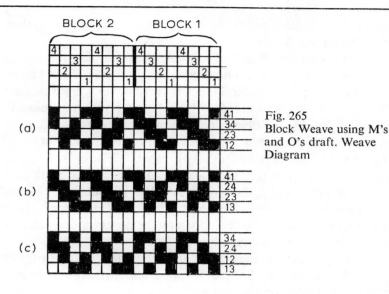

Fig. 265
Block Weave using M's
and O's draft. Weave
Diagram

(i) The classic way of weaving this threading is by lifting 13, 24 for one design block and 12, 34 for the other design block. This gives a design of plain weave and hopsack in checks. It will be understood that it is not very suitable for a weft-face weave, as a weft suitable for the plain weave areas will be too thin for the hopsack areas. But Plate 116 shows that it is just feasible. The pick-and-pick areas represent the blocks lifted on 13 and 24 and the intervening grey stripe the block lifted on 12 and 34. The characteristic distortion of the weft line is seen on either side of the grey stripe.

(ii) Fig. 265 (a) shows what happens if a 2/2 twill lifting is used. In the block threaded (1,2,3,4) there is naturally a normal twill, but in the other block, the weft is weaving plain weave and hopsack on alternate picks. This will give a slight difference of texture between the two blocks if just one weft is used, but if two wefts are used in an (A,A,B) colour sequence, the difference will be more apparent.

Plate 117 shows a sample woven in this way; the typical oblique lines of two colours are seen in the (1,2,3,4) block and an irregular spotted design in the (1,3,2,4) block. In the latter block, it is mainly the picks that have a hopsack interlacing that form the surface, i.e., virtually only every other pick is seen.

Fig. 265 (b), shows how the weaves in the two blocks can be reversed by lifting (13, 23, 24, 41). This is seen in the upper half of the plate, where the lifting sequence has been reversed to change the direction of the oblique lines.

There are many possibilities here, for in the (1,2,3,4) block, any of the many colour and weave effects described for 2/2 twill can be used and something quite different is bound to appear in the (1,3,2,4) block. This is hinted at in the photograph, where the (A,A,B) colour sequence has been changed to (A,B,B) in the middle of each design block. Luckily the two weaves beat down to the same extent, but any unevenness at the fell of the rug can be counteracted by reversing the weave areas (i.e., changing from weave (a) to weave (b) in Fig. 265).

(iii) Fig. 265 (c) shows the details of a block weave on this threading using two colours, pick-and-pick. The areas do not appear as solid colours, but as in Plate 118, where it is seen that in the white central block each white float is surrounded by a thin line of black, rather like the appearance of pebbles set on edge in cement. The same applies to the black blocks, the black floats being surrounded by white lines.

An interesting feature of this block weave is that the colours do not reverse on the back of the rug, a white block on the front is also a white block on the back. Examination of the weave plan explains this, see Fig. 265 (c). The surface of Block 2 is formed by the weft floats of pick 1 and 3, therefore it is colour A. But these two wefts float to an equal extent on the back of this block. So the back is also colour A. Colour B only weaves plain in Block 2 so is practically hidden by the floats on front and back; it only shows as the thin outlines mentioned above.

If the two colours were closer than black and white, this outlining effect would be less obvious and the blocks could appear as solid but variegated colours.

The variations described for the three-end block draft also apply to this block weave, thus a block can be converted from solid colour to stripes by changing the colour sequence from (A,B,A,B) to (A,B,B,B). This has been hinted at in Plate 118 where in three places spots appear due to a colour sequence change such as the above. Also three or four colours can be used.

Development. Shaft Switching

Again like the three-end block draft, this weave can be developed to give the possibility of free design, either using the construction in Fig. 265 (a) and (b) or in Fig. 265 (c).

It will be noticed from the threading that the only difference between the two blocks is the placing of the ends on shafts 2 and 3. In Block 1 they are in the normal sequence, in Block 2 in a reversed sequence, so some way has to be found of altering their order at will. The method used is a further development of the shaft-switching principle already described. It is a little more cumbersome, but feasible.

No ends are threaded on shafts 2 and 3, but the two ends which should be so threaded

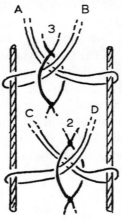

Fig. 266
Block Weave using M's and
O's draft. Shaft switching

are drawn in on either side of an empty heald on shaft 2 and an empty heald on shaft 3. See Fig. 266 which in a very diagrammatic way shows only the eyes of these two empty healds. Two string loops go through each eye, one encircling the right-hand end, one the left-hand end. These strings run up to their respective shafts and are knotted above them. The two on shaft 3 have been labelled A and B, the two on shaft 2 C and D.

Now if B is tightened and A is loosened, the left-hand end will move with shaft 3 and if C is tightened and D loosened, the right-hand end will move with shaft 2. Thus the ends will move as if they were threaded (1,2,3,4) as in Block 1.

But if B is loose, and A tight, and if C is loose and D is tight, the ends will become attached to the opposite shafts, and they will move as if the threading were (1,3,2,4) as in Block 2.

To avoid confusion use one colour yarn for the loops of B and C (which are always tightened together), and another colour for loops A and D. So at a changeover the two yarns of one colour are loosened and the two yarns of the other colour are tightened.

This manœuvre means that twice as much shaft switching has to be done, than was necessary with the three-end block draft, to change the threading. So designs will have to be carefully worked out to extract the maximum effect from the minimum of shaft switching.

For this particular weave the threading could be extended a little, thus (1,2,1,4,3,4) for one block and (1,3,1,4,2,4) for the other block. The floats will then be over three ends instead of two and they will beat down more easily, obscuring the plain weave to a greater extent. The first weave involving twill areas will not be possible with this extended threading.

PRACTICAL DETAILS

A warp of 4 working e.p.i. is suitable, with a weft of 2-ply carpet wool used three or fourfold.

2. SIX-SHAFT BLOCK WEAVES

Block weaves on six shafts are of two types, those which are further developments of the two-tie unit drafts and those which are based on three-shaft drafts.

Part 1. Six-Shaft Developments of Two-Tie Unit Drafts

A. Development of Three-End Block Draft

The three-end block draft described earlier can be extended onto any number of shafts. On four shafts and threaded in units of (1,2,3) and (1,2,4), two blocks were obtained or one block and a background. Each additional shaft used, means an additional block in the design, whose appearance is controllable independently of the other blocks. So with five shafts there are three blocks and with six shafts there are four blocks. Fig. 267 (a) and (b) show two of the many possible ways the threading units can be arranged. Only one repeat of each unit is shown but there could be any number of repeats. In Fig. 267 (a), a unit threaded (1,2,3) alternates with units on (1,2,4), (1,2,5) and (1,2,6). This will give the possibility of three separately controllable blocks on a background, as at Fig. 268 (a). Fig. 267 (b) is a pointed draft variation and can lead to interesting blocks of complex but symmetrical shape, as at Fig. 268 (b).

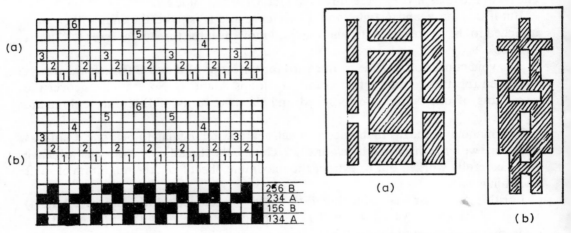

Fig. 267. (a) and (b) Two possible six-shaft developments of Block Weave using Three-End Block Draft

Fig. 268. (a) and (b) Types of design resulting from the drafts in Fig. 267

Two wefts are used pick-and-pick, exactly as in the four shaft version, but as there are four lifts for every possible combination of blocks, the lifts are numerous.

WORKING OUT THE LIFTS

Beneath Fig. 267 (b) is shown the weave plan when (134, 156, 234, 256), are the lifts. This brings colour A to the surface where the warp is threaded on (125) and (126) and colour B to the surface where it is threaded (1,2,3) and (1,2,4). So in the first lift, (134), shafts 5 and 6, which control the blocks where the weft of that pick is wanted on the surface, are not lifted. In the second lift, (156), they are lifted. The third and fourth lift are exactly the same as the first two but substituting 2 for 1, thus (234) and (256).

Similarly if the blocks controlled by shafts 3, 5 and 6 were wanted on the surface then the first lift would be (14) and the second would be (1356). The third and fourth would be (24) and (2356).

So the rule is that the first lift is 1 plus the shafts controlling the blocks *not required* on the surface, and the second lift is 1 plus the shafts controlling the blocks *required* on the surface (i.e., all the block-controlling shafts not lifted for the first pick). The third and fourth lifts are the same as the first and second, but with 2 instead of 1.

SPECIAL PEDAL TIE-UP

It will be obvious from this that, with a complex design, more lifts are wanted than there are pedals available to control them. So it is best to use a direct pedal tie-up, i.e., let each pedal control the lifting of only one shaft and by pressing a combination of pedals (and using both feet) all the lifts can be made.

A suggested tie-up for the design at Fig. 268 (b) is shown in Fig. 269. The right foot

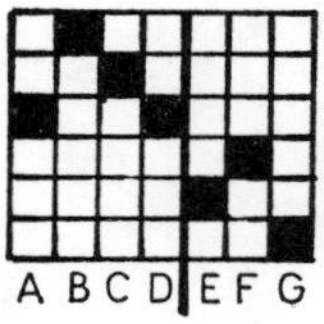

Fig. 269
Pedal tie-up for
weaving design in
Fig. 268 (b)

A B C D E F G

controls the lifting of shafts 1, 2 and 3, the left foot of shafts 4, 5 and 6. So the four lifts for the first part of the design, starting at the bottom in Fig. 268 (b), will be obtained thus:

Lift	....	Left Foot	....	Right Foot
1	....	—	....	G
13456	....	B+C+D	....	F+G
2	....	—	....	E
23456	....	B+C+D	....	E+F

For the next part, the two blocks at the foot of the motif, they will be obtained thus:

Lift	....	Left Foot	....	Right Foot
1346	....	A+B	....	F+G
15	....	C	....	G
2346	....	A+B	....	E+F
25	....	C	....	E

The tie-up at Fig. 269 will give all the lifts needed for the six-shaft version of this block weave, but if more than six shafts are used, a tie-up will have to be designed to suit the various lifts wanted, assuming that every possible lift is not wanted.

USING A DOBBY

A dobby loom can be used in a special way to produce all the possible lifts in this weave. Normally a dobby only gives a repeating design, there being as many lags as picks in the repeat. But in this method a non-repeating design of any size can be woven with a small number of lags.

The loom needs a little adapting. In front of the dobby-controlled shafts, hang two

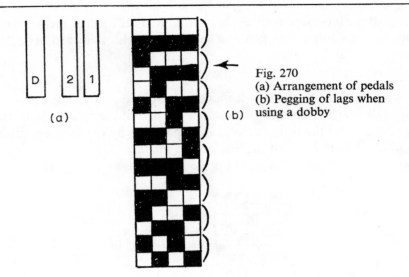

Fig. 270
(a) Arrangement of pedals
(b) Pegging of lags when
using a dobby

(a)

(b)

shafts on pulleys or a roller, so that when one is lowered the other is automatically raised. Attach two pedals to control these, putting them to the right of the dobby pedal, see Fig. 270 (a). Pedal 1 lowers shaft 1 and therefore raises shaft 2. Pedal 2 lowers 2 and therefore raises 1. Pedal 2 is also attached by a cord to the reversing lever of the dobby mechanism. So pressing pedal 2 also reverses the direction in which the chain of lags moves.

The warp is threaded normally. The two specially hung shafts count as shafts 1 and 2 and the dobby shafts behind are numbered from 3 upwards. So only the ends that control the blocks are on the dobby shafts. The other two-thirds of the warp ends are threaded on the two special front shafts.

The lags are pegged as in Fig. 270 (b). Each adjacent pair of lags (bracketed) controls one possible combination of blocks.

The sequence of lifting may seem complex but is quite easy to master as each foot stays down for two picks. Use the left foot for the dobby pedal, and the right foot for pedals 1 and 2. This means that the weaver must work seated.

⎧ Press dobby pedal+pedal 1—throw weft A.
⎪ Keep dobby pedal down, and press pedal 2—throw weft B.
⎨ Keep pedal 2 down, release dobby pedal and press again—throw weft A.
⎩ Keep dobby pedal down, and press pedal 1—throw weft B.

Keep pedal 1 down, release dobby pedal and press again—throw weft A.
This is the beginning of the sequence again.

Because of the way pedal 2 is connected to the reversing gear of the dobby mechanism, the chain of lags does not move continuously in one direction in the normal manner. It moves backwards one lag, forwards one lag, repeatedly presenting first one, then the other of an adjacent pair to the needles. Thus, as long as the above sequence is repeated, one combination of blocks will be woven. When the design dictates another combination, the lags can be moved round (by repeatedly pressing the dobby pedal alone, but of course throwing no weft) until the correct pair of lags is in the correct position in relation to the needles.

The shortest route to the pair of lags wanted may mean moving the lags in the reverse direction (i.e., press pedal 2, while repeatedly pressing the dobby pedal). A plan, showing the relative position of each pair of lags and what combination of blocks they give, should be hung on the loom and then the weaver can easily find his way about.

If the second pair of lags (arrowed in Fig. 270 (b)) are controlling the shafts, then the four lifts will be:

$$\left.\begin{array}{l} 2+456 \\ 1+456 \\ 1+3 \\ 2+3 \end{array}\right\} \text{Repeated ad lib}$$

(Remember that pedal 1 *raises* shaft 2 and vice versa.)

This gives a slightly different order to the four lifts from the normal, but the weave is practically identical.

The method has only been described briefly as not many weavers possess dobby looms. Those who try it will find that small refinements are necessary, e.g., a counterweight to make the reversing gear return to its normal position when pedal 2 is released. But once the system is working, it gives complete freedom of design with no repeats; and if four dobby shafts are used, as described here, only sixteen lags are needed to give all possible block combinations.

A really complex design with, say, eight controllable blocks, and therefore eight dobby shafts, will still need only relatively few lags. So using a dobby in this way makes it feasible to weave rugs with intricate designs, which would be quite impossible on a normal loom, due to the multiplicity of the required lifts.

B. Development of Four-End Block Draft

This draft can be extended in exactly the same way as described above. Again, each additional shaft gives another controllable block. Fig. 271 shows a possible threading on six shafts, giving four blocks. Plain weave will be obtained by lifting 12, and 3456.

The lifts for the floating pattern wefts will be of the same type as used above; i.e. 1 or 2 plus a selection of the other four shafts, depending on which blocks the weft is required to show in. Fig. 271 (a) shows two such lifts which will make colour A come to the surface in the areas threaded on (1,2,1,4) and (1,2,1,6). Fig. 271 (b) shows the lifts which will make colour A appear in the opposite areas. From this, the principle controlling the lifts will be understood.

All the four weaves described in the section on four-end block draft can be used.

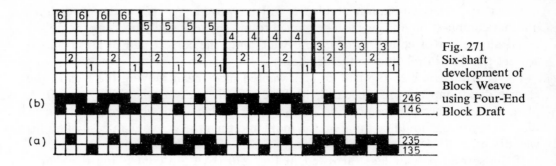

(b)

(a)

Fig. 271
Six-shaft
development of
Block Weave
using Four-End
Block Draft

C. Development of Six-End Block Draft

In exactly the same way six-end block draft can be extended to five or six shafts, see Fig. 272. Each extra shaft used gives another controllable block.

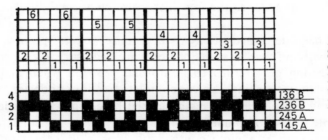

Fig. 272
Six-shaft
development of
Block Weave
using Six-End
Block Draft

The lifts to bring various combinations of blocks to the surface are the same as those described in detail for three-end block draft, except that their order is slightly different. In Fig. 272 are shown the lifts which will bring colour A to the surface in Blocks 1 and 4 (controlled by shafts 3 and 6) and colour B to the surface in Blocks 2 and 3 (controlled by shafts 4 and 5).

> *Note*—That in picks 1 and 2, shafts 1 and 2 are lifted in turn, plus those shafts which control the blocks where weft A is *not* required to show, i.e., 4 and 5. In picks 3 and 4, shafts 2 and 1 are lifted in turn, plus those shafts which control the blocks where weft B is *not* required to show, i.e., 3 and 6. So whichever of the block-controlling shafts are lifted for picks 1 and 2, it is the remaining ones which are lifted for picks 3 and 4. So another sequence could be (13, 23, 2456, 1456).

Part 2. Six-Shaft Block Weaves Based on Three-Shaft Weaves

Most of the weaves needing only three shafts can be converted into block weaves by threading some sections of the warp on the front three shafts and the intervening sections on the back three shafts, as shown in Fig. 273.

A. Block Weave Based on Double-Faced 2/1 Twill

The ends threaded on the front three shafts and those threaded on the back three shafts can obviously work independently of each other. Those threaded on (1,2,3) can be made to weave a double-faced twill exactly as in Fig. 208 (in the section on three-shaft weaves). In this, the sequence of:

$$12, 1, 23, 2, 13, 3$$
$$A \quad B \quad A \quad B \quad A \quad B$$

meant that colour B showed on the face and colour A on the reverse.

The exactly comparable weave on the back three shafts would be:

$$45, 4, 56, 5, 46, 6$$
$$A \quad B \quad A \quad B \quad A \quad B$$

where colour B again shows on the face. Now if these two weaves are combined, the lifts are:

$$1245, 14, 2356, 25, 1346, 36$$
$$A \quad B \quad A \quad B \quad A \quad B$$

and colour B will be on the face right across the rug and colour A on the reverse right across the rug. But they could be combined in such a way that the first lift of the front shafts' sequence and the second of the back shafts' sequence were used together, and then the second of the front and third of the back sequence used together, and so on, i.e., $\frac{12+4, \; 1+56,}{A \qquad B}$ etc. In this case colour B will be on the face in the areas threaded (1,2,3) and on the reverse in the areas threaded (4,5,6) and colour A will appear in the opposite areas. In other words a block weave will be produced, with each pick weaving as a 1/2 twill in one block and as a 2/1 twill in the next block.

In fact, in order to make the weaves on the two threadings join properly at the junction between blocks, a slightly different sequence has to be used, thus:

$$124, 146, 235, 245, 136, 356$$
$$A \quad B \quad A \quad B \quad A \quad B$$

but the principle is exactly as explained above. The weave is shown in Fig. 273 (a). Plate 119 shows a rug woven in this technique. Note the twill lines at the ends of the blocks. These are produced by using a pick-and-pick colour sequence for the weft coming to the surface at that point. Thus (A,B,C,B) will give twill lines of colour A and C in one block and solid colour B in the next block. Other weft sequences will give cross stripes in the blocks.

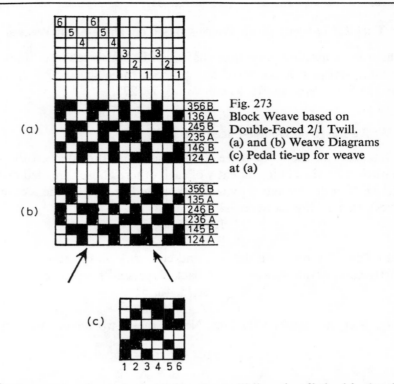

Fig. 273
Block Weave based on
Double-Faced 2/1 Twill.
(a) and (b) Weave Diagrams
(c) Pedal tie-up for weave
at (a)

The lifting sequence given above makes the twill lines in all the blocks slope up to the left. The lifting sequence at Fig. 273 (b) reverses the twill lines in the areas threaded on (4,5,6), see the arrows. If only one colour were used with this lifting sequence, the blocks would still appear to a slight degree, as the light would be reflected differently from the twill lines in adjacent blocks.

PRACTICAL DETAILS

A warp formula of 6 e.p.i., alternately single and double in the heald, therefore 4 working e.p.i. is suitable, with a weft consisting of 2-ply carpet wool used two or threefold.

If the pedals are tied up as in Fig. 273 (c) then the pedal sequence will be 1,6,2,5,3,4. This is the best way to arrange the tie-up, so that the feet are used alternately in some easily remembered pattern.

B. Block Weave Based on Three-Shaft Krokbragd

In the section on three-shaft Krokbragd it was noticed how different was the effect on the back and front of this weave. By expanding the threading onto six shafts, these two effects can be produced side by side on the front of the rug, as blocks. The threading is a pointed draft on the front three shafts for one block and a similar draft on the back three shafts for the other block, see Fig. 274.

The lifts shown in Fig. 274 (a) will give the tightly-woven 'right' side in the area threaded on the back three shafts (Block 2) and the loosely woven 'wrong' side in the area threaded on the front three (Block 1). The lifts shown in Fig. 274 (b) will reverse these effects.

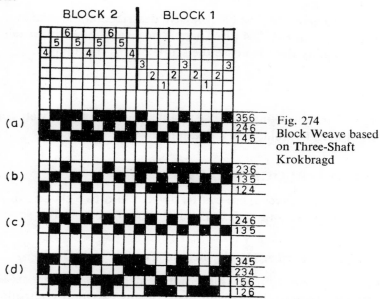

Fig. 274
Block Weave based
on Three-Shaft
Krokbragd

As in three-shaft Krokbragd, either of these lifting sequences is repeated over and over again, and the design results from the order in which one, two or three wefts are used. Note that in both sequences, the second pick is in plain weave right across. This pick will be hidden as it crosses a block of floats, i.e., Block 1 in Fig. 274 (a) and Block 2 in Fig. 274 (b); but it will contribute importantly to the design in the alternate blocks, i.e., Block 2 in Fig. 274 (a), and Block 1 in Fig. 274 (b). As picks 1 and 3 appear equally in both blocks, it is to this second pick that is due the chief difference in design between the two blocks. In other words, if one special colour is reserved for this pick, this colour will be very apparent in one block, but quite absent in the next.

A colour sequence of (A,B,A), will give warpway stripes of the two colours in Block 2 in Fig. 274 (a), but floats of colour A only in Block 1. See top row of blocks in Plate 120, where white is colour A. A colour sequence of (A,B,B) will give vertical lines of A on a ground of B in Block 2, and warpway stripes of the two colours in Block 1. See second row of blocks in Plate 120, in which the sequence has occasionally been changed to (A,A,B) to give the crossbars to the thin vertical lines. There are many other possibilities which the weaver can discover for himself, as suggested by the lower two rows of blocks in Plate 120.

Note—That in this sample the lifting sequence changes at the beginning of each new row of blocks. So in the top row, the extreme right block is an area of floats. in the second row this block is closely woven.

Plain weave on 135 and 246, see Fig. 264(c), can be used at the beginning and ending of the rug. A few picks of it can also be used as a bridge between the lifting sequences for the blocks.

This threading also gives the first block weave described in the section on four-end block draft. It is shown in Fig. 264 (d). There is no special merit in weaving it on six shafts, but its availability does increase the scope of this threading.

PRACTICAL DETAILS

A warp setting of 5 or 6 working e.p.i. is suitable, together with a weft consisting of 2-ply carpet wool used twofold. Use a floating selvage.

3. EIGHT-SHAFT BLOCK WEAVES

As with six shaft block weaves these can be divided into two classes, those that are further developments of two-tie unit drafts and those based on four shaft weaves.

Part 1. Further Development of Two-Tie Unit Drafts

The three weaves described under this heading in the section on six-shaft block weaves can obviously be extended to eight shafts, giving two more controllable blocks, making a total of six blocks. As there is no difference in principle, only of complexity, there is no need to deal with these in detail.

A. Double Two-Tie Unit Draft

A special case is the double two-tie unit draft, already mentioned in the last chapter, which has many possibilities. Details are shown in Fig. 275. Note that there are two ends on shaft 3 and on shaft 8 where the threading reverses. The threading could obviously be extended to more shafts. It is specially adapted to give a block weave in which the blocks are triangular or diamond-shaped. Any of the weaves described for four-end block draft can be used. Two will be described here.

(i) BLOCK WEAVE NOT REQUIRING PLAIN WEAVE

Fig. 275 (a) shows the lifts and weave plan to give an inverted triangle of colour B on a background of colour A. If on the 10th and last pick the lifts are reversed, a diamond will be woven.

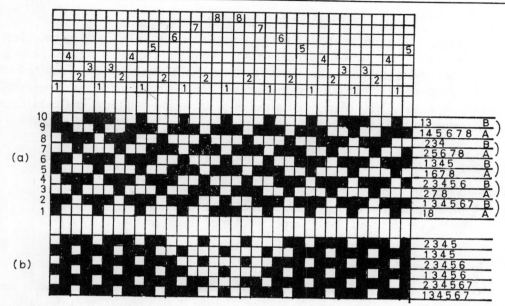

Fig. 275. Eight-shaft development of Double Two-Tie Unit Draft. Weave Diagrams with two weave plans

This will be a diamond with a smooth edge, as the top diamond in Plate 121. The next diamond down has a toothed edge and this is produced by weaving the picks in the order 2,1,4,3,6,5,8,7,10,9, and then reversing the order. The colour sequence is always pick-and-pick.

To make the hollow diamonds, change picks 5 to 10 to the following: 167, 13458, 256, 23478, 145, 13678.

Note—That when this is done with a smooth edged diamond, the contained diamond has a toothed edge (third diamond down from top in Plate 121); and when it is done with a tooth edged diamond, the contained diamond has a smooth edge (fourth diamond down).

As the bottom diamond shows, the angle of the side can be steepened by weaving the picks in this sort of order, 1,2,3,4; 1,2,3,4,5,6; 3,4,5,6,7,8; 5,6,7,8,9,10; etc. Plate 122 shows the reverse of this weave, which is rather unexpected. Colour Plate II shows a full-size rug, in which the draft has been varied to alter the spacing of the motifs.

Practical Details

Warp—5 working e.p.i.

Weft—2-ply carpet wool used threefold.

(ii) BLOCK WEAVE REQUIRING PLAIN WEAVE

The threading is the same as above. One pattern pick is always followed by two plain weave picks on 12, and 345678. Fig. 275 (b) shows a few of the many possible pattern lifts. Shafts 1 and 2 are raised alternately for these lifts, plus a selection of shafts 3 to 8. Plate 123 shows a small piece of this weave. The design is made up of areas of floats of the pattern weft (dark) and areas of plain weave (white) with the pattern weft showing through as spots.

Practical Details

Warp—5 working e.p.i.
Weft—for the plain weave, 2-ply carpet wool used singly.
       for the pattern weft, 2-ply carpet wool used three- or fourfold.

B. Three-Colour Block Weave

In a true triple cloth, three plain weave cloths with their own warps and wefts are woven simultaneously, one above the other, and the design results from the various ways these three cloths interpenetrate and come to the surface. There is always a third cloth in the pocket between the upper and lower cloths. But though in this present weave there are three wefts and they give three blocks of solid colour, the structure is far simpler than in a true triple cloth.

     There are basically two warps, see Fig. 276. One is threaded on shafts 1 and 2, it is

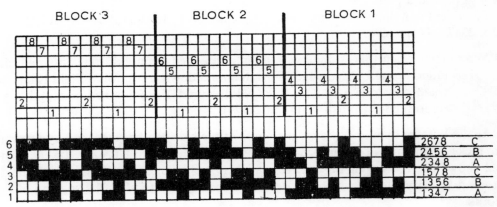

Fig. 276. Three-colour Block Weave. Weave Diagram

evenly spaced across the rug, and is the warp that comes to the surface to tie down the weft floats. Hence the inclusion of this draft amongst the two-tie unit drafts. The other warp is threaded on an extra two shafts for each additional block, i.e., on shafts

3 and 4, 5 and 6, and 7 and 8 in Fig. 276. This warp always lies in the centre of the rug. Of the three wefts being used, one passes over this central warp and appears on the face of the rug, another passes under it and appears on the back of the rug as in normal two-tie unit weaves, but the third weft which at this point does not come to either surface, interlaces in plain weave fashion with the central warp. See cross-sections in Fig. 277.

In Fig. 276, two repeats of each threading block have been shown. The six picks of one of the many possible lifting sequences is shown. Note that for picks 1, 2 and 3, shaft 1 is up and shaft 2 is down the whole time. The three lifts differ from each other only in the movements of shafts 3 to 8, (those controlling the central warp). It is the movement of these shafts which determines whether a pick will show on the front, on the back or be hidden in the centre of the rug. Fig. 277 (a) shows a cross-section of these three picks. For simplicity's sake, only one repeat of each threading block is shown. The circles represent the warp ends, each numbered according to the shaft it is threaded on. From this it will be seen that pick 1 will show on the back in Block 1, on the front in Block 2 but will be invisible in Block 3, as it is weaving with the central warp. The other two picks take a similar course.

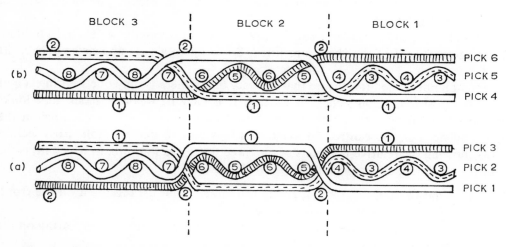

Fig. 277. Three-colour Block Weave. Cross-section of picks 1–6 in Fig. 276

For picks 4, 5 and 6, shaft 2 is up and shaft 1 is down the whole time. Again it is only the shafts controlling the central warp whose movement varies from pick to pick. Fig. 277 (b) shows the cross-section of these three picks. Pick 4 follows a similar course to pick 1, pick 5 to pick 2, and pick 6 to pick 3, but note that where each pick weaves with the central warp, it is now in the opposite plain weave shed.

So in any block of the design, one colour will show on the front and one on the back. These two wefts weave with the same warp, that which is threaded on shafts 1 and 2, and they appear as floats over five ends. Between these two wefts and completely hidden by them, the third weft lies, interlacing in plain weave order with the central warp. This central layer of cloth, besides dealing with the third colour, adds firmness to the weave, which otherwise consists of long floats. It is the manner in which this central warp is raised and lowered that controls the appearance of the colours in the blocks. There are many possible arrangements of the three colours, each of which requires six lifts, and it is better to understand the principle, than blindly to follow a printed list.

Looking at Fig. 276, the central warp for Block 1 is on shafts 3 and 4, that for Block 2 on 5 and 6, and that for Block 3 on 7 and 8. So these are the block controlling shafts.

For picks 1, 2, and 3, shaft 1 is always up.

For picks 4, 5, and 6, shaft 2 is always up.

For picks 1, 2, and 3, the rules for the block-controlling shafts are these:

In the block where the weft is to show on the front, do not raise the shafts.

In the block where the weft is to show on the back, raise both shafts.

In the block where the weft is to be hidden, raise the odd-numbered of the two shafts.

i.e., if weft is to show on front in Block 2, on back in Block 1, and be hidden in Block 3, then lift 1347.

For picks 4, 5, and 6, the same rules apply except that where the weft is to be hidden, the even-numbered of the shafts are lifted. So to make a weft appear as above, lift 2348.

When planning the lifts, ensure that in every block there is only one weft in each of the three positions (front, back or centre). It is easy to weave a block that looks correct on the front, but which will be found to have two wefts appearing on the back and none in the centre. To avoid this it is best to make simple cross-section plans showing the relative positions of the three wefts, see Fig. 278, in which (a) is the plan for the block arrangements shown in Fig. 276.

> *Note*—That (b) and (c), though giving the same colour arrangement on the front, differ from each other on the back.
>
> —that (d) shows one colour only on the front, the other two appearing on the back.
>
> —That (e) shows one colour appearing over two adjacent blocks.

As an example, the six lifts to give the weft arrangement in Fig. 278 (e) are:

$$A, 134$$
$$B, 13578$$
$$C, 1567$$
$$A, 234$$
$$B, 24678$$
$$C, 2568$$

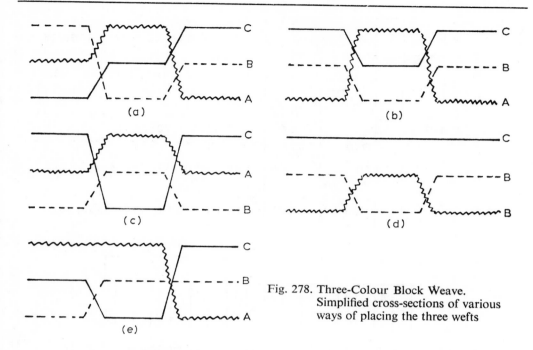

Fig. 278. Three-Colour Block Weave.
Simplified cross-sections of various
ways of placing the three wefts

Apart from different block arrangements, a great deal can be done by varying the colour sequences in a single block arrangement, i.e., not always using the sequence (A,B,C).

From the above it will be understood that the back and front of a rug in this technique may bear little relationship to each other, also that two rugs with the same design on the front may differ from each other on the back. Plate 124 shows a sample woven with a pointed draft, the threading blocks shown in Fig. 276 being used in the order, 1,2,3,2,1. Fig. 279 (a) shows how this was woven, giving the lifts on the right and the colour sequences on the left.

Note—That at the points marked with an arrow the lift sequence stays the same but the colour sequence changes.

No plain weave is possible with this threading but a one up, two down weave is produced by lifting 12, and 345678, and this can be used for starting and finishing the rug. The pick-up variation of this weave will be found in Chapter 9.

PRACTICAL DETAILS

Warp—9 e.p.i., single through a heald, therefore 9 working e.p.i.
Weft—2-ply carpet wool used three-fold.

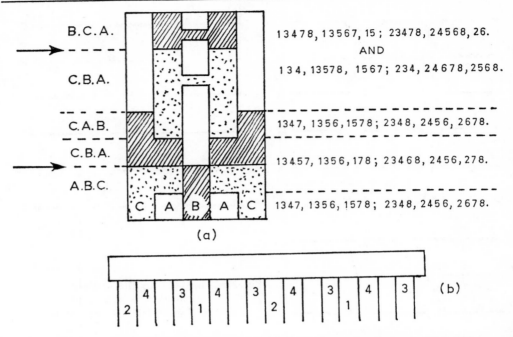

B.C.A.   13478, 13567, 15; 23478, 24568, 26.

AND

134, 13578, 1567; 234, 24678, 2568.

C.B.A.

C.A.B.   1347, 1356, 1578; 2348, 2456, 2678.

C.B.A.   13457, 1356, 178; 23468, 2456, 278.

A.B.C.   1347, 1356, 1578; 2348, 2456, 2678.

(a)

(b)

Fig. 279. Three-colour Block Weave. (a) Method of weaving design in Plate 123

The warp is sleyed in a 12 dents per inch reed, as shown in Fig. 279 (b), where each number refers to the shaft on which is threaded the end in that dent.

Note—That the ends on the block-controlling shafts (3 to 8) are threaded in alternate dents, i.e., at 6 e.p.i., and that the ends on shafts 1 and 2 are threaded in every fourth dent, i.e., at 3 e.p.i. So both the central and tie-down warps are spaced evenly and at their own particular set.

If the threading begins and finishes with an end on shaft 1 or 2 (as in Fig. 276), then all three wefts will catch at the selvage. It is best to start these three wefts from the same side, say, the right. Then, in the first three picks, they all move across to the left selvage, in the second three picks, they move back to the right. This gives a firm selvage showing all three colours in succession.

As the sample in Plate 124 shows, the warp is slightly visible. By beating very hard and using a finer weft it can be hidden. But the texture is a good one as described and there is no need to worry about the visible warp unless it interferes with the design.

Six-Shaft Derivative

It will be obvious from the above description that by using only six shafts a two-colour block weave could be produced. There would still be three wefts in use all the time, but only two of them would show on the front or the back at any point. The cross-section could be as in Fig. 280 (a) in which case the two colours in the design

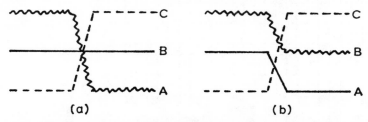

(a)   (b)

Fig. 280. Six-shaft version of Three-colour Block Weave. (a) and (b)
Cross-sections showing ways of placing the three wefts

(A and C) will be reversed on the back and the third colour (B) will lie hidden in the centre throughout the rug. This latter weft will only contribute to the structure, not to the colour, of the rug. Or the cross-section could be as in Fig. 280 (b), in which case colour C appears on both back and front of the rug, but colour A and B only appear on one side.

Four-Shaft Derivative

Similarly if only four shafts are used, a double-faced weave can be produced. It will still use three wefts, one for the front, one for the back and one hidden in the centre. No blocks can be woven.

Part 2. Development of Four-Shaft Weaves

All these weaves are produced on some threading which for one block is on the front four shafts and for the next block on the back four, as in Fig. 281.

A. Block Weave Based on Double-Faced 3/1 Twill

This is the eight shaft version of the weave described in the section on four-shaft twills. There it was seen (Fig. 228) that alternate picks floated over three ends under one, and under three ends over one, the former appearing on the surface all across the rug, the latter on the back.

When the weave is extended to eight shafts as in Fig. 281, the pick that is floating over three ends in one threading block floats under three ends in the next threading block. So it appears alternately on the front and the back of the rug, see pick number 1 in Fig. 281 (a). The next pick will take the opposite type of course, see pick number 2 in Fig. 281 (a). As the colour sequence is (A,B,A,B) this leads to blocks of the two colours, corresponding to the areas threaded on the front four and on the back four shafts.

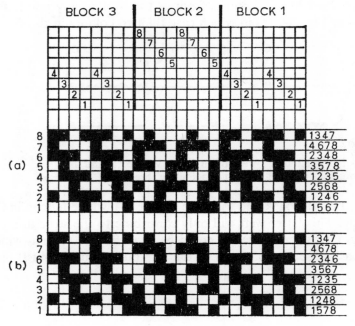

Fig. 281
Block Weave based on
Double-faced 3/1 Twill.
Weave Diagram with
two weave plans

The complete weave plan with lifts is shown at Fig. 281 (a).

As there are eight different lifts it will need eight pedals. As with the four-shaft version, the weave has a strongly twilled surface, and it will be noticed that the twill in Blocks 1 and 3 (threaded on the front four shafts) is the opposite direction to that in Block 2 (threaded on the back four shafts). It will also be noticed that the junction between one block and the next is 'clean cutting', i.e., every weft that passes over the last end in one block, passes under the first end in the next block, and vice versa. This gives a very sharp colour change at the junction between blocks.

Fig. 281 (b) shows the weave plan and lifts for the variation of this technique in which the twill lines in all the blocks are in the same direction. This has a clean-cut junction between Blocks 1 and 2, but not between Blocks 2 and 3.

Note—That only picks 1, 2, 5 and 6 are on different lifts, so it only needs the addition of four pedals to make both types possible in one rug.

Both of these weaves can be converted into broken twill by weaving the picks in the following sequence: 1,2,3,4,7,8,5,6. This gives an extremely tough but flexible rug; the same interlacement will be met in the chapter on pick-up weaves.

Note—That on this threading the block weave based on three-shaft Krokbragd can be woven by lifting. (1568, 2457, 3678) for one block, and (1245, 1368, 2347) for the other block.

PRACTICAL DETAILS

A warp set at 6 working e.p.i. is suitable, together with a weft consisting of 2-ply carpet wool used threefold. Use a floating selvage.

B. Block Weave Based on Four-Shaft Krokbragd

Normal four-shaft Krokbragd was not mentioned among the four-shaft weaves; because the floats on the back of the rug are so long, they make it impractical. But if it is used as a block weave, so that on each side of the rug blocks of close weave alternate with blocks of floats, it becomes feasible.

The threading, see Fig. 282, is a pointed draft on the front four shafts for Block 1, and a similar draft on the back four shafts for Block 2.

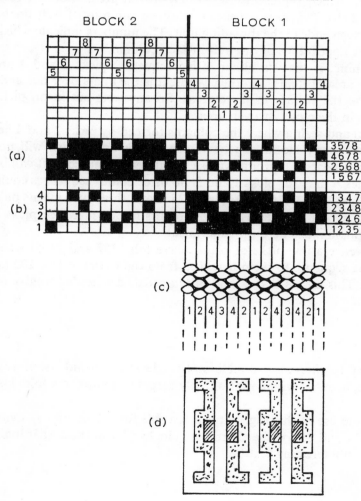

Fig. 282
Block Weave based
on Four-Shaft
Krokbragd.
(a) and (b) Weave
Diagrams
(c) Relationship of
picks to surface of
Block 1
(d) Possible motif
using three colours

As the weave plan at (a) shows, the shafts in the first threading block are lifted one at a time in broken twill order; and those in the second threading block are lifted three at a time in broken twill order. So each pick will float on the face in Block 1, and on the reverse in Block 2. Where it floats on the reverse it appears as a close weave on the surface. So Block 2 will be a closely woven area and Block 1 an area of floats.

The exact opposite is produced if the lifts in (b) are used, so this gives the alternating design block.

In the closely woven area, the four picks of the lifting sequence beat down to make what looks like two picks of plain weave. It is simple from the weave plan to work out which portions of this area are contributed by which picks. This is shown diagrammatically in Fig. 282 (c), which represents the closely-woven area, Block 1, seen directly above in Fig. 282 (b). This area consists of thirteen columns of weft floats, corresponding to the thirteen ends in the threading unit. The numbers indicate which pick is responsible for the appearance of the weft in each column.

Now the interesting thing, is that (in either lifting sequence) picks 2 and 4 are completely hidden in the area of floats. In other words, it is the floats over five ends (picks 1 and 3) that form the surface in these areas. So any weft put in on picks 2 and 4 will only appear in the closely-woven areas.

Looking at Fig. 282 (c) and seeing where the columns formed by picks 2 and 4 lie, it will be understood that many motifs can be woven in this area which will not appear at all in the areas of floats. To produce these, a different coloured weft will be used for pick 2 and/or pick 4 than for picks 1 and 3. So three colour sequences could be used, (A,B,A,B), (A,B,A,A) or (A,A,A,B). Plate 125 shows three such motifs on a full-size rug. Fig. 282 (d) shows another using two colours in one place for picks 2 and 4. There are many possibilities here for experiment.

It is a good idea to weave a few picks of plain weave (on 1357 and 2468) when changing from one lifting sequence to the other, (i.e., from the weave in Fig. 282 (a) to that in Fig. 282 (b)). This means that a total of ten pedals are needed to give all the possible lifts.

PRACTICAL DETAILS

A warp formula of 6 e.p.i., alternately double and single in the heald therefore 4 working e.p.i. is suitable, together with a weft of 2-ply carpet wool used twofold. Use a floating selvage.

The long floats limit the use of this rug, but it is feasible for a bedroom or living room rug. The rug is thick and heavy; the alternating blocks of floats and what looks like plain weave give it an interesting texture.

C. Block Weave Based on Plain Weave Double Cloth

HISTORY

Plain weave double cloth has a considerable history, both as the means of creating a strong double-thickness fabric and as the means of weaving intricate decorative fabrics. Early double cloths are known from Peru, Persia, India and from primitive peoples all over the world. In Europe its use as a floor covering dates from around 1735, when factories in Kidderminster started to produce carpets in this technique on hand looms. These carpets were woven on a 'barrel loom'. A drum above the loom had wooden pins or metal staples set in it, and as it turned it regulated the lifting of the shafts. A new barrel had to be made for each carpet design. Later the jacquard apparatus was used.

The carpets were called Kidderminster or Scotch, or two-ply carpets. The American name was ingrain. The surface was made up predominantly of the weft. Another type which was predominantly warp-face was called British or Damask Venetian. A later development added a 'stuffer' warp which bound the two cloths together but appeared on neither surface. Later still, a three-ply or triple ingrain carpet was woven, which was a true triple cloth, i.e., with three independent warps and wefts. Some of William Morris's carpet designs were produced in the latter technique. Denmark is one of the few European countries still producing double cloth carpets commercially. In the Kidderminster carpets, both warp and weft formed the surface of the rug, but it is a weft-face double cloth which is to be described here.

INTRODUCTION

In plain weave double cloth, two plain weave cloths are woven simultaneously, one above the other. The upper cloth has its own warp and weft, which interlace with each other, but which do not interlace with the elements of the lower cloth, and vice versa. So there is a space or pocket between the two cloths.

The structure can best be understood by looking at an expanded thread diagram, see Fig. 283. Cover the left half of the diagram, i.e., the part to the left of the arrows marked X. And look at the lower half of the diagram now left exposed, i.e., the part below the arrows marked Y. Here four ends are seen interlacing with four picks.

The ends threaded on shafts 1 and 3 (see top of diagram), are shaded, as also are picks 1 and 3. It will be seen that these shaded ends and picks interlace to form a plain weave cloth. This lies on top of a similar plain weave cloth formed by the interlacing of the unshaded ends and picks. For simplicity these will now be called black and white.

Note—There is no connection between these two cloths. The upper one could be lifted off to expose the lower one. In other words there is a pocket between the two cloths. This is indicated by a wavy line in the longitudinal section shown at the right.

So ends on shafts 1 and 3 and picks 1 and 3 form the upper cloth and ends on shafts 2 and 4 and picks 2 and 4 form the lower cloth.

Consulting the shafts above, it will be seen that the upper cloth is woven simply by lifting shafts 1 and 3 alternately. But the lifts for the lower cloth are a little more complex. Consider pick 2. This passes under both black ends (on shafts 1 and 3) and under one of the white ends on shaft 4. So the lift is 134. Similarly the lift for pick 4 is 123. In other words, for the picks of the lower cloth, all the ends of the upper cloth, i.e. the black ones, have to be lifted, plus alternate ends of the lower cloth.

Thus the lifting and colour sequence becomes

1, 134, 3, 123

A B A B

Now if this weave were continued without variation, the result would merely be two pieces of cloth on top of the other, perhaps joined at the selvages if the two wefts had been locked around each other. But if the position of the two cloths were reversed (so that what was the upper cloth now appears on the back, and vice versa), the pocket would be sealed off in a horizontal line at this point.

This is what happens after pick 4 in the right-hand exposed half of the diagram. The upper cloth formed of black warp and weft sinks to the back, and the lower cloth (white) rises to the top. This is seen most dramatically in the longitudinal section at the right. Note how the pocket is completely sealed off at the point where the warp ends change positions. In fact the black and white cloths pass right through each other at this point.

The lifts for picks 5 to 8, can be found by looking at the shafts above. The white cloth, now the upper one, is woven by lifting shafts 4 and 2 alternately. The black cloth, now the lower one, is woven by lifting both white ends plus one of the black ends, so the lift for pick 5 is 124, and for pick 7, is 234. So the sequence becomes

124, 4, 234, 2

A B A B

Thus on four shafts it is possible to weave plain weave double cloth and by varying the lifts to change the relative positions of the two cloths. This latter manoeuvre results in a horizontal, weftway, interchange of the two layers. So the visual result will be weftway stripes of black and white cloth, each stripe being a flattened tube with the opposite colour forming its rear wall.

To produce a vertical, warpway interchange of the two layers, i.e., to give the possibility of black and white checks or blocks, the threading must be extended onto eight shafts. This is shown in the left half of Fig. 283, which up to now has been covered to avoid confusion. The ends in this half are threaded on shafts 5 to 8. Look-

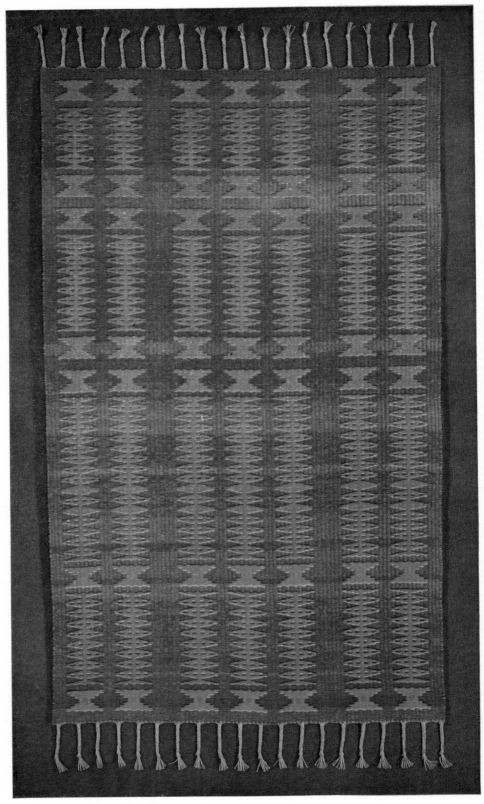

II. Weft-face rug in wool on linen warp, using a development of the Double Two-tie Unit Draft, see page 341

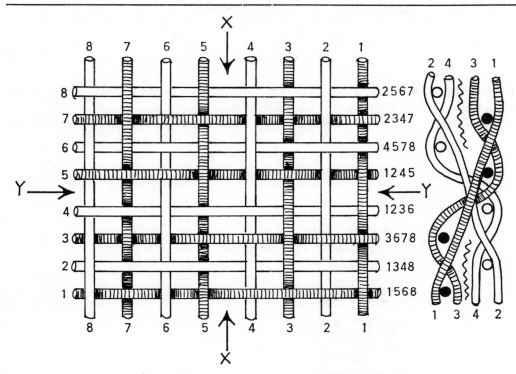

Fig. 283. Expanded view of Plain Weave Double Cloth

ing at the lower half, i.e., picks 1 to 4, it will be seen that the black cloth which was on the front when weaving with ends 1 to 4, is now at the back, and the white cloth which was at the back is now on the front. In other words, the four picks of weft change their relative positions as they pass from interlacing with the ends on the front four shafts to interlacing with the ends on the back four shafts (i.e., as they pass the arrow marked X), in exactly the same way as the four warp ends interchanged between picks 4 and 5. So the longitudinal section, at the right, which shows the warp interchange, could also serve as the diagram of weft interchange if turned through a right angle. Thus between the fourth and fifth end, this weft interchange seals off the pocket between the cloths in a vertical direction.

Consulting the shafts above, it will be seen that the lifts for picks 1 to 4, are

· 568, 8, 678, 6

A B A B

Looking upward, it will be seen that, as on the right-hand side, after pick 4 the two cloths have changed position. The black is now on the front, the white on the back. The lifts for picks 5 to 8 are

5, 578, 7, 567

A B A B

So combining the lifts worked out for the front four and the back four shafts, the sequence for the lower half of the diagram is

1568, 1348, 3678, 1236
A   B   A   B

If this is repeated, it will give a black cloth on the front in all areas threaded 1 to 4 and a white cloth in front on all areas threaded 5 to 8.

For the upper half of the diagram, where the colours are reversed, the sequence is

1245, 4578, 2347, 2567
A   B   A   B

The weave is shown in diagrammatic form in Fig. 284.

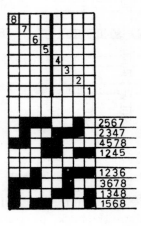

Fig. 284
Weave Diagram for Plain
Weave Double Cloth in
Fig. 283

WEFT-FACE PLAIN WEAVE DOUBLE CLOTH

In the above description, it was assumed that the two cloths were woven so that the warp and weft of both showed equally, i.e., so that two 50/50 plain weave cloths were produced, one with a black warp and a black weft, and the other with a white warp and white weft. These two colours alternated in both the warping and picking order. This is the type of double cloth used in the earliest Kidderminster carpets and in some modern decorative forms of the weave.

The situation is a little different if both upper and lower cloths are woven as weft-face fabrics, i.e., if the warp setting and weft count are such that the weft completely hides the warp. There is no longer any need for the warp to be of two colours as it contributes nothing to the surface of either cloth. The surface of both cloths is entirely made up of the weft. So the structure at any point is like two weft-face rugs lying one over the other.

(i) WOVEN ON FOUR SHAFTS

If woven on four shafts, i.e., like the right-hand half of Fig. 283, the two cloths can be interchanged as described above, by changing the lifting sequence from:

$$1, 134, 3, 123 \quad \text{to} \quad 124, 4, 234, 2$$
$$\text{A} \quad \text{B} \quad \text{A} \quad \text{B} \qquad \text{A} \quad \text{B} \quad \text{A} \quad \text{B}$$

Colour A will be on the surface in the first sequence and colour B in the second sequence. But the cloths (or, more accurately, the warps) can be interchanged, and yet the same colour can remain on the surface, simply by altering the colour sequence to B,A,B,A, for the second lifting sequence. Conversely the colour can be changed without interchanging the warps, simply by reversing the colour sequence at any point in either of the lifting sequences.

So it is a characteristic of weft-face double cloth, that an interchange of warps does not necessarily mean a change of colour, and vice versa. Thus a rug could be woven, all colour A on the front and colour B on the back, with occasional warp interchanges to give stability to the structure. Or a rug striped on the front and back could be woven, the front and back stripes being completely independent of each other, and also independent of the warp interchanges. These warp interchanges will appear as weftway depressions running across the rug. Between each warp interchange there is a pocket between the upper and lower cloths and this can be padded out with fleece or short ends of wool if so desired, to make a ridge across the rug.

Practical Details

To produce a double cloth rug of satisfactory weight, two thin rugs have to be woven one above the other. So if each rug has a warp setting of 4, 5 or 6 working e.p.i., the combined setting is 8, 10 or 12 working e.p.i. A suitable weft would be 2-ply carpet wool used double or single. The pockets in the structure of the rug are sealed at each point of warp interchange, but they are open at each selvage unless steps are taken to seal them here too. This can be done with a floating selvage round which passes the weft of both upper and lower rugs.

A rug of this type has not very much to commend it.

Many other double-faced weaves have already been described on three to six shafts, which are far quicker to weave. The only distinguishing feature here is the ability to form ridges, by filling the pockets. For these reasons it was not described among the four-shaft weaves.

(ii) WOVEN ON EIGHT SHAFTS

(*a*) *Blocks*

But when the weave is extended onto eight shafts giving a block weave there are more interesting results. The warp is threaded in groups of (1,2,3,4) and (5,6,7,8), but a slightly different interlacement is used than that explained in Fig. 283. Now, in Fig. 283, the black and white ends alternate in the warp. This means that the black weft has to weave with odd-numbered ends (black) whether it is forming the upper or lower cloth, see picks 1, 3, 5 and 7. Similarly the white weft has to weave with even-numbered ends (white).

But in a weft-face plain weave double cloth where the warp colour is immaterial, a weft can weave with odd-numbered ends when it is forming the upper cloth and on even-numbered ends when it is forming the lower cloth. This would imply that the weft of the upper cloth in two adjacent blocks would be weaving on even-numbered ends and that of the lower cloth on odd-numbered ends, or vice versa. This leads to one of the advantages of this interlacement, that one pick of appropriate plain weave can effectively seal off the pocket. For example, if the weft of the upper cloth in both blocks is weaving on even-numbered ends as in Fig. 285 (b), then one pick with the lift 1357, will seal the pocket and tie the two cloths together. The other advantage is that the join between adjacent blocks is cleaner. This is shown in Fig. 285 (a) and (b) where at the junction between threading blocks a filled square always comes up against an empty one.

The weave plan in Fig. 285 (a) shows four picks that will give a block weave in which both upper cloths are woven on odd-numbered ends (i.e., those threaded on shafts 1, 3, 5, and 7) so one pick of plain weave on 2468, will seal the pocket in both

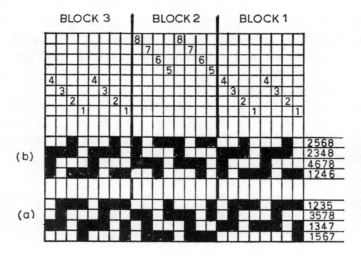

Fig. 285
Block Weave based on Weft-face Plain Weave Double Cloth. Weave Diagram with two weave plans

threading blocks. The colour sequence is (A,B,A,B). Fig. 285 (b) shows the weave plan which reverses the relative position of the warp ends, those weaving lower cloths in 285 (a) weave upper cloths in 285 (b) and vice versa. So changing from weave (a) to (b) also seals the pocket between cloths.

Fig. 286 shows a convenient pedal tie-up with two plain weave pedals, A and B, in the centre and the double cloth pedals arranged so that right and left feet work alternately.

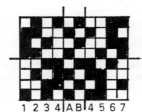

Fig. 286
Block Weave based on
Weft-face Plain Weave
Double Cloth. Convenient
pedal tie-up

1 2 3 4 |A B| 4 5 6 7

For weave (a) the pedals are pressed in the order 1, 4, 2, 5 and for weave (b) the pedals are pressed in the order 3, 6, 4, 7.

Design blocks of any width can be threaded, the smallest of course being of only four ends. In the warp direction it is wise to seal the pocket between cloths every few inches, either by changing the weave from (a) to (b) and back again or by putting in a plain weave pick (with a thinner weft). Otherwise the rug may not lie flat.

The obvious effects the technique gives are warpway stripes and alternating checks. These are not very interesting if both are woven in solid colours, as the texture of the weave is very fine (due to the close warp set of each cloth). So it is better to use blended colours in the weft or more than one weft for each block. Obviously any of the two-shuttle patterns (pick-and-pick stripes, cross stripes and spots) can be woven, either in the areas threaded on (1,2,3,4) or in those threaded on (5,6,7,8) or in both, see Plate 126.

Practical Details

A warp of 8 or 10 working e.p.i. is suitable, which gives 4 or 5 working e.p.i. for both upper and lower cloths. A weft of 2-ply carpet wool, used double or single respectively, is a suitable one to use. It might be assumed that a floating selvage would be best so that the weft from both upper and lower cloth caught round it. But this means that the floating selvage end has twice as many weft picks interlacing with it as do any of the other ends and this can lead to a bulky selvage which will not lie flat on the floor.

A far neater way is to begin and end the threading with two ends from what would be the next threading block; see Fig. 287 (a) where these extra two ends are encircled. If the main part of the threading is single in the heald, these two selvage threads will be double in the heald. Then weave normally with the two wefts. The effect of the

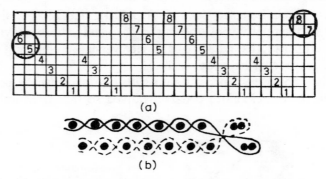

Fig. 287. Block Weave based on Weft-face Plain Weave
Double Cloth. (a) Threading for selvage (b) Cross-
section of selvage

extra ends is to produce a very narrow 'block' at the edge of the rug, which appears
as a line of the colour of the lower cloth. The pocket between its upper and lower
cloths is not closed in any way. So a cross-section of the right selvage would be as in
Fig. 287 (b). This gives a very firm edge.

(b) Ovals

It was mentioned above that the texture of such a rug is very fine, But if a much thicker
weft is used (i.e., 2-ply carpet wool used five or sixfold) a more interesting surface is
obtained. This means that the warp shows slightly in places, so it should approach in
colour that of the predominant weft.

In this weave, the pick-and-pick colour sequence is abandoned and several picks
of colour A (forming, say, the surface in blocks threaded on 1,2,3,4,) are followed by
several picks of colour B (forming the surface in the intervening blocks). The result is
that the colours can be made to appear as ovals, see Plate 127.

The basic sequence of pedals, using the tie-up in Fig. 286, is thus:

$$
\left.\begin{array}{l}
1,2,B,2,1,\text{—Weft A} \\
4,5,4,5,\quad\text{—Weft B} \\
2,1,B,1,2,\text{—Weft A} \\
5,4,5,4,\quad\text{—Weft B}
\end{array}\right\}\ \text{Repeat}
$$

The pick on pedal B, which is plain weave, ties the two cloths together. This pick
appears as a line of spots on both sides of the rug, so its use in a different colour
offers design possibilities. This pick also serves to separate the ovals of colour B.

A similar pick could be introduced in the middle of the oval woven on pedals 4
and 5.

Note—That the pedal before a plain weave pedal is repeated after it.

Plate 127 shows a few of the possibilities. It can be assumed the background colour is weft A, so the various ovals in black and white are produced by weft B.

The top oval is solid black. The next oval has an extra pick, so that it has five instead of four. It is woven in white, with the central pick (appearing as spots) in black. The next oval is all black, but it has a central plain weave pick which shows as a line of black spots in the intervening areas. The next oval has picks 1 and 4 woven with the background weft and only picks 3 and 4 with a different colour, white. These two picks appear as a wavy line. In between each of these above ovals there is of course an oval of background colour; these all fuse together visually to give the areas of solid colour between the columns of black and white ovals. The warp can be seen as light spots in the Plate. Plate 128 shows a full-size rug.

There is of course another pedal sequence which changes the relative positions of the warp ends. This, still referring to the tie-up plan in Fig. 286, is

$$
\left.
\begin{array}{ll}
6,7,A,7,6 & \text{—Weft A} \\
3,4,3,4 & \text{—Weft B} \\
7,6,A,6,7 & \text{—Weft A} \\
4,3,4,3 & \text{—Weft B}
\end{array}
\right\} \text{ Repeat}
$$

Changing from one sequence to the other will seal the pocket between cloths and do away with the necessity of the plain weave pick. It is best to carry out this change, half way through an oval, as indicated by the arrows, below:

$$
4, 5, 3, 4
$$
$$
\uparrow
$$

$$
\text{or} \quad 1, 2, 6, 7
$$
$$
\uparrow
$$

(c) *Block Weaves Based on the Analysis of Rameses' Girdle*

Interesting variations of plain weave double cloth are derived from the girdle woven for King Rameses III, about 1170 B.C. This remarkable textile, now in Liverpool Museum, is in two warp-face weaves which some think were done on tablets, others on a multishaft loom. The two weaves were analysed by Thorold Lee in 1913. One of these needed four shafts and eight different sheds, the other five shafts and eight sheds. The weaves to be described are obtained by turning the above weaves through a right angle so that they become weft-face weaves on eight shafts, and needing four sheds and five sheds, respectively. The details of the first weave are shown in Fig. 288 (a). The threading which is the same for both weaves is on (1,2,3,4) repeated ad lib, followed by two 'linking' ends on 1,2, then (5,6,7,8) repeated ad lib, followed by two 'linking' ends on 5,6. The four lifts are shown and in the weave plan these have been repeated twice to give a better idea of the structure.

Note—That these are the same four lifts as those in Fig. 285 (a).

To weave the sort of complex but small scale motifs present on Rameses' girdle, two or three wefts are used in special sequences, but the lifting sequence never changes. The distinguishing feature of these small motifs is that, though centred on one threading block, they spread across into the two adjacent threading blocks. See Fig. 288 (c) where the motif is centred on Block 2 (threaded on back four shafts) but spreads over into the blocks (threaded on front four shafts) on either side.

The weaving of these motifs can best be understood if a plan is made of how the four picks in the lifting sequence appear on the surface. This has been done diagrammatically in Fig. 288 (b).

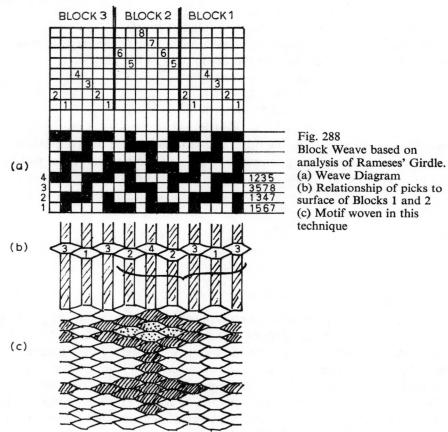

Fig. 288
Block Weave based on analysis of Rameses' Girdle.
(a) Weave Diagram
(b) Relationship of picks to surface of Blocks 1 and 2
(c) Motif woven in this technique

Note—That if Blocks 1 and 2 are taken together (bracketed in Fig. 288 (b)), the four picks come to the surface in six places and thus cover the six ends involved in the upper cloth. These six ends are represented by shaded lines. There are obviously another six ends woven in a similar way to form the back layer of cloth.

—That picks 1 and 4 only appear once and picks 2 and 3 both appear twice.

When beaten down these four picks make a solid line of weft, looking just like two picks of plain weave. To weave a motif, such as in Fig. 288 (c), the colour sequence will have to change frequently. Beginning at the bottom it is,

$$(A,A,A,B) \times 2$$
$$A,B,B,B$$
$$A,B,A,B$$
$$(A,A,A,B) \times 3$$
$$A,B,B,C$$
$$A,C,B,C$$
$$A,B,A,B$$
$$A,A,A,B$$

where A=the background colour
where B=the colour of motif
where C=the colour of the small diamond within the motif.

If the warp were threaded exactly as at the top of Fig. 288, motifs of the same size would appear all across the rug. But if some threading blocks had been extended, e.g., to $(1,2,3,4) \times 3$ followed by 1,2, then, $(5,6,7,8) \times 3$ followed by 5,6, the motif would be correspondingly wider in these areas, see Plate 129.

The back of the rug shows a completely different design. The relationship between the appearance of the four picks on the back and front is shown in Fig. 289 (a). This

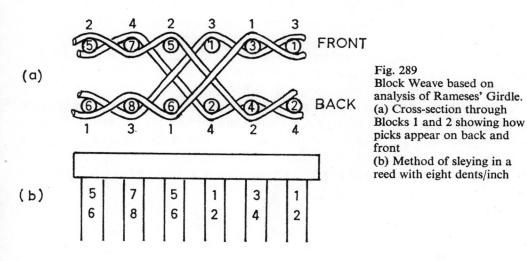

Fig. 289
Block Weave based on analysis of Rameses' Girdle.
(a) Cross-section through Blocks 1 and 2 showing how picks appear on back and front
(b) Method of sleying in a reed with eight dents/inch

represents a cross-section through the area of the rug bracketed in Fig. 288 (b), i.e., through an area threaded on a complete repeat of the pattern. The circles are the cross-sections of the twelve warp ends involved, and they are numbered according to the shaft they are threaded on. The four picks are also numbered where they come to the surface.

Note—That the picks 1 and 4 which only appear once on the front appear twice on the back, and picks 2 and 3 which appear twice on the front appear only once each on the back.

This causes the dissimilarity between the design on the two sides. Some colour sequence could be devised which showed similarly on both sides. Thus if picks 1 and 2 were colour A and picks 3 and 4 colour B, reference to Fig. 289 (a) will show that the two colours will appear as pick-and-pick stripes on both sides of the rug.

There is obviously great scope here for design, but only on a small scale. Plate 130 shows a rug woven in this technique.

The four lifts used give a plain weave double cloth so there is a pocket, running warpway between the two cloths in each threading block. To ensure that the rug lies flat, this should be sealed at intervals, either by a pick of plain weave (using a thin weft) or by interchanging the warp ends. In the latter case, the four lifts become (1246, 4678, 2348, 2568).

Hopsack can be woven by lifting 1278 and 3456; this is useful for the beginning and ending of a rug.

Practical Details

A warp with the following formula is suitable. 8 or 10 e.p.i., threaded single in the heald, therefore 8 or 10 working e.p.i. This gives 4 or 5 working e.p.i. for both upper and lower cloth, so a suitable weft would be of 2-ply carpet wool used two or three-fold for the first setting, and one or twofold for the second.

As Fig. 289 (a) shows, the warp ends tend to lie in pairs vertically above each other, and it is well to sley them in the same pairs. So if an 8-dent-to-the-inch reed is used, put two ends in every other dent, as shown in Fig. 289 (b).

A selvage threading similar to that described above is not a great help, because the weft sequence is constantly changing. So a floating selvage has to be used. Selvage ends are generally sleyed closer than the ends in the rest of the rug, but in this case sley them exactly as the rest of the rug, and this will in some way counteract the effects caused by the selvage ends interlacing with twice as many picks as do the other ends.

Variations

(1) *Four-Pick Weave*

By slightly changing the lifts, a weave can be produced that will show the same design on both sides of the rug.

Fig. 290 (a) shows a cross-section.

Note—The difference between it and that in Fig. 289 (a).

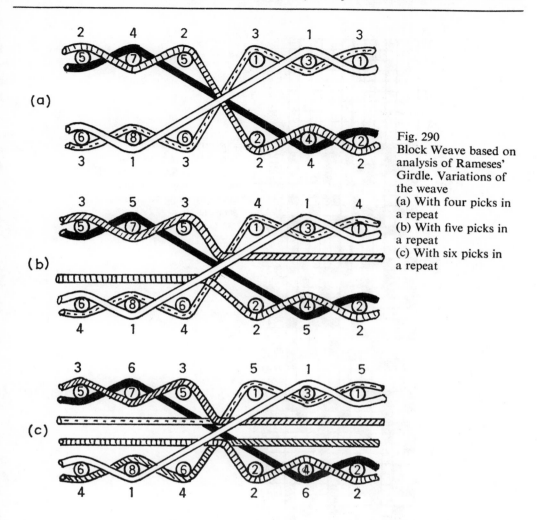

Fig. 290
Block Weave based on
analysis of Rameses'
Girdle. Variations of
the weave
(a) With four picks in
a repeat
(b) With five picks in
a repeat
(c) With six picks in
a repeat

Here all the wefts change from front to back of the rug, and vice versa, exactly at the same point. For this reason it is more difficult to beat down properly, so a 2-ply carpet wool used twofold as the weft is more suitable with an 8 working e.p.i. warp setting. The labelling of the picks in the cross-section shows the design will be the same on both sides.

The lifts are shown in Fig. 291 (a). The bottom four repeated or the top four repeated will give the same effect. Changing from one to the other interchanges the relative positions of the warps of upper and lower cloths.

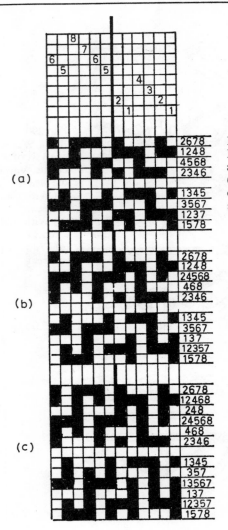

Fig. 291
Block Weave based on
analysis of Rameses' Girdle.
(a–c) Weave Diagrams
corresponding to cross-
sections in Fig. 290

(a)

2678
1248
4568
2346

1345
3567
1237
1578

(b)

2678
1248
24568
468
2346

1345
3567
137
12357
1578

(c)

2678
12468
248
24568
468
2346

1345
357
13567
137
12357
1578

(2)ˈ *Five-Pick Weave*

This is derived from the second weave found in the Rameses' girdle. Fig. 290 (b) shows a cross-section. If it is compared with Fig. 290 (a), it will be seen to be the same except that the second pick in Fig. 290 (a) has been replaced by two picks (numbers 2 and 3 in Fig. 290 (b)) one of which, pick 2, only appears on the back and the other, pick 3, only appears on the front. Where these picks are not visible on either surface they are floating between the upper and lower cloths. So though they contribute nothing to the surface at these points, they contribute to the thickness of the rug, padding out the pocket between the two cloths.

Note—If picks 2 and 3 are of the same colour, then the design on both sides will
be identical.

—By making these two picks of different colours, the two sides of the rug can
show a similar design but differently coloured in parts.

The two sets of lifts are shown in Fig. 291 (b). The weft should be 2-ply carpet wool
used twofold if the warp is 8 working e.p.i.

(3) *Six-Pick Weave*

This is an extension of the above weave, see Fig. 290 (c). Pick 4 in Fig. 290 (b) has
been split into two and appears as picks 4 and 5 in Fig. 290 (c). Pick 4 appears on the
back only and pick 5 appears on the front only, elsewhere they both float in the
pocket between upper and lower cloths.

Note—That only picks 1 and 6 appear on both sides of the rug, so here there is
more opportunity of varying the colours between the back and front of the
rug, though not of course of varying the motifs.

—The pocket has twice as many 'padding' picks as in the above weave, so
the rug is correspondingly thicker.

The two sets of lifts are shown in Fig. 291 (c). 2-ply carpet wool used twofold is
suitable as a weft if the warp is set at 8 working e.p.i. This will give a very firm rug.

D. Block Weaves Based on the Three-Weft Double-Faced Weaves

These are the eight-shaft developments of the three-weft double-faced weaves described in Chapter 7. They each had a weft for the front and a weft for the back of the
rug and a third weft which wove in such a way that it was hidden in between the other
two. There were two types which differed in that, in one weave, the third weft interlaced in plain weave order and, in the other weave, in hopsack order. The same
distinction carries through to the block weaves here described.

(i) WITH A HIDDEN WEFT IN PLAIN WEAVE

Fig. 292 gives the details of this weave. The threading is in groups on the back four
and front four shafts. These groups can contain any number of repeats of either
(1,2,3,4) or (5,6,7,8). The lifts and weave plan shown at Fig. 292 (a) give a block
weave. Note there is a three-colour weft sequence (A,B,C). This weave is best understood by the cross-section shown in Fig. 293. At (b) is a cross-section of picks 1 to 3,
at (a) of picks 4 to 6. The circles represent warp ends, numbered according to the
shafts they are controlled by.

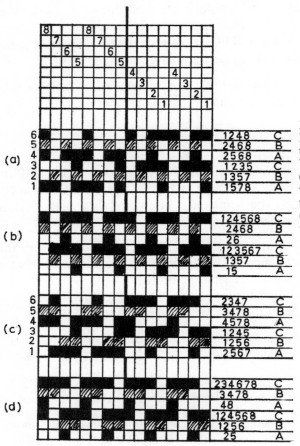

Fig. 292
Block Weaves based on three-Weft Double-Faced Weaves.
(a) and (b) Weave Diagrams with hidden weft in plain weave
(c) and (d) Weave Diagrams with hidden weft in hopsack

It will be seen that, as in the four-shaft weaves, picks 2 and 5 (dotted lines) are in normal plain weave. They are unaffected by the junction between blocks (indicated by arrows), and carry on from selvage to selvage. They contribute nothing to the surface of the rug as they are hidden by the floating wefts above and below them. The latter (colours A and C, indicated by white and black lines) are seen to change positions at the junction between blocks. What was the upper weft becomes the lower weft and vice versa, hence it is a block weave, with alternating blocks of colour A and C.

It is difficult with this structure to get a perfect join between adjacent blocks, and maybe there is a better solution than the one described above. The aim, of course, is to make the floating wefts change from an over-3-under-1 weave, to an under-3-over-1 weave (or vice versa), in as simple a way as possible at the block junctions.

Fig. 292 (b) shows the lifts that will give the same colour all across on the front and another colour all across on the back.

(ii) WITH A HIDDEN WEFT IN HOPSACK

Fig. 292 (c) gives the details of this variation. As the cross-sections in Fig. 293 (c) and (d) show, picks 2 and 5 weave in hopsack right across. The other picks take a different but comparable, course to those in the above weave.

Fig. 292 (d) shows the lifts that will give one colour all across on the front and another at the back. The pick-up varieties of these weaves will be found in the following chapter.

Practical Details

Warp—6 working e.p.i.

The weft for colours A and C should be 2-ply carpet wool used threefold. The weft for colour B should be 2-ply carpet wool used singly if it is to be quite invisible, or used twofold or threefold if it is required to show slightly on the surface. Use a floating selvage and start all wefts from the same side.

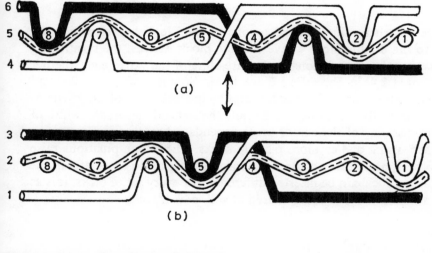

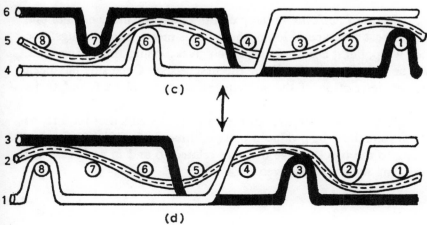

Fig. 293
Block Weaves based on
Three-Weft Double-Faced
Weaves.
(a) and (b) Cross-sections o
picks in Fig. 292(a)
(c) and (d) Cross-sections o
picks in Fig. 292(c)

9 · Weft-face Rugs in Multishaft Weaves

PART THREE: TECHNIQUES GIVING BLOCK DESIGNS CONTROLLED BY PICK-UP METHODS

INTRODUCTION

Each pick-up weave is structurally identical to one of the block weaves, which are themselves related to the double-faced weaves. In the block weaves, the positioning of the colour areas depends on variations in the threading of the warp, e.g., whether it is threaded (1,2,3) or (1,2,4) in Three-End Block Draft. So it is shaft-controlled and it cannot be altered once the warp is threaded, except by the technique of shaft switching. In the pick-up weaves, the threading is generally the same all across the width of the warp, and the positioning of the colour areas depends entirely on various manipulations of the warp, using one or more pick-up sticks. These manipulations raise some ends, lower others, and in fact control the warp exactly as do the shafts in the block weaves. But as the stick can be inserted differently for every set of picks, it is as if the threading of a block weave is being altered at will, pick by pick.

TWO METHODS OF PICK-UP

There are basically two ways of performing the pick-up; one is the more normal one and can be woven on almost any type of loom, the other is more suited to rugs, due to their widely spaced warp, but it needs a loom which gives a rising and falling shed. These two ways will be described in detail for the first weave. Once this has been understood, the shorter description of the subsequent weaves will be found to be sufficient.

It is difficult to classify the pick-up weaves by the number of shafts they require, as the identical weave can sometimes be produced on two, three, or four shafts. So they will be listed according to the block weave they are related to and in each case the various ways of producing them will be given.

1. PICK-UP VERSION OF BLOCK WEAVE USING THE THREE-END BLOCK DRAFT

It will be remembered that in this weave (the first one described in Chapter 8) it is the ends on shaft 3 or 4 which control the appearance of the weft either on the face or the reverse of the rug. So it is these ends that have to be manipulated in the pick-up. As mentioned above this can be done in two ways.

A. Centre Shed Pick-Up

(i) USING TWO SHAFTS

This method can most easily be understood by considering the two-shaft version of the weave.

Set up a two-shaft loom in such a way that *every third end is not threaded on either shaft.* Fig. 294 (a) shows the threading diagrammatically, where O signifies the position of an unthreaded end. The unthreaded ends are treated normally in the reed.

There are now only two possible sheds, shaft 1 up with shaft 2 down, and shaft 2 up with shaft 1 down. As the side views in Fig. 294 (b) and (c) show, these are both split, or double, sheds because the unthreaded ends naturally lie in the middle of the sheds, unaffected by the shafts' movements. In Fig. 294 (b) there is a half shed, A, above this central layer and a half shed, B, below it. The corresponding half sheds in Fig. 294 (c) are labelled C and D.

Two shuttles bearing black and white weft are used. The black goes through A, the white through B. Both are beaten and the shed is changed. The black returns through

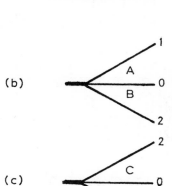

(a)

(b)

(c)

Fig. 294
Centre Shed Pick-Up version
of Block Weave using Three-
End Block Draft
(a) Threading Draft
(b) and (c) The two
available split sheds

C, the white through D, and both are again beaten. If this is repeated, a rug black on the face and white on the reverse will be woven.

Note—That there are two picks for every one change of shed.
—That the weave produced is identical to that shown in Fig. 211 in Chapter 8.

To pick up a design, attention has to be focused on the central layer of unthreaded ends. The shed as in Fig. 294 (b) is opened. Fig. 295 (a) shows a diagrammatic view of the central layer seen from above; for convenience, the uppermost layer of ends (those on the first shaft) have been omitted.

Enter a pick-up stick in the A shed (i.e., above the central layer), then pass it down through this layer into the B shed and then bring it back again up into the A shed. Turn it on edge and throw the black weft across in the shed so formed. In Fig. 295 (a) the stick is shown passing over the first three unthreaded ends, under the next three, and over the last three. Take out the pick-up stick and then using the black weft as a guide, re-insert the stick making it take the exact opposite course through the central layer. For convenience, this stage has been called pick-down as it is the opposite of pick-up. So the stick begins in the B shed, comes up into the A shed passing over the middle three ends and then drops back again into the B shed. It is turned on its side and the white weft thrown across in the shed so formed.

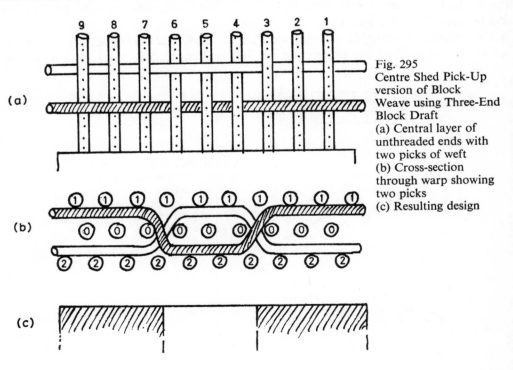

Fig. 295
Centre Shed Pick-Up version of Block Weave using Three-End Block Draft
(a) Central layer of unthreaded ends with two picks of weft
(b) Cross-section through warp showing two picks
(c) Resulting design

Take the pick-up stick out and beat the two wefts. The cross-section at Fig. 295 (b) (which indicates all three layers of the shed) shows the relationship of the two wefts to the central layer at this moment. They slip over each other so that the white only shows in the centre and the black at either side.

Change the shed and repeat the above procedure exactly. This is the complete cycle.

If the pick-up is continued exactly as in Fig. 295 (a), then the design would be as in Fig. 295 (c).

Note—That where the stick passes over the central layer, the following weft comes to the surface; where it passes under, the weft goes to the back.

—That when the pick-up stick is turned on edge for the first passage of the black weft, it is in effect raising unthreaded ends 4, 5, and 6, and lowering unthreaded ends 1,2,3, and 7,8,9. Shaft 1 is up and shaft 2 is down, so it is giving exactly the same shed as that obtained from a warp threaded $(1,2,3)\times3$, $(1,2,4)\times3$, $(1,2,3)\times3$, when shafts 1 and 4 are raised. Similarly the shed that the stick gives for the first passage of the white weft raises unthreaded ends 1,2,3 and 7,8,9 and lowers unthreaded ends 4,5, and 6. This is the same shed as lifting 13 would give on a warp threaded as above.

In the same way, the picked-up shed for the second black pick, corresponds to a lift of 24. And the shed for the second white pick corresponds to a lift of 23.

If this is understood it will be seen that the pick-up stick has taken over the function of shafts 3 and 4 in Three-End Block Draft. The weave structure obtained is identical in the pick-up and the block weave version.

—That the stick is always inserted twice in each shed; once for the black weft (pick-up) and once, taking the opposite course, for the white weft (pick-down). One weft, here the black, always acts as the leader, initiating any change in the design, the other merely follows. So the two wefts always work as a complementary pair. At any point in the cloth, one is forming an element of the design on the face and the other is forming a similar element but in a different colour on the reverse.

The great advantage of the pick-up method is that the course taken by the pick-up stick can be changed every time the shed is changed. Thus designs of any complexity can be woven, which would require a very large number of shafts if woven as a block weave.

It will be obvious from the above description that a loom which gives a rising and falling shed is necessary. So a two-shaft vertical rug loom, a counterbalanced and a countermarch loom will all be suitable, but a table loom will not. However, a table loom can be simply adapted for this technique. Fix an extra, raised, back bar. The

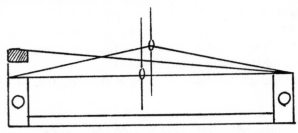

Fig. 296. Centre Shed Pick-up version of Block Weave
using Three-end Block Draft. Adapting table
loom to give split shed

unthreaded ends pass over this, while the threaded ends pass over the normal back
bar. As Fig. 296 shows, this gives the required split shed, as long as the extra back bar
is at the correct height. A jack loom is suitable as long as, in the shafts' position of
rest, the heald eyes are well below the line from breast beam to back beam.

(ii) USING FOUR-SHAFT COUNTERBALANCED LOOM

Thread the warp (1,2,3, 1,2,4) repeat, or in groups of (1,2,3) and (1,2,4) as for a block
weave. Immobilize the top roller or pulleys to prevent any movement of shafts 3 and
4 when shafts 1 and 2 are raised and lowered. Tie two pedals so that one lowers shaft
2 and therefore raises shaft 1, and the other lowers shaft 1, and therefore raises shaft
2. When either pedal is used, the ends on shafts 3 and 4 do not move and so they form
the central layer of the shed. Perform the pick-up as described above.

It is obvious that with this set-up, a shaft-controlled block weave can be combined
with the pick-up version, the latter being used occasionally to give variety to the fixed
colour areas of the block weave.

(iii) USING THREE OR FOUR-SHAFT COUNTERMARCH LOOM

Thread as above and tie up pedals as in Fig. 297 (a).

1 2 3 4 5 6
(a)

(b)

Fig. 297
Centre Shed Pick-Up version
of Block Weave using three-
End Block Draft.
(a) and (b) Pedal tie-up plans
for double countermarch loom

The convention for the tie-up diagram is thus:
black square=tie pedal to lower lam, i.e. the shaft is raised.
white square=tie pedal to upper lam, i.e., the shaft is lowered.
shaded square=do not tie pedal to either lam.
Thus pedal 3 is tied to the lower lam of shaft 1, to the upper lam of shaft 2 and is
not connected at all to the lams of shafts 3 and 4. Pedals 3 and 4 will give the two

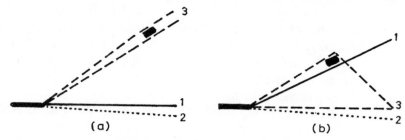

Fig. 298. Raised End Pick-up Method

split sheds for the pick-up. Pedals 1,5,2, and 6 will give the shaft-controlled block weave.

If the countermarch loom is threaded, (1,2,3) repeat, and the pedals tied as in Fig. 297 (b), then only the pick-up weave is possible (plus of course any purely three-shaft weave).

PRACTICAL DETAILS

The warp and weft settings are obviously the same as used for Three-End Block Draft, i.e., 4 working e.p.i. and 2-ply carpet wool used threefold. If the threading begins and finishes with two ends on shafts 1 and 2 (as shown in Fig. 294 (a)) the two wefts will catch at the selvage, providing that they begin from opposite selvages.

The pick-up stick should be of smooth wood, flattened so that when turned on its edge it gives a shed about 2 inches deep, and it should be pointed at both ends. When weaving samples or a narrow rug, the stick can be dispensed with; the shuttles themselves (preferably of the type used in netting) are threaded in and out of the central layer.

If a large piece of work in this technique is to be woven, it is an advantage to have the warp of two colours, the ends on shafts 1 and 2 in a dark colour, the ends of the central layer in a light colour. The latter are then more easily distinguished when picking up. A further refinement is to have threads of contrasting colour, spaced perhaps 2 inches apart, in the central layer. This makes the following of a design more easy and if ends have to be counted they do not have to be counted all the way in from one or other selvage.

B. Raised End Pick-Up

In this method the pick-up stick does the same manipulations with the same set of threads as above, but, instead of lying in the centre of a shed, these threads are raised to form the upper layer of a shed. Thread the warp (1,2,3) repeat, then the procedure is in the four following stages.

(i) Raise shaft 3. Pick-up with the stick in this raised layer of threads exactly as described above. So some of the threads on shaft 3 now pass over and some pass under the stick. This stage is shown in diagrammatic side view in Fig. 298 (a). The stick passes over the ends where the weft is to show on the front and under the ends where the weft is to show on the back.

Lower shaft 3, leaving the stick in position.

Raise shaft 1. The stick is naturally lifted by this new layer of threads. With it, are lifted all those ends from shaft 3 that, as a result of the pick-up, pass over the stick. Those that pass under the stick are not raised; they join the ends from shaft 2 to form the lower layer of the shed. Fig. 298 (b) shows a diagrammatic side view of this stage.

Throw colour A across in the shed directly under the stick. Lower shaft 1, remove the stick and beat.

(ii) Raise shaft 3 again. Pick-down with stick, i.e., make it take the exact opposite course through this raised layer of threads, going over where it previously went under and vice versa.

Lower shaft 3, leaving stick in position.

Raise shaft 1, and throw colour B across in the shed under the stick.

Lower shaft 1, remove stick and beat.

(iii and iv) Repeat the above two stages, but lifting shaft 2 instead of 1. So the whole process can be put in shortened form thus:

Raise 3, pick-up, lower 3, raise 1, weave weft A.
Raise 3, pick-down, lower 3, raise 1, weave weft B.
Raise 3, pick-up, lower 3, raise 2, weave weft A.
Raise 3, pick-down, lower 3, raise 2, weave weft B.

Note—The stick for this type of pick-up can be of small cross-section as long as it is fairly stiff. So a metal rod of $\frac{1}{4}$ inch diameter, tapered at both ends, is very suitable; or a flat metal strip, such as is used in rigid frame shafts for suspending the healds.

—In this type of pick-up the shed obtained is always shallow. When weaving a sample this is no inconvenience as a stick shuttle can easily be inserted into it and passed from selvage to selvage. But with a full-width rug, it may be necessary to insert the type of stick used for Centre Shed Pick-Up, turn it on its edge and thus enlarge the shed sufficiently for the shuttle's passage.

—The wefts work in pairs exactly as in Centre Shed Pick-Up. The pick-down is always the exact opposite of the pick-up. The design can be changed after every two picks if so desired, but never after only one pick.

—As in Centre Shed Pick-Up the stick is taking over the function of shafts 3 and 4 in Three-End Block Draft.

—This method is very suitable for table looms and jack looms.

VARIATIONS

(1) *In Picking Order*

Raise shaft 3, pick-up, lower 3, raise 1, weave weft A.
  Leaving pick-up stick in position, raise 2, weave weft A.
  Raise shaft 3, pick-down, lower 3, raise 1, weave weft B.
  Leaving pick-up stick in position, raise 2, weave weft B.
  Raise shaft 3, pick-up, lower 3, raise 2, weave weft A.
  Leaving pick-up stick in position, raise 1, weave weft A.
  Raise shaft 3, pick-down, lower 3, raise 2, weave weft B.
  Leaving pick-up stick in position, raise 1, weave weft B.

This gives a slightly different weave (in which spots of colour A show through an area of colour B and vice versa) but it has the advantage of only needing half the normal number of pick-ups.

(2) *In Colour and Lifts*

A sequence can be developed in which some picks are in normal shaft controlled sheds while others are in picked-up sheds, thus:

> Raise 1—weave weft A.
> Raise 13—weave weft B.
> Raise 3, pick-up, lower 3, raise 2, weave weft C.
> Raise 3, pick-down, lower 3, raise 2, weave weft D.

This will give Colour A all across on front, colour B all across on the back, and colours C and D only appearing where picked up. So the front of the rug will show areas of A striped with C and of A striped with D, and the back will show similar areas of B striped with D and B striped with C. Of course all four wefts need not be different colours. Two or three colours could be used in this way.

Practical Details

Exactly as for Centre Shed Pick-Up.

Two Pick-Up Methods Compared

(1) Picking up on raised ends is easier on the eyes than picking up in the middle of the shed, especially with a close set warp.

(2) Centre Shed Pick-Up always gives a good shed, as the stick used is turned on its edge for the passage of the shuttle. In Raised End Pick-Up, the shed is poor, so a second stick may be necessary to enlarge it.

(3) Using Raised Shed Pick-Up it is possible with some weaves to insert two picks of one colour after each pick-up. This is never possible with Centre-Shed Pick-Up, where every throw of the shuttle is preceded by its own individual pick-up.

2. PICK-UP VERSION OF BLOCK WEAVE BASED ON DOUBLE-FACED 2/1 TWILL

A. Centre Shed Pick-Up

This is only possible on a countermarch loom. Thread (1,2,3) repeat, all across the rug. Tie up pedals as in Fig. 299 (a), remembering a shaded square means that there is no pedal-to-lam tie at this point.

Fig. 300 shows the three different split sheds given by the three pedals with the above tie-up. Thus with pedal 1, ends on shaft 1 are raised, ends on shaft 3 are lowered, and ends on shaft 2 do not move at all, and thus form the central layer. The other two pedals give similar sheds, the ends from a different shaft forming the central layer in each case. The weaving sequence is thus:

Press Pedal 1—pick-up in the central layer, weave weft A.
               pick-down in the central layer, weave weft B.
Press Pedal 2—pick-up in the central layer, weave weft A.
               pick-down in the central layer, weave weft B.
Press Pedal 3—pick-up in the central layer, weave weft A.
               pick-down in the central layer, weave weft B.

Repeat.

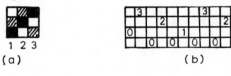

(a)   (b)

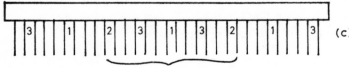

(c)

Fig. 299. Pick-up version of Block Weave based on Double-
        faced 2/1 Twill.
        (a) Pedal tie-up for double countermarch loom
        (b) Alternative threading
        (c) Sleying when using a pointed draft

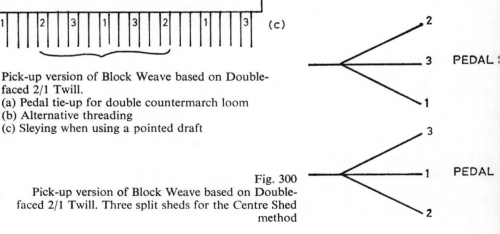

Fig. 300
Pick-up version of Block Weave based on Double-
faced 2/1 Twill. Three split sheds for the Centre Shed
method

Plate 131 shows a rug woven in this technique. The outlines of the rhomboid-shaped motifs follow the twill lines of the weave. If a motif with vertical, i.e. warpway, outline is woven, it will be found that this outline is in reality a succession of small angled teeth. The fact that the weave is a twill makes it impossible to obtain straight vertical colour junctions. This weave can be varied by threading as in Fig. 299 (b), but tying up pedals and weaving exactly as described. The centre layer of ends will now consist of the unthreaded ends (O) plus the ends threaded on one of the shafts. The wefts will now float over five instead of three ends, so the warp must be set closer, e.g., 6 working e.p.i. The extra warp ends add body to the rug, but do not affect the weave in any other way.

B. Raised End Pick-Up

Thread warp (1,2,3) repeat.
  Lift 1, pick-up, lower 1, raise 3, weave weft A.
  Lift 1, pick-down, lower 1, raise 3, weave weft B.
  Lift 2, pick-up, lower 2, raise 1, weave weft A.
  Lift 2, pick-down, lower 2, raise 1, weave weft B.
  Lift 3, pick-up, lower 3, raise 2, weave weft A.
  Lift 3, pick-down, lower 3, raise 2, weave weft B.

This is suitable for table and jack looms.

Practical Details

Warp—6 e.p.i., alternately single and double in the heald, therefore 4 working e.p.i.
Weft—2-ply carpet wool used two or threefold.

VARIATION USING A POINTED DRAFT

The weave can be varied by using a pointed draft on three shafts, i.e., 3,2,1; 3,2,1; 3; 1,2,3; 1,2,3; 1; 3,2,1; 3,2,1; etc. This enables diamond shapes to be picked up, the diamonds being centred on the reversing points of the threading.
  There are two sequences to be used:

(1) When a diamond is increasing in size.

Raise 1, pick-up, lower 1, raise 2, weave weft A.
Raise 1, pick-down, lower 1, raise 2, weave weft B.
Raise 3, pick-up, lower 3, raise 1, weave weft A.
Raise 3, pick-down, lower 3, raise 1, weave weft B.
Raise 2, pick-up, lower 2, raise 3, weave weft A.
Raise 2, pick-down, lower 2, raise 3, weave weft B.

(2) When a diamond is decreasing in size.

Raise 1, pick-up, lower 1, raise 3, weave weft A.
Raise 1, pick-down, lower 1, raise 3, weave weft B.
Raise 2, pick-up, lower 2, raise 1, weave weft A.
Raise 2, pick-down, lower 2, raise 1, weave weft B.
Raise 3, pick-up, lower 3, raise 2, weave weft A.
Raise 3, pick-down, lower 3, raise 2, weave weft B.

Naturally at the widest point of the diamond, a switch from one sequence to the other has to be made. Do this in such a way that the shafts lifted for weaving reverse their sequence at this point. Thus:

Pick-up and pick-down on shaft 1, weave on 2 ⎫
Pick-up and pick-down on shaft 3, weave on 1 ⎬ First sequence
Pick-up and pick-down on shaft 2, weave on 3 ⎭
Pick-up and pick-down on shaft 2, weave on 1 ⎫ Second sequence
Pick-up and pick-down on shaft 3, weave on 2 ⎭

Note—This means picking up twice with the same shaft raised (here shaft 2).

Practical Details

The warp setting is 4 working e.p.i. If a reed with 12 dents per inch is used, 3 empty dents follow every filled dent. But at the reversing points in the threading draft, leave only 2 empty dents between 5 consecutive ends, bracketed in Fig. 299 (c). This is to reduce the length of the otherwise overlong weft floats at these points.

3. PICK-UP VERSION OF ONE OF THE BLOCK WEAVES USING THE FOUR-END BLOCK DRAFT

A. Centre Shed Pick-Up

This can be woven in two ways.

(1) On two shaft loom, or using only two shafts of a multishaft loom.

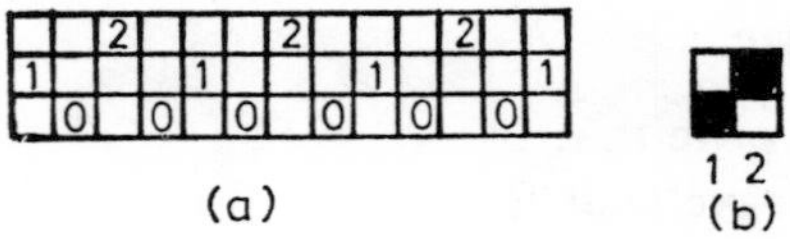

(a)

Fig. 301
Pick-up version of Block Weave
using Four-End Block Draft.
1 2   (a) Draft for Centre Shed method
(b)   (b) Pedal tie-up

Thread loom as in Fig. 301 (a), i.e., every other end is left unthreaded (O). Apart from the threading, this method is exactly similar to the first pick-up described in this chapter. So the sequence is:

Raise 1, lower 2, pick-up, weave weft A.
Raise 1, lower 2, pick-down, weave weft B.
Raise 2, lower 1, pick-up, weave weft A.
Raise 2, lower 1, pick-down, weave weft B.
Repeat. See Plate 132.

(2) Using four shafts on a counterbalanced loom.

Thread (1,3,2,4) repeat. Immobilize the top roller, to prevent any movement of shafts 3 and 4 when shafts 1 and 2 are moved. Tie pedals as in Fig. 301 (b). The sequence is:
Press Pedal 1, pick-up, weave weft A.
Press Pedal 1, pick-down, weave weft B.
Press Pedal 2, pick-up, weave weft A.
Press Pedal 2, pick-down, weave weft B.

The ends on shafts 3 and 4 form the central layer.

B. Raised End Pick-Up

Thread (1,2,3,4) repeat.
Raise 24, pick-up, lower 24, raise 1, weave weft A.
Raise 24, pick-down, lower 24, raise 1, weave weft B.
Raise 24, pick-up, lower 24, raise 3, weave weft A.
Raise 24, pick-down, lower 24, raise 3, weave weft B.

A variation of this is the following:

Lift 24, pick-up, lower 24, raise 1, weave weft A.
Lift 24, pick-down, lower 24, raise 3, weave weft B.
Repeat three or four times, then
Lift 24, pick-up, lower 24, raise 3, weave weft A.
Lift 24, pick-down, lower 24, raise 1, weave weft B.
Repeat three or four times as before.

The resulting weave has a ridgy surface.

4. PICK-UP VERSION OF BLOCK WEAVE USING THE SIX-END BLOCK DRAFT

A. Centre Shed Pick-Up

Thread as in Fig. 302 (a), i.e., every third end is unthreaded. The sequence is as follows:

Raise 1, lower 2, pick-up, weave weft A.
Raise 1, lower 2, pick-down, weave weft B.
Raise 2, lower 1, pick-up, weave weft A.
Raise 2, lower 1, pick-down, weave weft B.

See the section on this block weave in Chapter 8 for other possible colour sequences.

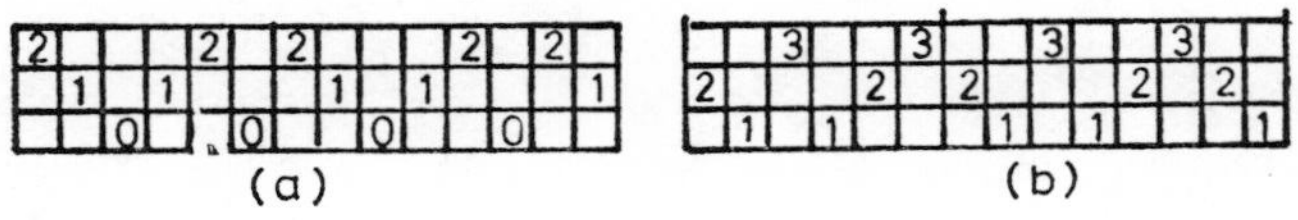

(a)   (b)

Fig. 302
Pick-Up version of Block
Weave using Six-End Block
Draft. Two threading drafts

B. Raised End Pick-Up

Thread on three shafts as in Fig. 302 (b).

    Raise 3, pick-up, lower 3, raise 1, weave weft A.
    Raise 3, pick-down, lower 3, raise 1, weave weft B.
    Raise 3, pick-up, lower 3, raise 2, weave weft A.
    Raise 3, pick-down, lower 3, raise 2, weave weft B.

    Alternatively the warp can be threaded on four shafts as for Six-End Block Draft in which case the pick-up is performed with shafts 3 and 4 raised.

Practical Details

The warp should have 5 working e.p.i., with a weft of 2-ply carpet wool used two or threefold.

5. PICK-UP VERSION OF ONE OF THE BLOCK WEAVES USING M'S AND O'S DRAFT

The pick-up method used for this weave is different from all the others described in this chapter.

A. Centre Shed Pick-up

Thread as in Fig. 303 (a), noting that two unthreaded ends always follow two threaded ends. As is normal with this type of threading, start and finish it with threaded ends. When shaft 1 is raised and shaft 2 lowered, the central layer of unthreaded ends will appear in pairs, with a definite space between each pair, see Fig. 303 (b).

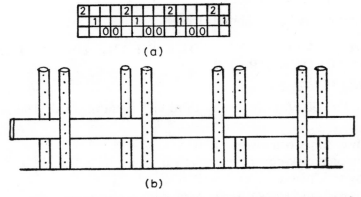

(a)

(b)

Fig. 303. Pick-up version of Block Weave using M's and O's draft.
(a) Draft for Centre Shed method (b) View of central layer
of threads

Now in picking up, the stick passes under either the right-hand or the left-hand end of *every* pair. In Fig. 303 (b), it passes under the left-hand ends of the first two pairs and under the right-hand ends of the next two pairs. How the pick-up is related to the appearance of the weft on the front or the back of the rug depends on which shaft is raised. The sequence is as follows:

(a) Raise shaft 1, lower 2.

Pick-up the left-hand end of each pair, where the weft is required on the surface, and the right-hand end of each pair where the weft is not so required.

Turn stick on its edge, and weave weft A in the shed so formed.

Withdraw stick and beat.

(b) Raise 1, lower 2, i.e., use the same shed.

Pick-up the exact opposite. Thus, pick-up right-hand ends where left-hand ends were picked up above and vice versa.

Turn stick on its edge and weave weft B.

Withdraw stick and beat.

(c) Raise 2, lower 1.

Pick-up exactly as done in stage (b) above, and weave weft A. This will not appear in the same position as weft B above, as might be supposed. But, because the main shed has been changed, it appears in a similar position to weft A in stage (a).

(d) Raise 2, lower 1, i.e., use the same shed.

Pick-up exactly *as* done in stage (a) above, and weave weft B. Again because the main shed is changed, this will appear in a similar position to weft B in stage (b).

The sequence is slightly complicated as the pick-up for weft A in stage (a) is the opposite of the pick-up for weft A in stage (c), and the same applies for weft B in stages (b) and (d). The pick-up could be made easier if all the right-hand ends of the pairs were one colour and the left-hand ends another colour.

B. Raised End Pick-Up

Thread (1,2,3,4) repeat.

The sequence is as follows:

(a) Raise 23, thus giving pairs of ends spaced out across the warp, as in the above method.

Pick-up left-hand end of each pair where the weft is required on the surface and the right-hand ends where it is not so required.

Lower 23, raise 4, weave weft A.

(b) Raise 23, pick-up the exact opposite, i.e., select right-hand instead of left-hand ends, and vice versa, lower 23, raise 4, weave weft B.

(c) Raise 23, pick-up as in stage (b), lower 23, raise 1, weave weft A.

(d) Raise 23, pick-up as in stage (a), lower 23, raise 1, weave weft B.

After each stage, remove stick and beat.

The two wefts work as a pair, so the design can only be changed after (b) or (d).

If at any point in the design, the same areas of colour are required for some distance it will save time to change to the following sequence.

(a) Raise 23, pick-up as required, lower 23, raise 4, weave weft A.

(b) With pick-up stick still in the above position, raise 1, weave weft B.

Remove stick and beat the two above picks together.

(c) Raise 23, pick up the exact opposite, lower 23, raise 1, weave weft A.

(d) With pick-up stick still in the above position, raise 4, weave weft B.

Remove stick and beat both picks together.

There are only two pick-ups in this sequence instead of four. Care must be taken in changing from one sequence to the other.

Plate 133 shows a sample woven in this technique. Like the block weave it is derived from, the technique gives a textile identical on the two sides; i.e., there is the same black shape on a white ground on both sides of this sample.

PRACTICAL DETAILS

Warp—6 e.p.i., alternately single and double in the head, therefore 4 working e.p.i. Weft—2-ply carpet wool used threefold.

6. PICK-UP VERSION OF BLOCK WEAVE BASED ON DOUBLE-FACED 3/1 TWILL

A. Centre Shed Pick-Up

(i) USING A COUNTERMARCH LOOM

Thread (1,2,3,4) repeat. Tie pedals as in Fig. 304 (a). This tie-up makes each pedal lower one shaft, raise another, and leave the other two shafts unaffected. The ends on the latter form the central layer. The sequence is as follows:

Press Pedal 1, pick-up in central layer, weave weft A.

Press Pedal 1, pick-down in central layer, weave weft B.

Press Pedal 2, pick-up in central layer, weave weft A.

Press Pedal 2, pick-down in central layer, weave weft B.

Press Pedal 3, pick-up in central layer, weave weft A.

Press Pedal 3, pick-down in central layer, weave weft B.

Press Pedal 4, pick-up in central layer, weave weft A.

Press Pedal 4, pick-down in central layer, weave weft B.

(ii) USING A COUNTERBALANCED LOOM

Thread (1,3,2,4) repeat, tie pedals as in Fig. 304 (b). Tie top roller of harness to prevent any reciprocal movement between front two and back two shafts. Because of this, when pedal 1 is used, shaft 1 is lowered and shaft 2 raised, but shafts 3 and 4 are unaffected and the ends threaded on them form the central layer. The sequence is exactly as above.

B. Raised End Pick-Up

Thread (1,2,3,4) repeat. The sequence is as follows:

Lift 13, pick-up, lower 13, lift 4, weave weft A.
Lift 13, pick-down, lower 13, lift 4, weave weft B.
Lift 24, pick-up, lower 24, lift 3, weave weft A.
Lift 24, pick-down, lower 24, lift 3, weave weft B.
Lift 13, pick-up, lower 13, lift 2, weave weft A.
Lift 13, pick-down, lower 13, lift 2, weave weft B.
Lift 24, pick-up, lower 24, lift 1, weave weft A.
Lift 24, pick-down, lower 24, lift 1, weave weft B.

The weave has a twilled surface; the motifs can run with the twill lines or against them. Like its parent block weave, this is an extremely good rug weave, tough yet flexible.

PRACTICAL DETAILS

Warp—6 working e.p.i.
Weft—2-ply carpet wool used threefold. Use a floating selvage.

7. PICK-UP VERSION OF PLAIN WEAVE DOUBLE CLOTH

This is the pick-up weave that has been most used in the past. Here the weft-face variety is described.

A. Centre Shed Pick-Up

(i) USING A COUNTERMARCH LOOM

Thread (1,2,3,4) repeat. Tie up the pedals as in Fig. 304 (a). The sequence is as follows:
Press Pedal 1, pick-up, weave weft A.
Press Pedal 2, pick-down, weave weft B.
Press Pedal 3, pick-up, weave weft A.
Press Pedal 4, pick-down, weave weft B.

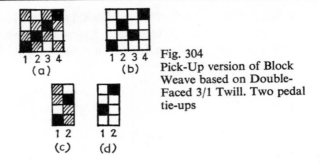

Fig. 304
Pick-Up version of Block
Weave based on Double-
Faced 3/1 Twill. Two pedal
tie-ups

(ii) USING A COUNTERBALANCED LOOM

Thread (1,3,2,4) repeat. Tie up the pedals as in Fig. 304 (b). Tie top roller of harness to prevent reciprocal movement between front two and back two shafts. The sequence is exactly as above.

B. Raised End Pick-Up

Thread (1,2,3,4) repeat. The sequence is as follows:
    Lift 24, pick-up, lower 24, lift 1, weave weft A.
    Lift 13, pick-down, lower 13, lift 2, weave weft B.
    Lift 24, pick-up, lower 24, lift 3, weave weft A.
    Lift 13, pick-down, lower 13, lift 4, weave weft B.

The weaving can be speeded up considerably by weaving two picks of A, then two picks of B, thus:

    Lift 24, pick-up, lower 24, lift 1, weave weft A.
    With the stick still in position, lift 3, weave weft A.
    Lift 13, pick-down, lower 13, lift 2, weave weft B.
    With stick still in position, lift 4, weave weft B.

The weave gives two completely separate weft-face plain weave cloths, one above the other. They are only joined at the perimeter of each colour area. So for the stability of the rug it is best to weave small units of design; or if large units are essential, break them up with stripes or spots of the other colour, thus tying the upper and lower cloths together.

PRACTICAL DETAILS

Warp—10 or 8 working e.p.i.
Weft—2-ply carpet wool used singly or twofold respectively.

For variations in pick-up methods for this weave, see *The Double Weave* by Harriet Tidball.

A Variation

A much simpler method of weaving is based on the fact that the warps of the two cloths, being invisible, do not need to interchange at horizontal colour junctions. So an upper warp can be used for *both* colour areas on the face of the rug and a lower warp for *both* colour areas on the reverse. In the following description, the upper warp consists of ends on shafts 1 and 3, the lower of ends on shafts 2 and 4.

A. Centre Shed Pick-Up

(i) USING A COUNTERMARCH LOOM

Thread (1,2,3,4) repeat. Only two pedals are needed, tied as in Fig. 304 (c). The two resulting split sheds are used in the normal way, thus the sequence is as follows:
    Press Pedal 1, pick-up, weave weft A.
    Press Pedal 1, pick-down, weave weft B.
    Press Pedal 2, pick-up, weave weft A.
    Press Pedal 2, pick-down, weave weft B.

(ii) USING A COUNTERBALANCED LOOM

Thread (1,2,3,4) repeat. Tie pedals as in Fig. 304 (d). If the top roller of the harness is tied to prevent reciprocal movement between the front and back two shafts, the two pedals will produce the same two split sheds as above. So the weaving sequence is exactly the same.

B. Raised End Pick-Up

Thread (1,2,3,4) repeat. The sequence is as follows:
    Lift 34, pick-up, lower 34, lift 1, weave weft A.
    Lift 34, pick-down, lower 34, lift 1, weave weft B.
    Lift 12, pick-up, lower 12, lift 3, weave weft A.
    Lift 12, pick-down, lower 12, lift 3, weave weft B.

PRACTICAL DETAILS

Warp—10 or 8 working e.p.i.
Weft—2-ply carpet wool used singly or twofold respectively.

This weave is the weft-face version of the warp-face weave known as One-Weft Double Cloth, described in Chapter 11.

8. PICK-UP VERSION OF BLOCK WEAVE BASED ON THREE-WEFT DOUBLE-FACED WEAVE.
With Hidden Weft in Plain Weave

A. Centre Shed Pick-Up

(i) USING A COUNTERMARCH LOOM

Thread (1,2,3,4) repeat. Tie up pedals as in Fig. 305 (a). The sequence is as follows:
Press Pedal 1, pick-up, weave weft A.
Press Pedal 1, pick-down, weave weft B.

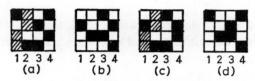

1 2 3 4   1 2 3 4   1 2 3 4   1 2 3 4
(a)   (b)   (c)   (d)

Fig. 305. Pick-up version of Block Weave based on Three-Weft Double-facedWeaves. (a) and (b) Pedal tie-ups for type with hidden weft in plain weave (c) and (d) Pedal tie-ups for type with hidden weft in hopsack

Press Pedal 4, weave weft C (hidden weft).
Press Pedal 2, pick-up, weave weft A.
Press Pedal 2, pick-down, weave weft B.
Press Pedal 3, weave weft C (hidden weft).

(ii) USING A COUNTERBALANCED LOOM

Thread (1,2,3,4,) repeat. Tie up pedals as in Fig. 305 (b). Tie top roller to prevent reciprocal movement between front two and back two shafts. The sequence is then exactly as above.

B. Raised End Pick-Up

Thread (1,2,3,4,) repeat. The sequence is as follows:
Lift 12, pick-up, lower 12, raise 4, weave weft A.
Lift 12, pick-down, lower 12, raise 4, weave·weft B.
Lift 24, weave weft C.
Lift 34, pick-up, lower 34, raise 1, weave weft A.
Lift 34, pick-down, lower 34, raise 1, weave weft B.
Lift 13, weave weft C.

With Hidden Weft in Hopsack

A. Centre Shed Pick-Up

(i) USING A COUNTERMARCH LOOM

Thread (1,2,3,4) repeat, and tie up pedals as in Fig. 305 (c). The sequence is as follows:
Press Pedal 1, pick-up, weave weft A.
Press Pedal 1, pick-down, weave weft B.
Press Pedal 4, weave weft C.
Press Pedal 2, pick-up, weave weft A.
Press Pedal 2, pick-down, weave weft B.
Press Pedal 3, weave weft C.

(ii) USING A COUNTERBALANCED LOOM

Thread (1,2,3,4) repeat, and tie up pedals as in Fig. 305 (d). Tie top roller to prevent reciprocal movement between front two and back two shafts. The sequence is then exactly as above.

B. Raised End Pick-Up

Thread (1,2,3,4,) repeat. The sequence is as follows:
Lift 12, pick-up, lower 12, lift 3, weave weft A.
Lift 12, pick-down, lower 12, lift 3, weave weft B.
Lift 23, weave weft C.
Lift 34, pick-up, lower 34, lift 1, weave weft A.
Lift 34, pick-down, lower 34, lift 1, weave weft B.
Lift 14 weave weft C.

PRACTICAL DETAILS

Warp—6 working e.p.i.
Weft—2-ply carpet wool used threefold for wefts A and B, and twofold or singly for weft C. Use a floating selvage, and start all three wefts from the same side.

9. PICK-UP VERSION OF THREE-COLOUR BLOCK WEAVE

A. Centre Shed Pick-Up

Thread as in Fig. 306 (a). Two unthreaded ends follow every threaded end. There are of course only two possible sheds, as shown in Fig. 306 (b), but three picks (three different colours) have to be inserted into each of these sheds. The sequence is as follows:

(1) Raise shaft 1 and lower shaft 2. Fig. 307 (a) shows the central layer of unthreaded ends (eighteen in number) seen from above; for convenience, the ends of

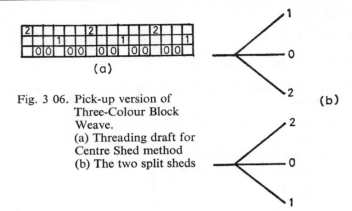

(a)

(b)

Fig. 3 06. Pick-up version of
Three-Colour Block
Weave.
(a) Threading draft for
Centre Shed method
(b) The two split sheds

shaft 1 have been omitted. Due to the method of sleying (see Practical Details), these ends are evenly spaced as shown.

Suppose, for simplicity's sake, that the three colours are required to show as in Fig. 307 (b), i.e., the right-hand third of the warp to have colour A on the surface, the central third to have colour B, and the left-hand third to have colour C. As explained (in the section on Three-Colour Block Weave in Chapter 8) in each of these areas one of the wefts shows on the surface, one shows on the back and one lies hidden in the centre, interlacing in plain weave order with the central layer of the warp.

So for weft A, pass pick-up stick from right to left over the first six ends, then make it interlace in plain weave order with the next six ends (under, over, etc.) then pass it under the final six ends. Turn it on its edge and weave weft A. See Fig. 307 (a).

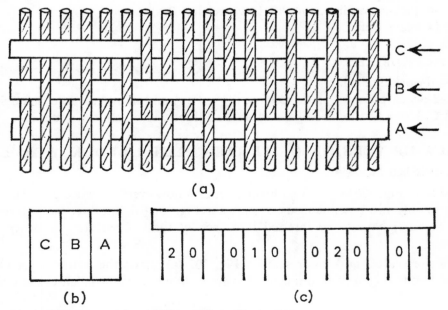

(a)

(b)

(c)

Fig. 307. Pick-up version of Three-Colour Block Weave.
(a) View of three picks in central layer of threads
(b) Colour arrangement
(c) Method of sleying warp

For weft B, pass stick under the first six ends, over the central six ends and interlace it in plain weave order with the final six ends (under one, over one, etc.). Turn it on its edge and weave weft B.

For weft C, start by interlacing it in plain weave order (under one, over one, etc.) with the first six ends, then pass it under the central six ends and over the final six ends. Turn it on its edge and weave weft C.

Note—That all the wefts pass from right to left.

(2) Now change the shed, i.e., raise shaft 2 and lower 1. Repeat the above three pick-ups, but wherever, for each weft, the stick interlaces with the central layer, make it do so in the opposite plain weave shed, i.e., over, under, instead of under, over. This is the complete sequence.

Reference to the description and diagrams given for Three-Colour Block Weave will show that for one colour arrangement on the surface there may be several possible ways of arranging the colours on the back. There can of course be no reversal of the colours on the back, because three colours are involved. So some skill and ingenuity is required in manipulating the colours to make both sides of the rug bear an acceptable design.

B. Raised End Pick-Up

Thread (1,3,4,2,3,4) repeat. The sequence is as follows:
    Lift 34, pick-up as explained above, lower 34, lift 1, weave weft A.
    Lift 34, pick-up as explained above, lower 34, lift 1, weave weft B.
    Lift 34, pick-up as explained above, lower 34, lift 1, weave weft C.
    Repeat, but lift 2 instead of lifting 1 (and of course use opposite plain weave shed in appropriate parts of pick-up).

In this type of pick-up, wherever the stick is interlacing in plain weave order with a section of the raised ends, its passage can be assisted by forming the appropriate shed, (i.e., by slightly dropping shaft 3 or 4). With a jack loom this will mean using two pedals (one raising 3, one raising 4) for the 34 lift; and of course using two feet. One foot is slightly raised to form the shed for the pick-up stick. If the right foot is raised when the three wefts are travelling to the right, and the left when they are travelling to the left, this will also overcome any confusion about which is the correct plain weave shed for the stick to enter.

PRACTICAL DETAILS

Warp—9 working e.p.i.
Weft—2-ply carpet wool used threefold.
    Sley the warp in a reed with 12 dents per inch, as shown in Fig. 307 (c).

Note—That the unthreaded ends are in alternate dents, i.e., at 6 e.p.i. and that the threaded ends are in every fourth dent, i.e., at 3 e.p.i. So both sets of ends are evenly spaced.

Begin and finish the threading on a threaded end. All three wefts start from the same side.

General Notes on Pick-Up Techniques Described in this Chapter

(1) From the point of view of experimenting with these techniques, note that five of them are possible on a straight 1,2,3,4, threading.

(2) Note that five of these techniques (including the Three-Colour Block Weave) can be woven on the simplest two-shaft vertical rug loom (using unthreaded ends and Centre Shed Pick-Up).

(3) Pick-up techniques are always slow. Their most economical use is in combination with shaft-controlled blocks. In other words thread the loom to give blocks and only use pick-up occasionally to rob the design of its regularity.

(4) It is simple to convert any shaft-controlled block weave into its corresponding pick-up weave.

Let the lifts for the block weave be:

$$13, 14, 23, 24$$
$$A \quad B \quad A \quad B$$

If they are considered in pairs, then it is the raising of shafts 3 or 4 which distinguishes the shed for colour A from that for colour B in each pair. So the pick-up is done with these two shafts raised and the sequence would be

Lift 34, pick-up, lower 34, lift 1, weave weft A.
Lift 34, pick-down, lower 34, lift 1, weave weft B.
Lift 34, pick-up, lower 34, lift 2, weave weft A.
Lift 34, pick-down, lower 34, lift 2, weave weft B.

As another example, let the lifts for the block weave be.

$$4, 134, 3, 234, 2, 123, 1, 124$$
$$A \quad B \quad A \quad B \quad A \quad B \quad A \quad B$$

Then the pick-up for the first two picks would be with 13 raised (because it is the raising of shafts 1 and 3 which distinguishes the shed for colour B from that for colour A), and the weft would be inserted with 4 raised. The pick-up for the next two picks would be with 24 raised and the weft would be inserted with 3 raised, etc.

So any new block weave encountered can be converted in this way into a pick-up weave.

10. PICK-UP METHOD USING A RIGID HEDDLE

All the pick-up weaves possible on a two-shaft loom, using unthreaded ends and Centre Shed Pick-Up, can also be produced on a specially adapted rigid heddle. This is not a feasible way of making rugs, but it provides a very simple way of exploring the techniques on a small scale.

The rigid heddles are made by blocking the dents in a reed with two lengths of wooden strips. Two of the longer strips put in a dent leave a small central eye, two of the shorter strips leave a large central eye. Some dents are left in their normal state. Fig. 308 (a) shows the various ways these have to be combined for the different pick-up weaves. Each bears the number of the pick-up weave as described earlier in this chapter. Two repeats are shown for each weave.

Set up a warp and thread one end in each dent. When the heddle is raised or lowered, there will be a split shed, see Fig. 308 (b). Whereas the ends threaded in the normal and small-eyed dents change position when the shed is changed, the ends in the large-eyed dents remain in the same central position. It is these ends (which correspond to the unthreaded ends in the methods described previously) which form the layer for the Centre Shed Pick-Up.

The pick-up is carried out on this layer, in the manner described under Centre Shed Pick-Up for each of the five weaves concerned.

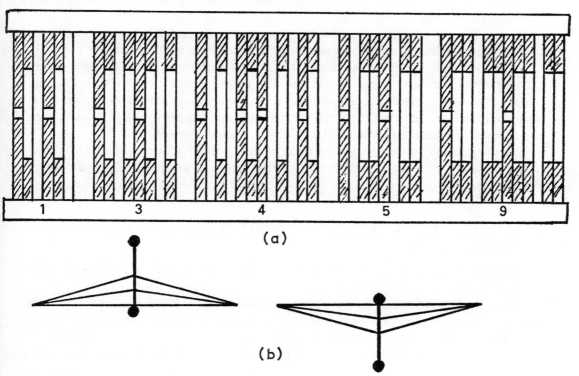

(a)

(b)

Fig. 308. Centre Shed Pick-up using an adapted Rigid Heddle.
(a) Blocking dents for various pick-up weaves
(b) The sheds obtained

10 · Weft Pile Techniques

INTRODUCTION

The many corduroy pile weaves to be described all stem from an original idea of the late Alastair Morton, R.D.I. This was to set up the loom so that the pile weft alternately weaves and floats for a certain distance all across the width of the rug. The distance over which the weft floats is always the same as the distance over which it weaves. This ensures that the weft is securely held and distinguishes the technique from other less practical methods. The floats are later cut to form the pile; hence it is a cut weft pile technique.

This process can be carried out in many ways and on any loom from a simple rug frame to an eight-shaft loom. There are two basic types, single corduroy and double corduroy, the latter being most used as it has the thicker pile. It is important to consider this as a technique in its own right, not as a time-saving substitute for knotting, or as a 'mock' rya. As will become clear, it has its own restricted but interesting design possibilities. It can give areas of pile and flat weave, it can give variations in pile length, it can give a double-faced pile rug, it can give a block design in two colours; and as all these are achieved by purely mechanical (i.e., loom-controlled) means, they are different in character from similar effects in a hand-knotted rug.

This chapter may serve as an illustration of how a single idea can be extended and varied in many directions, each extension and variation leading to different design possibilities. Many other ideas in this book could be treated in a similar way.

1. SINGLE CORDUROY ON NORMAL THREADING
A. Using Four Shafts

Single corduroy is Alastair Morton's original weave and the seed from which all other corduroy pile weaves have grown.

One and a half repeats of the threading are shown in Fig. 309. However many times the threading is repeated across the width of the warp, always add a half repeat at the end; thus the threading begins and ends with a group on the front two shafts. Three wefts are needed, one ground weft which is thrown in the two plain weave sheds (lifts

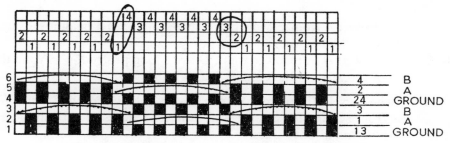

Fig. 309. Single Corduroy on four Shafts. Weave Diagram

13 and 24) and two pile wefts. The ground weft contributes nothing to the pile and is practically invisible in the finished rug.

As shown in Fig. 309, the sequence is:

Lift 13—Ground weft.

Lift 1—Throw pile weft A, from right to left. This pick weaves from selvage to selvage, weaving with the ends on front two shafts and floating over the ends on back two shafts.

Lift 3—Throw pile weft B, from right to left. As will be understood from Fig. 309, this pick stops short of either selvage, so a small portion is left protruding beyond the last raised group of threads on the right.

Fig. 310 (a) shows diagrammatically the stage now reached. Note that where weft A is weaving, weft B is floating and vice versa. So when beaten up they together make a pick of plain weave. The sequence continues:

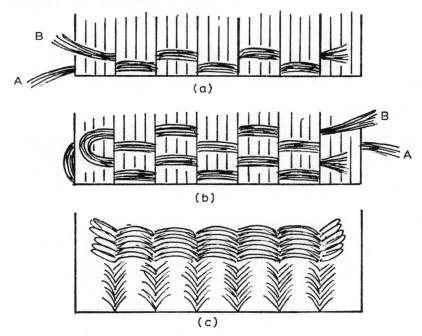

Fig. 310. Single Corduroy on four Shafts. (a–c) Stages in weaving

Lift 24—Ground weft.

Lift 2—Throw pile weft A from left to right. It floats and weaves in almost exactly the same positions as it did before.

Lift 4—Throw pile weft B from left to right. Leave a loop protruding beyond the last raised group of threads on the left. See Fig. 310 (b).

This is the whole cycle. Two picks of pile always follow a ground weft. Weft A always weaves from selvage to selvage; weft B never reaches either selvage and so leaves loops protruding at both sides.

Repeat the sequence several times and the woven rug will be covered with vertical columns of weft floats, with loops at both sides. See top of Fig. 310 (c).

Now cut the floats and the loops in their centres and there will be vertical rows of tufts as shown at bottom of Fig. 310 (c). (Methods of loop cutting are described in detail under Double Corduroy.)

This is the complete process.

Note—That the tufts are well spaced out. With a warp setting of 5 e.p.i., they will be 2 inches apart. So Single Corduroy does not give a close pile.

—That the length of pile can be controlled by pulling up the floats after each pile weft shuttle is thrown.

—That if weft A and B are different colours there will be vertical stripes of these two colours on the *back* of the rug, but all the tufts will consist of a mixture of the two colours, as each tuft has half its yarn contributed by weft A and half by weft B.

—Colours can be inlaid in the pile (see under Double Corduroy).

PRACTICAL DETAILS

Warp—5 working e.p.i.

Weft—ground—6-ply rug wool.

      pile—2-ply carpet wool used sixfold or thicker.

Normal selvage.

In all single corduroys there tends to be a point of weakness in the rug where the tufts spring from the background weave. This can be partly overcome by varying the sleying between each threading unit. If the ends are being sleyed singly in a 5-dents/inch reed, then the ends encircled in Fig. 309 are sleyed together in one dent.

B. Using Eight Shafts

A simple block weave is possible if the Single Corduroy threading is extended onto eight shafts. One way to do this is to alternate one and a half repeats on the front four shafts with one and a half repeats on the back four shafts as in Fig. 311 (a). The whole threading could then be Blocks 1, 2, 1, 2, 1.

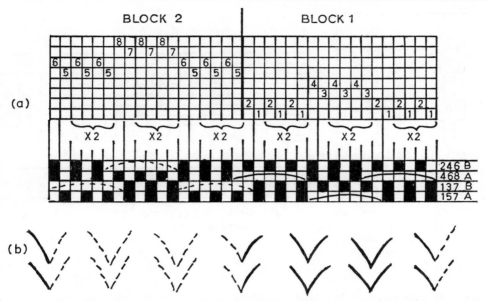

Fig. 311. Single Corduroy on eight Shafts. (a) Weave Diagram (b) Resulting pile

There is no ground weft required because the pile wefts act as the ground weft in the blocks where they are not forming pile. So there are only four lifts and the two pile wefts are used pick-and-pick as shown in Fig. 311 (a).

In the 1st pick, weft A gives a float in the centre of Block 1 (shown by curved line).

In the 2nd pick, weft B gives two floats in Block 2 (shown by curved dotted lines).

In the 3rd pick weft A gives two floats in Block 1.

In the last pick, weft B gives a central float in Block 2.

If this is repeated there will be vertical columns of floats of colour A in Block 1 and of colour B in Block 2. These floats, when cut, will give tufts as shown below, in Fig. 311 (b). Note that there are two solid colour tufts in each block; but at the junction between blocks there is always a tuft of mixed colours. This is typical of blocks in corduroy technique, whether they are shaft-controlled, as here, or inlaid. The two colours used are automatically blended into each other at the block junctions. It is impossible to produce hard colour junctions in a vertical direction; this is something only knotting will give.

Plate 134 shows a rug woven in this way. A colour sequence of (A,A,A,B) has been used between the blocks of colour. This gives floats of colour A everywhere except in the centre of Block 2 (consult Fig. 311 (a)) where colour B has a single float. The effect of these single floats, when cut, is to give a thin line of colour B joining the blocks of colour B. These lines are just visible in the photograph but are more obvious in Fig. 312. Similar lines could be produced in the centre of Block 1, with (A,B,B,B) or (C,B,A,B) colour sequences. Other variations will occur to the weaver.

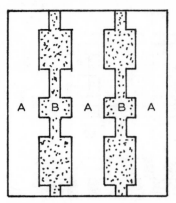

Fig. 312. Single Corduroy on eight Shafts. Variations in blocks by altering colour sequence in wefts

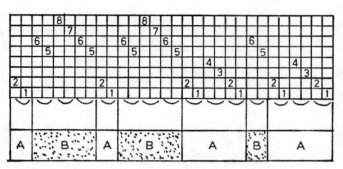

Fig. 313. Single Corduroy on eight Shafts. Alternative threading drafts

OTHER THREADING ARRANGEMENTS

(i) There need not be one-and-a-half repeats of the threading in each block. There can be just half a repeat. A threading of this type is shown in Fig. 313 where, for simplicity's sake, each bracketed pair of ends represents a half repeat. The blocks this will give are shown below.

(ii) There can be a whole number of repeats of the threading in each block. In this case the four lifts have to be slightly changed to (157, 135, 468, 248).

PRACTICAL DETAILS

Warp—6 e.p.i., alternately double and single in the heald, therefore, 4 working e.p.i.
Weft—2-ply carpet wool used seven or eightfold.
Normal selvage.

Of the four picks in the repeat all except the third reach both selvages. So a separate shuttle is needed for the third pick; this means two shuttles of colour A and one of colour B are needed throughout. As the wefts are so thick and there is no ground weft, this is a very quick type of rug to weave. The floats should be pulled up to increase the length of pile and so offset the wide spacing of the tufts.

2. SINGLE CORDUROY USING FOUR-END BLOCK DRAFT
A. Using Four Shafts

Three repeats of the threading are used in each threading block, see Fig. 314. Several weaves are possible, of which the following two are satisfactory.

(i) CORDUROY PILE ON CHEQUERED BACKGROUND

The lifts are shown in Fig. 314 (a).

Picks 2 and 3 produce the floats for the pile, weft B.

Picks 1 and 5 produce a weave in which weft A will come to the surface in some areas and go to the back in others.

Picks 4, 6 and 7 are in plain weave. If this weave is continued, it will give a pile of colour B on a background which is in blocks of colour A and colour B. To switch the colours in the blocks, lift 14 instead of 23, in picks 1 and 5. Plate 135 (top) shows a sample with a white pile on a background of black and white checks. Wefts A and C were white, weft B black.

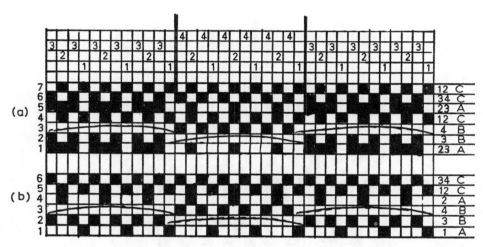

Fig. 314. Single Corduroy using Four-End Block Draft on four shafts. (a) and (b) Weave Diagrams

(ii) CORDUROY PILE ON BACKGROUND OF ANOTHER COLOUR

The warp is set up as for the previous example and the shafts lifted as in Fig. 314 (b).

Here, in picks 1 and 4, weft A takes an over 3 under 1 course across the whole width of the warp.

In picks 2 and 3, weft B floats to give the pile.

In picks 5 and 6, weft C weaves plain. If well beaten, weft A completely hides the other two wefts, so it is possible to have tufts of one colour springing from a background cloth of a completely different colour. (All three colours appear on the back). Plate 135 (bottom) shows this weave, with weft A, a grey-black mixture, weft B white and weft C black.

Both these photographs illustrate how the tufts of pile appear in very definite warpway lines. This is a characteristic of single corduroy.

PRACTICAL DETAILS

Warp—5 working e.p.i.

Weft—In both above weaves, A is 2-ply carpet wool used fourfold. B is 2-ply carpet wool used sixfold, and C is 2-ply carpet wool used singly.

B. Using Eight Shafts

Using eight shafts, a rug with alternating areas of pile and flat weave can be produced.

One complete repeat of the threading is shown in Fig. 315, with Block 1 on the front four, Block 2 on the back four shafts. Thread a whole number of repeats plus half a repeat (i.e., begin and end with a block on front four shafts).

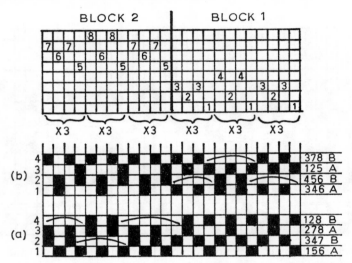

Fig. 315. Single Corduroy using Four-End Block Draft on eight shafts

The problem is to find a weave that will beat down equally in Block 1 and 2. The weave given repeats every four picks and uses two wefts, A and B, pick-and-pick. See Fig. 315 (a). On picks 1 and 3, weft A weaves over 3, under 1 with Block 1, but plain with Block 2. On picks 2 and 4, weft B weaves plain with Block 1, but gives corduroy pile floats in Block 2. *Note:* that the threading is condensed so the floats appear one-third of their real diagrammatic size. Structurally, the net effect of this weave is that a warp end weaving over 2 picks, under 2, alternates with an end weaving over 1, under 3, all across the rug. So there is bound to be a straight fell to the rug. Visually, the net effect is that Block 1 shows floats of colour A predominantly, and Block 2 is covered with long floats, which when cut, give corduroy pile. In Plate 136, weft A is dark grey and weft B is white, but they could perfectly well be the same colour. If two colours are used, the weave has an interesting check pattern on the back.

To change over the areas of pile and flat weave use the lifts in Fig. 315 (b). This has been done in the middle of the photographed sample.

PRACTICAL DETAILS

Warp—5 e.p.i.
Wefts A and B have to be the same thickness—i.e., both 2-ply used sixfold.
Use a floating selvage.

When using the lifts in Fig. 315 (b), there have to be two shuttles of weft B, as in pick 2 the weft does not reach either selvage; or one shuttle can be used and the weft repeatedly cut after pick 4.

3. DOUBLE CORDUROY

Double Corduroy was developed in an effort to produce a rug with thicker pile than single corduroy. It is the weft pile technique most used by hand weavers. With practice, a 3 foot × 5 foot rug can be woven in two days.

A. Using Four Shafts

The threading is shown in Fig. 316; it can be described as '6-end overshot blocks in twill order'. It is a threading that can be expanded and contracted. The one in Fig. 316 contains five ends on each shaft in one repeat. Earlier, in Chapter 7, a version with three ends on each shaft was described. There could be any odd number of ends on each shaft.

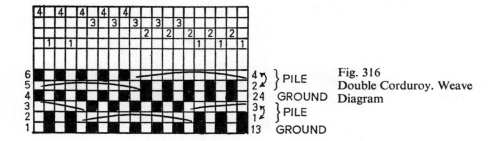

Fig. 316
Double Corduroy. Weave Diagram

Always thread either a whole number of repeats in a rug, or a whole number plus a half repeat. Splitting the repeat in any other way leads to unnecessary complications.

When threading, break the sequence up mentally into five-end groups, i.e., 12121, 23232, 34343, 41414. Always check that there are five ends on each shaft after each repeat is threaded.

As Fig. 316 shows, the lifts are identical with those used in single corduroy. But the great difference with this threading is that the weft floats in picks 5 and 6 do *not* lie vertically above those in picks 2 and 3. They take up an intermediate position. Upon this staggering of the floats depends the closeness of the pile and many of the design possibilities.

Of the six lifts in the sequence, two are in plain weave and are for the ground weft. The other four lifts are for the pile weft and each consists of a single shaft being raised.

With any of these four lifts, groups of five warp ends are raised at regular intervals across the warp. Between these groups the weft floats. Some of the initial difficulty encountered in weaving double corduroy stems from the four different types of shed these four lifts give. This is further complicated by the fact that the sheds are different for a rug with a whole number of threading repeats and for one with a whole number plus a half repeat.

(i) WITH A WHOLE NUMBER OF THREADING REPEATS

Reference to Fig. 317 shows that—

Lifting shaft 1, gives a pile shed with a warp group raised at both selvages.
Lifting shaft 3, gives a pile shed which has no warp group raised at either selvage.
Lifting shaft 2, gives a pile shed with a warp group at the right selvage, but none at the left.
Lifting shaft 4, gives a pile shed with no warp group at the right selvage, but one at the left.

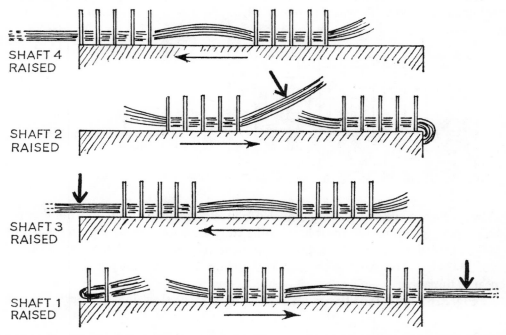

Fig. 317. Double Corduroy. Details of four pile sheds and four pile picks when woven with two threading repeats

Fig. 317 only shows what happens with two repeats of the threading, but the situation is obviously the same however many whole number of repeats are threaded.

Now imagine that a pile weft shuttle were thrown from left to right with shaft 1 up, and then the same shuttle thrown from right to left with shaft 3 up. There will now be a float of weft (arrowed in Fig. 318 (a)), emerging at the right selvage and disappear-

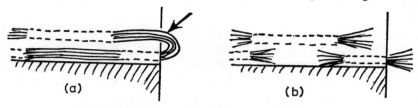

(a)   (b)

Fig. 318. Double Corduroy. Showing tufts at selvage

ing under the ends on shaft 3. When this is cut, it will give a small tuft protruding from this selvage, see Fig. 318 (b). To avoid this, a certain sequence of shuttle throwing must be followed. It is described below and shown diagrammatically in Fig. 317.

Lift 13—Ground weft, from left to right (not shown in diagram).

Lift 1—Pile weft, from left to right. Start at the left selvage. The neatest way to do this is to leave the end of the weft hanging out in the first space between raised warps at the left, see Fig. 317. Then take a separate piece of weft, half the normal thickness, loop it round the selvage thread and put it into the shed as shown. This only has to be done at the beginning and ending of a rug.

Cut the weft about 4 inches from the right selvage. Cutting points are shown in Fig. 317 with heavy arrows, the direction of the wefts by fine arrows.

Lift 3—Throw shuttle from right to left. This is the shed which reaches neither selvage. So leave a tail of weft protruding from the extreme right raised warp group and cut the weft about 2 inches beyond the point where it emerges from the warp group on the extreme left.

Lift 24—Ground weft from right to left (not shown).

Lift 2—Tuck in the weft end (cut at end of lift 1) under the first warp group at the right. Throw shuttle from left to right, leaving a tail protruding from the warp group on the extreme left, and cutting weft (as shown) in the space between warp groups nearest right selvage.

Lift 4—Throw shuttle from right to left. Leave a tail protruding from warp group on extreme right. Do NOT cut weft anywhere.

This is the whole sequence. When shaft 1 is lifted to begin the sequence again, the shuttle is already waiting at the left selvage, so it can be thrown straight across. The beginning procedure with half-thickness weft is not necessary.

Note—The above sequence has been designed so that **the pile weft shuttle is thrown** regularly from right to left and back again.

—The weft is cut at every pick except when shaft 4 is lifted.

—After a little practice the weft will be cut at just the right length, so that little is wasted.

(ii) WITH A WHOLE NUMBER OF THREADING REPEATS, PLUS A HALF REPEAT

Referring to Fig. 319, it will be seen that the four pile weft sheds are similar in type to those described above, but they are produced by raising different shafts, i.e., raising shaft 1 in Fig. 319, gives a similar shed to raising shaft 2 in Fig. 317, raising 3 in Fig. 319 gives a shed similar to raising shaft 4 in Fig. 317. So though the sequence of shuttle-throwing and cutting is identical, different shafts are lifted.

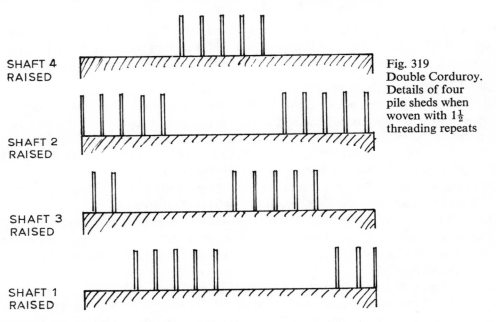

SHAFT 4 RAISED

SHAFT 2 RAISED

SHAFT 3 RAISED

SHAFT 1 RAISED

Fig. 319
Double Corduroy.
Details of four
pile sheds when
woven with 1½
threading repeats

Lift 24—Ground weft, from left to right.

Lift 2—Pile weft, from left to right. Start at left selvage as described above. Cut at right selvage.

Lift 4—Pile weft, from right to left. Cut beyond warp group at extreme left.

Lift 13—Ground weft, from right to left.

Lift 1—Tuck in end of weft cut when 2 was lifted. Throw shuttle from left to right and cut weft in space between warp groups nearest right selvage.

Lift 3—Throw from right to left, leaving end protruding at right selvage. Do NOT cut.

Repeat.

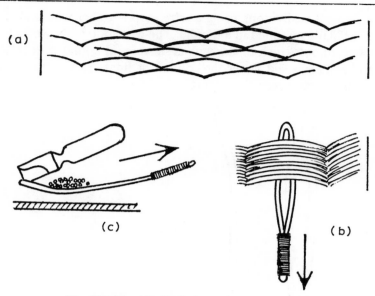

Fig. 320. Double Corduroy. Cutting the floats

So it will be obvious that Fig. 317 can be used as a guide when either type of threading is used. But when a whole number plus half a repeat is used, substitute lift 2 for lift 1, lift 4 for lift 3, lift 1 for lift 2, lift 3 for lift 4.

For either type of threading,

Note—The length of pile is controlled as weaving proceeds. If the shortest pile is wanted, simply throw shuttle and beat. If a longer pile is wanted, enlarge the weft floats by hand. Working from the selvage that the shuttle has just left, pull up two adjacent weft floats with the two hands to the required length, then move along one space and repeat. Do this right across the rug. This procedure also controls the tension of the pile weft in the places where it weaves. Remember that the pile will be half the length of the weft float.

The ability to weave a corduroy rug quickly depends largely on the ability to pull up the floats quickly and accurately.

Cutting Pile

When 2 inches or 3 inches have been woven, the surface of the rug is covered with a series of overlapping weft floats, see Fig. 320 (a). The only way to isolate a vertical column of floats from its overlapping neighbour in order to cut it, is to start at one of the selvages, and then work across to the opposite selvage, cutting each vertical column in turn.

The cutting is most easily done using a wire loop together with scissors or, better still, with a razor blade mounted in a handle. The wire loop is shown in Fig. 321. It is made of stiff wire, about ⅛ inch thick, bent as shown and bound with cord at one end to make a handle. This is slid under the column of floats to be cut, i.e., the column nearest one of the selvages, see Fig. 320 (b).

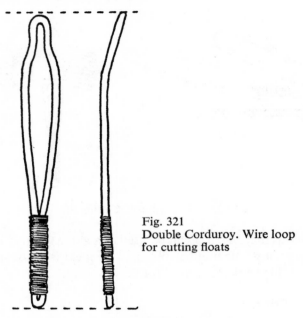

Fig. 321
Double Corduroy. Wire loop
for cutting floats

With scissors—Cut through the centre of the floats.

With a razor blade mounted in handle—put the tip of the blade in the wire loop where it projects beyond the last float, and pull both blade and wire loop in the direction of the arrow. Fig. 320 (c) shows this in side view.

In both these methods, raise the loop as far as possible above the ground weave. This puts the floats under tension so making them easier to cut and also lessens the chance of either cutting instrument nicking the ground weave.

Note—As the wire loop is slid under each column of floats, it should be forcibly moved from side to side. This helps to isolate these floats from those that overlap it, and helps the weaver to judge the centre of the float for cutting. If the loop will not move freely from side to side, this is a sure indication that an odd thread was left uncut in the previous column.

So the sequence of movements is:
  Slide loop under floats.
  Move side to side.
  Cut.

Slide loop under next set of floats, etc.

It only takes a matter of seconds to cut all the floats across the rug. It does not save time to weave a greater amount (say 5 inches) before cutting, as it is very difficult to manipulate the loop under so many floats.

If no wire loop is available, slide the index and middle finger of left hand under the column of floats from the far side (i.e., first pass them under the last-woven float). Open the fingers and with scissors cut the floats stretched tight between them.

Always cut after a plain weave pick, as this holds the pile weft firmly in place for the cutting. When all the loops have been cut, bang the rug with the hand to make the newly formed pile stand up. Then with sharp long-bladed scissors trim the pile level. This requires some skill as the scissors must be kept parallel with the surface of the rug and their tendency to dip downwards be overcome. It is a good idea as each portion of the rug passes from the breast beam to the knee bar, to give a final trim to the pile which is here hanging downwards and so displaying any discrepancies in length. As the weaver increases in competence, less and less trimming will be needed.

Weft Joins

Joins in the pile weft are made in the centre of a float (as in inlay, see later).

Joins in the ground weft are made by overlapping and bringing the two ends up into the pile. So no darning-in of weft is ever necessary (except at the very beginning and finishing of the ground weft). This contributes to the speed of the method.

PRACTICAL DETAILS

The warp setting and weft thickness depends on the length and closeness of pile required. Two typical examples are given:

Short Close Pile

Warp—6 e.p.i., single in heald, therefore 6 working e.p.i.
Weft—Ground, 6-ply rugwool.
    —Pile, 2-ply carpet wool, used sixfold.

Long, More Shaggy Pile

Warp—6 e.p.i., alternately double and single in head, therefore 4 working e.p.i.
Weft—Ground, 6-ply rug wool.
    —pile, 2-ply carpet wool used ninefold, or thicker.

Thicken the selvage ends in both types by starting with one treble and two double ends, as shown by the healds' eyes in Fig. 322 (a). If the corduroy was of the first type the next heald to the left will contain a single end, if of the second type a double end. Fig. 322 (b) shows how these selvage ends are sleyed in a reed with either 6 or 4 dents per inch.

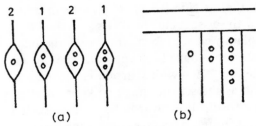

Fig. 322. Double Corduroy. Doubling and trebling of
ends at selvage

If a large corduroy rug is to be made by weaving strips and then sewing them together, the threading has to be slightly altered at each selvage. This is to maintain the even spacing of the vertical columns of tufts across the joins between strips.

Fig. 323 shows at A the threading of the right-hand strip. Its last group is cut short by two threads and becomes 4,1,4. At C is shown the threading of the left-hand strip, whose first group is reduced by three threads, to become 1,2. However many intervening strips there may be, they will all have a threading as at B. This has both its first and last groups reduced.

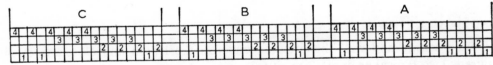

Fig. 323. Double Corduroy. Variations in threading when weaving strips to be sewn together

When sewn together, the 4,1,4, from one strip combines with the 1,2, from the next strip to make up a normal five-end group, and thus the tufts will be evenly spaced.

Note—That in Fig. 323 only one repeat of the threading is given for each strip. There would naturally be many repeats and only the first and/or last repeat would be reduced as shown.

Variations in Double Corduroy

(i) COLOUR

(a) *Warpway Stripes*

In the descriptions so far given, it has been assumed that only one pile weft has been used. But interesting things happen when two pile wefts of different colours are used in various sequences.

Consider the floats made by one repeat of the lifting sequence, as shown in Fig. 317. These are shown in Fig. 324 (a), the number over each float being that of the shaft lifted to give that float. When these are cut, they will give the seven tufts, shown in Fig. 324 (b). Now it is obvious that if, say, a black weft had been thrown when shafts 1 and 3 were lifted and a white weft when shafts 2 and 4 were lifted, the tufts will be alternately black and white. And if this sequence is continued, warpway lines of the two colours will result, as shown in Fig. 324 (c).

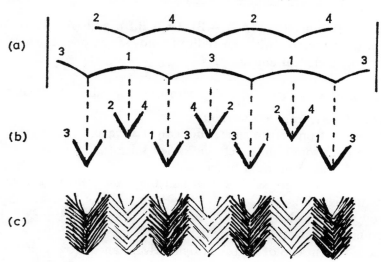

Fig. 324. Double Corduroy. Production of warpway stripes on the pile

Note—That these lines appear with simple shuttle throwing; they are inherent in the technique and so are one of the features to be exploited in corduroy rug design.

The stripes described are of equal thickness and they were obtained with an (A,A,B,B) colour sequence.

With a sequence of (A,B,B,B), stripes of solid B colour will alternate with stripes of an A–B mixture.

With a sequence of (A,A,A,B), stripes of solid A colour will alternate with stripes of an A–B mixture.

If the varying sequences are used successively as shown diagrammatically in Fig. 325, then elongated triangular shapes can be produced. These are seen in the photograph of a black and white double corduroy rug, Plate 137.

Because two shuttles are involved in various orders, the details given in Fig. 317 for one shuttle do not apply. There is in fact, a different sequence of actions for each

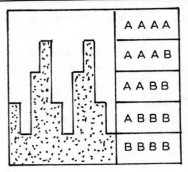

Fig. 325
Double Corduroy. Varying
widths of warpway stripes by
varying weft sequences

of the three colour sequences, (A,A,A,B), (A,A,B,B), and (A,B,B,B). When these
have been mastered together with the ability to move from one sequence to another,
there are no more technical difficulties.

AABB Colour Sequence—(warp threaded with whole number of repeats)

Lift 13—Ground weft, from left to right.
Lift 1—Pile weft A, from left to right, cut at right selvage.
Lift 3—Pile weft A, from right to left, cut at left selvage.
Lift 24—Ground weft, from right to left.
Lift 2—Start weft B at right selvage with half thickness weft, and throw shuttle to
    left, cut as in Fig. 317.
Lift 4—Throw weft B to left. Do NOT cut.
Lift 13—Ground weft, from left to right.
Lift 1—Tuck in the cut end of weft A at right selvage and throw shuttle of A to left.
    Cut few inches beyond left selvage.
Lift 3—Throw shuttle of A to right. Cut.
Lift 24—Ground weft, from right to left.

Note—That the shuttle of B is waiting at left selvage. The shed with shaft 2 lifted
    (the one that normally follows) cannot be used, as it has no warp group
    raised at left selvage. So reverse the order of the picks and:

Lift 4—Throw shuttle B, from left to right. Cut.
Lift 2—Throw shuttle B, from left to right. Do NOT cut.
    This is the complete cycle.

Note—There are eight pile picks in this cycle not four.
    —Lifts 2 and 4 can always be reversed if it makes the weaving simpler (as
    above). This also applies to lifts 1 and 3. The arrows in Fig. 316 are meant
    to indicate this interchangeability. As in neither of these pairs of lifts does
    one pick overlap the other, the weave is identical whether the order is normal
    or reversed.

—The two consecutive picks of weft B always go in the same direction—either both to the right or both to the left.

—A floating selvage is necessary.

AAAB Colour Sequence—(with whole number of threading repeats)

When there is only one pick of B to every three of A, it is easiest to put this in the shed with shaft 3 lifted, because this shed reaches neither selvage. So the sequence could be:

Lift 13—Ground weft, from left to right.
Lift 1—Weft A, from left to right, but do NOT cut.
Lift 3—Weft B. Cut.
Lift 24—Ground weft, from right to left.
Lift 2—Weft A, from right to left, cut at left.
Lift 4—Weft A, from right to left, do NOT cut.

The sequence is more complicated if, from the point of view of the design, the single pick of B is required elsewhere; e.g., in shed with shaft 2 lifted. Thus:

Lift 13—Ground weft, from left to right.
Lift 1—Weft A, from left to right. Cut.
Lift 3—Weft A, from right to left. Cut.
Lift 24—Ground weft, from right to left.
Lift 2—Weft B, from left to right. Do NOT cut.
Lift 4—Weft A, from right to left. Do NOT cut.
Lift 13—Ground weft, from left to right.
Lift 1—Tuck in end of A left hanging out at right selvage, throw shuttle of A from left to right, and cut it in the space between warp groups nearest right selvage. At this point neither the shuttle of A or a tail of A is protruding from either selvage.
Lift 3—Weft A, from right to left. Cut.
Lift 24—Ground weft, from right to left.
Lift 2—Weft B, from right to left, and cut.
Lift 4—Weft A, from right to left, and do NOT cut.
The shuttle of weft A is now back at left selvage ready to begin the cycle over again.

Note—That by substituting A for B, this also shows how to carry out the (B,B,B,A) colour sequence.

—If the above manœuvres are understood (and this can only really be done on the loom), the reader will be able to work out any other permutations of two or more colours for himself.

—That there must never be a weft float passing from selvage into the rug as shown in Fig. 318 (a). If there is, then some mistake has been made.

See under Inlaying Colours for an alternative way of weaving these colour sequences.

(b) Mixing Two Colours

A simple way of mixing two colours, A and B, in the weaving is to have a shuttle of each colour and weave them so that their floats appear in twill lines, see Fig. 326 (a). It is obvious that when these are cut each resulting tuft will have half its yarn from shuttle A and half from shuttle B, see Fig. 326 (b).

A colour sequence of (A,B,B,A,B,A,A,B) produces this twill arrangement. It is a very easy sequence to weave, as it involves less cutting than usual In fact it is the simplest two colour sequence.

Lift 13—Ground weft.
Lift 1—Weft A, from right to left. Do NOT cut.
Lift 3—Weft B, from right to left. Cut.
Lift 24—Ground weft.
Lift 2—Weft B, from left to right. Do NOT cut.
Lift 4—Weft A, from left to right. Cut.
Lift 13—Ground weft.
Lift 1—Weft B, from right to left. Do NOT cut.
Lift 3—Weft A, from right to left. Cut.
Lift 24—Ground weft.
Lift 2—Weft A, from left to right. Do NOT cut.
Lift 4—Weft B, from left to right. Cut.

(a)

(b)

Fig. 326. Double Corduroy.
Mixing two colours

Note—That in this sequence a weft coming out at the selvage is never cut.

(c) Inlaying Colours

In what has been described so far the pile wefts run from side to side of the rug. But it is perfectly possible to interrupt the normal pile weft and inlay a weft of another colour in its place. So blocks and motifs of one colour can be woven on a background of another colour. Fig. 327 shows this diagrammatically. Floats of a light-coloured weft are inlaid in the centre of a rug which consists mainly of a dark-coloured weft.

Fig. 327. Double Corduroy. Inlaying area in centre of rug

The junction between background weft and inlay weft is naturally in the centre of a float. The following sequence is a convenient one, as both shuttles keep up a left to right, right to left sequence, and each shuttle is used for two consecutive picks, thus avoiding the bother of repeatedly changing shuttles in a pick-and-pick sequence. It applies to a warp with a whole number of threading repeats. See Fig. 328 (a) where background weft is shown as black, inlay weft as white.

Lift 13—Ground weft.

Lift 1—Background weft, from left to right, leaving an empty space in the centre. Cut it at right selvage as normally done.
 Inlay weft, from left to right, filling the empty space.

Lift 3—Inlay weft, from right to left, weaving only where required in the centre.
 Background weft, from right to left, filling in the empty spaces on either side. Cut, as this shed reaches neither selvage.

Lift 24—Ground weft.

Lift 2—Tuck in pick of background weft at right selvage and throw background weft from left to right to meet it, cut it in space between warp groups nearest right selvage.
 Inlay weft from left to right.

Lift 4—Inlay weft from right to left.
 Background weft from right to left.
 Repeat.

Note—If the inlay area is very small, it is simplest to wind the yarn in a finger hank and just pass this under the raised warp groups where required.

—An inlaid block can never have hard vertical edges; there will always be two rows of tufts, in which background and inlay colour are mixed, interposed between the inlay area and background. These are shown by arrows in Fig. 328 (b) which represents a cross-section of the rug whose weaving is shown in Fig. 328 (a). An inlaid block can naturally have hard horizontal edges.

The width of an inlay area can be increased very gradually by altering only one of the picks in the sequence at a time. But this is complicated by the four positions the wefts lie in.

The dotted line down the centre of Fig. 328 shows the midline of the inlay area. It will be seen that whereas the inlays in the lower two picks are centred over this area, the inlays in the upper two picks are off-centre, one being to the left, one to the right. The difficulty can best be explained by describing the steps required to increase this inlay area in a symmetrical manner.

(1) When shaft 3 is lifted, inlay white weft under 3 instead of 1 warp group, i.e., the weft stretches further to left and to right, the other three inlays remaining the same. This will increase the width of the area by two white tufts (see Fig. 328 (b)

where there are five white tufts). In other words the two mixed tufts which flank the inlay area will move out one tuft.

(2) With shaft 2 lifted, inlay weft under one more warp group to the right and with shaft 4 lifted, inlay weft under one more warp group to the left. This will have exactly the same effect as the first move, i.e. the area increases in size by one tuft to right and one tuft to left.

(3) With shaft 1 lifted, inlay weft under four ends instead of two; i.e., the weft again stretches further to left and to right.

These are the three stages, which are repeated.

Apart from inlaying large areas, the technique can be used for smaller effects. A colour a little different from the main colour can be inlaid in very small amounts in odd places, to give variety and interest to the whole. Inlay can be used in conjunction with warpway stripes to break their regularity. See Plate 138 where the thick black lines are the result of inlaying black where white would normally be.

Note—The difference here between knotted and corduroy technique. The smallest unit in the former is a knot which appears as a spot; the smallest unit in a corduroy rug is a length of weft inlaid under one warp group and the two ends of this appear as two spots.

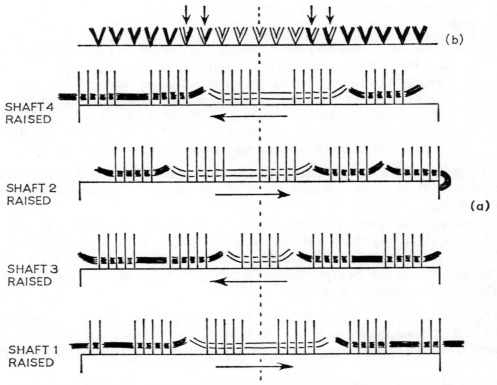

Fig. 328. Double Corduroy. (a) Details of four picks when inlaying (b) Cross-section of inlaid area

Sometimes it is essential to have a single spot of colour in corduroy (e.g., at the point where two angled stripes meet, see later). Fig. 329 shows how this is done. Half thickness pieces of background and inlay weft (dotted line) are linked together and then inlaid under a warp group.

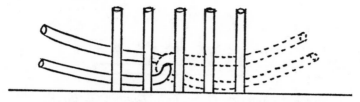

Fig. 329. Double Corduroy. Producing a spot of colour

The inlay principle can be used as a simpler way of managing the varying two-colour weft sequences than those already described. One weft, A, weaves normally (i.e., exactly as in Fig. 317). Where the colour sequence demands the other weft, B, this is inlaid but over as long a distance as possible, i.e., it stops just short of either selvage where colour A takes over. Because weft B never reaches the selvage it cannot confuse the normal shuttle sequence.

The advantages of this method are that the selvage is neater, as no floating selvage is necessary, and that it makes any conceivable colour sequence easy to weave. The drawbacks are that the wefts have to be cut more than usual and that the colour sequences are slightly altered close to each selvage.

(ii) PILE LENGTH

So far the description has concentrated on obtaining a level even pile. But the pile length can be altered either in the weaving stage (by pulling up the weft floats in varying degrees) or in the cutting stage (by cutting floats off-centre) or by a combination of these two methods. The effects produced in these simple (almost mechanical) ways, add a great deal to the possibilities of corduroy technique, especially when combined with two colours as explained below.

(a) *Alternate Long and Short Tufts*

If two consecutive pile picks are pulled up to give long weft floats and the next two pulled up to give short floats, and this is repeated, the situation shown diagrammatically in Fig. 330 (a) is reached. When these are cut in the normal way, the result will be as shown in Fig. 330 (b), tufts with alternate long and short pile. The long pile tufts will stand up as narrow ridges running the length of the rug.

It will be obvious that this type of pile will modify in an interesting way any warp-way stripes in two colours.

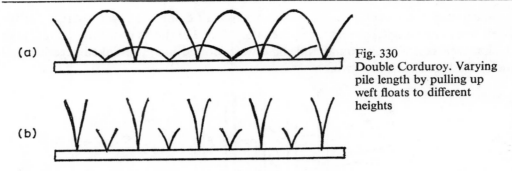

Fig. 330
Double Corduroy. Varying
pile length by pulling up
weft floats to different
heights

(*b*) *Cutting Two Adjacent Floats at Once, i.e., 'Double Cutting'.*

Because the vertical columns of weft floats overlap, it is easy to slide the wire loop under two adjacent columns. Starting at the right selvage, ignore the first column of floats (which is the one normally cut for a level pile) and insert the wire loop into the next available opening. This is marked X in the cross-section view in Fig. 331 (a). In this position, the wire loop will not be able to move from side to side as it did with normal cutting. Cut with scissors or razor. It will be obvious from Fig. 331 (a), that of the two columns of floats which are thus simultaneously cut, the right-hand one is cut to the left of centre (giving long pile) and the left-hand one is cut to the right of centre (giving short pile). If this is continued right across the rug, the net effect will be as shown in Fig. 331 (b), i.e., every tuft consists of long and short pile in equal amounts.

Note—As two columns are cut at once, there is only half as much cutting with this method.

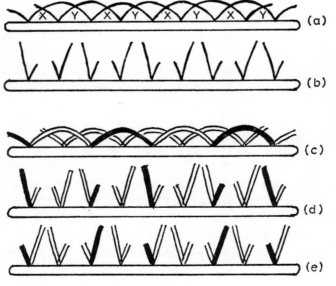

Fig. 331
Double Corduroy
(a–b) Varying pile length by
inserting wire loop
differently
(c–d) Combining above with
colour sequence of
(A,A,A,B)

When the rug is newly-woven or has just been shaken, this cutting tends to give warpway lines of short and long pile (as suggested by Fig. 331 (b)). But the general effect when the rug is in use is of an uneven shaggy pile, which has a more luxurious look than a level pile rug, although containing exactly the same amount of wool. This uneven character can be increased by sometimes cutting as described, and sometimes inserting the loop one opening to the right, marked Y in Fig. 331 (a).

These two positions for double cutting give interesting results when combined with two colours in an A,A,A,B, sequence. Fig. 331 (c) shows the cross-section where B is black and A is white. If these floats are cut in the X positions, then tufts appear as in Fig 331 (d). The long black pile will show on the surface of the rug, but the short black pile will be almost completely hidden. So the effect will be of thin warpway stripes of black on a white background, but at twice the normal distance apart. If the floats are cut in the Y positions, the tufts appear as in Fig. 331 (e). Where there was a short black tuft there is now a long tuft and vice versa; so the thin warpway stripe of black will appear in the intermediate position. Plate 139 shows these two positions of the black stripes clearly.

An interesting development is the production of twill lines in the pile. These result quite automatically from a combination of the two positions of double cutting with varying colour sequences in the pile weft.

A warp is threaded with a whole number of repeats plus three quarters of a repeat. This is so that the colour effects can be centred on the rug. There are four stages, in whose description the normal plain weave picks have been omitted for clarity's sake.

Stage 1: Lift 1—Weft A
Lift 3—Weft B
Lift 2—Weft A*
Lift 4—Weft B

Start double cutting to the left of the first tuft at the right selvage (i.e., in the Y position as described above), and continue all the way across the rug.

Stage 2: Lift 1—Weft A
Lift 3—Weft B
Lift 2—Weft B
Lift 4—Weft A*

Start double cutting to the left of the second tuft in from the right selvage, i.e., in the X position.

Stage 3: Lift 1—Weft B
Lift 3—Weft A
Lift 2—Weft B
Lift 4—Weft A*

Double cut as in Stage 1

Stage 4: Lift 1—Weft B
Lift 3—Weft A
Lift 2—Weft A*
Lift 4—Weft B

Double cut as in Stage 2.

Each stage can be repeated as many times as desired, and then cut, before moving on to the next stage. The angle of the twill naturally depends on this number of repeats.

Note—That the cuts are always made where a column of weft A loops overlaps a column of weft B loops.

—That if in the four picks with asterisks the colour is changed from A to **B,** the twill lines will appear thinner.

—That repeating any of the stages many times will give warpway stripes of equal thickness. These stripes will be twice the width of those obtained by normal cutting.

The rug in Colour Plate 111 shows twill lines produced in this way. Note that the lines have been confined to the centre of the rug by inlaying the appropriate wefts.

(c) *Cutting Floats Off-Centre*

Another development is to insert the wire loop normally (i.e., under one column of floats at a time), but to cut the floats either to the right or to the left of their midpoints.

Starting from the right selvage, cut the first two columns to right of centre and next two columns to left of centre and continue thus all the way across the rug. These cuts are shown diagrammatically in Fig. 332 (a); Fig. 332 (b) shows the resulting tufts,

Fig. 332. Double Corduroy. Varying pile length by cutting floats off-centre

two short alternating with two long. So this will give warpway ridges but of twice the scale of those obtained by method (a). The cutting is very simple and just as quick as normal cutting. The wire loop is inserted, moved from side to side and then pushed hard over to the right or left as required and the cut made in that position.

Starting from the right selvage the positioning of the cuts, described above was—to right, to right, to left, to left.

III. Corduroy rug with wool pile showing twill lines produced by double cutting, see page 416

Diagonal ridges, can be produced by varying this sequence thus:

right,right,left,left, (repeat ad lib)
right,left,left,right, (repeat ad lib)
left,left,right,right, (repeat ad lib)
left,right,right,left, (repeat ad lib)

The angle of the diagonal ridge will depend on how many times each of the above four sequences is repeated. If the sequence is reversed the diagonal will lie in the opposite direction. Ridges appearing as chevrons, diamonds, curves can all be cut on this principle. See Plate 140.

(d) *Combining Long and Short Floats with Off-Centre Cutting*

This method is a little more complicated, but enables the weaver to produce broad ridges of long and short pile. The sequence is as follows:

Lift 1—Pull up weft so that the floats are alternately very large and very small (and tight), see Fig. 333 (a). One way to do this accurately, is to pull up the floats to the normal extent and then go across pulling up every other float, taking in the slack from the intermediate ones.

Lift 3—Pull weft up normally.

Lift 2—Pull up weft as for lift 1, to give alternately large and small floats.

Lift 4—Pull weft up normally.

The floats will now look as in Fig. 333 (b), i.e., two columns of large floats, two of small and four of normal ones.

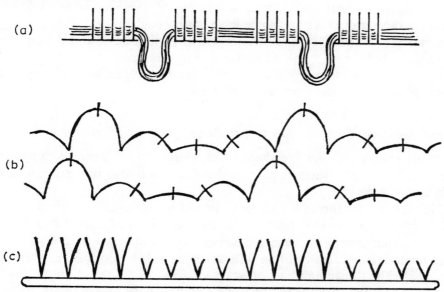

Fig. 333. Double Corduroy. Varying pile length by combining off-centre cutting with floats of different lengths

Now cut the extra large and extra small floats centrally, but cut the normal floats to right or to left of centre according as they lie to the right or left of an extra large float. If they lie immediately to the right then cut to the right of centre, etc., see Fig. 333 (b). So starting from the right-hand side in Fig. 333 (b) the cutting sequence will be:

centre, centre, to right, to right, centre, centre, to left, to left

and this will be repeated all across the rug. Fig. 333 (c) shows that this will give four short pile tufts alternating with four long pile tufts. So the rug will show warpway ridges twice the width of those obtained in method (c). As in that method, these warpway ridges can be made to lie obliquely.

The above four methods will give an idea of the range of possibilities in this aspect of corduroy technique. By extension or combination of these methods, the possibilities are further increased. Their use with two colour effects has only been touched on and is another large field for exploration.

(iii) THREADING DRAFT

(a) Shortening or Extending Whole Draft

It was mentioned at the beginning of this section that the threading draft could be shortened or extended, by diminishing or increasing the ends in each overshot block. If shortened, the vertical lines of tufts will be closer together, but the pile weft will weave for a shorter distance and so be less securely held.

If lengthened, the vertical lines of tufts will be further apart and the pile weft will be more securely held, as it will weave for a longer distance.

The pile can be the same length in both cases, because its length is controlled by the weaver's hands as the floats are pulled up.

(b) Extending One Block in Draft to give Areas of Pile and Flat Weave

The draft is made up of four overshot blocks. If any of these is considerably increased in size, while the other three remain unchanged it will lead to extra large floats in certain areas of the rug.

In Fig. 334 (a), the threading has been altered by increasing the block on shafts 3 and 4. This gives rise to long floats when the other two shafts viz. 1 and 2 are lifted. These extra long floats are cut in the weaving to avoid wastage of yarn. When the normal floats are cut, there will be tufts as shown in Fig. 334 (b), i.e., there is a flat area opposite the threading block of increased size. All that has been done structurally is to increase the width of the small area of flat weave that normally lies between two adjacent columns of tufts.

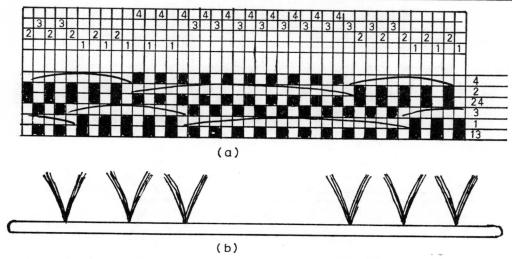

Fig. 334. Double Corduroy. Extending one overshot block in threading draft.
(a) Weave Diagram (b) Resulting tufts

By this means blocks of pile and flat weave of any desired width can be woven. As the positioning of these blocks is shaft-controlled, they naturally cannot be altered during the weaving of a rug.

(c) Pointed Draft giving Long and Short Pile

The pointed draft shown in Fig. 335 (a) (worked out by Pat Tindale) has forty ends in a repeat. Each shaft carries ten ends, these ends appearing as a single group on shafts 1 and 3, but as two 5-end groups on shafts 2 and 4. It is due to these features that two lengths of pile are produced. Fig. 335 (a) shows the weave plan, with normal length floats when shafts 2 and 4 are lifted, but double length floats when shafts 1 and 3 are lifted. These are shown in a cross-section of the rug in Fig. 335 (b).

It will be apparent that the arrangement of floats calls for a different method of cutting. Starting from the right selvage, insert the wire loop in the position marked X in Fig. 335 (b). It goes under a column of normal floats which is itself straddled by (and partly hidden by) a column of long floats. Both these sets of floats are then cut together. The wire loop then moves to the right and slides under a column of normal floats and cuts them (position Y in Fig. 335 (b)). Moving to the right it repeats its first manœuvre, i.e., cuts a set of long and normal floats together, and so on across the rug. The resulting pile is shown in Fig. 335 (c); a long tuft is always flanked by two normal tufts.

It will be obvious that this method can be combined with two pile wefts, i.e., the long pile could be a different colour from the short pile.

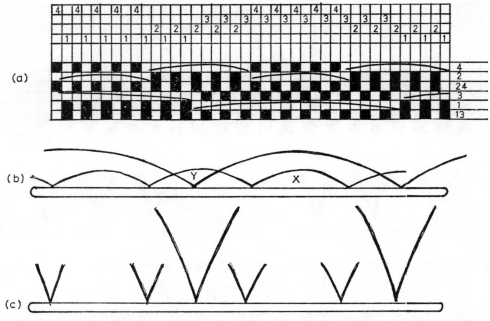

Fig. 335. Double Corduroy. Using pointed threading draft to give long and short pile

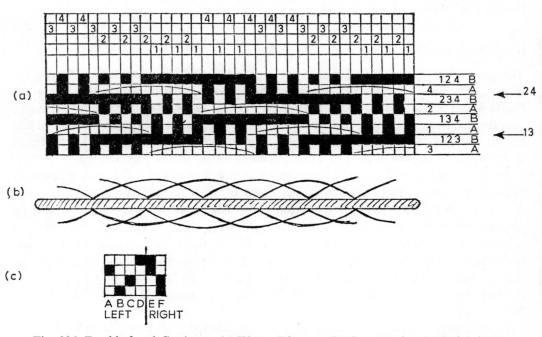

Fig. 336. Double-faced Corduroy. (a) Weave Diagram (b) Cross-section (c) Pedal tie-up

(iv) DOUBLE-FACED CORDUROY

It is obvious that if lifting one shaft at a time gives weft floats on the face of the rug, lifting three shafts at a time will give comparable floats on the reverse of the rug. Thus raising shafts 1, 2, 3, and 4, gives weft floats in four positions on the front and raising shafts, 123, 234, 341 and 412 gives similar floats on the back. The problem is to combine these two sequences in some order that gives a soundly constructed double-faced weave.

The lifts and weave plan of one solution are seen in Fig. 336 (a). The face floats are shown by curved lines as usual, and the reverse floats occur whenever there is a row of filled squares on the point paper. Both face and reverse floats are inserted in a broken twill order. Fig. 336 (b) shows a cross-sectional view.

The weave is quite sound as it stands, without any plain weave, but if two plain weave picks are inserted as shown by the arrows to the right, it will be further strengthened. This is a case where the weaving is simplified if the threading repeat is split in an abnormal way. In fact it is best to use a whole number of repeats plus threequarters of a repeat (i.e., end at left selvage with a group on shafts 3 and 4, as shown in Fig. 336 (a)). This enables a shuttle sequence to be established in which back and front pile wefts move in a regular and related manner. If shuttle A holds the face pile weft and shuttle B holds the reverse pile weft, the sequence is:

Lift 3—Shuttle A to the right. Cut.
Lift 123—Shuttle B to the right. Cut.
Lift 1—Shuttle A to the right.
Lift 134—Shuttle B to the right.
Lift 2—Shuttle A to the left. Cut.
Lift 234—Shuttle B to the left. Cut.
Lift 4—Shuttle A to the left.
Lift 124—Shuttle B to the left.

Both wefts have to be started at the left selvage in the normal way (using half thickness wefts as described before), at the beginning of the rug; thereafter they are only cut as indicated.

Even if the rug is to be the same colour both sides, a separate weft is necessary for front and back pile picks.

There are some problems dealing with the reverse pile picks.

(a) The weft floats cannot be pulled up in the normal way; but if the fingers are pushed through the warp, they can control the size of the floats adequately.

(b) Cutting the back floats. All the floats are left uncut on the back of the rug. When the rug is taken from the loom, stretch it, back side uppermost on a table or nail it to the floor and cut all the loops in this position.

PRACTICAL DETAILS FOR DOUBLE-FACED CORDUROY

Warp—5 working e.p.i.

Weft—2-ply carpet wool, used ninefold.

With a countermarch loom, ten pedals (two for plain weave) will be needed. With a counterbalanced loom use a direct tie-up and both feet. A neat method of tying up a jack loom is shown in Fig. 336 (c). The four left pedals are controlled by the left foot, the other two by the right foot. The sequence then is:

	Shafts lifted		Pedals used
	3	—	A
	123	—	A+F
⟶	1	—	B
	134	—	B+E
	2	—	C
	234	—	C+E
⟶	4	—	D
	124	—	D+F

Plain weave, A+B and C+D, can be inserted where shown by arrows.

(v) COMBINATION WITH OTHER PILE TECHNIQUES

(*a*) *Knotted Pile*

Pile can be knotted into the warp at any point, either to give additional colour or additional thickness of pile.

(*b*) *Cut Pulled-up Loops*

It may have occurred to some readers that the structure of corduroy pile could be exactly duplicated (though more slowly) by pulling up weft loops and cutting them. If the corduroy pile in Fig. 337 (a) and the pulled-up loops in Fig. 337 (b) are cut as shown, they will both give the identical result, viz. the pile in Fig. 337 (c). So these two methods of pile production are well suited to be combined.

Probably the most interesting application of this idea is to pull-up the loops half-way between the normal corduroy tufts. If this is combined with pile wefts in two colours, the resulting warpway stripes, already described, can be made to lie obliquely, see Plate 138. (The same structure can be achieved with eight shaft corduroy—see later.) Fig. 338 shows the four stages in this process and these will be described in detail.

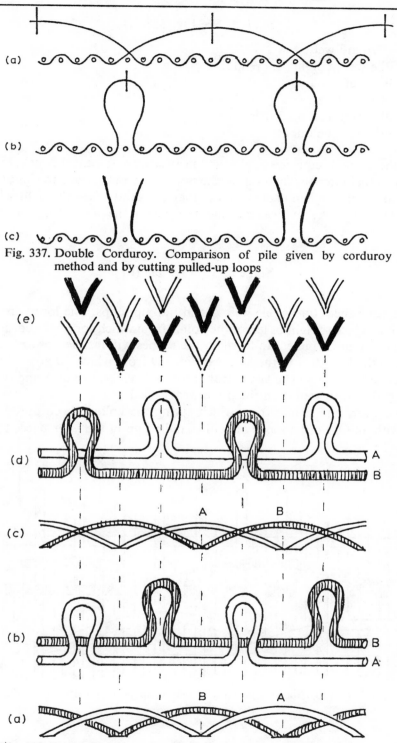

Fig. 337. Double Corduroy. Comparison of pile given by corduroy method and by cutting pulled-up loops

Fig. 338. Double Corduroy. Combining cut pulled-up loops with corduroy pile to give oblique colour stripes

Stage 1. See Fig. 338 (a)

Lift 13—Ground weft.
⟮ Lift 3—Pile weft, colour A. (White).
⟮ Lift 1—Pile weft, colour A.
Lift 24—Ground weft.
⟮ Lift 4—Pile weft, colour B (Black).
⟮ Lift 2—Pile weft, colour B.

This is the normal sequence to give warpway stripes. Repeat this, say, three times Arrange it so that after the final repeat the wefts run from selvage to shuttle (i.e., that there are no cut ends hanging out), and so that one shuttle is at the right selvage, and one at the left. This may involve reversing the order of the pile picks, hence the arrows above.

Stage 2. See Fig. 338 (b)

Lift 13—Ground weft.
Then in same shed, throw pile weft A and pull up loops. The loops are pulled up one warp interspace to right or left of the points from which spring the corduroy floats of the same colour. If pulled up to right, the stripes will incline upwards to right, if pulled up to the left, then to the left. See Fig. 339 from which all ground wefts have been excluded for clarity. The last repeat of four pile picks, two of A and two of B are shown, together with weft A in the plain weave shed.

Now the warp interspaces from which spring the colour A corduroy floats are labelled with an O. So the loops are either pulled up in the interspaces to the right

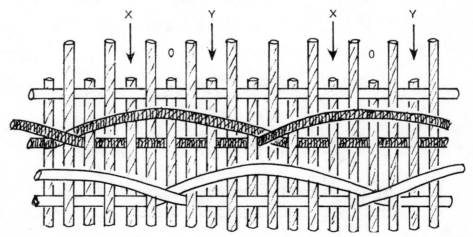

Fig. 339. Double Corduroy. Showing position for pulling up loops in relation to corduroy pile picks

(arrowed Y) or in the interspaces to the left (arrowed X). Or, if converging oblique lines, as in Plate 139, are wanted, then some of the loops are pulled up to left and some to right. In Fig. 338 (b) the loops are pulled up to the right.

Lift 24—Throw ground weft.

In same shed throw colour B and pull up its loops exactly halfway between the A colour loops. This is shown in Fig. 338 (b).

Repeat three times.

Stage 3. See Fig. 338 (c)

Lift 13—Ground weft.
Lift 1—Colour B.
Lift 3—Colour B.
Lift 24—Ground weft.
Lift 2—Colour A.
Lift 4—Colour A.

Repeat three times.

This is the corduroy sequence again but with colours reversed (see Fig. 338 (c)). As B is the last colour used in Stage 2 and the first used in Stage 3, there are two consecutive picks of B at the junction between these stages. End exactly as in Stage 1, with shuttles at opposite selvages and no weft ends hanging out.

Stage 4. See Fig. 338 (d)

Lift 13—Ground weft.

In same shed, throw colour B and pull up loops one warp interspace to right of points from which spring the colour B corduroy floats.

Lift 24—Ground weft.

In same shed throw colour A and pull its loops up half-way between B's loops.

Repeat three times.

This is the whole sequence, which can be repeated over and over again. When floats and loops are cut, tufts as shown diagrammatically in Fig. 338 (e) will be the result, forming black and white stripes running obliquely up to the right.

Note—Cut each stage as it is completed. It is easiest to cut the loops with scissors.

—Each stage can be repeated as often as wanted. Repeating each three times gives an approximate 45° slant to the stripes.

The thick black lines in Plate 138 were achieved thus:

In Stages 1 and 3 (corduroy sequences), by inlaying black weft, where white would normally go, in appropriate places.

In Stages 2 and 4 (pulled-up loop sequences), by pulling up black loops twice as close together as normal and pulling up no white loops in these areas.

It will be seen that this is quite a free way of designing in oblique stripes, as the direction of the angle can be altered at will. Although corduroy on eight shafts gives a much faster way of producing oblique stripes, it lacks this freedom.

B. Using Five Shafts

A corduroy can be woven on a five-shaft extension of the Spot Weave threading. The closeness of the tufts makes it a double corduroy, but this closeness is achieved without overlapping of the weft floats. The pile wefts weave for about the normal length (passing under six raised warp ends) but float for less than the normal distance (passing over only five ends instead of eleven). So the floats have to be well pulled up by hand to give a reasonable pile length.

The details are shown in Fig. 340 (a). Two plain weave picks with ground weft are followed by two pile picks labelled A and B. Then two more ground weft picks are followed by another two pile picks, C and D, in different positions.

The positioning of the four weft floats in the above repeat leads to interesting effects when two colours are used.

If, as shown in Fig. 340 (a), pile picks A and C are black and pile picks B and D are white, the resulting tufts would be as the top line in Fig. 340 (b). Continuing this

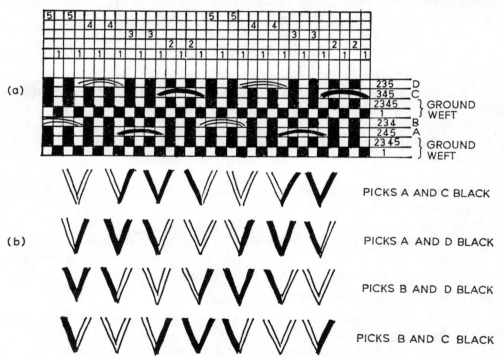

Fig. 340. Double Corduroy. Using a five-shaft draft.
(a) Weave Diagram
(b) Colour of tufts with different weft sequences

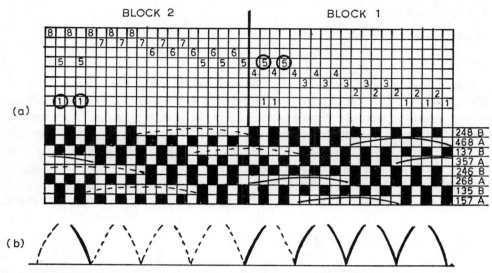

Fig. 341. Double Corduroy. Using eight shafts to give Single-Faced Block Weave.
(a) Weave Diagram
(b) Colour of tufts

sequence gives warpway stripes of black and white. But note how they differ from the normal four-shaft corduroy warpway stripes. Here there is a tuft of mixed colour interposed between each solid colour tuft. This makes the stripes appear wider and less clear-cut. See Plate 141 at bottom.

As Fig. 340 (b) shows, there are three other positions the black and white stripes can take up, depending on which two picks are black and which two are white. If these positions are used in sequence, the stripes will naturally lie obliquely, inclining up to the right or left, see Plate 141 (top).

It will be seen from Fig. 340 (a) that all the pile picks lie in sheds related to one of the ground weft sheds—viz. that given when shafts 2, 3, 4 and 5 are lifted together. It is only the two picks of ground weft with shaft 1 lifted that counter and lock these sheds. This leads to some untidiness at the selvages as the thick pile wefts are always entering and leaving the same shed and so passing over or under two ends. A floating selvage is of course necessary.

PRACTICAL DETAILS

Warp—6 e.p.i., alternately single and double in heald, therefore 4 working e.p.i.
Weft—Ground—6-ply rug wool.
    —Pile—2-ply carpet wool used ninefold.

C. Using Eight Shafts

(i) BLOCK WEAVE

(a) *Single-Faced*

The normal double corduroy threading is entered on the front four shafts and repeated ad lib to form the first block, the same threading is then entered on the back four shafts and repeated for the second block. See Fig. 341 (a). Where one block runs into the next, thread on the encircled shafts, i.e., end Block 1 on 4,5,4,5,4, instead of 4,1,4,1,4, and end Block 2 on 8,1,8,1,8, instead of 8,5,8,5,8. Alternate the two blocks across the warp, ending on the same block as the one that starts the threading.

As with the single corduroy block weave, there is no ground weft and the two coloured pile wefts (A and B) are used alternately. Fig. 341 (a) shows the lifts and the resultant weft floats. The tufts given by the latter are shown below in Fig. 341 (b).

> *Note*—There are two tufts of mixed A and B colour at the junction between the blocks.
> —The narrowest possible blocks (i.e., one threading repeat on front four shafts and one on back four shafts as in Fig. 341 (a)) give only two tufts of colour A, two tufts mixed, then two tufts of colour B.
> —Threading more than one repeat will increase the number of single-colour tufts, but not the number of mixed-colour tufts.

PRACTICAL DETAILS

Warp—4 or 5 working e.p.i.
Weft—2-ply carpet wool used ninefold.

The tufts are separated from each other in the warp direction by the thickness of the pile weft not forming tufts in that area. So the pile tends to be thin. This can be partly countered by pulling up the floats well and so giving a good length of pile.

(b) *Double-Faced*

This block weave has corduroy pile on both sides, the colours reversing on the back. So each of the two wefts has to form floats on the face in one block and on the reverse in the other block. Fig. 342 (a) shows the lifts and weave plan, and Fig. 342 (b) shows a cross-section with the resulting tufts. Where there is a colour A tuft on the front, there is a colour B tuft on the back and vice versa. Where there is a mixed colour tuft on one side, there is also a mixed colour tuft on the other side. As might be imagined, the shuttle sequence is a little complex and it is given in detail below. The sequence works best if the final repeat of Block 1 at the left edge of the rug ends on the 3,4,3,4,3, group, not the 4,1,4,1,4, group as is normal. So there is threequarters of a threading repeat at the left selvage.

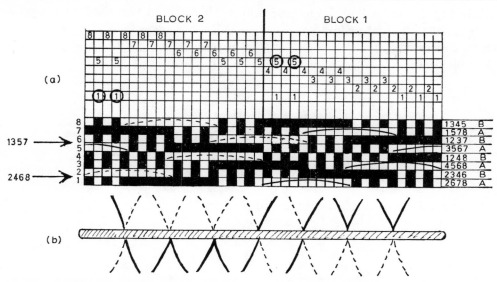

Fig. 342. Double Corduroy. Using eight shafts, to give Double-Faced Block Weave. (a) Weave Diagram. (b) Arrangement of tufts on two sides of the rug

Lift 2678—Weft A, from right to left. Start in normal way at right selvage. Cut at left.

Lift 2346—Weft B, from right to left. Start similarly at right selvage. Cut at left.

Lift 4568—Weft A, from right to left. Do NOT cut.

Lift 1248—Weft B, from right to left. Do NOT cut.

Lift 3567—Weft A, from left to right. Cut at right.

Lift 1237—Weft B, from left to right. Cut at right.

Lift 1578—Weft A, from left to right. Do NOT cut.

Lift 1345—Weft B, from left to right. Do NOT cut.

If this is followed exactly no floating selvage is necessary.

Note—There is no ground weft. But as shown by the arrows in Fig. 342 (a) a plain weave pick can be inserted (with shafts 2468 raised), between picks 1 and 2 and another (with shafts 1357 raised) between picks 5 and 6.

The tie-up for a countermarch loom is given at Fig. 343 (a). This would have to be altered if at any point in the design one colour all the way across on the face, with another colour all across on the reverse were wanted. With a jack loom the tie-up

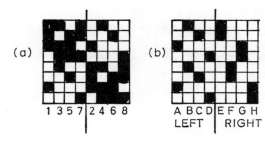

Fig. 343
Double Corduroy. Pedal
tie-ups for weave in Fig. 342

given in Fig. 343 (b) will do both these things. The left foot uses the four left pedals, the right the four right pedals.

The sequences are:

For block weave:

A+E

A+F

B+G

B+H

C+G

C+H

D+E

D+F

For one colour all across on back and on front:

A

A+E+F

B

B+G+H

C

C+G+H

D

D+E+F

PRACTICAL DETAILS

Warp—6 e.p.i., alternately 4 single and 1 double in heald, therefore 5 working e.p.i.
   (This fits in well with the threading, which is in five-end groups)
Weft—2-ply carpet wool, used ninefold.

(ii) TWILL CORDUROY

With four shaft corduroy, the tufts resulting from wefts thrown with shafts 1 and 3 raised, alternate in position with the tufts from wefts thrown with shafts 2 and 4 raised, i.e., there are only two positions for the tufts to emerge. If the threading is extended onto eight shafts as shown in Fig. 344 (a), there are four possible positions for the tufts. The threading repeat includes forty ends, five being on each shaft.

The lifts and resulting weave plan are shown in Fig. 344 (a). As in normal corduroy, a ground weft in plain weave is always followed by two pile weft picks. These pairs of pile picks have been labelled a, b, c and d in Fig. 344 (a). Fig. 344 (b) shows the resulting tufts similarly labelled; i.e., tuft, a, is the result of pile picks, a.

Note—That each pile weft weaves for twice the normal distance, therefore it is very
        securely held.

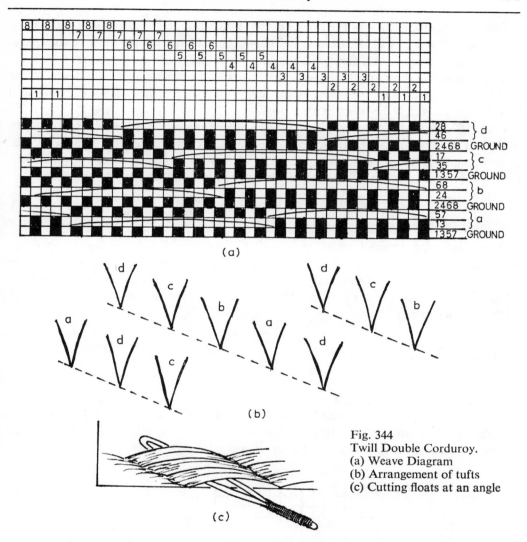

(a)

(b)

(c)

Fig. 344
Twill Double Corduroy.
(a) Weave Diagram
(b) Arrangement of tufts
(c) Cutting floats at an angle

—That it also floats for twice the normal distance, therefore it tends to give a long pile.

—That there is twice as much distance in a warp direction between one float and the next float in a similar position. Therefore the tufts are twice as much separated, warpway, as normal. The long pile (mentioned above) helps to make up for any resulting sparseness of tufts.

Now if pile wefts a,b,c,d were all different colours, the result would be warpway stripes of these four colours. This is one obvious possibility, but more interesting things can be done by using only two colours in different sequences.

The four positions of the tufts are exactly analogous to the four positions of the weft floats in a 2/2 twill. From this it follows that all the colour and weave effects obtainable with a 2/2 weft-face twill are also obtainable with twill corduroy.

These effects will naturally be on a far larger scale in corduroy and some of the more intricate ones will be blurred by the length of pile. But they all are possible, and so this is a very large field for exploration.

Plate 142 shows the two simplest colour sequences used in 2/2 twill, viz. (A,A,B) and (A,B,B).When applying these colour sequences to twill corduroy, remember that A or B, signifies 'two consecutive pile picks of A or B', since it needs two pile picks to make one tuft. So the colour sequences are really twice as long as written.

Cutting the Pile

This can be done normally starting at one selvage, and sliding the wire loop under each vertical set of floats, in turn. Or the wire loop can be slid at an angle under an oblique set of floats as shown in Fig. 344 (c). The latter method can be started anywhere, not necessarily at a selvage. It is probably easier to cut the loops centrally with the normal method.

PRACTICAL DETAILS

Warp—6 working e.p.i.
Weft—2-ply carpet wool used seven or eightfold.

The threading can be reduced to twenty-four ends (three on each shaft) as shown in Fig. 345. The only effect this has is to draw the tufts closer together in the weft direction. So it is more suitable if a short dense pile is wanted.

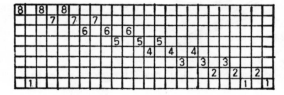

Fig. 345
Shortened form of Eight-Shaft
Double Corduroy threading

(iii) HALF CORDUROY

This is called Half Corduroy on analogy with half-rya and half-flossa techniques, which combine areas of flat weave with areas of pile.

The details are shown in Fig. 346. The threading is as for twill corduroy. The lifts and weave plan show that as usual one ground weft is followed by two pile wefts.

The floats are shown by lines. Floats produced when only one shaft is lifted are

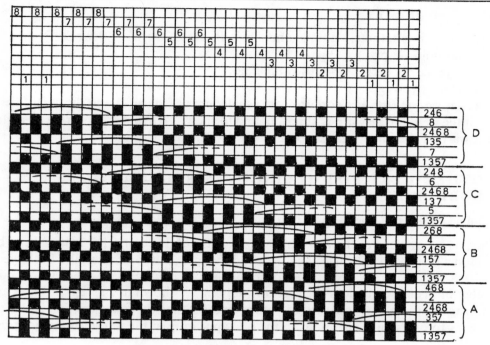

Fig. 346. Half Corduroy. Weave Diagram

exceedingly long and so are cut, during weaving, to save yarn. These are shown terminating in dotted lines.

The lifts have been grouped in sixes and, for convenience, labelled A, B, C and D. Each of these groups is a self-contained unit and can be repeated any number of times. The groups can follow each other in any order. If the weave were used exactly as shown, i.e., A,B,C,D, repeat, it would give alternating stripes of pile and flat weave which slope up to the left. They could be made steeper by weaving 2A,2B,2C,2D. The stripes could be made wider with the following sequence

$$(A,B) \times 2 \text{ or } 3 \text{ or } 4$$
$$(B,C) \times 2 \text{ or } 3 \text{ or } 4$$
$$(C,D) \times 2 \text{ or } 3 \text{ or } 4$$
$$(D,A) \times 2 \text{ or } 3 \text{ or } 4$$

Alternating checks of pile and flat weave result from repeating A many times, then C many times.

A pointed threading draft will vary the slope of the stripes across the warp. Using a D,C,B,A, sequence will reverse the slope of all the stripes. In other words it behaves just like a twill.

PRACTICAL DETAILS

Warp—6 e.p.i., alternately double and single in heald, therefore 4 working e.p.i.
Weft—Ground—6-ply.
  Pile—2-ply carpet wool used ninefold.
Use a floating selvage.

The flat weave parts of a corduroy are usually not weft-face, due to the great thickness of the weft. So the warp is almost bound to show. To avoid it appearing as spots, use a warp of the same general colour as the weft.

4. OTHER WEFT PILE TECHNIQUES RELATED TO CORDUROY

A. Inlaid Fleece or Other Long Fibre

Fig. 347 shows one of the ways that short lengths of fleece or other material can be inlaid in a plain weave shed, leaving their ends hanging out to form a pile. Each piece is passed under six raised ends, and overlaps the preceding piece as shown. An odd number of plain weave picks then follow (only one is shown in Fig. 347). Pieces are laid in again, using the same shed as before, but this time the inlay position is shifted two ends to one side. This results in the pile appearing in the intermediate position.

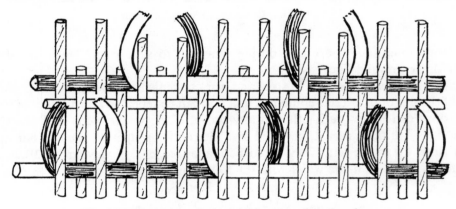

Fig. 347. Producing pile by inlaying short lengths of yarn

As each piece is laid in by hand, there is ample opportunity for varying colour sequences. If the pieces laid in are alternately of two colours, and the colours are made to shift sideways in each succeeding inlay pick (as do the black pieces in Fig. 347), then twill lines of the colours will be produced. At a less mechanical level, pieces can be inlaid to give blocks and motifs exactly as with inlay corduroy.

The structure of this technique is almost exactly similar to five-shaft corduroy and in fact the latter was derived from this technique.

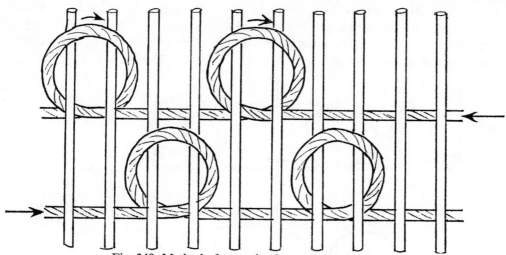

Fig. 348. Method of wrapping loops to be cut for pile

B. Cut Wrapped Loops

(i) An exactly similar structure to the preceding can be produced with a continuous weft as shown in Fig. 348. The technique is a modification of wrapped loops (see Chapter 6). With a shed open, the weft is passed forwards, under six raised ends, and backwards over two ends, forwards under six, backwards over two, etc. An odd number of picks of plain weave follow (not shown in Fig. 348). The looping is then repeated but, in this row, bring the weft out in the intermediate positions, so that the loops are staggered as shown. The loops are cut to give the pile.

(ii) An alternative method gives a structure very like normal double corduroy, except that no plain weave ground weft is required. In this the weft is passed forwards under ten raised ends and backwards over five, and this is repeated all across, see Fig. 349. The shed is then changed and the weft returns in a similar manner but making loops in the intermediate positions. The loops are cut to give pile.

Note—There are two thicknesses of the weft in both sheds, all the way across the warp. This is very obvious in the upper row in Fig. 349.

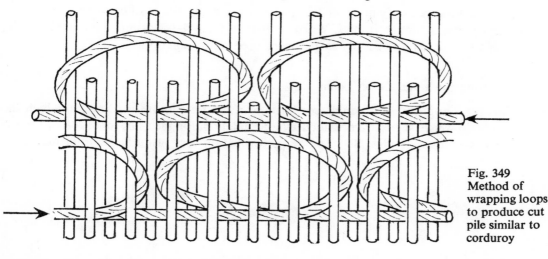

Fig. 349
Method of
wrapping loops
to produce cut
pile similar to
corduroy

Fig. 350 (a) shows the way to begin and end a weft, so that this double thickness is preserved right up to the selvage. Fig. 350 (b) shows how the weft is carried up from one row to the next in order to preserve this double thickness. Naturally if two colours are used in alternate rows it is simpler to begin and end each row as in Fig. 350 (a).

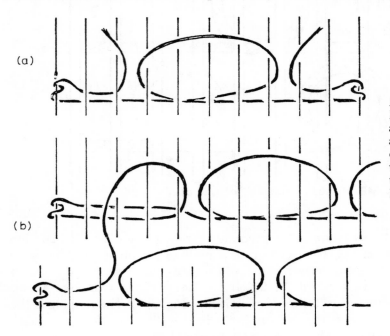

(a)

(b)

Fig. 350
Method of starting and finishing a row and jumping up from one row to the next when using wrapping technique shown in Fig. 349.

There are other possible arrangements of the loops. For instance, they could be made in twill order (in which case all the 2/2 twill colour and weave effects are possible—see Eight-Shaft Twill Corduroy), or in broken twill order or arranged as in twill on opposites. The technique is slow but very free. The absence of a plain weave weft makes it very simple to use.

PRACTICAL DETAILS

As these methods only need the two plain weave sheds, they can be carried out on the simplest looms or rug frames. Warp settings of from 4–6 working e.p.i. are suitable, with weft consisting of 2-ply carpet wool used six to ninefold.

C. Using Stick and Leash Loom

This is an application of single corduroy to a shaftless loom or frame, in which the two plain weave sheds are obtained by alternately pulling leashes forwards and twisting a shed stick on edge. So it can be performed on very primitive equipment.

Leashes are generally tied to a leash-rod, so that all the ends they encircle can be raised at once. But for this technique they are tied up in bundles of five leashes, so pulling up a bundle raises five ends. There should be an odd number of such bundles in the width of the rug.

The odd-numbered bundles have been labelled A, and the even-numbered ones B, in Fig. 351. A ground weft and two pile wefts (1 and 2) are necessary.

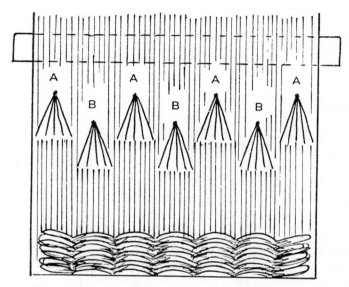

Fig. 351. Weaving Corduroy on a stick and leash loom

Start by weaving in plain weave, alternately twisting the stick and pulling up *all* the leashes for the two sheds. End with a pick in the leash shed, then the sequence is:

Pull A leashes only, and throw pile weft 1, start it at one of the selvages in the normal way. Note that it is lying in a normal corduroy shed, i.e., weaving for some distance then floating for the same distance.

Pull B leashes, throw pile weft 2. This pick floats where the previous one wove and vice versa. It reaches neither selvage.

Twist stick—ground weft.

Pull A+B—ground weft.

This sequence is repeated, pile weft 1 always weaving from selvage to selvage, pile weft 2 never reaching either selvage. The latter leaves small loops at each side as in single corduroy. Pull up the floats to the required size.

The floats and side loops are shown at the bottom of Fig. 351, and they are cut to form the pile.

All other details of this technique are as for Single Corduroy.

11 · Warp-face Rugs of all Types

INTRODUCTION

The warp-face technique has traditionally taken lowest place in the hierarchy of rug weaving methods. This is chiefly due to the fact that, when such a rug is woven in plain weave on the traditional two-shed rug loom, the design is limited to warpway stripes. But wherever hard-wearing properties have been the chief consideration, the warp-face technique has been chosen and used with success. Thus even today it is seen in the fabric for Bedouin tents, for carpet and storage bags and for simple, peasant rugs.

The technique is little used by present-day rug weavers, but when woven in non-traditional materials (e.g., mohair) and in weaves other than plain weaves, it has a great deal to offer. In addition, the speed at which a warp-face rug grows on the loom (with maybe only three picks per inch), commends it highly to professional rug weavers.

Whereas in weft-face rugs, the closely packed weft hides the widely spaced warp, in a warp-face rug it is the closely-crammed warp that completely hides the weft. This would suggest that a piece of weft-face plain weave rug could be turned through a right angle, making weft into warp and vice versa, and then be used as a guide from which to make an exact copy in warp-face technique. But this overlooks an important fact. It is impossible to weave a warp-face rug with the warp ends as close together as are the weft picks in a weft-face rug. With warps so closely set, shedding would be impossible. So the warp has to be opened to a setting that is practical and the consequent loss of weight in the rug made up by using a very heavy weft. Thus the warp-face warp bears some relation to the weft-face weft, being merely set differently; but the warp-face weft differs markedly from the weft-face warp, being far heavier.

Making these adjustments, almost every weft-face weave in which the wefts travel from selvage to selvage can be woven as a warp-face technique. So the field is large and awaits the weaver who learns the simple process of converting weft-face to warp-face.

1. GENERAL TECHNICAL DETAILS

A. Warping

Making the warp is designing the rug. Any colour stripes or changes in yarn will run the whole length of the rug, only being modified by the weave structure. So as much care and thought must go into this stage as goes into the selection of wefts when weaving a weft-face rug. If a block weave is to be used, this demands special sections in the warp in which two colours alternate, end-and-end. (See later.) No extra ends are needed at the selvages. The warp will be very bulky and should be made in 6 inch wide sections if a warping board or mill is being used.

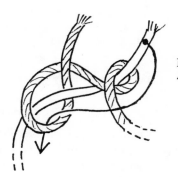

Fig. 352
A double weaver's knot

Knots should be avoided in the warp, especially with a slippery worsted yarn (such as belting yarn or mohair). Where knots are unavoidable, tie one of the double weaver's knots as a normal weaver's knot is bound to work loose in the weaving. Fig. 352 shows a simple one.

B. Beaming

Again due to its bulk, the warp presents problems in the beaming stage. If wound on normally with occasional warp sticks, the threads at either edge are bound to slip and spread when the full weaving tension is applied. Four large headless nails driven into the beam at each edge of the warp will prevent this from happening. Place the two sets of nails at exactly the correct distance apart, see Fig. 353 (a). A more professional way is to use two circular flanges of wood or metal which can be slid along the beam to the required positions and fixed. If the warp sticks are placed up against the nails, as shown in Fig. 353 (b), then the pull of the warp during weaving cannot shift them.

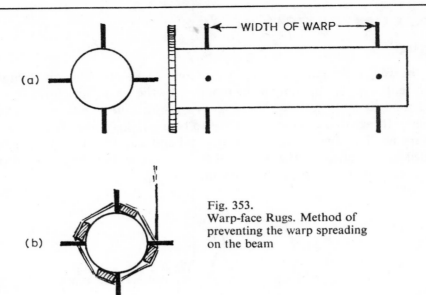

Fig. 353.
Warp-face Rugs. Method of
preventing the warp spreading
on the beam

C. Drawing-In

The unit of warp that is drawn through one heald may be one very thick yarn, or two, three or four thinner yarns. In either case, the healds must have large eyes (so string healds are preferable to wire) and a special threading hook will have to be improvised. The unit of warp is not doubled or trebled at the selvage.

D. Number of Shafts Used

With the warp settings suggested, shedding will be found almost impossibly difficult if only two shafts are used for plain weave, and especially if the yarn has tough, protruding hairs. So the threadings shown in Fig. 354 (a), which spread the ends over four, six, or eight shafts should be employed. In all these, plain weave results from raising

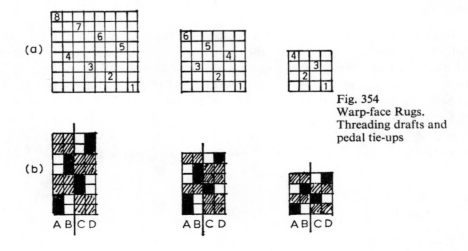

Fig. 354
Warp-face Rugs.
Threading drafts and
pedal tie-ups

alternately the back two, three or four shafts and the front two, three or four shafts. These threadings reduce the motion between adjacent shafts normally found with straight drafts. Other weaves can be similarly spread over all the available shafts.

E. Sleying

The choice of reed is a compromise. In order to clear the shed between picks, it would be ideal to have one warp unit in every dent. But the warp unit would probably stick in such a narrow dent, and moving the batten would be very difficult. So in order to have an easily-swinging batten, as many warp units as possible should go in a dent, e.g., three or four.

Two units in a dent is the usual compromise. Sley the selvage as the rest of the warp.

F. Tying to Front Stick

If 2 inch wide strips of warp are tied as with weft-face weaves, the knots will be impossibly bulky. So tie strips $\frac{1}{2}$ to $1\frac{1}{2}$ inches wide. Trim the warp ends after the knots are tied, to avoid an unequal build-up when the knots reach the cloth beam.

G. Pedal Tie-Up

To make the shedding easier with plain weave, have two pedals responsible for each shed. Then using two feet, press first one then the other, so that the actual shedding is divided into two actions.

The pedal tie-ups for a countermarch loom are shown in Fig. 354 (b). Remember that a filled square means a pedal-to-lower-lam tie, an empty square means a pedal-to-upper-lam tie, and a shaded square means no ties. The same plans can be used for jack looms if the shaded squares are disregarded. A four-shaft counterbalanced loom is tied as shown, again disregarding the shaded squares.

The left foot controls pedals A and B, and the right C and D. So one shed is obtained by pressing first A, then C; the other by pressing first B, then D. If the batten is swung after pressing A and again after pressing C, the shed should be clear.

H. Batten

The batten should be weighted as heavily as possible because a warp-face rug requires the hardest beat of any type of rug. In a weft-face weave, the batten has to force a slack weft between relatively rigid and widely spaced warp ends. But with a warp-face weave, the batten has to force a thick, tight weft as far as possible between closely-set warp ends.

In a weft-face rug, the beat-up is cumulative, i.e., the batten still exerts a compressing effect on picks about $\frac{1}{2}$ an inch from the fell. This is absent with a warp-face rug, where the batten only affects the actual pick it is driving home, and maybe the previous one.

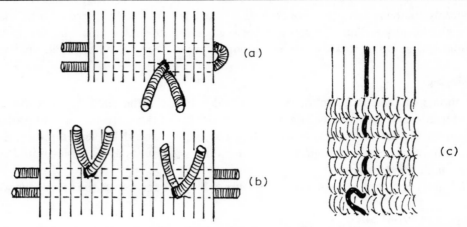

Fig. 355. Warp-face Rugs. (a) and (b) Beginning and joining wefts. (c) Correcting a loose end

I. Weaving

As the warp is closely set, it only requires two or three picks to space the ends out beyond the front stick. The Double Twined Edge is now worked across and the rug proper begins.

To start the weft, split it into two halves. Bring one half out of the shed about 3 inches from the selvage, in the space between two raised warp units. Take the other half around the selvage thread, back into the shed and bring it out in the same warp interspace as above, see Fig. 355 (a). In other words, the two halves do not overlap, as in a weft-face rug. In fact, if they did overlap they would make an obvious bulge in the weave. These ends naturally cannot be darned down a warp end; as they are firmly held by the closely set warp, it is perfectly safe to cut them off flush with the rug's surface.

Weft joints are made similarly with no overlap, see Fig. 355 (b).

There is no tendency for a warp-face rug to become narrower during weaving, so a temple is never necessary. In fact, if the weft is laid in loosely, the rug may increase in width. The weft should run straight from selvage to selvage at a tension sufficient to restrain this tendency of the closely set warp to spread. The best way to achieve this is the following:

Throw shuttle from right to left. Leave a !oop of weft at the right selvage.

Beat once to clear the shed. Draw the loop of weft into the shed by pulling on the weft at the left selvage; at the same time force the shed wide open at the right selvage with the right hand. The returning loop of the weft can then be correctly adjusted for tension and position. This is practically impossible, if the weft is simply thrown and beaten in one operation as with weft-face rugs.

Beat again.

With the batten still against the fell of the rug, change the shed in two stages (first pedal A, then pedal C).

Open the shed. If it sticks anywhere, ease it open with the hands, working between the batten and the shafts.

Push batten away and throw shuttle from left to right, leaving a loop of weft at the left selvage, as above. Beat. Adjust loop. Beat again.

This is the complete sequence of weaving a plain weave warp-face rug.

If, for any reason, an individual end becomes loose (e.g., caught by the shuttle), draw the slack down into the woven rug for a few inches, with the help of a needle point, see black end in Fig. 355 (c). Then darn the loop sideways into the weft.

Remember that as weft joins are so simple, it is best to use lightly filled shuttles which will easily negotiate the slightly troublesome shed.

Occasionally examine the back of the rug to make sure that there are no long warp floats. With a close-set warp, a small fault on the back of the rug gives no sign of its presence on the front.

After the final pick, repeat the Double Twined Edge and then cut the warp an inch or so beyond it.

2. WARP-FACE RUGS IN PLAIN WEAVE

A. Colour Blending

As the warp generally consists of several yarns used as one, the colour blending and colour plying ideas described for weft-face rugs can be used to add variety and richness to the warp.

B. Tied and Dyed Warps

The warp can be tied and dyed in two main ways.

(i) IN HANK FORM

This produces a haphazard mixture of two or three colours, as was used in some Peruvian warp-face weaves.

(ii) IN WARP FORM (See Fig. 356)

Make the warp on a frame, so that it can be stretched out full length though not necessarily full width. Insert a cross at both ends of the warp as it is being made. Bind the warp with thick cotton yarn where the dye is to be excluded, see Fig. 356. The crosses can be made use of during the tying. Thus, if, in one area, only the even-numbered ends are tied, it will produce a block of end-and-end cross stripes.

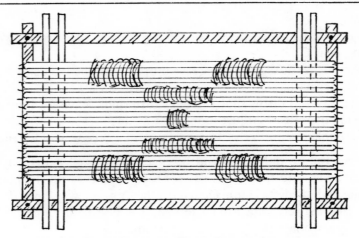

Fig. 356. Warp-face Rugs. Tie-dyeing warp on a frame

Tie both crosses and insert a string in the loops at both ends of the warp. Remove the warp from the frame and dye.

When dry, raddle and wind onto the warp beam of the loom. Only untie the binding cotton at the last moment, i.e., as the warp passes through the raddle, to avoid shifting of the warp threads.

Weave normally.

C. Warpway and Weftway Stripes and Spots

Three design elements are available when a two colour warp is used.

 (i) Warpway stripes, produced by a group of at least two ends of one colour in the warp.

 (ii) End-and-end cross stripes, produced by two colours used end-and-end (i.e., alternately), in the warp.

 (iii) Spots, produced by a warping order of (A,B,B) repeat, or (A,B,B,B) repeat.

 These will be recognized as the three elements produced with two colours in weft-face plain weave. If Plate 8, illustrating the latter, is turned on its side, it will show combinations of these three elements possible in warp-face weave. Note that end-and-end stripes in warp-face correspond to pick-and-pick stripes in weft-face. Plate 143 shows a section of a warp-face rug using all three elements.

D. Combining Thick and Thin Wefts

Wefts of different thicknesses can be used to vary the texture of the rug. It will be found that one weft has to be about three times as thick as the other, to make the difference apparent. One way to achieve this is to use a single shuttle, throwing one pick in a shed for the thin weft, but three picks in a shed for the thick weft (carrying the weft round the selvage thread at the end of the first and second picks).

When combined with a warp consisting of two colours, end-and-end, something very like a block weave can be produced.

Make a warp with, say, black and white, end-and-end. At certain points when threading, reverse the colour sequence by threading one of the colours in two consecutive healds.

Now open a plain weave shed and the raised threads will be black in some sections, white in others, the junctions between these sections being the points in the threading where the colour sequence was reversed. With the opposite shed open, the colours in these sections will naturally reverse.

Fig. 357 shows a small section of such a warp.

In the first shed, at the bottom, the eight raised ends consist of four black at the right and four white at the left. Throw a thick weft in this shed. In shed 2, in which the colours of the raised ends are reversed, throw a thin weft.

Repeat these two picks. The net effect is that shown in the lower part of Fig. 357; the right half of the warp is predominantly black, the left predominantly white.

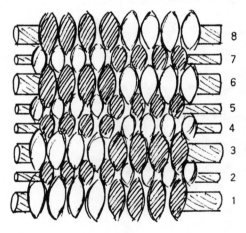

8
7
6
5
4
3
2
1

Fig. 357
Warp-face Rugs. Effect of using thick and thin wefts

In shed 5, which, according to the sequence, should contain a thick weft, throw a thin weft. This reverses the weft sequence, so that in the next four picks, the thick yarn lies in the opposite shed to that used in the first four picks, the same applies to the thin weft.

The effect of this switching of wefts is that, in the upper part of Fig. 357, the predominant colours are reversed, the right half now being white, and the left black. It will be obvious that the colours of these blocks will be reversed on the back of the rug. This type of weaving can be combined with areas in which both wefts are of equal thickness, so that end-and-end cross stripes are produced.

The technique is sometimes used in a plain weave structure, which has a predominant warp, but is not entirely warp-faced. In this case the weft's colour does contribute to the surface pattern. It can be a half-way stage between the two warp colours, which will lessen the contrast between the blocks, or it can be black or white which will emphasize one of the blocks. Rag strips are a popular weft for this technique.

E. Bringing Spots of Weft to the Surface

If in either of the plain weave sheds, the shuttle is floated over one raised warp unit, there will be a spot of weft showing at this point. Such spots can be moved sideways in successive sheds so that they join to form lines, or only put in alternate sheds in an end-and-end stripe, see Plate 144. However used, there will be a corresponding warp float on the back. This is best avoided by using two shuttles, each carrying half the normal thickness of weft. One is thrown normally from selvage to selvage, the other is thrown in the same shed but floats over warp units where spots are required. Fig. 358 (a) shows a section through such a shed. The normal weft is shown black, and the

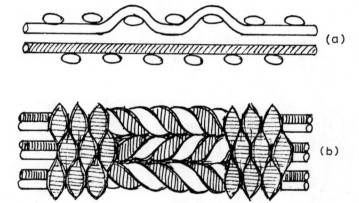

Fig. 358. Warp-face Rugs
    (a) Cross-section showing the bringing of spots to the surface
    (b) Combining weft twining with warp-face plain weave

spotting' weft is shown white. If the wefts are of two different colours, this gives the possibility of spots in two colours. Whichever weft is not floating as a spot lies in the normal shed and prevents the warp float at the back of the rug.

The same idea can be applied to other weaves. See Plate 145 where in three places the weft has floated over two adjacent ends in a warp-face twill weave. As the weft floats follow the direction of the twill, they have the effect of replacing the warp twill lines with weft.

This technique has no weft-face counterpart.

F. Combining Warp-Face with Weft Twining

Apart from a finish for warp-face rugs, weft twining can be used decoratively within the rug. A row, or rows, of twining from selvage to selvage not only alters the texture, but is one of the few ways of obliterating the warp stripes and introducing a new colour to the surface of the rug.

A further development is to introduce areas of weft twining on a background of warp-face plain weave.

Wind two shuttles using weft of half the normal thickness. Put both shuttles into a plain weave shed and bring them out of the shed at the same point. Then close the shed, and twine for a distance on the flat warp, using the two wefts on the shuttles as the two twining elements. Re-open the plain weave shed and put the two shuttles back into it, to emerge at the opposite selvage or at another point where a twined motif is required.

As Fig. 358 (b) suggests, any of the two-colour weft twining patterns can be introduced, if the two shuttles carry different coloured wefts. Plate 146 (top) shows a small sample in which one of the wefts was the same colour as the warp, so only the lighter colour shows in the twining area. The two wefts have been twined to give concentric diamonds. The warp in this sample was 6-ply rug wool set at 12 e.p.i., and the twining wefts (which embraced two warp ends between each half turn) were each of 2-ply carpet wool used fourfold.

A drawback that this technique shares with the following one results from the lack of warp take-up in weft twining. As there is considerable warp take-up in the surrounding warp-face weave, inequalities of tension develop quickly. So the twined areas must be small or alternated in some way so that the inequalities cancel each other out.

G. Combining Warp-Face with Weft-Face

This technique was developed by Violetta Thurstan in the Amria rug industry at Burg el Arab, Egypt. The principle is the same as for the last technique.

Use a weft a quarter to a third of the normal thickness. Carry it in a plain weave shed to the edge of the area which is to be weft-face, see Fig. 359. Then weave it across this area going over and under groups of warp ends. There may be two or three ends in a group, thus the working e.p.i. in the weft-face area are reduced from, say, 12 (the number in the warp-face area) to 6 or 4, and this reduction enables the weft to cover the warp. At the far side of the area, enter the weft into the normal plain weave shed, and carry it to the selvage.

Take it round the selvage thread, re-enter it into the same shed, as far as the weft-face area. Then weave it across this area again, but in the opposite shed, then enter the normal plain weave shed. Repeat these two picks, with the result that the warp-face

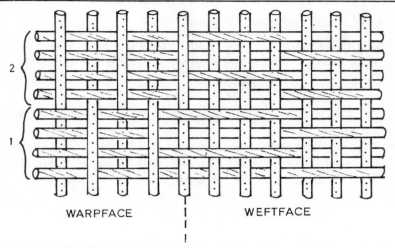

Fig. 359. Warp-face Rugs. Combining weft-face and warp-face plain weave

areas now have four picks in one shed, thus giving them their full thickness of weft, and the weft-face area has four picks in successive sheds. These two weaves should beat down the same amount.

Repeat the above four picks, but with the opposite plain weave shed in the warp-face area.

The position now reached, which constitutes one whole repeat, is shown very diagrammatically in Fig. 359. The warp-face area is to the left, with four picks in each of the two sheds (bracketed), the weft-face area is to the right with eight picks in successive sheds.

The outline of the weft-face area can be changed after every four picks, and this has been done in the motif shown in Plate 146 (bottom), but it can only shift three ends or a multiple of three ends at a time.

The weave can be made much easier if the warp is threaded so that the special theds for the weft-face area can be obtained by raising shafts. Fig. 360 shows such a shreading with the lifts and weave plan.

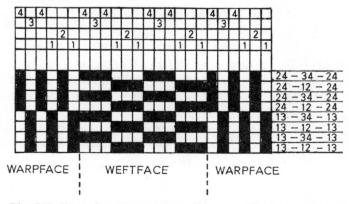

Fig. 360. Warp-face Rugs. Weave Diagram showing method of
combining weft-face and warp-face plain weave

Starting at the bottom of this diagram, pick 1 is woven thus.

Lift 13, carry the weft to the edge of the weft-face area and bring out to the surface.
Lift 12, carry the weft across the weft-face area and bring it out.
Lift 13, carry the weft to the selvage.

The other picks follow in a similar way, using the lifts given.
Any of the two shuttle patterns can be woven in the weft-face area.

H. Two Pick-Up Techniques Related to Plain Weave

(i) BEDOUIN SAHA TECHNIQUE

The saha is a dividing curtain in a Bedouin tent. It, and even the tent material itself, is often decorated with stripes of elaborate warp patterning. The technique used is the exact counterpart of the weft-face technique, called Skip Plain Weave, see Chapter 4.

It is carried out on the simplest of looms by the Bedouin women, and can be woven on any loom that gives the two plain weave sheds.

Set up a warp using two colours. Treat the two yarns (hand-spun goathair and cotton in the case of the Bedouin) as a single unit, both in warping and threading. So two yarns, one of each colour, goes in each heald. Sley the warp twice as close as is normal, because this is a form of double weave. No reed is necessary if a narrow sample is being woven. In the following weaving sequence, the yarns will be assumed to be black and white.

Open shed. The raised ends will consist of pairs of black and white threads. Pick up on a stick one thread out of each of these pairs, according to the pattern desired, i.e., pick up black where black is required, white where white is required. In Fig. 361 the white has been picked up from pairs 1, 2, 5 and 6, and the black from pairs 3 and 4. Turn the pick-up stick on its edge and carry the weft across in this picked-up shed.

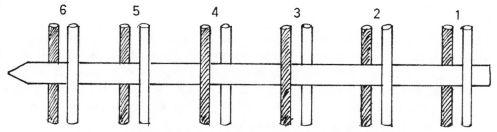

Fig. 361. Warp-face Rugs. Method of picking up in Saha technique

The threads not picked up (i.e., the white in the black areas of the design, and vice versa) drop to the back as warp floats.

Beat, and repeat the process with the opposite shed.

If no batten is used, beat with the shuttle in the opposite shed. To avoid twisting of the yarns in a pair, always pick up the black of a pair to the left of the white.

The design limitations found in Skip Plain Weave naturally apply here, i.e., use small motifs, or break up large units, to avoid overlong warp floats.

Structurally, this is a one-weft double cloth (see next section) in which the back cloth is left unwoven.

Plate 147 shows part of a saha. Motifs based on oblique lines will be seen to predominate. They come very easily to the technique; the stick merely moves its pick-up sequence one thread to the left or right in each successive shed.

This technique was developed for rugs by Violetta Thurstan in her Amria Rug Industry. These rugs were predominantly in normal warp-face plain weave but had perhaps lengthwise stripes in the saha technique. The problems of tension when such a rug was rolled onto the cloth beam did not arise, as they were woven on horizontal ground looms.

The technique can, of course, be woven in a less primitive way using four shafts. The warp is then made black and white, end-and-end, and threaded singly in the healds, using a straight draft. The two sheds for pick-up are obtained by raising shafts 12 and 34. Use a direct tie-up.

This method has three advantages:

(1) There is no tendency for adjacent black and white yarns to twist around each other in pairs.

(2) Areas with all one colour across the width of the rug can be woven by lifting, say, shafts 1 and 3 alternately for black to appear, and shafts 2 and 4 alternately for white to appear.

(3) The pick-up can be greatly aided by slight movements of the pedals. For instance, for the shed with shafts 1 and 2 raised, two feet are used on the appropriate pedals. Then, when picking up a white area, slightly drop the black ends out of the way, by releasing pressure on the relevant pedal; and do similarly for a black area.

(ii) ONE-WEFT DOUBLE CLOTH

This is a very ingenious development of the saha technique, by which the warp floats at the back are also woven, so that a completely-reversible two-colour design is possible. It is known from early finds in Peru and Egypt, where a piece dated about A.D. 400 was unearthed. Until recently it existed as a technique for weaving camel girths in the Sudan. It can be perfectly well woven on any two-shed loom, but the description that follows is for a four-shaft loom.

Make a warp with black and white, end-and-end. Thread it straight on four shafts, black on shafts 1 and 3, white on shafts 2 and 4. Sley twice as close as in normal warp-face.

For one colour all across the rug, lift the shafts thus, 1, 123, 3, 134, giving black on the surface, and 2, 124, 4, 234, giving white on the surface.

For areas of pick-up, use the following sequence.

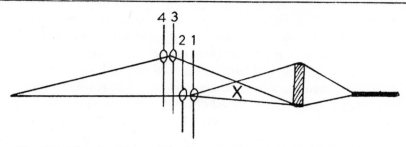

Fig. 362. Warpface Rugs. Side view of shed in One-Weft Double Cloth

Lift 12. Pick up colours as described for the saha technique. Turn stick on its edge. Throw weft from right to left, leaving the stick on its edge in this shed.

Lift 34. Fig. 362 shows a side view of the shed obtained. Return the weft from left to right in the small lower shed marked 'X'. The latter may need to be enlarged with another stick turned on its edge. Remove the pick-up stick and beat in the last two picks.

Pick up the second row of the design, still with shafts 3 and 4 raised. Turn the stick on its edge. Throw the weft from right to left, leaving the stick on its edge in this shed.

Lift 12. Again, there will be a small lower shed, through which the weft is returned to the right. Remove pick-up stick and beat.

Repeat this sequence.

Note—There are two picks for each change of shed.

—As this is a warp-face double weave, only one weft is necessary, its colour being immaterial. It is the interchange of warps from front to back that creates the design; the weft takes an unchanging course. So the pockets between back and front cloths are only sealed along horizontal colour junctions, not vertical. This makes it a far simpler structure than normal plain weave double cloth.

I. Practical Details for Warp-Face Rugs in Plain Weave

(i) Using 2-ply carpet wool as warp.

Use three threads as one (i.e., make the warp from three cones or tubes) and treat this treble thread as the unit in warping. A setting of from 10 to 12 treble ends per inch is suitable. The weft can be 6-ply carpet wool used three- or fourfold, or thick cotton or horsehair, or hemp of comparable thickness.

(ii) Using 6-ply rug wool as warp.

Though 6-ply rug wool may well contain exactly the same amount of yarn as three 2-ply threads, it has to be set at 12 e.p.i., at least, because it does not cover the weft as efficiently.

(iii) Using Belting Yarn and Mohair as warp.

Being more compact yarns, these do not cover the weft as well as carpet wool, so a higher warp setting is necessary, e.g., 48 e.p.i., treble in a heald, therefore 16 working e.p.i. These two types of yarn can be brushed during weaving to raise a pile, using either an old blunted pair of carders, or a specially made brush with very long, flexible wires and two handles. (See list of suppliers at end of book.)

Only raise the pile when the warp is under tension; so do it when a section has been woven and the warp is about to be turned on. It is very easy to over-raise mohair and weaken the yarn. Plate 148 shows the length of pile that can be raised with safety on a black and white mohair warp-face rug. Colour Plate IV shows a brushed warp-face rug of dyed mohair.

A good weft to give solidity to warp-face rugs in this section is 2-ply horsehair used threefold.

The traditional American warp-face rug, sometimes known as a drugget, was a lighter textile than those described above. It often had a warp of 2-ply handspun woollen yarn, set at 20 to 30 e.p.i., with a weft of a variety of materials, such as woollen yarn, rags and such.

If the Double Twined Edge is worked with 6-ply rug wool, then the group of warp ends embraced in each movement should consist of two treble ends of 2-ply carpet wool, or two ends of 6-ply rug wool, or three treble ends of belting yarn or mohair, when the above warp settings are used.

3. WARP-FACE RUGS WITH DISCONTINUOUS WARPS

The weft-face techniques described in Chapter 5 (meet and separate, and kilim) all depend on wefts that do not pass from selvage to selvage, but weave within a small area, i.e., discontinuous wefts. So to convert them into a warp-face structure involves either knotting together lengths of different coloured warp yarn so that they weave into a predetermined pattern, or the infinitely more painstaking Peruvian method of warp interlock. In the latter, a series of horizontal scaffolding wefts were first stretched on a frame and then between them, small one-colour warps were wound, each interlocking with the warp at either end of its own allotted area, and each being placed according to a design. These small warps were then woven, presumably with a needle, to carry the hidden weft from selvage to selvage. Neither method is a feasible one today for the weaving of rugs.

4. WARP-FACE RUGS WITH RAISED SURFACE DECORATION

The various techniques described in Chapter 6, i.e., soumak, weft looping, weft chaining and knotted pile can all be carried out on a warp-face plain weave background. Soumak and pile knots are best worked on the raised ends of a shed, not on the full thickness of warp. This is how the knotted motifs are worked on the warp-face Turkoman tentbands. In this way, if they are built up in blocks, there is no need for compensatory plain weave picks between the blocks.

5. WARP-FACE RUGS IN MULTISHAFT WEAVES

A. Converting Weft-Face Weaves into Warp-Face Weaves

(i) If both warp and weft take a similar course through the fabric, the conversion is simple. Thus in plain weave, both elements take an over 1, under 1 course; in 2/2 twill they take an over 2, under 2 course. When such a weave is turned through a right angle (making warp into weft and vice versa), the structure is identical, though in the case of a twill, the diagonal line will slope in the opposite direction.

All such weaves repeat on the same number of ends and picks, so their minimum weave plan will always be a square. For weaves of this type, e.g., plain weave, plain weave double cloth, hopsacks and many twills, the weaving directions are identical for warp-face as for weft-face, and the conversion is simply a matter of using different yarns and different settings. 2/2 twill is taken as an example.

2/2 *Twill*

All the colour and weave effects described in Chapter 7 for 2/2 weft-face twill, can be produced in a 2/2 warp-face twill. Where for instance, in a weft-face rug, the weft colour sequence is (A,B,A,B,A) repeat, the identical colour sequence is used in the warp. Because the warp of a warp-face rug is never as close as the weft in a weft-face rug, the effects will not be as clear cut.

Naturally, many different colour sequences can be combined in the same warp, and Plate 149 shows the different character that can be given to warpway stripes by using this idea.

The warp should be set a little closer than for warp-face plain weave. The weave is very suitable for rugs, being heavy and flexible and the shedding is easier than with plain weave.

Two interesting warp-face weaves can be arrived at by combining the lifting sequences of two twills.

(a) *Combining 3/1 and 1/3 Twill*

The lifts are 123, 2, 234, 3, 341, 4, 412, 1. If the warp is threaded straight on four shafts and each shaft carries a different coloured end, these colours will appear as four cross stripes. Both sides of the rug will be identical.

(b) *Combining 3/1 and 2/2 Twill*

The lifts are 123, 12, 234, 34, 341, 41, 412, 12. This gives a twill surface on both sides of the rug, but one shows longer floats than the other.

(ii) If warp and weft take dissimilar courses through the weave, and this applies to all block weaves and double-faced weaves, the conversion is a little more complex. It requires a small amount of work on point paper.

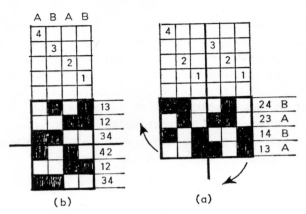

Fig. 363. Converting a weft-face Block Weave into a
warp-face Block Weave

Fig. 363 illustrates this process of conversion. At (a) is shown the minimum threading, weave plan and lifts for the simplest block weave. The weave plan is turned through a right angle (see arrows), and is shown in its new orientation at (b). This weave plan is then analysed. The weave is seen to be on four ends, all of which behave differently in their passage through the weave. So the threading is a straight draft on four shafts. This is written down above the weave plan. The four ends are coloured A, B, A, B, to correspond to the weft colour sequence in Fig. 363 (a). It is now simple to work out the six lifts that will give this weave, and these are written at the right, opposite the relevant pick.

Now, the right-hand half of the weft-face weave plan, represented one pattern block (threaded 1,2,3) and the left-hand half the other pattern block (threaded 1,2,4). And each of these blocks could be extended in the weft direction by repeating either 1,2,3, or 1,2,4, in the threading.

So the bottom half of the warp-face weave plan similarly represents one pattern block, and it can be extended in the warp direction by repeating the three lifts, i.e., 34, 12, 24, as often as desired. The top half represents the other pattern block, and it can also be extended at will in the warp direction by repeating the three lifts, 34, 12, 13, as often as desired.

So the warpway dimension of the blocks depends on how often the two sets of three lifts are repeated. Naturally, the blocks will appear only where the warp has two colours, end-and-end, so their weftway dimension depends on the extent of this colour arrangement in the warp.

The following general rules will be seen to apply to this example.

(a) The number of different lifts needed for the weft-face form of the weave becomes the number of different shafts for the warp-face form, and vice versa. For example an eight-shaft weft-face weave needing four different lifts becomes a four-shaft warp-face weave needing eight different lifts.

(b) The total number of lifts in the lifting sequence (often different from the above, as one or more lifts are repeated) of the weft-face form, become the total number of ends in the threading repeat of the warp-face form.

(c) As a corollary to the above, when a lift is used several times in the lifting sequence of the weft-face form, there will be a corresponding shaft used the same number of times in the threading repeat of the warp-face form.

(d) The weft colour sequence in the weft-face form, becomes the warp colour sequence in the warp-face form.

It will be understood from this example that sometimes a weave impossible in one form becomes possible when converted. Thus a weaver with only a four shaft loom, can convert an eight-shaft weave needing four lifts into a four-shaft weave needing eight lifts.

B. Block Weaves

In the field of block weaves, an interesting fact emerges. In their weft-face form, many block weaves have a feature in common and this is that they need only four lifts with an (A, B, A, B) colour sequence. So in their warp-face form, all these block weaves can be woven on a warp threaded (1,2,3,4) having sections with an (A, B, A, B) colour sequence. Alternatively, the warp could consist entirely of two colours, end-and-end, but with periodic changes in the colour sequence from (A, B, A, B) to (B, A, B, A) and back again. Both faces of the rug would then be completely covered with a counterchange arrangement of blocks. With a warp set up in either way, the following lifts will give the warp-face forms of six weft-face block weaves.

(*a*) *Warp-face Form of Block Weave Using Three-End Block Draft*

Lift (34, 12, 24,) repeat, for Block 1.
Lift (34, 12, 13,) repeat, for Block 2.
See Plate 150.

(*b*) *Warp-Face Form of Block Weave Using Four-End Block Draft*

Lift (34, 24, 12, 24,) repeat, for Block 1.
Lift (34, 13, 12, 13,) repeat, for Block 2.

(c) Warp-Face Form of Block Weave Using M's and O's Draft

Lift (34, 23, 14, 12,) repeat, for Block 1.
Lift (34, 14, 23, 12,) repeat, for Block 2.

(d) Warp-Face Form of Block Weave Based on Straight Three-Shaft Draft

Lift (34, 24, 12,) repeat, for Block 1.
Then lift 13, before changing to next block.
Lift (24, 12, 13,) repeat, for Block 2.
Then lift 34, before changing to next block.
Lift (12, 13, 34,) repeat, for Block 3.
Then lift 24, before changing to next block.
Lift (13, 34, 24,) repeat, for Block 4.
Then lift 12, before changing to next block.
Note that the four lifts which 'link' between blocks, correspond to the four 'linking ends' in the weft-face version. See Plate 151.

(e) Warp-Face Form of Block Weave Using Six-End Block Draft

Lift (34, 24, 34, 12, 24, 12,) repeat, for Block 1.
Lift (34, 13, 34, 12, 13, 12,) repeat, for Block 2.

(f) Warp-Face Form of Block Weave Using Single-End Spot Draft

Lift (24, 34, 24, 13, 24, 12,) repeat, for Block 1.
Then lift 24, before changing to the next block.
Lift (13, 12, 13, 24, 13, 34,) repeat, for Block 2.
Then lift 13, before changing to the next block. See plate 152.

In all these block weaves, it will be found that the weft on the reverse shows through on the face, far more than it does in the weft-face form. This is because in the latter, the two wefts involved slide one behind the other when beaten up, the face weft almost completely obscuring the back weft. Although the structure is identical in the warp-face form, this sliding cannot take place to any extent between adjacent warp ends.

In their weft-face form, the warp settings of these weaves were varied according to the length of weft float. A comparable adjustment is made in their warp-face form, a thinner weft being used in the weaves with a long warp float. This enables more picks to be woven to the inch and so reduces the length of the warp float.

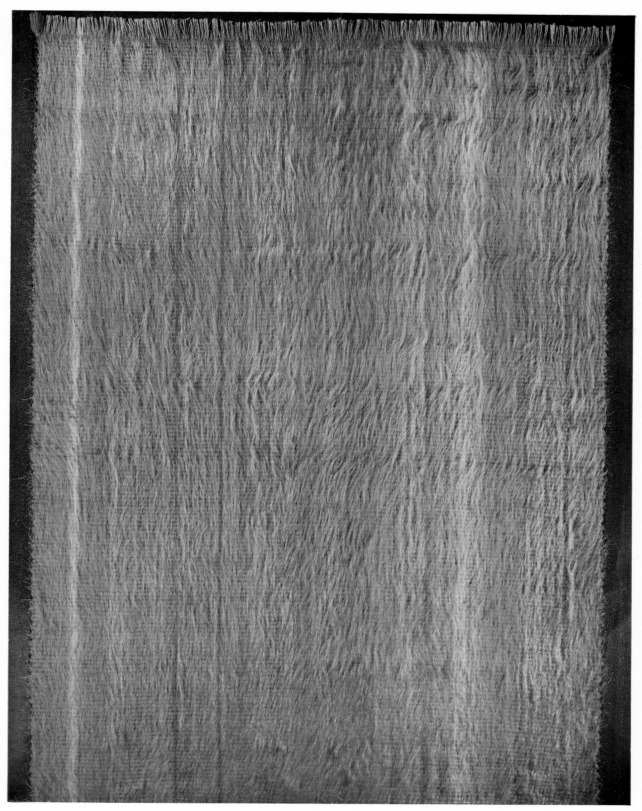

IV.   Warp-face rug with brushed surface, mohair warp and horsehair
      weft, see page 452

C. Pick-Up Weaves

It will be noticed that all the lifts in the block weaves are those of plain weave and 2/2 twill. As the warp in the relevant sections is of two colours, end-and-end, each plain weave lift will raise all the ends of one colour. It is the occurrence of one or other of these two plain weave lifts (once or several times) in the lifting sequence, that generally determines which colour comes to the surface in which block.

Thus in the weaves (a), (b) and (e) above, the lifts for both blocks will be seen to be identical, except for the substitution of 13 for 24 and vice versa. So the pick-up method for these three weaves must involve producing a composite shed which in part is that produced by raising 13 and in part that produced by raising 24.

Taking the first block weave above as an example, begin by lifting (34, 12, 24) repeat. Assume that the warp is so threaded that this brings a white block to the surface. Where the pick-up is to begin, stop after the pick with 12 raised.

Lift 24. This raises all white ends. Put a flat stick into this shed, but pass it over the raised white warp ends wherever black is wanted on the surface according to the design, i.e., wherever the two warp colours are to be counterchanged. Leave the stick in the shed close to the fell of the rug, and lower 24. Lift 13. This raises all the black ends. Pass a narrow rod *under* the raised black ends, wherever the previous stick floated *over* the white ends. Make sure the stick and rod are involved with the same number of ends, e.g., three, in Fig. 364. This pick-up is naturally done between the first stick and the reed. Lower 13.

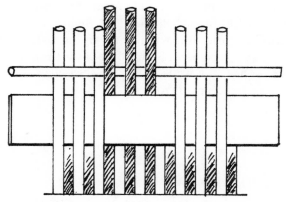

Fig. 364. Warp-face Rugs. Method of obtaining
pick-up shed with a stick and a rod

These two pick-ups have now to be combined onto one stick. Twist the first stick on edge and pull the rod as close to it as possible. Pass another flat stick into the very small shed under the rod. Withdraw the first stick and rod, and turn the second flat stick on its edge. This gives a plain weave shed, in parts of which black ends are raised and in other parts of which white ends are raised.

Throw shuttle across in this shed, withdraw stick and beat.

Lift 34, weave normally from selvage to selvage.

Lift 12, weave normally from selvage to selvage.

Lift 24, repeat the above pick-up sequence.

Lift 34, weave normally from selvage to selvage.

Lift 12, weave normally.

This is the whole sequence, which is then repeated.

Note that in this and other warp-face pick-up weaves, the pick-up is only done when either a lift of a 13 or 24 occurs in the normal lifting sequence for the block weave. In the above example, there is one pick-up for every two normal picks. So warp-face pick-up is fast when compared with weft-face pick-up, in which some form of pick-up is necessary for every pick woven.

In the sample shown in Plate 153, and woven exactly as described above, only nine actual pick-ups were needed to produce the diamond which is about 6 inches long.

Due to the lack of contrast between the two block areas, motifs have to be large to register. The fine intricate detailing possible with weft-face pick-up would be lost here.

Although block weaves and pick-up weaves have been dealt with in some detail, all the other weft-face multishaft weaves can be similarly converted. See Plate 154, for instance, which shows a Six-Shaft Shadow Weave woven as a warp-face structure. Some will create problems in their warp-face form. For instance, a weft-face weave with several wefts interlacing in such a way that their take-up varies, is simple to weave. But in its warp-face form, this will mean varying warp take-up and so two or more warp beams will have to be used. So in some cases the conversion is not worthwhile. But in all cases, converting weft- into warp-face gives the weaver a great deal of insight into the weave structures involved.

12 · Rugs in which both Warp and Weft contribute to the Surface

INTRODUCTION

Between the two extremes of warp- and weft-face structure, there are many structures some with predominant warp, some with predominant weft and some with an equal setting of warp and weft; and there are infinite gradations between these categories. With few exceptions, they share one characteristic, and that is, the use of stiff thick wefts (and sometimes warps) to make up for the solidity given by completely warp- and weft-face construction.

Such materials are

Coir (coconut fibre)

Sisal

Seagrass yarn

Rope

Raffia

Unspun hemp, jute or flax

Heavy cotton and jute yarns

Rayon tow

Long-stem plants, e.g., rush (which can be plaited)

Grasses

Due to the character of these materials, the textile produced comes into the category of floor-mats, rather than rugs.

1. EQUAL WARP AND WEFT SETTING

Into this group come mats woven industrially of coir and sisal. Warp and weft are identical, or almost so, and the weaves employed are hopsack and a variety of twills. A common coir matting is woven in its natural colour in 2/1 twill, the warp floats being on the top side of the mat as used. Sisal, which dyes excellently, is often used as warp and weft in more complex structures, e.g., colour and weave effects in sixteen-shaft twills. It is not a field much entered by the handweaver, as a specialized loom and warping technique is needed for such thick unyielding yarns. See Fig. 12 in Chapter 1 for a possible method of handling these yarns. But the handweaver may well design prototypes for industrial production. As the mats are simply normal cloth weaves much magnified, the design possibilities are similar to those in normal weaving.

Plate 155 shows an experimental piece with coir and sisal warp crossed by seagrass and jute weft in a hopsack weave. Plate 156 shows a piece with plastic tubing warp and seagrass weft interlacing in 2/2 twill.

Honeycomb and plain weave double cloth are two weaves that give a structure of such thickness that it is possible to make a practical rug of this type using wool as warp and weft.

Plate 157 shows a honeycomb-woven sample using 6-ply rug wool for both warp and weft (six ends and six picks per inch). The textile is thick and resilient, but the long warp and weft floats restrict its use somewhat.

Plate 158 shows a plain weave double cloth sample. The 6-ply rug wool warp is set at 12 e.p.i. and the weft is the same material used double. It is a simple four shaft draft, so the weave is a series of weftway stripes, between each of which the back and front warps interchange. The complexity of the design is due simply to the arrangements of the three colours in the warp.

2. WITH PREDOMINANT WEFT

This is the biggest group. All the wefts listed above can be woven into very interesting mats with a suitable warp.

The difficulty is that successive picks of such materials do not bed down with each other; due to their incompressibility, each lies separate and rod-like in its shed. So the warp has either to be very rigid itself and hold the wefts in place by that rigidity or very elastic and grip each pick so that it cannot shift.

An example of the former is seen in Plate 159 where a warp of plastic-covered wire (set at only 2 e.p.i.) weaves with a weft partly of a similar material but predominantly of seagrass.

Cotton is the most-used elastic warp. A 7/7s cotton yarn, or twine of similar thickness, can be set at 3 double to 3 quadruple ends per inch. Even with such an open setting (which is the minimum feasible one) the hard wefts cannot be used alone; however tightly they are beaten there will still be a gap between picks, unless one or more picks of some softer yarn are interposed. Plate 161 illustrates this point; a warp of 7/7s cotton is crossed by plaited rush and dyed coir. Between these materials are varying numbers of picks of a yarn similar to the warp. Because in this case there are always an odd number of these picks, it is always the same warp ends that float over the surface of the rush and coir, giving marked vertical lines. The same effect is seen in Plate 160 which shows a mat woven of dyed black sisal and unspun jute across a black and white striped cotton warp. The soft weft is here black cotton. Notice how the striped warp forms lozenge shapes of solid colour in the woven edge.

With an even number of intervening picks, alternate warp ends float over the stiff wefts. This effect is seen in Plate 162, where two picks of thick cotton lie between every pick of rayon tow, flax, and delustred rayon.

Plate 41 shows wrapped loops of coir yarn on a sample consisting of unspun jute, coir, jute and cotton yarn. The warp is of cotton.

Plate 163 shows a more complex weave. A striped cotton warp, grouped into sections of 8 ends on the front two shafts, and 8 ends on the back two shafts, is crossed by seagrass that passes over and under these groups. The other weft is the same as the warp yarn and interposes two picks of plain weave after each of the seagrass picks.

Practical Points

Selvages

Because the thick stiff wefts have to be carried up from pick to pick, the selvages are a problem in this type of mat, and they never have the neatness found in weft-face and warp-face rugs. But assuming the weft striping to be in some regular sequence, the unevenness of the selvage should at least be a consistent one.

A decision has to be made about the distance a weft can be carried up at the selvage. If the picks of one weft are, say, $1\frac{1}{2}$ inches apart, then its loops at the selvage are practical; but a wider spaced weft would be begun and finished each time it appears. This applies especially to materials like unspun jute and rayon tow, which quickly become hairy and untidy at the selvage. These considerations may influence the design to be woven.

If several weft materials are passing round the selvage, always place the thicker on the outside.

Weft Joins

It is difficult with some materials, e.g., plaited rush, to make weft joins invisible. In all cases taper the two wefts to avoid extra thickness at the point of the overlap.

3. WITH PREDOMINANT WARP

Strictly speaking, some of the weaves in Chapter 11 on warp-face rugs come under this heading (e.g., the block weaves) as the weft showed slightly.

Plate 164 shows a spaced warp matting sample. The warp is of bleached and natural hemp, end-and-end, and the weft of rope, coir, unspun jute and raffia. The stiffness of the wefts prevents the spaces in the warp from being points of weakness.

An interesting all-wool rug can be woven with 6-ply rug wool as a warp set at

12 e.p.i. It is lifted to give four picks of 3/1 broken twill followed by four picks of 1/3 broken twill, viz. (124, 134, 123, 234, 2, 1, 3, 4) repeat, using a weft about twice as heavy as the warp.

When taken from the loom, the rug contracts and both back and front surfaces show a series of weftway ridges. This gives it great thickness and resilience.

This chapter has not explored its subject systematically, an almost impossible task where so many varied materials can be woven in so many structures. But it has tried with a preponderance of illustrations to give an idea of what can be done.

13 · Weft and Warp Twining

Twining is not weaving, but as rugs can be made entirely from weft and warp twining and as weft twining in combination with other techniques plays an important part in rug weaving, it has been included in this book.

History

Twining is one of the most ancient fabric structures, and because it does not need a loom, it may well predate weaving. The astonishing finds at Catal Huyuk in Anatolia, which are presumed to date back to 6500 B.C., contain examples which seem to be twined. Better preserved, but still very old, examples come from Peru, the earliest being about 2500 B.C. The technique (which is also used in basket making) is distributed all over the world. It has been described as 'the most popular of all weaves on stretched warp threads'. (See Ciba Review No. 63 January 1948.) Primitive societies, where they still exist, use the technique extensively. It is still used in the making of horse girths in England. It was brought to a high point of decorative refinement by the weavers of the Chilkat blankets in S.E. Alaska and by the Maori weavers with their taniko cloth. Weft twining is essentially a hand technique; no device exists that can produce it or help in its production. The same applies to warp twining, except in the case of tablet weaving.

Of its many variations and types, only those suitable for floor rugs will be described here, i.e., weft-face and warp-face twining, but it is a technique which would repay exploration in relation to other less functional textiles, such as wall hangings.

1. WEFT TWINING

Introduction

Weft twining needs no sheds; the stretched warp is quite passive. Two or more wefts pass together across the warp, spiralling round each other and enclosing a warp thread between each half turn, see Fig. 365. So the wefts actually grip the warp. They lie like a plied yarn impaled by the warp. In Fig. 365 (a), the next movement is for weft A to be brought up across end 7 and passed behind end 8. Then weft B is brought

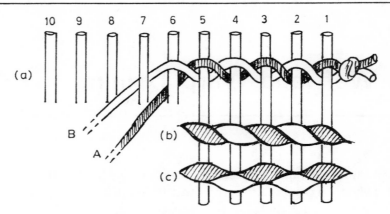

Fig. 365. Weft Twining. General Diagram

up across end 8 and passed behind end 9, and so on. The two wefts move alternately and each passes behind the next unused warp end.

Remembering that this is done on a closed shed, i.e., every warp end is included in the twining, it will be seen that one row of weft twining, see Fig. 365 (b), covers the warp to the same extent as two picks of plain weave, see Fig. 365 (c). The diagram brings out the essential feature, the '2-ply-yarn look' of a row of weft twining.

Just as a yarn can be either S-twist or Z-twist, so weft twining can be S- or Z-twist, and many of its design possibilities rest on this important fact. The diagram shows Z-twist weft twining.

A. Application to Rugs Woven on a Frame

Many Eastern rugs are made on a very simple vertical frame loom with no reed, so when starting a rug there is always the problem of spacing out the warp as evenly as possible. The most efficient way to do this, saving space and time, is to use one or two rows of weft twining. The beauty of the method is that it will work for almost any setting of the warp, for the thickness of the twining yarns controls the warp spacing. A fine yarn will give a closer set, a thick yarn a more open set. To make a decoration out of necessity, two different colours are sometimes used. They are knotted together at the right selvage, see Fig. 365 (a), and then twined across to the left selvage and again knotted, thus giving a small tuft at each side. Another row may be added. Though not needed at the finishing end of the rug, the twining is generally repeated there for completeness. Weavers making rugs on a frame will find this useful.

Occasionally a row or two of weft twining is found in Kilim rugs where an area of complex pattern abuts on an area of solid colour.

B. Two-Colour Weft Twining

(i) CONTROL OF COLOUR AND TWIST SEQUENCES

Its use in design, as opposed to its functional use as described above, begins to appear when several rows of weft twining using two colours are produced. There are several possibilities which depend either on the relation of colour sequence between successive rows or on the relation of direction of twining between successive rows.

If the row of twining is continued, as in Fig. 365 (a), to the left selvage, there is now a choice of two methods of turning the wefts to start the next row.

Fig. 366 (a) shows the method which brings the black of the second row over the white of the first row, and vice versa.

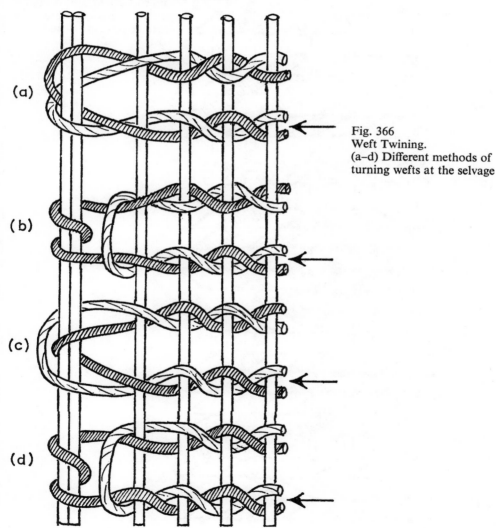

Fig. 366
Weft Twining.
(a–d) Different methods of turning wefts at the selvage

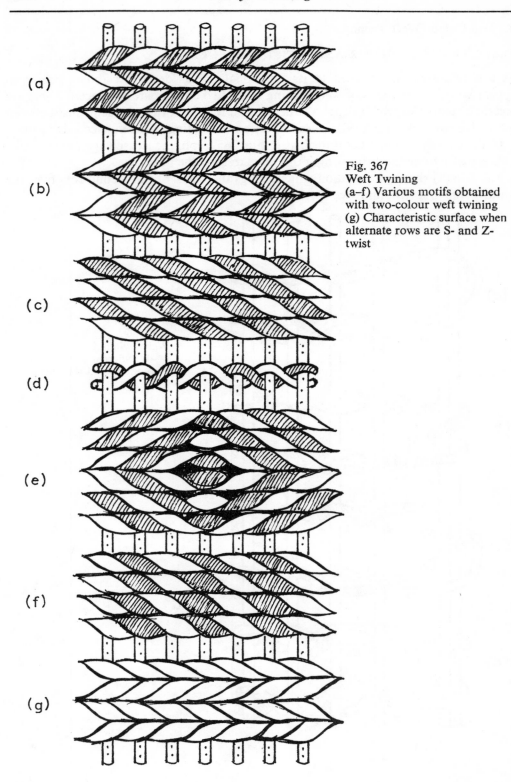

(a)

(b)

(c)

(d)

(e)

(f)

(g)

Fig. 367
Weft Twining
(a–f) Various motifs obtained
with two-colour weft twining
(g) Characteristic surface when
alternate rows are S- and Z-
twist

Fig. 366 (b) shows the method which brings the black over the black and the white over the white in succeeding rows. This incidentally is the method most often used when twining with two yarns of the same colour. Note its similarity to the pick-and-pick plain weave selvage.

In both these diagrams it will be seen that the twist of the second row is the opposite to that of the first row, it is S- instead of Z-twist. This is what normally happens; i.e., if the pattern of hand movements used in the first row is repeated in the second. The alternating rows of S- and Z-twist weft twining give a characteristic surface, even to one-colour weft twining, comparable with that found in soumak, see Fig. 367 (g). But it is just as easy after turning the weft at the selvage, to twine the second row in Z-twist, like the first; the hand movements are simply reversed.

Fig. 366 (c) shows how to produce a second row of Z-twist with the black yarn lying over the white yarn.

Fig. 366 (d) shows how to produce a second row of Z-twist with the black lying over the black and the white over the white. The twist can also be reversed at any point while twining a row, see Fig. 367 (d) in centre. This can be done many times across the width of the warp.

Using the twist variations and colour sequence variations described above, the following motifs can be produced.

(a) Checks

Turn the wefts at both selvages as in Fig. 366 (a) and a small pattern of checks as in Fig. 367 (a) is produced.

(b) Vertical Lines

Turn wefts at both selvages as in Fig. 366 (b), and zigzag vertical lines as in Fig. 367 (b) are produced.

(c) Twill Lines

Turn weft at both selvages as in Fig. 366 (c), and twill lines are produced as in Fig. 367 (c). These lines are a characteristic of weft twining and are often exploited in designing with this technique. The direction of twill line is naturally controlled by the direction of twining. If this is combined with reversing the twist in the middle of each row, concentric diamonds as in Fig. 367 (e) can be produced. Fig. 367 (d) shows how the twist and colour of the next row of twining in this pattern would be arranged. Note the reverse of twist in the centre.

(d) Vertical Lines

Turn weft at both selvages as in Fig. 366 (d), and vertical lines with serrated edge are produced, as in Fig. 367 (f).

Any of these motifs can naturally be combined with cross stripes, produced by twining two wefts of the same colour.

All these motifs are identical on the back of the fabric, except twill lines. Fig. 368 shows the front and back of a diamond in twill lines.

Fig. 368
Weft Twining. Front and back view of a diamond in weft twining

Although it is simpler to use the motifs all across the rug, with a little ingenuity blocks of differing motifs can be produced, side by side. Fig. 369 (a) shows a block of twill lines joining a block of checks. This is achieved by reversing the direction of the twist at the point of junction, but only doing this every other row, i.e., in rows 2 and 4 in the diagram.

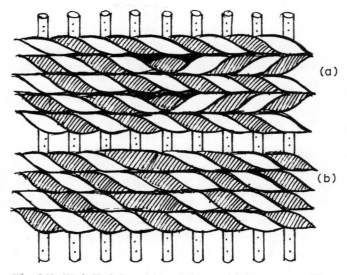

(a)

(b)

Fig. 369. Weft Twining. (a) and (b) combining two motifs

Fig. 369 (b) shows a block of twill lines joining a block of vertical lines. Here the twist is kept constant, but the changeover is achieved by making the two wefts twine around two, instead of one, warp end at the junction between the blocks. Again, this is only done every other row. With the help of these two examples, the reader will be able to work out other combinations of blocks.

Interesting rugs can be made of weft twining. The fact that it is a slow (but a very engrossing) process and needs the minimum of equipment, just a frame on which to stretch the warp, will recommend it to amateur weavers.

(ii) COMBINATION WITH PLAIN WEAVE

Apart from its all-over use, the technique can be used in stripes alternating with plain weave stripes, or more interestingly an area of weft twining can be surrounded by plain weave. Plate 165 shows an area of weft twining with an arrangement of twill lines on a background of plain weave in 2-and-2 stripes. Fig. 370 shows this in diagrammatic form.

Start with both wefts at the right selvage, see arrows in Fig. 370.

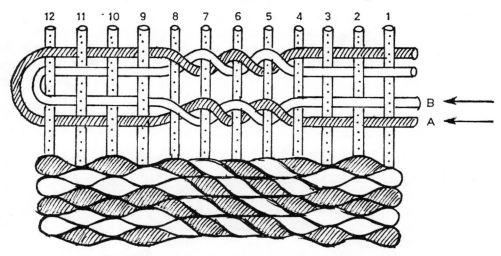

Fig. 370. Weft Twining. Combining plain weave and weft twining

Raise the even-numbered ends. Take A (black) across in this shed then bring it out of the shed, between the raised ends 4 and 6.

Raise odd-numbered ends. Take B (white) across in this shed and bring out between the raised ends 3 and 5.

Now with no shed open, i.e., on a flat warp, twine the two wefts encircling warp ends, 5, 6, 7 and 8.

Raise the even-numbered ends. Insert A into the shed down between the raised ends, 8 and 10, and carry it to the left selvage.

Raise the odd-numbered ends. Insert B into this shed down between the raised ends, 7 and 9, and carry it to the left selvage.

Both wefts have now arrived at the left selvage.

Repeat the above procedure for the return passage to the right, but reverse the colour sequence. In other words, start with B in the first plain weave shed instead of A, see Fig. 370. This is in order to produce the 2-and-2 stripes of black and white at each side; it also gives the colour shift in the twined area that makes twill lines possible. Note that both rows of weft twining have Z-twist.

From this description of a very simple example, it will be seen that there are many possibilities. There can be any number of twined areas across the width of the warp, and the shape and size of the areas is completely controllable. Also the plain weave areas can be either pick-and-pick or 2-and-2 stripes. Note the similarity between this technique and the twisted weft variation called Controlled Multiple Twisting, see Fig. 46 in Chapter 4.

(iii) ENCIRCLING ONE, TWO OR THREE WARP ENDS

A method of weft twining found in the island of Timor, Dutch East Indies, shows another application of the technique and suggests other directions for exploration in rug weaving. It is a two-colour weft twining and the design is partly the result of the positioning of each colour. But the important characteristic is that the twining wefts do not always encircle a single warp end, they can encircle one, two or three, depending on the demands of the pattern.

Fig. 371 shows how the twining is carried out to make the lower half of the motif seen in Plate 166. Note that rows are alternately S- and Z-twist, so it is unlike the

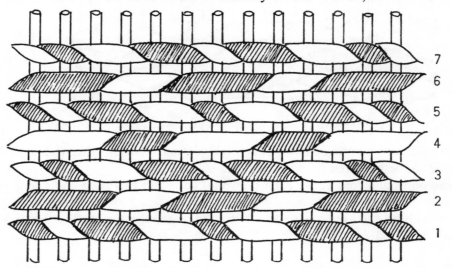

Fig. 371. Weft Twining. Producing design in two colours by varying number of ends encircled

diamond shown in Fig. 367 (e), which depends on a careful control of the twist in each row. This brings two advantages. Firstly, the design is completely reversible, though of course the colours are the opposite on the back. Where a black crosses over two warp ends on the front, a white must cross under two ends on the back. Secondly, the alternation of twist gives a far more lively, less mechanical quality to the line.

Note also that the sequence of warp ends encircled in rows 1, 3, 5 and 7, is identical, but the colours in rows 1 and 5 are reversed compared with those in rows 3 and 7. The same applies to rows 2, 4, and 6.

The motif described is symmetrical and geometrical, but a quite free design is perfectly possible as long as it observes the limitations of the technique. Such a design need not be planned in advance, but can be gradually created as row succeeds row. If working like this, remember the rather obvious fact that in order to have a float of one weft over three warp ends, the other weft must first pass under the same three warp ends; the unseen precedes the seen.

Due to the longer weft floats, this method gives a much looser structure than the normal weft twining. So in order to preserve a firm texture, the warp should be closer set or a thicker weft should be used.

This technique can be used all over a rug, or perhaps as a very intricate band at either end of a simply-coloured knotted rug, or in stripes alternating with plain weave.

(iv) TANIKO

The variety of weft twining developed by the Maori of New Zealand, and called taniko, depends on a complete turn of the two wefts between adjacent warp ends, see Fig. 372. As the wefts are of different colours, this has the effect of keeping one of them on the surface, instead of their appearing alternately as with normal weft twining. So in Fig. 372, black is on the surface over ends 1 to 4. But where the second colour, white, is wanted on the surface, a normal half twist produces the changeover as between ends 4 and 5, and thereafter white becomes the face weft.

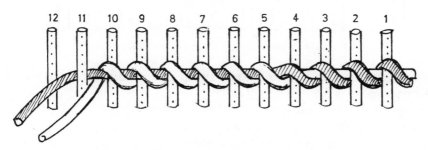

Fig. 372. Weft Twining. Diagram of Taniko

The weft not wanted on the surface, the back weft, is pulled tight after each twist and so takes a straight and invisible course on the back of the fabric. It is only the face weft which takes a serpentine course, see Fig. 372. This has the effect of tilting the face weft far more than in normal weft twining and it also makes the reverse of the fabric quite unlike the face.

The next move in Fig. 372 is to twist the white weft (face weft) behind the black (back weft). Then the black is passed behind warp end 12 and pulled tight. This is repeated for as long as white is wanted on the surface.

Note—That the face weft never passes behind a warp end, only behind the back weft.

The invisibility of the back weft depends on the correct warp/weft relationship, but more importantly on its being pulled tight.

The above description shows that taniko enables any two-colour design to be twined. Moreover areas of solid colour are not the only possibility, as any of the motifs in Fig. 367 (depending on a half turn) can be combined with them. See Plate 167. So the field is large and need not be confined to the triangles and diamonds found in Maori work.

More than two colours may be used in taniko. For instance with three-colour taniko, at any point in the design two colours are invisible at the back and the third is on the face. To change the surface colour, one of the two back wefts comes up to the face and the face weft drops to the back.

C. Three- and Four-Colour Weft Twining

Fig. 373 shows four-colour weft twining. Each weft passes over two warp ends and

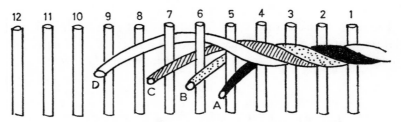

Fig. 373. Weft Twining. Four-strand weft twining

behind two warp ends, and all four wefts spiral around each other to make a 4-ply cord. The next move is for

A to go up over ends 5 and 6 and then behind ends 7 and 8,

B to go up over ends 6 and 7 and then behind ends 8 and 9,

C to go up over ends 7 and 8 and then behind ends 9 and 10, and

D to go up over ends 8 and 9 and then behind ends 10 and 11.

With a three-colour weft twining, the wefts go over two ends and behind one, so the back and front of the fabric are different.

Those familiar with tablet or card weaving will see that four-colour weft twining has the identical structure as four-hole tablet weave, but turned through a right angle, i.e., the warp and twisted weft of weft twining are related to each other in exactly the same way as are the weft and twisted warp in tablet weaving. So the many varied designs which result from the way the warp is made and arranged in tablet weaving are possible by ordering the twining wefts in a similar way. Here is another interesting field for investigation, though its use might be limited to narrow stripes.

D. Twined Tapestry

In the techniques described so far, the twined wefts go right across from selvage to selvage and the design is obtained by the relation of twist and colour in one row to that in the preceding rows. But a rug can be woven with many areas of solid colour. It is comparable with the tapestry technique but using weft twining, instead of plain weave. Each colour area has its own pair of twining wefts which pass from right to left and back again within the area, but never pass beyond its boundaries.

Rugs of this type are still made in Diessie, Ethiopia, by the Galla people. Plate 168 shows part of one of these rugs made of various shades of undyed sheep's wool. The vertical colour boundaries are managed in the neat way shown in Fig. 374, the selvages are of the type shown in Fig. 366 (b). Both warp and weft are of two 2-ply wool yarns plied together.

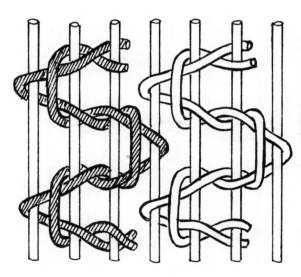

Fig. 374
Weft Twining.
Colour junction
found in Ethiopian
Twined Tapestry
rugs

The so-called Chilkat blankets, made by the Chilkat sub-tribe of the Tlingit, achieve an even greater freedom of design. They are technically similar, but the wefts are turned as in Fig. 366 (a), at the edge of each colour area. They use two different procedures at vertical colour junctions. Either what is in effect an extra warp is used which is woven in with the right-hand colour for a few rows then with the left-hand colour, or the colour junction is stepped slightly from side to side as in some of the Kilim methods. In either case the vertical colour junction is hidden under a row of vertical three-strand weft twining.

Using any of these joining techniques, almost any type of design can be twined. The difference between twined and plain weave tapestry is mainly the very pleasing surface texture of the former, which due to the alternate rows of S- and Z-twist is as in Fig. 367 (g).

As with plain weave tapestry, the twining can be done in a curve or at an angle to the warp.

The design is identical on both sides of twined tapestry.

E. Open Shed Weft Twining

In all the methods so far described, the twining wefts enclose all the warp ends in their passage from selvage to selvage, even though the number of ends enclosed between each half turn may vary. In other words, the twining was done on a closed shed.

But it can be carried out on an open plain weave shed, in which case the twining wefts only engage with the raised warp ends, see Fig. 375 (a). It will be seen that as each weft passes behind the warp it comes to lie in a plain weave shed (and does not float on the back in the usual way).

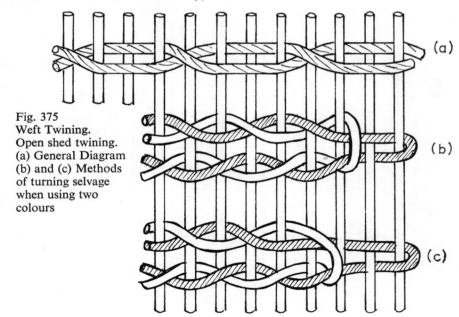

Fig. 375
Weft Twining.
Open shed twining.
(a) General Diagram
(b) and (c) Methods
of turning selvage
when using two
colours

The next line of twining is carried out with the opposite plain weave shed open, and so on. So the parts of the twining wefts not showing on the surface are actually forming a plain weave cloth with the warp. This is seen on the reverse. The technique could of course be combined with plain weave, one or more plain weave picks separating each twined row.

The technique has two points in its favour.

(1) The longer weft floats make possible larger scale motifs. These are achieved without the structural weakness that would result from similar length floats in normal weft twining. Thus, to get similar length floats to those in Fig. 375 (a), normal twining wefts would have to encircle four ends between each half turn, giving a very loose structure.

(2) The alternation of sheds between successive rows of twining makes it very easy to produce diagonals.

As this technique gives a mass of floats on the face of the rug and none on the back, there will be a tendency, for any large area worked in it, to curl when the warp tension is released. So it is only suitable for narrow cross stripes.

If Fig. 375 (a) is turned on its side, the connection between this technique and that of the Navajo selvage will be obvious. It is also related to Skip Plain Weave.

Turning Wefts at the Selvage

As there are plain weave sheds being used, it seems simplest and neatest to move from one row of twining to the next by making one of the wefts weave in these two sheds, and making the other 'jump up', missing the selvage altogether. See Fig. 375 (b) and (c), in which the wefts only pass behind one raised end as opposed to two, in Fig. 375 (a).

If both selvages are done as in Fig. 375 (b), there will be oblique lines of the two colours used, sloping up to the right, see bottom of Plate 169. If then both selvages are changed to the type in Fig. 375 (c), the oblique lines will reverse their direction, see Plate 169.

If the wefts are turned at one selvage as in Fig. 375 (b) and at the other as in Fig. 375 (c), then the colours lie on top of each other and make the vertical serrated stripes seen at the top of the Plate 169.

Note—That the plain weave selvages appear as stripes when oblique lines are being twined, but as solid colours when vertical stripes are being twined.

—That because the selvage is in plain weave, this gives the opportunity of strengthening the edge in any of the ways described for pile rugs in Chapter 6.

F. Practical Details

(i) STARTING AND FINISHING TWINING WEFTS

Starting

(a) One-Colour Weft Twining

Double the weft and centre it around the selvage, so that there are two equal lengths of weft to twine with, see Fig. 376 (a).

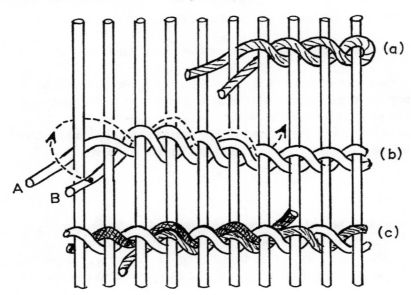

Fig. 376
Weft Twining.
Beginning, finishing
and joining wefts

(b) Two-Colour Weft Twining

Knot the two wefts together. Pass one weft under the selvage and begin twining, see Fig. 365 (a).

Finishing

Finish two-colour weft twining by knotting the two wefts together with an overhand knot in exactly the same way as it was started.

Finish one-colour weft twining thus. Push up the last row of twining so that the warp is exposed below it, see Fig. 376 (b). Take the weft which would be the next to move, if twining could continue further, i.e., B, in Fig. 376 (b). Turn it round the selvage and, making it follow exactly the course of weft A, twine it back towards the right for an inch or so, see arrow in Fig. 376 (b). Push the twined row down again and darn in the two ends.

(ii) WEFT JOINS

If twining more than one row, have the wefts in a finger hank, so that a great length does not have to be dealt with in each twining movement. When a weft join has to be made, twine with the new and old weft together for a short distance, treating them as one weft, before continuing with the new weft by itself, see Fig. 376 (c). Darn in the two wefts later as described in Chapter 3. To avoid a lumpy appearance, stagger the weft joins, i.e., do not join both black and white wefts at the same place.

(iii) WARP AND WEFT SET

For any particular thickness of weft, the warp should be set a little closer for weft twining than for plain weave. A too thin weft or too wide warp spacing will give a spongy texture and the rows of weft twining will easily slide up and down the warp. A too thick weft or too close warp spacing will give a very rigid structure, more boardlike than anything obtainable with plain weave. This is due to the lack of movement between warp and weft, the result of the weft's twisting around and gripping the warp.

As with most things in weaving, it is best to proceed by trial. If a certain weft yarn has been chosen, the problem is to find the warp set. Wrap about twenty ends of warp around a simple frame. Twine with the selected yarn for about four rows, pulling the yarn with the tension that gives the desired texture to the fabric. By the end of the four rows, the twining will have automatically spaced the warp correctly either pulling in or opening out the threads from the position they were in when twining began. Measure this new spacing and make a full-size warp accordingly.

The problem may be the reverse one of finding the thickness of weft that will suit the spacing of a warp already on a loom. Divide the warp mentally into four. Then on each quarter-width of warp, twine several rows, using a different thickness of yarn for each of the four areas. Then compare the areas. An area with too thin a yarn will have the warp ends pulled closer together than they are in the reed and will be of too soft texture. An area with too thick yarn will have the warp ends forced apart and will be too hard. Between these two extremes will be an area with the correct thickness of weft.

2. WARP TWINING

A. Tablet-Woven Rugs

The only practical form of warp twining for making a complete rug is that controlled by tablets or cards. Tablet weaving is a subject in itself and only aspects of the technique peculiar to the making of rugs will be mentioned here.

Tablet weaving is essentially a method of producing *narrow* ribbonlike textiles, so a rug can only be produced by weaving a series of these strips and joining them together. But these strips can be woven wider than is usual, if the tablet weaving is carried out on a warp mounted in a loom, not just stretched between two posts, or between the weaver and a hook on the wall.

Make a warp in the normal way up to 8 inches wide. 6-ply rugwool at 16 e.p.i. is a suitable setting. Then if four hole tablets are used, there are four tablets to every inch of width of the warp.
Beam the warp on the loom.
Remove the shafts, or slide the healds to either side, to leave a clear space in the centre.
Hang a 4 dents/inch reed here and sley the warp four ends to a dent.
Thread the ends through the tablets and tie to the front stick.

The function of the reed is to space the warp correctly; beat the weft with a flat stick in each shed. It is useful to have some flat surface for the tablets to rest on, as shown in Fig. 377. The tablets will probably have to be turned in sections, first the right-hand half then the left, and this surface steadies those not being turned.

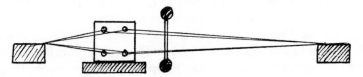

Fig. 377. Warp Twining. Tablet weaving on the loom

As the warp is fixed on the warp beam, weaves which do not continually build up twist must be used. So normal procedures but with periodic reversals of turning direction, and various double cloth techniques are suitable.
Begin and end the strips with the Double Twined Edge, described in Chapter 14.

B. Warpway Stripes in Navajo Selvage Technique

The Navjao method of strengthening the selvages on their rugs is well known. Two extra threads (thicker than the normal rug warp) are added at each selvage after the warp has been made. They are tied to the lower and upper cross bar. One of each pair of threads, A in Fig. 378 (a), passes over the shed stick. But the one that passes behind the stick, B in Fig. 378 (a), does not have a leash attached to it, thus differing from all the normal warp ends that pass behind the stick.
So when weaving begins, end A becomes the selvage thread, but end B never enters the weave and is left floating at the back. After $\frac{1}{4}$–$\frac{1}{2}$ inch has been woven, ends A and B are switched over, so A drops to the back and B now passes over the shed stick. For the next $\frac{1}{2}$ inch B is the selvage thread, and then A and B are switched again. They are

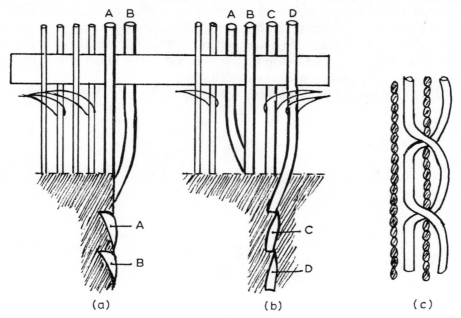

Fig. 378. Warp Twining. (a) Navajo selvage (b) Use of same technique to give warpway stripes (c) Longitudinal section

always twisted in the same way when switched, so they lie like a heavy 2-ply cord along the selvage. Naturally a reverse twist builds up in the threads above the shed stick, and periodically the threads are untied from the top cross bar to release them.

The same idea can be developed to give warpway stripes at any point across the width of a weft-face rug. It naturally needs a simple loom with a shed stick and leashes. It works well if the warp is thick and heavy, i.e., of wool rather than linen.

If a stripe is wanted front and back, at the same point in the rug, four ends have to be specially controlled at this point, see Fig. 378 (b).

Ends A and B are arranged exactly as in the Navajo selvage and they produce the stripe on the back. As shown in the diagram B is weaving and A is floating on the back.

End C passes behind the shed stick; end D passes in front of it. Both ends have leashes. This means that end C will weave normally, but end D will be raised in both sheds so will not be woven in, and thus it forms a float on the front.

To switch the ends, bring A to the front of the shed stick and drop B to the back, and bring C to the front and drop D back. Do this by sliding in a new shed stick from one side and switching the ends as they are encountered; then pull out the original stick. As with the Navajo selvage, the twist that builds up in these ends has to be periodically released.

Used thus it will be seen that the technique is a form of warp twining, hence its inclusion in this chapter. In fact it is the warp form of Open Shed Weft Twining, described earlier in this chapter. It differs from normal warp twining in that one of each pair is always embedded in the weave, so the twining ends actually only enclose every other pick. This is brought out in the very diagrammatic longitudinal section in Fig. 378 (c), where the picks are shown shaded.

Plate 170 shows a sample using this technique

14 · Rug Finishes

INTRODUCTION

When a rug is taken from the loom, it does not have to undergo any wet or heat processes to bring it to its final state, thus differing from many other textiles. But it always has the warp threads at both ends which have to be dealt with in some practical way to prevent the rug's unravelling. This chapter describes some of the many methods that can be used. Some are traditional, others are the result of experimenting with the ends of a rug, in an attempt to find new solutions to old problems.

There is no established nomenclature for rug finishes but names are needed for the purposes of reference in such a large field. Two of the following names are those used by Mary Atwater, others are related to the provenance of rugs which bear these finishes and others, which are of a more descriptive nature, generally apply to finishes which (as far as is known) are not used traditionally;—i.e., invented finishes.

A rug finish has two functions, (i) to prevent the initial and final picks of the rug from working loose and so unweaving and (ii) to prevent the exposed warp threads from fraying. So the finishes can be classified as weft protectors, warp protectors and warp and weft protectors (finishes which carry out both functions). These are now described.

All of these finishes apply to weft-face rugs, i.e., rugs which have, say, 6 to 12 e.p.i. One of the few practical finishes for warp-face rugs is described in the section called Specific Finishes.

1. WEFT PROTECTORS

A. Overhand Knots

The most universally applicable finish is a series of overhand knots. It can be used whatever the setting or material of the warp.

There is no lower limit to the number of ends to be included in one knot, except that very small knots are inappropriate on as tough a textile as a rug. The upper limit is the number of ends which make up an inch width of the warp; i.e., with a 6 e.p.i. warp, do not include more than six ends in one knot. If this number is exceeded, the rug may be pulled in at both ends and the weft may balloon out between the widely spaced knots.

It is important that the overhand knots be tight up against the last weft picks in the rug. One way to ensure this is to tie the knot loosely, then split the constituent threads in two and pull these two halves apart, as shown by the arrows in Fig. 379 (a). This

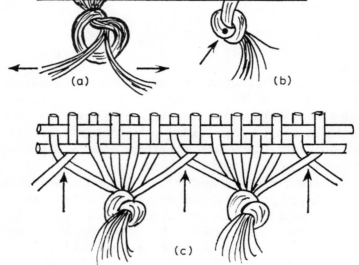

Fig. 379
Rug Finishes. Overhand knot.
(a) Method of tightening
(b) Introducing glue into the knot
(c) Preventing ballooning of weft between knots

manœuvre forces the knot towards the rug. Wherever an overhand knot is used in a rug finish either as a weft protector or as the final knot in one of the warp protectors, it should be tightened with great care. The only really successful way to do this is to pull each of the constituent ends separately. Some form of forceps (e.g., artery forceps), or pliers, are useful for gripping each end and applying a strong pull. Tightened thus, an overhand knot becomes a very compact hard mass and there is little chance of its working loose.

However, if the warp is of a springy wool yarn, such as belting yarn, the knot will soon become loose. For such warps put a spot of glue on the knot at the point arrowed in Fig. 379 (b); then as the ends are finally tightened, the glue is drawn into the centre of the knots and should hold all the threads together. Fig. 379 (c) shows how the ends that go into one knot can be selected in such a way as to prevent ballooning of the weft between knots. The arrows point to the positions where two ends are crossed over, thus locking the weft half-way between two knots.

For extra security a second overhand knot can be tied close up against the first.

B. Philippine Edge

This and all the other weft protectors are continuous knots that run without interruption from one selvage to the other. They all give ridges, some on the upper side as made, some on the lower. They all need a certain minimum number of ends in relation to their thickness. For example, a 7/7s cotton warp needs about 10–12 e.p.i., a 6/10s linen warp needs 6 e.p.i. or more, a 6-ply rug wool warp needs 4 e.p.i. If there are fewer or finer ends than the above, the finishes cannot be tied tight enough to be secure without at the same time drawing in the edges of the rug. If there are more or thicker ends, the finishes can be tied satisfactorily as long as the ends are grouped in twos or threes, and these groups used as the units in the various manipulations.

All the finishes can be tied either from right to left or left to right. The direction of tying given below are based on an endeavour to give the weaver's right hand the more complex or active part in the process.

The Philippine Edge is tied as follows:

Starting from the left, take the third end down to the left across ends 1 and 2 and then up to the right under these ends to emerge between ends 2 and 3, see Fig. 380 (a).

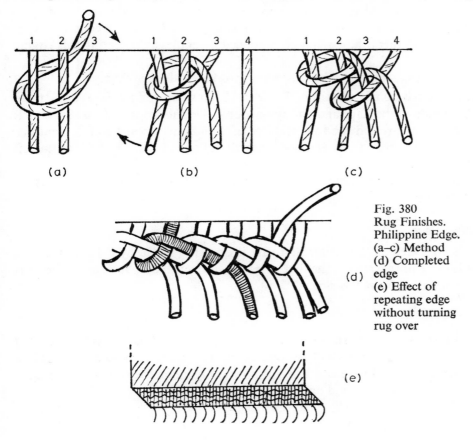

(a) (b) (c)

Fig. 380
Rug Finishes.
Philippine Edge.
(a–c) Method
(d) Completed
edge
(e) Effect of
repeating edge
without turning
rug over

(d)

(e)

This knot or hitch is much used in the weft protectors. In this case, the left hand holds ends 1 and 2 under tension and the manipulation of end 3, with its final tightening in an upward direction, is done entirely by the right hand. Note that in this knot all the bending is done by end 3; ends 1 and 2 run straight through it.

Swing end 3 down to the right of end 2 and discard end 1, see arrows in Fig. 380 (a) and (b). Now, holding ends 2 and 3 tightly with left hand, pick up end 4 with right hand and repeat the above knot. Swing down end 4 and discard end 2. See Fig. 380 (c).

This continues right across the rug always knotting one newly picked up end round the previous two ends and always discarding the left-hand one of these two. When the right selvage is reached, all the discarded ends hang down as a fringe and the final end (which has just been knotted) is brought down to join them.

The resulting ridge (see Fig 380 (d)) appears on the upper surface only.

One row of the Philippine edge is quite secure, but several rows can be made. If these are all done with the rug in its present position, the ridge will get progressively wider and will shift to the right, (as shown in an exaggerated way in Fig. 380 (c)). But if the rug is turned over for each new row and the finish is always begun from the left, the ridges will appear on both sides and there will be no sideways shift. This means that the final end knotted in one row becomes the first end in the next row. The knotted band so produced (with ridges on both sides) can be made as wide as is suitable for the rug. (In fact a fabric can be produced by endlessly repeating this edging technique).

There are variations of this technique which produce a thicker ridge:

Start as above but do not discard end 1 or end 2, so when end 5 is picked up, there are now four ends in the left hand to knot around. Tie this knot and discard end 1. Pick up end 6, knot around the four ends in left hand and discard end 2. Continue thus always picking up one new end and discarding the end that has been in the left hand longest.

Though this or similar variations give a thicker ridge, it is probably no more secure than the normal finish.

C. Damascus Edge

This edge is so called as the writer first saw it on a rug made by a Damascus rug weaver. It is done in two stages, the first of which starts at the right edge, so the ends have been numbered from this side.

(i) FIRST STAGE

Pick up end 1 and knot it around end 2, as shown in Fig. 381 (a). This is the identical knot to the one used in the Philippine edge. As in that instance, hold end 2 tight, as end 1 is pulled upwards. Leave end 1 in this position lying on the rug.

Pick up end 2 and knot round end 3, see Fig. 381 (b).

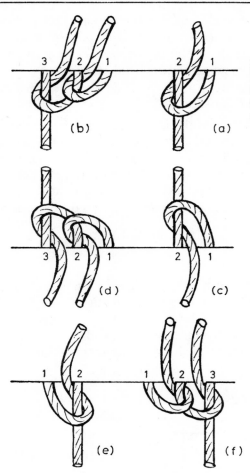

Fig. 381
Rug Finishes. Damascus Edge.
(a) and (b) First stage
(c–d) and (e–f) Two methods
of working second stage

Continue thus all the way across the rug. This produces a ridge on the back. The ends will now be pointing away from the weaver, i.e., in the wrong direction for a fringe; this is rectified in the second stage.

(ii) SECOND STAGE

There are two alternative ways of carrying this out, either (a) or (b).

(a) Without altering the position of the rug, start at the right edge and knot end 1 around end 2 in the manner shown in Fig. 381 (c). Then knot end 2 round end 3, and so on, all the way across. This produces a ridge on the front.

(b) Turn the rug over, and starting at the left edge, knot end 1 round end 2, then end 2 round end 3, as shown in Fig. 381 (e) and (f). This is the same manœuvre as in (a) but it may prove simpler to do.

In Figs. 381 (c)–(f), the first stage row of knots has been omitted for clarity's sake.

The result of the two stages is that a ridge is made on both sides of the rug and the free ends emerge from between them. It is one of the best looking of the simple finishes. Both stages can be repeated to make a wider band of ridges.

D. Half Damascus Edge and Related Finishes

A Half Damascus edge is just the first stage of the Damascus edge. The ends which are pointing away from the weaver are brought down and treated in one of the ways described under Warp Protectors. A half Damascus is a very quick efficient edge and is often used as a standard finish, as it takes no longer than overhand knots. A half Damascus finish can be repeated several times always beginning at the right. This duilds up quickly into a rather loose band. It is sometimes seen on Eastern carpets.

Related Finishes

(i) DOUBLE KNOTTING

End 1 is taken twice around end 2 as shown in Fig. 382 (a) and then pulled tight, see Fig. 382 (b). This is useful where there is barely enough quantity of warp. The double knot takes up more room than the single and helps to bridge the gap between one end and the next. If the single knot is normally made by rolling end 1 over end 2 with the right thumb, then the double knot is made by simply continuing the same movement a little further and takes no longer.

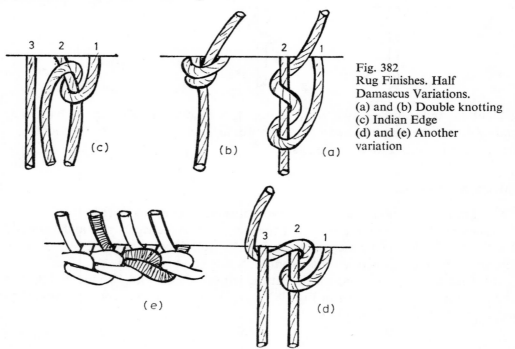

Fig. 382
Rug Finishes. Half
Damascus Variations.
(a) and (b) Double knotting
(c) Indian Edge
(d) and (e) Another
variation

(ii) INDIAN EDGE

This begins as a normal half Damascus edge, i.e., end 1 is knotted round end 2. But instead of leaving end 1 pointing away from the weaver, it is brought down again to lie between ends 2 and 3, see Fig. 382 (c). End 2 is now knotted round end 3, taking care that it passes in front of the discarded end 1. End 2 is now brought down between ends 3 and 4. The advantage of this method is that, though almost as simple as the half Damascus, it leaves the warp ends pointing in the right direction. It makes a ridge on the front. The rug can be turned over and the finish repeated.

(iii) ANOTHER VARIATION

Another variation begins as a normal half Damascus edge, but end 1 after knotting with end 2 is carried under end 3 and left pointing away from the weaver, see Fig. 382 (d). This is continued all across the warp. The result is shown in Fig. 382 (e). The next stage could be the darning of all these warp ends into the woven rug. (See under Warp Protectors.)

E. Looped Edges

When working a half Damascus edge with very long warp ends, it happened that instead of a warp end being pulled through the knot, a blind loop of warp was mistakenly pulled through. This suggested the following finishes based on loops.

(i) LOCKED LOOPS

Starting at the right edge tie the usual knot with a *loop* of end 1 around end 2, and pull it tight, see Fig. 383 (a). Bring up end 2 with the left hand, pass it through the loop (see Fig. 383 (b)) to the right hand, which pulls it tight, away from the weaver. With the left hand pull on the free end of end 1, thus tightening its loop around end 2.

Now bring down end 2 and knot with a loop of it around end 3. Pass latter through this loop, pull on end 2 to tighten loop.

Continue thus all across the rug.

The loop of each end is locked, and prevented from undoing, by the following end which passes through it. A ridge is formed on the front, see Fig. 383 (c) where one end has been shaded to show its course. If the rug is now turned over and the process repeated (again starting from the right), the result will be ridges back and front with the ends emerging from between them.

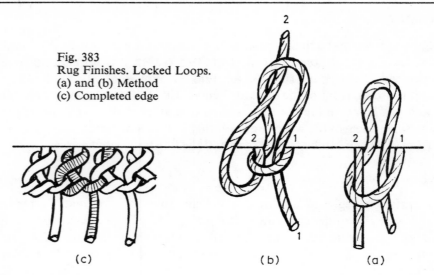

Fig. 383
Rug Finishes. Locked Loops.
(a) and (b) Method
(c) Completed edge

(c)   (b)   (a)

(ii) CHAINED LOOPS

This is done in two stages:

First Stage

Starting from the right, tie the usual knot with a loop of end 1 round end 2. Leave the loop lying on the rug. Now knot a loop of end 2 round end 3 and leave it and so on, all across the rug. There is now a loop from every end lying on the rug, with all the free warp ends hanging downwards, as shown diagrammatically in Fig. 384 (a).

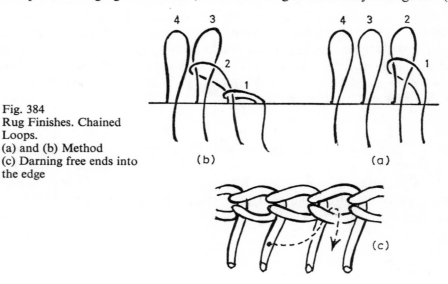

Fig. 384
Rug Finishes. Chained
Loops.
(a) and (b) Method
(c) Darning free ends into
the edge

(b)   (a)

(c)

Second Stage

This is the stage that gives the finish its name, as the loops are chained into each other exactly as in the chained weft loop technique in Chapter 6. Pass loop 2 through loop 1 (Fig. 384 (a)) and pull end 1. This tightens loop 1 round the neck of loop 2.

Now pass loop 3 through loop 2 and pull end 2, see Fig. 384 (b). This chaining and tightening of the loops is continued right across the rug until the left edge is reached. There the final end is passed through the final loop and that loop tightened to lock the whole row.

This finish gives a very pronounced ridge on the front. It holds the ends securely if the warp count is high enough. If not, the free ends can be darned, as shown in Fig. 384 (c) which represents an end-on view of the finish. Each end is darned upwards into the lower loop of the next knot to the right, as indicated by the arrow. As well as strengthening the finish, this makes the free ends lie in a better position.

The Second Stage of chained loops can be elaborated thus: Put loop 2 and 3 through loop 1, and pull end 1. Put loops 3 and 4 through loop 2, and pull end 2. Put loop 4 and 5 through loop 3, and pull end 3, and so on. This gives a thicker but less secure ridge.

Other ways of using these loops may be suggested by the method of finishing a frame-woven rug (see Special Finishes at end of chapter).

F. Maori Edge

This finish is used on Maori weft-twined fabrics. It gives a very neat rolled edge. It is structurally a cord running the width of the rug, made up of four warp ends, in the form of two 2-ply yarns plied together. At every half turn of this cord, one warp end is discarded and another brought in, so it remains of constant size. Despite its simple analysis, the finish is complicated to make and the description is best considered in two parts.

(i) THE START

This only has to be done once. See Fig. 385 (a)–(c). Starting at left, pass end 1 under 2, then pass 2 under 3, and then pass 1 under 4. There are now two ends pointing upwards and two ends pointing downwards. These are seen again in Fig 385 (d) where for clarity in the following description they have been relabelled A, B, C and D.

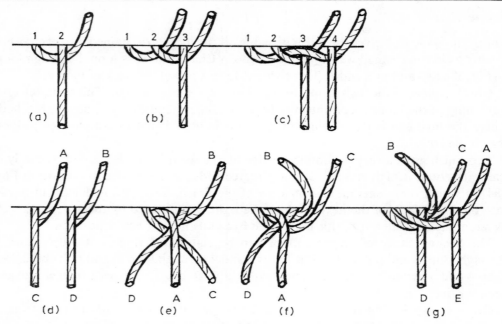

Fig. 385. Rug Finishes. Maori Edge. (a–c) Initial stages (d–g) Four stages of the finish proper

(ii) CONTINUATION

Now cross D over C, as close to the rug as possible, and bring A down over this crossing, see Fig. 385 (e). Hold this triple crossing tightly between the left thumb and index finger. With the right hand discard B to the left and bring up C to take its place, see Fig. 385 (f). Still with the right hand, bring up A under the next end, E; leave go of the crossing and tighten the finish by pulling C and A upwards and D and E downwards, see Fig. 385 (g). The sequence (e–g) is now repeated with these four ends; and the process is continued across the rug.

> *Note*—Each sequence ends with two ends pointing upwards and two pointing downwards; of these, one is a new end and the other three were involved in the last sequence. Thus each end is involved in four sequences and is then discarded.

Though this is a very secure edge, the rug can be turned over and the whole process repeated so that there are two rolled edges with the free ends merging between them.

G. Four-Strand Sennit Edge

This edge is structurally a four-strand square sennit (see Warp Protectors). As it proceeds across the width of the rug, new ends are constantly added to it and old ends discarded from it, so like the Maori edge (which suggested it) it remains of constant size.

Unlike other weft protectors it needs an extra piece of yarn. This should be longer than twice the width of the rug and depending on the warp setting may have to be thicker than the warp yarn. So it could be two pieces of warp used as one or some other yarn (perhaps the same colour as the weft).

Centre this yarn (shaded) over end 1 at the left edge of the rug, so that there are now two warp ends pointing upwards and two extra yarns pointing downwards, see Fig. 386 (a). Bring up the left-hand part of this extra yarn, pass it between ends 1 and 2 and bring it down so that it is now the right-hand extra yarn, see Fig. 386 (b).

Bring end 1 down, pass it between the two parts of extra yarn and carry it up so that it is now on the right of end 2, see Fig. 386 (c).

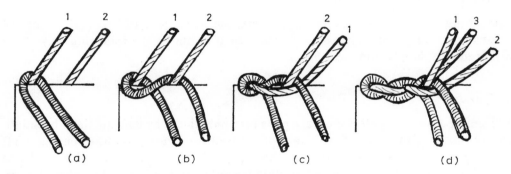

Fig. 386. Rug finishes. Four-strand Sennit Edge. (a–c) Method
(d) Stage reached when working the variation

Now discard end 1, and end 3, which should be found lying behind it, takes its place. So again there are two ends (numbers 2 and 3) pointing upwards and two extra yarns pointing downwards.

The two stages shown in Fig. 386 (b) and (c) are repeated; viz. lower left end between upper two ends to become lower right; upper left end between lower two ends to become upper right. Then end 2 is discarded and end 4 taken up in its place.

This process is repeated right across the rug. As it is only the upper ends that are discarded the extra yarn remains in the edge continuously from left to right selvage.

The following variation gives a securer edge, because each warp end is involved in four stages instead of two.

When the stage in Fig. 386 (c) is reached, do not discard end 1, but treat end 1 and end 3 as one unit for the next two stages. These are done exactly as described above, (the fact that one of the four ends is of double thickness making no difference at all), after which, the edge will look like Fig. 386 (d). Now discard end 1; bring in end 4 which for the next two stages will work as a unit with end 2. After these two stages, discard end 2, and bring in end 5, and so on.

> *Note*—Difficulty in deciding which of the pair of ends to discard may be resolved by pulling on them individually.
> —Neither of these finishes is easy.
> —The first can be tightened after it is made by pulling on the free ends one by one.
> —Probably the more complex sennits could be adapted as rug finishes; but the weaver should be familiar with them as entities in themselves before endeavouring to apply them in this way.

2. WARP PROTECTORS

After using one of the above weft protectors, the weaver is still left with a fringe of free-hanging warp ends. Unless these are treated in one of the following ways, they will gradually un-ply and wear away.

A. Darning

The simplest way to protect the warp ends is to hide them, by darning them back into the substance of the rug. After certain of the weft protectors, the warp ends are left pointing in the right direction to make this seem a simple and obvious solution. These are half Damascus (together with variation (i) and (iii)), Locked and Chained Loops, Maori and Four-Strand Sennit.

In all these cases, the fringe ends can be darned singly or in pairs for a distance of 1–2 inches into the rug.

Insert a needle (the type used for darning in weft ends is suitable) into the rug so that it slides down parallel with a warp end, then thread it with a wire loop, pull the fringe end into the rug, and cut it off flush.

> *Note*—This procedure doubles the thickness of warp in the last few inches of the rug, so it could be expected to make this part of the rug buckle or distort in some way. However, if in preparation for this finish, the weft is woven with a specially loose tension for the first and last few inches of the rug, this difficulty will be overcome.
> —As a further precaution darn the ends in a variable distance; so no two adjacent ends emerge at the same spot.

B. Overhand Knots

Overhand knots can be used in several ways.

(i) One of the commonest is to make several rows of knots, say three or four, the knots in one row receiving their ends from two adjacent knots in the preceding row and themselves contributing their ends to two knots in the succeeding row. See Fig. 387 (a). So the position of the knots in successive rows is staggered; this makes it possible for the knots to lie close together and so a thick finish with densely-packed knots can be made.

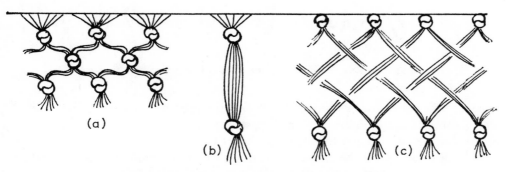

Fig. 387. Rug Finishes. Overhand knots as warp protectors

(ii) The overhand knot can be simply repeated at the extremity of the group of fringe ends as shown in Fig. 387 (b). Or these groups can be interlaced in some such way as shown in Fig. 387 (c) before the final knots.

C. Plaiting

A plait of any type makes a good fringe; due to its flexibility it lies well. A three-strand plait can be quickly made, (using two to four warp ends as one strand), if the fingers are used correctly. After the strands have been crossed two or three times, pull them tight to force the plait close up against the rug edge. There are many other more complex types (see *The Ashley Book of Knots*). Each plait can be finished off in one of three ways.

(i) With an overhand knot. Tighten it as described under overhand knots in weft protectors. This is very important as the knot is the first line of defence. Once it works loose, the whole fringe can begin to wear away.

(ii) With two half hitches. Split the constituent threads of the plait into two equal groups. Take the right half up behind the plait and then down through its own loop, see Fig. 388 (a). Tighten. Now take the left half up behind the plait and down through its own loop, see Fig. 388 (b); slip this knot below the first knot and then tighten. This gives a more compact finish than an overhand knot, see Fig. 388 (c).

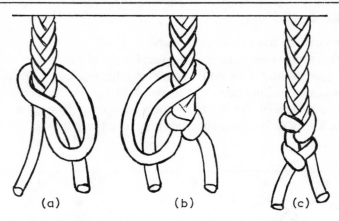

Fig. 388. Rug Finishes. Finishing a plait with two half hitches

(iii) If either of the above proves too bulky, the plait will have to be whipped. Fig. 389 (a) shows diagrammatically the neatest way to do this. Using a length of warp yarn, lay a loop of it down towards the end of the plait. Then bind the plait tightly, working downwards (in the arrow's direction). When this binding has covered about ½ inch of the plait, tuck the yarn into the loop as shown. Then pull on the end A, drawing the loop plus the yarn under the binding, see Fig. 389 (b). Trim both ends.

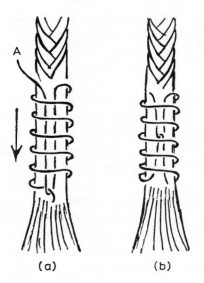

Fig. 389. Rug Finishes. Whipping a plait

D. Plying

Groups of warp ends can be plied, so that the fringe appears as a series of thick 2-ply cords.

Divide each group into two equal halves, and twist both in the direction that increases their twist. Thus if the final plying of the yarn was Z-twist, then add more Z-twist, see Fig. 390 (a). Because one half of the group is in the right-hand and the other is in the left, there is a natural tendency to impart opposite twists to the two halves, which has to be overcome. The two groups are plied with the reverse twist, i.e., S-twist in the above example, see Fig. 390 (b).

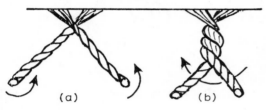

(a)   (b)

Fig. 390
Rug Finishes.
Plying warp ends

It is best to put extra twist into both groups simultaneously (rolling them between fingers and thumb), then make one half turn of plying and keep on repeating this for the whole length. This gives a better result than twisting each group separately right to its end and then bringing the two groups together and hoping they will ply.

Finish each plied end with one of the ways described under plaiting. If too much twist is added, the plied ends will not lie flat. If the warp yarn is very highly twisted to begin with, make the initial twisting in the reverse direction of the yarn's final twist.

E. Alternate Hitches

For the amount of ends involved in it, this gives a very bulky finish. An Alternate Hitch finish is at least twice as thick as a plied end containing the same number of threads. In addition, this finish uses up a greater length of warp than normal—i.e., the finish is less than half the length of the constituent threads. These two facts imply

(1) that it is useful wherever a large scale fringe is wanted, e.g., on a very large rug, where a normal fringe would seem out of scale.

(2) that it has to be prepared for. Extra long warp ends have to be left at both ends of the rug.

Divide the ends to be used into two groups, labelled A and B in Fig. 391 (a). Knot A round B as shown. This is the knot that occurs so often in the weft protectors. Hold B tight, as the knot is made. Then swing A down to the right. Now hold A tight, knot B round it and swing B down to the left, see Fig 391 (b). Repeat these two knots.

Fig. 391 (c) shows the appearance of this finish.

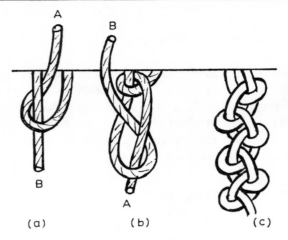

Fig. 391
Rug Finishes.
Finishing warp ends
with alternate
hitches

(a)   (b)   (c)

F. Four-Strand Square Sennit

Once the simplicity of a three-strand plait is passed, there is an almost endless variety of more complex intertwined finishes. Most of these are classed as sennits. Some are flat sennits (or braids) and are developments of the three-strand plaiting principle. Others are solid sennits and have characteristic cross-sections—e.g., square, triangular, circular, star-shaped. They may involve anything from four to sixty-one strands. Fig. 392 shows the simplest of this class, a four-strand square sennit.

Start with four ends, or four groups of ends, and cross them as in Fig. 392 (a). There are now two strands pointing down to the left (A and B) and two strands pointing down to the right (C and D).

The sennit is made in two movements.

(1) Carry the upper left strand, A, around behind the others, then forwards between the two opposing strands (C and D), and finally lay it below B, see arrow in Fig. 392 (a). So from being the upper left strand, A has become the lower left strand, see Fig. 392 (b).

(2) Carry the upper right strand (D), around behind the others, then forwards between the two opposing strands (B and C) and finally lay it below C, see arrow in Fig. 392 (b).

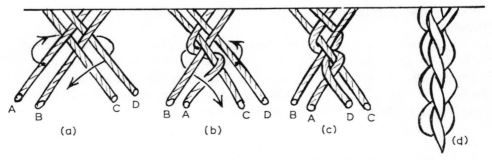

(a)   (b)   (c)   (d)

Fig. 392. Rug Finishes. Four-strand Square Sennit. (a–c) Method (f) Finished appearance

The sennit is now as in Fig. 392 (c). A and B have changed their relative positions, and so have C and D, but note that A and B are still both to the left and C and D still both to the right.

The above two movements are repeated; i.e., the upper strand from each side alternately is taken around the back, and then forwards between the two opposite strands to become the lower strand on its own side.

After each movement pull the right and left group firmly apart to tighten the sennit. Finish with an overhand knot or whipping. Fig. 392 (d) shows the completed sennit. If the strands are of two colours, then these can be made either to run longitudinally or spirally in the sennit according to their arrangement at the beginning.

The same principle can be applied to any even number of strands. Other sennits are more complex to make and can be found in *the Ashley Book of Knots*.

3. WARP AND WEFT PROTECTORS

A. Swedish Tapestry Edge

This is the simplest member of the class and has a limited usefulness. End 1 is darned down beside end 2 for about 2 inches and cut. End 2 is then cut flush with the edge of

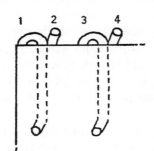

Fig. 393
Rug Finishes. Swedish
Tapestry Edge

the rug. End 3 is darned down beside end 4 and cut. End 4 is then cut. See Fig. 393. It is obviously not very secure, but is a neat way of finishing the edge of a rug which is then going to be turned under and sewn.

B. Woven Edge

There is very little evidence of ancient finishes as they are generally the first part of a textile to wear away. But there is a woven edge on a woollen fabric which was found in Denmark and dates from at least 1000 B.C.

The principle of the woven edge is that warp ends are one by one turned through a right angle and, acting as 'weft', are woven into the neighbouring warp ends.

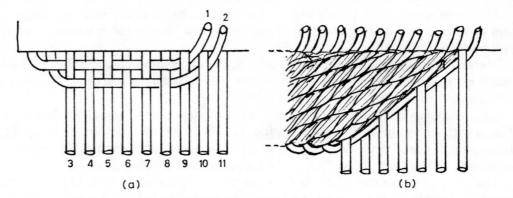

Fig. 394. Rug Finishes. Woven Edge. (a) General Diagram (b) Showing angled fell of the woven band

Referring to Fig. 394 (a), begin at the left edge of the rug and weave end 1 in a plain weave shed (over ends 2, 4, 6, 8 and under ends 3, 5, 7, 9), so that it emerges between ends 9 and 10. Then weave end 2 in the opposite plain weave shed (over ends 3, 5, 7, 9 and under ends 4, 6, 8, 10) so that it emerges between ends 10 and 11.

This is continued, the leftmost end always being woven in the next shed, for the same distance, and always emerging at one warp interspace beyond the last.

The woven band thus produced will gradually widen as each new end is woven, until a point is reached when the emerging end 1 is vertically over the next end to be woven (End 9 in Fig. 394 (a)). From then on the band will be of constant width, see Fig. 395 (a). Thus the width of the band depends on how far end 1 is woven in the first shed, as all subsequent ends follow its lead. In Fig. 394 (a) it is woven under four ends, but it could equally well have been under 3, 5, 6, 7, 8, etc. So the width of the woven band is easily controllable.

When the right edge of the rug is reached there will be about eight ends left with no warp to weave them into. These ends are made into a plait or sennit, and whipped, see Fig. 395 (a).

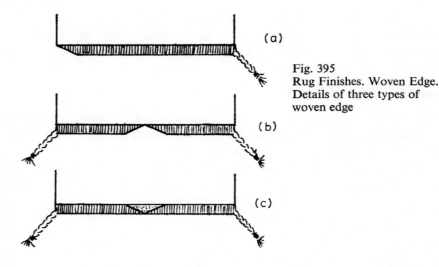

Fig. 395
Rug Finishes. Woven Edge.
Details of three types of
woven edge

The 'weft' must be laid in slackly so that, when pressed tightly home, it completely covers the warp. When this is done, it will be found that the fell of the woven band is not at right angles to the warp, but that it slopes towards the edge of the rug as shown in Fig. 394 (b). A rug fork or the fingers can be used for pushing the 'weft' into position.

A pair of tweezers or artery forceps are a great help in the weaving. Enter them from the right into the correct shed, then grasp the leftmost end with them and draw it back into the shed. If these are not available, carry out a similar manœuvre with two fingers of the right hand.

The emerging ends are cut about ¼ inch from the rug surface. If the rug is one-sided (i.e., a pile rug), carry out this finish with the rug upside down, so that the short cut ends will be on the underside. If the weaver considers the edge is not secure enough or if he is offended by the short cut ends, the emerging ends can be darned one by one back into the rug, and cut off flush with its surface.

The above is the basic method, but, as often happens with such a simple idea, there are many variations.

(i) VARIATIONS IN STARTING THE WOVEN EDGE

(a) *Starting at Centre*

The edge can equally well be started at the centre of the rug and worked in both directions. So there is a dip in the centre where the two woven bands start and there is a plait or some tassel at both corners, see Fig. 395 (b). Start by tying a half knot with the two central ends and then begin weaving, see Fig. 396 (a). The knot prevents

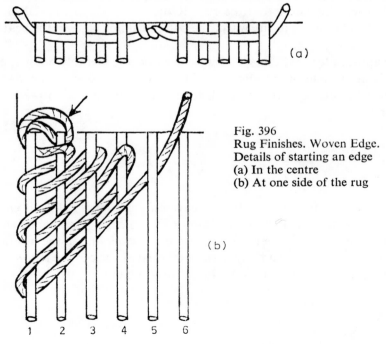

(a)

(b)

Fig. 396
Rug Finishes. Woven Edge.
Details of starting an edge
(a) In the centre
(b) At one side of the rug

1   2   3   4   5   6

the weft ballooning at this point. This edge is seen on the sample in Plate 14. To avoid the central dip, start by weaving a triangle in the centre with a separate piece of warp yarn (just like weaving a triangle in a kilim) and then continue as above. As long as the size of the triangle has been correctly judged, the woven edge will be perfectly straight, see Fig. 395 (c).

(b) Starting at Side

A woven edge can be started at one or other side of the rug, in such a way that the band is at full-width right from the beginning. This means building up a right angle triangle to counter the normal sloped beginning of the woven edge. The triangle can be woven either from an extra length of yarn or from one of the warp ends. Fig. 396 (b) shows the former alternative. The length of yarn is centred round end 2 (arrowed) and then woven to left and to right, always including one more end in its passage to the right. When the triangle is large enough, the yarn is made to emerge as shown. The warp ends are then woven in normally. So the next step in Fig. 396 (b) is to take end 1 under 2, over 3, under 4, over 5, and under 6. If the triangle is woven from a warp end, use end 2 and proceed exactly as above.

(ii) VARIATIONS IN WEAVING METHOD

A woven edge can be made at the final end of a rug, *as it is being cut from the loom.*

Cut the left-hand end, open a plain weave shed and weave the cut end in for a certain distance. Cut the next end, change the shed and weave the end in for the same distance. Proceed thus all across the rug. Remember that as the fell of the woven band is not at right angles to the warp, the batten cannot be used for beating. So use a rug fork.

It will be appreciated that this speeds up the work considerably but it can obviously be done only at one end of any rug. In a similar way, the edge can be made from the centre outwards, cutting two ends each time and weaving one to the right and the other to the left.

(iii) VARIATIONS IN WEAVE

(a) Two-Pick Woven Edge

There is no necessity for each 'weft' to weave only one pick before it emerges. Fig. 397 shows a stage in the making of a two-pick woven edge. The shaded end is woven to the right. When it meets the rug edge, instead of emerging in the normal way it is turned round the next warp end (arrowed), and weaves back to the left in the opposite shed. It then emerges at the outer edge of the woven band.

The first pick of the next end (unshaded) now enters the same shed as the second pick of the shaded end, see Fig. 397. It will then return to the left in the next shed.

Thus there are two picks in every shed, one passing to the right and one passing to the left. All the ends finally emerge at the outer edge of the woven band. If the weaving is secure enough they can be cut short here. Alternatively this finish could be considered just as a weft protector and the emerging ends then be plaited or plied.

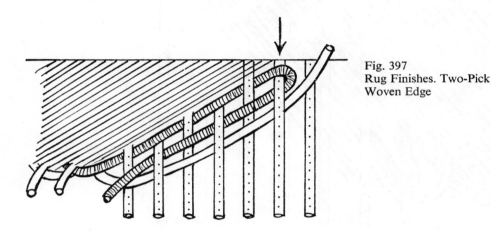

Fig. 397
Rug Finishes. Two-Pick
Woven Edge

(b) Three-Pick Woven Edge

Fig. 398 shows a stage in a three-pick woven edge. In this method the shed is changed between every pick. The shaded end is woven to the right with six ends (starting under the first), back to the left with five ends, and back to the right with five or six ends (depending on what is to follow). The next end (unshaded) does exactly the same.

> *Note*—There is only one pick in every shed. The final pick is woven with six ends (as is the unshaded end) if the emerging end is to be cut short or darned into the rug. In some Swedish finishes, it is woven with five ends (as is the shaded end), pushed through to the back in the space marked X, and subsequently darned outwards. A needle is inserted along the nearest warp thread, the emerging end threaded into it and drawn out, so that it now protrudes from the outer edge of the woven band. These ends are then plied or plaited, thus treating the woven edge merely as a weft protector.
>
> —That the second pick weaves with one less end than the first. If it wove with the same number it would form a loop at the outer edge that could work loose. If however the ends are to be darned outwards as described above, they will catch and secure these loops—so in this case, the thread could weave six picks to right, six to left, six to right.

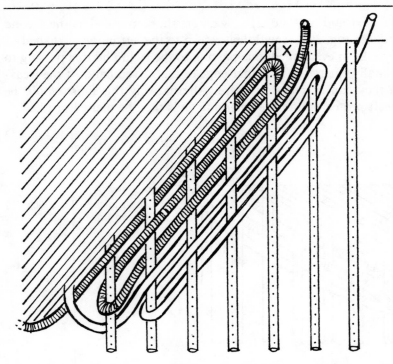

Fig. 398
Rug Finishes.
Three-Pick Woven
Edge

Because in these variations the threads interlace two or more times with each other, they can achieve the same security by interlacing with fewer ends than are involved in a normal woven edge. Thus a three-pick woven edge in which the 'weft' weaves with four ends in each pick, is probably just as secure as a normal (one pick) woven edge in which it weaves with twelve ends. A related feature is that a two- or three-pick woven edge in which the 'weft' weaves with a certain number of ends, will be much wider than a one-pick woven edge weaving with the same number of ends. The extra width is the result of the increased angle of the fell of the woven band.

To ensure a straight edge to the rug, some weavers first knot the warp in pairs and then regard these pairs as the unit in weaving the edge. When this is done with a two- or three-pick woven edge, the 'weft' as it turns between the first and second pick is caught between the knot and the rug, see Fig. 399.

Fig. 399
Rug Finishes.
Detail of Woven Edge

(iv) VARIATIONS IN COLOUR

If the warp is striped, the colours will appear as lozenges in the woven edge, see Plate 161.

C. Twined Edge

Just as the last finish is based on the idea of weaving warp into warp, this is based on the idea of twining warp about warp. (Reference to Chapter 13 on Twining is advised at this point.)

Start at either side of the rug or in the centre. In Fig. 400, the twined edge begins at the left side of the rug. The twining can be either S- or Z-twist, or a combination of the two. Assuming it is to be Z-, start by twisting ends 1 and 2 as in Fig. 400 (a). These two ends are now going to twine with six warp ends.

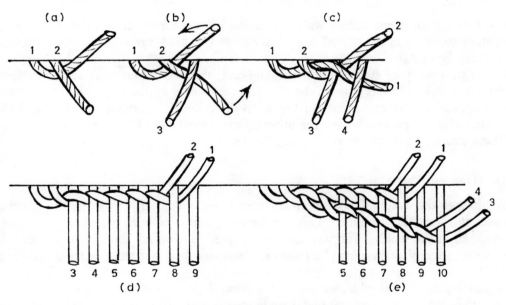

Fig. 400. Rug Finishes. Twined Edge

Bring end 3 down between the twining ends, as in Fig. 400 (b). Lock it in position with another twist of the twining ends (arrows in Fig. 400 (b)), then bring end 4 down between them, see Fig. 400 (c). Carry on thus until six ends have been brought down (these are ends 3–8 in Fig. 400 (d)). The two twining ends emerge, as shown, in adjacent warp interspaces.

Now twist ends 3 and 4 as in Fig. 400 (a), and use them as the twining ends for the next row. They will twine round the next six ends (numbers 5–10), and emerge in the next two warp interspaces, see Fig. 400 (e). Continue thus across the rug; and deal with the emerging ends by cutting them short or darning them into the rug.

> *Note*—That each row of twining reaches two warp ends to the right of the former.
> —When twining to the right, hold the two twining ends in the right hand and bring the warp ends down between them with the left hand. With practice the right hand can twist the two ends without shifting its grip.
> —As each row is twined it will tend to slant down towards the twining hand (right), see Fig. 400 (e). So on completion, force it up against the previous row.

Due to its structure a twined edge is very strong, but it is naturally slower to make than a woven edge.

Variations

(*a*) *Twist*. With a one colour warp, variations of the direction of twist can make a subtle patterning in the twined edge. But ensure that such variations will not prevent the edge lying flat.

(*b*) With a warp of two colours, end-and-end, the two-colour weft twining effects can be produced in this edge. If the edge is done exactly as described, the two colours will appear as stripes running in the warp direction. By varying the twist and the colour which begins each row, the other effects described in Chapter 13 are possible. These can lead to very interesting rug finishes.

D. Wrapped Edge

Again with the wrapped edge, warp is worked into warp, but in this case the working takes the form of wrapping. This can be analysed as soumak which is alternately wrapped in the locking and non-locking manner. But unlike soumak, row succeeds row without any intervening plain weave. It was seen on a tent-hanging from Bokhara.

Starting at the left edge, wrap end 1 around 2, as shown in Fig. 401 (a). Tighten this, then wrap end 1 around end 3, as shown in Fig. 401 (b). These two wrappings, one of the locking, one of the non-locking type, are repeated with an odd number of ends (five in Fig. 401 (c)). The odd number ensures that the row finishes with a locking wrap, from which the end emerges as shown. If Fig. 401 (c) is turned over, it may be easier to see that wrappings of the locking and non-locking type are being produced alternately. Now pick up end 2 and do exactly the same as above, i.e., start with a locking wrap.

Fig. 401 (d) shows the edge when these two rows have been pressed down tightly.

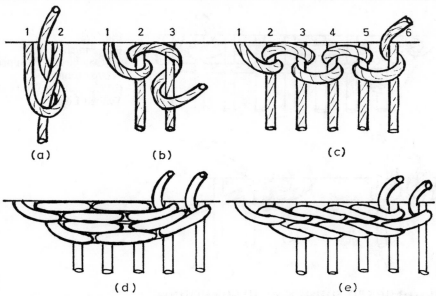

Fig. 401. Rug Finishes. Wrapped Edge. (a–c) Method (d) Completed edge (e) Variation

Note how the positions of the soumak loops alternate rather like bricks in a wall. The edge is continued thus, right across the rug. The reverse of this edge is quite different, consisting of narrow ridges made by the soumak 'wefts' as they wrap around successive warp ends.

It is important to keep the passive elements (the warp ends) under tension as the wrappings are made, also to make the latter at a tension that will not distort the warp ends from their true parallel position.

A possible variation is the following. If only the locking wrap (Fig. 401 (a)) is used and repeated, say, six times, a slightly different edge is produced. This could be called a locked soumak edge. The wrapping can be made round an odd or even number of ends, but always round the same number in each row. As Fig. 401 (e) shows it resembles the twined edge. The back of this edge is identical with the back of the normal wrapped edge.

E. Combinations of Woven, Twined and Wrapped Edges

(i) STARTING OR ENDING A WOVEN EDGE WITH A LOCKED SOUMAK

See Fig. 402 (a). Starting a woven edge thus, gives a very firm border to the band. Finishing it thus, gives it additional strength, especially if the emerging ends are cut short.

> *Note*—How the 'weft' passes over two warp ends, after the initial wrapping and before it enters a plain weave shed. This helps the bulk of the wrapping to bed down into the weaving below it.

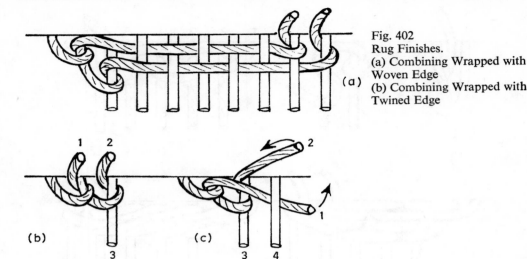

Fig. 402
Rug Finishes.
(a) Combining Wrapped with Woven Edge
(b) Combining Wrapped with Twined Edge

(ii) USING LOCKED SOUMAK AS DECORATION

One row of locked soumak (using two 'wefts' as one), introduced in a woven or twined edge, makes an obvious ridge. Such ridges can either have a rhythm of their own or be related to some design element in the rest of the rug.

Or an all-over texture can be made by alternating, say, two twined or woven rows with one soumak row.

(iii) STARTING A TWINED EDGE WITH TWO LOCKED SOUMAK WRAPPINGS

Begin by wrapping end 1 round 2 and end 2 round end 3, see Fig. 402 (b). Then bring end 1 across to the right, and behind end 4, see Fig. 402 (c). Now continue twining, i.e., twist ends 1 and 2, as arrows, and bring down end 5 between them.

These are only a few of the many ways, both functional and decorative, in which the various warp-into-warp finishes can be combined.

F. Woven Edge Using Extra Warp

This is one of the most complex but satisfying of rug finishes. It involves setting up a narrow warp (about 2–3 feet longer than the rug is wide), and holding it close up against the edge of the rug. It is then woven using the rug's warp ends as its weft. Each warp end goes in one shed and back in the next and then is discarded. It shares this latter shed with the next warp end. Thus each shed contains two warp ends which

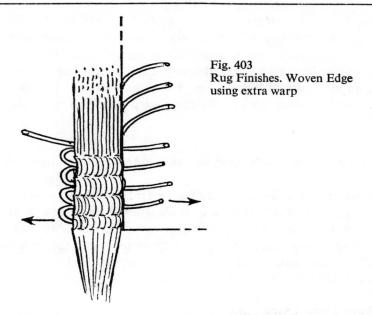

Fig. 403
Rug Finishes. Woven Edge
using extra warp

move in opposite directions. The discarded ends are cut off or darned into the rug. See Fig. 403.

This, in brief, is the method, but its carrying out presents some problems, mostly to do with tension.

The narrow warp has to have some shedding mechanism. This can be a rigid heddle or stick and leashes, in which case the warp will have a warp-face plain weave structure. Or it can be tablets, in which case the warp will have the characteristic twined warp structure of tablet weaving. As the warp is quite separate from the rug, it gives a good opportunity for introducing not only new colours, but also the neat intricacies that tablet weaving is capable of.

When the warp is made, it is stretched (perhaps between pegs mounted on a table's edge). Now the rug has to be stretched as well so that both extra warp and rug contract an equal amount when the process is completed and the rug is laid on the floor. One way to do this is to fix a temple so that it stretches the edge of the rug that is to be worked. The width at which the temple is set is something that has to be found by trial and error and will, of course, depend on the relative elasticity of the rug's weft yarn and the extra warp yarn. The temple can be relaxed at intervals during the weaving to see whether the rug and the woven edge contract equally or whether the temple has to be reset to overcome any inequality. The temple is useful in another way. If the ends as yet unwoven are turned back under the temple, they are prevented from fouling the shed of the extra warp.

It is difficult to weave the extra warp so that it is tight up against the rug's edge. So leave a loop of each 'weft' at the outer margin of the woven edge. Every 6 inches or so, tighten the first pick then the second pick of each 'weft' in turn; i.e. first pull on the loop (arrow to left in Fig. 403), then pull on the emerging end (arrow to right in Fig. 403). This brings the woven edge as close as desired to the rug.

The extra warp yarn can be identical with the rug warp or be the same yarn dyed; or it can be another material altogether. But remember that the soundness of the finish depends on how this yarn and the rug's warp yarn grip each other.

WHEN USING TABLETS

Set the tablets so that each is twining the warp in the opposite direction to its neighbour.

If the woven edge is beating down too far, i.e., if the edge is becoming shorter than the attached rug, turn the tablets once or twice without inserting a 'weft'.

A neat way to begin and end a tablet-woven extra warp is to weave a few inches in a circular manner. Using a separate weft, always enter it into the shed from the same side. Tightening the resulting weft floats, one by one, causes the braid to curl up into a tube, the right and left selvages meeting. See Plate 10.

G. Twined Edge Using Extra Yarn

Taniko Edge

This method uses extra yarn, which is twined round the warp ends. It is a Maori finish.

Take two pieces of yarn each of which is about three times the width of the rug. Double each piece over and loop the two doubled pieces into each other, so that the two pieces join as in Fig. 404 (a). For clarity, these have been shown black and white, but there is no need for them to be in different colours.

Centre the looped yarns round the selvage of the rug, as in Fig. 404 (a). Cross the white and black yarns over and, in so doing, pass the white through the black. Tighten by pulling apart, see Fig. 404 (b). Pass the black yarns behind end 2, see Fig. 404 (c). Bring down the last warp end (i.e., end 1) behind end 2, see Fig. 404 (d). Cross the black and white yarns back again, this time passing the black through the white, see Fig. 404 (e). Tighten them. Tighten the warp ends by pulling ends 1 and 2 in opposite directions (arrows). The process is continued: pass white yarns behind end 3, bring down end 2 behind end 3, cross black and white yarns over and tighten, and so on. As the yarns are crossed over, always separate the left-hand pair and pass the right-hand pair between them.

The completed edge is shown diagrammatically in Fig. 404 (f). It will be seen that the edge is structurally two rows of weft twining, which are produced simultaneously by this method. The emerging ends are cut off or darned in.

VARIATIONS

(i) As it stands, the edge is not very secure. So at the stage shown in Fig. 404 (d), knot end 1 and 2 together. Use a half knot as shown in Fig. 404 (g) or add another twist to it. This greatly increases the practicability of this edge.

(ii) A further strengthening is achieved if after each of the above knots is tied the last discarded end is brought up and laid beside the knot before the black and white yarns are crossed over. So these yarns are now twining round three thicknesses of warp instead of two, and the warp ends are now emerging from the outer margin of the edge. Fig. 404 (h) shows the serpentine course taken through the edge by one warp end. The emerging ends can safely be cut flush with the edge, to give a very neat if tedious finish.

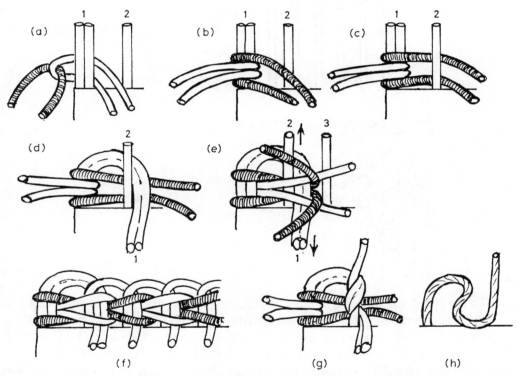

Fig. 404. Rug Finishes. Taniko Edge. (a–e) Method (f) Completed edge (g) and (h) Variations

The thickness and material of the two twining yarns is obviously crucial. They have to be such that when the edge is made firmly enough to secure the warp ends, it lies flat without curling or buckling.

H. Specific Finishes

(i) FOR A RUG WOVEN ON A FRAME WITH A FINITE WARP

Rugs are sometimes woven on a warp that has been stretched between nails on the upper and lower crossbar of a rug frame. When such a rug is finished, it has loops of warp, not cut threads, at both ends, those at the starting end probably being shorter.

Warp loops produced thus, or in any other manner, can be finished in the following way. See Fig. 405 (a).

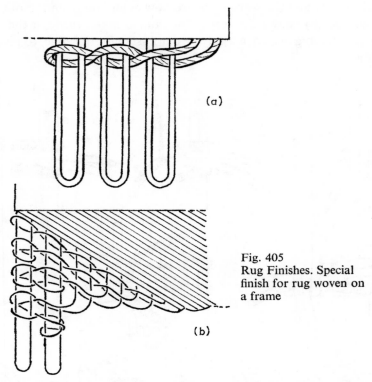

Fig. 405
Rug Finishes. Special
finish for rug woven on
a frame

Take the first loop at the right edge of rug. Pass the second loop through it. Twist the first loop (in the direction suggested by the twist of the yarn) and pass the third loop through it, twist it again in the same direction and pass the fourth loop through it. Continue until the end of the loop is reached, see Fig. 405 (a). Then do exactly the same with the second loop, third loop, and so on. The result is a twined edge, but with no emerging ends.

When the opposite edge of the rug is reached, double the loops back on themselves as shown in Fig. 405 (b). This can probably be done until only two loops are left, which can then be knotted together or one can be darned down beside the other.

This is a very sound edge, because there are no cut warp ends to work loose.

(ii) FRINGELESS FINISH FOR A KNOTTED RUG

A fringeless finish is often wanted on a long pile rug and one of the simplest and neatest is the following:

Begin and end the rug with about two more inches of plain weave than are required to show. Then with the rug, pile downwards, do a half Damascus edge.

Cut the free ends about 1 inch long.

Fold an inch or so of the rug back onto itself, thus making a longitudinal pocket (marked X in Fig. 406 (a)). Push the free ends into this pocket and sew the folded piece to the back of the rug, as indicated by the needle. These stitches will be hidden by the pile of the rug.

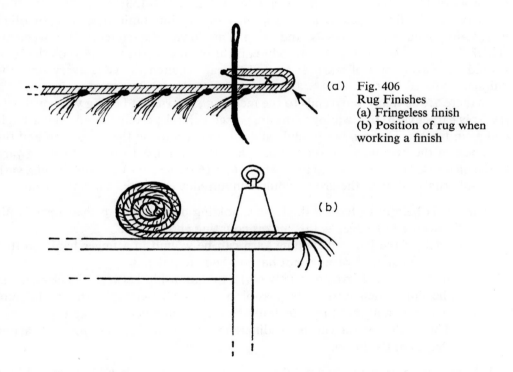

(a) Fig. 406
Rug Finishes
(a) Fringeless finish
(b) Position of rug when
working a finish

(b)

It is quite difficult to make a straight fold especially with a wide rug. So as the rug is being made, some weavers put in a row of weft chaining or two picks of another colour at the point where the fold is to be made (see arrow in Fig. 406 (a)) to act as a guide. This can be decorative as well as functional.

(iii) FOR WARP-FACE RUGS—DOUBLE TWINED EDGE

Because of the great bulk of warp to be dealt with at the ends of a warp-face rug, any of the normal finishes are far too clumsy. It is interesting that wherever textiles of this type are made, the weavers have almost always arrived at the same solution to the problem—and that is to insert two or more rows of weft twining.

Two rows can be inserted at the same time if a modification of the Taniko Edge is used.

Always make this edge on the loom if possible. So before the weaving begins, make the edge on the tightly stretched warp. Then weave the rug, and make a similar edge beyond the last pick. The rug can then be cut from the loom and needs no further finishing. If another rug is to be woven on the same warp, leave a short gap and repeat the process. This edge is seen on the samples in Plates 150–153.

Carry out the finish exactly as in Fig. 404 (a)–(e) but omit stage (d). In other words, do not cut any warp ends, and bring them down. The sequence of movements is therefore: open left pair and pass right pair through, pass the pair now on the right behind the next group of warp ends, and repeat. Tighten the edge every time the pairs are crossed over.

As there are so many warp ends to the inch (e.g., forty-eight belting yarn or thirty-six 2-ply carpet yarn) the twining yarns are passed behind a group of ends, not a single end as in taniko. The number of ends in a group depends on the warp yarn and the thickness of the twining yarn. As an example if the warp has forty-eight belting yarn to the inch (used three as one; so there are in fact 16 treble e.p.i.) and the twining yarn is a 6-ply rugwool, then the group would contain nine ends (i.e., three treble ends).

Note—It is helpful to have a thick stick holding a plain weave shed open while working this edge, as this makes counting ends easier.

—Each of the pairs of twining yarn can be wound in a finger hank, so that great lengths of yarn do not have to be manipulated.

—In order to achieve an exactly correct relationship between the elements in the finish, remember it is possible to use two twining yarns of different thickness and that they can embrace varying numbers of warp ends.

—The twining yarns can be of different colours, which will appear as arrow shapes in the finish.

When the far edge is reached, tie the four threads in an overhand knot and tighten it against the last warp group. Two rows of this edge look well on a wide warp-face rug; work one from left to right and the other from right to left, so that there is an overhand knot at both edges.

1. General Remarks

(i) A rug must be firmly held and at a suitable height, if the finish is to be done comfortably and efficiently. A good method is to place it rolled up on a table, with a heavy weight on it and with its edge protruding slightly beyond the table, see Fig. 406 (b). The table's edge can act as a check on the straightness of the rug's edge. While working the finish, concentrate on doing everything with an even tension.

(ii) The weaving of a rug always begins and ends with a few picks of thick yarn. These are not part of the actual rug but merely act as a temporary weft protector after the rug is cut from the loom and before it receives its real finish. These picks are kept in place with a few temporary half knots in the warp.

Only remove these picks as the finish is being worked. For example, a Philippine edge starts at the left selvage, so slide these picks out, freeing a few warp ends at this point only. Work the edge as far as possible, then free more warp ends. In this way, the final (or initial) picks of the rug proper never get a chance to shift from their correct position as woven. This is very important in a wide rug.

(iii) There is always a tendency for a rug to be pulled in slightly at either end of the finish. This leads to a rounding of the rug's corners. This can generally be overcome, if in working the finish the doubled or trebled ends at the selvages are split, and their constituent ends worked singly.

(iv) For all these finishes, there are certain ways of holding and manipulating the warp ends that will make for quickness and efficiency. They have been omitted from this chapter, partly because they are so difficult to describe and partly because every weaver has his own slightly different way of doing things; to discover that way is one of the pleasures of mastering a new technique.

(v) These finishes can be practised (and new ones tried out) on a magnified rug fringe. The latter is made by fastening 1 foot lengths of thick cord, about $\frac{1}{2}$ inch apart, to a strip of wood which can be clamped to a table. If a new finish works on this contrivance, test it next on the real thing.

Bibliography

Achdjian, A. *Le Tapis*. 1949. Paris.

Allard, Mary. *Rug Making, Techniques and Design*. 1963. Chilton Books, Philadelphia.

Amsden, Charles Avery. *Navaho Weaving*. 1949. University of New Mexico Press. Reprinted and revised by Rio Grande Press, Glorieta, New Mexico.

Ashley, Clifford W. *The Ashley Book of Knots*. 1948. Faber and Faber, London, and Doubleday, New York.

Aslanapa, Oktay. *Turkish Art and Architecture*. 1971. Praeger.

Aslanapa, A. *Turkish Arts*. Istanbul.

Beaumont, Robert. *Carpets and Rugs*. 1924. Scott, Greenwood & Son.

Von Bode and Kühnel, *Antique Rugs from the Near East*. 1958. Textile Book Service, Metuchen, New Jersey.

Brinton, R. S. *Carpets*. 1934. Pitmans Common Commodity Series.

Bronson, J. and R. *The Domestic Manufacturer's Assistant*. 1817. Reprinted by C. T. Branford. U.S.A.

Collin, Maria. *Gamla Vävnader och Deras Mönster*. 1928. Stockholm.

Crowfoot, Grace. *Coptic Textiles in Two-faced Weave with Pattern in Reverse*.
  The Sudanese Camel Girth. Kush, vol. iv, 1956.
  The Tent Beautiful. Palestine Exploration Quarterly, April 1945.

Cyrus, Ulla. *Manual of Swedish Handweaving*. 1956. C. T. Branford. U.S.A.

Dreczko, Werner. *Teppiche Europas*. 1962. Aurel Bongers, W. Germany.
  Teppiche des Orients. 1962. Aurel Bongers, W. Germany.

Dunn, Eliza. *Rugs in their Native Land*. 1910. Fisher Unwin.

Edwards, A. C. *The Persian Carpet*. 1953. Duckworth, London, and Humanities Press, New York.

Emery, Irene. *The Primary Structure of Fabrics*. 1966. Textile Museum, Washington.

Emmons, George T. *The Chilkat Blanket*. 1907. Memoirs of the American Museum of Natural History, Vol. III, Part IV.

Gallinger and Del Deo. *Rugweaving for Everyone*. 1957. Bruce Books, New York.

Grierson, Ronald. *Woven Rugs*. 1952. Dryad Press, Leicester.

Haack, Hermann. *Oriental Rugs*. 1960. Faber and Faber.

Hald, Margarethe and H. C. Broholm. *Costumes of the Bronze Age in Denmark*. 1940. Copenhagen.

d'Harcourt, Raoul. *Textiles of Ancient Peru and their Techniques*. 1962, University of Washington Press.

Hoffmann, Marta. *The Warp-Weighted Loom*. 1964. University Press, Oslo, and Textile Book Service, Metuchen, New Jersey.

Hopf, A. *Oriental Carpets and Rugs*. 1962. Thames and Hudson, London.

Hosain, Ali. *Oriental Carpets*. ACO DRUCK GMBH, W. Germany.

Ingers, Gertrud. *Trasmattor*. 1955. I.C.A. Sweden.
Nya Mattor. 1959. I.C.A. Sweden.

Jacoby, Heinrich. *How to know Oriental Carpets and Rugs*. 1952. Allen and Unwin. 2nd Edition 1967, Textile Book Service, Metuchen, New Jersey.

Jacobsen, Charles. *Oriental Rugs, a complete guide*. Charles Tuttle, Vermont.

James, George Wharton. *Indian Blankets and their Makers*. 1920. Chicago. Reprinted by Rio Grande Press, Glorieta, New Mexico.

Kendrick, A. F. and Tattersall, C. E. *Handwoven Carpets, Oriental and European*. 2 vols. 1922. Benn Bros. Ltd., London.

Kent, Kate Peck. *The Cultivation and Weaving of Cotton in the Prehistoric Southwestern United States*. 1957. The American Philosophical Society.
The Story of Navaho Weaving. 1961. Heard Museum of Anthropology and Primitive Arts.

Kuhnel, Ernst and Bellinger, Louisa. *Cairene Rugs and Others Technically Related: 15th–17th Century*. 1957. Textile Museum, Washington.

Larson, Knut. *Rugs and Carpets of the Orient*. 1966. Warne. London.

Lewes, Klara and Hutton, Helen. *Rugweaving*. 1962. Batsford, London, and Branford, Newton Centre, Massachusetts.

Lewis, G. G. *The Practical Book of Oriental Rugs*. 1920. J. B. Lippincott & Co.

Mead, S. M. *Taniko Weaving*. 1952. A. H. and A. W. Reed, Wellington, N.Z.

Mera, H. P. *Navaho Textile Arts*. 1958. Laboratory of Anthropology, Santa Fé, New Mexico.

Mumford, J. K. *Oriental Rugs*. 1901. London.

Murphy, W. S. *The Textile Industries*. 1910. Gresham Publishing Co., London.

Nisbet, H. *Grammar of Textile Design*. 1916. Scott, Greenwood & Son.

Nooteboom, C. *Quelques Techniques de Tissage des Petites Iles de la Sonde*. 1948. Rijksmuseum voor Volkenkunde, Leiden, Holland.

Reichard, Gladys. *Navaho Shepherd and Weaver*. 1936. New York. Reprinted and revised, 1968, by Rio Grande Press, Glorieta, New Mexico.

Ropers, H. *Les Tapis d'Orient*. 1962. Presses Universitaires de France.

Sirelius, U. T. *The Ryijy Rugs of Finland*. 1962. Helsinki.

Sylwan, Vivi. *Svenska Ryor*. 1934. Stockholm.

Tattersall, C. E. C. *Notes on Carpet Knotting and Weaving*. 1920 and 1961. Victoria and Albert Museum, London.

The Carpets of Persia. 1931. Luzac & Co., London.

Tidball, Harriet. *The Double Weave, Plain and Patterned*. 1960. Craft & Hobby, Pacific Grove, California.

The Handloom Weaves. 1957. Craft & Hobby, Pacific Grove, California.

Tomlinson, Charles. *The Useful Arts and Manufactures of Great Britain*. About 1850. London.

Tovey, John. *The Technique of Weaving*. 1965. Batsford.

Watson, William. *Textile Design and Colour*. 1946. Longmans, London.

Wyatt, M. D. *Industrial Arts of the Nineteenth Century*. 1851. London.

Suppliers of Equipment and Yarns

The following suppliers are all prepared to deal with handweavers and will send their products anywhere in the world.

SUPPLIERS OF WEAVING EQUIPMENT

Gunnar Anderssons, Vävskedsverkstad, Oxberg, 792 00 Mora, SWEDEN.
General suppliers of all weaving equipment, including shuttles, temples, looms, rya and flossa guide rods and knives. Also 'ski shuttles', called *mattstickor, no 69c* in catalogue.

Walter Arm, 3507 Biglen, SWITZERLAND
Looms of all types, shuttles, temples, rug forks and a small electrical doubling machine. A special carpet loom, up to 2 metres wide, is made, with underslung batten and 4 shafts with countermarch action; also a vertical 2 shaft tapestry loom with a pivoted batten and full-width pedal; both can have either sectional or warp beams.

Peter Collingwood, Old School, Nayland, Colchester, ENGLAND.
Wire loops for cutting corduroy.

K. Drummond, 30 Hart Grove, London, W.5. ENGLAND.
Wooden 'ski shuttles'.

Dryads, Northgates, Leicester, ENGLAND.
Suppliers of weaving equipment to schools, including vertical rug frames and looms. Also solid metal and lead-weighted wooden rug beaters. Small celluloid tablets.

Föreningen Hemslöjden, Box 433, Boras, SWEDEN.
The Ulla Cyrus loom. An excellently designed countermarch loom, with overslung batten and specially strengthened beams. Suitable for all but the heaviest rug weaving. Order direct from the maker, Arvid Kristiansson, Hallstorp, 510 12 Oxaback, SWEDEN.

'Harris' Looms, Northgrove Road, Hawkhurst, Kent, ENGLAND.
Makers of the 'Maxwell' multishaft floor looms, which are strong enough for rug weaving and of the 'Harris' table looms (up to 16 shafts) which are very suitable for weaving rug samples.

Anders Lervad and Son, Askov, pr Vejen, DENMARK.
Excellent looms of all types. A special carpet loom is made from $2\frac{1}{2}$–6 metres wide, but the normal looms are strong enough for rug weaving. Also vertical rug looms,

tablets, and a good range of shuttles and strong temples. Detailed catalogue sent on request. Lervad (UK) Ltd, Vernon Building, Westbourne St, High Wycombe, Bucks, ENGLAND is a subsidiary firm catering for the United Kingdom and Ireland.

Manchester Metal Works, 368/376 Bury New Road, Salford M7 9BS, Lancs, ENGLAND.
Strong metal skeiners, swifts or ryces of many types and sizes, some specially designed to take heavy yarns, such as carpet wool. Also tension units and other devices available.

Vävstolsfabriken Glimåkra AB, S–280 64 Glimåkra, SWEDEN.
Suppliers of a good range of weaving equipment, including a very solid rug loom made up to 3½ metres wide. The warp and cloth beams are of metal and are turned by geared handles. The breast beam, knee bar and back bar are also of metal. Sliding seat and two sets of pedals for the wider sizes. Other looms made which are also strong though incorporating less metal. U.K. agent is Baddy's Bookshop, 165 Linthorpe Road, Middlesbrough, Yorks, ENGLAND. Catalogue sent on request.

SUPPLIERS OF YARNS

All the following suppliers will send samples and price lists free of charge, unless otherwise stated. The minimum quantity that each firm will sell of one type of yarn is given where possible.

Warp Yarns

Barbour Threads Ltd, Hilden, Lisburn, Co. Antrim, N. IRELAND.
Linen and synthetic seaming twines in various plies. Minimum quantity=12 lbs.

Blackstaff Threads Ltd, P.O. Box 134, Belfast BT14 7EP, N. IRELAND.
Will spin to order any type of flax yarns; minimum quantity = 200 lb. Carry a stock of 6/10s lea flax twine, very suitable for rug warps.

Bridport-Gundry Ltd, Bridport, Dorset, ENGLAND.
Specialize in the manufacture of a wide range of twines, spun from flax, hemp, nylon, polypropylene and polythene. Minimum quantity=2 lbs. A heavy spun nylon rug weft yarn can be produced to order.

Mersey Yarns, 2 Staplands Road, Liverpool, L14 3LL, ENGLAND.
Good range of cotton, hemp, jute and ramie yarns and twines; heddle twine and loom cord; jute and flax fibre for spinning and weaving purposes. (This firm has taken over the supply of yarns formerly sold for handweaving purposes by H. & J. Jones and Southwick and Case.)

Pymore Mill & Co Ltd, Bridport, Dorset, ENGLAND.
Flax rug warp in various counts, e.g., 3/12s, 3/8s, 3/6s on 1 lb tubes.

Weft Yarns

Borgs, S–22104 Lund, SWEDEN.
Suppliers of all types of yarns, including many grades of linen rug warp. Amongst weft yarns for rugs are:
Nöthårsgarn, 100% wool singles yarn.
Afghangarn, very high quality lustrous worsted for rya rugs.
Frostagarn, more normal quality worsted for rya rugs in many colours.

Craftsman Mark Yarns, Broadlands, Shortheath, Farnham, Surrey, ENGLAND.
A range of yarns specially spun for handweavers. Includes a 2-ply rug wool in white, natural grey and natural black, about 40 yds per ounce. Also 6/10s lea rug warp. Minimum quantity=1 lb.

A. K. Graupner, Corner House, Valley Road, Bradford BDI 4AA, ENGLAND.
2-ply rug wool, approx: 2/50s, in white and in various grey mixtures. Also, when available, odd lots of other rug yarns which may be dyed, natural, all-wool or blends.

Hyslop Bathgate & Co, Galashiels, SCOTLAND.
2/2½s worsted yarn in white and 25 colours, about 700 yds per lb. A soft yarn but suitable for some types of knotted pile and corduroy. Sample card sent on request. Minimum quantity=one hank (¼ lb).

Julius Koch, Nørrebrogade 52, Copenhagen, DENMARK.
Supplier of handweaving yarns of all types. Very large colour range of a 2-ply yarn (five natural greys and over 150 dyed shades) called ryegarn, which is suitable for both pile and flat weaves. Also about 80 dyed shades of a singles coarse wool (nöthårsgarn) suitable for flat rugs. Small charge for samples.

Multiple Fabric Co Ltd, Dudley Hill, Bradford BD4 9PD, ENGLAND.
2- and 3-ply horsehair yarns, belting yarns spun from camel hair, grey hair, white wool, white and black mohair. All supplies in oil on tubes. Minimum quantity= 5 lbs. Special carding brushes for raising surface of warpface rugs.

Norsk Kunstvevgarn A/S, Homborsund 4897, pr. Grimstad, NORWAY.
The best spinner of Norwegian Spaelsau wool. Excellent 2-ply yarns in four different counts, including kunstvevgarn (tapestry yarn, about 3,000 metres per Kgm) aklegarn and ryegarn (about 450 metres per Kgm). The latter is a very heavy, solid yarn of a type not offered by other spinners. Also ullspissgarn, a coarse singles wool yarn similar to Nöthårsgarn. All types available in white, five shades of grey (from pale to almost black) and about 20 dyed shades. Minimum quantity=one hank (about ¼ lb).

Weavers' Shop, Royal Carpet Factory, Wilton, nr. Salisbury, Wilts, ENGLAND.
A good range of 2/55s carpet wool in white and dyed colours. Minimum quantity= ½ lb. Wool can be specially dyed, if not less than 20 lbs of one colour is required. Small charge for samples. Also mixed thrums, suitable for knotted pile.

Index

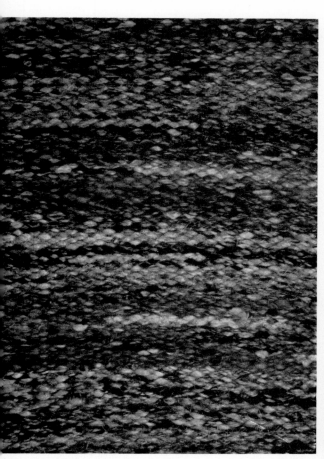

1. Sample with handspun weft of rayon, hemp and jute.

2. Rug with tie-and-dye weft giving a repeating design.

3. Sample with tie-and-dye weft giving a non-repeating design.

4. Twisted wefts. Area of spots on a background of lines.

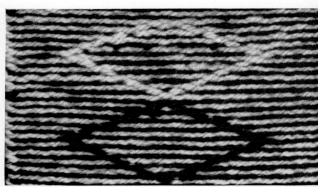

5. Twisted wefts. Diagonal lines on a background of horizontal lines.

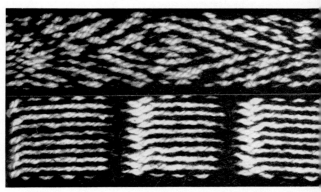

6. Twisted wefts. Vertical lines on a background of horizontal lines and concentric ovals.

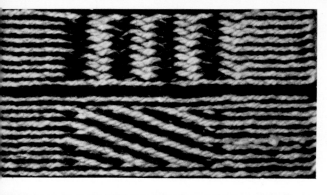

7.
Twisted wefts. Oblique and vertical lines produced by controlled multiple twists.

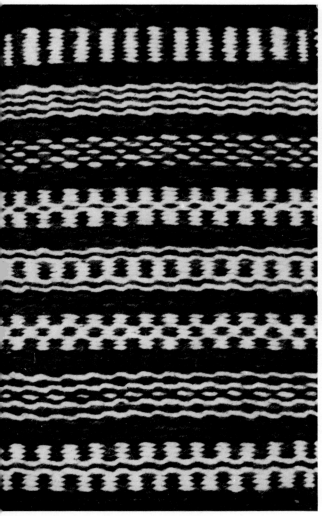

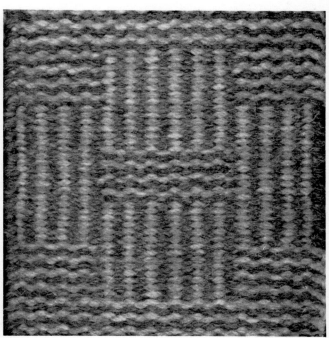

9. Crossed wefts in contrary motion. Area of pick-and-pick stripes on a background of cross stripes.

8.
Combination of pick-and-pick stripes, cross stripes and spots.

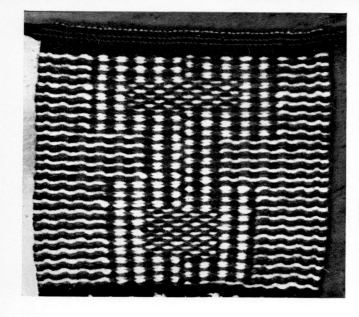

10.
Crossed wefts in
contrary motion.
Using 3 wefts.

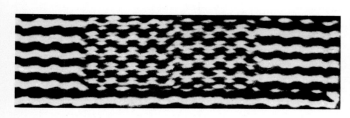

11.
Crossed wefts in
contrary motion.
Using 4 wefts.

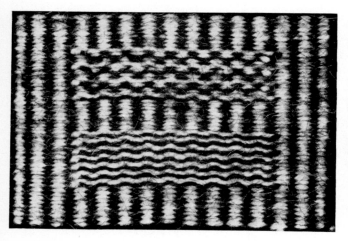

12.
Crossed wefts in
parallel motion.
Two types of blocks.

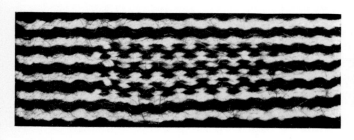

13.
Crossed wefts in
parallel motion.
Block on background of 4-and-4
stripes.

14. Skip plain weave.

15. Skip plain weave. Part of rug woven by Rosemary Bruton.

16. Skip plain weave. Middle Eastern textile using 3 colours.

17. Weaving letters and figures at the end of a rug.

18. Meet and separate weave. Two methods of interchanging left- and right-hand colour.

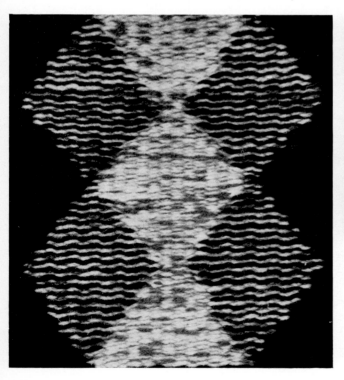

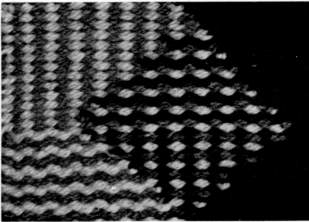

20. Meet and separate weave. Using 3 colours with clasped weft method.

19. Meet and separate weave. Using 3 colours.

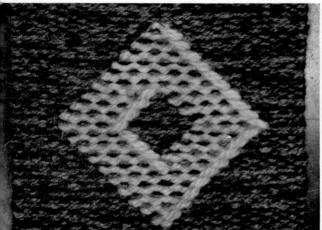

23. Compensated inlay. Using 2 wefts.

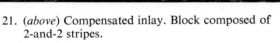

21. (*above*) Compensated inlay. Block composed of 2-and-2 stripes.

22. (*below*) Compensated inlay. Block composed of 2-and-1 stripes.

24. Compensated inlay. Using 2 wefts in one block, to give oblique jump-up ridge.

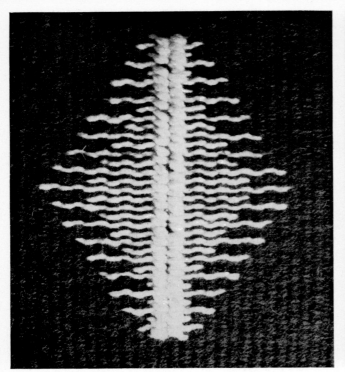

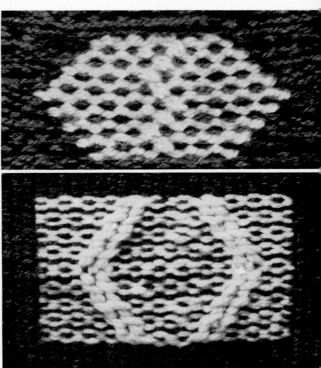

25. Compensated inlay. Using 2 wefts in one block, to give vertical jump-up ridge.

26. (*above*) Compensated inlay. Using 2 wefts in one block, to give jump-up spots.

27. (*below*) Compensated inlay. Using 4 wefts in one block.

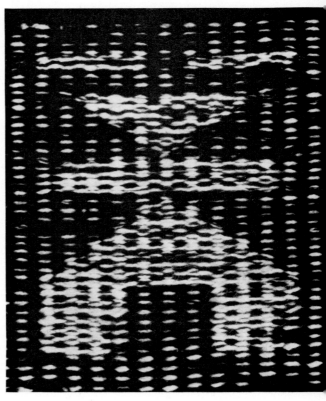

28. Compensated inlay. Producing several blocks with one weft.

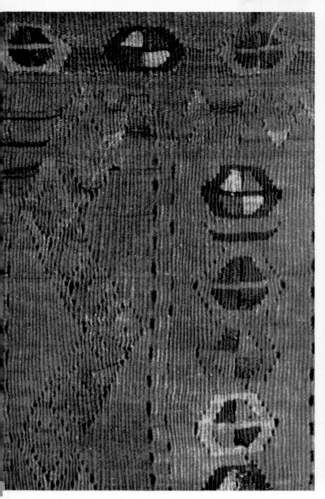

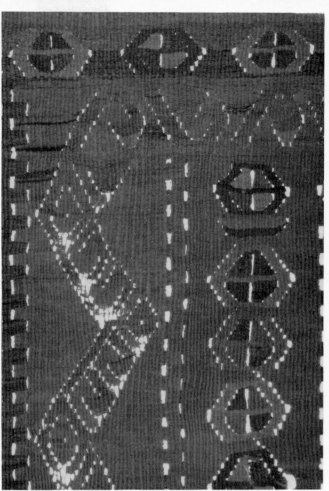

29. Part of a rug in kilim technique.

30. Same rug as in Plate 29 photographed against the light to show the slits between vertical colour junctions.

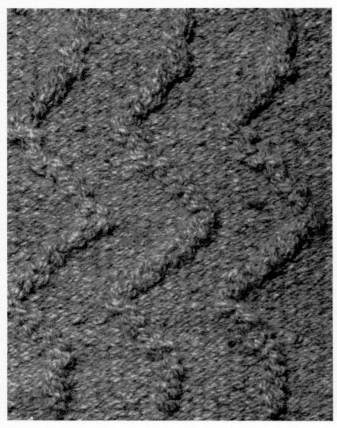

31. Double interlocked tapestry. Vertical ridges obtained by using several wefts of the same colour.

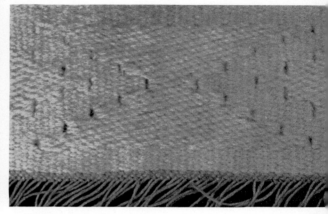

33. Tapestry of weaves.

32. Diamond twill tapestry.

34. Part of Middle Eastern saddlebag in soumak.

35. Vertical single soumak with areas of cut pile.

37. Weft chaining. Part of rope, sisal and cotton mat.

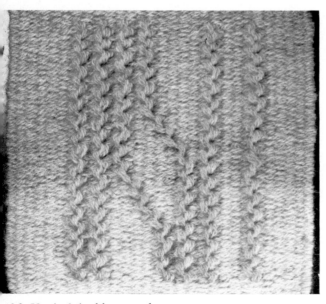

36. Vertical double soumak.

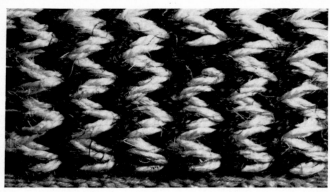

38. Weft chaining. Using 2 wefts alternately.

40. Chained loops. Sample in black and white wool by Kathryn Hiltner.

39. Weft chaining. Using 2 wefts to give blocks.

41. Wrapped loops. Sample using cotton, coir and unspun jute.

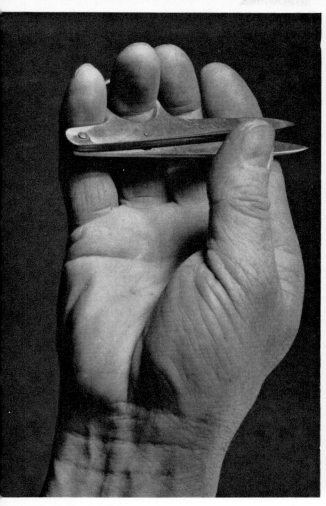

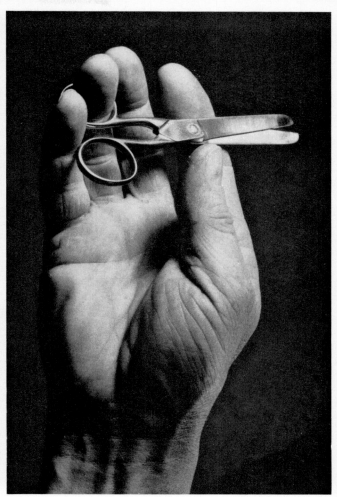

42. Holding weaver's scissors.

43. Holding normal scissors.

44.
Double-faced weave
using pointed 3-shaft
draft.

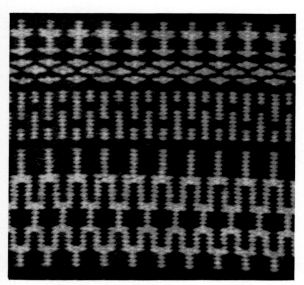

45. 3-shaft Krokbragd.

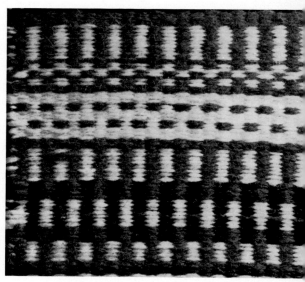

46. 3-shaft Krokbragd, showing the reverse of the sample in Plate 45.

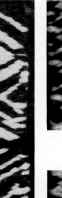

51. Straight 2/2 twill. 10-pick colour sequence.

47. Straight 2/2 twill. Using 2 and 3 colours.

52. Straight 2/2 twill. 12-pick colour sequence.

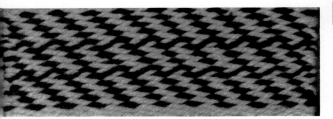

48. Straight 2/2 twill. 5-pick colour sequence.

49. Straight 2/2 twill. 7-pick colour sequence.

50. Straight 2/2 twill. 9-pick colour sequence.

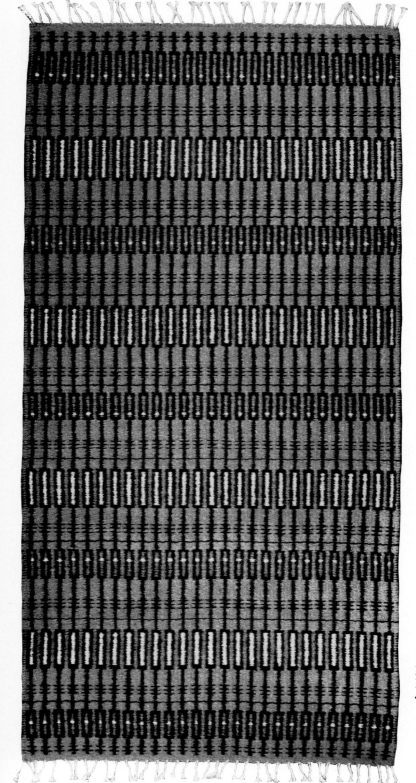

53.
Broken 2/2 twill.
Rug using various
4-pick colour sequences.

54. Broken 2/2 twill. 5-pick colour sequence.

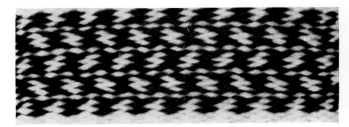

55. Broken 2/2 twill. 7-pick colour sequence.

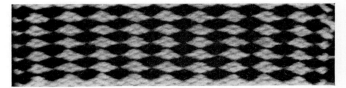

56. Broken 2/2 twill. 8-pick colour sequence.

57. Broken 2/2 twill. 8-pick colour sequence.

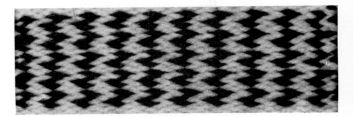

58. Broken 2/2 twill. 12-pick colour sequence.

59. Broken 2/2 twill. 12-pick colour sequence.

60. 2/2 twill, 'woven on opposites'.

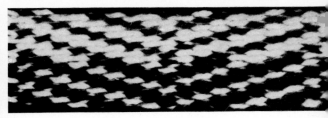

63. Skip twill repeating on 8 ends. 2/2 twill lifts with 3-pick colour sequence.

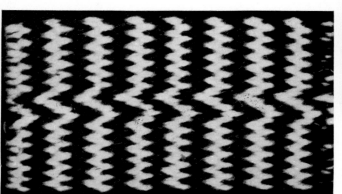

61. 2/2 twill, 'woven on opposites', with extended lifting sequence.

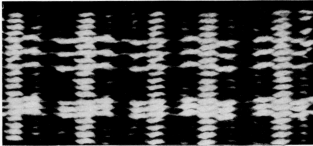

64. Skip twill repeating on 8 ends. 2/2 twill lifts with 4-pick colour sequence.

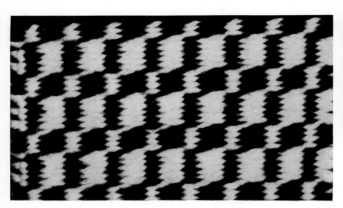

62. Straight 2/2 twill, using only 3 lifts.

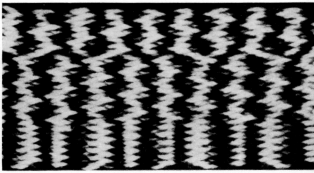

65. Skip twill repeating on 8 ends. 2/2 twill 'woven on opposites' and plain weave.

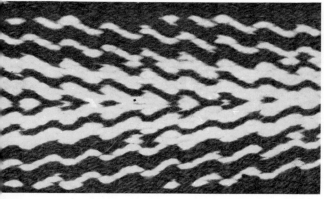

66. Skip twill repeating on 16 ends. 2/2 twill lifts with 3-pick colour sequence.

70. Skip twill repeating on 24 ends. 2/2 twill lifts with 12-pick colour sequence.

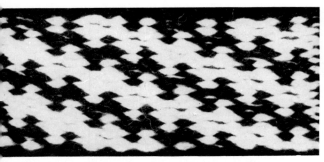

67. Skip twill repeating on 16 ends. 2/2 twill lifts with 12-pick colour sequence.

71. Skip twill repeating on 24 ends.

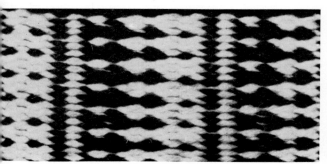

68. Skip twill repeating on 16 ends. 2/2 twill lifts with 7-pick colour sequence.

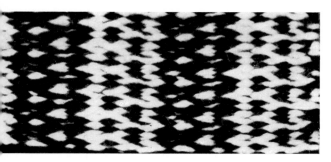

69. Skip twill repeating on 16 ends. Broken 2/2 twill lifts with 12-pick colour sequence.

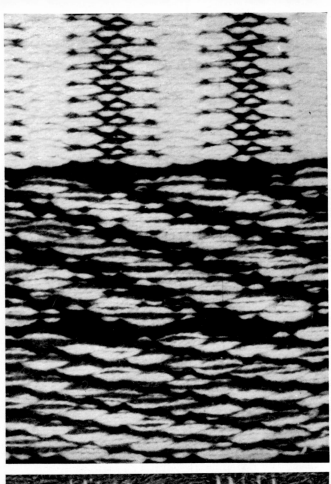

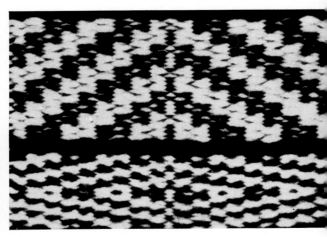

72. Twilled overshot blocks. Three methods of weaving.

74. 4-shaft weft-face shadow weave.

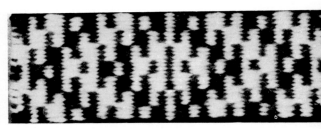

75. 4-shaft weft-face shadow weave.

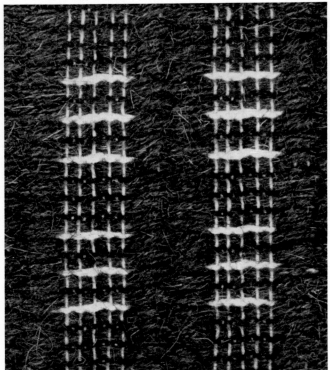

76. 4-shaft weft-face shadow weave.

73.
Twilled overshot blocks. Warpway stripes.

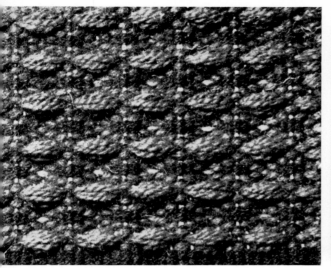

77. 4-shaft honeycomb.

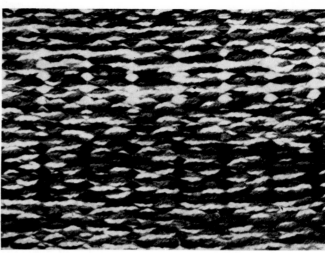

80. Single-end spot weave.

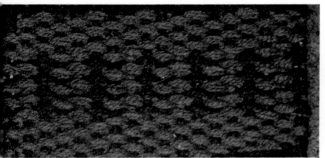

78. Single-end spot weave.

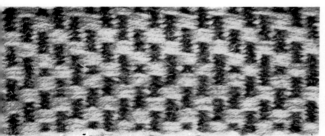

79. Single-end spot weave.

81. Alternated 2-shaft blocks. Sample by
Marjorie de Linde.

82. 2/2/1/1 twill. Straight lifts with 4-pick colour sequence.

83. 2/2/1/1 twill. Straight lifts with 5-pick colour sequence.

84. 2/2/1/1 twill, 'woven on opposites'.

85. 2/2/1/1 twill.

86. 2/2/1/1 twill. Broken twill lifts with various colour sequences.

87. 1/3/1/1 twill.

88. Combination of 1/3/1/1 twill with 3/1/1/1 twill.

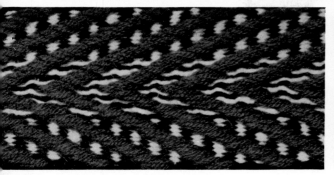

89. 3/3 twill.

90. Combination of 3/3 twill with 2/2/1/1 twill.

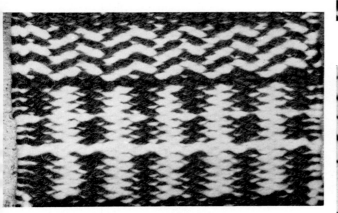

91. 6-shaft weave based on 3-shaft weave in Fig. 211.

92. 6-shaft weft-face shadow weave.

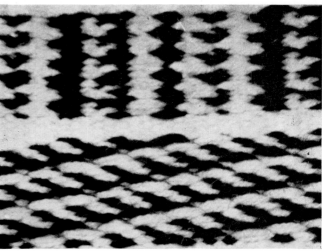

93. 6-shaft skip twill. Two methods of weaving.

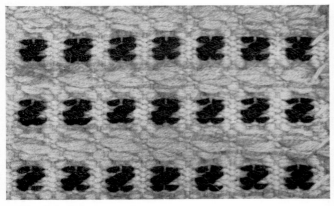

94. 6-shaft honeycomb.

95. Double two-tie unit weave.

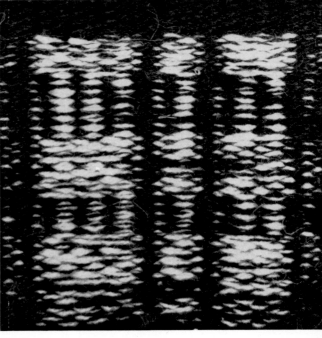

97. 3-end block draft.

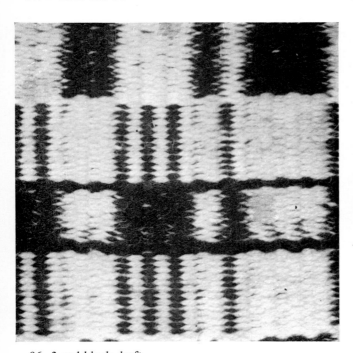

96. 3-end block draft.

98. 3-end block draft. Rug showing areas where shafts have been switched.

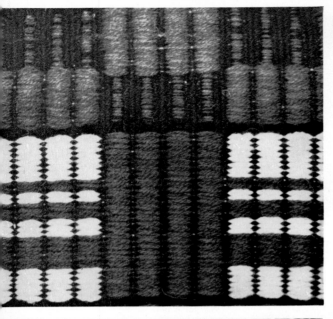

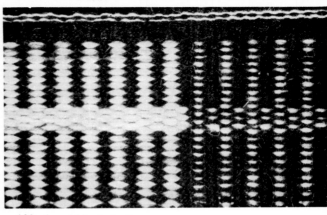

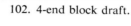

102. 4-end block draft.

99.
4-end block draft. Methods of weaving.

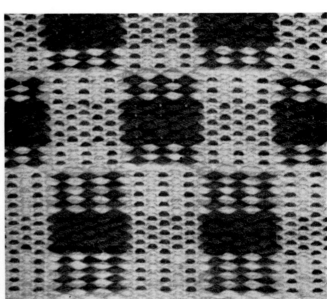

103. 4-end block draft.

100.
4-end block draft.

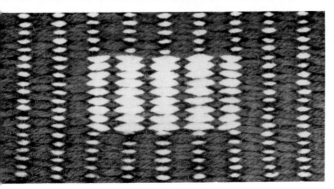

101.
4-end block draft.

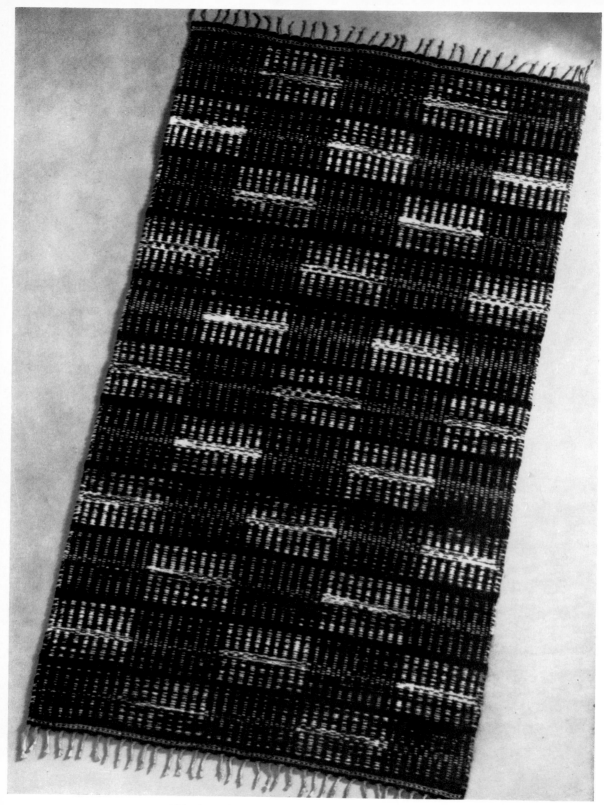

104. 4-end block draft. Rug in black and white.

105. 6-end block draft.

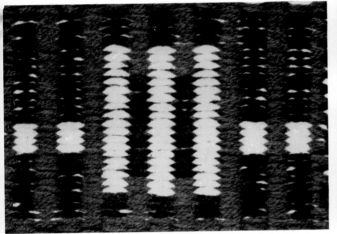

106. 6-end block draft.

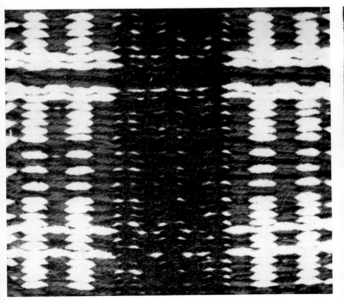

107. 6-end block draft.

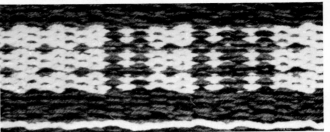

108. Draft based on single-end spot weave.

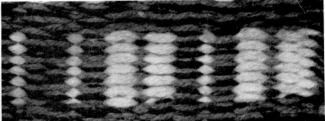

109. Draft based on single-end spot weave.

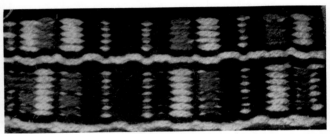

110. Draft based on single-end spot weave.

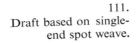

111.
Draft based on single-
end spot weave.

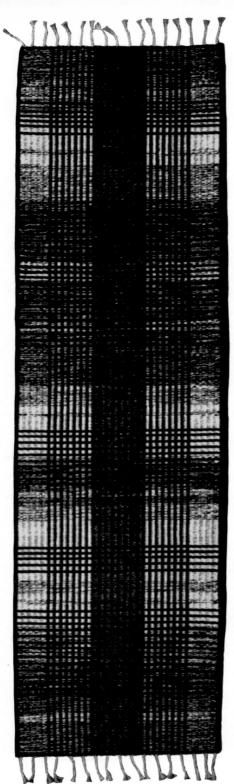

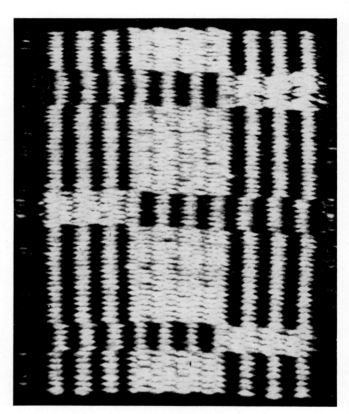

113. Draft based on straight 3-shaft draft.

112.
Draft based on straight 3-shaft draft.
Rug in black and whites.

114. Draft based on straight 3-shaft draft. Rug in black and
reds.

115. Draft based on straight 3-shaft draft.
Rug with design produced by shaft-switching.

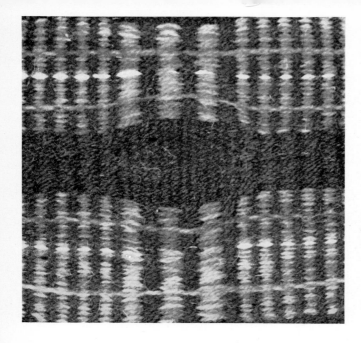

116.
Traditional M's and O's
draft. Sample showing
distorted weft.

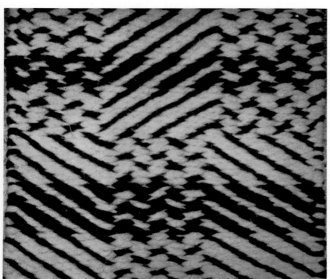

117.
Traditional M's and O's
draft.

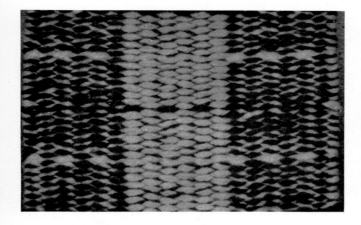

118.
Traditional M's and O's
draft.

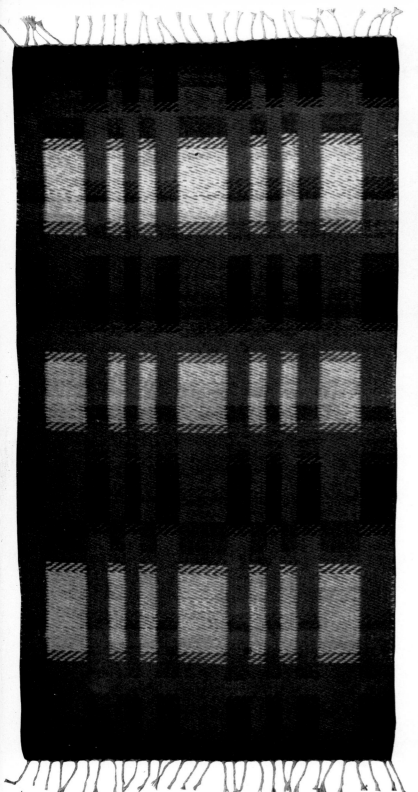

120. Block weave based on 3-shaft Krokbragd.

119.
Block weave based on
double-faced 2/1 twill.
Rug in greens.

121.
Double two-tie unit
weave. Various ways of
weaving diamonds.

122.
Reverse of sample in
Plate 121.

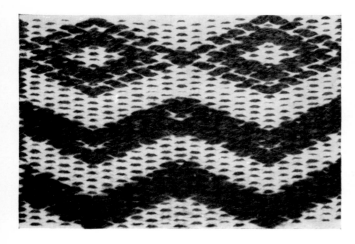

123.
Double two-tie unit
weave.

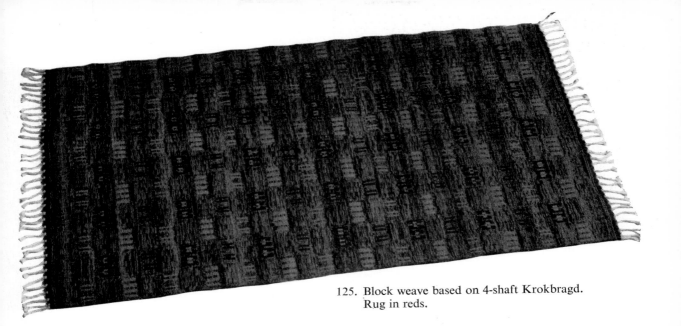

125. Block weave based on 4-shaft Krokbragd.
    Rug in reds.

126. Plain weave double cloth.

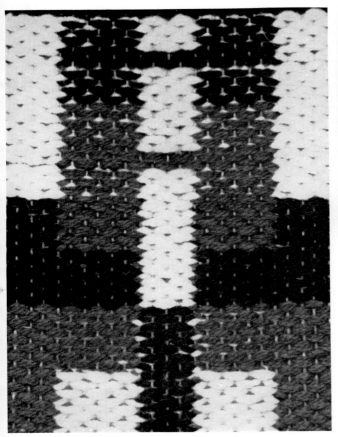

124.
Three-colour blockweave.

128.
Plain weave double cloth.
Rug in yellows
showing ovals.

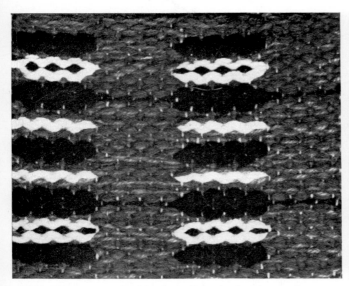

127. Plain weave double cloth. Sample showing various ovals.

129. Block weave based on the Girdle of Rameses.

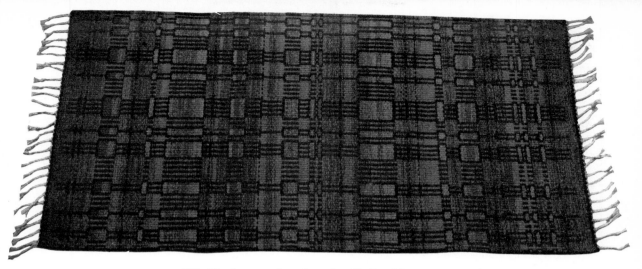

130. Block weave based on the Girdle of Rameses. Rug in blues and purples.

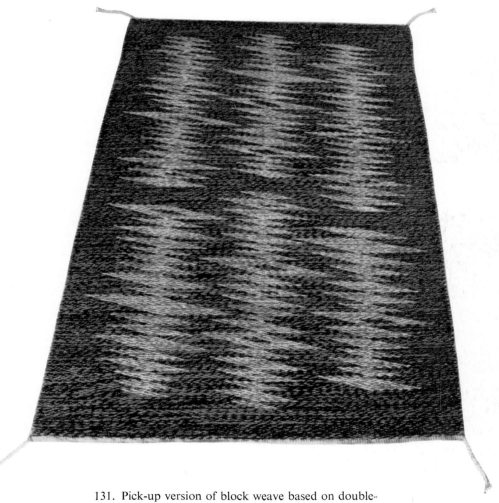

131. Pick-up version of block weave based on double-faced 2/1 twill.

134. 8-shaft single corduroy. Rug in reds and pinks.

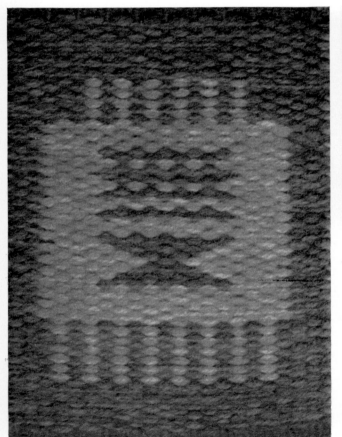

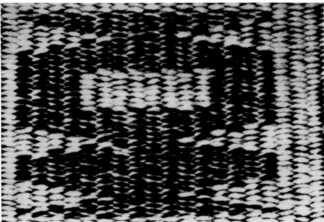

133. Pick-up version of block weave using M's and O's draft.

132.
Pick-up version of block weave using 4-end block draft.

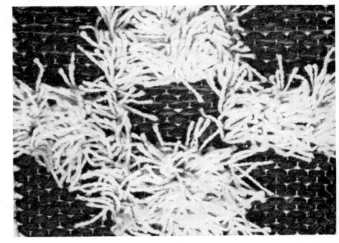

136. Single corduroy using 4-end block draft, on 8 shafts.

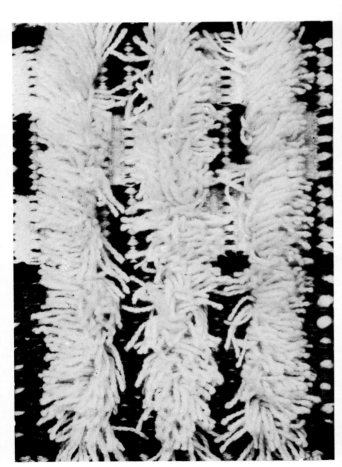

135. Single corduroy using 4-end block draft, two ways of weaving on 4 shafts.

137. Double corduroy. Rug in black and white.

138.
Combination of double
corduroy and cut pulled-
up loops. Rug in black
and white.

139. Double corduroy. Effect on warpway stripes of 'double cutting'.

141. Corduroy on 5 shafts.

140. Double corduroy. Cutting floats off-centre to give oblique ridges of long and short pile.

142. Twill double corduroy.

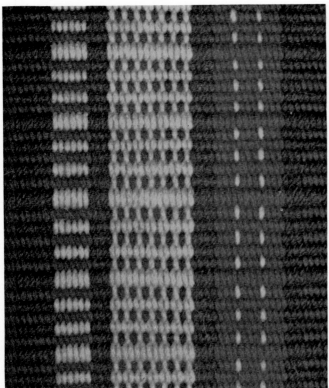

143. Warp-face plain weave.

145. Warp-face twill. Weft brought to the surface.

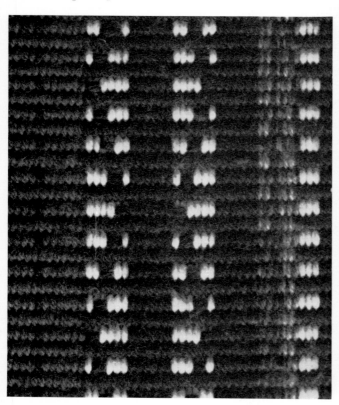

144. Warp-face plain weave. Spots of weft brought to the surface.

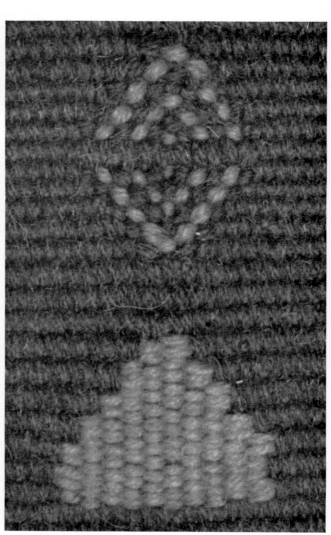

146. Warp-face plain weave combined with weft twining and weft-face plain weave.

147. Part of a Bedouin saha.

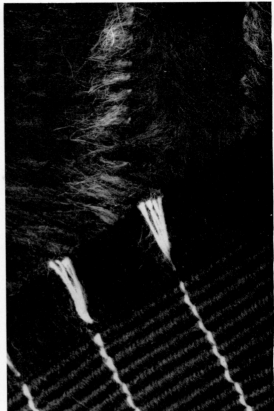

148. Mohair warp-face rug showing raised surface and unraised reverse.

149. Warp-face 2/2 twill, with various colour sequences in the warp.

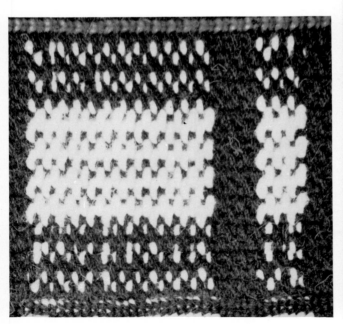

150. Warp-face form of block weave using three-end block draft.

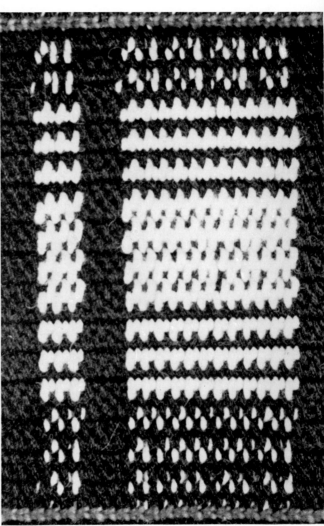

151. Warp-face form of block weave based on straight three-shaft draft.

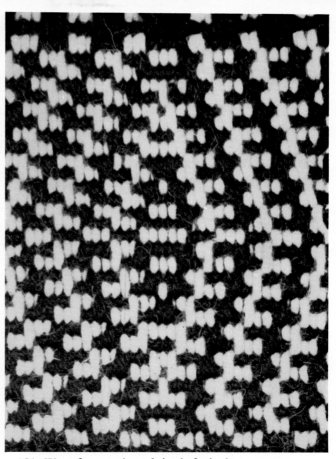

152. Warp-face form of block weave using single end spot draft.

154. Warp-face version of six-shaft shadow weave.

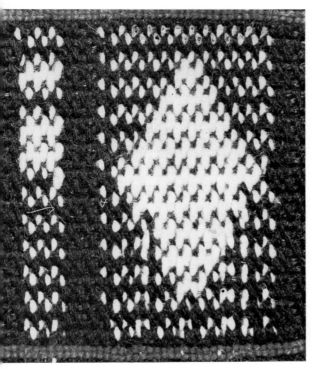

153.
Pick-up based on weave shown in Plate 150.

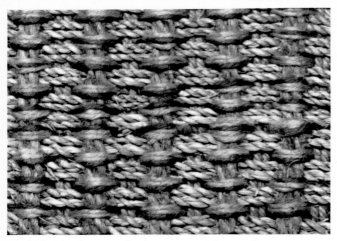

155. Matting sample. Seagrass and jute weft across coir and sisal warp.

156. Matting sample. Seagrass weft across a warp of plastic tubing, 2/2 twill.

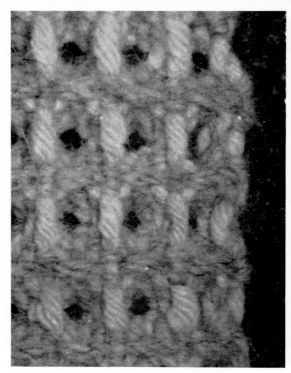

157. Honeycomb weave, warp and weft being 6-ply rug wool.

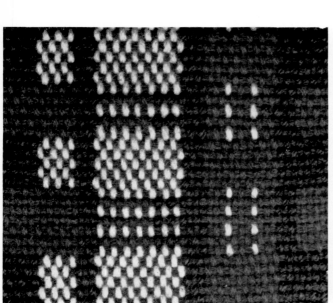

158. Plain weave double cloth, warp and weft being 6-ply rug wool.

159. Matting sample. Seagrass weft across warp of plastic-covered wire.

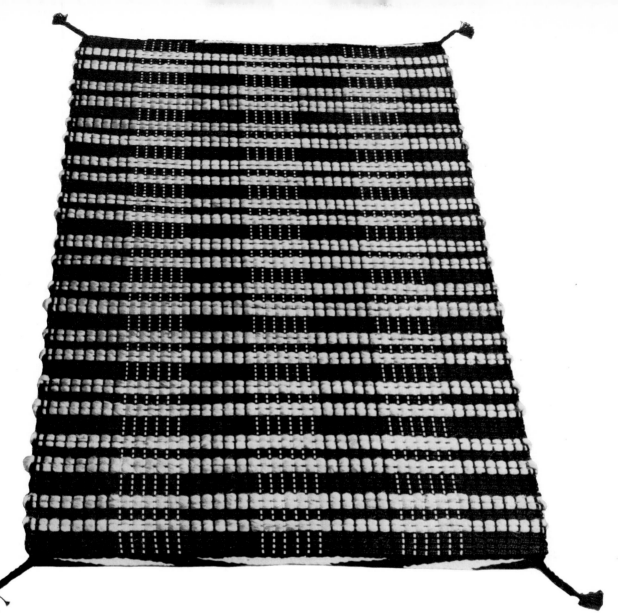

160. Mat woven of unspun jute, dyed sisal and cotton.

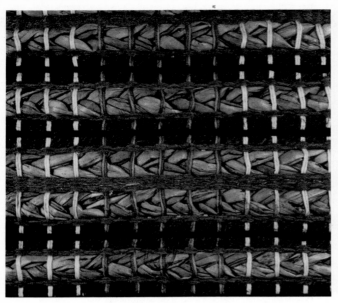

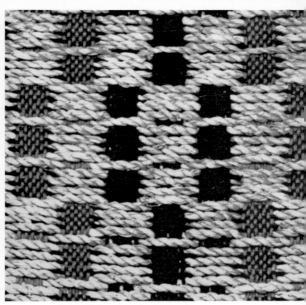

161. Matting sample. Plaited rush, dyed coir and cotton across cotton warp. Woven by Brian Knight.

163. Matting sample. Seagrass and cotton across cotton warp threaded on alternate two-shaft blocks.

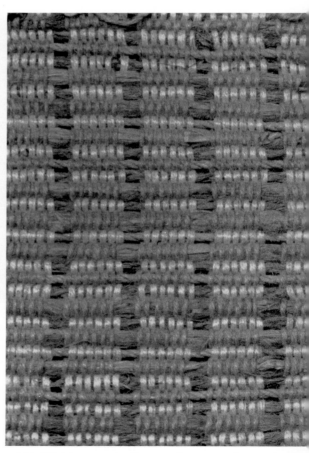

162. Matting sample. Rayon tow, unspun flax, unspun delustred rayon and cotton across linen warp.

164. Matting sample. Rope, coir, unspun jute and raffia across a spaced hemp warp.

165. Block of weft twining on a background of 2-and-2 stripes.

166. Weft twining. Wefts encircling 1, 2 and 3 ends.

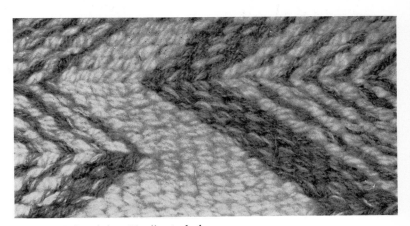

167. Weft twining. Taniko technique.

168. Weft twining. Part of rug in twined tapestry, from
Abyssinia.

169. Open shed weft twining.

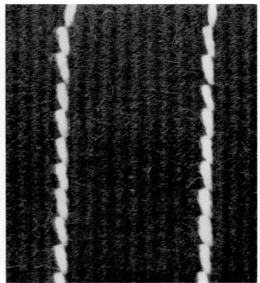

170. Warpway stripes in Navajo selvage
technique.